Reader's Digest

GREAT
BIOGRAPHIES

*Reader's
Digest*

GREAT
BIOGRAPHIES

*selected
and
condensed by
the editors
of
Reader's
Digest*

The Reader's Digest Association, Inc.
Pleasantville, New York
Cape Town, Hong Kong, London, Montreal, Sydney

READER'S DIGEST CONDENSED BOOKS

Editor-in-Chief: Barbara J. Morgan
Executive Editor: Tanis H. Erdmann
Senior Managing Editor: Marjorie Palmer
Managing Editors: Jean E. Aptakin, Thomas Froncek, Herbert H. Lieberman
Senior Staff Editors: Anne H. Atwater, Joseph P. McGrath, James J. Menick,
Angela H. Plowden-Wardlaw, Ray Sipherd
Senior Editors: Dana Adkins, M. Tracy Brigden, Catherine T. Brown,
Linn Carl, Thomas S. Clemmons, Maureen A. Mackey, John R. Roberson
Senior Associate Editor: Catharine L. Edmonds
Associate Editors: Christopher W. Davis,
Ainslie Gilligan, Julie E. Sanders
Senior Copy Editors: Maxine Bartow, Claire A. Bedolis,
Jeane Garment, Jane F. Neighbors
Senior Associate Copy Editors: Rosalind H. Campbell, Jean S. Friedman
Associate Copy Editors: Jeanette Gingold, Daphne Hougham, Tatiana Ivanow,
Marilyn J. Knowlton, Charles Pendergast, Joan R. Wilkinson
Editorial Administrator: Ann M. Dougher
Art Director: Angelo Perrone
Executive Art Editors: William Gregory, Soren Noring
Art Editor: George Calas, Jr.
Associate Art Editor: Katherine Kelleher
Art Research: Marcelline Lowery, Todd D. Victor
Director, Book Rights: Virginia Rice

CB INTERNATIONAL EDITIONS
Managing Editor: Gary Q. Arpin
Associate Editors: Bonnie Grande, Eva C. Jaunzems, Antonius L. Koster

The credits and acknowledgments that appear on pages 639–640
are hereby made part of this copyright page.

FIRST EDITION

Library of Congress Cataloging-in-Publication Data
(Revised for volumes 13-15)
Reader's digest great biographies.
1. Biography. I. Reader's Digest Association.
II. Reader's digest. III. Great biographies.
CT101.R42   1987   920'.02   86-29816
ISBN 0-89577-259-0 (v.1)   ISBN 0-89577-329-5 (v.13)

Printed in the United States of America

Contents

A PILLAR
OF IRON

A CONDENSATION OF THE BOOK BY
TAYLOR CALDWELL

ILLUSTRATIONS BY STANLEY W. GALLI

Cicero was called "Rome's angry man."
The ambitious and the greedy could count him
their enemy. For as Rome thundered down the
bloody road to tyranny, it was Cicero—
the statesman and golden-tongued orator—who
valiantly sought to defend her against her foes. . . .

Against Catiline—
    charismatic but evil to the core.

Against Julius Caesar—
    a friend not always to be trusted.

Against Mark Antony—
    an enemy who bore watching.

Over the years, many great men of the ancient
world would cross Cicero's path. And women,
both noble and decadent, would touch his life.
For Cicero *was* Rome, and her history
was his history—until, one day, someone
marked him for murder.

CHAPTER ONE

Marcus Tullius Cicero winced when the hot plaster was placed on his chest by his physician, and in the somewhat pettish voice of a semi-invalid he demanded, "What is that stink?"

"Vulture's grease," said the physician. "Two sesterces a pot and guaranteed to allay any inflammation." Slaves stirred up the coals in the brazier and M. Tullius shivered under his blankets.

"Two sesterces," he repeated with gloom. "What did the Lady Helvia say about that? A frugal wife is excellent, but I resent being numbered on the household accounts between the kettles and goat cheese." He coughed heavily.

"Aha, the cough is much looser," the physician said, pleased. He looked at the thin dark face on the white pillows. The features were kindly, the chin undetermined. Marcus Tullius was a young man, with the somewhat passive hands of the scholar.

He heard footsteps and winced. His father was approaching, and his father was an "old" Roman. He closed his eyes and pretended to sleep. He loved his father but found him overpowering, with his old-fashioned beard and all his tales about the family. The father, also Marcus Tullius Cicero, entered and leaned against the bed. "So my son again retreats to his bed when the Lady Helvia becomes too dominant! I hear she has suddenly taken to *her* bed. Is the child due, Phelon?"

"Any day. I will go to her at once." Phelon hurried from the room.

"Marcus," the old father said, "I know you are not sleeping. Do not try to delude me."

M. Tullius opened his eyes. "Is she about to give birth?"

"There is a scurrying in the women's quarters, and the midwife has put on her apron; but as this is the first child no doubt it will be some time before it is born."

"Helvia does all things with dispatch," said M. Tullius.

"Still, she is subject to the laws of nature."

"Not Helvia," said M. Tullius.

As the old father chuckled, the midwife came in and bowed. She said, "The birth is imminent, masters."

The old father flung back the covers from his cowering son. "A woman," he said, "wishes the presence of her husband when she gives birth, especially a patrician like Helvia. Marcus, arise."

A fur cloak was brought and wrapped over M. Tullius' narrow frame, and his father marched him into the windy, cold stone hall.

There was no attendant at the door of the women's quarters except a very old woman who had been Helvia's nurse. She glared at the intruders.

"My child is suffering," she said in a rusty voice. "And who is at hand but slaves and a male physician! In my day no male doctor approached a lady in her travail; it is disgusting."

"Open the door, slave!" said the old father.

Lira pushed open the door and shook her finger at the old father. "This child will be a boy. When my lady's pains began, I saw a flash in the sky like lightning, and a cloud shaped like a mighty hand holding a scroll of wisdom. This child will make the name of Cicero known.'

She shuffled aside, and the two men entered the room. Three young female slaves were standing aimlessly near the window, Phelon stood by the bed, and the midwife was dropping a handful of wood chips on a brazier. Helvia lay in bed, her account books all about her. She saw her visitors and frowned.

"Marcus, your bookkeeper is illiterate—or a thief," she said.

"Oh, gods!" muttered the old father.

"I rose from my sickbed, my love," Marcus said, "to be with you at this hour."

"You are always in a sickbed, Marcus. If you would ride daily or snare rabbits with me, you would be rugged as I am. But what is that vile odor?"

"Vulture's grease," said Marcus. "On my chest."

She wrinkled her nose. "Carrion. And, without doubt, very expensive. How much?" she demanded of Phelon.

"Two sesterces," Phelon admitted.

Helvia rolled over, reached for an account book and inscribed the sum. She studied the book, frowning. She had beautiful gray-blue eyes with thick lashes. Her nose was slightly aquiline, and her large mouth as full and guileless as that of a child. She was only sixteen and, though a daughter of the noble Helvius family, she was often busy in the kitchen or the barns.

For a moment her young face was contorted, and the physician bent over her solicitously. "It is nothing," she assured him impatiently. Then she flushed and looked embarrassed. "I fear the child is here."

The old father hastily left the room. The physician thrust his hand under the blankets. M. Tullius fainted. The physician cried, "The head!"

With no more effort than that, a boy was born on the third day of January to Marcus Tullius Cicero and his wife, Helvia. He was named Marcus Tullius Cicero also.

"THE CHILD HAS your noble father's expression, my lady," said Lira, four days later.

Helvia looked critically at the babe in Lira's arms, swaddled in white wool. She opened her bodice and put the child to her breast. "He is the mirror of my husband. He has a distinguished appearance." She considered the account books again. "Ten more linen sheets! We shall be bankrupt!"

Lira said obstinately, "Am I ever mistaken? A hero has been born. The Jews, lady, are expecting a hero. It is in their prophecies. And at Delphi, I have heard, the Oracle spoke of the Great One who is to appear. There have been portents. The priests murmur of it in the temples."

Helvia said, "He seems more like a lamb born before its time, or a little goatling without hair."

"There will be magnificent events in Rome when this is a man!" said Lira.

MANY YEARS LATER, the child, Marcus Tullius Cicero, wrote to a friend, "It was not that my mother, Lady Helvia, was avaricious as I have often heard it meanly remarked. She was simply thrifty, as were all the Helvii."

He often thought of the modest household near Arpinum where he had been born, for there lay his sweetest memories. After his naming, to avoid confusion, his father was addressed as Tullius; the grandfather roared that he himself had lost his name after the birth of his grandson. "I have heard the very slaves speak of me as 'the old father'!"

Helvia thought him unreasonable. She said to Tullius: "*My* father is of a better temper. My mother will permit no roaring in the household. Once she hurled a dish of sauced fish at my father's head when he became intemperate at the table."

"What did your father do?"

"He wiped the sauce and fish from his head with his napkin," said Helvia. "What else could he do?"

"He did not object?"

"My mother was larger and stronger," said Helvia. "*Your* mother did not assume authority when she married your father. It must be done at once, my mother told me. Later, a man is less tractable. I had a wise mother." But Helvia's staff of authority was tipped with serenity. Rarely was she disturbed and she performed all her duties to perfection. Her husband was grateful for a placid household in which he could retreat to his library and write poetry.

The family lived on a river island near Arpinum, but they were Roman citizens. The blackly glittering mountain stream Liris joined the small river Fibrenus to form their island. It lay about sixty miles from Rome, and the people there spoke of polyglot Rome disdainfully, for in Arpinum the spirit of Cincinnatus and the old Roman Republic still lived. In Arpinum, people remembered the days when a Roman was fearless and free, revered the gods and practiced the virtues of piety, charity, courage, patriotism and honor.

The Cicero family belonged to the middle class. None of them had held high office, and so none could ride in an ivory chair. But the old father boasted that the Ciceros belonged to the equestrian class—men who, by law, must be of good birth and reputation, with some property.

Little Marcus, though slender as his father and subject to fevers, walked alone at the age of eight months, and at two had mastered a formidable vocabulary, the result of his father's visits to the nursery. Tullius, even under the fierce eye of old Lira, had dandled the babe on his knee and taught him to speak in the accents of a learned man. Marcus would listen to his father gravely, his small face tight with concentration, his rare smile sweet and dazzling when Tullius made a little jest. He had Tullius' fine brown hair, gentle chin and sensitive mouth; but he also had his grandfather's resolute air and the calm steadfastness of his mother.

To Helvia, a household perfectionist, the child was a little lamb who needed strength, firm handling and no pampering.

THE SWEET AND spicy autumn lay on the island, and cool mists floated in the immense branches of the oak trees. The poplars were bright golden ghosts, fragile as a dream, and the waters ran wildly and darkly along the banks of the island, those cold and brilliant waters which Marcus was to remember all his life and whose mysterious colloquy was always in his ears.

Tullius stood on the riverbank and heard the laughter of little Marcus near at hand. He walked toward the sound and found old Lira sitting with her back against a tree, watching as Marcus tried to catch butterflies. Tullius paused to watch his firstborn with pleasure. The child was clad in a blue woolen tunic; little drops of sweat matted the fine hair into ringlets on his brow. Marcus ran to his father with glee.

"We were about to return to the house, master," Lira said grimly, and began to struggle to her feet.

Tullius put his hand on the child's damp curls as he said, "Leave my son with me for an hour longer."

She stumped off, glowering, and Tullius sat down on the warm grass, pulled his child into his lap and kissed him.

My son, Tullius thought, what will the world of men do to your spirit, which is now as a cup of clear water? Will they taint it? Or will you be stronger than your father, and surmount them with words like burning swords? Will you tell them that power without law is chaos, and that law does not come from men but from God?

The child raised his hand and touched Tullius' cheek, and Tullius felt a comforting, a promise. It is only my imagination, for he is still a babe, thought Tullius, yet his hand on my cheek is like a father's and not a child's.

Tullius lifted his eyes to the sky and prayed as the "old" Romans prayed, not for wealth for his child or for fame and glory, but that his son would be a man; strong in patriotism, pious, courageous, a protector of the weak, just, temperate and honorable. Tullius offered his child to God.

LITTLE QUINTUS, BROTHER of Marcus and four years his junior, was at birth much larger than Marcus, heartier and noisier. He had his mother's curling dark hair, her lusty coloring and her plumpness; and he had a stentorian voice. The robust child looked like a miniature soldier, and the old father, who was disappointed in the reserved and gentle-mannered Marcus, rejoiced in him. By the time Quintus was a year old the brothers were friends and companions. Quintus followed Marcus everywhere and doted on him.

Tullius thought it was time for Marcus to learn Greek, the language of gentlemen. So he journeyed to Antioch, and returned with a poet and scholar, Archias, to teach his son. Archias, who called Rome "the nation of grocers," as did all Greeks, was at first dismayed by the simplicity of the household, its crude statues and uninspired country meals. However, Marcus' perceptiveness and sweet nature had not been exaggerated by a fond father. The poet settled down on the island and conceived a lifelong attachment to his pupil.

Marcus soon learned Greek and spoke it as if it were his native language, and Archias was delighted. He was secretly an agnostic, but he wisely did not impair the boy's natural piety. In fact, it was Archias who taught the boy to pray to the Unknown God, for he found Him easier to believe in than the multitude of Grecian and Roman gods.

Archias had spent two years in Palestine. "Many Jews," he

told Marcus, "are expecting a Saviour, a Messiah. They expect this Saviour to make clear to them God's will with regard to mankind, so that never again can man go astray. They also believe that man's soul is immortal; but their God, Jehovah, is not beautiful and gay as are the Greek gods. He seems of a most unpleasant temper."

But Marcus thought of the Messiah of the Jews with excitement. "He is the Unknown God," he said.

At six, Marcus was writing poetry, but despite Archias' hopes he did not become a true lyric poet. However, he began to write marvelous prose, and would read what he had written in a powerful and eloquent voice that enchanted his teacher.

When Marcus was nine, his family decided to move to Rome, partly because of Tullius' health, partly to allow Marcus to study in a school with other boys as well as with Archias. Marcus was elated, but young Quintus said, "I am satisfied here. And Grandfather is sorry he is going to Rome, which is wicked and crowded and full of smells." Dropping the subject, the two boys raced out onto the warm summer grass.

Quintus threw a ball to his brother. "Catch!" he shouted.

"I am tired," said Marcus, and sat down on a stone.

Quintus had never been tired. He waited impatiently in front of Marcus on his sturdy brown legs, his yellow tunic blowing back on his thick thighs.

The boy was as handsome as Helvia with his curly black hair and square, highly colored little face. He could swim better and climb faster than his brother. Yet he considered his accomplishments as nothing before those of his adored Marcus. He looked at his brother now, his eyes brilliant, and said, "I shall be a general in Rome."

"Good. I shall be a lawyer. Perhaps someday a consul!"

Quintus did not know that the two elected consuls headed the Roman government, but he gazed at Marcus admiringly. "You shall be whatever you wish," he said. He scowled and held up a brown fist. "And let that man beware who stands in your way!"

Marcus laughed and tugged at his brother's curls with affection. Quintus began to climb the tree under which his brother sat. Twigs rained down on Marcus' head. Then, from the green leaves above, his brother called, "Catch me!" and Marcus obligingly but awkwardly began the ascent. Finally, stretching as high as he could, he seized Quintus' sandal and then his sturdy calf.

Then he slipped. Instantly Quintus reached down and seized his brother's hand. Marcus dangled from it like a swinging fruit. He looked below and clenched his teeth. "Do not be afraid, Marcus," Quintus said. "Grasp my hand tightly, and I will climb down until you can drop safely."

Marcus was too frightened to utter a sound. He felt himself being lowered, inch by inch, as the strong child above him descended, holding by one hand to the branches of the tree. When Marcus was close enough to the ground he dropped into the deep grass and rolled. Quintus fell on his knees beside him, full of anxiety.

Marcus sat up and laughed. "You are a Hercules, Quintus," he said. Many years later he remembered that day vividly, and he thought his heart would break with the remembrance.

"I had the happiest of childhoods," he would write later. "I had a father who was wise and good, a grandfather who taught me never to compromise with evil, and a steadfast mother, patient and calm. I had Archias, my dear teacher. And I had Quintus, my beloved brother."

The grandfather found a modestly priced but commodious house on the Carinae, the southwestern hip of the Esquiline Hill in Rome. It was of a modern style, Pompeian-red mortar with a white tile roof. The neighborhood was no longer fashionable, as prospering families were moving to the Palatine Hill.

While the grandfather haggled with the agents, Tullius wandered outside to gaze down upon the pulsing city. The sunset stood over it, murky and lurid. It was a most vehement city! Steep and narrow streets raced up and down the seven hills, surging with crowds of hurrying Romans, in a constant roar of clattering vehicles and shouted oaths and threats from their drivers. There was a smell of burning and the stench of sewers.

Tullius saw a child watching him from the lawn of the house next door. He appeared to be about Quintus' age.

"Greetings, master," the boy said in a high, piercing voice.

It was not polite for a child to address an adult first, but Tullius murmured, "Greetings." The child came nearer. He had a pointed, lively face, with dancing black eyes and black hair.

"Are you buying the house, master?" he asked.

More bad manners. "I do not know," said Tullius. "What is your name?"

"My name is Gaius Julius Caesar, and my father is named the same and my mother is Aurelia. I go to the school of Pilo. Do you have any little boys?"

"I have a little boy your age: Quintus Tullius Cicero. My older son, Marcus, is nine."

Julius laughed raucously. "Cicero! You are named *Chick-pea!* It is a plebian name. My name is very old and noble. And your Marcus is not too old for me, though I am but five. My best friend is eleven. His name is Catiline, and he is also a patrician."

It was foolish to feel stung at the words of a child, but Tullius said, "We are not plebs," with annoyance. The child whistled derisively as Tullius went back into the house.

MARCUS WENT TO the school of Pilo, a Greek freedman, and was also tutored, with Quintus, by Archias. Little Julius Caesar invaded the Cicero house freely. Helvia slapped him as readily as she did Quintus, and Julius would only laugh. The grandfather found cronies in the city, and would drive his carriage to the Forum to exchange stories of old campaigns. But Tullius longed for the island.

Marcus, too, longed for Arpinum, though he also loved Rome for its life and bustle, for the temples, the lofty pillars bearing the statues of heroes or deities, the mighty steps rising from street to upper street, the government buildings, the circuses, the clangor of traffic, the vociferous, roaring voice of power. He was a Roman, living in Rome. He waked with excitement to each new day.

But he did not like his school. Pilo had a slavish respect for the boys of noble family. To those of plebeian origin he was condescending.

Though he came from the country, Marcus was advanced beyond his age. Placed with older boys, he came to hate that great friend of Julius Caesar, Lucius Sergius Catiline. Lucius was an extremely handsome boy, and a natural leader. He carried himself as if aware of his beauty and charm. But Marcus sensed that Lucius was corrupt, while all that Marcus was—generous, patient, kind—aroused Lucius' enmity and contempt.

At first Marcus could not believe that the eleven-year-old Catiline could really be a close friend of the five-year-old Caesar. But Julius adored Lucius, and Lucius was his protector in spite of his frequent blows. Julius laughed the loudest when Lucius baited Marcus, calling him "the bumpkin," because he knew no gossip, no lewd stories, and did not laugh at the pain of others. As a man, Lucius was to say to Marcus, "I hated you, Chick-pea, the moment I saw you."

Soon all the boys made Marcus the target of their jokes. There must be something wrong with me, he told himself. He had always had the assurance of a dearly loved child. Now this became less certain.

Marcus was to write, "It is wrong to bring children up in an atmosphere solely of family affection, without enlightening them that beyond the safe walls of home there lives a world of godless, dishonorable men. For when an innocent youth encounters the world of men, he suffers a wound from which he will never recover."

He and Julius walked to school together. When away from his idol Julius was good company and a great wit, much older than his years. Already he was ambitious and shrewd, gaily exploiting his fellows, and most particularly Marcus. He always wanted to be foremost, but there was much that was good in him—humor, and sudden surges of generosity. He liked Marcus, who could always be coaxed out of a few pennies at recess when the vendor came to the school with sweetmeats and small pastries.

One day Catiline saw Marcus putting a pastry into Caesar's hands. "Why, Julius," he said, "are you so stricken by poverty that you receive gifts from an inferior?"

Catiline had as little money as Julius did. "What is an inferior?" Julius said impudently. "One who has no money."

Lucius' eyes flashed dangerously. He struck Julius' hand so that the pastry fell to the street, and then hit Julius' face viciously. Julius kicked Lucius in the shin and the other boys gathered around, amazed, for no one had ever objected to Lucius' cruelty before. Now he threw Julius on the pavement and kicked him. Julius howled, and Lucius, laughing, lifted his foot again.

Marcus could feel all the weeks of pain and humiliation gather into a knot of loathing in his chest. "Stop!" he said, his face pale. He put himself between Lucius and his victim.

Lucius stepped back with astonishment, for he was older and heavier than Marcus, and an expert boxer. "You dare to defy me?" he said, and struck a foul blow. Marcus bent over in anguish and Lucius was on him in a flash. Forgetting honorable fighting in his pain and hatred, Marcus brought up his knee in Lucius' groin. Lucius staggered and Marcus kicked him with all his strength. Lucius collapsed on the ground.

The boys shouted, "Foul!"

"You did not think it foul when he attacked *me* foully!" Marcus cried. Pilo, hearing the commotion, hurried outside and dragged Marcus into the school while the other boys followed.

"Lucius kicked me foully," cried Caesar pathetically. "And then he hit Marcus and Marcus protected himself."

"Is that the truth?" Pilo asked the other boys.

Catiline spoke. "No, it is a lie."

The boys could not look at each other. Their faces reddened. They loved the popular Lucius, who loved no one. Pilo understood instantly, but he too loved Lucius, and if he punished Marcus there would be no reprisals, for Marcus was no tale-bearer. So he thrashed Marcus severely before the class, and the boy took the lashing in silence. When Marcus returned to his bench the boys could not raise their eyes to his face.

That night Julius told his mother, Aurelia, and the stout little lady went at once to Helvia in outrage. Helvia sent for Marcus. "Remove your tunic," she said. Marcus did so, and Helvia inspected the welts on his young body. She said, "You will not return to that school."

"Mother," Marcus pleaded, "that would be shameful. The boys would laugh at me for a coward."

Aurelia nodded with approval. "He speaks as a Roman," she said. "You can be proud of him."

"I was always proud of him," said Helvia, to Marcus' surprise. She smiled at her son.

Aurelia fished at a golden chain about her short, rosy neck and pulled up a medal of Pallas Athena. "The goddess of wisdom and law," she said. "You are worthy of it, Marcus." She put it in his hand.

"I am proud," Helvia repeated. She kissed his cheek.

Marcus wore Aurelia's gift all his life. Years later he showed it to Julius under very special circumstances.

Meantime, the enmity between Cicero and Catiline grew prodigiously, and Marcus' life at school became even more miserable with the entrance of Cneius Piso and Quintus Curius, who became Lucius' devoted friends, joining him in his contempt for Cicero.

Piso was a patrician, a haughty, fearless boy with fair hair, gray eyes and deceptively girlish mannerisms. Curius was a tall, sullen, dark-faced youth, an intellectual and the heir of his rich grandfather.

Julius, now almost nine, laughed at them. "Curius has a beautiful cousin named Livia," he said to Marcus. "Lucius wishes to marry her." Fortunately, Curius' father decided to have all three boys privately tutored. Marcus was overwhelmingly relieved: I will never encounter them again, he thought. When he heard, later, that they had gone to study in Greece, Rome seemed cleaner for their absence.

The year after Catiline and his companions left the school, a new student appeared, a pleasant-looking, alert boy of fifteen, Noë ben Joel, the son of a rich Jewish banker. He became a general favorite, for he was affable and, though he could mimic anyone, his jests were never cruel or vindictive. He was also a formidable scholar.

"Why so grave?" he asked one day, coming on Marcus alone in the schoolroom. He had a basket in his hand and lifted the white napkin that covered it. "Hamantaschen," he said. "Have one. Have two!" Marcus took one of the pastries filled with sugared fruit, and they talked of a play Noë was directing, one of Aristophanes'. Marcus had declined a part in the play.

"I would feel foolish," he explained.

"But you are going to study law," Noë said. "How will you face the courts if you are afraid to stand up and speak? A successful lawyer is always an actor. You have, in fact, the bearing of an actor. It is not that you are flamboyant, but your voice and eyes are very compelling, and you speak with authority and eloquence."

"I?" said Marcus, amazed.

"You." Noë nodded. "I myself will produce and write plays, even though my father beats his breast and threatens to take me back to Judea where I must grow a beard and marry a fat Jewish girl and have ten sons, all rabbis. I am no mean actor, but a sincere actor, like you, my grave Marcus, is beyond rubies. You do not appreciate yourself. Does your father beat you very much?"

"My father? He is the sweetest of men." Then he told Noë about his family. "And I have a brother, Quintus," he ended, his eyes passionate with love.

Noë was touched. "I see we have no Cain and Abel here." And he told him of Adam and Eve and their sons.

Marcus said, "Noë, tell me of your Messiah."

"There are now portents of His coming. He will deliver Israel from her sins, so say the rabbis, and be a light unto the Gentiles. And he will give Israel rule of the earth, including Rome and all her legions."

"So small a country?" said Marcus, feeling a Roman's incredulous surprise.

"A pearl, however small, is more valuable than a handful of the most polished glass," said Noë, feeling a Jew's pride.

MARCUS ANNOUNCED THAT when he was invested with the toga of manhood he wished to take the Greek goddess Pallas Athena, whose amulet he wore, rather than the Roman Minerva as his patroness. The grandfather roared his horror, but Helvia said, "He is fifteen years old, no longer a child, and must make his own decisions."

The investment would take place the next spring. Lists were made of guests to be invited, and Helvia chose the flax from which to weave the robe, which, since Tullius was a knight, would be of white with a purple strip. March 17 was the day on which all youths of approximately Marcus' age assumed the toga, so it was a national festival. Priestesses of Bacchus would offer white-honey cakes to the god on their behalf, hundreds of cattle would be sacrificed, and a long procession would accompany them to the Forum. There they would be ceremoniously presented to their countrymen, and henceforth would be citizens of Rome. They would then return to their homes for a feast, during which even the boys themselves were permitted to become drunk. Knowing his mother's frugality, Marcus doubted that *anyone* would be drunk at his own feast.

CHAPTER TWO

THE FAMILY WENT to the island for the summer. Here, among the sacred oaks and poplars, Marcus began to write his first true poetry, though he despaired of ever being able to put into words the color of the sky and waters, the intricate green of leaves, the fragrance of grass and flowers. There were large thoughts moving in his head, and he spoke of them to Archias one warm and golden day as they wandered beside the river.

Archias said, "May I give you some advice which will serve you well all your life? Man is a creature of reason. Beware, Marcus, of the excitable man, for he has lost his reason! The truly civilized man is immune to fashions in thought, and to emotional storms. Be reverent before the wisdom and traditions painfully garnered through the centuries."

He picked up a leafy twig and held it out delicately on the cushion of his thumb. "Balance," he said. "It is the law of nature. Let that man beware who disturbs it."

Later, the grandfather sought Marcus out. "It is time," he said, "for me to put into brief words the things a young man must know."

Marcus privately doubted the brevity of the grandfather's words, but he courteously put his cloak on the grass for the old man. The grandfather shook his head with a mention of rheumatism, and leaned on the staff which he recently affected, stroking his beard. He studied Marcus' grave face with pride, but he kept his face stern. One should never let the young know of one's approval.

"A man owes it to his manhood," he said at last, "to be prudent, honorable, frugal and courageous. The coward is more to be feared than the evil man. Beware of the mendicant, the dependent. They destroy empires. They will," said the grandfather with bitter sorrow, "eventually destroy Rome, as they destroyed other nations."

"Yes," said Marcus soberly.

"In our history," the grandfather said, "there have been times of danger when we needed swift action, unfettered by law. So we appointed dictators. But we removed temptation by denying them honor and luxuries, and as soon as they had done what they must, we removed their power. The day of the dictator is almost upon us again—this time the dictator of prolonged, illimitable power. My grandson, it is your duty to hold back these evil men. Remember, it once took only two heroic men, with Horatius, to stand on a bridge and save Rome. Swear by our gods and by the name of Rome that no one shall reach her heart and halt it."

Marcus lifted his hand, praying that he would have courage, and swore solemnly. He would never forget his grandfather's words.

That night Marcus sat with his father, Tullius, in his pleasant, lamplit library, with the rolls of parchment and vellum about them. Marcus looked unhappily at his father's haggard face. He said, "You seem sick, my father."

Tullius replied, "It is only my usual malaria, Marcus. Do you think me dying? Not yet!"

But his voice was weary. In what words could a man tell his son that he was tired of living? It would be a lie, thought Tullius, to say that my life has been burdensome and now I wish for my rest. I have spent a serene life and have known no heartbreak. Why am I tired of living?

Suddenly he thought: I am weary for God! I long for my true home! The thought flooded him not with melancholy but with exultant joy. His drawn face filled with radiance, and seeing this Marcus was afraid. It was as if his father had withdrawn from him to a place he could not follow.

Then Tullius lifted his goblet and saluted his son with the sweetest of smiles. "To you, Marcus; may God be with you always."

In a voice now youthful and eager he went on, "Marcus, you will have duties in this world, but your first duty is to God. To a good man, happiness in this world is of no importance, for this is not our home. A good man can find happiness only when he joins God forever, after death."

Marcus placed his hand on his father's bony knee. Tullius laid his fingers over it.

"Once Rome was strong with faith, patriotism and justice—God, country and law. Now we have a republic. Aristotle said: 'Republics decline into democracies, and democracies degenerate into despotisms.' When you discover a man who seeks power, expose him, Marcus. If a man seeks office because he wishes to enslave the people with promises of luxuries they have not earned, expose him. And never forget that without God man is nothing."

Tullius was suddenly exhausted. He closed his eyes, and prayed for his son.

THE NEXT MORNING Helvia dismissed her maids and said to Marcus, "Sit down. I must talk with you." Though Helvia was only thirty-two, she had grown plumper. Her massive breast pushed against her yellow stola, and her waist was thick. She looks like Ceres, thought Marcus—the mother of the earth.

"Your grandfather and your father and your tutor have talked with you," she said. "Now you must have a woman's wisdom. Men have dreams; women live in reality. What would my men do if I left my kitchen and sat at their feet? Their plates would be empty. In spite of their dreams, men are tremendous eaters."

Marcus laughed, and Helvia laughed with him, comfortably.

"Your grandfather is all patriotism and your father thinks only of God, but if a dish is undercooked they both reject it with distress. What patience women must have with these child-like creatures! Yet a woman cannot step into a man's shoes without throwing life into upheaval." Helvia continued, reaching for a length of linen and beginning to apply her busy needle. "If she has no household arts, she is no comforter to her husband. If she neglects her children for games, politics, sports or the marketplace, her children reflect her disorder."

"But you, Mother, are interested in business and investments," said Marcus.

"So I am. But only to invest prudently, unlike fanciful men. My son, a word of advice to you now. Remember that a man is known by his control of his appetites and his devotion to family. He does not lose his temper easily. He rejects all things which reflect badly on his country, his gods or his family. Above all, he does his duty."

Years later Marcus wrote, "I received different advice from my tutor, my grandfather, my father and my mother. Yet in essentials they did not disagree, but like the four petals of the wild rose made a perfect flower. Blessed is that man who had a wise tutor, a stern grandfather, a spiritual and tender father and a prudent mother!"

THE SEASON WAS early autumn, and it was near sunset when Marcus noticed on the bridge leading to the mainland from the island the figure of a maiden. A slave from the household? A wanderer from Arpinum? He sauntered toward the girl.

She was leaning on the stone ledge, and turned to look at him idly, as if he were the intruder.

"Greetings," said Marcus, setting foot on the bridge.

"Greetings," she responded in a soft clear voice. She looked at the river, then at the island. "It is beautiful here," she said, and smiled. She was tall and graceful, with an air of assurance and dignity, and near his own age. He thought he had never seen a girl so lovely. Her long auburn hair seemed to catch fire around her face. She had eyes of deep blue, and her mouth was as full and fresh as raspberries.

"I am Marcus Tullius Cicero," he said, staring openly.

She smiled. "I am Livia Curius. I am visiting friends in the town of Arpinum. This is your island, is it not?"

"It is my grandfather's."

Then Marcus remembered Quintus Curius, the formidable dark youth who was Catiline's friend. "Is Quintus Curius your cousin, Lady Livia?" he asked.

"A distant one," she said. "I am betrothed to Lucius Sergius Catiline. I believe you were schoolmates."

He thought: Betrothed! He said, "Lucius and I are enemies. You must know that, Lady Livia."

"Yes, I know. As I also know that Lucius is a liar—but a delightful liar. And as I also know that he is marrying me because I am an heiress. Let us talk of pleasanter things."

Aware of his rudeness, yet with an undeniable urgency, he asked, "Why are you marrying Lucius? You say he is a liar."

"But a *delightful* liar." She was laughing. "And is he not marvelous in appearance? Moreover, my guardians have ar-

ranged the marriage, and what have I to say? I exchange money for a great name."

A sensation of calamity came to Marcus. He wanted to seize the girl's arm and shake her and tell her she must not marry Lucius. But she was gazing at him with coolness, as if affronted. Then, suddenly, dimples flashed about her mouth.

"Show me your island," she cried, and raced down the bridge. She stood on the bank as he followed, and then, laughing, ran like a wood nymph. Marcus followed her into the forest. She was nowhere in sight. Had he dreamed her? He looked about him through the dim aisles of poplars and oaks and cypresses.

"Livia?" he called. There was no answer. "Livia?"

He looked up and saw her perched on a high branch of a tree laughing down at him, her green dress vivid, her palla like mist floating about her. She called gleefully, "Catch me!"

Marcus was up on the first branch before he realized it. The girl bounded higher, revealing smooth young calves and thighs, and seeming to climb without effort. Soon she was at the top of the tree, swinging lightly. She looked out at some distant scene and began to sing in a soft voice. Marcus gazed up at her, full of wonder. Never had he met such a strange and delightful creature, full of fantasy, clothed in secrets. Her palla lifted and blew in the wind, her hair was a glow of fire, and Marcus, for an instant, was conscious of an aloneness that separated him from her.

"It is dangerous up there," he said. "Shall I help you down?"

Without effort she came down through the branches, balancing gracefully, as lightly as a falling leaf. She passed him, then stood as if waiting, and Marcus, following, wondered if she waited for him or for some call beyond his ears.

He stood beside her. They did not speak, but a sense of peace and fulfillment came to Marcus. He took her hand. Finally he asked, "What were you singing? It was like the sound of the wind, or a fountain at night."

"It is my own song. They say I am a very peculiar girl."

"Then I am peculiar also," said Marcus.

The girl smiled at him. "Yes," she said. "Were you not, I would not be with you now." Her young breast lifted. "I have never told anyone why I sing my song. My dear mother had a mortal disease. While she was dying my father plunged his dagger into his breast and died with her. They thought I did not see them, but I stood in the doorway in the moonlight. I was five years old then. When my father was dying he held my mother in his arms, and they died with their lips together. My father said, 'Where you go, my beloved, there will I go also.' I sing my song to them in the Elysian Fields. My mother was only twenty and my father a year older. I do not grieve for them, for not even the gods could part them."

She pulled her hand away and raced back to the bridge.

"Will you come again, Livia?" he called, but she did not answer. He was left alone in the forest, to wonder again if the brief and baffling encounter had occurred at all.

At dinner that evening he was unusually silent. He thought about the girl's betrothal to Catiline. A marriage between a dryad and a wolf! He put down his knife and stared at his plate.

"What is it, Marcus?" asked Tullius.

But Marcus could not speak. There are times, he thought, when there is no communication, even among those who love.

Quintus said, "Marcus is in love." And he grinned delightedly at his brother.

"Nonsense," said the grandfather. "He knows no girls."

I am in love with Livia, thought Marcus, and suddenly he was taken by ecstasy and then by desolation and a sense of loss.

CHAPTER THREE

THE LONG-ABUSED provinces were now in rebellion because of the discrimination Rome practiced against them, and the family wondered if they might be safer in the city. Marcus half listened to the agitated discussions in the family circle, while each day he haunted the bridge and the forest paths where he had seen Livia. He began to think that he had dreamed her.

Where does fantasy end and reality begin? he would ask himself. He could believe in wood nymphs and apparitions very easily. There were intellectual men, like his tutor Archias, who scoffed at omens and portents, yet admitted there was a vast area beyond the sight and ear of man. He longed for Livia, fantasy or no fantasy: it was useless to tell himself that it was impossible to love an elusive girl, a weird, laughing, indifferent girl he had seen but once.

Then one day he came upon her. She sat under a tree, singing softly to herself—blue-eyed Livia in a white dress with a mantle of blue wool over her shoulders and a blue silk cloth rippling over her hair. He looked at her and it seemed that all creation rushed to this spot and held its breath, waiting.

"I have been here every day but you never found me," she said. "What were you looking for as you dreamed and walked?"

"You," he said. "Why did you not speak?" He sat on his heels and looked at her, afraid that she would disappear.

"I do not speak to men who ignore me," she said. Then she laughed. "I was in the trees, and watched you from above. I was behind a trunk, and you passed me. But you did not find me!"

She was not a girl like the others he had seen in the women's quarters or on the street. He had been stirred by them, but it had been a passing emotion which had embarrassed him later. He looked at Livia with the most urgent longing and passionate love, without embarrassment, forgetting everything else.

"You came, but hid from me," he said, enchanted. "Why?"

Her mood changed and she was serious. She let leaves slide through her fingers. "I do not know," she answered. "Who are you? You are not rich or noble. You are, as my cousin has said, of no consequence." She gazed at him candidly. "Then why have I come here all these days to see you even if you did not see me? I do not know. Why did I tell you about my parents? I never speak of them to anyone. Why do I think of you when I awake, a youth I spoke to but once? Tell me, Marcus Tullius Cicero."

"You have seen me searching for you. Why did I search?"

She considered. "It is because you speak like me, and think like me. When I am with you I am not conscious that you are another being. This is what my parents must have known."

She held out her hand to him, and he fell on his knees. A scarlet oak leaf drifted down and settled on the girl's left breast and lay there on the whiteness of her clothing like a splash of blood. Marcus was a Roman, and Romans are superstitious. He stiffened. The leaf resembled a bleeding wound.

"What is it, Marcus?" asked Livia.

He took the leaf, and she watched, bewildered by his pallor as he flung it from him. "It was only a leaf," he said. He clasped the girl's hands firmly; he could hear his heart in his ears.

The girl said, "Has a god whispered to you?" and suddenly she pulled her hands from his, jumped to her feet and ran through the forest. He followed her. She waited on the bridge, leaning over the parapet and watching the green water.

"Listen to the rivers sing," she said as he joined her. "They are singing of the mountains, of nymphs and satyrs and Pan." She began to sing with the rivers a strange murmurous song.

"You must not marry Lucius Catiline," he said. "He is evil. He will cause you suffering. That I could not bear, Livia, because I love you."

She shook her head. "I have been betrothed to him since I was ten years old. Now I am fourteen, of an age to marry. You are not yet a man. You must not speak of this again."

Marcus was desperate. "But you declared that we felt for each other what your parents felt!"

Her face clouded. "What has that to do with marriage? My mother was betrothed to another when, against the wishes of her parents, she married my father. She offended the gods, and she died. I dare not invoke the wrath of the gods, Marcus."

"You will invoke calamity." Marcus gripped her arm. "I have premonitions."

The girl made the sign against the evil eye. She said, "You frighten me." She pulled from his hand and ran down the bridge to the mainland, her clothing whirling in the wind.

Foreboding sickened him as he thought of Catiline. He returned to the island and walked miserably along the bank. Whom could he consult? Then he thought of his mother. She knew the great families of Rome.

He found her among her slave girls, spinning wool for winter blankets. She saw his face, dismissed the girls kindly, then remarked, "You are troubled. What is it, my son?"

He sat near her. "Do you know the Curius family, Mother?"

"Not closely. What have they to do with you, Marcus?"

He told her of Livia, while her spinning wheel hummed. She frowned slightly at the mention of Catiline, and when he had finished she dropped her hands in her lap and fixed her beautiful eyes on him.

"You will not be a man until spring," she said, "yet you are in love. I speak no ridicule. I saw your father in my father's house when I was no older than your Livia. I fell in love at once. He seemed a young Hermes to me."

"Hermes? *My father?*" said Marcus.

"I, too, was young," she said, smiling. "And I was free. But your Livia is betrothed. Troth is not pledged lightly in Rome."

"But she does not know Lucius," Marcus said wretchedly.

"Women know more than you think. In any case, that girl is not for you, Marcus. Because of her mother's tragedy, she is afraid to love. She does not love Lucius—and therefore she prefers him to you. If she married you, she would live in terror of your death. Besides, children inherit their parents' passions. There is violence in your Livia, a recklessness which was her father's. No, Marcus, she is not for my son."

"I love her," he said. "I shall die if she marries Lucius."

"What nonsense." Helvia began to spin again. "Men do not die for love. Your Livia will become a matron, but to you she will remain forever young, unconquered, beautiful. The gods grant that you never encounter her later, surrounded by children and gossiping with her friends!"

Each of her sensible words was a stone falling on Marcus' heart. "I shall never forget Livia," he said.

"Do not forget her, then. But there is more to a man's life than the love of women. Marcus, you must become a man." She recalled the slave girls, and Marcus left the women's quarters in anguish.

Livia never came to the island again. In the meantime, the situation in the provinces grew even worse and the family— since, unlike most in Arpinum, they were Roman citizens— returned to Rome.

YEARS BEFORE MARCUS was born, the desperate people of the provinces of Italy had tried repeatedly to redress their wrongs under Rome. They could not vote, yet they were taxed more than Roman citizens. A Roman consul could plunder them at will. Without Roman citizenship, they were like dogs at the disposal of their masters.

But the sturdy rise of the middle class in the provinces had aroused the fear of the Roman leaders, for, if they were once possessed of the vote, they could control taxation, force the aristocrats to practice the ancient virtues of Rome, and compel the idle Roman mobs to work or go hungry. When the Senate disapproved a bill enfranchising Italians outside Rome, the Social War broke out. Some of the provinces formed a confederacy to secede from Rome, march on the capital, and form a new nation. A new state, Italica, was set up, and the ancient laws of the Republic were revived. Roman fortresses were seized and new banners lifted. An air of joy and freedom blew over Italy.

"GOVERNMENTS USE NATIONAL emergencies to destroy liberty," said the grandfather. "We now have new taxes which will never be lifted, for once government imposes a tax it finds excuses to retain it forever. And the mobs of Rome—do they care for freedom? They do not know the meaning of this war. Politicians and greedy mobs—this has been the history of all doomed republics."

Rome was full of riot and disorder, for the war rang close beyond her walls. There was little social life, and Marcus was driven in upon himself. He wrote poetry, and thought of Livia Curius. When he could make his way among the seething mobs of Romans and refugees, he went to the Temple of Venus. He sacrificed doves, and prayed at the altar of the deity of lovers. The clangorous city about him, the banners, the hurrying legions carrying their eagles and their fasces, the galloping of couriers' horses, the air of haste and disaster, all became dreamlike to Marcus in his pain. "He needs a tonic," said Helvia, and she brewed herbs and administered them to her son. Even Quintus, his beloved brother, could no longer amuse him. Quintus had joined Marcus at Pilo's school, and had become something of a leader because of his amiability, his self-assurance and his excellence in sports. He brought home gossip about the Caesars—they had moved to the Palatine Hill, and Julius' father was a high official, a praetor, of the senatorial party.

"Julius comes to fencing school, at another hour than yours," Quintus said to Marcus as they walked home one day. "He is still a boaster. All that relates to Julius is noble—too awesome for a common mind to appreciate. He is a bad fencer, but few can approach him in words. His voice is like honey."

The dull February day was darkening, and torches, lanterns and tapers were scurrying up and down the steep and narrow streets. Suddenly Quintus caught Marcus' arm and pulled him into a doorway, for a detachment of soldiers were marching up the hill, ironshod sandals clanging on the stones, drums beating, banners flying. Their faces fixed and unseeing, they rushed by the two youths in the doorway with a sound like thunder. Quintus' eyes sparkled in the flare of the torches. "I wish I were old enough to be a soldier," he said.

"I am glad you're not old enough to murder Italians."

"It is for the preservation of Rome," said Quintus.

"It is for the advancement of despotism," said Marcus.

They went on in silence. Then Quintus touched his brother on his arm. "Do you know that you sadden the house? Father has not risen from his bed for days, yet you have not visited him."

"Days?" And I did not miss him, thought Marcus sorrowfully.

"He has been bled several times," said Quintus. "And you barely touch your plate at dinner. You distress our mother."

Marcus was ashamed. He could not overcome his pain, but he could endure it decently. That night, as he ate his frugal dinner with his grandfather and his brother, he forced himself to notice things. His mother and two slave girls ministered as usual to the men at the table, but Marcus saw that there were lines between Helvia's remarkable eyes. He noticed, too, that the overseer, always stationed in the hall, had disappeared. When had that happened? Also, there was one oil lamp on the table instead of two. I have seen nothing, he thought, for I have seen only Livia, and neglected those dear to me. "How is my father tonight?" he asked his grandfather.

"He is not improved from yesterday." The grandfather added sardonically, "But you do not know how he fared yesterday."

Marcus colored. "I have been engrossed. I beg forgiveness."

Helvia took compassion on her son. "We must be more frugal," she said to Marcus. "The value of our investments has declined. Had it not been for war we would have prospered, but only those concerned with military supplies are making fortunes these days. I fear you will not study in Greece, my Marcus."

"I will be a general," said Quintus. "Then I will be rich."

Helvia smiled fondly at her favorite. The grandfather rose after a brief invocation of the gods and left the room, and Marcus followed him. He went first to his own *cubiculum*. Hating himself, he knelt beside his narrow bed and prayed for his family. But he prayed without fervor. He beat his head on his bed and muttered aloud in agony, "If only I could forget Livia! Am I a child, that I cannot control my emotions?" Tears fell on his clasped hands. Finally he rose and went to his father.

Tullius had had his meager supper, and lay exhausted. A smoky lamp burned on the wall; a chest of small belongings stood against another wall, and there was a chair. He turned his head feebly as Marcus entered, and smiled with radiant sweetness. "My son!" he said, like one who greets a returning traveler.

When Marcus inquired about his health, his father said, "It is my malaria. Do not fear. I shall not die. I shall see you with these eyes when you are a great man, with your wife beside you, and your children."

Marcus looked into those fever-stricken eyes and saw the powerful spirit in them. His misery lifted. His father would live. He talked to him of his school and of his future, and then Tullius fell suddenly into sleep.

Marcus blew out the lamp, drew the coverlet over the thin breast and went back to his chamber, but could not sleep. He lay listening to the sleepless roar of the mighty city. He thought of her vast subject territories, her millions of subjects, her tremendous power. As she now struggled with her own people, Roman banners on distant fortresses were being eyed with speculation. If Rome was divided the jackals would move upon her, though she had been the most benign ruler in history, though she had brought peace, the *Pax Romana*, to a world simmering with war.

Suddenly Marcus heard a hoarse groaning, and then a faint and strangled cry. His first thought was of his father, but when he reached Tullius' *cubiculum* he heard no sound from within. He ran on down the narrow hall to his grandfather's room, threw aside the curtain and entered. It was dark, and Marcus hurried back for a lamp and held it high over his grandfather. The old man was sitting up in bed, his eyes rolling wildly.

"I am dying," he said in the faintest of voices.

"No!" said Marcus, in terror. He shouted for Phelon, the physician, who slept nearby.

THE CYPRESS OF mourning stood at the door of the house of the Ciceros.

"You are only sixteen, Marcus," said Helvia. "Nevertheless, you are now the man of the family."

His grandfather had died in his arms, and it was only then that Marcus had realized how the old man had stood in the family like a great oak among saplings. Now the oak had been felled, and the ritual of death had to be observed: sacrifices made, prayers said, money distributed to the poor, offerings made for the prayers of the vestal virgins. There were visitors to be greeted, condolences to be endured, the grandfather's will to be read; and his ashes to be preserved and, someday, taken to Arpinum.

Marcus felt some bitterness against his father. Tullius had wept like a child and hidden his head under his coverlets. When Marcus visited him in his *cubiculum* now, Tullius only extended a thin trembling hand for help, for reassurance. It was some time before the distraught youth could bring himself to touch that hand, which should now be the firm rudder of the family and not the hand of a child.

Helvia did not advise her son. She was an "old" Roman. The sooner a youth became a man the better. She laid her books before him and referred him to the lawyers and the bankers. Noë's father, Joel ben Solomon, was one of them. Marcus felt weak and vulnerable at first, but soon his wings grew strong. "We must live sparely," he told Helvia.

Quintus left school to study with Archias, who insisted upon remaining without pay. Marcus himself would start his law studies in a few weeks. One day Helvia said, "Marcus, we must arrange for your betrothal. I have a girl in mind—Terentia. She will bring you an excellent dowry. She is twelve, so the marriage can take place in two years."

Memory flamed into fire. "No!" cried Marcus.

"Why so vehement? Is it possible you are still thinking of

Livia? Aurelia Caesar says her marriage to Lucius Catiline is to take place this summer."

Marcus felt sick. "It does not matter," he said at last, in a low voice. "I shall never forget her, nor marry anyone else."

Helvia shrugged. "We shall see," she said. "Meantime, I have arranged for you to study law with Scaevola, the augur and pontifex maximus. To study with so high an official is a privilege you owe to my father, who is his friend."

Helvia drew from her secret account to provide the proper ceremonies when Marcus assumed the toga of manhood. Marcus pretended interest in the ceremonies. The toga lay on his shoulders like iron.

CHAPTER FOUR

YEARS LATER MARCUS wrote of the Caesar family: "They loved no one but themselves, and at no time did they forget their own advantage. By this magic they convinced everyone that the Caesars were uncommon, and deserving of honor."

Aurelia, Helvia's friend, invariably brought the young Julius Caesar with her when visiting the Ciceros. Marcus found Julius, now twelve years old, irritating but amusing. There was no rumor in the city that the boy did not know—or invent. So when Julius spoke of Livia's approaching marriage to Catiline, and then mentioned Catiline's prowess with complaisant ladies of Roman society, Marcus discounted the tales. Was not Livia enough for any man?

Julius said, "Livia is virtuous as well as beautiful. But she is very strange. He is strange himself. They share the same blood. I believe they are third cousins."

Marcus remembered, now, the extraordinary blue of Lucius' eyes, like Livia's. But he said to himself, It is only the color and the shape. There is nothing of the Catilines in Livia.

The wedding was in less than four weeks, and now Marcus' agony returned.

Early summer heat had come upon the city. Sunlight glittered from the soldiers' armor and helmets, and chariots stood motionless, wheel to wheel, while drivers cursed the traffic. One day, as Marcus moved slowly through the litters, chariots, horses and people, he saw the cool dark entrance to the Temple of Venus. It was a refuge from the heat and crowds, and he darted within. The coolness and the scent of incense were delightful. He looked at the goddess on her altar, and her great calm beauty assuaged his wretchedness. Candles burned before her like stars.

Many girls, approaching marriage or in love, stood before Venus, offering up their prayers. Doves fluttered in their hands. Their chaperons stood beside them, severe in their mantles.

Suddenly Marcus froze like a statue. He saw Livia. The candlelight flickered on her pale cheek and exquisite profile; she held the sacrificial doves close to her breast. Behind her stood an elderly lady, soberly but richly clad.

Marcus began to breathe quickly. Joy burst over him; promise and hope bloomed again.

The priests moved among the worshipers with baskets in which they gathered the doves. A faint sound of lutes filled the temple, and the softest of singing. The girls and women prepared to leave. Marcus, shaking as if with fever, moved to the portico and waited until Livia and her guardian appeared. The girl's face was aloof.

"Livia," said Marcus. She started and glanced up. Her lips trembled, her blue eyes brightened. He said urgently, "Livia?" He stretched out his hand and touched hers. She shivered, then stood mute.

"Who is this impudent person?" asked the older woman. Her eyes swept over Marcus' modest toga.

"He is my friend," said Livia.

"Eh?" the guardian said in her parrot voice.

"My aunt is deaf," Livia said to Marcus. She put her lips to her aunt's ear. "Marcus Tullius Cicero!"

"I know no Cicero!" shouted the aunt.

Livia said to Marcus, "I am sorry that your grandfather died. I am sorry—" She drew a quick breath, and her blue eyes were full of pain. "Marcus, we must go."

"Livia," he pleaded.

"What do you wish of me?" the girl cried despairingly.

"I cannot forget you. I live only by the thought of you," said Marcus.

The aunt was tugging at Livia's arm, her old eyes fixed angrily on the interloper.

"Forget me, Marcus," Livia said.

"That is beyond me. Livia, tell me that you think of me. I come here often to pray that Venus will have mercy on us."

"I pray that I will love Lucius," said Livia sternly. "I beg of you, Marcus, depart from me." She gathered her filmy cloak about her, turned to her aunt and took her arm. They passed Marcus and did not glance back.

He leaned his forehead against a pillar and wept. If only I were rich and powerful, he thought in his agony. If only I had a great name! But I am nothing, nothing.

MARCUS' MENTOR, SCAEVOLA, had an enormous round bald head, no discernible neck, three vast chins, a huge belly and short legs. He had a small, intellectual, satyr's face and a voice like a bull, and an intense zest for life. His minute blue eyes overlooked nothing. He accepted the evil in man with good humor. He thought sincere men fools; those who believed man capable of virtue even greater fools. To him law was a game even more exciting than his beloved dice.

Once he said to Marcus, "You quote your grandfather copiously. He must have been a remarkably innocent as well as a good man. You have been with me in the courts. Did you believe my clients innocent? One in a thousand! Tell me, why do you want to be a lawyer, anyway?"

"Because I believe in our Twelve Tables of Law. I believe that all men have a right to be represented before their accusers. You said yourself, master, that one in a thousand clients is innocent. Is it not enough that one man escapes injustice?"

The old man belched loudly and scratched himself. "You will have no clients if you take only those you believe are innocent!" He shook a thick finger in Marcus' face. "You are wasting your money studying with me."

"Do you wish me, then, to leave?" asked Marcus.

"No. I have had all life's amusements save one. I have never seen an honest lawyer." He laughed uproariously.

The Social War ended in a series of concessions by Rome to the provinces, only to be succeeded by a new war in the Middle

East with Mithradates. Meantime, Scaevola plied Marcus with books and took him on an endless round of the courts. Once he said to Marcus, "You have a presence, which is invaluable in law. But remember that a lawyer must also be confident. You must tell yourself that Marcus Tullius Cicero is an important man.

"Also, if you value your future, never let your personal opinions be known. Say, 'Yes, you are correct. But on the other hand—' and smile agreeably. Compromise, pander, but never offend." Then he shouted irascibly, "Confusion on you! I have lapsed from my own conviction, which is to have no convictions. Begone!"

THAT AFTERNOON MARCUS' fencing class met. The fencing school was famous, patronized not only by boys but by army officers. When Marcus opened the door he felt a blast of warmth from sweating bodies. The air was filled with shouts and the admonitions of the teachers, and with the clash of guarded swords. Gaius, the master of the school, moved about from group to group, watching, advising.

Marcus removed his mantle and long tunic, and stood in a short wool tunic. He took his sword from its peg on the wall and looked about for an opponent. Three young officers in full armor stood with their thumbs in their leather belts, joking together. One of the three took off his helmet, and Marcus' heart lurched as he recognized Lucius Catiline, and then his companions, the slight Cneius Piso and the grim, dark-faced Quintus Curius.

Lucius looked like a young Mars. When Gaius paused before him, Lucius clapped the fencing master affectionately on the shoulder.

"There is not one here that I would recommend to my general," Lucius said. It was an insult, but Gaius only smiled.

"You were one of my best fencers, Lucius," he said. "Why do you not show my pupils your talent?"

"No, no!" cried Lucius. "These are only schoolboys! We but paused on the way to dinner." He looked about him with his smiling charm, and then his eyes reached Marcus.

The smile became ugly. "Ah!" he exclaimed. "There is one we

know! Look, Piso, Curius. I seem to remember those undistinguished features."

"It is the Vetch, for a certainty," said Curius.

"Chick-pea!" said Piso, and they burst into loud laughter and stared at Marcus, who could only stare at Lucius while the sword in his right hand shook as if it had a life of its own.

"You have frightened him, Lucius," said Piso.

Lucius replaced his helmet and strolled toward his old enemy, then paused before him, looking him up and down.

"I thought, Gaius, you accepted only men and boys of good family, and not such as—this." He extended his booted foot and tapped Marcus on the knee with it.

Marcus slapped aside the foot with the flat of his sword.

The room fell silent. Then Lucius Catiline drew his sword, and the sound was a clash in the silence.

Gaius caught his arm. "This is my school, not an arena, Lucius! Are you mad?"

"It is but an animal," said Piso with contempt. "Let Lucius run him through, and then bury him in your garden."

Gaius shouted, "Would Lucius Catiline, an honorable man, murder a pupil of mine who has a foil on his sword?"

"Give me one like his," Lucius said through his teeth. He lifted his hand and struck Marcus across his cheek. "There is my challenge, Chick-pea." Quickly he stripped to his short tunic. Gaius thrust a foiled sword into his hand, and he fell at once into a strong and graceful posture of attack.

Teachers and pupils lined the walls, leaving an open space about the antagonists. Their swords crossed at once. Lucius was a trained soldier, one of the most notable swordsmen in Rome, while Marcus was more than two years younger, much lighter and no athlete. He felt the strong, steady pressure of Lucius' sword on his, but he experienced no fear. They sprang apart, their swords whistling, and then Lucius, as if with disgusted impatience, moved his sword like a thin streak of lightning and the guarded point stung Marcus' left shoulder. Lucius Catiline laughed with delight and his friends raised a cry.

He is reckless, thought Marcus. I will goad him. Suddenly bending his knees, he reached under Lucius' shield and struck him full in the chest. Lucius actually fell back. Then, as he lunged forward again, Marcus deftly stepped aside, and Lucius ran several paces into emptiness. "What?" said Marcus, tauntingly. "Did you see a mirage?"

Lucius turned white with fury. Losing his head, he plunged his sword at Marcus' face and the younger man struck it aside with an easy motion. I am dreaming, thought Gaius. What is wrong with Lucius, who won all the prizes in this school?

Lucius Catiline was now wild with mortification. He ran at Marcus so fiercely that Marcus fell back, stumbled, and was stung several times. Lucius pursued him, smiling again, sure of victory. But now Marcus recovered dexterously. Their swords crossed halfway up the hilts. Marcus said, "Did they not teach you better on the field, or did you fight with unarmed men, or maidens?"

At this, Lucius struck the floor with his sword, disengaging the foil on its tip, and Gaius shouted, "No, no! This is fencing, not murder!" The sword came, naked, at Marcus' breast, and fear touched him as he realized that Lucius Catiline meant to kill him. He fell back, and struck the guard from his own sword. Now they faced each other with flickering death.

"Wretch!" cried Marcus. "Liar! Coward!"

Lucius Catiline smiled. He was now so sure that he made a deadly mistake. He lunged, and his foot slipped. Instantly he felt a sting in his right shoulder. Before he could recover, Marcus' sword was at his throat and he was on one knee. Marcus' sword flashed, hurling aside Lucius' sword, and then the point returned to Lucius Catiline's throat.

The room roared. Gaius came plunging forward, but Marcus said quietly, "Let one man move and I run Catiline through." He added to Lucius, "I will kill you in a moment. But I must enjoy the thought first."

Lucius' arms were bent backward and he was supporting himself on the palms of his hands. He looked up into Marcus' face and saw the hatred, and he knew he was about to die. He said, "Kill me. Have done with it."

The point edged into his flesh. Catiline did not wince. And then Marcus saw Lucius' eyes in their full intense blue, and they were the eyes of Livia. Marcus' own eyes filled with tears. He stepped back, withdrawing his sword. He could not speak.

"Noble fighter! Gracious victor!" shouted Gaius. He flung his arms about his pupil, weeping with joy and relief.

Teachers and students all raised their voices in salutation, and Piso and Curius came to their friend, helped him to his feet and pressed a kerchief against his bleeding throat. But Catiline put them aside. Mockingly, he saluted Marcus. "I felicitate you, Chick-pea."

Years later Marcus said with anguish, "Livia, Livia! I should have killed him."

CHAPTER FIVE

"TOMORROW YOU PRESENT your first case to the Senate," Scaevola said to Cicero. "I have informed a number of my friends, and they will be there to applaud you."

"If I win," said Marcus.

Scaevola's eyes narrowed. "A lawyer must not permit himself an 'if.' Now, Marcus, you cannot appeal to any established law in the case of your client, Persus. As you know, he was a small farmer with a wife, two young children, and three slaves who assisted him on his farm. But he fell on evil times and could not pay his taxes. The tax gatherers have seized his property and imprisoned him, and are prepared to sell him and his family into bondage, according to the law for a bankrupt."

Marcus said, "That evil law should have been repealed. It has remained for decades on the books without being enforced."

"When that law appeared on the books, centuries ago," said Scaevola, "it was to discourage profligacy and irresponsibility, and it was never enforced because the people were frugal and their rulers humane. Now the people are profligate and irresponsible, and their rulers are tyrants."

Marcus sat down and stared at the table. "I shall appeal to the humanity of the Senate."

Scaevola rocked with laughter. "Humanity? The Senate? You are mad! You are appealing to a hungry lion to release a gazelle. I look upon this case as an exercise for you. I hope only that the Senate will applaud you."

Marcus flushed. "I shall rescue my gazelle." He went into Scaevola's library, and sought again and again an avenue of justice for Persus and his wife, Maia. At noon, he went to the Temple of Athena and prayed before the altar of the Unknown God. "Surely, you are Justice," he whispered. "Surely, you will not abandon your children."

He returned to the house of Scaevola. A rich litter was before the door and Noë ben Joel was emerging from it with a white and desperate face. When Marcus ran to him, Noë tried to speak. Then he burst into tears. "My father!" he groaned.

A FEW MONTHS BEFORE, Joel ben Solomon had summoned his son and said, "I gave your sisters large dowries, for God did not see fit to endow them with the countenances of angels. The dowries and the loss of many of my investments have depleted my coffers, and I can no longer help you produce your unprofitable plays. Therefore, I have arranged a marriage for you with the daughter of Ezra ben Samuel. Her dowry—"

"She resembles a camel!" cried Noë. "She is older than I! No dowry could persuade a man to marry her!"

"She is only twenty-four, which is not elderly. A camel? She is no Bathsheba, but she is gentle and of much virtue."

"A camel," said Noë desperately.

"Speak not so. Her nose could be more shapely and her eyes larger, but she has excellent teeth."

"A man does not take a wife for her teeth. She is fat."

Joel said, "It seems to me that you are not purchasing a wife. Leah is purchasing a husband. You."

Noë wanted to tear his hair. However, Leah's income would mean that he could still produce plays.

Marcus had been a guest at the wedding. He thought Noë had done his bride injustice. Leah was too plump, but she had a charming smile and gentle manners, and when Noë arrived at the Cicero house one evening two months later, Marcus noted that he was less lean and had a more contented expression.

BUT NOW NOË'S face was streaming with tears. He told Scaevola and Marcus his story. A number of senators had made investments which Joel had recommended. Now, because of bad times and their own profligacy, they found themselves heavily in debt to Joel. So they announced that Joel had not carried out the transactions for which they had paid in full, and they had had him thrown into prison for this pretended embezzlement. Joel's family was in despair. The daughters' husbands had gone to the senators offering a magnificent sum as payment in full, but the senators had laughed at them.

Scaevola listened, like a huge fat toad in his chair, to Noë's story. Good, he thought, this will at last teach this young donkey Cicero—for whom I have an unaccountable affection—to distrust this government. He said, "Marcus, you will find a strongbox under my bed. Noë, write on this papyrus the names of the senators your in-laws saw this morning."

When Marcus returned with the box Scaevola patted it paternally. "When the wicked attack you, do not attack them honestly. Discover their secrets." He unlocked the brassbound box, removed scrolls and studied one. He glanced at Noë's list and nodded.

"This senator poisoned his wife," Scaevola said. He plucked out another scroll. "My dear senator!" he exclaimed. "You shock this leathery old heart! You have seduced the young wives of four of your devoted colleagues in the Senate! Tut, tut. If they learn of this they will murder you."

He studied several other scrolls, then impaled Marcus with a malevolent eye. "I have brought these matters to the attention of these senators before," he said, "and on several occasions my house has been broken into. Now they know that these dossiers are only copies."

Noë said, "How did you obtain this information?"

Scaevola rubbed his finger and thumb together. "Gold! I have the best spies in Rome."

He summoned messengers and addressed a respectful letter to each senator, reminding him discreetly of his information and urging that the charges against Joel be removed. He had no information about two other senators. To them he wrote, "I am in possession of a secret of yours which distresses me. I would like to confer with you about it."

Noë said, "Has no senator ever challenged you?"

"Never," said Scaevola. "These senators will wonder what secret I have stumbled upon." He winked at Noë.

"My grandfather believed," Marcus said with a sad smile, "that

I could help to rescue Rome and the rule of law. I shall still try."

"Good," said Scaevola. "That is why I have prophesied that you will not die peacefully in your bed."

Now that his father was to be rescued Noë could smile. He said, "I have been occupied lately, Marcus, and so have had no opportunity to coach you as before. Stand up now and show me how you intend to present yourself to the Senate."

Marcus hesitated, embarrassed. Then he reminded himself that an advocate should be prepared to address any audience at any time. He rose. His slender shoulders straightened, his face flushed with outrage, and his eyes glowed. Before he could say a word the others applauded.

Then Noë pointed to Marcus' legs. "A longer robe," he said. "Marcus' legs are not his best feature. It must be faultless as marble and fastened with a severe yet expensive pin. I have the very robe you need. Your shoes must be white as the robe, to indicate unsullied justice." He put his head on one side, critically. "A girdle, too, of finely wrought silver. Ah, and I have a magnificent ring."

"They know I am but the son of a poor knight."

"Then they will wonder who is your unknown but powerful client," said Noë. He leaped to his feet and circled Marcus, as if preparing an actor for a role, lifting Marcus' elbow, dropping a shoulder, turning the chin. And, as Scaevola watched, his diffident pupil became a statue of avenging, youthful justice.

ARCHIAS HAD RELUCTANTLY departed for the house of another client, persuaded to do so by Helvia, since he had become a painful reminder of their present state and all they owed him. So Tullius taught Quintus each morning and, as Helvia had secretly hoped, his health improved.

Through Quintus, whom he still saw often, Caesar sent to Marcus an ivory and silver rod of authority to hold when he addressed the Senate. A slave of Joel's brought gifts from Noë, wrapped in white silk, with a letter. It said: "Rejoice, dearest friend! My father has already been delivered from prison! I will be present tomorrow to watch you. You have my prayers."

Helvia watched Marcus unwrap Noë's gifts. She was thirty-seven now, and there was an occasional thread of gray in her abundant black curls. But she was as composed as ever, an "old" Roman matron whom life could never overcome. She could not restrain her admiration for the toga and adornments Noë had sent. When Marcus was attired in them, she stood back to admire him. But she sensed that something had unnerved her son. She said, "Are you afraid that you will forget your address?"

Marcus was holding up a ring Noë had sent. He stared at it emptily.

"I am not going to give the address I memorized," he said. "I shall simply let myself be moved by the power of Athena."

Helvia considered that most imprudent: the gods did not always come when summoned. "You think that wise, Marcus?"

He spread his hands out helplessly. "I do not know." He opened his small treasure chest, took out the amulet of Athena that Aurelia Caesar had given him, and hung it about his neck.

THE NEXT DAY, as Helvia sat back to regard the toga she had draped on her son, a slave appeared in the doorway to announce, with excitement, that a rich litter was awaiting the noble Cicero, carried by four magnificent slaves. Marcus and Helvia both ran to the doors. There was Noë beside a litter with curtains of fine blue wool embroidered in silver. He came to bow over Helvia's hand.

"Did you expect to walk to the Forum, like a peasant?" he asked Marcus.

"Cincinnatus walked to the Senate," said Helvia, but she smiled as she turned back to the house.

When the young men were in the litter, Noë said, "My father owes his life and reputation to you, Marcus. Scaevola helped him only for you. Scaevola loves you like a father, and it hurts him that you are so unworldly. He wants to protect you with knowledge of this world."

Marcus thought about this. "No," he said. "Scaevola is a roaring bull. Nevertheless, he loves justice." He pulled aside the curtains and stared out at the violent sunlight on the red and yellow buildings, at the hurrying throngs. Noë tried to divert him.

"I have some gossip for you," he said. "Catiline is with General Sulla, in Asia, fighting Mithradates."

Marcus said, "I had hoped he was dead."

"Unfortunately, no. Lucifer protects his own, a practice I highly recommend to the Almighty, who seems less conscientious in these matters. Unfortunately, Catiline is one of Sulla's favorite officers. If Sulla ever rules in Rome, he will be in a fine position."

The litter entered the Forum down the steep slope of the Sacred Way, and Marcus' breath came faster. He fumbled for the amulet under his tunic. The Forum was all vast, colorful, uproarious confusion. Temples, basilicas, porticos, government buildings, banks crowded in upon one another. Chariots churned amid a turmoil of litters and people.

Only lawyers and officials were permitted within the Senate. Those who had already tried cases, or were about to, stood near the entrance surrounded by clients and well-wishers. A few, like the famous Scaevola, could bring chairs inside. The rest sat outside, with small awnings held over their heads by slaves.

Scaevola's entourage today included Julius Caesar, Quintus and Archias, now famous for his poetry. Marcus and Noë went to Scaevola at once and he smiled faintly at his pupil. "Greetings, Marcus," he said. "We are splendidly arrayed."

Caesar said, "Marcus, since you are about to do battle, I have invoked Mars on your behalf." He turned to a youth who stood beside him with alert gray eyes. "This is my friend Gnaeus Pompey. He has been fighting with General Sulla in the East."

Pompey bowed to Marcus. "All success," he said.

"Take your place," Scaevola said, waving Marcus to a line of four lawyers waiting to be called.

There were only thirty senators present, and it alarmed Scaevola that Senator Curius was among them, a most evil man, and the father of Cicero's old enemy.

Scaevola listened to the proceedings for a time, and then beckoned to Noë, who bent over him. Scaevola whispered, "Your parents must return to Jerusalem. If I died tonight, who knows if my son would have the courage to use what I have used?"

"The old story of the Jews again," said Noë, frowning. "We must leave at once?"

"Yes. Ha! Our Marcus is now second in line."

Marcus had begun to tremble. Huge though the Senate Chamber was, the heat was frightful.

Three broad marble steps stood along two sides of the chamber, and on these sat the senators on chairs, formidable in their white robes, golden girdles and armlets, and scarlet shoes. At one end of the chamber was a platform with a huge marble chair cushioned in velvet. Here the small, dark consul, Cinna, sat in state.

In the center of the floor stood Marcus' manacled, emaciated client, Persus, and his more lightly chained wife and children. They gazed beseechingly at Marcus, their faces wet with tears. Marcus went to Persus and laid his hand gently on the prisoner's shoulder.

"Be of good hope," he said.

The aedile was droning, "Prisoner, one Persus, plebeian, his wife, Maia, and his children, a boy, ten, a female, six. The charge is failure to pay his taxes. The farm of Persus has been seized in part payment, also his three slaves."

"Surely there is a lawyer for the prisoner," said Senator Servius, an "old" Roman of distinguished appearance.

"Marcus Tullius Cicero," said the aedile, "son of a knight, student of the pontifex maximus Scaevola."

"His qualifications are accepted," said the old senator.

"Is this advocate a Roman citizen?" Curius said in an acid voice.

The question was superfluous, and Curius knew it. Servius said with vexation, "Certainly!" And seeing that he was no friend of Curius, Marcus took heart.

Servius leaned forward to observe him and Marcus smiled. Instantly his face was dazzling.

The aedile said to Marcus, "What is your plea, master?"

"Not guilty," said Marcus.

"The law is specific," said Curius.

"Have you no respect for law, Cicero?" Servius said.

"Lords," said Marcus, in a fervent voice which rang through the chamber, "I respect no evil law, even though it exists. Who can embrace evil simply because it exists?"

Scaevola nudged Noë and smiled.

Marcus resumed, his eyes flashing. "Is it not the foundation of Roman law that the government is not more than the people? If the government is guilty of evil, is it not the duty of a people to restrain it and punish it?"

"Gods!" groaned Scaevola.

Marcus' face flushed with passion. "Romans," he said, "have taxed themselves from the first days of the Republic for useful

purposes. But our tax laws were not passed to purchase an idle rabble with free food, free shelter and free circuses!"

He paused for breath, and there was silence in the chamber. Then Marcus went on: "We are taxed not only for the idle but to maintain legions abroad in the name of the Roman Peace—the *Pax Romana*—which will fall into dust whenever it pleases our allies. Are these people worth the heartblood of our nation? Let us remember the intentions of those who wrote this law, and let us beware of those who use it today. The first were heroes. Those who use it today are criminals."

"Treason!" muttered Curius.

"They will kill him," groaned Scaevola. "For he has spoken the truth."

Cicero held out his hand to the Senate. "My lords, a just law brings order, liberty and prosperity. It nourishes patriotism. A just law deserves our obedience. But if a law brings fear and slavery, then it is an evil law, upheld by evil men. If this be treason, lords, accuse me."

He brought forward his client, Persus.

"Look upon this man, lords. He has never sought power. He loved his peace, the sun on his few acres. He is the ancient strength of Rome; he is Rome herself."

Suddenly Marcus could not restrain his tears, and the senators watched, some with bitter faces, some with shame, as he spoke. "Look upon your fellow Roman, lords. He is a victim of these gold-devouring wars, just as you are. He had a young son who died in the Social War, just as some of you had. But *he* lost all he had in this calamity! Only the Fates prevented you from being born with his destiny!"

"Treason!" cried Curius, and started to his feet. "Dog! You have taunted us with your lies and your insolence!"

Servius rose also. He said to Curius, "You lie yourself, Curius. He has spoken truth. And may the gods defend him."

A great mob had gathered at the doors. There were shouts of "Noble Cicero!" "Free the oppressed!"

"Sit down," said Servius to Curius. "You know how easily aroused is the Roman rabble. This man can destroy you with his tongue."

Curius sat down, but he clenched his hands on his knees and regarded Marcus with hatred, and there was murder in his eyes.

Marcus flung out his arms and advanced a step or two toward the senators. "Lords, it is said that the gods love a merciful man. Be magnanimous. Let the news of your kindness reach the gates of the city, and beyond. What arouses admiration most in the breast of the people but goodness, mercy and justice? For no matter how base a man is, he still adores virtue."

The consul, Cinna, rose and all rose with him. He said: "Cicero, this law will be removed only when Romans, aware of their extreme peril, demand that it be removed. In the meantime, I recommend that this family be set free and all we have taken be restored. Of what use are more beggars in the streets?"

He looked at Persus and his wife and children, who had fallen to their knees, and he said, "Go in peace."

Cinna stepped from his high platform and moved without a glance through the aisle of the senators, who stood like statues on each side as he left the chamber. On seeing him the people shouted, "Hero! Hercules!"

The senators followed him out in a dignified body and were gratified to be saluted as heroes. Marcus remained behind to congratulate his clients. He gave them his meager purse.

Persus wept. "I will send you two kids, blessed master!" Roman lawyers did not receive fees from clients, only gifts if the beneficiaries were grateful.

Marcus said, "Then send them to my island in Arpinum, if you can spare them."

As he thought of Arpinum he was filled with nostalgia. It was now peaceful there, and Helvia had opened the house. Marcus stood in meditation and looked up to find himself alone, confronting the vast statue of the blind goddess of justice, her scales in her hands.

He thought: She wears a blindfold so she will not be swayed by appearances. She is impartial. That is the meaning of law.

CHAPTER SIX

MARCUS LEANED AGAINST an oak tree in the spring sun that flooded Arpinum and reread a letter from Noë ben Joel, now in Jerusalem with his family. Noë wrote:

"I delight in your increasing success. Fortunate it is that you have obtained clients who can enrich you with gifts! My own plays are received here with acclaim, and we have just celebrated the first birthday of my son, Joshua. The Roman proconsul, a friend of my father, attended the festivities. He presented my son with a beautiful Roman sword. My father was uncertain how to express his gratitude—if he possessed any—but as usual I was swift with my fluent tongue and the innocent Roman was pleased.

"I have sought out prophecies of the Messiah for you. Isaiah writes: *For a Child is born to us, and a Son is given to us, and the government is upon His shoulder, and His name shall be called Wonderful, Counselor, God the Mighty, the Father of the world to come, the Prince of Peace.* He will be, Isaiah says, a light unto the Gentiles. But the prophets say He will not come with the cloak of celestial majesty, so who will know him? Is it possible that I shall see Him, and you? Dear friend, be cautious. Do not arouse more animosity than you can afford. We send our blessings."

Marcus smiled as he rerolled the letter. Although Cinna was a tyrant, Noë's concern for him was ludicrous. He was only a modestly successful young lawyer, with a small, windowless office for which he paid Scaevola a small but regular fee. The room was stifling and stank of sweat, parchment, damp stone and burning oil. "The odor of learning," said Scaevola.

Marcus looked at the rushing river, lemon-colored in the light of spring. The town of Arpinum, across the river, seemed drenched in shadowy gold as it climbed hills still brazen from winter. Spring was again celebrating life.

He looked at the bridge that led to the mainland, and he thought of Livia. He thought of her as he remembered her more than ten years ago, with her glowing hair and strange blue eyes. As his mother had prophesied, she remained forever young to him, safe from sorrow and change. He had learned to shut his mind from her.

But there was something about the light today, the descending sun, the scent of the earth that made her a breathing presence. If he turned his head quickly, he would see her again, like a dryad under the trees.

"Livia!" he said aloud.

He did not hear the stealthy glide of a boat near him, the hushed footsteps. When he felt iron arms suddenly seize him he struggled, outraged.

52

There were four men in hooded cloaks about him. One of them struck him sharply in the face. Another said angrily, "No, there must be no bruise on him, no sign! Restrain yourself." The voice had a Roman accent.

Cicero looked down at the strong hands holding him and noticed that one bore a handsome ring.

A wad of cloth was forced between his teeth, and for the first time he thought: Death. He struggled and fear gave him strength. Once he actually broke from his captors, but they seized him again. They began to strip him, carefully, as if they wished not to tear his garments, which they laid neatly on the grass. One man reached for the amulet Aurelia Caesar had given him so long ago, but another said, "No, he would not remove his amulet while swimming."

Then Marcus understood: he was to have an accident. He was lifted into the boat, and the men rowed to the middle of the river. Marcus was overwhelmed with terror. The current was swift, and the river, fed by icy springs from the mountains, would be paralyzingly cold. Even Quintus, the mighty swimmer, never ventured into the river until summer.

The rowers turned broadside to the current to hold the vessel, and the men regarded Marcus without animosity. "Drowning," said one, "is not an unpleasant death. Be grateful that we did not disembowel you."

They slowly slipped his body into the water; then, quickly, one pulled the gag from his mouth. Before he could shout they had pushed his head under the bitter water. He closed his mouth and held his breath. The river instantly numbed his flesh, and his lungs began to strain. In some way he must tear himself loose from their grip. He pretended to go limp, and as he had hoped, the hand that gripped his hair relaxed. Instantly, he wrenched his head down and forward; his heart thundered in his breast as the current seized him and he was swept away.

But now he must breathe for his life's sake. He came to the surface, drew in a breath with a strangling sound and heard a yell. His would-be murderers had seen him. They rowed toward him, and when the boat was almost upon him he let himself sink below it. Above him, he saw the shadow of the boat and swam deeply away from it.

He needed air again. At last he struggled to the surface and drew a groaning breath. The boat at once swung about in pursuit. Again, he waited until they were almost upon him, and let himself sink.

How long could this game continue? Wearily he let himself be carried by the current toward the main river. Light flashed behind his eyes, and his body no longer tortured him. He was like a cloud, floating mindlessly.

Then a savage tug at his throat lifted his lips above the water, and he was coughing and choking in the blessed air. He saw that a great uprooted tree had lodged in the rocks at the bottom of the river. A branch had caught his amulet and lifted him so that his face emerged.

He turned his head. Twilight was falling rapidly. The boat, tiny now, was being rowed toward the bridge. He saw it land at Arpinum and saw the little figures pulling it up on shore. Then they were lost in the thickening dark.

He clutched the tree to relieve the tug of the chain on his neck. He said aloud, "You cannot remain here; you will die of exposure." Nevertheless, it demanded all his courage to cast free and swim toward the island, against a current which seemed a limitless wall he must climb.

He swam doggedly, and prayed. And then a heavier darkness was near him: a rock, and the shore. He walked through the shallow waters and reached the beautiful dry land. He fell upon it, kissing the earth.

IN THE DISTANCE HE HEARD the shouts of searching slaves and saw the glimmer of a lantern. So they had discovered his clothing! He called out in a soft voice, and they came joyfully to him. Athos, the overseer, fell on his knees and embraced him, saying, "Master! We thought that you had drowned!"

"I was set upon by men who wished to kill me. They tried to make it appear that I had drowned. I must return to Rome at once. Two of you remain with me. Order the others to bring me clothing, my sword, my best horse and my purse."

He rested in Athos' arms, and closed his eyes. A slave threw his rough woolen cloak over Marcus' shivering body. Athos chafed his hands. "Master, let me ride with you!" he said.

Marcus shook his head. "Your absence might be noted. Once I am in Rome, you can be certain I will not go unguarded!" He was remembering the magnificent ring on the finger of one of the hooded men. Someday he would discover the man by that ring.

The army had seized all the best horses for the war. A poor, docile plow horse arrived, led by a slave, and another slave brought clothing and food.

Athos helped Marcus to dress. He put on his sword, patted the horse to reassure it, and climbed into the saddle. He leaned down to embrace Athos. "Pray for me," he said, and rode away, trying not to remember how long was the way to Rome.

He did not halt until the horse was panting and lathered and it was near dawn. Then he dismounted, led the horse into a forest, and slept with his sword in his hand.

He awoke to full sunlight, ate some bread and cheese, and in a few minutes was on the way again. He was just beginning to breathe more easily when he heard the thunder of horses behind him. He spurred his horse into a copse. As the riders came nearer, he heard the rumble of a chariot, and a detachment of legionnaires swept by him, their banners waving. Within the chariot sat a centurion in his cloak and glittering helmet.

Marcus rode back onto the road and shouted. The legionnaires slowed and the chariot halted. The bearded centurion scowled.

"Hail!" Marcus lifted his right hand in a military salute.

"Hail," said the centurion without notable enthusiasm.

"Marcus Tullius Cicero, of Rome," Marcus said, smiling. "May I have safe passage with you into Rome?"

The centurion looked suspiciously at his humble cloak and tunic. "Why are you abroad these dangerous days, and alone?"

"A sensible question, but alas, I am not a sensible man," Marcus said hastily, aware of the other's unfriendliness. "My brother is a centurion, now in Gaul—Quintus Tullius Cicero. My grandfather, Marcus Tullius Cicero, of Arpinum, was a veteran of many wars."

The centurion began to smile. "I remember him well. When I was a subaltern, he was my captain. A noble soldier. Why are you not a soldier?"

"I am a lawyer. But I will volunteer my time in the legions."

The captain grinned. "You are a liar, Cicero," he said. "You are no horseman. Who is your mentor in the law?"

"The great pontifex maximus Scaevola," said Marcus.

"My dear old friend! What a scoundrel he is!" The centurion moved on his seat. "I am Marcius Basilus. You may as well ride with me. And let us be gone; you have delayed me enough."

When Marcus walked into his house the next day, Scaevola cried, "You rascal! What is this I hear from my old friend Marcius Basilus, that he encountered you on the road in vagabond attire, with a limping horse and the face of a criminal in flight?"

"Let me tell you," said Marcus, seating himself, and Scaevola listened with incredulity while Marcus told him his story.

"But Marcus, I have always said you were as harmless as a dewdrop! Whom have you offended?"

"None who would carefully plot my death. I do not engage in politics, nor am I rich, with greedy heirs. I have never intrigued for or against Cinna. I have betrayed no woman."

"Your assailants, you said, appeared to be men of culture. Tell me about that ring."

Marcus said, "One of them wore a ring of heavy gold in the form of two serpents whose mouths were joined together by a large emerald, an intaglio of Diana holding a crescent moon."

"Hum." Scaevola's brilliant little eyes fixed themselves keenly upon Marcus. He said, "They will soon know that you escaped.

Your danger is still extreme." He pulled his lip. "You have not irritated our young Julius, have you?"

Marcus smiled. "No. We are the dearest of friends."

"Do not underrate him. He has developed epilepsy, and after a seizure recently he spoke mysteriously of a strange vision. In any case, you need a guard." Scaevola bellowed and a tall, powerful young Nubian appeared, armed with a dagger. Scaevola pointed to Marcus. "Syrius," he said, "behold your new master. Leave him not for an instant."

Syrius bowed, lifted the hem of Marcus' tunic and kissed it.

"You need not feed Syrius," Scaevola said. "He lives from betting on the races. Instead, force him to share his ill-gotten gains with you." He waved at Marcus as if vexed. "Why do you devour so much of my time? Go."

The attempted murder remained a mystery, and Marcus doggedly pursued his law career.

THE SOCIAL WAR continued sporadically all over Italy, but the Romans accepted it fatalistically. Such fatalism had never been part of the Roman nature, which was pragmatic, materialistic and optimistic, and Marcus felt with alarm that his countrymen had begun to accept an Eastern philosophy.

One day Scaevola brought him a new client. He said, "Here is a strange one. I cannot bring myself to defend him."

The client was a sturdy, middle-aged man named Casinus. He employed forty men in a metal factory which made artifacts of every kind, from plowshares to the most intricate jewelry, as well as shields and swords for the government. But now he had been ordered by Cinna to cease the production of all but war materials. "My jewelers have delicate hands, trained over long years, master," he told Cicero. "I will not send my artists into pit and foundry!"

Marcus said, "A Roman citizen can be conscripted during a national emergency."

"But a competitor of mine, Veronus, has been exempted! He has approached one of my foremen, Samos, with a large offer. My jewelers love Samos, and would follow him."

Marcus said, "I would like to see Samos."

Samos was frightened when Cicero asked if he would testify.

He stammered, "Veronus has hinted to me that if I do so it will go ill with me."

Marcus frowned. "I will take your case, Casinus. Samos, I promise no harm will come to you."

He maneuvered in the next days to place his case before a noble magistrate, but this proved impossible. Because of the rumor that Sulla would soon return to Rome in triumph, the patricians, who had stood against Sulla, were preparing for flight. Only petty bureaucrats planned to remain.

Marcus reluctantly called upon Caesar, who had only a few months ago married Cornelia, Cinna's daughter. Caesar professed to adore Cornelia and to be devoted to Cinna.

Julius greeted Cicero affectionately. He was very elegant these days. His toga was of the finest violet linen, beautifully embroidered. His black hair was perfumed, his lips bright red. Marcus hoped he had not tinted them in the depraved new fashion. There was certainly kohl around his mischievous black eyes!

Cicero looked about at the large, elaborate house. Lamplight shone on tables of lemonwood and ebony. Oriental carpets bloomed on the marble floors. There was a splashing of fountains.

"Let us go into the gardens," Julius said.

Marcus was taken aback by the splendor of cypresses and flowering, scented trees, fountains, marble nymphs and satyrs. Beyond the gardens the hoarse voice of Rome rumbled insistently, like a giant who muttered in his sleep.

A female slave of marvelous beauty brought them wine as they sat on a marble bench. Julius embraced the slave's waist with a negligent arm. "Is she not delightful?" he asked. Marcus did not look at the girl, and Julius laughed. "I forgot you were an 'old' Roman," he said.

Marcus asked, "Will you keep all this when Sulla returns?"

"He will not dare to return," said Julius.

"No doubt Cinna has assured you of that."

"My father-in-law is a man of wisdom. Did he not choose me as his son-in-law? But, Marcus, I do not flatter myself that you are here to renew sweet acquaintance. You have a purpose. Has it aught to do with the fact that you have a bodyguard with you?"

Marcus decided that it was time to abandon prudence and confide in Julius, though Scaevola had warned him not to. As he told Julius of the attack upon him, the smiling face became still and intent. Marcus showed him the amulet and said, "Had your mother not given me this, I should be dead."

"They must have been mad," said Julius in a peculiar, low voice. His face was hard and dark. "How could you harm them?" he continued, as if questioning himself.

"Who are they?" asked Marcus.

Julius averted his head. "I do not know."

Marcus said, "One of the men who attacked me wore a magnificent ring, two golden serpents joined at the mouths by a large emerald. Is it possible you know its significance?" Julius shook his head. "Scaevola said he believed I was potentially dangerous to someone. To whom, Julius?"

The younger man turned, smiling and gay again. "To whom could so kind and amiable a man be dangerous?" he asked. "You are a lawyer, an 'old' Roman—" He paused, and the smile left his face. Then Marcus was startled at Julius' sudden laugh, for it was not mirthful. "Therefore, though you are eloquent, you are dangerous to no one! Why did you seek me out tonight?"

Marcus was perturbed. But he told of his search for a magistrate who would not be swayed by the oppressive government. "I ask only justice for my client," he said. "Veronus has bribed someone. Are we to be ruled by favor and extortion?"

His voice filled the garden with indignant fervor. That eloquent voice had the power to move the heart. I see now, thought Julius, why it was judged he must die. Nevertheless, though I am one of them, he must not die.

"My dear Marcus," he said, "I shall find you your magistrate, and I shall come myself to the Basilica of Justice to hear you defend the equal application of Roman law to every man." He clapped Marcus on the shoulder. "All will be touched to the heart by your eloquence."

But after Marcus left, Julius wrote hastily to his friends, warning that Cicero must not be allowed to move hearts with his eloquence.

TWO DAYS LATER, Casinus came rejoicing into his office. "The order has been withdrawn!" he cried in jubilation. "Ah, what wonders you have accomplished!" Marcus read the order of withdrawal. He could not understand it. He was not a lawyer before whom a bureaucrat would cower. He took the parchment to Scaevola.

"To whom have you spoken of this case?" Scaevola asked.

"Only to you, and Julius Caesar."

Scaevola's fat face tightened. "What else have you told him?"

"I told him of the attempt on my life. I disobeyed you."

"I see," said Scaevola, and dismissed him.

Marcus went to tell Julius that the order had been withdrawn.

"So it was a mistake from the beginning," said Julius with an innocent face. "But matters are somewhat chaotic these days."

He insisted on having Marcus share wine with him. Nightingales sang to the moon-drowned night, and suddenly Marcus was mysteriously relieved of the nervousness which had haunted him since the attack in Arpinum. "I shall never forget your kindness," he said, his heart warm with love for Julius.

Julius became grave and quiet, and Marcus looked at him questioningly as the younger man stared into his wine cup. At last Caesar said, "No, you will not forget. All others might, but you will not, Marcus Tullius Cicero."

THERE HAD BEEN no letter from Quintus for some time, and Marcus and his mother were anxious. One afternoon he went to the Temple of Mars to say a prayer on behalf of Quintus. When he emerged, great storm clouds were gathering like enormous armies over the city, and the Forum was plunged in gloom. Marcus and the Nubian, Syrius, started to hurry home, but they had hardly reached the Temple of Vesta when the storm broke with ferocity. Marcus fled inside. Shafts of fiery lightning lit up pillars, floor and altar.

Marcus leaned against a marble wall, and his arm touched another arm. He turned his head, and lightning illuminated the eyes of Livia Catiline. In the blaze of light her large blue eyes reflected a cold, meaningless ruin: there was no recognition in them. Her face was also empty and pale as sorrow. So would she look at the hour of her death, untenanted, forsaken.

A few people near the altar murmured prayers. The thunder prowled savagely outside, and a few small votive lights burned.

Marcus felt the icy sweat on his forehead. Surely this silent woman was not Livia!

The storm was retreating now as fast as it had come. Suddenly sun drenched the Forum outside and the worshipers at the altar left, with mutters of relief.

Marcus turned and faced Livia. He pushed back her hood, and his hand brushed her silken hair. She looked at him with those awful eyes which held no recognition. She had not aged: she had been frozen in her early youth. Then he heard the faintest murmur: "Why do you weep?"

"For you, Livia, my beloved. And for me."

"Do not weep," she said indifferently. "I have shed all the tears there are. I have had a message from—him. He will soon return with Sulla—to me, and to our little son. Where shall I flee? Where shall I hide my child?"

"Livia, what has he done to you?"

"He took my life from me. Why does he not die?"

Marcus embraced Livia, holding her tightly to his breast. What had Catiline done to this nymph of the forest? "Come with me, beloved," he said. "I will hide you, protect you."

"My child," she whispered, not even hearing him. "He is with his uncle in the house where we live. I am mad; they laugh at me. I cannot flee without my child, for then he would die also. There is no pity in Catiline. He will divorce me, and I shall never see my child again. Nor is there shelter for me. Not anywhere, not anywhere."

"Livia, have you no relatives, no friends?"

"They all believe me mad," the faint voice continued. "They will rarely let me see my little one, who cries for me. I hear him crying in the night, but the door is barred to me. Listen! He is weeping for me now!"

She lifted her head and stared wildly before her. "I must go!" she cried. "My child is calling me!"

She slipped through his hands like a shade. He shouted, "Livia! Livia!" and followed her. The Forum was crowded again and she vanished among the throngs.

Syrius, whom he had forgotten, came to Marcus' side and looked into his desperate face. "Master," he said quietly, "let us go."

Followed by the slave, Marcus roamed the streets of Rome blindly, and did not come to himself for a long time. When Helvia saw his face she knew something terrible had happened to her son, but she asked no questions. She let him go without words to his *cubiculum*, and then she questioned Syrius.

So, she learned, he had not forgotten Livia. Helvia was full of pity—and also of impatience. But she was a wise woman and she greeted her son the next morning in a tranquil tone and spoke of casual things. She looked into his eyes, bloodshot and sleepless, and she mentioned that the garden would produce many excellent fruits this year.

CHAPTER SEVEN

MARCUS DINED WITH Scaevola at noon, as usual, but he hardly touched the boiled meat, onions, artichokes and fruit. His face was drawn and his eyes were red.

Finally Scaevola said, "You are troubled, Marcus. I suspect it is a woman. This is stupid of you, so I do not ask your confidences lest I lose my respect for you. In any case, there are more disturbing matters. I heard, this morning—and the city is quaking with the news—that Cinna was murdered a short time ago in a mutiny while challenging Sulla's advance on Rome. Now we shall have Carbo as consul. He is no improvement."

Marcus looked up, surprised. Scaevola nodded grimly. "You despised Cinna. Yet we have had worse consuls. Cinna at least distrusted Caesar and the *populares* party. Carbo is a fool. And he suspects I favor Sulla. Already I am threatened by his friends. Who knows when I shall be assassinated?"

"Nonsense," said Marcus. "Do you not hold the sacred office of pontifex maximus? Who would lift a hand against you?"

"Many," said Scaevola promptly. "Certainly Carbo. Then let us consider Sulla. He is a cold and ruthless genius. If he in turn seizes Rome, the mobs will have met their master. Sulla will not spare his enemies, especially the *populares*—the 'democratic' party of your friend Caesar. Julius is already in hiding in Carbo's house, but he will not escape Sulla."

Scaevola ate a handful of grapes, and ruminated. "I *do* have a weakness for men who know their own minds, like Sulla. So I am in danger. Being a wise man, I have survived so far by not engaging in politics, for no one can restore the Republic anyway. Man never learns from the history of nations which died in the past.

"Speaking of our leaders, Marcus, I have come upon a strange thing. You remember Pompey? The young man who was with Julius at the Senate? I saw him a month ago near the Senate doors. He was wearing a ring such as you described when you were attacked."

"No!" Marcus exclaimed incredulously.

Scaevola nodded. "I wonder if Julius has such a ring."

"Impossible," said Marcus. "Julius shook his head in bewilderment when I described it, and said he knew no one who possessed such a ring."

"And you believed Julius," said Scaevola with amusement. "He manipulates truth admirably, so that it serves his purpose. I think after all that he will survive Sulla."

Marcus shook his head. "I cannot believe that Julius, whom I love, was responsible for the attack on my life."

"I did not say he had plotted against you! But this ring must symbolize a secret brotherhood, of which he is probably a member. Julius' house on the Palatine is filled with stolen Egyptian treasures; one of them is a small pillar of bronze on which coils a golden serpent, like the ring you saw, with a brilliant crystal in its mouth. In Egypt, the serpent is sacred and is endowed with marvelous powers, including prophecy and strength. It is the guardian of those on thrones and those who hold scepters. It is the nature of the serpent to move in darkness, silent and remorseless, to accomplish its ends."

"It is all coincidence," said Marcus stubbornly.

Scaevola sighed. "You will believe nothing ill of those to whom you are attached. Marcus, remember one fact: there has been no further attempt on your life. Someone interceded for you, or you would be dead by now. I believe it was Caesar. But Catiline is among Sulla's followers, so you may still be in danger."

Marcus half rose to his feet, his hands clenched. "I despise myself. I should have killed Catiline." And, bursting into tears, he told his mentor of Livia.

Scaevola's gross face was compassionate. He said, "You have

vowed to kill Catiline. That is ridiculous. Balk him, frustrate him, deprive him of his ambitions and desires. Then he dies, not one, but a thousand deaths."

"Who am I?" said Marcus despairingly. "I am powerless."

Scaevola rose. "You are many things. I feel the stirring of prophecy in me. You will do what you desire to do. I feel that in my bones."

That night, in the steaming heat of the city, Scaevola was being carried in his litter to the house of his son. He was by nature a fatalist; therefore, when his slaves screamed in terror and the curtains of his litter were torn aside, and the litter dropped to the street, he made no effort to defend himself. By the light of a lantern he saw the faces of his assassins and recognized them. He did not utter a word. Stabbed to the heart, he died as imperturbably as he had lived.

"Hail, Carbo!" cried the murderers, brandishing their daggers. They fled into the darkness.

When Marcus heard the news the next morning, his grief overwhelmed him. Since Quintus still had not been heard from, he felt utterly alone. He went into Scaevola's office and looked at the marble table, the books, the scrolls; the chair of carved ivory, teak and ebony. One of Scaevola's sons came to him. "He was devoted to you, Cicero," said the son. "He has bequeathed to you fifty thousand gold sesterces, this chair, his books of law, and the slave Syrius."

Marcus could not speak.

"He shall be avenged," said the son. "Do not weep."

But the murderers were never discovered. Senators and tribunes expressed their horror, but few appeared at the funeral. It was Cicero who delivered the funeral oration. He said, "A patriot has been silenced forever! There were three assassins, it has been said. No—there was a nation of assassins. We assented to this death by apathy, greed, cowardice and lack of patriotism."

Now, while Sulla fought his way to Rome, Carbo ordered the death of all who were suspected of sympathy with Sulla. Caesar said to Carbo, "Scaevola should not have been murdered. I advised against it. There are outcries against you, my friend."

"And who is raising the loudest cries against me? That plebeian lawyer, your dear friend Cicero! I say he must die."

"I say he must not. If he dies, I shall avenge him."

Carbo's eyes narrowed. "You threaten me, Caesar?"

"We are in mortal danger," said Julius, "and there is work to do. Let us not descend to wanton butchery."

Carbo regarded the elegant and smiling young man evilly.

As Sulla approached Rome, the city became an armed camp, swept with winds of fear. Mindless mobs milled through the streets. Rumor shrieked that when Sulla triumphed there would be free grain, meat and wine.

Factions sprang up overnight; there was rioting. And the gates of Rome opened constantly to admit crowds of refugees and wounded soldiers. News finally came. Carbo had fought a fierce battle with Sulla near Clusium, and had fled in defeat. The mobs ran wild. Shops were looted. Armed guards, ready to kill, surrounded the larger business establishments, but the mobs mocked them.

Soon Caesar received a letter which made him smile. His friend Pompey, fighting with Sulla, had captured Carbo and put him to death.

SULLA CAME FROM a poor but patrician family. He believed in power, but he hated senators who took bribes. In many ways he was an "old" Roman. His enemies called him half lion, half fox.

He entered Rome during a frightening thunderstorm, wrapped in his cloak, riding his magnificent black horse, and followed by his soldiers. As he reached the Sacred Way, the Temple of Jupiter was struck by lightning and the pillars and the walls rose in flame and fell to the earth in crashing fragments.

Sulla, at a little distance surveyed the roaring fire, and the howling tens of thousands who had gathered to welcome him were stilled into terrified silence. He said to his officers, "You observe that Jupiter has lit a torch to guide me!"

One officer, the firm-faced, impassive Pompey, thought of his friend Caesar, whose patron was Jupiter. Was this a portent? Pompey's position in Rome had been equivocal; he had pretended to be anti-Sulla, but he had served Sulla as a spy and had joined Sulla's army during the last stages of the war. Pompey knew many things about Julius—and Julius had much information about him.

Catiline also watched the fire and smiled as he felt the serpentine ring on his finger. This, he thought, was only the beginning. All that Catiline hated would be at Sulla's mercy now.

Sulla touched his horse and turned it as the remains of the Temple of Jupiter sank into embers.

TERROR NOW FILLED Rome. Its gray, hushed voice was on every threshold; in the temples, and the colonnades. Sulla killed implacably and methodically. He had posted five thousand proscribed names in the Senate, but there were thousands more known to none except the bereaved. Even the mobs were quiet, appalled by the presence of death everywhere.

Marcus had many clients, even in these days, but he had no friends. An invisible cleft had long since widened between himself and Tullius. Marcus had so many silent terrors of his own that often he could not endure his father's petulant voice, his insistence that he be assured that all was well with this world. Even Helvia wept, though she tried to be calm.

Sulla had proclaimed freedom and peace, but men were afraid to speak to one another in confidence.

"I will refill our bankrupt treasury," said Sulla, so men withdrew their savings from the banks and hid them in their gardens.

"Justice, at last!" cried Sulla, and the citizens were afraid of each new dawn. Thousands of Romans fled the city.

One winter dusk, Cicero entered the Temple of Justice and went to the empty white altar of the Unknown God. He prayed silently. Why do You delay Your birth? Evil rides triumphantly through the streets of Rome. Why have You denied us Your salvation?

The altar glimmered in the half-light; Marcus pressed his cheek against it. "Help us," he said aloud.

Scaevola had once told Marcus, "We shall not be lost as a nation until the College of Pontiffs is seized by a tyrant and made to serve his will."

Now Sulla had declared himself head of the pontiffs. He spoke only as directed by the gods, he said, and the pontiffs did not denounce him. He appointed his favorites to the Senate, increasing it to six hundred members. Some were prosperous businessmen, for he wished to gain their favor. Contrary to ancient Roman law, which laid all power in the hands of the public assembly, the Senate was given power over that body. Sulla had destroyed the constitution with a stroke of his pen.

That year the festival of the Saturnalia was very subdued. Sulla ordered tremendous amounts of food to be given to the people and arranged for magnificent public games. The people accepted it all, but they were filled with apprehension.

The month of Janus was extraordinarily cold. Marcus heaped coals upon the brazier in Scaevola's office, which he now occupied. The blue woolen curtains were drawn tightly over the windows even at noonday, but the floor was like ice, and the chill seeped through his fur-lined shoes.

Now he had students of his own, and he was kind and patient with them. He told them: "Law must prevail or our humanity will be lost. There are natural laws of God which can never be changed. Let us study them."

One day one of his students came to him in terror and cried, "Master, a centurion wishes to see you!"

Marcus said, with a calmness he did not feel, "Request the centurion to enter."

A young man in armor came in with a clangor of ironshod shoes, and raised his right arm stiffly in salute. "Greetings, Cicero," he said. "I am Lepidus Cotta, commanded to escort you to dine with General Sulla. At noon, which is now."

"It is impossible," Marcus said. "I am to present an important case in the Basilica of Justice within the hour."

The centurion's jaw dropped. He said, "Master, shall I return to Sulla and give him that reply?"

"I have had two postponements of my case, Cotta. In the interest of my client I think it best that I present it now, without fail. Then I will go to Sulla."

"We have a litter awaiting you," Cotta said.

So I am not to die—at least not immediately, Cicero thought. Escorted by Cotta, and accompanied by Syrius, he went out and entered the warm litter awaiting him. Four slaves in scarlet mantles lifted it, soldiers surrounded it, and they marched off, Syrius running behind.

Seeing the litter, the magistrate was awed and respectful as Marcus presented his case. He signed the papyrus with a flourish and imprinted his seal upon it. Marcus marched out with his helmeted escort.

At Sulla's walled house the guards saluted, and a ruffle of drums announced Marcus. They went through a marble hall into a spacious room with a floor of black and white marble. The furniture was of lemonwood and ebony inlaid with ivory. A man at an immense table lifted his head, frowning, when Marcus entered. "Greetings," Sulla said, and yawned.

He was in his middle fifties, lean, browned, leathery, with very black eyebrows as straight as daggers over the palest and most terrible eyes Marcus had ever seen. He thrust aside a mass of scrolls on the table, dismissed the centurion, and sent Syrius off to the kitchens. Then to Cicero he said, "Seat yourself. You must be content with a soldier's meal. You have never been a soldier?"

"No, lord. But my brother, Quintus, is a centurion in Gaul. My parents and I have not heard from him for a long time—we fear he is dead."

Sulla looked at him with a curious expression. "Death is the companion of soldiers," he said.

"It is the companion of all Romans," Marcus said.

"And particularly now?" said Sulla. He was actually smiling.

Marcus did not reply. Sulla said, "I have heard much of you from my dear friend Scaevola. Did he never speak of me to you?"

"He said that you were preferable to Cinna and Carbo."

Sulla was amused. "He was discreet. I was his friend from youth. As my agent, he was more valuable to me than a legion. And you, whom he loved, never suspected it!"

"No, lord." Marcus felt suddenly weary. "So that was why Carbo had him murdered."

"Scaevola knew I was inevitable, and the lesser of two evils. Also, he loved me. He had no greater love, except for his family and his country. And I myself loved Scaevola."

Marcus heard the tremor of genuine emotion in the soldier's voice. "Your grandfather was my captain," Sulla went on. "Rome is poorer for his death. She has been growing poorer every year as her heroes have died. But they were old-fashioned heroes. We live in a changing world, and they would not change."

Marcus said, "On every hand I hear the excuse that we live in a changing world!"

"People love slogans and always believe that change means progress. We must not disillusion them." His teeth flashed in a broader smile. "I admire you, for you are a brave man like your grandfather. Ah, my other guest has arrived."

Marcus turned, and started with astonishment. There, smiling gaily, was his old friend Julius Caesar. He rose, and Julius seized him by the arms. "My dear Marcus!" he exclaimed. "I never see you without joy and pleasure!"

"And I never see you without amazement," said Marcus, but he could not help smiling.

Julius laughed. "Why, here we are at home, you and I!"

Cicero's suspicions about his friend returned to him. Caesar was a member of the *populares* party, which advocated the democracy Sulla detested. Julius should be Sulla's mortal enemy. But why should he expect him to have principles?

Julius took a chair as slaves brought in a table laid with a linen cloth and gilt spoons and knives, and trays of food and wine. Sulla poured wine into three goblets, then spilled a little in libation. "To the Unknown God," he said.

Marcus was amazed. He also poured a libation to the Unknown God, and felt a spasm of pain and longing.

Julius said, "To Jupiter, my patron."

"Whose temple was destroyed," said Sulla. "I have announced that Jupiter wishes a far more magnificent temple. We shall have a lottery to finance it, which will please the masses—and the frugal also, for they know we are bankrupt."

Marcus ate in silence. As he listened to Julius' jocular exchanges with Sulla, whom he obviously amused, he wondered again why he had been brought here.

They had just finished their dinner when the door opened and Caesar's friend Pompey entered in uniform. He saluted Sulla, then turned his broad, impassive face to Marcus. "Cicero, law and order are now restored. At the last, law must rely upon military discipline to support it."

He sat down and poured wine, and Marcus noted that he did not wear the serpentine ring. Marcus said, "The work of the lawmaker is not less glorious than that of the commander."

"So speaks the civilian," said Pompey disdainfully.

"I speak as a Roman," said Marcus with quiet anger.

Surprisingly, Sulla said, "Cicero can be trusted." Is it possible that they were afraid of me? Marcus asked himself incredulously. "Julius told me," Sulla went on, "that you have always mistrusted the masses, Cicero."

"I distrust uncontrolled emotion, lord. If man is to rise above beasthood he must obey just law. The people have souls and minds! I ask that rulers appeal to these things, not to base appetites!"

"I am pleased to find a man who loves the laws of Rome," said Sulla. "I have restored the law. I have restored the Republic. I have delivered my people from lawlessness."

We do not speak the same language, thought Marcus with despair. But now Sulla was smiling his cold smile. He said, "Cicero, I have news for you. Your brother, Quintus, is under my roof."

Marcus' first emotion was shock. Then joy ran through him. He rose. "Where is he?" he cried.

Sulla said, "Sit down, Cicero, and let me tell you. Quintus fought with me to the very gates of Rome, and there fell. He was taken to a farmhouse and cared for by my own physician, but his life was despaired of. Then only two days ago there was new hope, and, since I look upon him as a son, he was brought to this house. He is still in danger, but my physician now believes that he will survive."

Marcus said angrily, "My parents and I have lived in agony for nearly a year! Why did we not have letters from Quintus? Or a word from you?"

Sulla cut through Cicero's protest. "Have you forgotten that the consuls thought of me as a traitor? If they had known Quintus was my loyal officer, they would have visited their revenge on your whole family. Your brother would have died, had not Catiline come to his rescue. He had been unhorsed, but Catiline slew his attackers. Is it therefore not time, Cicero, to forget your boyish disagreement with Lucius Catiline?"

Marcus put his hands over his face. "I am grateful to Catiline," he said at last. "May I see my brother?"

Julius rose. "Dear friend, I shall take you to him."

He led Marcus into the atrium as the outer door opened, admitting a white swirl of snow. A young woman entered gaily, throwing back her hood to reveal curling masses of golden hair and the face of a beautiful but wicked child.

"Divinity!" cried Julius. He kissed her white hand.

The girl's laughter was like a tinkle of lutes. "Who is this?" she demanded in the sweetest of voices.

"Marcus Tullius Cicero. Marcus, the Lady Aurelia."

Marcus knew of her. She was a rich and licentious young woman, twice divorced. "Where is Lucius?" she asked Julius.

"He will be here in a moment," he said.

"Lucius Catiline?" said Marcus.

Quickly, Julius took his arm. "You want to see Quintus," he said, and he added, "Sulla is also named Lucius."

He guided Marcus to a magnificent bedchamber with a wide bed strewn with fur robes. Marcus gazed at the face on the silken pillows. He could not believe that this emaciated man was his beloved Quintus. He dropped to his knees and laid his head beside that of the unconscious man. "Quintus," he said. *"Carissime*, it is Marcus."

Slowly Quintus' eyes fluttered open and the head turned. Marcus bent his ear and heard a sigh. "Marcus?"

"Beloved Quintus," said Marcus. "Rest. Sleep." He held the cold hands between his warm palms.

The lips stirred again, in a shadow of Quintus' amiable grin, and suddenly the soldier sighed with contentment and fell asleep. Marcus felt a compassionate hand on his shoulder and heard a voice. It was the physician. He said, "He will live. Go, and give your mother the joyous news."

CHAPTER EIGHT

ONE DAY WHEN Cicero returned from the courts a clerk told him that a mysterious lady had come to see him about her will. "She would not leave her name," said the clerk. "When I told her you were not here she lifted her hands in resignation, and she departed like one who has been refused a last reprieve. I did not see her face. But one lock of hair escaped her hood; it had a glorious color."

Cicero's heart jumped. "Hair like an autumn leaf?" he said. "Yes, master," said the clerk. "And her voice was sweet."

Livia, thought Marcus. Rumor said that Catiline had spent the last of his fortune, and all of his wife's. He lived a profligate life with his friends Piso and Curius, and now he was infatuated with the dissolute Aurelia Orestilla, who would marry him if he divorced Livia. But divorce meant he must return Livia's dowry, which he could not do.

Marcus dismissed his clerk. If Livia were divorced she would be free for another marriage. Now he knew that the fury of his love had only waited under his self-control. Should he send her a message? But what if it had not been she?

Suddenly he thought of Aurelia Caesar. Forgetting his lawyer's prudence he wrote to her: "In confidence, I have reason to believe that Livia Catiline came to my office today. Dear friend of my mother, can you give me any enlightenment?"

He waited in his office until the answer finally came that evening. Livia and her son were visiting relatives near Naples. Aurelia added, "Livia has been strange for a long time. It was thought by those who loved her that she should rest in the country."

The letter devastated Marcus. He could deceive himself no longer. Without Livia, he was nothing. As he was borne home in the litter he could now afford, he closed the curtains so he would not see the faces on the street. He struggled within himself, telling himself to be a man.

Quintus was at home, recovering rapidly. As usual, he was surrounded by friends. They were like bear cubs, Marcus thought, laughing and cursing as they diced on the blankets. (In fact, Catiline, Quintus said, called him Bear Cub.) They thought Marcus a serious elderly man, though he was but a few years their senior.

He wished to avoid their callow youth and noise today. He went to his *cubiculum.* He had begun a long series of essays for his publisher. He swept the scrolls from the table, as if he could not bear the sight of them.

WHEN, ONE MORNING, Cicero's clerk announced a visit from Caesar and Catiline, the old hatred shook Marcus; but he motioned to his clerk to admit his visitors.

Julius was magnificently attired in purple and gold, with Catiline, in a crimson cloak and glittering golden ornaments, beside him. Caesar embraced Marcus. Then Catiline held out his hand. Mechanically, Marcus stretched out his own. But in the second before encounter both dropped their hands. The space between them was like an unsheathed sword.

"Greetings, Cicero," said Catiline. "How is our Quintus?"

"Well," said Marcus. "I thank you for that, Lucius."

Catiline smiled. "We are soldiers. I love your brother."

Marcus turned to Julius, who had seated himself. Julius said, "We are here on a matter of importance, Marcus. You are the tenth lawyer we have visited this morning. Gods, we are weary! Will you not offer us wine?"

"You are in difficulties, I trust?" said Marcus. He struck a bell.

"It is only that we need information, and the other lawyers had none."

Syrius entered and poured wine. Catiline and Julius drank deeply, but Marcus could not bring himself to drink with Catiline. He touched the rim of the goblet to his lips.

"What is the information you require?"

"The matter of a will. Or a will not made," said Julius.

Marcus' heart had jumped violently. "Whose will?"

"It is a sad story," said Julius. "The will of Lucius' wife, Livia. Do you know of such a will?"

Marcus could not speak for a moment. He knew they were watching him like tigers. He said, "I know of no such will."

"You were never a liar, alas," said Julius. "Therefore, I must believe you."

"But if I had seen a will," Marcus said, "I would have said, 'My clients' affairs are confidential.' "

"So," said Julius. He lifted a brief from the table. He scanned it carelessly and burst out laughing. "A lady wishes to divorce her husband because he has dallied with her sister! How small-minded! After all, it is a family affair!"

"Put down my briefs!" said Marcus with fury.

"My apologies," Julius said. "Curiosity is an old vice of mine." He folded his arms and relaxed, but now his stare was hard on Marcus.

"Not one of the other lawyers had been visited by Livia. Were you?"

The question was sudden and fierce, for all its quiet.

"How could it be possible for Lady Livia to visit me, when she is not in Rome?" Then Cicero was aghast, for a look flashed between the others.

Catiline spoke softly. "It is true that she was away. But she returned. How did you know she had been absent?"

"Rumor," said Marcus, wanting to kill him.

Catiline arched his brows. "Did you know Livia?"

"When we were children. She visited in Arpinum." Marcus clenched his fists on his knees.

"The sweet memories of childhood," sighed Julius. "Lucius, let us go. There are other lawyers to question."

"I believe," said Catiline in a deadly voice, "that this lawyer knows something. Cicero, did my wife visit you here?"

Marcus arose. "Had she done so I would not tell you."

"Then she visited you," said Catiline, and his hand stole to his sword. "What did she say to you, Cicero?"

"Are you threatening me?" cried Marcus, shaking with rage. "Do you wish another engagement, Catiline?"

Julius put his hand soothingly on Cicero's arm. "Forgive Lucius," he said. "He has suffered a great sorrow."

"Livia?" Marcus whispered.

"Had you not heard?" asked Julius, and now there was genuine compassion in his tone. "She has been mad for many years. Did she not appear strange to you, even as a maiden? Did she tell you that when her mother died her father killed himself? And one of her aunts committed suicide, and also her grandmother? Livia was mad."

"That is a lie," said Marcus. "Livia was a lonely orphan, the child of tragic parents. But she is not mad."

Julius said, "Livia has been under the care of physicians for a long time, and they have sworn to her condition. Do not embroil yourself in this, or hope for vengeance, Marcus. It is too late for Livia. Two nights ago she poisoned her son. Then she stabbed herself, and died."

Marcus felt the stillness of despair. He could see Livia as she had been in the forest, seated beneath a tree, a scarlet leaf like a stain of blood on her bosom. He thought: She is at peace, at last.

Julius spoke to him urgently. "The slaves say that several nights before Livia killed herself and her son she muttered of lawyers, and her will. Then one day she disappeared, and returned in a state of incoherent distress. She never spoke rationally again. Marcus, Lucius must discover if she consulted a lawyer and made a will. Who knows what absurdities she might have written in it, what baseless accusations? She had nothing to leave. She had been ruined by the wars. It is a measure of her madness that she did not know this."

Marcus turned to Catiline. He spoke hoarsely. "Livia wished to divorce you. In that case, you would have had to return her dowry, so she wished to dispose of it in case of her death after her divorce. But you had already dissipated her dowry. Livia's divorce action would have revealed this. Therefore you had to prevent her divorce action until you could have her certified as mad. When you learned she had tried to consult lawyers, what was left to you but murder?" His voice rose. "You murdered her!"

Julius stood up, as if shocked to the heart. "Marcus!"

Marcus rose and pointed at the silent Catiline. "Guilt is on his face! He poisoned his son! He plunged his dagger into Livia's innocent heart, and then placed it in her hand! What did you do then, base Catiline? Did you flee to friends, who would establish that you were with them while your wife and child were dying?" He swung to Julius. "Are you one of them?"

"He was indeed in my house!" exclaimed Julius. "And so was General Sulla."

"I call you to witness, Julius," said Catiline, "this vicious libel by a man who has always hated me!"

"Let us be calm," said Julius. But his face was pale. He looked for a long moment at Catiline.

"There is a redress for libel, Catiline," Marcus said. "Will you bring suit against me? Or will you arrange my 'suicide' also?" He turned to Julius Caesar. "Julius, I have loved you since you were a child, though I have not been deceived by you. I beg of you that you speak the truth."

Julius said, "Marcus, I swear to you that Lucius was with me and others when his wife died. A messenger came to tell us the news."

"And when had Catiline arrived at your house?"

"I am prepared to swear, and others with me, that Catiline had been with us for several hours."

"Then," said Marcus, "this has been discussed among all of you, before you even came to me." He lifted his arms in despair. "Is there no God to avenge this murder of a young woman and her child?"

Julius said, "Marcus, you have uttered a calumny against Catiline on no evidence save your own emotions. I knew Livia for many years. She was irrational and distraught, and it was not her marriage to Catiline which made her so. As for Catiline's attachment to Aurelia Orestilla, he has not sought to hide it. His marriage was a calamity. When he returned to Rome, his wife shrank from him as from the jaws of Cerberus."

"She had reason to be afraid. She told me how much she feared the return of Catiline." He held out his hand. "Julius, in the name of honor, in the memory of our long friendship, stand with me to bring a murderer to justice."

Julius took Marcus' hand. "If murder had been done, I would stand with you. But I am certain she killed her child and herself. Let this unhappy girl rest in peace; intemperate accusations will do her no good. To preserve her honor, we have given out that the two of them perished of tainted food."

Marcus said, his eyes blazing, "He who lives by the sword shall die by the sword. I say to you both: You will die as Livia died, in your own blood!"

Catiline and Caesar were transfixed by his eloquent eyes. Both made the sign of protection against the evil eye, and fled.

CHAPTER NINE

PEACE ENFOLDED THE island; only the sounds of distant cattle, the occasional bark of a dog, the cries of birds and the splashing of water stirred the quietude. But Noë ben Joel, blinking in the sweet sunshine, thought, The country is disquieting. It makes man realize the noisy discord he brings into this world. The earth is joyously one with God, like a temple at dawn before man profanes it with his presence. I prefer the city, where I can delude myself that I am Jehovah's crowning achievement.

He looked for Marcus and found him sitting on a bank looking at the water, his face shadowed by sorrow. But when he saw Noë he smiled with pleasure.

Noë sat on the grass beside him. "When will your next book of essays be ready?"

Marcus moved restlessly. "I do not know. My publisher is impatient. Writers are only commodities to him."

"Without a publisher you could not afford this island."

"True," said Marcus. "But I also took your father's advice. I bought land and a villa or two, which are now very valuable. And I have received three magnificent legacies from grateful clients."

Noë coughed significantly. "I too have been fortunate! The great actor Roscius has consented to appear in my play. He is a scoundrel and a mountebank, but the ladies of Rome adore him."

"Roscius!" Marcus exclaimed. "Why, he can command his own fee!"

"He did," said Noë ruefully. "He is as penurious as a Spartan. Women have bought him villas, chariots, slaves and jewels. What a face he has! He has but to stride along a street to make every vehicle stop."

Marcus was amused. "How can you afford such a prodigy?"

"I cannot," said Noë. "He has robbed me. Now I must have an additional forty thousand sesterces before my play opens in Rome. But I shall make a profit of five times as much! Marcus, I have written a stupendous play. I have a copy with me for you to read. Then I am offering you a part interest in Roscius."

Marcus groaned. "How much?"

"Twenty thousand sesterces for one third of the godlike Roscius. Such an opportunity will never come to you again!"

"For which I devoutly thank the gods. Did you come here only for this? Ah, I have hurt you, dear friend. I only jest. I will write you a draft on my bank tonight."

Noë said, "This Roscius would not meet with the approval of the old men in Jerusalem, who despise beauty of body and prefer the beauty of soul."

Marcus seized his friend by the arm. "Noë, do you still expect the Messiah to be born?"

"In the Sacred Books it is written, *Who is she that looketh forth as the morning, fair as the moon, clear as the sun, and terrible as an army with banners?* Holy men now seek the Mother of the Messiah everywhere. They declare that they will know her by her beauty and her majesty. But her Son will be known by an act of faith only."

Marcus considered. "By an act of faith only? That is too much to ask of mankind. We, with our feet plunged deep in earth, to rise like birds into a light unseen? To fling ourselves on the winds of trust? It is too stupendous an act for men."

Noë said gently, "Trust in God is not vain, Marcus. I have seen the transfigured faces of the old men in Jerusalem when they speak of Him. I must believe like them, or I must die." And marveling, he went on, "I did not know how much I believed until this very instant!" He added, "If you wish, you may withdraw your promise to buy one third of Roscius."

Marcus burst out laughing and Noë thought: He is alive again. God be thanked.

Helvia heard the young men's laughter as they approached the farmhouse, and she closed her eyes a moment to thank her patroness, Juno, for this mercy to her sorrow-darkened son. Quintus returned from the fields and stopped to listen with disbelief as he stood in his rough herdsman's tunic of gray cloth. He nodded happily and thought, My brother has returned to us.

NOË BEN JOEL'S play *The Fire-Bearer* was based on the legend of Prometheus, who stole fire from Heaven. It was a magnificent success, and by the time Quintus returned to the legions Marcus was receiving pleasant sums from the production.

Just before the Saturnalia, Cicero's publisher, the Greek Atticus, visited him in his office.

Marcus greeted the stout, jovial young man. "Have you and the law collided?" he asked. "Perhaps you have published a book which one of Sulla's grim censors has pronounced a danger to youth?"

"In a manner of speaking, yes. But the book is not lewd; it is merely honest. It was written by an old soldier, Cato Servius, a captain under Sulla."

Marcus was interested. "Ah, the great soldier who lost his

sight and his left arm while fighting with Sulla. I have read his book. It was written with fire and passion, in behalf of the old Roman virtues and against oppressive government. It demanded a return to national solvency and industry and patriotism. I thought, when I read it, Rome is not yet dead when such a man can write and be published. But not once did the book denounce Sulla."

"Sulla leaves much to his captains and his bright politicians. Cato's book has fallen into their hands, and Cato is now in the Mamertine prison, charged with treason. The penalty asked is death, and the prosecutors are Caesar and Pompey. I have come to ask you to defend him."

"I will do what I can," Marcus said.

Together they went to the prison where they found Cato lodged in a comfortable room reserved for respected public men who had annoyed the government.

Cato was a man about sixty, of a poor but patrician family. His wife had brought him a huge dowry and a deep love. Now he had no wife, his sons had died in the wars, and his fortune had been confiscated. But he sat with dignity before a small stove, wearing full uniform. He turned his blind, scarred face toward his visitors and said in his irascible soldier's voice, "Who has entered?"

"Atticus," the publisher said, "and Cicero, a lawyer."

Servius extended his hand. "Greetings, Atticus. But why should a soldier who has done no wrong need a lawyer? I laughed in the faces of those who read out my 'offense' against Rome. Sulla must be laughing now as he reads the letter I sent him this morning. I thought my release had come when you entered—but Sulla is very busy these days. One understands that."

Atticus and Marcus exchanged glances.

The publisher said gently, "Cato, Sulla signed the order for your arrest."

Cato fell silent. Then he beat his bony knees with his clenched fist. "I do not wish to live in a Rome no longer the home of honorable men!"

"You have two young grandsons," Marcus said. "Will you leave them a disgraced name? A man does not live only for himself, but for his descendants. You must defend yourself. You must fight for Rome."

"I wrote my book so my grandchildren could live in liberty." He paused. "Cicero, can you restore my name?"

"It is possible I cannot save your life, lord. But I will, with the help of Pallas Athena, clear your name."

Cato's proud lips quivered. "That is all that matters."

When Cicero returned to his office he wrote Caesar: "I have undertaken the defense of Cato. Remember, Julius, that his convenient death in the Mamertine would set indignant rumors afloat among his soldiers."

Then he wrote a letter to Noë and sent him a copy of Cato's book.

Upon reading the book, Noë thought for a long time. Then he went to Roscius' villa. He said to the actor, "I have a matter to discuss with you."

"That means money," said Roscius, his violet eyes narrowing.

"No. I am offering you glory and honor, Roscius. As you know, an actor is not considered the equal of a gladiator in Rome. But when an actor becomes a hero, even Romans bow before him."

"This sounds very dangerous to me," said Roscius.

"Roscius, you have an opportunity to be a greater hero."

"Are you plotting my death?" said Roscius. But he listened with profound attention as Noë spoke. He took Cato's book and scanned a page or two. Then he began to pace up and down. Finally he stopped before Noë and glared at him. "Sulla will have me murdered!" he said.

But actually, within him, his actor's soul was afire. This was an opportunity no actor could resist, and at last he agreed. Noë left him with a high heart.

Marcus, while this was taking place, received a visit from Caesar.

"Dear Marcus!" exclaimed Julius. "I have neglected you! You are looking in good health." Then his smile faded. "These are dangerous days, *carissime*."

Cicero called for wine, and the two men drank in silence. Then Julius made a grimace. "I must send you some wine from my own cellars," he said. "It is not that you are poor. You are comparatively rich."

"I save my money. Why did you come, Julius?"

"Because I have discussed your letter with Sulla. To keep Rome at peace, we must present an image of power abroad. You are endangering that with your defense of Cato, which will inflame the mob. Cato is now quite mad. We do not deplore patriotism, but these old soldiers, who have been deranged by battle and suffering, rant wildly and cry ruin. But, Marcus, we are willing to make concessions. There are grumblings in the city about Cato. We will return his military honors and his fortune and let him go in peace."

"And the people will then acclaim Sulla for his compassion, but Cato's name will be dishonored forever."

"What is a name?" asked Julius.

Cicero flamed into anger. "To Cato it is the whole world. He cares for honor, a word you do not know."

"I am a sensible man and I move with the times. You will not move from the past."

"The past is also the present and the future. The nation that forgets that is doomed."

Julius said, "We are prepared to offer you a magnificent sum for your withdrawal from the case."

"I do not want Sulla's money. Let him restore Cato's name."

"That is impossible." Julius stood up. "I told Sulla you would be obdurate. I bear his invitation that you dine with him tonight so he may lay his case before you."

"If I refuse?"

"I would not recommend that," said Julius softly. "What a fool you are, Marcus! It is sunset. I now order you to accompany me to Sulla's house."

SULLA MET CICERO in the atrium of his house, and led him and Julius into the dining hall like a fond father. The other guests were Cicero's old enemies, malicious Piso and surly Curius, together with Pompey and the wealthy Crassus. They were reclining on divans about the table, drinking wine from Grecian goblets and sampling dishes of anchovies, pickled fish, sausages in a pungent sauce, and squid floating in olive oil and spices. Between the divans were chairs, occupied by pretty girls in sleeveless, brightly colored robes. Sulla, in a throne-like chair at the head of the table, was straight and military.

Cicero sat between Pompey and Julius. He had not known that Sulla had a passion for wanton girls and lewd conversation, but the dictator was enjoying himself as the girls chattered and squealed, leaning over to kiss their dimpled white shoulders.

"I see that our friend Catiline is not here," Marcus said.

Sulla's eyes filled with amusement. He said, "No, he is enjoying the embraces of his bride tonight."

"I thought that he was mourning the murder of his wife."

Julius laughed loudly. "What a jester Marcus is!" he exclaimed. He nudged Marcus sharply in the ribs with his elbow. "My general, your wine must be potent."

"Not as potent as my outrage," said Marcus.

"Let us discuss pleasanter matters," said Sulla, as slaves brought in a roast suckling pig on a silver platter, broiled fish, vegetables and sauces, and poured more wine. "I thought we would have an amiable dinner."

"I assume I am here for a purpose," said Marcus. "To discuss my defense of Cato before the Senate."

Sulla was no longer smiling, but he spoke kindly. "Julius has told you of our offer. Why are you stubborn? Cato is sick; he has not long to live." He lifted his hand. "You will speak of the dishonor. Public dishonor, my dear young friend, is not the stigma it was once in Rome. And men have short memories; the grandsons will not suffer."

"Cato and his grandsons revere their honor more than their lives. I shall protect them with all the law I know."

Piso and Curius laughed aloud, and Julius clapped derisively.

"Heroic words!" said Curius. "Worthy of a Chick-pea."

"Worthy of a Roman," said Marcus. "But who is here who understands what that means?"

"I," said Sulla. His angry voice filled the room and he pointed a thin brown finger at Marcus. "Consider this Rome of ours, Cicero. Once the forebears of our senators walked barefoot to a rude wooden chamber to indicate their humility before the people, the gods and eternal law. They spoke in country accents, with manliness, justice and pride. Look upon their inheritors! Would our senators today give up a fraction of their power or their fortunes, or one of their mistresses, to save Rome?"

"No," Marcus said desolately.

"Consider the politicians! Will they exhort the electorate to virtue and thrift? Will they face the mobs of Rome and say, 'Be men and not idlers?' And your own middle class, Cicero. Will they relinquish the profits of war and demand peace? These fat men! Will they stand in the Forum and tell the people the fate of Rome unless they return to virtue and thrift?"

"Before God, no," said Marcus.

"Cicero, for years our subsidized farmers have sold their grain to the government, to feed the slothful mobs. The farmers are happy: it is nothing to them that our treasury is bankrupt. And if a hero told the mobs that the government would no longer give them food and amusements, they would murder him. Now let us consider the 'old' Romans like yourself. Are there a dozen who would pledge their lives, their fortunes and their sacred honor* to re-create the old Rome?"

Marcus' lips were white. He shook his head. "They are afraid to lift their voices."

Sulla's face was black with passion. "Cicero, look upon me, the dictator of Rome! If one hundred men whom I could honor had met me at the gates and had said, 'Lay down your arms, Sulla, and enter the city on foot as a Roman citizen,' I would have obeyed in thankfulness. There was not one man to challenge me. I would, even now, try to restore Roman law and virtue. But a dead nation cannot rise again. I tell you that worse men will follow me!"

He lifted his goblet and stared about him, at the silent young men and the empty-faced women. "These, Cicero," he said, "are the Rome of tomorrow."

Julius said, "Lord, you do us an injustice. We love Rome."

Sulla threw back his head and laughed long and loud. It was a frightful sound.

Marcus stood up, and waited until Sulla's laughter had died. When he had the general's attention he said in a quiet voice, "Lord, I stand indicted before you. I was not at the gates to challenge your entry. I was a coward. I must remove my guilt.

---

*Patrick Henry quoted these actual words of Sulla, whom he admired.

For that reason I must defend Cato—and through him defend the Rome I betrayed."

He bowed. Then in silence he walked from the room.

Sulla said sadly, "There goes a Roman, marked for death."

"A traitor," said Curius with contempt.

"A fool," said Piso. "A baseborn fool."

"A man of emotional, hasty judgments," said Julius.

"A man," Sulla said.

CHAPTER TEN

JUST BEFORE HE was to defend Cato, Marcus dined with Roscius and Noë in the actor's gem of a house.

"Politicians," said Roscius to Cicero, "must be mountebanks, or they are not politicians."

"I am not yet a politician," said Marcus. But he was coming to realize that to save his country law was not enough, even the grandeur of Roman law.

"My dear friend," said Roscius, "all lawyers are incipient politicians, and both professions require acting. It is not what they say, but how they say it. One of my early mentors had the ability to count to ten in so moving a voice that spectators burst into tears."

He studied Marcus. "You have a proud air," he said. "But in defending Cato you must appear broken. You must wear mourning, and lean on a staff, and there must be a kerchief in your hand to wipe your tears away." He lifted his hand as Marcus began to protest. "Listen intently to me, dear friend!" And as he spoke, Marcus forgot his indignation and began to laugh.

Marcus gave exclusive thought to the case of Cato Servius in the next few days, but nothing he wrote pleased him. He went to his father and explained all to him.

The emaciated Tullius listened with passion. "You say it is possible to save Servius' honor. But you must save his life also, for which you despair. What you save of the true Rome today will be remembered by a few, and they will hand the lamp of truth down through the ages to other men, to light the darkness."

Marcus put his hands on his father's shoulders and bent and

kissed his cheek. "You are right, my father," he said. And he marveled again that one so secluded and timid could strike so directly at the heart of a matter.

CAESAR SAID TO Catiline, "Did you know that Cicero has written Sulla to say that he will *denounce* his client Cato before the Senate? He has respectfully prayed that Sulla be present."

"No! It is not possible!" Catiline said incredulously. "Then he is not so formidable! He is a trickster, but he would never dare humiliate Sulla before the Senate."

But Caesar said, "Cicero is afraid of nothing. . . ."

As Julius was saying this, Marcus sat knee to knee with Cato in the Mamertine prison. "I cannot do this," Cato said.

Marcus said wearily, "I am asking you to do nothing dishonorable. The gods expect men to use their intelligence. You must meet your enemies on their own ground."

That night Marcus went to his parents and told them his strategy. To Marcus' astonishment, Tullius began to laugh, at first faintly, and then with huge, gathering mirth. "It is a marvelous comedy!" he exclaimed.

Sulla, alone the night before the Senate would hear the charges against Cato, considered Marcus' extraordinary letter with a strange emotion. Then he, who did not believe in the gods, went to the shrine of Mars in his atrium and lighted a candle before the statue. He said aloud, "There are soldiers who never bore a sword, and brave men who died in no battle."

DURING THE NIGHT snow fell, white and heavy, over the great city. Caesar, riding in his fine litter with Pompey, said with satisfaction, "There will be few of the mob in the Forum this day."

But they were disagreeably astounded, for a veritable ocean of humanity was roaring into the Forum, and the steps of the Senate were packed. The litter was halted and Julius sent a slave with a staff to try to breach the fortress of human flesh. Then the fortress suddenly parted and a company of mounted soldiers appeared, led by Roscius the actor. Following them on foot was a turbulent river of soldiers carrying the banners of their legion.

"Roscius, with Cato's accursed soldiers!" cried Caesar.

His litter proceeded, then was halted again. Suddenly trumpets shattered the air on the rise of the Palatine Hill, and there was a thundering of drums. Soldiers with drawn swords pressed back the screaming mobs, and through the corridor they made came a pounding of hoofs and the rumbling of a chariot leading a detachment of armored horsemen. And in that chariot, alone stood Sulla, dictator of Rome, bareheaded and clad in golden armor and golden tunic, a scarlet cloak rippling from his shoulders.

The Romans loved the spectacle. Their tyrant, whom they had rarely seen, appeared magnificent and heroic to them, and they raised their voices in an echoing roar.

Julius yelled with laughter. "Roscius has a rival!" He laughed until his face dripped tears. Then his dark face became contorted and a line of foam appeared at the edges of his lips.

Pompey shook him fiercely. "Control yourself!" he cried.

The sacred illness, as epilepsy was called, was rarely to be halted by an effort of will, but somehow Julius unclenched his fists and focused his eyes. He drew a quiet breath, then said, "We are here." He alighted from the litter and made his way to the Senate steps.

The mob, seeing Julius, roared their joyous approval, for they loved his gaiety and youth. He bounded up the steps and Pompey followed more slowly. They sat down in the Senate Chamber as, surrounded by his soldiers, Cato was led in, his white head high. He held out his helmet to a soldier, and acknowledged those present by touching his breast with his right fist. Then he bent his stately head to Sulla.

"Lucius?" he said.

Sulla moved as if stricken. "Cato," he said at last to his old comrade-in-arms. He added, "Where is the advocate of Captain Cato Servius?"

"Here, lord," answered a confident voice, and Cicero entered. To the Senate's astonishment, he was clothed in mourning, with ashes on his forehead.

Sulla's mouth twitched in anger. "What is this garb?"

"Lord," said Marcus, humbly, "I am in mourning for my client's crime."

"You admit, before trial, that your client is guilty?"

"I am not completely familiar with the alleged crimes."

"By the gods, read the roll to him," exclaimed Sulla.

So Julius rose and held up a scroll. He intoned the crimes: high treason, subversion, seeking the overthrow of lawful government, insurrection, incitement to riot, contempt of authority.

"Speak, Marcus Tullius Cicero," said Sulla.

Cicero lifted his hands with Roscius' own gesture of pleading, and Roscius, standing by the door, nodded with satisfaction.

"I do not know of these crimes," said Marcus. "But I know of a greater crime."

Sulla considered Marcus. He looked around at the senators and at the soldiers, and then he saw Roscius in his magnificence. His face darkened. "Are you responsible, Cicero, for this tremendous assemblage in the Forum today?"

"Lord, this is a case of tremendous importance to the people of Rome. You, lord, have been libeled. Your name has summoned them here."

At an arranged signal a bellow of sound arose and spread to the furthermost reaches of the Forum. "Hail, Cicero! Cicero!"

Sulla contemplated Marcus darkly. "It is not my name they are screeching. Cato, are you responsible for the appearance of your veterans, in defiance of this court?"

"No, Lucius!" exclaimed the old soldier.

Marcus said, "They have come as a tribute to their old commander, lord. Is it not moving?"

"I do not find it moving," said Sulla.

The soldiers gathered at the doors were watching Sulla. He recalled that Roscius, that infernal actor, was a patron of the veterans and had built two sanitoria for them. For a moment Sulla was moved. It would have gratified him if his bankrupt government could have done what Roscius had done. Finally he looked at Julius, whose eyes were mirthful. "You are the prosecutor, Caesar. Speak!"

Julius rose and struck a statuelike attitude, holding a copy of Cato's book high above his head. He said to the senators: "In this book, Cato Servius has accused his government of tyranny and the perversion of our hallowed constitution.

"Our noble dictator Sulla has labored to restore the constitution and all we had lost under men like Carbo! This is a painful labor, and these are dangerous days. During them, no excited voice must rise, or we shall fall into chaos again. Therefore, there is treason in this book!"

Cicero said, "May I ask you to read an excerpt from the book which illustrates the point you are—attempting to make?"

Julius hesitated. "We are all acquainted with this book."

Marcus said, "Are the senators familiar with this book?"

An old senator said, "We are."

"Would you then mention a passage which offends you?"

The old senator flushed. "I will not repeat treason."

Marcus said, "Caesar, may I again request that you read a section you found objectionable?"

Julius turned some pages as dead silence filled the chamber. Then he began to read:

" 'Let that nation beware which regards its ruler as a divinity, ostracizing those who differ from him, hailing all that he does and deluding themselves that he is superior to those who have elevated him.' "

"That is an attack on Sulla!" cried the old senator.

"How was it possible for Cincinnnatus, the father of our country, who said that four hundred years ago, to refer to Sulla?"

A great laugh burst from the soldiers, and the crowds outside caught it up. Sulla said, "There is no treason in the quotation."

Cicero said to Caesar, "Pray continue."

Caesar looked at Sulla for a signal, but Sulla's expression was unreadable. Caesar began to quote again:

" 'There are times of dire emergency when power is given to one man, but that time must be limited and the man scanned sleeplessly. Should he say, *I am the law,* depose him at once.' "

There were shouts of "Treason!" but Sulla said, "That also is a quotation from Cincinnatus." He raised his hand to hide a smile.

Watching Sulla, Caesar felt relieved. He said, "Let us leave the deathless words of Cincinnatus. We are all familiar with them."

"Continue, Caesar, with other readings," said Marcus.

Julius darted an inscrutable look at Cicero. Inwardly hilarious, he riffled the pages of the book and read a passage on the superiority of the educated, the landowners and the nobility to the common man.

The old senator said, "This is defiance of the democracy which Sulla has established!"

Marcus shook his head sadly. "Cato was quoting Aristotle."

Julius said with affected irritability, "It appears that Servius' book is composed almost entirely of quotations from great patriots and philosophers."

Cicero said, "Is it illegal to quote honored sources?" He raised his arms in a gesture of anguish. "Yes, unless a man who does so gives credit! Cato implies he is the author of these noble utterances. Therefore, he is guilty!" As if in remorse, he dropped his arms and bowed his head. "Woe unto me, I must accuse my client of a crime! Plagiarism! And I ask that he be punished.

"What is the punishment? Let me read it to you, lords: 'The offender shall be fined from one hundred to one thousand gold sesterces.' I leave the judgment in your merciful hands." He bowed humbly to the Senate, and then to Sulla.

Sulla seemed to be repressing mirth. "We have a serious infraction of the law here," he said. "Senators, what is your judgment?"

They stared at each other. The old senator said, "Two hundred sesterces' fine," and the rest muttered agreement.

Sulla said, "It is done. I order that Cato Servius' lands and fortune be restored to him, and that he be set free."

Cato turned his blind eyes to Sulla. He said bitterly, "Unless my old general forgives my—crime, I shall fall on my sword."

Sulla rose from his chair and descended the steps with slow majesty. He embraced Cato, his terrible light eyes filled with tears. "Henceforth, Cato, you are under my protection," he said. "I forgive you. Go in peace."

Cicero's friends gave the signal. Now the crowd screamed, "Hail, Sulla! Hail, Cicero! Hail!"

Cato said in a voice only Sulla heard: "You are still a tyrant, and the enemy of my country."

Sulla whispered, "Blame me not, Cato. The people willed it so." And Cato returned his embrace with understanding.

SULLA SOON RESIGNED his dictatorship, and a year later died. The consul, Marcus Lepidus, a friend of Pompey and a member of Caesar's *populares* party, managed to become dictator.

Caesar was in his first military post in Asia Minor. He wrote Cicero, "Though Lepidus is rich, you surely were not referring to him when you quoted Aristotle: 'Great office should not be bought, for this makes wealth of more account than nobility in a politician.' I feel a premonition that I shall soon look upon your face. In the meantime, may my ancestress, Venus, grant you a desirable maiden for a wife, and her son, Cupid, pierce your heart with his arrow."

Cicero put down the letter. He was in his late twenties, but he still could not forget Livia, though years had passed since her horrible death. She remained passionately young and elusive as a dryad.

Helvia had managed to marry Quintus to Pomponia, sister of the publisher Atticus. Quintus had the reputation of being a blustering soldier, but Pomponia soon succeeded in conquering him. It was a scandal in the family that Quintus had become a typical modern Roman husband—afraid of his wife.

Roscius, the rascal, was now in Jerusalem. "No doubt seeking forgiveness for his many crimes, especially against me," Noë wrote. "He is growing the Jewish beard, he writes me. I prefer to believe he is growing a centaur's tail and hoofs."

Cicero had become rich from the many cases he had won, but though he was not fool enough to despise riches, it seemed to him that his external life was a dream, and that the only realities were his memories of Livia, his studies, his poetry and his thoughts. He had developed rheumatism, and his endless work and increasing pain began to overcome him. One hot summer day he collapsed in his office, and his physician was called. He said, "You must rest. Go to Greece, to the shrine of the great physician Asclepius, who is reputed to cure the afflicted in dreams. Your rheumatism simply reflects the pain in your soul."

Before he was well enough to travel, Caesar and Pompey arrived to see him. "Dear friend!" Julius cried, leaning over the bed to embrace him. "I returned to Rome only yesterday, and heard of your illness but an hour ago."

"And I heard that Lepidus had put a price on your head," Marcus said. "Has no one attempted to assassinate you?"

Julius began chattering gaily, a habit of his when he wished to conceal his thoughts. "I am no threat to Lepidus," he said. "He belongs to my party, and my friend Pompey helped elect him. Besides, I have given up politics. I am a simple soldier."

Marcus laughed, and the two young men laughed with him. He saw that Pompey was regarding him with kindness, and this startled him. Then he noticed the serpentine ring on Pompey's hand. He averted his eyes. "Lepidus is a tyrant," he said. "At least Sulla forced the idle mobs to work or go hungry."

He leaned back wearily and closed his eyes. Suddenly a whirling chaos was before him, with strange half-seen forms and faces. Then they began to take shape. Without opening his eyes he murmured, "Not one of the three of us in this *cubiculum* will die peacefully in his bed."

"Who will betray me?" Caesar asked softly.

Marcus whispered, "Your son."

"I have no son," said Julius.

"And I?" said Pompey. "Who will kill me?"

"Your best friend," said Marcus in a faint voice.

Julius said, "He has many best friends." He took Cicero's cold hand. "Who would kill you, Marcus?"

"I do not see their faces," Marcus whispered.

He fell into a deep sleep as the curtains parted and Helvia stood on the threshold, her anxious gaze on her son. "He is much better," she said, seeing their disturbed expressions. "Soon he will be able to go to Greece."

"He spoke very mysteriously to us," said Julius.

"Marcus is superstitious," Helvia said indulgently. She reachéd under the pillows and brought forth a small silver object. The young men regarded it with horrified repugnance, for it was the cross of infamy, the top curved into a loop to hold a chain.

"It was given to him by an Egyptian merchant who was his client," said Helvia, replacing the cross. "It came from the tomb of an ancient pharaoh. We know it is the sign of the infamous death of the worst criminals, but the merchant told him that it was the sign of the Redeemer of mankind, prophesied eons ago, and he honors it as the sign of the redemption of man. He awaits the birth of a son of the gods."

Julius was smiling broadly. "Are the gods coming down from Olympus again for fresh romps?"

But Pompey did not smile. He looked back over his shoulder in fear as he and Julius left the sickroom.

In the litter, Julius noticed the ring on his friend's hand. "How imprudent of you!" he exclaimed. "Marcus recognized that ring! In revenge, he deliberately frightened us." Then he smiled admiringly. "He is more subtle than even I knew."

"IT IS EASY enough for you to counsel patience, Julius," said Catiline. "You are only twenty-three. But I am six years older."

The young men were sitting on a marble bench in the garden of the Caesar house on the Palatine, drinking honey-sweet wine. Peacocks strutted and spread their fans, and the scent of jasmine rose on the air.

"Now we have Lepidus," Catiline went on. "The Senate is weary of him, for he restricts their power and favors the people. He will soon be banished to Gaul. Then what of us?"

"One observes and considers. One throws the dice."

Catiline laughed. "Your dice are always loaded, Julius. Beware of losing your friends."

Julius looked offended. "What friends have I lost?"

"Cicero told you that you will be betrayed. He is plotting against you."

"Cicero? You are mad."

"He prophesied my murder. He is vindictive."

"He said my *son* would kill me. Have I a son? No."

Catiline smiled. "What of little Marcus Junius Brutus?"

Julius' face became cold. "You defame his mother, and his father, who is my friend."

Catiline moved cautiously on the bench. "Cicero haunts me," he said. "He is powerful now, and becoming interested in politics. He may challenge us."

"He is very sick. He may die."

"Let us, then, end his pain."

Caesar carefully put down his goblet. He said, "What do you recommend, Lucius? Poison?"

Catiline's eyes shifted like the flick of a snake's tongue. "Poison is a woman's weapon."

"Ah, yes. Livia employed it. I should have remembered. Lucius, it is true that I love Cicero for many reasons which

would seem absurd to you. Still, if he rose in my way I would dispatch him; yet he has powerful friends in Rome, and his brother is a soldier. Do you think they would all accept his death meekly? Let us not complicate our affairs."

As Catiline had prophesied, Lepidus was banished to Gaul by the Senate. But he stopped in Etruria and raised an army of disgruntled veterans. Defeated by Pompey, he escaped to Spain, where he was mysteriously murdered. The Senate solemnly announced that he was a noble soldier who had become deranged. They ordered public mourning for him.

CHAPTER ELEVEN

MARCUS WAS VISITING Atticus at his house in Athens. "I have heard," he said to Atticus, "that Greek buildings were erected not to please the eye of man but the eye of God. That is why they are so marvelous, so fascinating. Rome was built only for the glory of man."

The hot dry climate of Greece and a trip to the Temple of Asclepius at Epidaurus had restored Cicero's health. The temple was the final refuge of the hopelessly afflicted, and its priests were notable physicians.

The place was not only a shrine but a whole community. The inn at which Cicero, Quintus and Syrius stayed was a two-story structure of some one hundred and fifty rooms, the largest building in the sanctuary. It accepted the very poorest, who slept in the stables or under the porticos, as well as the rich; and rich and poor were served the same simple food, for the divine Asclepius, son of Apollo, loved all men. Outside the sanctuary also were small structures where the desperately sick and the pregnant were visited by the priest-physicians, for no one near death or about to give birth was permitted inside.

The sanctuary lay in a shallow valley surrounded by low hills, while above it all arched the incandescent blue of the Grecian sky. This was surely the land of Apollo, filled with depthless light, insistent and burning.

Sometimes Cicero thought that Greece was the Eden of which Noë ben Joel had spoken. From this land had flashed the light that had illuminated the wilderness of the Western world and given it art and philosphy.

Rome's cynical power had depressed Cicero. Now he thought of the words of Epictetus: "Know yourself. Take counsel with the Godhead. Without God put your hand to nothing!" And what of my unhappiness? thought Cicero. Epictetus again had an answer: "If any be unhappy let him remember that he is unhappy by reason of himself alone. For God has made all men to enjoy felicity and the constancy of God."

QUINTUS AND SYRIUS carried Marcus to the temple, for he could barely move because of the pain in his joints and muscles. Servants of the god bathed him in curative waters and dressed him in a white robe, and he sacrificed on the altar, where a great gold and ivory statue of Asclepius sat on a throne. His face expressed compassion and wisdom; one hand was on his staff and the other on the head of a serpent, while a dog lay humbly at his feet.

Marcus was laid upon his assigned pallet and a priest came to him with a cup in his hand. "This is a distillation of willow-tree bark efficacious in the treatment of rheumatic diseases. It will relieve your pain." Marcus drank the potion, which was acrid and vinegary.

As the sun sank, the clouds of incense were transformed into billows of deep purple. Then the temple was lit only by the scarlet light on the altar. Some patients, lying on their pallets, groaned, and priests moved among them, speaking soothingly and administering medicine. Other priests began a chant to Asclepius, their voices rising in majestic cadences.

Have mercy, God, prayed Cicero silently. He fell asleep.

The next morning he awoke to sunlight, feeling marvelously refreshed, for his body, though still weak, was without pain. The priests were already moving among the awakening patients, carrying tablets in their hands on which they recorded dreams.

When one priest came to Cicero, he said, "I did not dream at all."

"That is the best of sleep," said the priest, and gave him another potion. "Nightmares are the travail of the mind."

"I am well. Will this continue?"

The priest said, "We do not know the cause of the rheumatic

diseases, but we know that the rheumatic is a melancholy man, and the frustration in his soul is reflected in his locked joints. The spasmodic muscles, too, indicate the passionate struggles of the tormented spirit. Cicero, if your mind rests in peace your body will so rest. Pray that God will bless your efforts and leave all else in His hands."

It was true, Marcus reminded himself, that even if Rome passed away, God would remain, and all His plan for humanity. On the other hand, God would not interfere if man was bent on destruction, for He had given man free will. Therefore Cicero could not cease his personal fight on evil, for those who fight evil are the soldiers of God.

When Cicero left the temple, after leaving an offering in gratitude, the fierce dry heat of the sun made him blink. He sat alone in the inn for a long time, meditating, and when he emerged his face was peaceful.

The next day he left with Quintus and Syrius for Athens.

LUCENT LAND! THOUGHT Marcus, as he sat in the car driven by his brother, which raised great clouds of white, iridescent dust. To the right the Aegean was a royal purple, running with silvery light. To their left rose the cypress-wooded hills. They passed meadows filled with sheep and cattle, orchards of twisted, silver olive trees, little cities, each crowned by a templed acropolis, and villages crowded with white cube-shaped houses. At noon, they dined in a quiet inn on cold mutton, a spicy salad, brown bread and cheese and honey, and looked at the glowing sapphire sky of Greece.

They set off again, Quintus driving the fine black horses, and Syrius riding a white horse at the side of the car.

Quintus sang ribald ditties and Marcus drowsed, lulled by the sound of wheels and hoofs. The car was rolling along the empty road when Marcus woke to the ring of hoofs behind, and saw two hooded horsemen swiftly overtaking.

What magnificent white horses! he thought. Then he became anxious. The road was narrow here, and the embankment down to the sea was steep and stony. If the horsemen intended to pass the car they must go in single file. "Fools!" said Quintus, and Syrius dropped behind a little.

The horsemen came faster, as if the car before them did not exist. Syrius shouted and Quintus pulled on the reins. Then one horseman fell behind the other and they swept past the car in a rush of dust and thunder. They met beyond the car and slowed their pace. The air was full of blinding dust.

Like a flash a long spear shone in the hand of one of the horsemen. He flung it, and it struck one of the horses in the breast. The horse reared with a whinny and fell in his traces; and the car crashed onto his body. The other horse reared, tore loose from the car and raced off. As the car upended, Quintus sailed through the air, fell and lay still, and Cicero was hurled to the road, his forehead making savage contact with the level stones.

Syrius had seen the flash of the weapon and had pulled back. He was able to control his horse and whirl it about. But then he felt a deathly pain in his chest as a spear impaled him. He fell from his horse and sprawled dead in the dust.

Now all was quiet. The horsemen halted at a distance and looked back.

"Let us make sure," said one, preparing to dismount.

The other horseman hesitated. He heard the sound of distant hoofs.

"No!" he exclaimed. "They are all dead. Not even Quintus, with his thick head, could have survived that. And someone is approaching! Hurry!"

They swung their horses and plunged off the road across the meadows.

Quintus, protected by his helmet, was only stunned. He rose, spitting out blood, and saw Syrius' horse standing trembling near his body. In an instant Quintus was in the saddle, spurring the horse after the attackers, sword in hand.

He did not see another company of men who were now approaching the wreck with exclamations of dismay. They dismounted, and saw at once that Syrius was dead. Cicero's face was bleeding and his left arm was obviously broken, but he was breathing. The merchants began to minister to him.

"Thieves!" said one of them.

"How fortunate we came before they could complete the killing!" said another.

"Who is that pursuing the murderers? Look! He has overtaken them!"

They shaded their eyes from the sunset to stare at the little black figures wheeling in a death struggle. One horseman broke away, leaving his companion to struggle alone with the soldier. Quintus plunged his sword into the lone horseman's side, and the man tumbled to the ground. Quintus bent over him.

"Brave man!" cried one of the merchants.

MARCUS AWOKE TO discover himself in bed, with the bruised and wounded Quintus sitting beside him. His left arm, which throbbed like a fire, was bound to his side. He stared blankly at his brother's discolored face.

"Quintus!" he whispered.

Quintus started upright in the big oaken chair in which he had been drowsing. His swollen mouth spread in a smile. One tooth was missing. His left arm was bandaged.

"We are alive," said Quintus, "and that is all that matters. I must make a sacrifice to Mars, who saved us." He told Marcus briefly what had happened.

"My poor Syrius," Cicero said, weeping.

"The merchants brought us to this inn," Quintus said, "and three of their servants are now guarding our door, for they understand now that we were set upon by murderers, though it was intended to appear an attack by thieves."

"Who were the attackers?" said Marcus.

Quintus reached into his pouch and showed Marcus something small and glittering. "Do you recognize this? I took it from the dead hand of one of the assassins."

Marcus blinked at the jeweled serpentine ring in his brother's hand, and he could not speak.

Quintus flung it on the table. "It is obvious that your death is greatly desired."

"You did not recognize either of them, Quintus?"

"No, but they were Romans."

Safe in the home of Atticus, on a hill facing the Acropolis, Marcus wrote to Caesar in Rome: "I am returning this ring, taken from the dead hand of one of two horsemen who attacked me on the road from Epidaurus to Athens. I have loved you as a brother and I cannot believe that you are responsible for this second attack. But I am sure you know the persons who wish me dead. I shall never forgive those who caused the death of my devoted Syrius. Show the ring to your friends, Julius, and inform them that their blood will wipe out the blood of a slave."

In Rome, Julius sat at his table with his friends. The ring which Marcus had sent him lay on the table. Julius looked at the men who surrounded him.

"I have told you all," he said, "that Cicero is under my protection. One of you has flouted me. Catiline? Crassus? Piso? Curius? Pompey?"

Each shook his head.

"The Chick-pea is of no importance," snapped Catiline.

"Once you protested to me, Catiline, that Cicero was dangerous and should die. Have you changed your opinion?"

"Yes." Catiline smiled beautifully. "You convinced me."

"I have observed that none of you is wearing his ring tonight. I have also observed, Curius, that you wince if you move suddenly. Were you wounded by Quintus?"

Curius' dark and surly features were cold with anger. "I was wounded in a duel with the husband of the lady I love."

"I have not seen you for three weeks, Curius."

"I was recovering from my wounds."

"And the husband of the lady—he survived?"

"He is recovering."

Julius stared at him. "You told me once you did not know Quintus. So if he saw your face he would not have known it."

Curius struck the table violently. "You are accusing me of a lie, Caesar!"

Julius was not disturbed. "One here is guilty of the attempt on Cicero's life. I warn you again, if he dies, apparently in an accident, or is poisoned—a woman's weapon, is it not, Catiline?— I shall not rest until he is avenged."

Marcus sat on a stone seat in Atticus' garden and looked at the Acropolis. He was both depressed and exalted at the vision— depressed that man was now so little, and exalted that man could be so great. What was the power of empire compared with this?

Sunk in meditation, he started when burly Quintus brought him some newly arrived letters. "I am to be a father!" Quintus shouted. "Rejoice with me, Marcus!"

Marcus rose and embraced him and kissed his cheek. "Let us pray you will have a fine son," he said.

Quintus swaggered boyishly up and down the garden paths. He said, "My son will be a brave Roman."

Marcus did not suggest that the baby might be a girl. For a moment he was envious of his brother. Casual love, which was all he had, was no love at all. A man needed a woman who would love him above all others, keep his house and bear his children. For the first time, he thought seriously of marriage.

"You have not read your letters," said Quintus.

Marcus opened a letter from his mother. She reviewed Marcus' investments and advised the sale of some holdings. Tullius, she said, was less secluded, he now had a few congenial friends who had given him an interest in the public games. The olive groves and vineyards were bearing well.

She added, "I still wish you would take Terentia to wife. She is a patrician and her sister, Fabia, is a vestal virgin, which augurs a blessing on the marriage. She has a large dowry and is in all ways a desirable wife, though not young. Her intelligence would delight you, Marcus. It is true that she has not the beauty of her sister, but beauty is often cursed."

Marcus said to Quintus, "Do you know Terentia?"

"Hah!" said Quintus. "Her sister, Fabia, is remarkably lovely! What glorious eyes, what magnificent golden hair, what—"

"We were not speaking of Fabia, but of Terentia."

Quintus thought, his lips puckered. Then he said, "She is a friend of Pomponia. Her appearance does not come readily to my mind, but I recall that her voice was amiable and her demeanor retiring—truly 'old' Roman. She is of a mild countenance, like my Pomponia. But I suspect these soft-spoken women. Pomponia has a tongue like a viper."

"It would please our mother if I married Terentia."

"You? Marry? This is a grave matter." Quintus seated himself on the parapet. "When you marry your whole life is changed. No more freedom, no more adventure."

Marcus concealed his mirth. "You do not recommend it."

"There is not a husband, however handsome and virtuous his wife, who does not often wish he had never laid eyes on her!"

"Ah, traitor! I consider Pomponia adorable, and you the most fortunate of men! If Terentia resembles Pomponia—"

"She does," said Quintus in a sad tone.

"Then I will give the matter the most earnest thought. My new house on the Palatine needs a mistress."

MARCUS AND QUINTUS remained at the house of Atticus for six months. Marcus took lessons in elocution and rhetoric, and read philosophy at the school of Ptolemy. The sad mists which had enveloped his mind lifted, and he was happy with the joy of full maturity and acceptance. He wrote his mother that he would be glad to marry Terentia.

A few days before he left Athens a servant announced an Egyptian merchant, Anotis, one of the party that had come to Marcus' rescue on the road from Epidaurus. Marcus received him on the terrace. He said, "Noble Anotis, you did not linger so we could thank you for saving our lives. How can we repay you?"

Anotis smiled. "I did not know at first that we had helped the famous lawyer Marcus Tullius Cicero." His shining gray eyes were fixed on Cicero's face. "I helped undress you while you were unconscious, and saw a strange object about your neck, on a chain ornamented with the holy falcon of Horus." He paused. "Though a merchant, I was trained in the ancient mysteries."

"Ah," said Marcus, bringing forth the scarred silver cross. "The Egyptian who gave me this told me it is the sign of the Holy One who shall be born to men."

Anotis touched two fingers to his lips, then reverently to the cross. "It is so," he said.

"I wear it as a promise," said Marcus, "and as a hope. Does this represent the Messiah of the Jews?"

Servants had brought a table to the terrace and now they began to serve the noonday meal. Marcus and his guest lifted their goblets, and then poured a little wine in libation to the gods.

"Let me tell you," said the Egyptian as they dined, "of Holy Isis, our Mother. She was the spouse of Osiris, who was murdered and who rose from the dead in the springtime of the year."

Anotis drew a gold medallion from under his robe. "Behold the Holy Mother and Child," he said. On the medal appeared a beautiful little painting of a sweet-faced young woman with a child in her arms. "The sign of Horus was not only the falcon but also the cross, which represents Resurrection. The worship of Isis and Horus has ceased now the Greeks are in Egypt. But our priests have foretold that a Messiah will be born of woman in another country."

Anotis sighed. "There is not a race which does not have the legend that the Holy One will appear on this earth. Therefore God must have imparted this occult knowledge to all nations. But I no longer believe that Isis is the Holy Mother and Horus her Holy Child. My medal is but a prophecy of the Holy One."

Marcus said, "The Messiah is to come. But when?"

Anotis said, "Some of our priests are still hidden in Khem, our sacred land, and as I am of a priestly family I am admitted to their temples. They tell me of great portents and omens."

"Tell me!" Cicero cried. "I hunger and thirst for hope!"

The Egyptian bowed his head. "It is unlawful for me to reveal all that has been told me. Nevertheless, because of that holy amulet you wear I will tell you that the priests have seen a woman clothed with the sun, bright as the morning, crowned with stars and with a serpent under her foot. She is great with child. She is very young, but in her eyes are all wisdom, beauty and tenderness. When the priests saw this vision quivering with intense light above the altar fires they cried aloud: 'Isis! She comes again!' Her Son will not delay much longer. Let us pray that our eyes will behold Him."

They rose and stood side by side, gazing at the Acropolis. Anotis said, "When He comes, who will recognize Him? There is but one thing certain, that He will never pass from the minds of men as Horus did." He took the medallion from his neck and gave it to Marcus. "Wear it in faith, Cicero. I came to give it to you. Her name is not Isis, nor His name Horus. Their names are still hidden in Heaven."

WHEN THE TWO BROTHERS RETURNED to Rome after two years in Greece and Asia Minor, they found Helvia a plump matron with whitening hair, but with her old sturdiness of spirit and tranquillity. Tullius wanted to hear about Greece, but only the Greece of his dreams, where gods walked the streets of Athens and men spoke in poetry. My father, thought Marcus, wants to believe that Athenians have none of the concerns of ordinary humanity. Marcus was as usual annoyed by his father's innocence, and annoyed with himself for his own annoyance.

Julius Caesar called upon Marcus at once with his usual affectionate exuberance. "Ah, how I have missed you!" he cried.

"I hope you warned your friends with the serpentine rings of what I told you. Julius, what have you been plotting?"

"I plot nothing. I live, enjoy, love, sing." He looked at Marcus with his brilliant black eyes. "Your house on the Palatine is very handsome. Did you know that Catiline is now your neighbor?"

Cicero did not rise to the provocation, and Julius drank some wine and said boyishly, "Ah, this is excellent! Your taste has improved since you sojourned in Greece!" He looked into the depths of the goblet. "I hear a rumor, which I trust is absurd, that you are to marry Terentia."

"What is wrong with Terentia?" asked Marcus.

"She is not the wife for you. Her air is mild but it conceals granite. She dresses soberly, and her hands are large like a man's. Never marry a woman with masculine hands! And she is uncomfortably shrewd. There is not a day that she does not make transactions in the city. And she is still a virgin, at her age!"

"You convince me she will be an excellent wife and mother."

To Marcus' astonishment Julius became very serious. "Do not marry her, Marcus! She will make you wretched. A man needs laughter and sweetness—a woman who is at once a mother, a companion and a shy nymph. Terentia has a violent temper and unwomanly ambition."

"Julius, tell me the real reason for this solicitude. Is there someone else dear to you who wishes to marry her?"

"No! None will have her!"

"I will judge my marriage for myself."

"I foretell disaster." Julius paused. "Have you seen her sister, Fabia, the vestal virgin? She is very beautiful, and as sweet as balm. But I must not speak so," said Julius, his eyes sparkling, "for is it not blasphemous to speak of the vestals as ordinary women? Moreover, a vestal caught in unchastity is buried alive, and her lover beheaded."

"But this has nothing to do with Terentia," said Marcus. "Let us not discuss my future sister-in-law, dear friend."

Julius had been watching him closely. Now he appeared satisfied and relieved, which puzzled Marcus. The two friends embraced, and before leaving Julius said, "I still foretell disaster if you marry Terentia."

This conversation partly determined Marcus to marry his mother's choice. And when old Archias, his beloved tutor, died, Cicero had a sense of bereaving time and the impermanence of living. If he did not marry and have sons there would be nothing of him to remain for the future.

CAESAR SAID TO Catiline, "Let us go into your gardens so we may converse where your lovely Aurelia will not hear us."

They found a secluded spot in a grotto full of moonlight like poured honey. Catiline was now thirty-two, but he still looked like Adonis, though the lines about his mouth were depraved and there were times when Julius wondered uneasily if he had not inherited his ancestors' madness.

"Have you persuaded Chick-pea to relinquish the fair Terentia?" Catiline asked.

"Unfortunately, no. Your wife, Aurelia, has also failed with Terentia. She hinted that Cicero lacks virility and has secret vices, but Terentia is obstinate."

Catiline said, "Aurelia is becoming curious about my wanting her friend not to marry the Vetch, though I have told her it is because I hate him."

"Lucius," Julius said, "your infatuation with Fabia is dangerous, even calamitous. I beg of you, relinquish your pursuit of her! If evil, or even joy, comes to her in your arms, she will confide in Terentia. And neither Terentia nor Cicero will spare you."

Catiline rose and began to pace the scented grass. He said in a low voice, "I still insist Cicero must die, if necessary, to prevent that marriage."

"Do not weary me again with that! Are you a man, or a youth

enthralled by passion? We have too much at stake. I beseech you, forget her."

"No," said Lucius, and shook his head over and over. "She is in my blood. I must have her or I shall die."

That would not be a bad idea, Julius thought, though Catiline was valuable for his following in the Roman underworld.

Catiline turned on Julius as if he had read his dark thoughts. "Well?" Catiline said. "Is the secret brotherhood ever to move? Let us strike and have done with it."

"What we propose is too enormous, too tremendous for hasty action," Caesar said.

He left then. When he looked back once, Catiline was staring after him with a black and enraged expression.

HELVIA AND MARCUS went to see Terentia, who lived with her guardians.

"You must try to make a good impression," Helvia said. "Terentia looks upon me already as a mother. Your grandfather would have approved of her too, though I fear she intimidates your father. He told me that Terentia resembles me." Helvia smiled. "Am I so formidable?"

Cicero kissed his mother's cheek. "If she resembles you, then she has already won my heart."

The hot summer evening had drawn to dusk, and low dark clouds were streaming over the sky. Cicero and his mother were conducted to the garden where Terentia and Fabia sat on a marble bench. They rose, and at that moment a flash of brilliant lightning lit the air. Marcus saw Fabia glowing in it like a dream of Astarte.

Never had Cicero seen so lovely a woman. She was tall and graceful, and her veil only partially concealed the web of shining hair that fell to her shoulders. Her trusting eyes, almost as golden as her hair, were shadowed by thick lashes, and her expression was sweet and childlike. She stood meekly, her hands clasped before her; untouchable, divine.

"Terentia," said Helvia, pinching her son's arm. "My son, Marcus Tullius Cicero."

Marcus started, and turned in confusion to his hostess. He bowed.

Terentia already had a matronly figure. Her complexion was pale, and her brown hair was dressed severely. Her clear brown eyes were her best feature: they revealed character and intelligence. She wore no jewels, and her hands were big. My wife, thought Marcus, feeling depressed.

A sister vestal virgin arrived for Fabia almost immediately, and they left. Terentia said, "My dear Fabia wished to look upon you, noble Cicero." Her brown eyes were truly lovely in their deep affection for her sister.

"I know how dear she is to you, Terentia," said Helvia.

"It was a great honor to the family when Fabia became a vestal," Terentia said. "Men of the noblest families desired to marry her, but she has always been devout."

The clouds had turned livid and the wind rose. Helvia took Terentia's arm maternally and led her toward the house. "You will observe, my dear Terentia," she said, all too audibly, "that my son is awkward with women. That is because he is a scholar."

Terentia glanced back at Marcus, her eyes kind and warm. It was evidently all settled. He had no choice in the matter.

The first drops from the clouds were falling when they reached the portico. Suddenly Marcus thought of Livia and could have wept.

THE BETROTHAL WAS very sensible and without illusions. Marcus was to write later to Atticus: "It set the tone of my marriage." Cicero gave Terentia many gifts, according to custom, and Terentia told him that she would prefer useful gifts for their new home. He discovered a dismaying lack of humor in the young woman. Her learning was practical. She liked to discuss business and hear about Marcus' influential friends in the city.

She had an attitude of sisterly affection toward him. Once he took her hand and then kissed the bend in her plump arm. She turned very red, gave him an outraged look, and drew her sleeve down.

Am I repugnant to her? he asked himself dismally. He bluntly put the question to his mother, who arched her brows.

"Did you expect sophistication from Terentia?" she asked him reproachfully. "She will be the good keeper of your purse and hearth. You will never be dishonored by her. What more can a man expect of a woman?"

The marriage was "old" Roman. Terentia was arrayed in the traditional white linen, fastened with a woolen girdle tied in two knots, beneath an overrobe of pale yellow. Her hair was bound in a crimson net under a bright orange veil with a wreath of marjoram and verbena. She wore no jewelry but a collar of finely spun silver which Marcus had given her. She would have preferred the traditional iron or copper collar.

Tullius, who had hoped a god from Olympus would intervene to save Marcus, felt wretched. As he glimpsed Terentia's strong features through her veil, he wanted to cry to his son, Fly, while you have time!

A ewe was sacrificed to the gods, and the augur declared that the omens were auspicious. The couple exchanged their vows before the augur: *"Ubi tu Gaius, ego Gaia."* ("Where thou goest, Gaius, there go I, Gaia.") Then friends and relatives raised a cheer and congratulated the couple.

Fabia was not present at her sister's wedding, for vestals took no part in festivities. But she had sent her prayers and a touching letter which Terentia read at once. Her face softened, and suddenly she was charming and young. She turned to Marcus and laid her head on his shoulder, and he vowed that he would love and cherish her.

The feast lasted until long after night fell and it was time to take the bride to her husband's house. Musicians, led by torch-bearers, marched before the couple and sang discreet songs, not the naughty ditties of modern Roman weddings. Nor were there dancers and fauns in the procession, and no coins were tossed to passersby, as was now customary. It was all very solemn.

At Marcus' fine new house the threshold had been spread with a white cloth, signifying that a virgin bride was to pass over it. Marcus put his arms about Terentia, lifted her to carry her over the threshold, and staggered, for she was surprisingly solid. He was sweating in an unseemly manner when he eventually got her into the house. The bridesmaids followed, carrying Terentia's distaffs and spindles, and singing in praise of a matron's virtues.

Terentia was sure and composed when the chief bridesmaid finally took her by the hand and led her to the nuptial chamber.

The curtains had no sooner fallen over the door than the guests abruptly left Marcus to the delights of his bed. Where there had been singing and voices there were now the ruins of a last libation and half-eaten cakes.

The lamps flickered. Soon it would be morning.

Never, surely, had there lived so reluctant a bridegroom, Marcus said to himself. If I close my eyes, he thought childishly, and then open them, I will discover I have had a nightmare. He could not recall Terentia's face or form. A strange woman awaited him, who had gone with steady serenity to the nuptial chamber, as no doubt she went to her banks.

Then Marcus threw back his shoulders. He thought, I am years older than that poor girl, who is probably quaking in my bed and staining my pillows with her tears. He strode manfully into the bridal chamber.

A fragrant lamp burned dimly near the bed. Terentia was fast asleep in a modest shift of white linen whose sleeves reached to her large wrists. She slept deeply and soundly, as a child sleeps, her braided hair spread on the pillows.

Marcus undressed, lifted the blankets and lay down beside his wife after blowing out the lamp. He put his hand on her shoulder and sought her lips.

Terentia came awake not with love but with vexation, and caught his hand in a very competent grasp. "It is late," she said firmly, "and I am weary. Tomorrow, Marcus."

Outraged, and burning with humiliation, he wanted to strike her. He decided he would divorce her at once and return her to her counting houses and bankers. Then suddenly the humor of the situation overcame him and he burst out laughing. Settling himself comfortably he fell asleep, still chuckling.

At some time before morning Terentia must have taken his hand, for when he awoke he found his fingers clasped with hers. He was touched, and kissed her drowsy cheek.

Later Terentia responded to her husband with competence, as she did all things. Love was no more significant to her than her other affairs, but it had its place in her life, and must be attended to. Moreover, it was her duty, and she valued duty above all.

Marcus could not decide whether she loved him or not; but he was sure she was his friend.

CHAPTER TWELVE

"THAT ACCURSED CHICK-PEA!" exclaimed Catiline. "He is now a politician! Who knows where his career will end? I have always known that he was a threat to us."

"A mere quaestor," said Julius, "the lowest of magistrates. And he is being sent to Sicily, which in my opinion is Hades. Unfortunate Cicero! Besides, at his age he expected a son, and Terentia has presented him with a daughter. Let us speak of more important matters. Such as the rumors in Rome. And Fabia."

Catiline's expression changed. "What of Fabia?"

"Cicero says that the girl often visits her sister. You wished him murdered to prevent his marrying Fabia's sister, yet he apparently knows nothing. Am I to congratulate you on your discretion?" Catiline was silent. Julius said insistently, "Lucius, I hear that Fabia looks pale, and that a few days ago she fainted before the fires of Vesta and her sisters had to bear her away. The people thought it an omen of disaster. Does this concern you, Catiline?"

Catiline's terrible eyes flashed. "You are insolent, Julius! The days lately have been hot; the maiden fainted. On this small premise you build a tower of lies. You spoke of rumors. What other rumors?"

"She weeps at night, among her sister vestals, and wakes groaning from dreams, accusing herself of unnamed crimes."

"Ah, you sleep among the vestals!"

Julius sprang to his feet, struggling to control his emotions. He said, "There must be no more of Fabia, Lucius. If she has succumbed, desert her at once. If she has not, forget her.

"Now, there is another matter. It is rumored that you are an associate of Spartacus and the slaves whom he is inciting to revolt. Catiline, the time is not ripe. A revolt of the slaves will not lead us to power."

"Something must," Catiline said bitterly. "Too many years go on." He left without a farewell.

TERENTIA BELIEVED THAT no room in her house should be sacred from her. She came without knocking into the library, where Cicero was busy with an essay.

He said with as much severity as he could muster, for he was fond of his wife, "I have asked you, dear Terentia, not to invade my library."

"Pish," said Terentia. "What are you writing? Obscure essays for idle men!"

"What is wrong now?" asked Marcus in a resigned voice.

"I am planning the dinner you wish, but I notice that your guests are only lawyers and businessmen; none is of real importance. Only men like Caesar, Pompey, Crassus, or Catiline can advance your political career."

Marcus leaned back in his chair. "Julius is too adroit. Pompey is heavy, and I need not tell you again how I loathe Catiline. Crassus made himself rich through the confiscated estates of unfortunate men who were against Sulla. Now he buys offices for himself and his friends."

"All politicians buy offices," said Terentia.

"I do not," said Marcus angrily.

Terentia shrugged. "Well, do you insist on those dull men for all your dinners? Or will you take my advice?"

"Next time, we will ask those you consider important," Marcus said kindly. "Except Catiline."

She was relieved. She smiled maternally. "Do you wish to see Tullia before she sleeps?"

They went to the lamplit nursery. Tullia crowed at her father and held up her little arms. He saw his own face in hers, and he lifted her in his arms and kissed her.

"Sweetheart," he said. The child caught a lock of his hair in her fist and pulled it happily. Terentia regarded father and child with pride. She put her hand on her husband's shoulder, then leaned her cheek against it. He was very strange. But he was virtuous and famous.

When Cicero returned to his library his overseer announced that Caesar and Pompey the Great were waiting for him.

They came in with the well-being that comes from the bottle. "You must pardon our late intrusion, dear friend," said Julius, embracing his unwilling host. "We have brought an invitation from Licinius Crassus, who spoke of you gloriously tonight. He wishes you to dine with him a week from today, before you leave for Sicily."

"No," said Cicero. "I despise Crassus."

"Crassus was the dear friend of Sulla. He has a letter from him which he wishes to read you. It concerns you, dear Marcus."

Marcus hesitated, for he knew Crassus' dinners were depraved. But he was curious about the letter.

"I will attend the dinner," he said at last, "for I should like to read the letter from Sulla."

CRASSUS WAS A patrician, a short, heavy and muscular man in his forties. He loved nothing but himself and money. And now that he was the richest man in the Republic he found himself restless, and longed for power. So he became a philanthropist, and flattered the mobs by upbraiding the wealthy for their selfishness and lavishly distributing his own ill-gotten gold.

Marcus had never seen so gorgeous—or so decadent—a house as that of Crassus. It was filled with the sound of fountains and the fragrance of perfume. The slaves had been chosen for their youth and their beauty; the long hair of both youths and girls was caught up in jeweled, golden nets. Many of them were naked. Nubian slaves, tall and brilliantly black, moved about the rooms with plumed fans. Hidden by a carved ivory screen, musicians played and girls sang.

The guests wore wreaths of flowers, the tablecloth was gold, and the linen napkins were bordered with woven gold. There were wealthy men and politicians at the dinner, but no women except the beautiful nude slaves who refilled the goblets.

"I hope, Cicero," said Crassus, in his rough but compelling voice, "that you are enjoying my poor dinner."

"I am overcome. Do all champions of the common people dine so magnificently?"

Crassus considered him from under his thick black brows. "I should like to see all Romans live thus. Do they not deserve the fruits of their labor? Alas, they are deprived of their honest luxuries."

"By the government, no doubt," said Marcus. "The privileged. The greedy. The exploiters of the people."

Crassus pretended to take his irony as sincerity. "Romans are worthy of the best the world can produce."

"The riches of Croesus would not be sufficient, lord, to give each Roman what I see here tonight."

"True. But there is a middle way between luxury and poverty. The answer is equal distribution of land. All land should be owned in common."

"Our constitution guarantees the right to private property."

"I am not disputing that. Do I not uphold the constitution?"

He is not a fool, thought Marcus; therefore, these foolish utterances have a design. He observed that everyone was listening to Crassus with approval as he continued, "Alexander dreamed of a united world, as I do, too. One government, one people, one law. We should work toward that goal."

"Why? We would then destroy the infinite variety of humanity. Who has the insolence to say our way of life is the best? We Romans have no authority to impose our wills upon others. If their way is good, then all will eventually recognize it."

Crassus thought, Catiline is right: he should be murdered. Out loud he said unctuously, "Cicero speaks rightly. He is a true Roman."

He removed a scroll from beneath his rich garments. "I have a letter written to me by Sulla before he died. I wish to read it to you, Cicero. He says, 'Among those you can trust is Cicero. Cultivate him! He will never betray his country or his gods. If Rome can be saved, it will be by Cicero and those like him.' "

Cicero was moved. He reflected that Sulla could not have written so to a man who was a threat to his country. He said, coloring, "I am not worthy of such praise."

Crassus embraced him. "Let others judge of that, Cicero. I ask only that you pursue your honorable way and that you advise me when I request it."

When Cicero had gone, and he was alone later with Julius and Pompey, Crassus said, "It is fortunate that he did not demand to see that letter. It was not written in Sulla's hand."

"You read it so eloquently, even I thought it was from Sulla," Julius said. "Are you convinced now that Cicero is harmless?"

Crassus considered. "I am convinced that I deceived him. Let him live."

MARCUS DISCOVERED THAT he loved Sicily, that island of wild bronze mountains, stony earth and violent sun. He liked the poor but volatile people; he admired their struggle with their fierce land, and their seamanship. Though they hated Romans, from the first they had loved and trusted Marcus. His door was open to them at all times, and he was patient with complaints and always tried to right a wrong.

He found peace living alone in his little villa. He wrote frequently to his parents and Terentia, who had stayed in Rome with Tullia. He heard in return that Crassus was growing in power, and Julius and Pompey were his counselors. All were disturbed because of the increasing signs of rebellion among the slaves led by Spartacus.

A month before his departure from Sicily he received a letter from Terentia, filled with grief:

"My darling, my adorable sister, Fabia, is dead by her own hand. She had defiled the sacred fires of Vesta. Who was her partner in this abominable crime? The one you warned me against, dearest husband: Catiline! My heart is broken. Why did she not confide in me?

"After her death Catiline was seized and brought to trial, but Caesar was his advocate. Caesar swore that Catiline had never once gazed upon Fabia, and Aurelia testified that her husband never left her side at night. Catiline was adjudged guiltless, but all Rome knows the truth. Who will avenge my Fabia, who now lies in a shameful grave? Most of all, I fear for her soul, for she broke her vows of chastity. I can write no more for I am blinded with tears."

Marcus crushed the letter in his fist, filled with hatred and the lust to murder. There were murderers for hire in Rome!

But he seemed to hear the voice of old Scaevola: "Deprive him of his ambitions and desires. Then he dies a thousand deaths."

Marcus raised his hand and renewed his vow that Catiline would be destroyed.

CHAPTER THIRTEEN

MARCUS STROKED TERENTIA'S hair as she wept in his arms. "It will take some time, but be sure I shall avenge Fabia," he said.

"I fear for your safety," Helvia said. "Catiline is dangerous."

"I will not die until it is fated," Marcus said. But, being prudent, he resumed his fencing lessons and wore a dagger at all times. Through friends, he kept informed of Catiline's comings and goings. Surely, Catiline had an Achilles' heel through which he could be wounded.

In the meantime, Marcus rejoiced in his little Tullia. She had his features, his curling brown hair, his wit and amiability. No son could have been dearer to him than this daughter.

Marcus' fame as a lawyer grew. He was given the high post of curule aedile, at the urging of Caesar and over Catiline's protest.

The crucifixion of thousands of the slaves who had rebelled under Spartacus had made Rome uneasy. Though Romans were not easily moved to pity, many were the sons of freedmen, and many more might be sold into bondage if they fell into debt. Marcus had without success intervened for the condemned slaves. He was never to forget the sight of their piteous crosses. Though he could not save the lives of those crucified, he did help others who were seized later. He said to Caesar, "Do you want a revolution? I am nearer the people than you are, and I hear mutterings."

"Cicero is invaluable," said Julius to Crassus. "He has the ear of the people." And Crassus then freed the slaves still in prison.

Terentia was overjoyed that as a curule aedile Marcus had an ivory chair and the privilege of placing his own bust in his atrium, thus acquiring nobility. She engaged a famous sculptor to carve his bust in marble, and invited friends to the unveiling. She could not understand Marcus' reluctance.

"You are afflicted with the worst of affectations—false modesty," she said.

Marcus left the greater part of his law work to his young lawyers and clerks now, for his duties were pressing. He established the first public library in Rome. He supervised temples, public buildings, the markets, the streets, the annual games and religious festivals.

It was the games which worried him, for Romans had become accustomed to splendid extravagance. A curule aedile, besides using public funds, was expected to contribute from his own pocket. Cicero made some cautious economies and persuaded Noë to mount some spectacles which delighted the public. Roscius, alas, had mysteriously left for Jerusalem.

He was learning that politics was a tightrope on which he

must dance with apparent ease. But he also discovered that he liked politics; he was alarmed when he discovered himself feeling a secret sympathy for the dead Sulla, and even for Crassus. He did not know that his integrity was a facade that concealed the activities of the secret brotherhood. People knew that he would not be a curule aedile if it were not for Crassus and his friends. They concluded that Crassus too was virtuous.

Marcus had large offices in a public building near the Forum. He was encountering the most irritating people for a politician with conscience: those seeking his influence in government contracts. He wrote to Atticus, "Manufacturers and builders and all other suppliers offer me bribes. I approve only the best. They consider this folly, but I live without their approval."

He had to attend many public dinners and he was often feasted by Crassus, Caesar and Pompey. He had to admit that scoundrels were frequently far better company than virtuous men. This offended his sense of rightness: scoundrels should be repulsive, the virtuous charming.

He recalled that Noë had once quoted to him: "The children of darkness are wiser in their generation than the children of light." He would add to himself, And more attractive. The children of light wore heavy countenances and grieved over the evil in the world. Let us hope they receive a reward after death, he thought. They certainly do not receive it here.

Gradually Cicero became aware that some enigmatic evil was stirring in Rome, like a shadow seen only through the corner of the eye, or like the movements of rats in cellars. Yet on the surface all seemed prosperous and calm, and the populace said the great games had never been better.

REFUSING TO SIT down, Cicero stood before Crassus' table as he dined with Caesar and Pompey. Crassus regarded Cicero evilly, Julius smiled to himself and Pompey gazed at his jeweled hands.

"I do not understand your vehemence," Crassus said. "What is it to you that Catiline is praetor?"

Cicero said, his face deeply flushed, "To give him high office is to make a leopard the guardian of sheep. The man, by nature, is a disaster! He is a friend and patron of the most despicable elements in Rome. He is not a lawyer; he has never held a lower office. He is corrupt and vicious. Are these now qualifications for praetor?"

Crassus said, "Catiline is much loved. Many people are pleased that he is praetor."

"Whom has it pleased?"

"Calm yourself," said Pompey. "Of what crimes has Catiline been convicted? None. Of what does his ill fame consist? Adultery? A man can deceive his wife but remain loyal to his country. A man may be extravagant in his household, but I have observed that such men are frugal in government."

This was a long speech from the usually taciturn Pompey. Cicero looked into his calm eyes and saw there only tolerance and liking. He said, "We all know Catiline is a criminal."

Crassus, enraged, cried, "You are insolent and arrogant, Cicero. As curule aedile, you are responsible to me. Do you wish to be relieved of your public duties?"

Cicero was too aroused to heed the threat. He said to Crassus, "In the course of those very duties I would encounter Catiline in the courts. He would be my superior, and he would thwart any just cause if I were involved in it."

"I doubt it," said Julius. "After all, there is public opinion to be considered. Catiline would not dare to rule against you through malice."

He turned to Crassus. "May I confide a secret to our embattled Marcus, lord? Yes."

He smiled at Cicero. "We have warned Catiline that when he encounters you in the courts he must follow the law, dignity and reason."

Some mysterious exchange had occurred between Crassus and Julius. Crassus' tone was mild when he said, "Catiline's term is but two years. Who knows but what you, Cicero, will succeed him."

They wish to silence me, thought Marcus.

Julius was laughing lightly. "Catiline is indolent. He will rarely appear in court or bother to study a case."

"Then why was he made praetor?"

They did not answer him, but only smiled faintly.

Marcus looked from one silent face to the other, and his mind raced. He went on, "So it is true that you owe him something. Anyone who owes Catiline anything is guilty of a crime against his country."

Crassus' face was white with rage. "You dare accuse me of treason?" He shook his clenched fist and half rose from his jeweled chair. Julius, terribly alarmed, seized his arm and almost thrust him back.

"Do not order my murder," said Marcus, with a bitter smile. "You may believe that Romans are no longer disturbed by assassinations, but I have influence."

"You forget," said Pompey, in a peculiar voice, "that if you were assassinated it would be very easy to declare that you had been a traitor. The people would accept the explanation. They hate being disturbed."

Cicero saw that Julius and Crassus were regarding Pompey with disfavor. Then they looked into each other's eyes and a question was asked and answered.

Julius smiled charmingly. "We will tell you the truth, Marcus. Accept it or not. We despise Catiline, but we dare not ignore him. Not only gutter rabble and petty criminals would follow him, but rich men who desire despotism and patricians who despise the Republic. It was because Catiline controls these elements that he was appointed praetor."

"So it was blackmail," said Marcus.

"True," said Caesar.

Marcus fell into a chair; his chin dropped on his breast. Finally he said, "It must still be possible to rid ourselves of our enemies and restore the Republic."

Pompey said in his calm voice, "We must deal with reality. Even our grandfathers knew the Republic was declining."

"If I were to found a new nation," Julius said, "I would make it a benevolent despotism."

"The man on horseback," said Marcus.

"He survives longer than any republic, and his nation with him. Republics need too much self-discipline and virtue."

Marcus stood up slowly. "My reason tells me that you speak the truth. Nevertheless, my spirit insists that I must fight that truth." He turned to go, then added to the three silent men who were regarding him with strange expressions, "Do not let Catiline cross my path."

When he had left the room, Crassus said, "We need our noble white facade no longer. Let it fall."

"We need him more than ever," said Julius. "There are murmurs against Catiline. I have said to many, 'Would Catiline be praetor if Cicero had objected?' Let Cicero die and the storm will be upon us."

"If any assassination is planned," said Pompey, "I recommend Catiline as the victim."

Crassus said, "We stand between a man of virtue and a man of evil. By the gods, I do not know which is the more dangerous."

FOR A CONSIDERABLE time Cicero enjoyed comparative tranquillity, which at times made him uneasy. He wrote to Atticus, "I have entered into what some consider the golden middle years, the years that fly and leave no trace."

He did not encounter Catiline, who, at forty, remained as beautiful as a statue, though he now drank heavily and rarely appeared in court, leaving his work to deputies. Marcus began to think that Crassus, Caesar and Pompey had rid themselves of a dangerous man by giving him power that he was unable to exercise. He congratulated them in his mind for their cleverness.

Meantime, Crassus pursued a middle way and the sun was peaceful on a prosperous Rome. "A fine age in which to live," said veterans of many holocausts, with thanksgiving.

But one day Noë came to him. "I leave for Jerusalem soon," he said to Cicero. "Rome is not for a middle-aged man who has nightmares, and I have them."

"Do not be absurd," said Cicero uneasily.

"A Jew knows when the knives are loose in the scabbards. I beg of you to retire to Arpinum."

"So you have advised me for years. Yet I live in peace."

"I hear much talk of you and that young politician Publius Clodius. And—this is probably gossip—his sister, Clodia. Alas, how scandalous are tongues!"

Cicero's face became uncomfortably red. "Oh, Publius," he answered with an air of carelessness. "One of those eager young men in politics, resounding like a struck drum, all noise and air."

Noë said, "Do you believe the rumor that Clodius, when prosecuting Catiline for extortion, was bribed to acquit him?"

Cicero looked pained. "I do not believe Clodius accepted a bribe. He may have been convinced that Catiline was innocent."

Noë noticed that Cicero did not mention the lovely, witty but notorious Clodia. He knew that Terentia had become increasingly greedy and ambitious, and that Cicero and she now lived more or less as strangers. Gossip said that Cicero had once slapped his wife before slaves, and that she had thrown a platter at him.

Cicero changed the subject. "You will return someday?"

"No. I shall write you often. Perhaps you will visit me. I have all the money I need, and now that my children are of an age to marry I believe they should know their ancient traditions."

He began to laugh. "I still cannot believe that our greedy, posturing actor Roscius has become an Essene monk! God can light a fire in the most improbable men. Roscius has assumed the name of Simeon, and says that he will not die until he has seen the face of the Messiah. He often goes to the Temple in Jerusalem, staring at the faces of all babes who are brought before the altar."

"I should have thought it of anyone but Roscius."

It came to Cicero that each year saw a diminishing, through death, or exile or change, of his own life. "When *you* go, Noë," he said, "do not come for a last embrace. I do not wish to know the day."

So Noë did not tell him that he was leaving two days later. When he took his departure he could hardly refrain from weeping, for he thought that never again would he and Marcus meet in this world. "You have my prayers," he said.

"It is said that when a man grows older he begins to think more of God," Cicero said. "But it is not true. I was afire with the love of God when I was young. Now I rarely think of Him."

"The world intervenes. We are exhausted with our efforts merely to live," said Noë. "A man should be able to retire at thirty-five, so that he may devote his mind and soul to God."

Marcus sat in the sunset garden after Noë left, and tried to remember. Not an echo rose in him. Then he began to think of Clodia. He smiled and went in to dress for dinner at her house, where there was always laughter, intelligent companions and music. It was rumored that Clodia had recently taken Mark Antony, a very young man, as one of her lovers, but Cicero did not believe it.

In the house, he found his father waiting for him in the atrium. There were days when he forgot that his father even existed, and he was always startled to see his thin shadow on the marble walls or hear his light and timid voice.

Tullius' hair was white, his figure gaunt; only his large brown eyes remained alive. He began to speak rapidly, as if to catch Marcus' attention. He said, "My dear son, I must talk with you. It is most necessary."

Marcus could not control his impatience. "I am late. I am to dine—"

"I know. You are always late, Marcus. You always have appointments." The old man's face was sad. "Marcus, I feel I must speak to you."

"Well?" said Marcus, with resignation.

"We have all lost you, even your daughter, Tullia," said Tullius with humility.

"I do not know what you mean, my father," said Marcus. He looked at the water clock. He must bathe and array himself; it was already late. "Can we not continue when I return?"

"I never hear you return," said Tullius imploringly. "When I awake in the morning you have already gone. When you are at home, you have clients or guests."

"I am a busy man. I have a family to support, and public duties. Now, what is this 'necessary' thing?"

Tullius looked with grave intentness at his son. "I have forgotten," he said, and stood aside to let Marcus pass.

Marcus hesitated, feeling a vague sorrow. His father, for some reason, was a reproach to him. He did not like reproaches; he received too many from Terentia. He said with impatience, as if defending himself, "This is a different world than the world you knew, Father."

"It is always the same world," said Tullius. "You will discover that to your own anguish before you die."

It was very late when Cicero returned that night. He yawned and thought of his own bed with pleasure. Then, as he alighted from his litter, he saw the bronze doors of his house were open and flooded with light, and that lamplight gleamed at all the windows.

He thought of his daughter, Tullia, and his heart jumped. He hastened into the house to be met in the hall by a weeping Terentia, who fell on him like a fury.

"While you lay in the arms of your harlot," she screamed, "your mother died!"

HELVIA'S ASHES WERE LAID WITH her father's. The funeral meats had been eaten, the cypress planted at the door, the guests departed. There had been a multitude of mourners, including all the Helvii and the Caesars. Quintus and Terentia wept, but Tullius and Marcus were dry of eye, for they mourned the most.

On the fourth day Marcus sat again in his favorite spot in his garden, beneath the myrtle trees. His father, seated with Terentia not far from him, appeared like a shade himself.

"I have lost more than a wife," said Tullius. "I have lost a mother."

And that is true, thought Marcus. Always you have depended on others, crying for love and protection. But I will not be a father to you. He did not know why he felt so bitter toward his father except that he must turn on someone to alleviate his own suffering.

He said, "Doubtless, Father, you would feel more comforted if you lived with Quintus and his family. He is more like my mother than I am."

Tullius studied Marcus in silence. Then he said, "So be it." He groped weakly to his feet and moved away.

"Have you no filial feeling?" Terentia cried. "You have driven your father from your house. He who does that is cursed!"

"Had he wished to stay, he had but to say the word. My door is not closed to him. He will be happier with Quintus, and always be an honored guest here."

"I do not understand you. You are not the man I knew," Terentia said. She was fat now, and her brown hair had lost its luster. She has the ugliest hands I have ever seen in a woman, thought Cicero. He felt weary to death.

"Do you wish me to divorce you?" asked Terentia.

"If you wish."

"Do you care for nothing?" she exclaimed.

"I try not to care. That is the only way I can endure."

"Endure what?" Terentia was outraged. "Are you poor, deprived, homeless, wifeless, childless? No! You are rich and famous. You want for nothing. You will soon be praetor. Yet you speak of enduring! Beware, Marcus, that the gods do not take back their gifts from one so ungrateful!"

Marcus did not answer.

She said, "I shall not divorce you, for divorce is wicked. Besides,

I shall not deprive Tullia of her father, whom she adores. Despise me and reject me, as you have done for many years. You will find me here to welcome you, when it pleases you to notice me."

He was moved to pity and shame. "Believe me, Terentia, I shall always regard you as my wife, the mother of my daughter, the heart of my household. If I do not talk with you, it is because I cannot."

She began to smile through her tears. "So my father often told my mother—'I cannot talk with you.' Men are like children who believe their thoughts are too mighty to be communicated. In reality, they are very simple, and easily understood by women."

CHAPTER FOURTEEN

MARCUS HAD WORKED to have Quintus made a magistrate, yet now he seemed more ill-tempered every day. "Is it because Pomponia exasperates you?" he asked his brother. "What woman does not exasperate her husband! You have a son. You are rich. What is it that you wish?"

Quintus said with a scowl, "I do not think you are safe, Marcus. You think me ambitious, but I am ambitious only to protect you."

"I know," said Marcus, greatly moved. "But still, you have not explained your bad temper."

Quintus flung his arms wide in despair. "I do not know!" he exclaimed. "But affairs in Rome are so complex, and I am a simple man! Why do not matters remain black and white, good and evil? And I am troubled about our father. He grows more removed day by day. He is like a shade in my house, and Pomponia complains. He hardly knows he is a grandfather. He says he is troubled because you compromise."

"He never compromised because he never took a stand," said Marcus, with that inner spasm of pain he always felt when his father was mentioned. "Do you think it easy for me to endure Caesar and all his friends? But they exist in my world and I must endure them." He tried to divert his brother's thoughts. "I will soon seek to be consul of Rome," he said.

Quintus eyed him with sudden grimness. "Do you not know the rumor? It is said that Catiline will be consul."

ROMANS, BEING MATERIALISTS, were suspicious of men of intellect. They loved Cicero for the justice he dispensed as praetor; they could not forgive him his books, though few read them. The intellectuals who did read them argued about them. Cicero dealt in "duty" and "patriotism" and "honor" and "law" as if these were immutable values. Was anything more ridiculous? But others of the intellectuals felt their consciences aroused—which simply made them angry with Cicero.

Cicero did not believe the rumor Quintus had repeated. The thought of the monstrous Catiline being consul of Rome was incredible. Crassus, Caesar and Pompey were not madmen. They would not further the aims of a totally irresponsible man who might then destroy them.

Cicero proposed to some friendly senators that Catiline be brought before the Senate for questioning. They looked at him uneasily. What proof did Cicero have of his activities?

"The time to be prepared is during periods of tranquillity," Cicero wrote Atticus. "The methods I suggest for the safety of Rome bring accusations that I am losing a sense of proportion. My friends believe that our constitution is invulnerable. They tell me that Catiline's following is a very small minority!"

PUBLIUS CLODIUS WAS devoted to his sister, Clodia. Her husband, Caecilius Metellus Celer, came of a distinguished family; but after a few months with her he had gone back to illicit companions and pleasures. Clodia then took lovers, but she was fastidious in selecting them.

Among her favorites was Cicero. Since she possessed not only beauty and charm but an excellent mind, there were many nights when Cicero sat with her until dawn discussing philosophy and politics and the fate of man. He considered her a dear friend as well as a mistress. He bought her jewels and filled her house with flowers.

Clodius learned much of what was going on in Rome from Clodia. One day she said to him, "You know Mark Antony. He is a valorous young soldier, but he has the mind of a boy. He adores your friend Caesar. Why this is I do not know, for I mistrust and dislike Caesar."

She paused and studied her brother with her great black eyes.

"I have heard a rumor from my guileless Mark Antony."

Clodius became alert. He was of the serpent-ring brotherhood, but he was not close to Crassus, and he knew only what the others wished him to know.

He said, "No one would trust a constant talker like Mark Antony. You can rely on nothing he repeats."

"He tells me that Cicero's murder has been arranged for the first part of the month of Janus, when the new consuls are to take office."

Clodius was disappointed. He laughed. "What nonsense! He is under Caesar's protection."

"He was. But Mark Antony is Caesar's favorite. During one of Caesar's fits of epilepsy he babbled to him of the murder of Marcus. He wept and struck about him and screamed that he was helpless. Catiline had demanded it, and Crassus no longer would prevent it."

"Nonsense," said Clodius again. "Mark Antony is only a silly babbler."

But he was alarmed and angry. How could Cicero be warned? To go to him openly and tell him of the plot—which Clodius still did not entirely credit—would be to betray those to whom he had taken the secret blood oath of brotherhood and would ensure his own murder.

He said to Clodia, "Why do you yourself not warn Cicero of these rumors?"

"Cicero would scoff at them as women's gossip." She smiled. "I love Marcus in my fashion. Let nothing evil occur to him. If your friends can destroy him with impunity, do you think they will hesitate to murder anyone?"

When he returned to his house Clodius sent an anonymous letter to Cicero.

TULLIA ADORED HER father and silently took his side in Terentia's furious disagreements with him. Now she felt betrayed by Marcus, for Terentia was pregnant. Tullia knew this sense of betrayal was ridiculous; but she still felt it. She had not yet fully learned compassion, nor understood the bonds which hold a man and wife together despite bitter controversy.

One cold evening, shortly before the month of Janus, Tullia

came into the library where her father was writing. Marcus kissed her cheek. She sat down, serenely conscious that he loved having her with him. He put down his pen, smiled at her and said, "I have been considering who might, in the future, be an appropriate husband for you, my child."

"I am content to remain with you all my life, Father," she replied in her gentle voice.

He shook his head. "That cannot be. Blessed will be the man who takes your hand in marriage."

He took up his pen to write again, and Tullia sat in her chair, reading. A cold draft blew the curtains at the windows, and the great house was silent.

Aulus, the overseer, knocked at the door and entered. "Lord," he said, "I have here a letter from a mysterious person, cowled and cloaked, who would not show his face. He implored you to read this."

Cicero took the letter and opened it. He read: "Beware! Your murder is plotted by those you know during the first week of the month of Janus. Guard your household. Go nowhere without an armed escort."

Tullia had never seen so frightful an expression on his face. "Father?" she said.

He tried to smile. "It is late, child. I wish to be alone." He said to Aulus, "Conduct Lady Tullia to her apartments and command an armed slave to sleep on her threshold. Let other armed slaves sleep at each door. And send a slave to bring my brother here." He turned to Tullia. "Do not be unduly alarmed, my daughter, but let it be as I say."

When he was alone he reread the letter. He was not especially surprised. If his murder was plotted, then Rome was in dreadful danger also. He was deep in thought when Aulus entered again, with a troubled face, and said, "Lord, another mysterious personage has arrived. He also is cowled and cloaked, and his face hidden. He begs for an audience with you. Alone."

"He is armed?"

"Only with a dagger, lord."

"Have him give you his dagger; then admit him."

A moment later Aulus brought in a tall figure, swathed and silent. When the two men were alone, the visitor threw back his hood and Marcus saw the broad, impassive face of Pompey.

"It must not be known that I visited you tonight," Pompey said. "But you are in danger of assassination."

Cicero gave him the letter. "Did you send this?"

Pompey read the letter. He was breathing as if he had been running. "So," he said. "You have another friend, and what he writes is true. Your death has been plotted, and I do not wish to see you dead."

Pompey leaned toward Marcus and spoke in a low voice. "I am married to Caesar's daughter, Julia. Nevertheless, I mistrust and fear him. He did not easily give his consent to your murder. In truth, he is distracted and has left the city for his villa."

"Why did he consent?"

"He was left no choice by Catiline, who threatens us with his rabble. Catiline believes you stand in the way—"

"Of whom?"

"Of all of us." Pompey rubbed his lips with his hand and went on, as if to himself: "I never trusted any of the rest. I am a soldier. If power is to be seized, let it be seized openly, in the way of a soldier, not with a slave's plot and sly murder. They planned to move—" He stopped. "After your death."

"How were they to move, Pompey?"

Pompey stood and pressed his clenched fists on Marcus' table and stared at him. "By murdering the newly elected consuls and making Catiline a consul of Rome. They—we—have waited long enough for power."

"Do they not fear the anger of the people of Rome?"

Pompey threw back his head and laughed. "Cicero, Cicero! The people forget their heroes almost before their ashes are cold. I tell you, loved though you are, that you could be murdered tomorrow and a week from now your name would not be spoken. I came because I mistrust Caesar and fear for myself if this miserable plot succeeds. Also, because I honor you."

Pompey put on his hood again. "I leave the solution in your hands. Forget I visited you. Remember only your safety. And Rome." The door closed after him.

When Quintus arrived a few minutes later, his cloak was sprinkled with snowflakes. Marcus asked him, "How many trusted soldiers can you command?"

The color left Quintus' face. "A legion," he said. "However, I would trust only twenty men with my life. Or yours." He took his brother in his arms and said fiercely, "Tell me!"

THE PATIENT SNOW was falling over the vast city, in a silent veil of white. It fell over an abandoned quarry in a section of the Trans-Tiber used for rubbish disposal. Here outlaws gathered. The pit of the quarry was lit by scores of smoking, flaming torches which caught the fierce profiles of mantled men, steam

The Roman Empire in the Time of Cicero 106–43 B.C.

rising from their damp woolen garments. Some of the fitfully illuminated faces were patrician; many were savage and coarse.

Catiline stood on a great rock, in military garb, and surveyed the men below him. He kept his hand on his short sword as he began to speak.

"I have gathered you here tonight, comrades, to tell you that our hour has struck! Before another moon has waned your signal will be given, in the name of Rome and freedom and justice!

"What is our government today? Privilege for a few! Slavery

for the many! Scorn for the noble freedman, the worker, the humble! Advantage for the powerful! I tell you that the lowest slave in the house of the rich is better fed than the average Roman! Is that justice? No!"

The men roared back to him: "No! No! No!"

Dogs! thought Catiline. You will tear a path through flesh for me to advance. Serve me well, dogs. He raised his hand as if taking an oath.

"Comrades! The signal will soon be given! Prepare yourselves for the day! For me, power to protect you; for you, gold and liberty and loot! Rome is ours!"

The mob swarmed about Catiline, kissing his hands, his knees, his feet. His fellow patricians embraced him. Among them was Publius Clodius.

THERE WERE FEW abroad as Cicero and Quintus, accompanied on horseback by twelve officers, rode out of the city in the early morning light. They reached the country house of Julius Caesar where the guards, after one glance at the horsemen and their leaders, opened the gates and watched the company wheel rapidly up to the house. Quintus alighted first, ran to the carved bronze door and struck it mightily with his armed fist. When Marcus alighted and joined his brother his face was haggard.

The door swung open and Julius' mother, Aurelia, appeared, her stola hastily draped over her plump figure. She stared at Marcus with fearful eyes. "What is this, at this hour?"

Cicero tried to smile reassuringly. "Dear Lady Aurelia," he said, "we must speak to Julius. Do not be alarmed."

"But you have brought soldiers!"

Marcus bent and kissed her cheek. "There are robbers about these days, and we set forth when it was hardly light."

The young and beautiful Pompeia, Caesar's second wife, glided into the atrium. Her long pale hair streamed down her back, and her face was pale as a lily. She wore a long lavender robe hemmed with gold, and despite the hour she was fragrant and composed. "Dear Marcus," she murmured, as he kissed her hand, "it is delightful to see you again." She smiled bewitchingly. "My poor Julius is unwell! He has had several seizures."

Quintus replied harshly, "We must see him." Aurelia put her hand to her shaking lips.

Pompeia said, "He is not confined to his bed. Let me conduct you to his audience chamber." She led them there, then left them.

Caesar soon entered, clothed in a long robe of crimson wool. He was gaunt but he smiled gaily. He embraced Cicero as gratefully as if Marcus had rescued him from danger. "I cannot tell you how happy I am to see you!" he said. "But what is this I hear? You have come with a detachment of cavalry."

Cicero's nerves were raw. "Julius, you are not under arrest—yet. But let us be done with lies and evasions. Let us speak to each other like men, for a change."

Julius sat down as if suddenly undone, and Marcus seated himself in an ebony chair. Quintus remained standing. "I have come on this information," said Cicero, and he tossed the anonymous letter to Caesar, who continued to smile. Then, as he read, his face tightened and he became paler than death.

"This letter seems mad to me. What enemies do you have?"

"You, Julius?"

Julius looked incredulous. "I, Marcus? Do I—"

" '—not love you as a brother?' But brothers have murdered each other. Do you wish me dead, Caesar?"

"Never, never!" Julius groaned.

"I know now that there is a plot to kill our elected consuls in the first week of January. I was to be murdered first."

Julius got to his feet. "I swear to you I know nothing of this. You have brought me an unsigned letter and expect me to take it seriously?"

"You take it seriously enough. It is possible that I cannot oppose you or stop the ruin of my country. But I can destroy you. If Quintus thrusts his sword into you now, who will reproach him? I have only to reveal my knowledge of your plots to have the people unanimously acclaim my brother."

Cicero's eyes met Julius'. They locked and held each other. Quintus moved a step closer, his sword half drawn. Then Julius smiled. "It is possible that Catiline has conjured up such a plot. If so, he shall be warned."

"Listen well to me, Julius," said Quintus. "If my brother dies, or the consuls are murdered, the army will seize Rome."

"And that," said Cicero, "would not be the best fate for Rome. I have refrained from arresting you and your companions because I fear the rule of the military even more than yours."

JULIUS SAID TO the conspirators: "It was a hasty plot, a miserable one, as Pompey warned us. It was your impatience, Catiline, which forced us into it. We shall succeed, eventually, but not by childish recklessness."

"I cannot wait," said Catiline. "I have alerted my followers."

But Julius ignored him. "I am glad Cicero discovered it. He has done us a service. Still, I am interested to know who sent him that anonymous letter."

He looked around but none acknowledged it.

Later, when Caesar was alone with Crassus and Pompey, Crassus said, "Am I dictator, or am I the tool of these reprobates?"

"A dictator, dear lord," said Julius, "collects reprobates as a ship collects barnacles. We will scrape them away when they have served their purpose."

WHEN TULLIA WAS born, Cicero had still felt there was hope in the future. Her birth symbolized to him the continuity and promise of life. Now Terentia again lay in labor and Cicero tried to feel some interest in the coming child. But he shrank from the thought of his second born, begotten in sadness.

He sat in his gardens and did not hear the physician approaching him. He started when the man spoke. "Lord, Lady Terentia has given birth to a son! She asks for you."

A son! thought Cicero, rising and going into his house. My son, Marcus Tullius Cicero.

Terentia, triumphant and appearing almost young again, greeted him with joyous tears and showed him the child. "Marcus!" she cried. "I—we—have a son!" There was no sadness, no doubt, no fear in her.

Cicero looked at the face of his son and thought, The child resembles my grandfather! The bright wing of forgotten hope touched his heart. Romans were still being born.

Grateful clients, relatives and friends sent lavish gifts to the baby. Caesar came with a purse of rubies, an awesome gift, in the nature of a peace offering. Pompey arrived with a present, and the perceptive Cicero noticed that he and Caesar greeted each other indifferently. Then Pompey said to Julius, "Where is your slave, that fatuous young Mark Antony?"

Cicero heard a clash of swords in the voices, though Julius answered the insult lightly. Marcus was reminded of their plot, and it seemed to him that his infant son was threatened. Alarm lifted like a black wing before his eyes.

Julius said, "What does our augur see that has made him pale?"

"I was considering how dangerous a world this is into which I have brought a son."

Julius said, "It was dangerous to our fathers, also."

"They did not have traitors in Rome," said Cicero, and then was appalled at the words he had uttered.

Pompey and Caesar exchanged a glance, and all at once the coolness between them disappeared, and they laughed. "Our dear Marcus!" exclaimed Julius. "He is obsessed with plots. I know of none, Marcus."

"Nor do I." Pompey's gray eyes were veiled. So, thought Cicero, this time I shall not be warned.

ONE COLD AUTUMNAL dawn, Cicero received an imperative summons from his brother, Quintus. Tullius was on his deathbed and unconscious. Cicero rose, not believing the news: from his earliest childhood his father had been expiring. But he went to the house of Quintus on the Carinae, shivering in his litter.

Tullius was already dead. He lay on his bed in the small *cubiculum* which Cicero himself had occupied in his youth, and his face was not the face Cicero remembered. It was calm, remote, cleansed of the dust of living and all its pains.

Marcus bent and touched his father's cold hands with his lips. He murmured a prayer for his spirit, but felt it a mockery, for his father had no need of his prayers. He had lived a sinless life and had never been part of the world he had thankfully deserted.

He turned and left the chamber with a calm Quintus resented.

But in the days that followed he was struck by the inconstancy of life and its fragility. His own existence was less secure because his father no longer existed.

CHAPTER FIFTEEN

Noë ben Joel wrote from Jerusalem to congratulate his friend on being elected consul of Rome, the mightiest office of the mightiest nation in the world.

"How I rejoice!" he said. "You claim that you received the support of the senatorial party only because they feared the deranged Catiline, who was also a candidate. You defame yourself with this modesty; even venal senators can sometimes be moved to support a wise man. Nor did you believe that Caesar's party, the *populares,* would cast their votes in your behalf, for you are convinced that they prefer rascals. Yet those whom you mistrusted elected you! You are greatly beloved, for all your shyness and reserve.

"God has strange ways of manifesting Himself when He realizes that a nation is in grave peril. I like to believe that He intervened in your behalf to save Rome. I prophesy the name of Cicero will never pass away so long as history is written.

"I heard that Caesar has been named pontifex maximus and praetor of Rome. You regard this with misgivings, but God, whose ways are mysterious, often uses villains as well as good men for His purposes.

"You say your son is already a prodigy at the age of two. How can he be otherwise with such a father?

"I rejoice with you in your beautiful daughter's marriage to the patrician Piso Frugi. Though you express misgivings, I detect in them the natural jealousy of a father for his beloved daughter.

"You fear Catiline's obscurity, for you say it is better to have an enemy in full sight. But the fact that Caesar, and Crassus himself, supported you for consul should reassure you.

"You ask me again of the Messiah. The Pharisees send priests up and down the length of Palestine searching for the Mother and the Holy Child, while the worldly Sadducees laugh at them. Each night I look to the heavens and ask: 'Is He born at this hour? And where shall I find Him?' "

Terentia, now wife of the consul, glowed with elation. She was the noblest lady in Rome. Her magnificent litter, carried by four Nubian slaves, was saluted on the street. Her house on the

Palatine was thronged with patrician ladies seeking her intercession on behalf of their husbands. Graciously, she presented the petitions to Cicero, and could not understand his annoyance. Often she wondered how a "new" man had attained such high estate. She came to the conclusion that he owed it all to her.

Tullia, alarmed, considered her mother mad but her young husband, Piso, laughed merrily. "Your mother is becoming old; permit her to have her conceits."

C. ANTONIUS HYBRIDA, a wealthy, middle-aged patrician, was consul with Cicero. He was much loved for his easy tolerance. He believed that man was naturally good and that only circumstance or environment distorted him. Catiline was a friend of his, and a fellow patrician, and Antonius admired Catiline's sophistication and lightheartedness. He also discounted the vile and wicked things he heard of his friend.

Antonius heartily agreed with Cicero that the budget should be balanced, the public debt reduced, assistance to foreign lands curtailed, and that the people should not depend on the government for their subsistence. But when Cicero produced facts and figures showing how all these things must be accomplished, through austerity and discipline, Antonius was troubled.

"But this [or that] would be a hardship on this [or that] class," Antonius would say. The people were accustomed to circuses and free grain, he argued. Were they not citizens of the richest nation on earth? Antonius suggested higher taxes to continue such expenditures.

Cicero sighed. "Hundreds of thousands of good citizens now labor under unbearable taxes," he said. "A little more pressure and the backs of these faithful horses will break."

That night Catiline called on Antonius, who was delighted to embrace him, for Catiline would not point at documents and talk of economy, a most disheartening subject of conversation. They sat in Antonius' library, laughing and gossiping. But Antonius became aware that Catiline was pale, with a terrible fixity in his magnificent eyes. He said, "Are you well, Lucius?"

"Well enough," said Catiline. "Do not think I brood on my failure to become consul." He rose and shut the bronze door of the library. Then he stood in silence, his strong legs apart, glittering with jewels like a sparkling statue as he meditated. "And how do you find the Chick-pea," he said at last, "who bites every coin, whether his own or the treasury's?"

Antonius smiled uneasily. "Cicero is realistic," he replied. "I was taken aback to discover how insolvent we are. I tell him that our nation is sound at heart, but he is not optimistic."

"He is a vulgarian who would have us return to the barefoot days of Cincinnatus. I have a better way to save Rome. A heroic way, in the Roman spirit." He turned his blazing eyes on Antonius. "Are you valorous, Antonius? I think you are. Well, the Vetch is right in one matter: the fall of Rome is inevitable, unless we remove the ambitious and avaricious from power and restore the proud Republic. You know Sulla's general, Manlius?"

Antonius sat as if struck across the face. All that he had heard of Catiline returned to him, and he thought, It is quite true.

"Manlius," Catiline went on, "is beloved by the veterans. He has pleaded with Cicero to increase their piteous pensions. Cicero has refused. Shall we abandon them to starvation?"

Antonius forced himself to meet those deranged eyes. "Cicero has increased the veterans' allowances. He wishes only that the young and able-bodied ones support themselves."

"He lies! Tens of thousands of veterans are in despair at this very moment. They are with Manlius, in Etruria. And when Manlius appealed for the proposed law to give veterans public lands, who opposed it? Cicero!"

Antonius said, "But under the proposed law, not only the veterans were to be given land, but the Roman mobs who wish only, according to Cicero, to resell it at a profit."

"Who has more right to land than the Roman people? They are with us. So are many senators, and all who feel a responsibility for the common good." Catiline shook his fist violently. "Once Cicero is destroyed, you and I, Antonius, shall be consuls of Rome." And he unfolded the whole story of the conspiracy.

ANTONIUS HURRIED TO tell Caesar, Crassus, Clodius and Pompey the strange story of Catiline's visit. "I can only believe," he ended, "that Catiline has become deranged."

"It is true that he is mad, my poor Antonius," Crassus said, meditatively chewing a fig, "but the story he told you is true.

We hoped that with his growing madness he would lose his following. We should have had him murdered."

Antonius stared, aghast. "Murdered!"

Crassus said gravely, "These are desperate times. Yes, we knew of Catiline's plot, but we did not know when he would move. All Rome will honor you for telling us, and also for telling us of his plot against Cicero. Let me make sure I understand. You are to send a message to Cicero next week imploring him to see you at once on a matter of great importance. Cicero will naturally inform his guard that you are expected. You would enter with hooded bodyguards—actually Catiline and some followers. They would slay Cicero." Crassus looked with contempt at the wretched man before him. "Would Catiline have permitted you to live to betray him, Antonius? No. You would have died an instant after Cicero died."

Antonius looked at Crassus speechlessly; the thought had not occurred to his credulous mind. Crassus said, "Fortunately, you are not the man Catiline judged you to be. We will go to Cicero at once, and tell him of the nearness of disaster. The hour has come to expose Catiline. Cicero is the only man who can do it."

Cicero sat with the leaders of Rome in his cold library, long after midnight. After Antonius finished speaking, he said, "Who made Catiline a threat against Rome, Antonius? These men who sit with you now." He looked at Caesar, his eyes blazing. "The tiger who roamed your garden is now within your house, Julius. I have called Catiline a traitor, but you are traitors also."

"Marcus," said Julius. "Let us be done with recriminations. We must work together to halt Catiline."

Cicero began to write quickly. He said, "I will summon Catiline to appear before the Senate to answer charges of treason."

Catiline, receiving the summons next morning, laughed with delight. Arraying himself in a scarlet toga, he was carried in his litter to the Senate Chamber. The suddenness of the summons assured him that only a quorum of the senators would be present, many of them his friends. Cicero would be derided and banished! Absorbed in his vengeful thoughts, he became aware that his litter had not moved for some time. He held back the curtains and glanced out.

He was stunned. The Sacred Way was lined with soldiers,

shoulder to shoulder, shield to shield. It was the legion of Quintus, whose life he had saved so many years ago. Behind them, a multitude of men poured into the Forum in a voiceless tide, like silent wolves.

Catiline let the curtain of his litter fall. For the first time he was full of foreboding. How had Quintus assembled his legion in so short a time? Who had summoned the crowds to the Forum?

He alighted from his litter. Not a single hail greeted him. He looked into thousands of impassive eyes, and they looked back at him silently. He heard the slap of his own boots, and his knees began to tremble as he mounted the marble steps of the Senate Chamber; but he held his head high and his face expressed contempt. The senators sat quietly as he entered. None looked at him but Cicero. The eyes of the two men met as once their swords had met.

Cicero rose. For this day we have both waited many years, he thought. Here was the murderer of Livia, the murderer of his own son, the traitor, the destroyer Cicero must destroy if Rome was to live. "Lucius Sergius Catiline!" And his voice was like a trumpet as he read the charge of treason and conspiracy. "Your crimes are known. If you have an advocate, call him forth!"

Catiline felt alone, but he smiled coldly at Cicero, as one smiles at an insolent inferior. "I have no advocate, Cicero," he said. "I have committed no crime. Produce your witnesses."

From the multitudes outside came the sounds of a vast murmur. Catiline thought, Animals! Slaves! Suddenly excited, he thought of the day when he would have this rabble at the tip of his sword, and this Senate would prostrate itself before him. He smiled. "The law demands that an accused man be confronted by witnesses." He surveyed the Senate. "As I am not under arrest, and charged only with vague crimes which I repudiate, there is nothing to hinder me from leaving this chamber. Lords, I will remain out of deference to you."

Cicero said, "You deny the truth which all Rome knows. I will not produce witnesses—though I have them—because of the danger to them. You have conspired with felons and the disaffected to overthrow Rome. You have conspired to murder me one night next week. Do you deny this?"

Catiline looked at Antonius. "The allegation is absurd."

Then Cicero raised his great voice in his most famous words: "How long, O Catiline, will you abuse our forbearance? Do you not perceive that your conspiracy is known to all here assembled? Alas, what degenerate days are these! The Senate is well aware of the facts, but the criminal still lives! Lives? Yes, and even comes arrogantly to this Senate, and with ominous glances marks down every single one of us for massacre!"

There were angry shouts outside: "Death to the traitor!" and Cicero went on to remind the Senate that Catiline and Manlius had established a military base north of Rome. As consul, he could order Catiline's arrest and execution; with a bitter glance at Crassus and his friends, he added that he would not take that step at present. Then he lifted his hand to point implacably at Catiline.

"You will perish in the end, Catiline, but not until it is certain there is no one in Rome who does not admit the justice of your execution. Meantime, many vigilant eyes and ears will keep watch over all your actions. Abandon your sword! All is known." And, as Catiline paled, he mentioned one meeting, in Laeca's house, in the Street of the Scythemakers. "I see there are present in the Senate itself," he went on, "certain of those who met you there, your accomplices in your insane and criminal adventure! Merciful gods! What is the government under which we live?"

Cicero dropped his hand to his side and tears appeared on his cheeks. He looked again at Catiline and his amber eyes glowed like embers. "Quit Rome, Catiline. Take with you your associates. Free the city from the infection of your presence. There is not a man in Rome, outside your band of conspirators, who does not fear and hate you. Get you gone, Catiline. Get you gone!"

Cicero walked down the steps from his chair and the Senate rose in respect. With Quintus clanging in his armor by his side, he reached the door and heard the thunderous shout: "Hail Cicero, savior of Rome! Hail to the hero!"

That night Catiline left for Etruria. When he reached Manlius he said, "The Slave Holiday will soon be upon us. We will strike then."

Cicero delivered the second and third orations against Catiline in his absence, and among those who listened with burning hearts was Marcus Porcius Cato, one of the leaders of the senatorial aristocracy and a devoted admirer of Cicero. He persuaded the cautious Cicero to arrest some of Catiline's lieutenants, patricians all, who had remained in the city to show their contempt of Cicero.

Cato said, "They must be arrested or the people will wonder why known enemies of the state remain free. I know this is legally dangerous, but there are times when one must confront danger."

When Cicero had them thrown into prison as conspirators against Rome, the people went mad with praise of him.

ONE NIGHT WHEN Caesar was in his library trying to read, but overcome by foreboding, his overseer came to tell him that Catiline urgently desired to speak to him. Loosening his dagger in its sheath, Caesar ordered that he be brought in. "Greetings, Caesar!" cried Catiline as he entered. His beautiful, depraved face was alight with exultation as he held out a jeweled hand.

Caesar hesitated, then took it. It seemed feverish and tremulous, as though Catiline were vibrating with inner fire. Catiline flung himself uninvited into a chair. "Why are you here?" Caesar said. "Rome is dangerous for you now!"

"It was the city of my fathers before the Ciceros ever saw it!" exclaimed Catiline. "Shall Rome be deprived of her own son? Dear friend, sweet friend, faithful friend," he went on in a deadly voice, "I have come to thank you for your courageous support. Because of it, I may be inclined to mercy—later."

"Catiline, leave Rome," Caesar said, ignoring this. "Do not tempt the Fates. Tomorrow, Cicero speaks against you in the Temple of Concord; he may ask for your execution."

"Caesar—faithless friend, treacherous enemy—I have warned you before. Should a single hair of my head be harmed, you shall go down with me. Tomorrow we shall destroy Cicero, for I shall have an advocate."

"And who is this reckless advocate?"

Catiline burst out laughing. "You, Caesar."

Then Catiline was no longer laughing. He advanced on Caesar, his fist clenched. "There are many virtuous and patriotic senators who do not know the whole truth about you. Shall I enlighten them? Do you think Crassus will then save you and the others of our brotherhood?" He laughed again. "And do not think to have me murdered as I leave here. I have a guard waiting."

"You have no patience, Lucius," Caesar said in rising alarm.

"Had you not abandoned our plan, you would still be one of us when we seize Rome in an orderly fashion. But—"

He halted at Catiline's wild gesture of contempt. "Caesar, I care nothing for Rome! It shall be cleansed by fire, and on the cooling embers I will build a city of marble where a slave shall forever remain a slave, a patrician a patrician, and an emperor an emperor." He rose, put his fur cloak over his shoulders. "Tomorrow, noble advocate, you will defend me."

After he was gone Caesar hastily summoned a slave and sent messages to Cicero and the brotherhood. Then he sat until the blue dawn appeared at his windows, considering what to do.

CATILINE MUST DIE, thought Cicero the next morning, and his chief followers with him. There is no other way to save Rome. I hate violence—but when my country is in desperate danger, I must strike.

The Senate was already waiting to consider the fate of Catiline's lieutenants, and the Forum was filled with a huge mob. Cicero could see Catiline, with his beautiful, idle smile, seated near the door, and he remembered Noë's tales of Satan, the archangel of death and destruction, who was of awesome beauty.

Cicero began to speak in a voice like a trumpet: "My lords, we are here to discuss the fate of the lieutenants of Catiline, conspirator against our country. I am here as the advocate of Rome." Urgently he described Catiline's plan, now confessed by his lieutenants, to burn the city and massacre them all. Then he pointed suddenly at Catiline. "Behold the traitor who has designed our doom! I knew his plots, lords. But even I never imagined that he and his followers were engaged in a conspiracy so vast. It cannot be stamped out except by severe measures, taken without delay. In the name of Rome, I demand death for Catiline and for his lieutenants!"

Outside the temple the people raised a mighty cry: "Death to Catiline! Death to the traitors!"

The senators were silent as statues as they looked at Cicero, tall and slender in his white robes. He began to speak again. "In all my years of public service I have asked no magistrate, nor the august Senate to condemn any man man to death. Only a man bereft of manhood can rejoice in the extinction of another, even an enemy, or feel triumphant at the sight of a bloody battlefield, even if his own nation has conquered. The true man, surveying a battlefield, must bow his head and pray for friend and foe alike—for all were men. But now we are faced with the most dire of choices: Catiline dies, or Rome dies!"

Catiline looked at Cicero with a derisive smile. And as Cicero returned his gaze, between them stood the misty form of a young woman who had been done hideously to death.

Then Caesar rose. "My dear friend Cicero has spoken eloquently and with patriotic fervor," he said. "Patriotism is to be honored. It is only its excess which is to be feared."

Cicero looked at him in outrage, and Julius raised his hand in protest, as if Cicero had cried out. He said: "Let Catiline speak in his own defense."

Catiline stood and as if at a signal the torches flared and flooded him with bloody light. He bowed to the Senate. "Lords," he said, "I, Lucius Sergius Catiline, patrician of Rome, warrior of Rome, have been accused before you of conspiracy and treason! I, Lucius Sergius Catiline!" He paused, as if what he had said was so incredible that he was stunned. "My ancestors," he went on, "served their country, as your ancestors did. As did I. Look upon my scars, received in the service of my country!"

He rent the top of his toga and showed his chest crossed with the scars of old wounds, and the memories of old soldiers stirred within the senators. "Has Crassus, Caesar, or Pompey, or the noble Clodius, risen to denounce me, their comrade-in-arms? No! Not a single voice has denounced me. Save one."

He pointed to Cicero. "And who is the man who accuses me? A man born near Arpinum, a Roman only by courtesy. He prates of law—but it was my ancestors who wrote the law." Catiline struck his breast with his clenched fist. "This son of tradesmen dares to accuse me—me!—of treason. He is consul of Rome; he has risen from poverty to riches. It is not enough. He wishes to be a patrician. Failing that, he would destroy what he can never attain."

He turned the blue fire of his eyes on Cicero with scorn and loathing. "Lords, I can endure this lowborn man no more. Remember our common blood and ask yourselves if I could be guilty of the crimes of which I have been accused by this

Cicero!" He flung himself into his chair, his breast heaving.

Quintus gripped his brother's arm and found it as rigid as stone. Cicero's face was white. His stare was fixed on Catiline.

Then in the profound silence Caesar rose again and addressed the Senate. "Lords, we have heard the accuser and the accused. Catiline's words strike to the heart of every proud man. But, lords, we have the confessions of Catiline's own lieutenants, freely admitted by these patricians themselves.

"These days are not the days of our fathers, alas," said Julius sadly. "Life was simpler in those days. A man knew his duty to his country, and politics were not as complex as they are now. Out of confusion, even out of good will, one may be duped by beguiling tongues. Shall we call a man's confusion treason? Or shall we call it deplorable, but have compassion upon him?"

Crassus suppressed a smile, Pompey's eyes narrowed and Clodius moved uncomfortably. But the young Cato looked upon Caesar with horror as he continued: "Catiline's lieutenants, eager to escape punishment for their own crimes, may have exaggerated. Let us grant that Catiline listened to them and dreamed mad dreams. He has been wounded in the service of his country and suffered fevers in foreign lands; these are enough to affect a man's judgment. If he was confused by younger, ardent men, does that constitute treason? Perhaps. Perhaps not. Nevertheless, it *does* call for a penalty, and I demand it."

He looked at Catiline, whose head was now bowed in dejection.

"Let him go forth!" cried Julius, as if tortured by indignation mixed with pity. "Let him spend the last years of his life in exile, recalling that his fellow Romans were moved to compassion and spared him." With this, Julius sat down and covered his face with his hands, as if to hide his tears.

Oh, Julius, Cicero thought, I hoped that at the last you would stand with your country. Now all is lost.

Then young Cato rose, with eyes unafraid. He came to stand beside Cicero.

"Caesar, famed soldier!" he said. "Son of a great and honored house! You know that what Cicero said is truth! Tell me, Caesar, why do you speak softly in behalf of traitors? Must there be an excuse for traitors, that they were duped, confused? Or are they what you know they are—traitors and renegades with a full knowledge of their crimes?"

As Cato continued, the senators and the people were so struck by his passionate honesty that they did not notice that Catiline had disappeared, melting away through the throngs. Only Caesar saw his stealthy exit and he—who had been holding his breath—smiled with relief.

Again the temple was invaded by a thunderous roar from the people: "Death to Catiline and all the traitors! Death! Death!"

The faintest of smiles passed over Cicero's features, and the senators knew they had no alternative. The oldest of them directed his somber eyes upon the consul and said: "Death to Catiline and his conspirators."

But Catiline was, at that very moment, riding furiously through the gates of Rome to join the old and honorable general, Manlius.

MADNESS, CICERO HAD once said, has a terrible grandeur of its own, and it was this grandeur which fascinated those who loved Catiline. He had no restraints, no mercy.

Manlius said to him, "I have seen too much violence and death. Let us first bargain with the rulers of our country."

But Catiline said wildly, "I have no country! I shall have one only when I seize Rome!"

He struck almost at once, with a mixed army—patriots he had seduced, Manlius' skilled soldiers, and a rabble of freedmen, runaway slaves and traitors. Rumor ran in fright to Rome: Catiline was on the march, and there were tens of thousands of his sympathizers within the city.

Quintus was with an army sent to intercept Catiline. But Catiline turned his forces north to drive his way across the Apennines into Gaul. He had not the slightest doubt of success. Riding along the ranks of his huge, straggling army often equipped only with sharpened staves, he carried a blood-red banner on which was embroidered the ancient arms of the Catilines. With his beautiful, exultant face, he seemed like a god to his men.

The two armies finally approached each other on a broad plain, the heavy war chariots with snapping banners rumbling and thundering ahead of the legions, the officers leading them on horseback. The pale but dazzling sun struck on scarlet and gold banners and on thousands of gilded shields, making a little sun of each of them. Quintus' blood was stirred; but then his simple heart was struck as with a fist of iron, as he realized that he was eager to kill the man who had risked his own life to save him. He prayed that it would not be he who would kill Catiline.

"Charge!" Quintus cried, and the army sprang forward. Catiline's men saw the glittering wave rushing upon them and wavered, but did not break. In the shock of the wild and terrible meeting, horses flung themselves against horses, men against men, and the earth quaked. Chariots wheeled and churned about the foe. The air was filled with shouts and groans, the shrieks of horses, the thuds of colliding armored bodies.

Catiline's men fought like lions, for there would be no quarter given. But the men of Rome fought even more tenaciously. They had their nation to defend; the enemy were defending nothing but themselves.

The frightful encounter was over as swiftly as it had begun. Gasping for air, Quintus searched about him for his general, and could not see him. A mound of dead lay before him: the slaughter on both sides had been terrible. Then suddenly Quintus saw Catiline lying on the ground in a puddle of his own blood.

He descended from his horse and went to the fallen man. The helmet had dropped from the noble head, and a wind stirred the thick dark hair. The blue eyes, which had terrified and fascinated so many, stared at the sky sightlessly. Quintus shuddered, for Catiline's eyes were glazing, but the savage soul struggled to see through the closing veil of death.

"Catiline?" said Quintus, and he lifted the flaccid hand near him. The spirit struggling to be free from Catiline's flesh paused a moment to listen. Then it saw Quintus' face, and the faintest smile touched the gray lips.

"Quintus," Catiline whispered; and, smiling, called him by the affectionate nickname he had once given him: "Bear Cub." The dying fingers tightened on Quintus' hand. "Farewell!" The white lids closed.

Quintus wept. He thought, I thank the gods that it was not my hand that slew him! He looked at Catiline's hand and saw the serpentine ring of the deadly brotherhood. He forced himself to remove it and dropped it in his pouch to give his brother. Then he lifted a fallen Roman banner and covered Catiline's body with it. For, at the end, Catiline had not died ingloriously.

BUT IT WAS NOT yet the end. Cicero knew that every conspirator with Catiline must be exterminated, though he shrank from the slaughter. General Manlius had fallen on his own sword, and Cicero was grateful that the brave old soldier would not have to suffer an ignominious death. With the wiping out of the conspiracy, more patricians became Cicero's mortal enemies.

Clodius said to Caesar, "I shall not forget this Cicero whom I once honored." But Julius shrugged. "We still need him."

Clodius had a small dark face with black eyes so wide apart the malicious said he looked like a frog. His eyes gleamed now. "Mark Antony swears a vendetta against Cicero because his stepfather, Lentulus, was one of Catiline's lieutenants. Cicero has made enough enemies to form a company."

Terentia said to Cicero, "My friend Julia, widow of Lentulus, ostracizes me, as do other widows of the conspirators. Our son-in-law finds doors closed to him. What future will be your son's?"

"Rome's future, if any," said Cicero. He thought sadly of divorcing Terentia, for her complaints and recriminations were more than he could bear now. Catiline's conspiracy had involved more great families than he had realized. He now knew that Lentulus had been assigned by Catiline to assassinate all the senators. Now these very senators—and the people—muttered that Cicero had been too harsh in his destruction of the conspiracy!

CHAPTER SIXTEEN

SPRING WAS RADIANT at Arpinum, and the air was sweet. Sometimes, especially when the moon was large, Cicero evaded his bodyguards and visited the places where he had met Livia. Then the sound of the river was unbearably musical and full of memories. He was growing old, but she was eternally young, and she was a blessing to his spirit.

He received a letter from Noë ben Joel, who was now a gray-bearded grandfather. "The wise men at the gates tell me that 'something has moved' in Heaven, but what it portends they do not say. Has something quickened in the blood of the House of David, as prophesied? I see our old friend Roscius in the Temple. As each young mother brings her man-child in to offer him to the Lord, he peers at the infant, then turns away with disappointment, muttering, 'No, it is not He.' "

Marcus had not thought of the Messiah of the Jews for a long time, so fearful had been the strain upon him. It was easier to think of Him in the golden peace of the island. If He ever, indeed, were born, surely He would come to a little hamlet. Socrates had said, "Out of cities grows confusion. In the hamlets, philosophy can flourish."

It was with regret that Cicero had to leave for Rome. And it was ridiculous that, as consul and therefore guardian of Rome's "morals," he was now forced to prosecute Clodius for adultery with Pompeia, Caesar's wife.

He said cynically to Julius, when Caesar visited him to discuss the case, "Pompeia's conduct has never been exemplary. Whom do you wish to marry this time?"

"I wish only to divorce Pompeia," Julius said. "Caesar's wife must be above suspicion."

Cicero mused, his eyes fixed on Julius' face. "Has Clodius become dangerous to you, with his ambitions?"

"What nonsense! Clodius is only a tribune." He rose to leave, then paused. "I have asked you before, Marcus. Join Crassus and me. We have mighty plans for the future. I should like you to be one of us."

"There is a Greek saying," Cicero said. " 'If a man is dangerous, induce him to join you and thus disarm him.' "

Julius suddenly became grave. "I shall not ask you again, dear comrade. Therefore, reflect."

After he had gone Marcus considered Caesar's words with alarm. Despite the fresh hostility against him, he had not believed himself in much danger of assassination, for Catiline was dead, and most of the conspirators with him. Yet Julius' black eyes had contained a deadly warning.

There was growing talk, too—instigated, Cicero thought, by young Mark Antony—that Cicero had violated the bill of rights by not granting Catiline's lieutenants a trial by jury. Cicero had to admit, privately, that this was true. But he had feared that the trials would lead to riots.

Now the case against Clodius must be pursued, for the scandal had had an astonishing impact on the Roman people. Clodius, wearing female garments, had invaded Caesar's house during the celebrations of *Bona Dea*—the Good Goddess—when no man should be present. Then he and Pompeia had been caught in "flagrant behavior" by Aurelia, Julius' mother.

Cicero remanded Clodius for trial and Clodius, of course, pleaded not guilty. A witness swore that on the night of *Bona Dea* Clodius had been with him in the country, ninety miles from Caesar's house. Cicero called Julius as a witness, but Caesar emphatically declared that he knew nothing personally of the case. Finally Cicero himself was called as a witness by the prosecuting magistrates. He testified that he had seen Clodius in Rome barely three hours before the *Bona Dea* ceremonies.

To Cicero's incredulous horror, the jury voted, thirty-three to twenty-five, that Clodius was not guilty. There could be only one answer: they had been bribed, and Caesar himself had somehow been induced not to press his case.

And now one thing was wholly certain: he had made an enemy of Clodius.

AT THE END OF his term as consul, Cicero appointed his friend Antonius Hybrida as governor in Macedonia. Scandalous reports soon reached him that Antonius was guilty of oppression and extortion, but he refused to believe this and at Antonius' request prepared to defend him when he was recalled to be tried.

Then he was stupefied to learn that Antonius had written senatorial friends that Cicero had commanded him to share the spoils plundered from Macedonia! Evidently he hoped to implicate Cicero and thus escape a great measure of guilt himself. Meantime, he was still writing affectionately to Cicero thanking him for his acceptance of the defense.

In despair, Cicero withdrew from the case. He trusted few men again. The animus against him in Rome had become so fierce that his law practice declined and he was forced to discharge his clerks. The Senate did not dare to censure him formally, for he still had a small coterie of devoted friends. Besieged and beleaguered, he sometimes thought of death; but he recalled the words of Noë ben Joel: "Suicide is man's ultimate hatred of God."

He was surprised one day in his library by a visit from Julius Caesar. He said to the younger man sourly, "What! I thought you no longer remembered my name!"

Julius laughed and embraced him affectionately. "How is it possible for me to forget you, my childhood mentor, the man whose honor can never be questioned?" He sat.

"It is being questioned incessantly," said Cicero.

"Bah," said Julius. "The mob acclaims; the mob denounces. One ignores them. Now, I am here to ask your help. I am a candidate for consul. Will you speak for me?"

Cicero stared at him incredulously. "You are not serious!"

"I am. A consul is elected by a minority of fastidious men who throw their votes to one candidate. Crassus and Pompey and I have also formed a triumvirate. Crassus and Pompey have resolved their quarrel."

Marcus was stunned. "Triumvirate?"

"Certainly. Dictators are not popular with Romans, and to meet our complex problems today one man is not sufficient, anyway. I will represent the masses, Crassus will attend to financial problems, Pompey will govern the military."

"An infamous oligarchy, such as destroyed Greece!" Cicero's heart had begun to thump. "No! By the gods, no!"

"Hardly an oligarchy," said Julius. "The Senate and tribunes will have the power to remove any or all of us. Is not this most excellent for Rome?"

Cicero groaned. "Rome is lost. So this is your plot!"

"There is no plot," said Julius kindly. "And again I ask for your help." He stood up, and leaned his palms on the library table. "Marcus, it will do you no service to oppose me."

Cicero's eyes burned on Julius. "I will lay bare what I know about the three of you! You shall not win, Julius."

Julius struck the table with the flat of his hand. "Then you may as well fall upon your sword, Marcus. I came today to warn you that Clodius and Mark Antony, among others, have vowed to destroy you." He gazed at Marcus with mingled exasperation, anxiety and love. "Oppose us and you are ruined."

Marcus knew that Julius spoke the truth. He opened a small casket on the table and brought forth a ring and spun it between himself and Caesar. "Do you recognize this?" he asked.

Julius took the serpentine ring in his hand. Marcus smiled. "This time you cannot return the ring to its owner, unless you cross the Styx. Take it. It profanes my house. And, Julius, I will use what little power I still retain to oppose you."

Julius said, "Then, Marcus, farewell—for you are standing on the abyss." He dropped the ring in his pouch and left.

THE NEXT DAY Caesar withdrew his support of Cicero, and within a few days the Senate passed a bill which Clodius had introduced exiling anyone who had put Roman citizens to death without due process of law. The Senate summoned Cicero before it, and he was solemnly censured for having requested the death penalty for Catiline and his lieutenants. Cicero pointed out that the senators themselves could have rejected his request. He also protested that no one could be punished by a law passed after the alleged crime. But it was useless. He left the Senate with dignity; but when he was in his litter he had the sensation of unreality which is the cloak that despair wears. He must leave his beloved country and live at least four hundred miles from Rome!

He had an alternative to exile. He could fall upon his sword. But he had a family. He went to his library, sank down upon a couch and pressed his hands over his face in a stupor of profound grief until he became aware of a thunderous knocking at the door. He opened it to be met by the pale faces of his wife, his daughter and his brother.

Terentia cried, "You would not listen to me! You were so sure of your own might! And now you have brought disgrace and ruin upon your family." She burst into furious sobs and gazed at her husband with rage and misery.

But Quintus came to Cicero and put his hand on his shoulder, and Tullia kissed his icy cheek. "I shall go with you, dear Father," she said.

Embracing her, Cicero said, "None of you must go with me. Terentia, this house is forfeit, with all I have. But what you have inherited and what I have given you over the years is yours. In the morning I will take with me what I can carry, and leave. To go with me would be treasonous for a legionnaire, Quintus; and Tullia must remain with her husband, who will work with you for my recall." He kissed Tullia. "Beloved child, do not forget me, and ask Piso to help me. It is all you can do."

THE LONG AND melancholy journey into exile almost destroyed Cicero. As he halted briefly at the villas put at his disposal by his friends, he would recall that he was both homeless and penniless; not even his books remained. Nor could he live as an exile, far from all his dreams and memories, the ashes of his forefathers, his mother's tomb. "All else is nothing, but the hills of home," he wrote to Atticus, "and the sound of the dear beloved tongue."

He heard from family and friends that Quintus, Piso, and Terentia's powerful family were raising a storm of indignation about his exile among the fickle Romans. He heard that Clodius and Pompey were now bitter enemies, that Caesar used and despised both, and that Pompey and Crassus looked upon each other "through crossed swords." He heard that Calpurnia, Caesar's new wife, was a soothsayer and a woman of awesome tempers. But he felt no interest. The mind which had once embraced a world had shrunk to the size of his own suffering ego, and he had decided that he must take his own life. His letters made his friends fear he had lost his mind.

He reached the villa of a friend in Salonika, which looked upon the Aegean and the silver mountains, amid the lovely simplicity of Ionic columns casting purple shadows; the aromatic air of Greece, the vast silky azure of the sea. But Greece could no longer enchant the exile. He had planned to die here, but now he feared to have his ashes become one with this alien dust, and blow in this blue and ardent air.

The overseer at the villa, Adoni, a man of considerable learning, had heard much of Cicero. When the exile, who seemed to age day by day, sat like a blind man in the brilliantly colored gardens, Adoni brought him delicate viands and pointed out to him the white walls foaming with scarlet flowers. But the smell of the roses around him reminded Cicero only of his own lost gardens.

One day Adoni said to him, "Lord, a ship has arrived from Palestine. The Jews have excellent silvers, bronzes and silks, and marvelous fruits; and always, always, they write books. Shall I go to the port and see what I can find for you?"

Cicero, who desired nothing but Rome, felt Adoni's kindness. "Go to the port, Adoni," he said. "But remember that I have little money. Be prudent."

At sunset Adoni returned with two visitors.

THE SKY WAS pure gold that evening; the sea ran with gold, and every leaf in the gardens was gilded. And in the drenching golden light Cicero sat on a marble bench under the myrtle trees, like the statue of a dying man. His eyes, once so compelling, seemed drained of color; his face, once so furrowed with secret laughter and humor, was the face of a lost and seeking shade: for now he felt that God was indifferent—or did not exist.

The approaching visitors gazed at him with consternation as they entered the gardens. One of them cried out, "Marcus!" and Cicero looked up indifferently. He saw a tall, slender, middle-aged man with a long gray beard, and brown eyes which were both soft and probing. He wore a robe of saffron embroidered with gold and silver; and an Egyptian necklace with tassels of gold and emeralds was about his throat. Weeping, he embraced Cicero.

"Marcus, dearly beloved friend," he said. "Do you not remember Noë, your friend, your brother?"

"Noë!" cried Marcus, his face lighting up. "It is not possible! I thought even God was dead."

"God lives, therefore the world still lives."

Noë sat down beside his friend, and Marcus took one of his hands and held it tightly. "And see," said Noë, "here is another old friend of yours, Anotis the Egyptian. We met in Jerusalem, and when we discovered that you were our friend we became friends also." Noë's voice was soothing but clear as he tried to reach that besieged and distant spirit. "I heard from friends in Rome that you were in Salonika, and Anotis and I decided to visit you. And here we are, our eyes gladdened to behold you once more."

"Anotis," said Marcus, in a faint and troubled voice. He looked at his other visitor, so tall and lean in his crimson and green robes. He saw the clear gray eyes, the dark aquiline face, and the pointed, grizzled beard. "Anotis! Anotis!" cried Marcus, and he burst into tears.

"We Jews were also driven from our land and were captives,"

said Noë, as the three men sat together. "Hear what David says: *By the rivers of Babylon, there we sat down, yea, we wept, when we remembered Zion.* And God remembered the exiles and restored them to their own country. So He will restore you, Marcus, in His own good time."

Noë had brought Cicero a tiny silken and silver replica of the Sacred Scrolls, the Torah. Anotis had brought him the golden figure of a woman crowned with stars, her body great with child. He said, "The Chaldean priests have told me a strange thing. Their astronomers now watch for a stupendous Star which will lead the holy men to the birthplace of Him who shall save the world and deliver us from death. For so it has been promised to all men who have ears to hear and a soul to listen."

During the days of the men's visit, Marcus' worn face became younger: it was as if he had been newborn. He spoke buoyantly, as a young man. He opened the books in the library and read to his friends in Greek. He spoke eagerly of what he hoped to accomplish when he was recalled to Rome. He boasted of his children, his brother, his friends. At night he wrote new essays. The servants rejoiced to hear his ringing voice. "Oh!" Marcus would exclaim to his friends. "God is good, that He sent you to me, when I looked for nothing but death!"

"That is because He has need of you," they would answer.

"Tell me again of the Messiah," Marcus would say. "I had forgotten Him."

"Despite what the Pharisees declare," Noë said, "the Messiah will not come with silver trumpets and thunder, but will be born as the humblest and the meekest. He will endure an agonizing death, as the Sacrifice for sinful man. How shall we know Him? Surely God will reveal Him."

"We have His sign, the Cross," said Anotis, "and this we have had for many ages."

Marcus listened avidly, and in his heart he said, Forgive me, that in my exile I doubted You and forgot You.

When his friends left, he accompanied them to the port. As the great winged ship fell below the horizon he was again filled with sorrow; but then he thought, They are not gone. We say "Farewell," but in another harbor they say, "Here they return."

CHAPTER SEVENTEEN

"SUDDENLY THE WHOLE city demands Cicero's recall," said Julius Caesar to Crassus and Pompey. "If we are magnanimous, the people will hail us."

"I say yes," said Pompey, and raised his thumb. But the storm of protest had angered Crassus, and it was only when it became dangerous to resist that he gloomily gave in. It was decided to so confuse the issue that no man could know who had forced Cicero's recall. Pompey wrote Cicero stating that he worked sleeplessly for his recall. "But," he added, "it now lies with Caesar." The Senate turned down a motion for his recall, but restored his civil rights and rank, and Atticus wrote, "It seems that all Italy desires your return; but Clodius still hates you, and he is very powerful."

Atticus did not add that Cicero's brother, Quintus, had been set upon in daylight, in the Forum, by the minions of Clodius and had barely survived.

Finally Pompey, who despised the mob, addressed them in the Forum, urging a vote—a *lex*—to recall Cicero and appealing to their decency and honor, which he privately considered they did not possess. No member of the terrible triumvirate, whom all men feared, had heretofore spoken to the people, and the mob was flattered. They voted in favor of Cicero's recall, momentarily forgetting Clodius, their master.

Clodius strove to regain control of his followers, but this time the people did not follow him. For, though he had bribed them often enough, Pompey had aroused the latent instinct for decency in them. The exile was over, and Tullia met her beloved father on the shores of his homeland and threw herself in his arms. He put her from him gently, and knelt down and kissed the sacred earth.

HIS PROGRESS TO Rome was triumphal. Magistrates crowned him with laurel; farmers and their families lined the roads, strewing flowers in his path, and every hamlet and town along his passage declared a festa in his honor.

The twenty-third night of his journey, he sat in a flower-filled chamber in a large villa near Rome while Tullia laid out his ceremonial robes for his entrance into the city the next day. For the first time, he noted that she appeared more fragile and delicate than he remembered. Her slender face was very pale. He was alarmed. "Tullia!" he said. "This journey has wearied you."

She tried to smile. Then all at once she burst into tears and threw herself into his arms.

"Tell me!" he cried. "What is wrong with my darling?"

Then, at last, he heard of the death of his devoted son-in-law, Piso, who had worked valorously for his return. Tullia was brokenhearted.

"I have been so blind!" said Cicero. "I should have seen how stricken you were. But no! I was listening too hard to plaudits for myself!" He forgot his joy in his mourning, but Tullia finally persuaded him that Piso would wish him to rejoice; for Piso's sake he must do so tomorrow.

He was awakened at dawn by a triumphant blast of trumpets. From his window he saw Quintus' legion surrounding the villa, banners unfurled. Beyond them was a gilded chariot, sent for him from the Senate, and a mass of people who had come from Rome to gather in his train. The procession began, trumpets, drums and cymbals leading, officers on their prancing black horses, and then Cicero and Tullia in the shining chariot, and behind them tens of thousands of dancing, screaming, clapping men and women. New rivers of humanity flowed into the procession all along the Appian Way. The sun had raised half a red rim against the eastern sky, and now scarlet light in the east towered upward like a conflagration. Tullia saw something ominous in the bloody light, for it was reflected on Cicero's white toga and in his eyes; and the dust rising under the running feet was scarlet. Shaken with fear, as if she had glimpsed a procession in Hades, Tullia reached out to touch her father's arm.

All at once the uproarious scene sparkled into other colors as the sun mounted. The walls of Rome could be seen, and above them the city itself, red, flaming gold, gleaming umber, light green and blue, all its tiled roofs afire as if a thousand bonfires had been built upon them to hail the hero.

Tears rushed into Cicero's eyes as the whole Senate, in white and scarlet robes, met him at the gates, with the tribunes and the magistrates. Julius rode on a great white horse through the

ranks of the legionnaires to Cicero's chariot, and leaped in like a youth to embrace him. Then Pompey rode beside the chariot and Crassus trotted at the head of the procession, as if he were the hero. The soldiers at the gates raised their trumpets and the whole world went mad with cheering and cries; and all was covered with clouds of dust, golden red in the morning sunlight.

Then Cicero addressed the senators, who wept when he began, "This day has been equivalent to immortality." He had been the victim of these very men, yet elation lifted his soul and he felt young again, for these were Romans, and he was again a Roman. He launched into a panegyric of the Senate and of the Roman people, and everything seemed outlined with radiance.

At Atticus' house on the Palatine, Cicero forced himself to embrace his wife and to thank her for her efforts on his behalf. He rejoiced in his son, in whose face, red-cheeked and merry, he fancied he discerned wisdom and all other virtues. But when he was shown to his sumptuous apartments, he recalled that he now had no house of his own, and that Clodius had built on the site a temple ironically dedicated to liberty.

Before sunset, Cicero went to see Quintus, still suffering from his wounds. Sitting beside his brother, he learned of the true state of Rome.

Pompey held unprecedented military power. There was a serious shortage of grain, for Sicily and Egypt had had poor harvests, and the merchants had raised their prices enormously. Clodius had now formed gangs of malcontents and trained them as an army which only he could control: they had actually stoned the Senate while it was in session. The people, as usual, cared for their bellies rather than their liberties, and it was easy to influence them.

In short, Cicero reflected with dismay, little or nothing had changed in Rome.

CICERO BEGAN TO campaign for the restoration of his property. He appealed to the College of Pontiffs, who held religious responsibilities; for to destroy the temple Clodius had erected on the site of his house on the Palatine Hill might be blasphemous. The pontiffs declared that Cicero had been deprived of his property through malice and enmity; it could, therefore, be returned to him.

The consuls let out contracts for the demolition of the temple and the rebuilding of Cicero's house, and offered money—though less than their actual worth—to pay for Cicero's villas, which had also been destroyed.

But Clodius was not subdued by authority. When the first snow fell, he commanded his lawless bands to destroy what had been rebuilt of the house. What could not be dismantled was burned.

Then, in open daylight, when Cicero was going down from the Capitol on the Sacred Way, Clodius in person attacked him with his cutthroats. Fortunately, Cicero was attended by a large body of police and the rabble was dispersed.

Titus Milo protested this "outrage against law and order" before the Senate. As a consequence, Milo's house was burned to the ground.

Caesar was now pursuing the Gallic wars with young Mark Antony as his first officer, but he frequently returned to Rome to keep an eye on his enemies. One day Cicero went to his villa. Julius received him with his customary ebullience and summoned his new wife, Calpurnia. She was a young woman, tall and very thin, dressed in purple embroidered with gold Grecian keys; both she and Caesar affected purple. Her long straight hair was black and she had an angular face, white as bone. Her large dark eyes burned, and her thin mouth grimaced and trembled constantly. The first impression was of ugliness; the next, of frightening, unearthly beauty. She gazed almost fiercely into Cicero's eyes, and her face changed as if she were about to burst into tears. In silence, she seated herself.

"My dear Calpurnia," said Julius, "is my right hand. I trust her implicitly."

Cicero came to the point bluntly. "You, the triumvirate, could outlaw Clodius and his murderers if you desired. You suffer Clodius only because he will create so much disorder that the triumvirate can declare an emergency and seize total power in Rome. Then Pompey, with his legions, will move upon Rome, creating a military dictatorship."

"Plots again?" said Julius with amusement. "You were always a victim of your own imagination."

But Calpurnia cried in anguish, "I warned Julius! He is pursuing a dangerous course. It will end with his murder!" Her eyes were wide and glittering and she was breathing as if in terror.

Julius' laugh was gay. "I swear that the two of you are the most dismal of augurs! The triumvirate wishes only peace and prosperity for Rome. Let Clodius riot and shout with his gangs in the street. Is it not wiser to permit such demonstrations than to suppress them and drive them underground? After they have shrieked themselves hoarse, they return to their homes in high good humor."

"After burning houses, stoning the Senate, killing harmless men and defying the police."

Julius shrugged. "These are not the old days when dissent was quickly suppressed. Besides, Clodius has been reprimanded."

"And secretly encouraged," said Cicero.

Calpurnia was wringing her hands. "I have dreamed that Julius was dying of many wounds! Marcus Cicero, you are his friend. Add your voice to mine." The tears ran down her cheeks.

"Do you desire to be king of Rome?" asked Cicero.

Julius reached for his wife's hand and patted it. "We are a republic, not an empire, Marcus," he said.

Cicero shook his head. "You and your friends were the executioners of our Republic, Julius. But there still live Romans who love freedom. Move to take the crown and you will die."

Julius rose. He caught Cicero's arm. "Have you not learned through suffering? Be done with meddling, and let your final days be serene. I give you this advice because I love you."

Cicero flung off his arm. "Let my country die without a word from me, a protest?" He kissed Calpurnia's hand, and departed.

CICERO'S NEW HOUSE on the Palatine was not so grand as his former one, nor was it filled with treasures, for the Senate, though voting for the "full return" of Cicero's fortune, had set its own estimates. Terentia was dissatisfied and querulous, as if she deserved better of the world, and especially of her husband.

In the month of Janus, Quintus departed for Sardinia as one of Pompey's lieutenants, but before he left he had a talk with his brother. "Be resigned, Marcus," he said. "We shall never see the Republic again. Turn your energy to your books. Seek pleasures. Acquire a mistress; dine pleasantly; drink good wine. Better not to stare too fixedly at life, but to enjoy what it has to give."

"I prefer to end as a man, and not a surfeited animal," said Cicero with anger. "We have a greater destiny than that of a beast. If we did not have such a destiny, mysterious though it is, we would not yearn for it and for the knowledge of it."

Quintus said gravely, "Spare your family further misery. Caesar loves you in his fashion—but do not annoy him, Marcus." He embraced his brother and left. He doubted that Cicero would take his advice.

Cicero began his monumental work, *De Republica,* on the nature of human society and the state. He did his duty as a senator, reopened his law offices, loved his children, endured his wife, tried for contentment with his friends. But he could not keep silence while his country fell into the abyss. "There is active evil, such as supporting evil men and traitors," he told his friend Cato, "and there is passive evil—not speaking when a man should speak—and that is the worst."

He appeared before the Senate to oppose Clodius' bid for office. He asked his friends' help and was aghast at their shrugs, the words of tolerance for Clodius, now often seen in company with Caesar. "But we are living under a tyranny," said Cicero.

His friends spoke of their prosperity and laughed. "If this is tyranny, give us more of it!" they said. Clodius was elected in spite of all the evidence against him.

Meantime, Cicero wrote proudly to Atticus: "Young Marcus needs a goad to assert himself, but is this not true of all incipient philosophers?" He did not know that Marcus was lazy, greedy and self-indulgent. Terentia secretly encouraged him in his habits, delighted that her son did not resemble his father; that he was a gentleman and not a vulgar dissenter.

Tullia came to her father and shyly announced that she wished to marry the young patrician Dolabella, who had loved her long before she had married Piso. Cicero believed the house of Dolabella was idle and dissipated, but he was reconciled when, after the marriage, he saw Tullia's happiness.

LATER, ATTICUS WAS to write young Marcus: "Your father was Rome, and her history was his history. All those whom men account great touched his life. They brought evil and blood and despair on their country; he brought valor and virtue. They succeeded. He did not succeed. But in the final accounting, who knows but that such a man's defeat is victory?"

"You are a pillar of iron," Noë wrote Cicero. "Long after polished marble has crumbled, the iron of justice remains. Without such as you, dear Marcus, man would be no more."

After Clodius' victory, Cicero resolutely shut Roman politics from his awareness. He could fight no longer. He wrote some of his noblest books, which were to survive the ages and warn men yet unborn of dangers to their own countries. He had long conversations with his son, young Marcus, and mercifully did not know that the boy listened to him with a sober face but with inner mockery. He visited his daughter and his beloved island. His law business began to flourish and he found his coffers filling.

Then to his astonishment he was appointed to the Board of Augurs, a well-paid and dignified life office. The Board was composed of agnostics who disputed with the College of Pontiffs on religious doctrines. A disagreeable thought came to Cicero, though he was pleased with the post: The pontiffs had always shown him friendliness, while the augurs contended often with the college. Did Caesar wish to reconcile the augurs and the pontiffs through him? Caesar said: "Why not accept the manifest truth, dear Marcus, that the gods moved to have you appointed?"

Cicero thought many of the augurs' prophecies absurd, but he was enough of a mystic to believe that the future was indicated to a few souls, and he took his new duties seriously. An augur divined from signs in the sky and from the flight of birds. In the presence of a magistrate, the augur would designate with his official staff the place for his studies, usually a hill. There he prayed and sacrificed at night under the shelter of a tent, observing the heavens and asking for a sign. He reported any sign to the magistrate, and it would then govern the affairs of Rome to a great extent. Fortunately for Rome the augurs had been singularly free from corruption.

The birds of good fortune were the eagle and the vulture; the malign were the raven, the crow and the owl. Their flight, their cries, their manner of taking food were interpreted by rules. Augurs also divined from the behavior of animals in the field or from animals slain for sacrifice. A client might request an augur to prophesy on a proposed venture. If, for instance, the augur reported lightning in the sky, the client did not act the next day.

Caesar wrote to Cicero that he had a plan in mind and asked him to consult the sky on a certain night. Cicero therefore went outside the city walls with a magistrate and swung his staff in a circle. The staff suddenly appeared to have a life of its own; it tugged him forward, then plunged into the earth. Cicero's heart began to beat with dread. "I shall set up my tent here," he said.

That night the purple heavens were crowded with flashing stars; they seemed a portent to Cicero. I am being ridiculous, he told himself. I am projecting on nature my own forebodings.

The magistrate sat in respectful silence at his side, his stylus and tablet ready for notes, and for some reason Cicero began to think of Noë's account of Elijah and the fiery chariot which had borne the prophet to Heaven in a whirlwind. Then he started, and his flesh turned icy, for suddenly, imposed on the furious white radiance of the stars, there had appeared a great and blazing chariot drawn by four blazing horses! In the chariot stood Julius Caesar crowned with laurel, holding glittering reins and laughing with a terrible, exultant laughter. In his uplifted hand a sword, twisted and turning like fire, reached to the zenith. On his left shoulder stood a mighty eagle with eyes like jewels, and behind him blood-red banners appeared. All was movement; the horses raced, the sparkling wheels of the chariot churned.

Then on Caesar's head shone a crown. The black eagle lifted its wings and uttered a frightful cry. A beautiful woman, her flowing black hair crowned with golden serpents, appeared, and Caesar lifted her into the chariot, and there was thunder.

"What do you see, lord?" asked the magistrate, aware of Cicero's pale and staring face. But Cicero did not answer.

The vision remained. Then from the right appeared a flock of ravens, owls and crows, each carrying a dagger in its mouth. They circled Caesar and the woman, and the woman disappeared. An enormous soldier appeared before the galloping horses, his sword pointed at Caesar. Caesar lifted his own sword and struck him down. The soldier's place was taken by an empty throne, and Caesar raced toward it. But the birds of ill omen circled closer. They fell upon Caesar, with the daggers in their mouths, and slashed him with many wounds, and he collapsed in the chariot.

The magistrate could feel the augur shudder, for now Cicero

saw the open gates of Rome with triumphal arches; a fair young man with a crown was driving his chariot through them. Then through the gates hordes of bearded men rushed in, striking death on every side, and Rome collapsed slowly, its white walls turning gray as swirling mist crept over the site.

Now in the semidarkness a mighty dome appeared like a sun, while from its summit rose a golden fire that formed a cross. From the doors of the walls beneath came men clothed in white, speaking the words, "Peace on earth to men of good will."

But as the last man emerged a dark and crimson confusion began to form before him. He faced blackened heavens tongued with flame and rolling balls like suns.

"Lord, have mercy on us!" cried the men in white, and there was the sound of mountains falling, and whirlwinds.

Cicero fainted. Much later he wrote Caesar: "I have seen auguries which defy my power to describe. Julius, refrain from your dreams. You will surely die." The letter angered Julius.

CHAPTER EIGHTEEN

CRASSUS WAS AN old man and had never been a soldier, but when the Parthians, in Asia Minor, turned against Rome it was he who led the Roman armies. He was killed in battle. Now Pompey alone confronted Caesar in the struggle for power. Caesar built his great bridge across the Rhine and then invaded Britain; but he still appeared unexpectedly in Rome on occasion, and it was said that he was borne there by Jupiter himself.

Effervescent and amusing, he often visited Cicero when he came to Rome, and he made Cicero smile, for all his care. "You are but four years younger than I, Julius," he said, "yet you are a youth. What is your secret?"

Julius pretended to ponder. Then his face sparkled with laughter. "Myself," he said. "I love myself; I adore myself; I contemplate myself and I am in ecstasy. How, then, can Rome refrain from giving me homage?"

Cicero stopped smiling. "Do not underestimate Pompey," he said. "Respectable men revere him, for he is honest." He went on, remembering his vision, "Julius, if you were in danger I would defend you with my life. When I see you, I see the face of the little schoolboy who took my hand for protection, and made me laugh when I was serious. Do not try Romans too far."

Caesar embraced him, his face sober now. "In all Rome I trust only you," he said. "Our lives are bound up together, Marcus. So dissimilar, we yet are like the Gemini."

IT WAS INEVITABLE that the Romans should love Caesar for his wit and his vices; it was just as inevitable that they should not love the more virtuous, tedious Pompey. Young Titus Milo and Clodius were running for office. Milo campaigned with the words, "Romans need no soldier or despot to control them." Clodius used the slogans: "Caesar and Clodius for the People!" "Free corn for the needy!" One day on the Appian Way Milo's men were assaulted by Clodius' rabble. During the struggle Clodius was slain.

As usual, it was all forgotten within a few days. The great games were approaching, and there was wild betting on gladiators, wrestlers and races. One day the daily newspaper posted on the walls of Rome reported that a revolt in Gaul led by one Vercingetorix had been crushed by Julius Caesar, who was remaining in Gaul to restore order. Pompey, seizing this advantage, announced himself sole consul. "The lion and the bear will soon be at each other's throats," Cicero wrote to a friend.

Meantime he could find no peace in his family. Terentia was even more captious and restless; Quintus, an admirer of Caesar's, kept urging his brother to forget politics; and Tullia was not happy in her marriage to Dolabella after all. Her manner was listless, though she smiled and said she had no complaints.

Then Cicero received a letter from Leah, the wife of Noë, sadly announcing the death of her husband. "He recalled you with his last breath," she wrote. "He asked me to repeat to you the words of Isaiah: *Fear thou not, for I am with thee; be not dismayed; for I am thy God."*

"Why do you weep?" asked Terentia.

"The earth is poorer," said Cicero. "It has lost a good man."

CICERO, IN HIS fifties now, was sent as governor to the province of Cilicia. He took young Marcus with him, for he had become aware that Terentia's influence was injuring their son.

He found that Cilicia had been looted by his predecessors. But in a few months he could write to Atticus: "A number of states have been released from debt by my efforts. Not one penny of expense has been imposed upon them in my government."

Pompey and Caesar were now deadly enemies. Pompey controlled the Senate, which had become fearful of Caesar's ambitions. The legions were half for Pompey, half for Caesar. Pompey asked Caesar to hand over his army. With humor, Caesar proposed that *both* he and the government give up their armies.

When Cicero returned to Rome he went to Julius. "Cannot this whole dangerous nonsense be halted?" Cicero said.

Julius said sadly, "Pompey is a militarist. They acclaim me in Rome as the mightiest soldier of them all, but I was never at heart a soldier. Pompey thinks cold iron is the way to govern a country. That suet-head affronts me."

"Julius, you never spoke the truth in your life," said Cicero, and Caesar laughed.

The Senate now named a date on which Caesar must lay down his arms or be declared a public enemy. Caesar at once rejoined his devoted legions, a refugee.

The weather was particularly vicious that year. Military operations during winter were usually suspended in any case, and Pompey, who had little imagination, believed that Julius would be inactive. But winter meant nothing to Caesar.

All else is violent history. Caesar gathered his legions in Gaul and started down the Adriatic coast to Rome. Violating a very ancient law of the Republic, which forbade any general returning from the wars, with troops under arms, to cross the river Rubicon, he passed over the tiny river on the northern border of Italy. "The die is cast!" he shouted to his soldiers. The northern towns were with him, and he ran down the coast like fire with his cheering legions. Pompey's legions surrendered to Caesar, and then joined his forces.

Pompey fled to Macedonia to raise new legions. Against the advice of Quintus, Cicero went to Durazzo to join him, since Pompey was on the side of the law. He understood he was risking his life, but he no longer cared. Although as a man of peace he must go to Pompey, he could not relinquish his affection for Julius, and his dreams were haunted by memories of childhood.

Languishing in the sullen and restive camp at Durazzo, Cicero was in despair. He wrote his brother that Pompey was "a poor statesman and a rotten soldier." Finally he fell ill in both mind and body. In a dream he saw Pompey on a battlefield, in a mighty struggle. Then he saw a hand reaching out in a bloody darkness, with a serpentine ring upon it, and it gave a dagger to another hand. Cicero awoke, crying that he must warn Pompey; and Pompey's physician, who was caring for him, dared not tell him that Pompey was even then in battle with Caesar.

Cicero slept again. Now he found himself in a garden of bright flowers and towering oak trees. He caught a glimpse of a slight figure running across a marble bridge toward him. He opened his arms mutely, and Livia fell into them. Her kisses were like jasmine honey on his lips. "Dear love," he said, "I have had a most terrible dream. I dreamed that you were dead and I was old and brokenhearted."

"Dearest love," she replied, in the voice he had never forgotten, "be comforted. Heaven is astir. Soon we shall join our hands and wait."

"For what shall we wait?" he asked, holding her.

"For God," she replied, smiling at him. She gently extricated herself from his arms and the scene faded. He cried wildly, "Livia! Livia, my love!" But he was only in a mist, bereft and terrified.

He awoke and found the physician still at his side. "You have slept well and long," he said cheerfully. "And I have good news. Our troops have driven Caesar off. He is retreating south, to Thessaly, pursued by Pompey."

Marcus thought of Julius, who would be executed as a traitor, and wept, for it is the weakness of humanity that it must love even when love is undeserved.

But during Cicero's convalescence, terrible events followed one upon another. Caesar defeated Pompey in the famous battle of Pharsalus, and Pompey fled to Egypt where he was murdered. When Cicero was told what had transpired, he said, "My dream was true. Now we are utterly lost."

So far as Cicero was concerned, the disastrous civil war was over. Cato and Pompey's sons urged him to take over the struggle against Caesar, but he refused and decided to return to Rome. Caesar still loved Cicero, and sent word through Dolabella, Cicero's son-in-law, that he would embrace him as a friend. Then Caesar went to Egypt to destroy the remnants of Pompey's legions, and word came that the aging man was having a love affair with young Cleopatra, who wished to destroy her brother Ptolemy and assume his throne.

Cicero landed at Brundisium, at the southern end of the Appian Way. His beloved daughter, Tullia, joined him there. Always frail, she was now seriously ill. She had decided to divorce the profligate Dolabella. Meantime, Terentia wrote that young Marcus was "displaying some marks of dissipation, doubtless due to the desertion of his father." Cicero pined for Rome, but Caesar had left Mark Antony, an enemy of Cicero, in command there. Cato, much loved by the Roman people for his virtue and manliness, had committed suicide rather than "permit my eyes to gaze on tyranny in the city of my fathers."

The climate of Brundisium made Tullia worse, and he left with her for one of his Tusculan villas, where the air was salubrious. There, he wrote Atticus, he would be able to forget the world and permit the world to forget him.

In Tusculum he knew the last peace he was ever to know in his life. The country air restored his health, and he persuaded himself that it was of benefit to Tullia, also. He wrote a number of splendid, vigorous books here.

During this time Caesar destroyed all his enemies in Africa and Spain. He defeated Ptolemy and elevated Cleopatra, by whom he now had a son, to the throne of Egypt. He was in his late fifties, yet his energy seemed boundless.

Tullia fell gravely ill and Cicero decided that no matter what happened to him he must take her to the doctors in Rome. He told Terentia to leave his house on the Palatine. He had never loved her, and for this he blamed himself; but her complaints and contempt for him were intolerable and he had decided to divorce her immediately. As for young Marcus, he must study in Athens, where the philosophical climate would help him forget his dissipations and become a man.

In Rome, the physicians informed Cicero that Tullia's death could only be delayed, and he began to move through his days like one in a nightmare. He was sixty-one, and he moved like an old man; but his spirit still shone indomitably from his strange eyes, and his smile could still be charming. In the autumn he went to Arpinum with Tullia. There, in the blue shine of the autumnal days, his daughter was dying, his sweetness, his very life. She never complained, and her smile was always tender, her remarks amusing. She played with the lambs and petted the horses. Never in her life had she made a peevish remark; never had she been mean or small. One so lovely, he thought, must be coveted by God for His Isles of the Blessed.

One day, breathless and white, she rushed into his library. "I have seen a phantom! The most mysterious of women!"

Cicero rose and hastily forced a goblet of wine into her frail hand. "Be calm," he implored her. "You have seen but some wandering slave girl."

She shook her head vehemently. "She was no slave girl! She had hair like a shining autumn leaf and she came across the bridge and paused near me and gazed at me."

Cicero's heart began a wild plunging. He could not speak.

"She looked toward the farmhouse as if she knew you were there, my father, and smiled to herself like one with a secret. Then she stretched forth her hand to this house and smiled and beckoned. I was frightened, and she must have known, for she fled across the bridge again and was lost among the trees."

Livia! Cicero's spirit seemed to spread wings.

"Was she a sign of ill omen?" Tullia said.

"No." He could not say, She is the core of my life, and my soul yearns for her. He said, "Was there nothing else about her that you remember?"

She shivered. "There was a stain on her breast like blood."

Livia wished me to know beyond all doubt, Cicero thought. He kissed his daughter, and comforted her. He was a Roman, and skeptical, and he had almost forgotten God; but when he thought of Livia he was young again, and immortal.

WHEN THE WEATHER became sharp he took Tullia to Rome. She was put to bed and never rose again. Her eyes grew larger as her flesh dwindled, and Cicero visited her each midnight to be sure that she still lived. Her eyes blessed him and she seemed to be trying to comfort him. The slaves said she slept constantly, but her father had only to approach her chamber for her to awaken.

One night as he sat beside her he fell into an exhausted sleep. The lamps burned low. Suddenly he heard Tullia cry, "Father!" He started awake; the lamps flared up. Tullia was standing beside him, fresh with life, her face glowing with joy. Incredulous, he stretched out his eager hand to her, but she evaded him. Without sound, but looking over her shoulder, smiling at him, she sped through the door. He heard her call, "I am coming!"

All grew dark before him. Then he felt his shoulder being shaken and looked up to see a weeping slave girl. Starting violently, he turned to the bed; Tullia lay there, still and white, a small mound under the blankets. He fell to his knees and laid his cheek against hers.

CHAPTER NINETEEN

CAESAR HAD RETURNED to Rome in triumph. He was no longer young, but virility and power radiated about him and where he moved the air crackled. One day in late summer he visited Cicero, accompanied by the handsome, swaggering Mark Antony, and Marcus Brutus, who gossip said was Caesar's son. Caesar embraced Cicero. "My dear old friend!" he exclaimed. "Your sorrow must be great." He looked about the cold, empty house. He thought of the overwhelming loneliness which had induced Cicero into a brief but disastrous marriage with his gay young ward, Publilia. Apparently the marriage had been only an episode, a dreamlike gesture on the part of the abandoned man.

Julius went on in a loud voice, "You have been alone too long! It is time to live again!"

Cicero looked into Caesar's eyes and saw there the child he had once protected, but he could only say with a wan smile, "It is not the time for me. But you now have all you wish, Julius."

Julius' eyes shifted. Then he clapped Cicero on the back exuberantly. He said, "Not all! Not entirely."

Later Cicero told himself that it was only his imagination that Brutus' face had darkened. Mark Antony was smiling his glowing smile; he looked like Mars himself, ingenuous and brave.

Unable to bear Rome, Cicero went to the dear island which was haunted by all he loved. There he wrote his greatest books;

among them, *On the Nature of the Gods, On Old Age* and *On Friendship*. A false spring came, warm and soft. The rivers shouted as they ran and patches of greenness appeared. The slave girls wove in the open portico, and ancient Athos hobbled out to look at the young lambs.

Cicero had few law cases now, but some were to be heard during the ides of March, so he returned to Rome not knowing he would never again see Arpinum. No one was in the house on the Palatine save the slaves and the old overseer, Aulus, a freedman, for Cicero freed all slaves after they had been in his service for seven years. A gray rain falling outside whispered in every room of the cold house. His footsteps slapped on marble as he walked from room to room.

A visitor was announced and, to Cicero's surprise, Marcus Brutus entered. Cicero ordered wine, and Brutus sat down, saying in the intense voice of a young man who is disturbed: "I have seen a letter of yours to Caesar in which you say he must summon all his powers 'to restore the Republic.' "

"True," said Cicero.

"Do you know what Caesar did when he received your letter? He laughed, and said, 'Our Cicero returns to dreams of youth!' But, like you, I wish the Republic to be rebuilt. Now Caesar says Sulla was stupid to give up his dictatorship. Though Caesar refused a crown, it was only because he felt the time was premature. He has betrayed all of us, including you. Denounce him in the Senate, Cicero! Denounce him to the people!"

"Are you mad? I would be murdered on the spot. If I believed that in laying down my life I could save Rome, I would do so at once. But it would be of no use."

Brutus said contemptuously, "Your age speaks, not your spirit." He stood up with the furious swiftness of youth. "I ask only one thing of you now: do not interfere with what younger, more determined men swear to accomplish."

Cicero said tiredly, "With joy, Brutus, I give into your hands my fading torch. May you be more successful than I was."

Surely it was only the flickering lamplight that made Brutus' smile so terrible. "We receive the torch," he said. "We shall light up Rome with it!" He bowed and left without another word.

The next morning Calpurnia, white-faced and in tears, said to

Caesar, "I had a frightful dream—I saw you murdered, Julius. If you love me, remain at home. Do not go to the Senate today!"

He embraced her indulgently. "Sweetheart, I have business there." He patted her cheek and left for the Senate. It was meeting in a hall next to the Theater of Pompey, instead of the Senate Chamber, for few would be present at this routine session.

Caesar had reached the supreme point in his life. His friends had assured him that the crown would again be offered him; this time he must accept it. By sunset he would be the first emperor of Rome. His beloved Cleopatra was at his villa in the suburbs with his son, Caesarion, and he regretted that Octavius, his nephew, would inherit his crown, and not Caesarion. Julius smiled and waved to the people, who hailed him, and his legion marched beside his litter, the March sun shining on their helmets. The hour had come.

Quintus came early to the house of his brother that morning. As they breakfasted together, Cicero became aware that Quintus was unusually quiet. "Is something wrong?" he asked.

Quintus' voice was harsh. "Do you know that Caesar is appearing before the Senate today, asking for new 'reforms'?"

Cicero studied him. "I thought you and Caesar were now friends."

"I love my country," Quintus said. "Go to the Senate meeting with me today," he added. "You may—hear something which will rejoice you."

"Nothing that Caesar can say will rejoice me." But Cicero looked through the open window at the glowing day. It would be good to see the teeming Forum in the exuberant Roman spring. He said, "I will go with you, Quintus."

Senators were moving through the columns of the Theater of Pompey when the brothers reached it. Cicero, alighting from his litter, saw Caesar walking up the steps, surrounded by his friends. He called, "Julius!" and Julius turned and waved to him affectionately as he went within.

Cicero and Quintus were not far behind. They halted when a curious flurry and confusion began ahead, and a vehement sound of voices. "What is it?" asked Cicero. Quintus was staring before him, his hand on Cicero's arm. Cicero, his heart suddenly pounding, shook off his brother's hand and moved forward.

Then he saw the upraised and reddened daggers flashing in the light of the sun, and heard the uproar of screams and shouts. Quintus caught his arm again but Cicero fought him off. He reached the spot where Caesar was lying on the white stones, bleeding from a dozen wounds. He was staring up at his assassins and his clouding eyes sought the face of but one. He said in a faint breath, "You, too, Brutus?" Then he died at the foot of Pompey's statue.

Brutus raised his bloody dagger exultantly as Cicero dropped to his knees beside the dead man. Gently, he moved Caesar's cloak which half concealed his face. He and Julius were alone, and they were children again. He began to weep. "You would not listen," he whispered. "No, you would not listen."

HAD QUINTUS KNOWN that this would happen today, on the ides of March? Cicero never wanted to know. He visited Caesar's widow and held her hand. He looked at the statues of the Gemini, and thought of Caesar's words. Yes, their lives had been entangled together.

Young Mark Antony took strong charge in Rome. He read Julius' will, standing behind Caesar's bier on the steps of the Forum. Caesar had left his gardens to the people for a public park, and to every citizen a sum of money equal to many weeks' wages. Caesar's assassins were never named. The ranks of the powerful drew together.

Antony was made consul of Rome, and all his acts were conciliatory. But Cicero disliked Antony for his flamboyance and insolence: Antony had spent public funds lavishly to woo the people, used Caesar's money to pay his own debts, and forged documents to prove his actions were Caesar's will. Late in the year, Cicero delivered the first of his great "Philippics" against him. The senators were transfixed by his fiery eloquence. He ridiculed Antony so that even senators who supported him had to smother laughter. It was reported that Antony was so enraged that he remained drunk for days: "The last refuge of the violent and uncertain man," Cicero said.

Antony now accused Cicero of having been among the conspirators who had assassinated Caesar. This provoked Cicero into his second Philippic, denouncing Antony as a coward and a liar. Meantime Octavius had won the loyalty of the legions which became his private army. He had also mysteriously gained support of the financial leaders in Rome—and of Cicero, whom he wooed.

Quintus tried to restrain Cicero, pointing out that as a constitutional lawyer he ought to denounce Octavius, who appeared determined to bring on a civil war with his private army. "Octavius is the lesser of two evils," Cicero said stubbornly. "He is young, but intelligent, and wants no war. Antony is a fool." So the bemused orator cried to the Senate: "Nothing is dearer to Octavius than peace! Nothing more important to him, lords, than your authority, nothing more desirable than the opinion of good men!"

When Octavius heard of this he laughed aloud, a rare demonstration for him. "My uncle Julius overestimated him," he said. "I find him absurd. Nevertheless, he serves me well."

Quintus cried to Cicero, "Do you know what you are doing? Antony will be forced to save himself by declaring civil war and attacking Octavius!"

The terrible drama was drawing to an end. Gathering his legions, Octavius crossed the Rubicon. The Senate panicked and he entered Rome in triumph. Antony, resigned to the inevitable, embraced his old enemy. All who opposed them, Octavius said, were enemies of the people. Wholesale massacres took place, and Cicero fled to his villa at Astura, on the Bay of Antium, south of Rome. The whole Cicero family, in fact, was proscribed. Quintus planned to join Cicero with young Quintus; then the three would join young Marcus in Macedonia.

Now the city of his fathers was closed to Cicero forever. He was an old man, and his heart was broken. He had lost everything; at the end he had been unable to save his country. He had lived only for law and for Rome. They were dead.

The villa at Astura had never been intended for winter use. Now gales struck the white walls so they trembled, and sleet swept the villa until its floors and walls were dank and chill. Cicero huddled in his cloak with blankets about his feet. "He still lives," complained the shivering slaves to each other, for they knew that they would be freed at his death.

"Shall we kill him ourselves?" asked Philologus, whom Cicero had freed as a youth and had educated. "Then when his brother comes we can say, 'Alas, he died by his own hand.'" But the slaves were afraid of Quintus.

It was well that no news came to the lonely villa, for Quintus had already been murdered. Young Quintus would not reveal his father's hiding place even under torture, so to save his son further suffering Quintus revealed himself, and was slain with the young man, and at the last moment father and son had gazed into each other's eyes with affection before they died.

One ashen twilight when Cicero dozed in his chair, he suddenly heard the urgent voice of his brother: "Marcus! Leave at once for Macedonia!" He started awake and stared about him.

"Quintus!" he cried wildly. He went from room to room, calling his brother in a desperate voice. Then he forced himself to think. Voices from afar were often carried to loved ones, to warn them. Quintus must be in mortal danger. He must go to Macedonia at once and there await him. He summoned Philologus and told him the decision. "Seek out my brother," he said, "and tell him that I have gone before him."

But the next morning the seas were furiously high. The impatient Philologus persuaded him to take a shore boat to Gaeta, near his villa at Formiae, where he could find a ship for Macedonia. So the distraught man did. Arriving at his villa, he was greeted by a handful of sulking slaves, who had planned to abandon the Ciceros and return to Rome as adventurers. Philologus helped his master to bed and then promised the slaves that their lord would soon be dead. "His sands have run out," Philologus said.

Cicero fell into a prostrated sleep. He did not know when he first became conscious of light and warmth. A light more brilliant than the sun, but softer and all-enveloping, warmed his icy flesh to life. Slowly the shining golden light parted like a curtain and from between pulsating folds a hand was extended, its fingers beckoning. It was at once the hand of a youth and a father, cherishing, protecting. Seeing it, Cicero's heart rose up in joy and humility. And then he heard a voice: "Fear not, for I am with you. Be not dismayed, for I am your God. When you pass through the waters I will be with you. When you walk through the fire you shall not be burned. For I, the Lord your God, hold your right hand."

The light faded and the hand withdrew, and yet Cicero was no longer cold, no longer abandoned. He fell into a sweet sleep.

The next morning he arose and the slaves were astonished at the life in his face. But the seas were higher than the day before, and his attempt to board a ship for Macedonia failed. It is Plutarch who gives the most eloquent account of Cicero's last day:

"There was at Gaeta a chapel of Apollo from which a flock of crows rose screaming, and made toward Cicero's vessel as it rowed to land. This was looked upon by all as an omen of evil. Cicero, entering his house, lay down upon his bed and the crows settled about the window with a dismal cawing. One of them alighted upon the bed and with its beak tried to draw the cover from his face. His servants, seeing this, blamed themselves that they should do nothing in their master's defense, while brute creatures came to take care of him in his undeserved troubles. Therefore, partly by entreaty, partly by force, they took him up and carried him in his litter toward the sea.

"But meantime the assassins were come, with soldiers. At the villa, it is said, an emancipated slave named Philologus informed them that the litter was on its way to the sea through the wood. They hurried to the place where he was to come out. Cicero saw them and commanded his servants to set down the litter. Then he thrust out his head and, stroking his chin, as he used to do with his left hand, he looked steadfastly upon his murderers, his person covered with dust, his hair untrimmed, his face haggard. Most of those that stood by covered their faces while Herennius, a centurion, cut off his head. Then by Antony's command he cut off his hands also, by which the Philippics had been written. When Antony saw the head and hands he cried out, 'Now let there be an end to our proscriptions!' He commanded them to be fastened up over the rostra, where the orators spoke, a sight which the Roman people shuddered to behold, and they believed they saw there, not the face of Cicero, but the image of Antony's own soul."

Cicero's mutilated body was hastily buried where he had been assassinated. The freedman, Philologus, was thrown the golden amulet of Aurelia. He hung it, laughing, about his brown neck. But when he was also given Cicero's cross, he threw it from him with a cry of loathing.

It is said that Fulvia, Clodius' widow, maliciously drove a pin through Cicero's dead tongue, the heroic tongue which had defended Rome so valiantly. Finally a soldier knocked the skull from its post and kicked it aside.

FORTY-THREE YEARS LATER the event Cicero had so yearned to see came to pass, and the hour for which he had longed.

As Rome thundered down the bloody path to tyranny, a little Jewish maiden stood in the tiny hamlet of Nazareth one calm spring evening, in the last of the sunset's glow, and breathed in the warmth of the air and the new scent of jasmine. She was very young; and she was the delight of her parents' hearts. Her hair flowed down her straight back, and her blue eyes—for she was a Nazarene—looked serenely at the heavens, and she prayed with humility and joy to the Lord her God, the Protector of her house, which was the ancient House of David.

She stood on the roof of her parents' home as she prayed, her hands folded together, and the headcloth on her small head was white, for she was a virgin. Her coarse dress was as blue as her eyes, and her childish feet were bare.

Suddenly she knew that she was not alone, and she started, full of fear. The sunset air about her palpitated with a light brighter and clearer than the sun. And in that light she saw a great Angel with radiant wings.

It is possible that in the shining halls where the just waited to be admitted through the gates of a Heaven which had so long been closed, Cicero waited also. It is possible that he, too, heard the mighty Annunciation which shook the ramparts of Heaven, and the golden pillars, and struck fire along all the corridors of the dark and gloomy earth!

"Hail, full of Grace! The Lord is with you! Blessed are you among women!"

THE
FITZGERALDS
AND THE
KENNEDYS

The
Fitzgeralds
and the
Kennedys

An American Saga

A condensation of the book by

DORIS KEARNS GOODWIN

The Fitzgerald family rose to power through the brawling back room of big city politics. The Kennedys rose to power by amassing a vast family fortune. And when elegant Rose Fitzgerald married hard-driving Joe Kennedy, the two dynasties converged powerfully on the American scene.

With their radiantly gifted children, they were, to us, simply the Kennedy clan. Yet at the height of their glittering celebrity, they became the closest thing to royalty America ever enjoyed. Their lives seemed to be the stuff of which legends are made. But fate—a merciless fate—took a hand, and when all their aspirations came finally to rest with that "brightest sun," young Jack Kennedy, he found the weight of it sometimes too much to bear.

This is a big sprawling tale of our most famous first family, and despite its utter honesty, the Camelot legend remains . . . just as the reader hoped it would.

BOOK ONE

THE
FITZGERALDS
(1863–1915)

1

THE IMMIGRANT WORLD

O N THE TWELFTH OF February, 1863, on a morning described in the Boston newspapers as "below freezing" and "cloudy" with a cold wind blowing hard from the north, a tiny boy, John Francis Fitzgerald, not yet one day old, was carried by his father to St. Stephen's Church for baptism.

For the father, Thomas Fitzgerald, the rushed baptism reflected the extreme fragility of life in the North End, the immigrant quarter of Boston, where three infants out of ten died before the age of one. Believing that an unbaptized child would be a little soul howling in the night, forever prevented from entering the kingdom of heaven, Thomas had arranged for the baptism within twelve hours of the baby's birth.

The journey to the church from the wooden tenement on Ferry Street in which the baby had been born took the father and son through a maze of narrow alleys and dark lanes. Emerging onto Hanover Street—the bustling, congested center of commerce in the North End—they passed dozens of narrow storefronts housing apothecaries, grocers, saloonkeepers, watchmakers, tailors, all just beginning a long day of work. Finally, the father and child came to a large majestic structure that stood in commanding and elegant contrast to the crowded surroundings.

St. Stephen's Church, one of the most beautiful Catholic

churches in Boston, had been commissioned in 1802 as a Congregational church by wealthy old Boston families. Designed by the city's most famous architect, Charles Bulfinch, this stately red brick structure with its Doric columns boasted a splendid classical interior, perfectly proportioned, its every detail related in perfect harmony to every other. But its life as a church of Boston's elite had not lasted long. With the onrush of Irish immigrants into the narrow cobblestoned streets near the wharves, the North End had become Boston's most densely populated slum. The old Protestant families had fled to Beacon Hill and the Back Bay; their Bulfinch church had been sold to the Catholics.

Thomas Fitzgerald, who had been through the baptismal ceremony with his first three sons, understood that when he arrived at the church he was to knock on the door and then wait outside with the baby and the baby's sponsors, Sam O'Brien and Susan McGowan. Inside, the parish priest, the Reverend Charles Rainoni, made ready the holy oil and balm, the salt and the natural water for the sacrament of baptism.

Once his preparations were completed, Father Rainoni, attired in a flowing white surplice and a long purple stole of embroidered silk, advanced to the threshold of the church, where he asked the name of the child to be baptized. The selection of a name was a serious task. People believed that a child would be protected by the saint whose name he bore, and that he would develop that saint's characteristics. Other considerations also prevailed, such as the desire to honor a close relative or to substitute the newborn for a child that had died. Thus, the Fitzgeralds' first son, born in 1858, was named Michael after both Michael the Archangel and his paternal grandfather, Michael Fitzgerald; later, after the baby died, another Michael was christened in 1864. The next son, James, was named for both Saint James the Apostle and for Thomas' younger brother, James, while Thomas Junior obviously carried on his father's name. As for the name John, it was said at the time that if parents wanted a son to be a great writer or a great orator, he should be named after John the Apostle, the author of the mysterious Book of the Apocalypse, or after the golden-mouthed Saint John Chrysostom. History does not record which ancestors Tom and Rosanna had in mind in choosing the name John. But once the name was chosen, it would be passed on for generations to come.

When the name had been announced, Father Rainoni put a grain of blessed salt into the mouth of the infant, as emblem of true wisdom and prudence, as in the Biblical reference to the "salt of the earth." Then, by solemn prayers, the priest cast from the soul the devil under whose power all humans were born by original sin. "I exorcise thee in the name of the Father and of the Son and of the Holy Ghost."

That much of the ceremony was performed in the entry of the church, but now that the devil had been cast out and the infant was worthy to enter into God's place of worship, the priest brought him inside to the baptismal font and anointed him with holy oil, representing the inward anointing of the soul by divine grace. Then, with both godparents holding the child, the priest poured water upon the infant's head three times in the form of a cross, saying, "John Francis Fitzgerald, I baptize thee in the name of the Father and of the Son and of the Holy Ghost."

FROM WHAT IS KNOWN of the texture of the daily life of the Fitzgerald family and their neighbors in the North End, it is easy to understand the magic of the Catholic Church. Against the clamor of the teeming streets—where Thomas Fitzgerald worked from dawn to dusk as a peddler—the church provided a hushed and solemn refuge where one could find that rarest of possessions in a city slum—privacy. Inside, there was the gleam of brass candlesticks; there were pictures, music and stately ceremony. There was the fine smell of aging wood and the fragrance of burnt incense. Amid the rich surroundings of his church, an immigrant's mind could soar high into the realm of hopes, away from the world of hunger, dirt and despair, away from the tyranny of the here and now to a promise of life eternal. In one of the standard nineteenth-century spiritual books Catholics were told: "You may be a poor man—striving for a poor living, you may . . . feel envious sometimes to see your Protestant friends so much better off in the world's way . . . but there is something you possess which our poor friends with all their wealth cannot purchase—the true religion of Jesus Christ."

Acceptance of one's position—the central message for Catholics then—was a religious dictum that reinforced the self-denying and pessimistic view of the world that the Irish peasants had carried with them across the Atlantic. In the New World, this gospel of acceptance was to bear bitter fruit, for of all the immigrant nationalities in Boston, the Irish fared the least well, beginning at a lower rung, rising more slowly on the economic and social ladder than any other group, and accepting conditions that few other people would have tolerated. Yet the story of the Fitzgerald family is the story of the slow escape from the grind of mere subsistence. It is a tale not of acceptance or resignation but of gradual progress and achievement and an ever expanding horizon.

THE HOME AT 30 Ferry Street to which the Fitzgerald party returned after the christening consisted of two doorless rooms no larger than closets, with straw pilings that served as beds, and a kitchen twelve by ten feet. Behind a makeshift wall lived a tailor, his wife and their two children, and next to them a laborer, his wife and their three children. On each of three floors, the same pattern prevailed: nine families separated only by the thinnest of walls and a dark stairwell.

The Fitzgeralds, at least, were on the top floor and their kitchen fronted onto the street, providing them with sunlight, a considerable advantage in their struggle for survival. Of all the ills associated with tenement housing, insufficient light and air, especially on the lower floors of tenements, was cited as the primary cause of death and disease. Nevertheless, John Francis Fitzgerald long remembered his family's description of the warmth and the pleasure of their Ferry Street kitchen on a sunny day. And it was in that kitchen on the twelfth of February, 1863, that the Fitzgeralds held the customary christening dinner, to which the parish priest, the baby's sponsors and the family's relatives were invited.

Evidently lack of space did not prevent the assembling of the whole Fitzgerald clan, including the baby's paternal grandmother, Ellen Wilmouth Fitzgerald, Thomas' three younger sisters, Bridget and Hannah, both married with children, Ellen, who was about to be married, and—central to the story of the Fitzgeralds' rise from poverty—the youngest brother, James, a forceful young man of twenty-five, with dark blue eyes and a deep, gruff voice.

As in the old country, the christening of a baby was considered one of the central events of a person's life, occasioning a large, joyous celebration. But this particular christening held a special importance, for on that day an agreement was reached that changed the direction of Thomas Fitzgerald's life. It was then that he decided to go into business with his brother James and to build his family's future in the old North End.

A broad-chested, powerfully made man with a handsome face and a ruddy complexion, Thomas Fitzgerald, or Cocky Tom as he was commonly called for his having one cocked eye, had lived in Boston for seven of his forty years. Yet the city had remained for him an alien and forbidding place, not his home but a way station until he could save enough money to move his family to the open lands of the Midwest, where once again he could till the soil, the only livelihood he ever wanted, the only labor he considered worthy of a man. Born in the little farming community of Bruff, in the boggy countryside of western Ireland, Thomas was brought up to be a potato farmer. To share in cultivating the soil created among the men of Ireland and of the Fitzgerald family an unbreakable bond with each other and—they thought—with the land.

John Fitzgerald later said that when he listened to his father talk about his childhood in Ireland, he thought there must be no more wonderful place in all the world in which to grow up. For though the family slept on a mud floor in a one-room thatched cabin on a tiny plot of rented land, they had all the food, warmth and companionship they needed to feel spirited and gay. But then the potato, the country's main crop, had failed. The blight of 1845, which caused the failure of four successive crops, sentenced one out of every six peasants to death by starvation. Before the Great Famine, as it came to be called, the Irish had regarded the idea of leaving their country as appalling. But now, in desperation, they made their way out of Ireland by the tens of thousands. In the first major exodus, in 1846 and 1847, hordes of panic-stricken peasants simply fled on the great "coffin ships," so named because of the great numbers who died on board. The poorest class of farmers went first, but when two succeeding crops also failed, even the better and more energetic farmers readied themselves to leave. It was in this second wave of emigration, which lasted roughly from 1848 to 1855, that the Fitzgeralds came to America.

Family tradition has it that James, the youngest boy, came first and Thomas later, clinging to the family's land until there was absolutely no hope of survival. "As I heard it told," second cousin Mary Hannon Heffernan recalled, "James came over as a little boy in 1848 or 1849 with his uncle Edmond and his first cousin Mary Ann, Edmond's daughter. He was only ten or eleven at the time and he got desperately sick on board the ship. Everyone was terrified that the captain would think it was typhus and simply throw him overboard. Then, near the end of the voyage, they ran into a terrible storm with winds so high that the ship turned itself completely around, and they were sure they were headed back to Ireland."

It is a fragmentary memory, yet powerful in its suggestion of the severe emotional dislocation, the internal terror, experienced by millions of immigrants sailing across an unknown

North End

ocean to an unknown land. For many of them, the church was the only salve for their anxiety, but others, the Fitzgeralds among them, found a powerful substitute in the prevailing American ideology, the ideology of opportunity and success.

FAMILY TRADITION HOLDS that when Thomas Fitzgerald first arrived in Boston, he accompanied his cousin Mary Ann and her new husband, Michael Hannon, to the little community of Acton, west of Boston, where he worked as a farm laborer in the hope of saving enough money to buy his own plot of land. But his meager wages kept him living so close to the margin that by 1857 he had moved back to Boston, where he became a street peddler along the wharves and docks of the immigrant district, tramping up and down the crowded streets, selling the day's catch of codfish and haddock.

That he became a peddler seemed at first a fortunate choice, for in the days before retail stores, there was money to be made in peddling. His five years at this work, however, coincided with his marriage and the rapid growth of his family. He was married in 1857 to Rosanna Cox, twenty-three, at St. Stephen's Church. Although Thomas was already thirty-five, he soon made up for lost time: in the first five years of his marriage, four sons were born.

The costs of feeding and clothing his family were high, yet before six years had passed he had saved what he needed to move his family to the Midwest and purchase a farm. Then, just before he planned to leave, there came the christening dinner for John Francis, where, Thomas later said, he received an offer from his younger brother James to stay in the city and become his partner in running the small grocery store that James had recently purchased at 310 North Street. If Thomas would contribute his savings, they could expand the stock and operate the store together as grocer and clerk.

Though that idea failed to correspond to any vision of happiness Thomas had hitherto entertained, he accepted his brother's proposition. From that moment on, the city became his permanent home, the locale in which the lives of all his children would be played out.

When asked later why he had given up his vision of a life in the country, Thomas listed three reasons: his wife, his relatives and his church. The Irish had always been a highly social people, and once they had tasted the close life in the city, with friends and relatives on every corner, the women especially were unwilling, or afraid, to give it up. Then, too, there was the fear of losing their church and of finding themselves in a faraway place without a priest close by. Though these explanations centered mainly on the fear of leaving the familiar for the unknown, it is reasonable to suppose that Thomas also felt there was something special in his brother's character, an uncanny instinct for business, which would lead him someday to achieve considerable success. And Thomas was right, for eventually James became one of the wealthiest men in the North End.

It was said that James, of all the Fitzgerald children, adapted the most readily to the challenge of life in the New World. His first job was that of an assistant in the very grocery store he would eventually own and operate for fifty years. Always alive to necessity, he educated himself in the arts of weighing, measuring, reckoning, bargaining and even purchasing, and by the time he was sixteen he had risen to the responsible position of clerk. Then, in his twentieth year, James met his future wife, Julia Adeline Brophy, and after they were married, James developed a business relationship with his wife's uncle Cornelius Doherty, one of the most successful grocers in the North End. The city records show that in 1862, when James was twenty-four, he received a sum of more than $1,000 from Doherty, and that same year James became "the grocer" at 310 North Street. It is reasonable to assume that Doherty's loan helped him to purchase the store.

As a grocer, James had an advantage over native competitors. Immigrant women preferred to patronize those merchants who spoke Gaelic. But the best money in the grocery business came when the grocery doubled as a saloon, when it could minister to the needs of the women by day and the men by night. Such was the rationale behind the partnership that James offered to his brother Tom, for with Tom's savings James would stock his store with beer, gin, whiskey and wine, while at the same time keeping his barrels filled with the conventional supplies of sugar, flour, potatoes, crackers and kindling wood.

As a combination grocery-groggery, 310 North came to serve as an informal social center for neighborhood folk. It was, as well, the locale for some of young John Francis Fitzgerald's earliest memories. Shopkeeping in those days was a family business; whenever she could—that is, whenever her state of pregnancy allowed—Rosanna Fitzgerald worked with her husband in the store, while in the back, John and his brothers were left to play amid the wooden casks and the barrels of flour. John later recalled that he "loved the sense of being right in the middle of everyone, where everything was happening." The traffic would begin soon after dawn, with neighborhood women streaming in to fill their cans and jugs with flour and milk for the morning meal. Then, in the afternoons, they were back again for more flour and their daily supply of meat. Thus the store at 310 North began to prosper.

If the store did well by day, it thrived by night as the neighborhood men, home from a day of hard work, began to drop in for drinks. A saloon at that time was not simply a bar. According to one study done at the time, the typical saloon supplied "many legitimate wants besides the craving for intoxication. It is the workingman's club, in which many of his leisure hours are spent. In winter it is warm, in summer cool, at night it is brightly lighted. It is not enough to say that the sense of discomfort pervading the dark tenement house, with its tired, unkempt wife and restless children, leads to its use. No, at bottom, it must be a craving for fellowship underlying the unrest of the workingman's hours that draws him into the saloon."

AMONG THE IRISH, it has often been said, there are only two types of drinkers: alcoholics, who give in completely to liquor's seductive appeal, and teetotalers, who guard themselves completely against it. In this context, it is curious to note that of the nine sons eventually born to Thomas and Rosanna, three followed their father's path to success by entering into some aspect of the liquor trade, while three ended up as heavy drinkers and died young. It seemed as if the blessings that had accrued to some family members as a result of the liquor trade had brought a curse upon the others, as if the profits built upon the backs of stumbling men had exacted a price in the ledger of family accountability. "Whenever anything bad happened in the family," a Fitzgerald relative remembered, "my mother would sigh deeply and then with fear and bitterness in her voice she would say, 'It's the curse of the liquor money. I know it.' "

By the fall of 1866, Thomas had accumulated enough money to enable him, with his brother's assistance, to buy a three-story brick tenement at 435 Hanover Street and move his family into larger quarters there. For the first time in his life he was a property owner, and the experience of signing the papers provided him with a great feeling of accomplishment. Years later, John Fitzgerald remembered his father saying that "beyond his family, nothing he had done before or since meant as much to him as that small white document that testified to the fact that Thomas Fitzgerald at the age of forty-four was finally the owner of his own home."

The change from tenant to landlord increased the degree of control Thomas was able to exert over the physical conditions of his family's daily life. In their new quarters, behind a storefront that Thomas would eventually convert into his own grocery store, the family boasted a parlor with two windows, and a kitchen heated by a coal stove; and, for the first time in their married life, Tom and Rosanna enjoyed the privacy of their own bedroom, separated by a flight of stairs from a big room in which all the children slept, with their beds lined up dormitory-style. But while the Fitzgeralds could spread out on two floors, four families, at least twelve people, on average, occupied the uppermost floor as boarders, living huddled together behind a jumble of thin walls. There is no way of knowing how Thomas treated his renters, but stories abound that, once in possession of property, the Irish landlord, "like an apt pupil . . . collected rents with the same avidity as the Yankee owners had from him." And we do know that with the money he earned, Thomas soon was able to buy two additional tenements, at Four Webster Place and 379 Hanover.

Though Tom Fitzgerald never became as wealthy as his brother, he did master the struggle for existence. For with food and shelter guaranteed, his children experienced the small pleasures of life—a bed with a mattress, a bath at the public bathhouse, the chance for an education—that broadened their horizons and transmitted to them a feeling of power at odds with the dominant fatalism so characteristic of the slums.

2

GREAT EXPECTATIONS

THE FITZGERALD BOYS eventually numbered nine, with two boys older and six of them younger than Johnny. But Johnny was always the smallest. Always in motion, always struggling to reach a position of vantage, he battled with his puny body as with a reluctant animal that had to be mastered. Every night, when all his brothers had gone to sleep, he would complete one hundred sit-ups on the wooden floor in front of the lined-up beds. In the morning, before sunup, he would venture outside to the alleyway behind his house and drag his body through an ordeal of exercises to strengthen his muscles and build his stamina. For he intended, despite his size, to become an athlete and compete with his oldest and tallest brother, Jimmy. He decided to become a runner, and worked at it with all his energy.

In choosing to overcome his physical inadequacy and not simply give in to it, he exhibited a familial trait that would show itself again and again in succeeding generations. Wherever he went, he ran: to school, on errands through the crowded streets, along the dingy waterfront. So complete was his concentration, so resolute his will that it was only a matter of time until he began winning races against his brother Jimmy and then against the neighborhood boys as well. Week after week he found himself pitted against boys taller and more coordinated than he, but they ran without his urgency or his sense of purpose, and as a result he was always the first to cross the finish line.

More than fifty years later, John Fitzgerald still felt proud of his accomplishment. "We used to run on the cobblestones of Hanover Street and I could always beat any of the boys. One year I won the half-mile distance cup in Boston. I was a champ."

Thus developed a confidence in the mastery of his will over his body which would, he later claimed, affect the course of his entire life. "I attribute my good physical condition, my mental alertness and the consequent capacity for work to an athletic youth." It was not the individual victories that mattered; it was the sense of his potentiality being fulfilled and completed, the knowledge of what could be accomplished when his whole mind and body were directed toward a task. It was a knowledge he would put to good use in his first job as a political organizer.

Fitzgerald's special qualities as an organizer manifested themselves early on. Since there was not a single playground in the North End, the children's games took on a makeshift quality: contests to see who could climb the corner lamppost in the shortest time or kick a can up a hill in the fewest kicks. But stickball, played with a rubber ball and with a broomstick for a bat, was forbidden because of the crowds on the streets, and policemen, brandishing clubs, patrolled the area to enforce the decree.

Undeterred, Johnny moved the game to an open space at Union Wharf and made friends with the cop on the beat. Together they worked out a system where the boys were allowed to play undisturbed for nearly an hour each day.

Beyond games and athletics, much of Fitzgerald's childhood revolved around helping his mother with his little brothers. For some reason it was Johnny and not his older brothers, Jimmy and Tommy, who took on this particular role, and relatives universally remember him with a rush of warmth as "the one who taught the others how to swim, how to play ball and how to whistle through their fingers," "the one who kept the whole family together."

Fitzgerald's characteristic approach to life was also evident in his first reaction to school. When he was five years old, still too young for the first grade, he became curious to know about this institution that kept his older brothers away from home all day. One morning he followed them to school and stationed himself beneath a small open window. Crouched on his knees, he listened to the morning's routine. First he heard a teacher reading from the Bible, then some singing, and a recitation period in which each child was called upon to stand and read aloud. While the recitations were taking place, Johnny saw a small boy running down the street, late for school. Through the open window, he traced the sound of footsteps as the latecomer raced into class. There was a moment of stillness and then a strange clapping sound followed by a succession of screams so loud and horrible that Johnny closed his eyes until they finally stopped.

That corporal punishment was used in the primary and grammar schools of the day is confirmed by the record and from the memoirs of any number of distinguished Bostonians from Henry Adams to Henry Cabot Lodge, all of whom regarded their early educational experiences with hostility and disdain. Yet the system affected the child of the slum far more deeply than the child of means, who had many other outlets for learning. And for the Irish Catholic child there was the additional problem of a system that was Protestant and openly prejudiced against Catholicism. Boston's William Cardinal O'Connell described his early years in the Lowell, Massachusetts, schools in the 1860s as "a perfect torture." He wrote:

> We sensed the bitter antipathy . . . which nearly all these good women in charge of the schools felt toward those of us who had Catholic faith and Irish names. For any slight pretext we were severely punished. We were made to feel the slur against our Faith and race . . . our inferiority to the other children, blessed with the prop of Protestant inheritance and English or Puritan blood.

The fear that Johnny experienced on that morning thus had a strong basis in reality. But the determined boy refused to be dominated by his fear. He peeked through the window to see the villainous woman. With black hair pulled tightly back from her long, thin face, with a long black dress and black shoes, she looked to him like a wicked witch. But he summoned his courage, and when school was dismissed for lunch he followed her to a local grocery store. From the doorway he heard her voice as she talked with the owner, and he was surprised at how soft it sounded. Then he saw her lean down and pat the head of a little girl who darted out from behind the counter. When the teacher turned to come out, Johnny turned and ran home. But the next week he followed her every day into the store until she finally smiled and asked him his name. From that moment on he knew he was safe, and all that summer he looked forward to school.

The young boy, it is clear, already possessed an unusual ability to charm potential enemies and to respond to things that troubled him by moving toward them rather than backing away.

Once Johnny started school, his positive approach and his enthusiasm were contagious, and his teachers responded in kind. At the end of three years, he was promoted to the Eliot Grammar School, a significant achievement attained by few students from the North End.

ON THE LATE AFTERNOON OF January 27, 1870, the Fitzgerald household was filled with a general rejoicing. After eight sons, Rosanna Fitzgerald had given birth to a fair-skinned, blue-eyed little girl. They named her Ellen Rosanna, and her proud father said she was "as beautiful as an Irish morning." The child was watched over with special care. "Every time she got a fever, my mother was sure she was going to die," John Fitzgerald recalled. "Later I wondered if it had been a premonition."

Rosanna's anxiety was not uncommon in the Irish community at that time. So many mothers had seen one or more of their children die of smallpox, typhus or cholera that they interpreted the early symptoms of any illness as a prelude to death. Also the mortality rate for children born in Boston in the 1870s was alarmingly high—higher, in fact, than in any other city in the United States. Still, young Ellen Fitzgerald was, as the winter gave way to the balmy days of April and May, "in the bloom of health." But then, in the sweltering first weeks of August, the dreaded disease of cholera came to the North End.

The cause of cholera was not yet known, but experience had taught that it attacked the poor, living in crowded, unsanitary conditions, in a much larger proportion than the rich. In the North End it killed more than eighty children in twelve days. As Rosanna watched the disease spread down Hanover Street, its fatal progress marked by the appearance of a black ribbon on the door of each stricken house, she made every effort to protect her family. She would not allow anyone to eat any fruit or meat that was not personally inspected by her, and she hung newspapers over the screenless windows to keep out the flies thought to carry the disease. Yet, despite her precautions, cholera struck the one Fitzgerald who was least able to fight back: little Ellen Rosanna, six months old. Within one day, the child was dead.

That the Fitzgerald family was deeply affected by the loss of this little girl is clear from the length of time John Fitzgerald held on to his memory of her short life. The parents found solace in the belief that Ellen's death was just the beginning of her eternal life in a far better world. But young Johnny responded with frantic activity. He entered a swimming contest at Lewis Wharf, and with all the neighborhood children watching, he came in first. "I felt it was important to do something great to take away the sadness," he later said, "and winning the swimming meet was the only thing I could think of to do."

IN THE AUTUMN OF 1871, Johnny entered the Eliot Grammar School, one of Boston's oldest schools. Entering with him were a hundred and eighty boys from three different primary schools. Of these, only thirty-five, John Fitzgerald among them, were to graduate six years later. The explanation is simple: by the final year of grammar school, a majority of students had to quit school and go to work—a choice fully understood and even expected in a community that depended upon the labor of its children to survive. For those who remained, the curriculum and the teaching were on a high level. To qualify to teach in such schools, aspiring teachers had to pass a wide-ranging examination in psychology, music, Latin, geography, English and American history, civil government and the principles of education. And though student learning was still largely through recitation, the teachers were well equipped to move beyond it to stimulate the children's curiosity and interest. Fitzgerald responded well, and family tradition has it that he graduated near the top of his class and emerged as a natural leader among his peers.

IN SEPTEMBER 1877, when he was fourteen, Johnny obtained a license to hawk newspapers on the streets of Boston—a lucrative business for those willing to stick to it through the bitter cold of winter and the steamy heat of summer. And Johnny stuck to it. A sturdy youth, courageous and defiant, with a ruddy complexion and clear blue eyes, he had a curious, receptive mind, and he was full of self-confidence.

With the passing years, the immigrant newsboy of the nineteenth century has acquired a picturesque image. At the time, however, educators and reformers alike despaired at this most visible form of child labor, arguing that the "indiscriminate handling of money and the contagion of the street often undermines the character and health of these boys," placing them "constantly in the way of temptation" and "leading them directly into crime." Moreover, the late hours "bring them to school tired out and altogether unfitted to do the classroom work." But Johnny was in a different position. Since he had finished grammar school, all elements of his vibrant personality moved in one direction: toward the goal of making money. Already a sophisticated student of human nature, he was ready to respond to the fascinating range of characters he encountered each day. From childhood he had loved the sport and gossip of political life; he had listened for hours to the men talking politics in his father's store; now, as he stood on the street, his papers under his arm, his voice calling out the headlines, he experienced himself as a participant in that larger world.

Getting up at three o'clock in the morning, he would be first in line to pick up his papers at each newspaper office—at the *Traveler,* the *Advertiser,* the *Journal,* the *Herald,* the *Post* and the *Globe.* At this early hour, the offices were filled with people— editors, reporters, office boys—milling around the tall rotary press that stood in the center of the printing room. Naturally gregarious, brimming with curiosity and a love of adventure, Fitzgerald responded to the pace, the noisy atmosphere and the continuous talk. But as much as he might have enjoyed staying around, he understood that a newcomer's only hope of turning a profit was to arrive on the streets early. For in contrast to the "regular" newsboys, who had established corners and habitual customers, the newcomers were obliged to sell their papers by roaming up and down the streets, a far more difficult task. But Johnny evidently went about his relationship to the city streets in the right spirit. He walked everywhere, up Tremont and down Charles, up Washington and down Beacon, and his wanderings took him into strange new parts of the city and introduced him to new types of people.

Johnny's diligence and enthusiasm met their reward. According to his own account, he was often the first of the newsboys to sell out his entire bundle of papers. At the same time, with his uncanny faculty for making friends, he developed a network of new relationships. The job was all that he had expected it to be and more, and years later, when he became the publisher of a weekly paper, he maintained that his experiences as a newsboy had taught him "more about the business of publishing than any of those fancy colleges across the river."

EVENTUALLY, JOHNNY ACQUIRED a regular corner. It was the choicest in the city of Boston—the corner of Park and Beacon streets, facing the benches and the grassy space of the Common in one direction and, in the other, the front of the State House, with its familiar gilded dome. The corner had belonged to a neighbor, a tall, spare boy named Fred, who appeared to Johnny as a heroic figure, for the most energetic and enterprising of all the newsboys, he supported his widowed mother, grandmother and five sisters and brothers from the earnings of his stand.

Johnny made it a practice each morning to fall in line with Fred as he gathered up his bundle of papers on newspaper row, and at night he would end up by Fred's corner so they could

Beacon
Street

walk home together. Soon they became friends, spending many of their free hours in each other's company. Then, in the middle of January, 1878, Fred fell sick with tuberculosis—or consumption, as it was commonly called. His body wasted away to a skeleton, yet he refused to stay in bed, understanding only too well that once a boy had worked a corner regularly for a period of time, it became his stand and all the other newsboys recognized it as his. But the moment a boy stopped coming regularly, his stand was up for grabs.

Johnny responded by taking responsibility for both his own and Fred's bundles of papers. All Fred had to do was drag himself to the corner at the start of the day so his presence could be noted; then he could go home and stay in bed while Johnny took care of the rest by working double time. This went on until one particularly cold morning when Fred, pale and shivering with fever, collapsed. Johnny propped him up and took him home. He was put to bed, and though he tried every morning until the February morning when he died, he never could get up again.

Eventually, the corner of Beacon and Park became Johnny's, and now for the first time he saw "the other Boston"—the clean, cultured world of Beacon Hill, a world aloof and inhabited by Yankee elite later referred to as the Boston Brahmins. Beacon Street—aptly described by Oliver Wendell Holmes as "the sunny street that holds the sifted few," was right in the middle of the most aristocratic quarter of the city. With stately Mount Vernon Street, gracious Chestnut Street and quaint Pinckney Street nearby, Johnny observed entire neighborhoods filled with splendid, spacious mansions of quiet dignity. He was astonished at the beauty of their elaborate arched entrances and large bay windows, at the profusion of silk-hatted, liveried coachmen in open victorias, carrying elegantly attired couples to parties—the gentlemen resplendent in frock coats and high hats, the ladies in lace shawls and billowing dresses. For a child of the slums, this was a glimpse of happy privilege at the highest pitch. And as the ways of the Brahmins became familiar to him, this familiarity would color his ambitions and his hopes and open up for him a vision of a world whose pleasures and privileges he would crave as long as he lived.

In truth, Johnny had confronted these Bostonians before.

From earliest childhood he had participated in the legendary snowball fights on Boston Common between the North Enders and the Beacon Hillers of which so many Brahmins later boasted in their memoirs. On the one side were the manicured young gentlemen in woolen suits, Eton collars and caps; on the other, a motley assortment of Irish youths, looking bigger and tougher in their worn and shabby coats and ill-fitting caps, their sheer presence inspiring fear in the hearts of the upper-class boys. Yet these ritualistic contests were not as one-sided as they seemed. Living close to Boston Common, the Beacon Hillers had an advantage: they could prepare their snowballs the day before, leave them to freeze overnight and carry them to the field of battle. Then, in the midst of combat, a direct hit could draw the blood of one of the "muckers," as they called the Irish boys. But in the end the Beacon Hillers were generally defeated by the North Enders.

JOHNNY'S YEARS ON THE corner of Beacon and Park witnessed the waning days of an extraordinary period in the history of Boston's elite. From the beginning of the century through the Civil War, Boston had enjoyed a position as the merchant trading capital of America, a dominance made possible in part through the great speed of her native clipper ships. Prosperity in shipping had fostered prosperity in manufacturing, and Boston flourished. Moreover, in its moment of economic triumph, the city also possessed unchallenged authority in the cultural world as well, with an extraordinary concentration of intellectuals, writers and poets all flowering in the same time and place. The wondrous parade included Ralph Waldo Emerson, Nathaniel Hawthorne, Henry David Thoreau, Henry Wadsworth Longfellow, John Greenleaf Whittier and Louisa May Alcott, to name a few, and this unusual coherence of literary and intellectual life can be traced in part to the remarkable pattern of living established in Boston and existing nowhere else in the United States.

Like Renaissance Florence, early nineteenth-century Boston had a leading core of wealthy citizens who lived in town, intermarried, patronized the arts and letters, interested themselves in local institutions and still believed in public responsibility. It was this ideal that produced in Boston, more than in any other American city, a culture in which the life of the mind was accorded a dignified and important place. It was this tradition that led New England's men of commerce to dedicate large portions of their money to learning—to the building of libraries, the endowment of universities, the support of free lectures and the publication of books. And when a Brahmin family had accumulated a certain wealth, it would, often enough, step out of business altogether and try to accomplish something in politics, public service, education, medical research, literature or the arts: the Lodges had two Senators, a poet, a museum director; the Lowells a jurist, an educator, an author, a judge, a historian, an astronomer, a president of Harvard and two poets; the Peabodys an educator, two professors, an architect, a headmaster and a poet. And then, of course, there was the incomparable Adams family, which included a patriot-governor, two Presidents, a diplomat, a historian and a writer.

Always in touch with the currents of contemporary life, these families produced a vigorous leadership caste that directed the destiny of their city and their nation with self-confident vigor.

Of all the cities Charles Dickens visited in America, he reserved his highest praise for Boston, "where the tone of society [was one] of perfect politeness, courtesy, and good breeding," and where, he concluded, "I sincerely believe the public institutions and charities are as nearly perfect as the most considerable wisdom, benevolence and humanity can make them."

Through his readings in school, Johnny Fitzgerald developed a heroic image of Boston's "merchant princes" who had built their fortunes out of their own enterprise and then turned their energies back to the benefit of their city. In his fertile imagination, he could see himself doing the same thing. Even as a young boy he felt that his history and the history of Boston were magically intertwined, that the heritage of the patriots and the abolitionists, the clipper ships and the counting houses, belonged to him as much as it did to anyone else.

Yet already the city's days of dominance were fading. With the end of the Civil War, the interior of the continent rapidly sprang into life. A wholly new America was shaping itself—a vastly expanded America in which the balance of power, population, wealth and productivity was rapidly shifting to the West. Of all the great cities of the East, however, Boston alone failed to create a substantial trade connection with the West. Without a direct link to the new markets, the city's foreign commerce languished. The ships from Canton, from Calcutta, from Russia and from Africa began to change their routes, sending Boston's trade into a decline. And with the decline in trade went a marked decline in Boston's manufacturing position.

Many old Bostonians liked to point to the massive influx of immigrants in the mid-nineteenth century as the reason for Boston's decline. For years, they argued, Boston had retained a remarkably homogeneous population. In the aftermath of the Civil War, however, as industrialism and immigration pressed forward with a speed that seemed to leave all the old landmarks behind, the old Bostonians despaired and withdrew into themselves. The comfortable, aristocratic world they knew—a world in which the leading families spent most of their time together, went to the same schools and shared the same religion—was slipping away. For them the postwar industrial world of humming mills and smoking factories represented the triumph of materialism and unabashed vulgarity, the loss of traditional standards, the end of dignity.

The influx of Irish immigrants did indeed cause dramatic changes. In the long view, it spoke of a richer and more varied culture for Boston. But at the time it must have been wrenching for old Bostonians to witness the transformation of their cherished, well-ordered city into a slum-ridden metropolis. The once fashionable North End was the first section to give way; then the West and South Ends were destroyed as well. The narrow and crooked streets, where Sam Adams, John Quincy and other patriots had dwelt, lost their familiar character. Tenements mushroomed. Revolutionary-era landmarks disappeared. Gone from the city was the atmosphere of quiet repose and the ideal of a shared community life.

The old Bostonians, overwhelmed, retreated to the higher and more rarefied ground of Beacon Hill and the Back Bay, where, in the seclusion of their elegant town houses, they were able to forget the slums, the immigrants and the vulgar industrialism engulfing their city. Among them, the ideas, customs and social standards of the British aristocracy assumed enormous importance, affecting everything from literary taste to taste in clothing, from the custom of afternoon tea to the cotillion and the hunt balls. By stressing tradition, lineage and decorum, the Brahmins could believe they held their position by right of birth, thus tying themselves to one another and separating themselves forever from the parvenus and the foreigners.

Paradoxically, just as the days of Brahmin intellectual, industrial and political supremacy were drawing to a close, Brahmin social life was reaching its zenith, shining down to us even now like a masterpiece of art, a portrait in pastels of polite ladies drinking tea, of sporting gentlemen in silk top hats, of calling cards and soft gaslit drawing rooms and cotillion balls. Insulated in its privileges, ideas and habits, still commanding a very large portion of the wealth, prestige and social standing, Brahmin society became even more difficult to penetrate.

It was this fleeting moment of high privilege and exquisite social form that young John Fitzgerald caught sight of in 1879 from his corner at Beacon and Park. Looking up at the lighted windows, he pictured the people inside, sitting beside a bright fire, talking and sipping wine, and he wanted more than anything else in the world to share in their company. Indeed, he was afforded one interior glimpse of a Beacon Street home when, one cold evening, he saw a large, kind-faced Irishwoman, laden with bundles, trying to negotiate her way up the slippery street. Offering to carry her packages home, he found that her destination was 31 Beacon, a large, elegant red brick mansion across from the Common. She was the second cook, and since the master was away, she invited Johnny in for a warming cup of tea.

Seated in the servants' kitchen, flushed with excitement, Johnny was fascinated to see the large number of servants required to keep the place functioning: a butler, a footman, a valet, two cooks, a housemaid, a parlormaid, a lady's maid. Never shy at moments like this, he asked to see some of the rooms upstairs. When he was shown the children's playroom, he found it an "extraordinary sight, filled with the most elaborate wooden toys you could ever imagine . . . beautifully carved miniature soldiers and horses, hand-painted boats with movable parts, wood-burning locomotives and bright-red fire engines." Then and there, he later remembered, "I made a promise to myself that someday, when I had children of my own, I would be in a position to give them all the toys that these children of privilege had enjoyed."

Johnny learned that the owner of the house was the distinguished Henry Cabot Lodge, a proper Bostonian whose name Johnny would hear more and more frequently. For surprising as it would have seemed to him then, the incidents that would shape the course of his life, his destiny and that of his children, would intertwine over and over with the figure and the family of Henry Cabot Lodge.

FOR ALL HIS FASCINATION with the glittering world of Beacon Hill, Fitzgerald's social life remained where it had always been, in the Irish North End. From all accounts, the Fitzgerald family, with its nine boys, was an extraordinarily close one. Then suddenly, in the spring of 1879, the family experienced a wrenching transformation. That winter Rosanna had given birth to her twelfth child, a baby girl, whom she named Mary. Family history records the pregnancy as a difficult one, and four days after birth the baby died, her death certificate simply listing "debility" as the cause. When two months later, still weak and tired, Rosanna found herself pregnant again, her endurance gave way. On the morning of March 10, 1879, the story goes, Thomas took all the boys to a church picnic at Caledonian Grove, a popular picnic ground on the outskirts of Boston. Rosanna, not feeling well, stayed at home. In the afternoon, a man came riding through the North End bearing the false news of a dreadful accident on the train carrying the picnickers to Caledonian Grove. Upon hearing the story, Rosanna collapsed, and two hours later she died, grieving for a family she thought she had lost. She was forty-eight. On her death certificate the cause of death is given as "cerebral apoplexy," a term used at the time to describe a sudden shock.

Years later one of Fitzgerald's favorite memories was of sitting at his mother's feet listening to the story of her girlhood days in Ireland. He loved her description of the rolling green hills and the happy life she had led on the farm before the famine came. And then the hard resolution to leave it all—relatives, neighbors and homestead—to seek whatever life she could find in an unknown and faraway land. To a child it was a great romance, an adventure story without equal.

Seen from a less romantic perspective, however, her life story suggests a perpetual weariness, for she typifies an epoch in which constantly pregnant women literally worked themselves to exhaustion. A fitting remnant to her memory stands in a grassy plot at Holy Cross Cemetery in Malden, just north of Boston, where a tiny stone marker bears her name and the simple epitaph MOTHER.

IN THE MONTHS THAT followed Rosanna's death, there grew in Thomas Fitzgerald the ambition that one of his sons should become a doctor. He had seen his first little girl die from cholera and his second die after only four days of life. But with the death of his wife, a longing had stirred in his heart. If someone in his family did something big in the field of medicine, could discover a cure for the terrible illnesses that had taken his little girls from him, then, perhaps, some solace could be found.

There was no question that John was the one to fulfill his father's dream. Among the boys, he alone had the brains, talent and drive to commit himself to four years of high school and three of medical school. But it would entail considerable sacrifice—in the loss of John's income to the family and also in the cost of the textbooks and supplies. As the story is told by one of Thomas' grandsons, the decision was a collective one. "Thomas and all the boys got together and decided to send Johnny to school. In an age when mutual help by family members was essential for survival, they all got behind him and gave him the shove." Thus a new life began for Johnny in September, when he entered the musty halls of the prestigious Boston Latin School.

The Latin School, founded in 1635, had been championed by proper Bostonians as a truly public institution where the sons of the humblest artisans could read Virgil beside the sons of the most aristocratic citizens. By the time Johnny arrived, however, the Brahmins were in full retreat from their democratic ideals. With the exploding immigrant population placing its sons in minority positions in the public system, the Brahmins put their energies into founding private schools where their sons could be enrolled from birth and educated with people of their own class—preparatory schools like Middlesex, Groton, St. Paul's and St. Mark's.

So it happened that when John Fitzgerald arrived at the Latin School, he was surrounded by an ethnically mixed group of bright and ambitious students—Irish boys wishing to be lawyers or doctors, Jewish boys wishing to be professors, Yankee Protestant boys whose families were unable to afford prep school. For the first time in his life, Johnny had to work hard just to keep up with his class. In the process, in listening to lectures on Shakespeare's plays and Milton's poems and in being called upon to translate Homer's *Iliad* and Cicero's orations, his mind was deepened and stretched. Here, too, he developed his oratorical skills and practiced the art of debating.

In June 1884, along with thirty other students from an entering class of one hundred and three, Fitzgerald passed the school's demanding final examinations and was graduated. So highly regarded was the Latin School diploma that he was admitted directly to Harvard Medical School without having to pass the entrance exams or to present a college diploma.

While he was pursuing his first-year courses, Fitzgerald continued to live at home, where he was active in neighborhood and church organizations, finding time for both his studies and his social life. But there is no record of his performance at Harvard Medical School that first year, since, two weeks before final exams, his father died and the medical career of John Francis Fitzgerald came to an abrupt end.

It was pneumonia that took the sixty-two-year-old Thomas Fitzgerald's life. His last will and testament, signed on May 19, 1885, the very day of his death, was an unusual one for an old-country Irishman; instead of giving his entire estate to his oldest son, James, it decreed that all real estate and personal property "be divided equally among all my children, share and share alike," and that none of the real estate be sold until the youngest child (Henry, age ten) reached twenty-one. In this way, the dying father ensured that his nine sons would have a home as long as they needed one.

Thomas had not had an easy life. Forced to leave the land of his birth and the farm of his youth, having settled for the city, he had seen three of his children die and had lost his wife at an early age. Nor had he achieved fame or fortune. The short account of his life that the Boston papers ran the day after he died simply said, "He was a plain, frank, noble-hearted man, open of speech and upright in his dealing."

3

THE BOY POLITICIAN

AFTER HIS FATHER'S death, Fitzgerald needed help. Five of his nine brothers were still under age, and with his older brother James already the father of three small children, and with Thomas, twenty-four, receiving only $2.50 a day as a clerk, the only course of action seemed to be to split the family and send one or two of the younger boys to live with relatives. Johnny wanted to keep the family together, but he did not see how he could do it. In his predicament, he turned to the most respected man in the district—the neighborhood political boss, Matthew Keany.

From their earliest years in America, the masses of Irish immigrants in the cities had developed a characteristic style of politics known as machine politics or the ward boss system. Built on the inability of existing governments to meet the demands of the immigrant poor, the ward boss system was a shadow government at the local level, a supplementary power structure in which immigrants willingly gave their votes and their loyalty to local political bosses in exchange for all manner of help. In time, as the local bosses gained more power in more city neighborhoods, the Irish in Boston, New York and Chicago virtually took over the Democratic Party at that level.

Fitzgerald found the bluff and genial Matthew Keany behind a desk in his headquarters, the back room of his grocery store at One Prince Street, one of the most prosperous groceries in the city. A steady and industrious man, large and husky, with wavy dark hair, a thick walrus mustache and bushy eyebrows, Keany was the undisputed boss of the North End. Over the years thousands of men and women had entered this room in search of assistance. By Keany's word, a widow could be provided with food, an aspiring peddler issued a permit, a destitute father given a coffin to bury his infant child. Keany already knew Fitzgerald to be a promising young man, having observed the organizational work he had done for the church and for neighborhood groups. Now he listened as Johnny spoke of his terrible fear that in the wake of his father's death he and his brothers were going to be separated. But, Fitzgerald added, he had a plan. He would leave medical school, take a job and hire a housekeeper so that the family could stay together in the Hanover Street home. The only question was, could the boss help him find a good job?

Fitzgerald's request put Keany in a difficult position. On the one hand, Keany had observed long before this crisis that the young man's most absorbing passion lay with politics rather than medicine. On the other hand, Keany felt honor bound to his late friend Thomas—whose will he had witnessed only three days before—to help this boy become a doctor. To Fitzgerald's request for a job, therefore, Keany offered instead the money for school plus an additional sum to pay a housekeeper. But the boy was not to be driven from his decision, and once Keany realized it, he changed his tack. If Fitzgerald really was determined to stop school and get a job, why not start as an apprentice to the boss? The work would be a means of making money and the chance to study politics, if such a thing appealed to him. Keany had barely finished making the offer when Fitzgerald threw his arms around him and said he'd report for work the following morning.

So Fitzgerald began to study ward politics, to study first the men in a district—their family relationships and their social organizations; their needs and their willingness to trade their votes for the satisfaction of those needs, and their capacity for loyalty. And there was no better place to learn than at Matt Keany's headquarters, where all summer long he helped dispense the hundred and one favors that spread the boss's influence like a huge spiderweb over the entire district. Many of his assignments involved him with the scores of Irish associations already familiar to him—St. Stephen's Church, the Charitable

Irish Association, the Neptunes Associates—and he learned which men in each organization could be counted upon to help implement the boss's orders; in the process, he began building a political force that would later become the foundation of his own substantial success. Then, in the autumn as the elections drew near, the technical part of Fitzgerald's learning began. He came to understand the machinery of the party organization— the primaries, the nominating conventions, the campaigns, the elections—and all the intricate procedures involved in the filing of nominating papers, the printing of party ballots and the final rounding up of votes on election day.

Fitzgerald long remembered the pride he felt when the boss first designated him a ward "heeler," one of the chosen few whose responsibility it was to ensure that only the "right" party members attended the meetings where delegates were chosen for the nominating conventions. Each September, the boss drew up a list of the voters in the ward who were on the right side, and the heelers were dispatched on primary day to round them up. If the heelers did their job well, the handpicked meeting invariably supported the boss's slate of delegates. And as long as the slate of delegates was kept intact, the choosing of nominees for public office was entirely automatic.

Since it was the city committee's practice to order the names of candidates on the ballot in the same sequence in which their nominating papers were filed, each ward leader wanted *his* candidate's papers filed first. More than any other practice, this one, the rewarding of the first group through the door, produced the most absurd demands on the heelers. But Fitzgerald accepted the challenge with the delight of a natural competitor, and his exploits grew legendary. It was said that on one occasion, while a rival leader's forces were keeping an all-night vigil at the door of the city committee headquarters, Fitzgerald climbed a tree and came down through a skylight, and so was first to present his slate's nominating papers.

As a reward for filling the post of heeler so well, Fitzgerald was advanced to the speakers' bureau, where he gave rousing speeches on behalf of the boss's nominees. In an age when the people looked to politics for their entertainment and when campaigns resembled carnivals, Fitzgerald's dramatic presentations touched all the proper chords. So effective was Little Fitzie, as he came to be called, that the boss moved him rapidly up through the ranks, giving the young man a view of the ward system at every phase. But it was during the final phase, the elections, that Johnny came up against the hardest test of his early political education.

On election day, Fitzgerald was to be a "checker" at the precinct headquarters—to sit where the voters deposited their ballots into the ballot box and determine exactly how each voter voted. In those days, each party printed its own ballots. Although the law prescribed that these be printed on plain paper, the parties evaded the law by using different shades of white, ranging from shiny white to cream. Thus the checker could determine which party's ticket the voter was using by noting the shade of the ballot he slipped into the box. This year, as it happened, there were two men, the boss's man and a rival candidate, running for the same office, and there was talk that some North Enders were going to defy Keany and vote for the opposition. Keany was determined to catch any defectors early in the day, as a warning to the rest of the voters. These men had accepted his favors; all he asked in return was their vote. Loyalty demanded it.

The checker's job was to watch voters as they slipped their ballots into the box, and identify defectors by raising an arm. The punishment could then be administered immediately. If, for example, the defector had a job supplied by the boss, he would be fired on the spot; a defecting saloonkeeper would be fined for staying open after hours; an unfaithful merchant would be boycotted. And everyone would understand that the action was the result of one man's word.

Fitzgerald had no trouble with the system, harsh as it seemed. But on this day he was faced with an agonizing dilemma. It chanced that one of the men to vote against the boss's candidate was the uncle of the newsboy Fred, the friend of Fitzgerald's youth. After Fred's death, his uncle had come to live with Fred's family in the North End. Boss Keany had found him a job on the docks, and he had done well by his dead brother's family. Fitzgerald had kept in close touch with him, but on this occasion, when he saw the man approach, he dropped his head, fearing the worst. As the uncle picked up his ballot, he merely glanced at Fitzgerald, a glance Fitzgerald would remember all his life.

Years later, Fitzgerald recalled that as he discovered that the uncle was a defector, he became conscious of a loud throbbing in his heart. If he turned the man in, all would be lost for Fred's family. Yet he felt that his first loyalty had to be to Matt Keany. To desert Keany was to lose everything he'd been working for. Drawing a deep breath, he raised his arm, then turned back to his work.

Try as he might, he could never block from his mind the sight of the boss's heelers as they swarmed about the uncle to let him know that his job at the docks had vanished, that there was nothing else in the city he was qualified to do.

The reward for Fitzgerald's faithfulness came several months later when the boss secured for him a position in the Customs House, a job that provided the substantial sum of $1,500 a year plus benefits. It also had an additional benefit: now that he had a regular income, Fitzgerald was finally able to think of marrying the beautiful Josie Hannon, the girl with whom he had been in love since the first day they met.

MARY JOSEPHINE HANNON—Josie—had been just thirteen on the September Sunday in 1878 when fifteen-year-old Fitzgerald first saw her. That morning the Fitzgerald family had come by train to spend a day at the Hannon farm, in the country town of Acton, twenty-five miles west of Boston. Mary Ann Hannon, Josie's mother, was Thomas Fitzgerald's cousin; it was with her and her husband, Michael, that Thomas had lived when he first came to America. Having always loved the country, he wanted his boys, too, to grow up with a knowledge of country life.

John Fitzgerald would remember the details of this September day until the end of his long life—the simple beauty of the countryside, the smell of the cool, fresh air and the first sight of the young girl who would eventually be his wife for sixty-one years.

She was standing at the sink in the kitchen of the family's farmhouse, and as John Fitzgerald later wrote, "The first time I saw her, I knew this was it."

Josie was a beauty. She had lustrous black hair drawn up in a swirl, a slender neck, a clear white complexion and dusky-rose cheeks. She looked out upon the world with dark, shining eyes, and, perhaps most arresting of all, she stood perfectly erect, her slender figure tall and graceful. Years later, even up to her ninetieth birthday, her grandchildren would remark on the dignity of her bearing. Josie was an unlikely match for Fitzgerald. At fifteen, he was small of stature with a large handsome head and husky frame, his entire figure molded by action, his voice full of energy. Josie's manner was one of composure, with a stillness about her that balanced his exuberance. As Fitzgerald remembered it, no sooner had she smiled hello than she withdrew from the room, scurrying upstairs with a faint rustling of her long skirts. Fitzgerald did not see her again that day. He spent the afternoon picking apples with her brothers, Michael and Jimmy. But he had already decided that this girl would someday be his—a decision that would meet with substantial opposition.

The most immediate barrier was Josie's extreme shyness, a trait that stayed with her throughout her life. "Father was an extrovert," Rose Kennedy recorded in her memoirs. "Mother was innately rather shy and reserved . . . happiest with friends and close members of her family." In the months following their initial meeting, as the Fitzgerald family continued to make regular trips to Acton, a relationship slowly developed between Johnny and Josie, and over time, the wellsprings of Josie's character, so different from Fitzgerald's, must have seemed less mysterious to him. But it is doubtful whether he understood then the depth of her reserve or whether he ever contemplated the possibility that beneath her shyness lay a deeper chill, a permanent shadow brought on by the troubled course of her early life.

JOSIE, BORN IN ACTON in 1865, was the sixth of nine children. Before she was born the Hannons had seen their eldest son, John, die at age six from "inflammation of the lungs" and the next oldest son, Edmond, die at five of "brain fever." Still left when Josie was born were Ellen, nine, Michael, five, and James, two.

Although the Fitzgerald family had also suffered its share of bereavements, the Hannons experienced death and sorrow beyond the average and through causes harder to accept than childhood disease. A third daughter, Emily, was born to them, and after that a fourth daughter, Elizabeth, who became Josie's favorite sister. One sunny December afternoon when Elizabeth was nearly four, she eluded eight-year-old Josie's watch and, with a friend, walked down to the edge of a nearby pond. By the time Josie realized that Elizabeth was missing and her father ran down to the pond, it was too late. The two little girls had drowned.

"This was something the family never got over," said Mary Heffernan, daughter of the oldest Hannon girl, Ellen. "My mother was still haunted years later by the image of her father, half mad with grief, carrying the girls in his arms to the little playmate's house."

Four years later, when Josie was twelve, the last child, a son, was born to her parents. Named John Edmond after his two dead brothers, he grew up fearing that his name had brought a curse upon him, a fear that was sadly realized when he was thirteen. Walking his mother to the Acton train station one morning, he caught his foot in a track just as a train was pulling in. He only had time to get his body out of the way, but his leg was mangled and had to be cut off. Still, despite a heavy artificial leg, John Edmond would live out a full life, the only one of the Hannon boys to do so.

A different and more fatal curse fell upon the two older sons. Michael Hannon, Jr., twenty-one, died in 1881 of "congestion of the lungs," and Jimmy died in 1889 at the age of twenty-five of "consumption." But the family history records the real cause as alcoholism. "It's the curse of the Irish," Mary Heffernan said, "always has been and always will be." And so it happened that five out of the nine Hannon children died, leaving only three girls and a crippled boy.

It is, of course, impossible now to know in detail the impact of these tragedies on the family, but later accounts suggest that over the three living girls there hung forever a pall of sorrow and withdrawal. Yet into this home, darkened by the shadows of death, John Fitzgerald brought energy, sunshine and, finally, for Josie, escape. "I can see how John F. must have impressed

Josie," niece Geraldine Hannon said. "He was a great character, a diamond in the rough, a man of such incomparable force. And he was always cheerful, always talking, talking to anyone and everyone."

"She could not help being intrigued by him," Josie's daughter Rose suggested. "It was a clear case of opposites attracting." For his part, Fitzgerald interpreted Josie's reserve as a personal challenge, and it kept him coming back to her year after year.

More than his visits to her house, Josie enjoyed the time they spent away from Acton. There was something proud in Josie, almost haughty, that kept her from enjoying the simple life of the little farming town. Though they owned their own home, the Hannons were among the poorest residents in Acton. While visiting Fitzgerald in Boston, however, Josie shared in a manner of life larger and more plentiful than her own. On each of her visits Fitzgerald would give her a present of clothing or a piece of jewelry that he picked out himself. Always generous, he enjoyed nothing more than the knowledge that through him this beautiful somber young girl was beginning to flower.

Slowly their intimacy ripened. They took long horseback rides together over the country hills, and on horseback Josie proved herself—in spirit and in skill—more than Johnny's equal. "My mother loved riding," Rose Kennedy recorded in her memoirs. "Riding sidesaddle at a gallop, [the horse's] mane and tail flying, and her own long, dark hair streaming behind her. She was magnificent."

It is not certain when John Fitzgerald proposed to Josie, but possibly it was sometime in 1887, more than two years before the marriage actually took place. The stumbling block was the opposition of Josie's parents to the idea of her marrying her second cousin. According to Catholic canon law at the time, second cousins required a dispensation to marry. Although such dispensations were usually fairly routine, it seems that for the Hannons, more than canon law was at stake. Their real fear was that by marrying within the family Josie would produce retarded and weak children. There was no way for Fitzgerald to allay this fear, but over time his persistence simply wore down Josie's parents. Once they agreed to the marriage, an official dispensation was granted. After eleven years of waiting, John Fitzgerald refused to wait any longer. The wedding was set for September 18, 1889, at St. Bernard's Catholic Church in Concord. The Concord *Enterprise* reported:

> The marriage of Miss Mary Hannon and Mr. J. F. Fitzgerald . . . was solemnized in Concord on Thursday last. Elegant wedding gifts were presented by Mr. Fitzgerald's associates in the Customs House, from the Neptune society and classmates in the Boston Latin School.

After a honeymoon in the White Mountains of New Hampshire, Fitzgerald took Josie back to his family's home on Hanover Street, where six of his brothers still lived. It is easy to imagine the difficulties for the new bride. Whereas John Fitzgerald flourished in the dormitorylike conditions of Hanover Street, Josie, who valued solitude and privacy, could not find it. But two months after their honeymoon, she learned she was pregnant, and the exultant father-to-be decided it was time for them to move into a place of their own. The Fitzgerald family had earlier purchased a building at Four Garden Court Street, and it was to this three-story red brick house that Fitzgerald and his pregnant wife now moved.

Unlike most men, who long for a son, John wanted a daughter. Perhaps it was because his own household had been without a female since the death of his mother ten years before. In any case, his wish came true on July 22, 1890, when Josie gave birth to a healthy, strong little girl. She had her mother's clear white skin, dark hair and finely chiseled face, and it is said that John Fitzgerald was so excited that he ran up and down the streets of the North End, knocking on his neighbors' doors to tell them the happy news.

The girl was named Rose Elizabeth in memory of her grandmother Rosanna and her mother's little sister, Elizabeth Hannon. From the first time her father held her in his arms she was *his* little girl; his love for her, he later told a friend, was greater than any feeling he had ever known, and into little Rosie he poured all his magnificent hopes and enthusiasms and all his remarkable vitality.

WITH THE BIRTH OF his first child, Fitzgerald decided the time had come to move into elective politics. Having left the Customs House to set himself up in the insurance business with his youngest brother, Henry, a business that benefitted greatly from his many contacts, he could take the time to run for office. With Boss Keany's backing, he chose to stand for the common council, the lowest branch of the city government, a body of seventy-five men, three elected from each of the twenty-five wards. Fitzgerald's name appeared on the chosen slate of three for Ward 6, and his victory was assured. But even Keany was surprised when the returns revealed that his young apprentice had gathered more votes than either of his two fellow victors.

Fitzgerald used the council's sessions to argue for the creation of a public park in the North End, so that the children who were dying of contagious diseases in the slums might have "a chance to get a breath of God's pure, fresh air." He ran into substantial opposition from members who lived in the better parts of the city. But, powered as he was by memories of his childhood, he never gave up; with his oratorical flair, the more he spoke, the more votes he gathered. After two months, the council authorized $350,000 for the creation of the North End Park on Commercial Street. It was a triumphant moment.

While Fitzgerald was making a name for himself in the common council, Matthew Keany was taken ill, and political leaders in Ward 6 began jockeying to determine who would inherit the kingdom Keany was leaving behind. For Fitzgerald, this was a difficult time. The loss of Keany would be the loss of a second father, a kindly mentor. Yet ambition compelled him, even as he spent his days at Keany's bedside, to spend his nights gathering friends and allies in a quest to take over the leadership of the ward.

Keany died on February 27, 1892, and in the confusion that followed, Fitzgerald became the new boss of the North End. How this came about was a mystery. "Fitzgerald is as different from Keany as crème de menthe is from New England rum," one reporter observed. "He is in a class by himself . . . a blend of audacity, vigor, force and perseverance." At twenty-nine, he was viewed as a boy by some, but he knew exactly whom to approach for support and how best to make that approach in a district that was changing. For the Irish were now moving to better neighborhoods, and the North End was becoming home to thousands of newer arrivals, mostly Italians and Russian Jews. Fitzgerald, with his supreme confidence and his instinct for power, was arguably the only man who could hold the machine together, the only bridge between the old politics and the new.

As the new boss of the North End, Fitzgerald lost no time in nominating himself for higher office, boldly skipping the state house of representatives to stand for a seat in the state senate. Gathering together the members of his newly formed organization, which he called the Jefferson Club, Fitzgerald announced that he intended to run against George McGahey, the power in neighboring Ward 7. He could be assured of Ward 6's support to balance McGahey's support in Ward 7, but when Fitzgerald sought and won the support of Martin Lomasney, the boss of Ward 8, the outcome of the race became a foregone conclusion. When the election took place in the fall of 1892, Fitzgerald became one of the youngest senators in the State House.

These were turbulent years, years that saw Massachusetts take the lead in shaping progressive legislation to respond to all manner of social evils brought about by the Industrial Revolution. As a state senator, Fitzgerald voted with the progressives on bills relating to the rights of the working people, including bills to provide minimum wages for manual labor and to limit hours for women and children working in factories and sweatshops. Soon he began to emerge as a major figure in the state.

Then, in the fall of 1894, Fitzgerald decided to seek the nomination for the House seat in the solidly Democratic Ninth Congressional District, the same district from which his grandson would launch his political career half a century later. It would be an uphill battle all the way, for the incumbent, Joseph O'Neil, had served his district well, proving himself both an effective errand boy for Boston businessmen and a rich source of patronage for the local bosses. But O'Neil had little sympathy for the radicalism of many Irish laborers; to him, moderate reforms seemed the safer route.

The year 1894, however, was not one for moderate solutions. In the wake of the Wall Street panic of 1893, a serious economic depression had set in, marked by bank failures and factory closings and widespread unemployment. Claiming to represent the poor and downtrodden against established leaders who had broken their ties with the slums, Fitzgerald stepped in at just the right moment. He canvassed every ward, taking a message of hope to the streets, appealing to the voters to "give youth a chance." Everywhere he went, his loyal cadre of friends bore torches, roman candles and horns, which turned his arrival into a triumphal parade. Yet, for all his derring-do, Fitzgerald never could have succeeded had it not been, once again, for the support of Martin Lomasney, who controlled the city machine.

The polls closed at midnight, and by morning, when the votes were tallied, the astonishing result was clear: John Fitzgerald had defeated Joe O'Neil to become the Democratic nominee for Congress.

All through the campaign, Fitzgerald had been careful to say nothing that would offend the ward bosses backing O'Neil. On the contrary, he frankly confessed that he regretted he could not have their support for himself. To prove his point, he set out on the morning of his victory to visit with each opposing boss—P. J. Kennedy, Jim Donovan and Joe Corbett. "Now that the fight is over, P.J., let's shake hands," Fitzgerald said at Kennedy's home in East Boston. And they did, but before Fitzgerald left he spotted P.J.'s sandy-haired, blue-eyed son. With his customary warmth, Fitzgerald lifted the child onto his lap and gave him a lollipop. If this story is true, it is the first recorded meeting between John Fitzgerald and his four-year-old daughter's future husband, Joseph Patrick Kennedy.

Compared to the nomination fight, the general election was easy, but Fitzgerald never let up. The baffling economic conditions had spawned a rash of strikes, which in turn gave birth to a nativist movement among those who were convinced that immigration was responsible for the industrial unrest and that the time had come for a general restriction on all new immigrants. The nativists bore a strong anti-Catholic tinge, and in speech after speech Fitzgerald denounced it as "a secret society which was stabbing in the back a certain loyal class of citizens." It was an effective approach. On Election Day, November 6, 1894, Fitzgerald emerged as the new Congressman from the Ninth District, the only Democrat from Massachusetts.

In 1895, when Congressman Fitzgerald arrived in Washington, D.C., the city was still southern in atmosphere, with a leisurely pace, tree-lined streets and spacious parks and squares. Congress was in session only four or five months a year, and like most Congressmen, Fitzgerald chose to live in a boardinghouse, leaving his family at home. As he had done during the campaign, Fitzgerald spoke out eloquently against what he perceived as a tide of anti-Catholicism in the Congress; he also became a leading proponent of continuing America's policy of unrestricted immigration.

At that time, the movement to restrict immigration had found its ideal spokesman in the person of Henry Cabot Lodge, the Republican Senator from Massachusetts. At the age of forty-six, Lodge was well on his way to becoming one of the most powerful figures in Washington. A brilliant historian from Harvard, Lodge personified the Yankee gentleman, the scholar-in-politics. Tall and slender, with a Vandyke beard and a serious demeanor, he had served four terms in the House before assuming the Senate seat. To him, the earlier immigrants—the British, Irish, Scandinavians and Germans—represented a totally different and higher class of people from the hordes of Italians, Greeks, Hungarians and Poles now coming to America. These "new immigrants," he argued, were desperately poor, displaced persons who congregated in eastern cities, aggravating problems of health and housing and threatening "a great and perilous change in the very fabric of our [Anglo-Saxon] race." To shut out the undesirables, Lodge introduced a literacy bill requiring that all entrants to America should know how to read or write in their own language. It was the perfect exclusionary device, and in the end the bill passed the Senate by a vote of 34 to 31.

When the bill was introduced in the House, Fitzgerald rose to speak in opposition to "the insidious arguments" that would have excluded his own mother from entering the United States. It was a speech he would always be proud of, though there was no doubt when the vote was taken, the sentiment of the House went the other way. Years later Fitzgerald liked to tell the story of his meeting Henry Cabot Lodge in the Senate chamber shortly after the speech.

"You are an impudent young man," Lodge reportedly said.

"Do you think the Jews or the Italians have any right in this country?"

"As much right as your father or mine," Fitzgerald responded. "It was only a difference of a few ships."

President Cleveland eventually vetoed the literacy bill, thereby keeping America's doors open for twenty more years. It was a courageous decision on his part, and its effect, as Fitzgerald correctly observed, "was to bring millions of immigrants to these shores who would otherwise have been kept out."

WHILE FITZGERALD WAS dividing his time between Washington and Boston, Josie remained at home with her growing family. Two years after Rose was born, a second daughter, Agnes, arrived, and then a boy, who was named Thomas after Fitzgerald's father. These were difficult years for Josie, since Fitzgerald was seldom at home, and she longed to live in the country near her family. Fitzgerald agreed, and in 1897 they moved to a large wooden house in West Concord. Set back from the road on a little hill, the house boasted a broad veranda, a glassed-in conservatory and a sizable tract of land. Best of all, it was only two blocks from the street where her brother John Hannon lived and a ten-minute carriage ride from her parents' home in Acton.

"These were wonderful years," Rose recalled of the six years in Concord, "full of the traditional pleasures and satisfactions of life in a small New England town." During this time, Josie gave birth to two more children: a son, John Francis Fitzgerald, Jr., and a daughter, Eunice. As the oldest child, Rose enjoyed a privileged status, though she later admitted that sometimes her mother was so busy with each new baby that she didn't have much time for her. Yet Josie, a deeply religious woman, did drill her children regularly in their catechism lessons and talked to them about the fasts and feasts of the church. In contrast, Fitzgerald was, in Rose's words, "so deeply involved in the affairs of the world that he took religion for granted without thinking much about it." Although a directive was issued by the Boston archdiocese commanding all Catholic parents to send their children to Catholic schools, Fitzgerald sent his to the Concord public schools, believing that the public schools were the training grounds for success in the world.

The grammar school young Rose attended was small, with five teachers and one hundred and ninety pupils, but from the start, Rose proved herself a hardworking and intelligent student. "Some children will study less if their father is in an important position," she later observed, "thinking they can get by. I studied more because I thought I was more conspicuous on that account."

For a girl who adored her father as much as Rose did, Fitzgerald's long absences from home must have seemed interminable. Decades later, she could still remember "the absolute thrill" of driving in the carriage to meet her father when he arrived from Washington at the train station in Concord. "To my mind, there was no one in the world like my father. Wherever he was, there was magic in the air."

4

A MOST ENERGETIC MAYOR

AFTER SERVING THREE terms in Congress, Fitzgerald publicly announced that he did not want to run again. He seemed to be stepping out of politics, but he was, in fact, preparing the way to reach his real goal—the mayorship of Boston. He knew, however, that if he wanted a future in the Democratic Party, he had to move his family back to Boston. "Mother loved Concord," Rose recalled, and Fitzgerald stayed in the country as long as he could. But in 1903 he decided that the time had come to return to the city. Fortunately, he had enough money by then to afford a large mansion at 39 Welles Avenue in Dorchester, which Josie soon came to love. Perched on a hill, with a curving driveway, the gracious house boasted a mansard roof with a turret, big parlors, a solarium, a library, a billiard room and a music room.

The money for the house had come from Fitzgerald's purchase of a small Catholic weekly, *The Republic*. Under its previous owner, the paper had been steadily losing money, and Fitzgerald managed to buy it for only $500. From his earlier experiences as a newsboy, he knew that the success of a newspaper depended on its advertising revenue, and that advertisers considered women their main customers. "I accordingly made the paper more readable to women by publishing society notes," he said. Moreover, as a powerful city boss, Fitzgerald was in an excellent position to sell ads to Boston's biggest advertisers, and in a few short years his energetic promotion built a dying enterprise into a thriving business.

The Republic, however, was merely a way station on the road to the mayorship. Even as early as 1901, the Boston papers observed that a strong movement for Fitzgerald as mayor was beginning. But Patrick A. Collins, one of the most respected men in Boston politics, was in office, and Fitzgerald dared not oppose him for reelection. So the years went by until September 1905, when the fifty-year-old mayor contracted pneumonia and died.

Collins' sudden death precipitated a wild contest for his successor. With the Democratic primary only eight weeks away, Fitzgerald moved immediately to mobilize his machine. He assumed that Boss Martin Lomasney would be with him. But as it happened, the other ward bosses, anxious to eliminate Fitzgerald's rising star, came up with the one candidate who could tear Fitzgerald and Lomasney apart—Ned Donovan, Lomasney's closest friend.

Fitzgerald was stunned by Donovan's entry into the race, but soon recovered his poise. He decided to run a solo campaign against the whole system of bossism. "I am making my contest single-handedly," he shouted, as crowds roared with delight,

Mayor Fitzgerald shares a reviewing stand with President Taft.

"against the machine, the bosses and the corporations." Linking himself to progressive reformers, he promised "to banish graft and jail the grafters."

On the stump, Donovan was no match for the magnetic Fitzgerald, who averaged more than ten speeches a night. For weeks, reporters observed, Boston "throbbed with excitement" as Fitzgerald whipped the crowds into a frenzy. On primary eve, he spoke in each of the twenty-five wards and ended his tour in his old hometown ward "surrounded by a procession of cheering and yelling constituents."

On primary day, Fitzgerald gave the regular Democratic machine the worst beating it had suffered in many years. Yet, ward politics being what they were, all the Democratic leaders save one patched up their differences with Fitzgerald, and he won the general election handily. His victory, he proclaimed, marked the dawn of a new era.

INAUGURAL DAY, JANUARY 1, 1906, dawned bright and clear. The people of Boston, inspired by the abounding vitality of their youthful new mayor, turned out by the thousands to watch the festivities. Outside city hall an immense crowd had congregated; inside, the city council chamber was crowded to overflowing. The air was filled with conversation and anticipation. Finally the "monster automobile" containing Fitzgerald, his elegantly attired wife and their five "exuberant" children appeared. There was "wild applause," the newspapers reported; Fitzgerald's "countenance fairly shone with pleasure."

To continued ovations, the inaugural party entered city hall. In the chamber, a prayer was offered by the pastor of St. Stephen's, the North End church where John Fitzgerald and all his brothers had been baptized. Then the chief justice administered the oath, making Fitzgerald the thirty-fifth mayor of Boston.

At last he began his inaugural address. "What we need above everything else," he suggested, "is a reawakening of civic pride," a return to the days of Boston's dominance, a return to the days when Boston was "a beacon to the whole American nation." Fitzgerald characterized the economic situation of Boston as one of "stagnation." The time had come, he urged, for a new leadership caste, men who would manage the city's enterprises "with imagination." With the moneys of the city treasury at his disposal, he intended to create "a bigger, better and busier Boston," its wharves alive once more with the bustle of commerce, its streets humming with new factories, schools, hospitals and public buildings, its landscape dotted with new parks and playgrounds, baths and gyms.

The speech went on for fifty-seven pages. At the end, amid a roar of enthusiasm, Fitzgerald smiled his great dimpled smile and left the chamber.

Celebration filled the remaining hours of inaugural day. There was a family luncheon at the Quincy House, a large banquet for the board of aldermen and the common council and, later, dinner with his brothers and a few intimate friends. Fitzgerald returned to his home on Welles Avenue tired and happy. Just before he dropped off to sleep he thought of the one thing that would have made his inauguration perfect: he wished that his parents had been with him to share in his pride at becoming the mayor of Boston.

IN THE FIRST WEEKS of his administration, Fitzgerald seemed to be everywhere—filing economic-reform bills before the council, announcing evidence of collusion between a group of milk dealers and inspectors, calling for a new boulevard along the Charles River, leading the grand march at the firemen's ball, and greeting a steady stream of visitors in a working day that began before sunrise and ended well after midnight. "I never went home to dinner once during my administration," he later claimed, "except on Sundays and holidays."

The administration Fitzgerald headed was divided into forty-four departments, from the health and library departments to the parks and water departments. Thus a man who had had no formal business training was all at once responsible for an organization that employed twelve thousand people and spent $100,000 a day.

But the new mayor had made an auspicious beginning. The press wrote stories on his dress, his voice and his dancing; they portrayed him as charming, well mannered, funny and impetuous. The only concern expressed in these early weeks was that even his abnormal energy might have its limits. Despite the warnings, however, Fitzgerald kept up the pace. He absolutely loved the job, savored the hectic routine. Basking in the admiration of friend and foe alike, he no doubt thought that he could accomplish things no other politician could, by combining good government with practical politics.

But whatever such vision Fitzgerald may have held, the very nature of the political machine that had brought him to power and sustained him in office made it impossible for him to work objectively for the public interest. The machine was built upon rounding up votes. For half a century it had used the public payroll to finance itself, dangling contracts, appointments and jobs to attract and bind party workers together. And in the end, despite his brave new words about ending corruption and graft, John Fitzgerald was the offspring of this machine. He may have run for mayor as an outsider, but he had liberally given promises of jobs in exchange for support in each neighborhood. Now these people had to be brought into the city government, and their numbers far exceeded the positions under the mayor's control. For a short period, Fitzgerald's ingenuity proved equal to the task. For some supporters he provided "provisional" or "emergency" appointments to civil service jobs, which then became permanent once they were on the payroll. For others he created a host of novel job categories that conveniently fell outside the civil service listings: tea warmers, brick slingers, watchmen to hire other watchmen. Inevitably, there were cries of outrage from the Good Government Association and the various progressive papers. "The payrolls are padded by the employment of scores of men who do not labor," the Boston *Journal* reported.

An even stronger outburst of criticism followed Fitzgerald's departmental appointments. He used the positions as he earlier had said he would not do—as rewards for his political supporters. His new superintendent of streets was James Doyle, a pub keeper who had recently been expelled from the legislature for election fraud. James Nolan, a popular liquor dealer in East Boston with no knowledge of building construction or repair, was made superintendent of public buildings; John Leahy, a whitewasher and furniture polisher, became superintendent of sewers, a post that called for a civil engineer; and a saloonkeeper replaced a doctor on the board of health.

While reform organizations railed against these appointments, saying they left the city in the hands of men "without education, training or experience," Fitzgerald survived the initial flurry of criticism. The general public, still regarding patronage as the natural order for a democracy, rallied around their activist mayor, and for the first months of his administration he enjoyed widespread popularity. More in the public eye than any other man, he captivated audiences with his plea for a "bigger, better and busier Boston," charmed reporters with his swift repartee and his affable manner, and astonished many by his mastery of the details of his office. So much did the political life of the city center upon the mayor that when he went away in August for his summer vacation, the press and "half the city" traveled with him.

FOR IRISH CATHOLIC families in Boston at the turn of the century, the most popular vacation place was Old Orchard Beach, Maine, a summer resort built along one of the longest beaches on the Atlantic Coast. Known as "the city of the sea," with hotels and cottages thickly crowding the waterfront, Old Orchard was described in a contemporary guidebook as "the typical watering place for those who detest the name of solitude." It was packed with "shops, cafés, fruit stands, shooting galleries, bazaars without end." For the sociable Irish, it was the ideal resort.

Fitzgerald first took his family to Old Orchard in the early 1890s when Rose was still an infant, and year after year they returned. It was there at the age of five that Rose Fitzgerald first met a seven-year-old boy named Joseph Patrick Kennedy, eldest son of P. J. Kennedy. And it was there, a decade later, in

1906, that Rose's romance with Joe Kennedy began. A student at the Boston Latin School, the tall, sandy-haired Joe was as confident in his striking good looks as Rose was in hers. Talkative, clever, driving and masterful, he had, Rose recalled, a smile "that seemed to light up his entire face from within."

They went well together, these two—they shared a vital ambition to live life to its fullest. Born to conquer, they had each grown up as the favored child in a favored family, secure in the love and admiration of friends, proud of the honors won in school. Rose was consistently at the top of her class while Joe was elected president of his and captain of the baseball team.

"I shall always remember Old Orchard as a place of magic," Rose Kennedy said when she was nearly ninety years old, "for it was the place where Joe and I fell in love. It was a magical place for our parents as well, because so many of their friends and relatives went there. They all . . . took cottages right near one another and they visited back and forth constantly."

As Boston drowsed in the heat that summer of 1906, life at Old Orchard was a whirlwind of activity, with Mayor Fitzgerald, not surprisingly, at the center of the whirlwind. Various dispatches describe him playing baseball, going for his daily swim, giving impromptu speeches. "Hardly a day passed," the press reported, "that Fitzgerald did not have visitors from Boston." To the cottage he had rented at Old Orchard came a majority of the city's ward leaders: Timothy Coakley, Joe Corbett, P. J. Kennedy, Jim Doyle. In Old Orchard, as in Boston, however, Fitzgerald spent far more time with his six brothers than he did with any politician. Wherever the mayor went, he was accompanied by Jim, Eddie, George, Mike, Joe or Henry, and it was then that journalists began good-naturedly to refer to the Fitzgeralds as "the royal family." Irish to the core, by turns affectionate and raging, rowdy and wise, the Fitzgerald brothers acted as extensions of the mayor's power, distributing patronage, delivering orders and bearing messages.

John Fitzgerald was probably most involved with his oldest brother, Jim, though their relationship was often stormy. The best-looking, most self-sufficient of the Fitzgeralds, Jim was an extremely wealthy man and an influential one. But the brothers were not the least alike. John was conspicuous, loud and chatty;

Jim was invariably cool and distant. Yet if Jim was sparing with his emotions, he was generous with his money. At different times he gave financial support to each of his brothers: to John for his campaigns, to George and Eddie to set up businesses, to Henry to buy a cigar manufacturing plant.

John Fitzgerald seemed most relaxed with his youngest brother, Henry, for here the bond was between two similar natures, both avid for work and ambitious for power. Their partnership dated back to John's first foray into the insurance business, when he recognized how clever Henry was and put him in charge of all patronage activities in the North End. Then Henry married and bought a house in Dorchester, only half a block from his brother's. The two families grew up as one, and when Fitzgerald became mayor, Henry became, it was said, the second most powerful man in the city.

Of the middle brothers, Eddie was the most gregarious, the most unconventional and, in many ways, the most endearing. Described as "a wonderful character" and "a natural politician," he was generous and caring, and prospered as the owner of several taverns and a hotel.

George, a brewery salesman, was a milder edition of Eddie, but more conventional and more reserved. A shrewd business-man, he was already doing well when he married Lizzy, "a dazzling beauty." Relatives remember heads turning as the handsome couple strolled along the beach at Old Orchard.

Michael, just one year younger than John, was a policeman when his brother became mayor, and his work brought him into contact with all manner of people, which gave him a perspective on city life that his brother greatly valued. In return, the mayor secured for Michael the position of health inspector.

Of all the brothers, Joe, five years younger than John, had the hardest time making his way. Genial and good-natured, he had returned from the Spanish-American War with a form of malaria in which the parasites had localized in his brain and left him, in the words of relatives, "a little dippy." He was unable to secure work on his own, so John found him a job delivering the daily traffic report from the Warren Avenue Bridge to city hall.

There were, to be sure, disadvantages for the mayor in having his brothers so visible in city affairs. Their errors could not be easily repudiated or ignored; disgruntled politicians would claim that "the Fitzgerald dynasty" had appropriated to itself a king-like power. But as John saw it, his brothers had always been his closest friends and he needed them now more than ever.

"THERE WAS ONLY one problem with our summers in Maine," Rose Fitzgerald Kennedy recalled; "they never lasted long enough." It is little wonder that, at seventeen, Rose wanted time to stand still. At that age she seemed to have everything a girl could have: an open, ardent nature, a radiant complexion; a fine figure and plenty of new clothes; a strong, active mind and abundant opportunity for stimulating conversation. She was her father's chosen companion, with privileged access to all manner of political and social events, ranging from box seats at the ballpark to the head table at banquets. As one of her companions recalled, "We all stood in awe of her. She lived in a special world of infinite possibility."

A remarkable photograph, taken at about this time, shows her seated on the edge of an air duct on the deck of a ship, her face flushed with excitement. There are the fine cheekbones, the square chin and the straight nose, features which, with maturity, would become the handsome and familiar face of the Kennedy matriarch; but there are also the dancing smile and the bright eyes of an untamed and unbroken spirit, a captivating image of budding womanhood.

All through her girlhood years, in contrast with her mother's experience, Rose had been encouraged to express herself, had been expected to have intelligent opinions. She had devoured books on history and politics, and, one reporter wrote, "she displays depth and strength of mind rarely found in so young a woman." At the time, her ambition was still of a general nature: to be one of the best, to move in a world of challenge. Her dreams of her future focused

Every inch an American beauty: Rose sits for her portrait aboard ship.

on a college education, and from there a career, perhaps in music or politics.

The college Rose had chosen was Wellesley, twelve miles west of Boston, and with her intelligence and her grades she was accepted for admittance in her junior year of high school. She persuaded three of her close friends to apply to Wellesley too, and when all of them were accepted, there was great rejoicing.

It would have been difficult for Rose to choose a college more in keeping with her temperament. Founded in 1875 for the purpose of giving young women an education equivalent to that of the best colleges for men, Wellesley was noted for its exceptional curriculum, its elite student body and its extraordinary faculty. Courses were offered in political economics: in the industrial history of the United States and England, the development of modern socialism and the regulation of trusts. One teacher was nationally recognized as a leader in the campaign to abolish sweatshops. Another, Emily Greene Balch, was a powerful force in the settlement-house movement and would later win the Nobel Peace Prize. Together, these women inspired a generation of Wellesley students. For a young girl like Rose Fitzgerald, there was probably no better school in all of America. However, while Rose was happily anticipating her college experience, there was a movement under way that was to have calamitous results for the Fitzgerald family.

It began simply enough on July 30, 1907, with the election of former Mayor Nathan Matthews as chairman of a newly created finance commission, which had been established by the state legislature in response to "the uneasy feeling in the community that waste and extravagance were flourishing" in Boston. The city treasury had become a field for exploitation by contractors and politicians. Thousands of dollars were being wasted each year through the excess prices paid to favored contractors and to operators of streetcar lines; suppliers of gas, light and coal; providers of telephone services. These contractors then returned the favor by financing the party machine from their swollen profits. Pressured by reformers to investigate, the state legislature named a seven-man commission and gave it broad powers. In addition to former Mayor Matthews, it included as secretary, J. Wells Farley, a young, energetic lawyer, and as counsel, Michael Sughrue, a former district attorney and expert in criminal practices.

Perhaps Fitzgerald assumed that this committee, like most such bodies, would merely hold an occasional meeting and issue a dull report, and there it would end. But events took a very different turn. At the conclusion of their first meeting, the commission's members decided to meet again at nine o'clock the following morning, and again the following day and the day after that. Like impatient hounds on the scent of game, they decided not to wait to issue an official, polished report, but instead to run with each set of findings, "so long as every line was weighed and tested to be sure that it told the truth."

The first report, issued on August 7, 1907, called on the mayor to withdraw his improvident appointment of eight unnecessary deputy sealers in the department of weights and measures. Over successive weeks a batch of reports was issued, and for once in his life Fitzgerald said very little. From the sands of Old Orchard came only the flat comment that he would look into the matters when he returned home.

But back in Boston in September, Fitzgerald faced a far more troubling announcement: the commission had scheduled a series of public hearings on the manner in which his new supply department had let out contracts for coal. The supply department, originally created to solve the problems of inefficiency, waste and corruption, consolidated all of the city's purchases into one central department, so that the mayor's office, for the first time, could scrutinize all payments made from the city treasury. The centralized purchases would also, Fitzgerald had said, "secure lower prices for our city," especially in its enormous coal purchases. The superintendent of the supply department, a man named Michael Mitchell, was one of Fitzgerald's closest and oldest friends, and Fitzgerald trusted him completely. If the commission had any evidence against Mitchell, it would surely implicate Fitzgerald as well.

A large man with broad shoulders, bushy hair and a thick black mustache, Mitchell radiated warmth and goodwill. Over the years, he had grown almost as attached to Fitzgerald's family as he was to Fitzgerald himself. "We simply adored him," Rose remembered. "He was always so kind, so interested in everything; he reminded me of a big, comfortable teddy bear."

When Fitzgerald first approached Mitchell about becoming superintendent of the new department, Mitchell had expressed substantial reservations. While he had been successful as an undertaker, he felt he was not prepared to superintend nearly one million dollars a year for the purchase of materials ranging from coal and oil to flagstones and drainpipes. It was, in fact, only by appealing to Mitchell's loyalty that Fitzgerald finally persuaded him to accept the position, with the understanding that the mayor's office would be involved in all the major decisions. Now, as Fitzgerald received word of the impending public hearings, his thoughts ran back to Mitchell's original hesitation, and an ominous sense of foreboding passed over him.

The sessions, known as the Coal Graft Hearings, opened on a rainy morning in September. In the meeting room the atmosphere was charged with excitement. The first witness, George P. Koch, was chief clerk in the supply department and worked directly under Mitchell. Under questioning by Counsel Sughrue, Koch admitted that he could not give a single instance where a major coal contract had been advertised for bid and awarded to the lowest bidder, though the law required it.

The afternoon session resumed with Mitchell on the stand. He was anxious about the hearing, he later told a friend, not because he had done anything wrong but because he feared the commission would find out the truth—that he had never really taken hold of the department, that he had left all the major decisions to the mayor and his brothers. Sughrue made the most of Mitchell's discomfiture, taking every occasion to expose his ignorance of his job. Finally, Mitchell admitted that five contracts were let to Maurice Klous, the agent for the W. C. Niver Coal Company, without public advertisement—though just why Klous had been chosen above all others Mitchell could not say. Then Sughrue produced a letter, which, he suggested, illustrated the motivating force behind the lucrative contracts Mitchell had made with Klous. The letter, written by Klous to James Donovan, former superintendent of streets, was presented as the tip of the iceberg. In it, the coal contractor promised to deliver at least 300 votes for Donovan's candidate, representing "the employees of this company and as many more as our combined efforts will secure for him."

The next afternoon, back on the stand, the hapless Mitchell faced a barrage of technical questions about the poor quality of the coal Klous had supplied. Artless, incapable of feigning, Mitchell was forced to acknowledge that he knew very little about coal. At this startling admission a burst of coarse laughter ran through the room. Sughrue, sensing victory, brought an end to the testimony, and Mitchell left the stand, a beaten man.

The mayor's aides had listened in dismay to the hearing. Elections were coming up, and Mitchell's continued presence in the administration could damage Fitzgerald's hopes for reelection. Mitchell's resignation was the only answer. But Mitchell's friends were telling him to remember that he had done nothing wrong, that he must stick it out in order to vindicate himself and restore his good name. Mitchell's friends were probably right; had he told the commission how his department really worked, it would have been clear to all that he was simply a stand-in for the mayor. But when Fitzgerald asked him to resign, Mitchell promptly agreed. "Mitchell's loyalty to the mayor was simply unbelievable," a friend later recalled.

Although Fitzgerald's failure to support Mitchell angered Mitchell's many friends, it is unlikely that Fitzgerald ever regarded his actions as a betrayal. Just as he had given loyalty to Matthew Keany under difficult circumstances, so Mitchell was now exhibiting that same loyalty to him. As soon as the hearings were over, Fitzgerald told a friend, he would make sure that Mitchell had everything he needed to resume his rightful place within the community.

IF FITZGERALD SEEMED at first to escape the baleful effects of the hearings, their melancholy shadow spread over Rose in a most unexpected way. The first indication of trouble came at a family discussion in early September, just before Rose was scheduled to begin Wellesley. Fitzgerald's face set hard, his voice determined, he looked directly at Rose and said that he and her mother had decided she was too young for Wellesley. She had been enrolled instead at the Academy of the Sacred Heart in Boston. That was it. No further discussion.

Rose was startled and confused, but she never said a word in protest. In her experience, a daughter simply did not argue with her father. It did enter her mind, however, that there was betrayal in his words—that there was more involved in her father's decision than just her youth. And her apprehensions were not misplaced; for her father had indeed had a permanent change of heart about his daughter's college. And the fact was that his decision reflected a concern for *his* needs and not hers.

It seems that the Archbishop of Boston, William O'Connell, had heard that Rose was planning to attend a Protestant college. O'Connell was very upset, fearing the impact on other Catholic girls, and he conveyed his displeasure to the mayor. Fitzgerald was anxious to please this powerful man, especially at a time when the commission hearings were already imperiling his position. Accordingly, he agreed to shift his daughter from Wellesley to the Academy of the Sacred Heart.

It is impossible to overestimate the importance of this event in Rose's maturing sensibilities. When asked at the age of ninety to describe her greatest regret, she was silent for a moment and then, with a bitterness she did not often allow herself to betray, she said, "My greatest regret is not having gone to Wellesley College. It is something I have felt a little sad about all my life." One cannot help feeling that through this experience Rose suffered an injury that went deeper than the loss of a college. Until this moment, John Fitzgerald had been the unquestioned center of her universe. For seventeen years he had offered her everything, telling her she could do or be whatever she wanted. Now he was telling her, in essence, that she was only an appendage to his political needs.

Yet Rose smothered her feelings of resistance and bowed to her father's powerful will. In mid-September 1907, while her three friends were busy unpacking their trunks at Wellesley, she boarded a streetcar to begin her year as a day student at the Sacred Heart Convent. But it was as if a mask had fallen, allowing her to see her father for the first time. Though they would remain the closest of friends all their lives, a barrier had been raised, a detachment forged, which would allow Rose, when the time came, to go against her father on a matter of even greater importance—the choice of a husband.

THE CONVENT SCHOOL that Rose entered that fall was one link in a chain of many first-rate academies run by the Sacred Heart Society for the daughters of the Catholic aristocracy. Following a pattern laid down by the original Sacred Heart Society in France, the academies were the same the world over. Their curriculum, as Rose later characterized it in her memoirs, was "unusually concerned with the practical things of this world. It was assumed that the girls when they married would be devoting their lives to *Kinder, Kirche, Küche* (children, church, cooking)." It was further assumed that they would have servants do all the actual work, but in order to instruct and supervise the servants and to run an efficient household the girls were taught cooking, needlework, first aid, packing, preparing for journeys, writing orders to shops, and the other arts of housewifery.

It was not easy to enter this system from the outside, Rose discovered. There was a fundamental contrast between her previous college preparatory courses at Dorchester High and the schooling she received at the convent. Never again would knowledge be presented to her objectively, for its own sake; never again would the subjects she studied be approached from various points of view, considering all sides of the matter. As she observed years later, "The world in which I found myself was very different from the world I had known."

ON OCTOBER 8, 1907, three weeks after the humiliating hearings that resulted in Superintendent Mitchell's resignation, George Koch, the clerk in the department of supplies, was found in his lodgings with all the doors and windows locked and the gas jets open. What inner torment lay behind Koch's decision to take his life cannot be known. If, however, Koch intended to take his secrets with him to the grave, his plan misfired. His landlady, having detected the smell of gas, found him unconscious but still alive, and an ambulance hurried him to City Hospital.

The next day, J. Wells Farley, the finance commission secretary, went to the hospital to see Koch. Farley evidently established a feeling of trust in Koch, and the story Koch told him described a state of municipal affairs in which bribery had become so endemic that few public officials could escape its corroding influence. The prices paid for contracts, he said, were often double or triple the going rates, with the excess profits being divided between the individual contractors and the politicians or middlemen who made the lucrative deals possible.

In the course of his hospital-bed confession, Koch listed contractors from whom he had obtained gifts and money—including Maurice Klous, the infamous agent for the W. C. Niver Coal Company, and a Mr. Patrick Bowen, acting on behalf of Maher Brothers, who furnished flagstones to the city at well over the market price. Having obtained these damaging admissions, Farley made an attempt to widen the circle of guilt. And although he failed to establish a direct link to Fitzgerald, the sensational interview became the basis for a new set of hearings and a grand jury investigation of Michael Mitchell and Thomas Maher, senior partner in the Maher Brothers firm.

Upon hearing of Koch's testimony, Fitzgerald immediately suspended the clerk and issued a statement expressing his great surprise that Mr. Koch "had received money in connection with the discharge of his duties." Fitzgerald then went on to criticize the commission for releasing the testimony at a public hearing just a few days before the municipal election.

The commission's timing was indeed hardly an accident. As the battle lines had developed, the Republicans had chosen a conservative Yankee, George Albee Hibbard, as their candidate for mayor. The former head of the local Republican machine, Hibbard pledged that, if elected, he would "clean up the mess" in Boston's city government. Still, had the election been a straight two-way contest between the Democratic and the Republican machines, Fitzgerald would have emerged the victor. But also in the race was John A. Coulthurst, a reform candidate running as an independent. Coulthurst, a relative newcomer to politics, appealed to the Democratic voters embarrassed by the public dishonor stamped upon their municipal government, and when the voters went to the polls on December 10, 1907, Coulthurst stunned party professionals by amassing enough votes to give Hibbard a narrow plurality over Fitzgerald.

For a man who had never before lost an election, Fitzgerald

faced his first defeat cheerfully. "We held a conference a little while ago," he said with a broad smile on his face, "and began our planning for the next election." And, "in a way," he added, "the defeat will be a good thing . . . since it will allow me more time with my family."

5

"GUILTY AS CHARGED"

WITHIN TWO weeks of his defeat Fitzgerald, along with Mitchell, Maher, Koch and Bowen, were summoned to appear before a grand jury to give testimony in regard to the flagstone contract. The task of the grand jury was to hear the state's evidence with regard to the flagstone fraud and then to decide whether Mitchell or anyone else should stand trial.

By far the most sensational happening of the probe came when Mayor Fitzgerald made his appearance before the grand jury. "As nearly as can be learned," the Boston *Journal* reported, "it was the first time in the history of the city that a mayor has been called as a witness before the indicting body."

During his nearly four hours of testimony, Fitzgerald told the grand jury that he had approved the flagstone contract because Mitchell told him that the Maher brothers were the only ones who could supply the stone and that the prices had gone up. Afterward, in public comments, Fitzgerald stated positively that the city had been "fooled" in the flagstone contract into paying double the going price. He refused, though, to accept any responsibility for the situation, declaring that as the head of the administration he had to rely implicitly on the integrity and ability of his department chiefs.

From the tone of this and other statements it is clear that Fitzgerald had decided to place the responsibility for the flagstone deal on the shoulders of his best friend, Michael Mitchell. Although no one believed that Mitchell had received a cent of money, it was he who became the scapegoat of the whole sordid affair.

Fitzgerald's betrayal of Mitchell, it was later argued, may have come about because Fitzgerald believed that the grand jury would never indict his friend. In Boston, in those days, it was widely understood that politicians could control the grand jury, and since the jury's deliberations were secret, Fitzgerald doubtless assumed that no one on the outside would ever hear the testimony he gave. As it happened, however, this particular grand jury defied all expectations and came back with no fewer than eight indictments, including those of Thomas Maher and Michael Mitchell, who were charged jointly with a series of larcenies aggregating $28,000.

When the indicted men arrived at police headquarters to be placed under arrest, they had to make their way through the huge crowd of spectators, holding up their arms to shield their faces from photographers. The experience was an agonizing one for Mitchell, for the arrest stripped away his reputation for honesty. Yet it must have been a time of anguish for the defeated mayor too. For despite his confident declaration that he would run again, he must have known that Mitchell's upcoming trial was certain to cast a shadow upon his first administration. So would the continued probe by the finance commission, which was determined to find something on him so that he could never occupy the mayor's chair again.

Hoping to shield his family from the vicious struggle that lay ahead and the chance that he might be charged, Fitzgerald made up his mind to take his family on a vacation to Ireland, England and France. He also decided to send his two oldest daughters, Rose and Agnes, to boarding school in Europe, where they would be enrolled in the Sacred Heart Convent at Blumenthal, Holland.

Rose Kennedy later recalled that when her father first told her she was going abroad to study for a year, she reacted with dismay; it seemed so far away from her family, her friends and her growing romance with young Joe Kennedy, whom she had been seeing steadily since the previous summer at Old Orchard Beach. But the more she thought about the trip, the more excited she became.

After a "glorious send-off party" at the dock, attended by scores of prominent politicians and churchmen, the Fitzgeralds sailed for Europe on July 18 aboard the S.S. *Cymric,* which Rose said was "as comfortable and as nice as a house."

Landing in Liverpool, the family took the train to London, where they spent five hectic days taking in English architecture and history. On August 1 they crossed the Irish Sea to Dublin. As an old man looking back, John Fitzgerald would remember this first trip through Ireland as the high point of his travels, recalling vividly his visit to the small farmhouse in Bruff where his father, Tom, had been born. Seen through the sentimental eyes of an immigrant's son returning to the homeland, the area around Bruff appeared "indescribably lovely."

From Ireland the Fitzgeralds traveled to France, Switzerland and Brussels and then to Holland, where Rose and Agnes were placed in the convent school at Blumenthal.

Upon his return to Boston, Fitzgerald found that the district attorney, John Moran, the man who held Michael Mitchell's fate, and Fitzgerald's, in his hands, had contracted tuberculosis. As autumn turned to winter, Moran's condition failed, and on February 5, 1909, the district attorney died.

Moran's death gave Fitzgerald and Mitchell the precious gift of hope. The next district attorney was to be elected in November. If luck ran with the Democrats, the new man might be a friend and the case might never go to trial. In the meantime, Governor Eben Draper chose Arthur Hill, "one of the mildest and least aggressive looking men in the city" as acting district attorney. "Innocent, green, and boyish looking," he was, in the words of one reporter, "the last man one would pick for a successful prosecuting attorney."

Pretty soon, however, the politicians were astonished to find Hill bringing case after case to trial, and winning verdicts of guilty in each of them. As *Harper's Weekly* observed, "the climax of excitement came when Mitchell and Maher were placed on trial," charged with conspiracy to defraud the city.

The trial opened on a stifling Monday afternoon in June before an overflowing crowd of politicians, reporters, sketch artists, messengers and spectators. All the seats available in the high-ceilinged chamber of the superior court had been taken, and still the curious kept coming; they stood in the corners and sat on the windowsills and on the benches in the corridors.

With the jury in the box, District Attorney Hill made his opening statement, outlining the government's case: that the defendants had conspired together so that crosswalk flagging, which had been purchased from another dealer at thirty-three and a half cents a square foot, had been bought for sixty-seven cents a square foot, the result being that the city was defrauded.

Six witnesses were then sworn in, including the former mayor. The man who would cross-examine them was Daniel Coakley, a feisty Irishman who was Mitchell's lawyer. Flamboyant and glib, Coakley combined his law practice with an active interest in politics and he and the mayor had become friends. But for many months now reporters had detected "a noticeable coolness" in their relationship. What lay behind this break was Coakley's strong feeling that Fitzgerald had betrayed Mitchell, a feeling that Coakley would keep in harness during the course of the trial; but once the trial was over, Coakley's anger would become an obsession—with disastrous results for Fitzgerald's political career.

On the second day of the trial, Michael Cuddihy, whose firm had held the flagstone contract before Maher Brothers, was called to testify. He said that when the contract was taken from him and awarded at double the price to Maher Brothers he was still willing to sell at thirty-three and a half cents per square foot. He went to see Mitchell, but Mitchell told him that he must see the mayor.

Next, District Attorney Hill placed Farley, the former finance commission secretary, on the stand. Under cross-examination, Farley was led to recall an interesting exchange with Maher in which Maher had said, "I am a Catholic and I say that as true as there is a God in heaven, I never paid Mitchell any money." At that, Mitchell's taut body relaxed for the first time in days. However, the next witness, Mitchell's former assistant, George Koch, testified that on at least three occasions he had pointed out to Mitchell that the price of the Maher contract was double the old price.

Then came the dramatic moment that everyone had been waiting for: the testimony of the prosecution's star witness, ex-Mayor Fitzgerald. Having built up his case for the conspiracy in slow and painstaking detail, the district attorney now hoped to clinch his argument with the man whose grand jury testimony had unquestionably been the most damaging to Mitchell and the other defendants. Hill, however, failed to consider that Fitzgerald possessed a mind shrewder than his own.

All through his initial testimony, from his first to his last moments on the stand, Fitzgerald maintained a remarkably cool countenance. In answer to the preliminary questions, he listed his occupation as newspaper publisher and told of the work of the supply department leading up to the appointment of Mitchell.

"What experience had Mitchell that fitted him for this position?" Hill asked.

"He had had business experience as an undertaker," Fitzgerald replied.

"His business as an undertaker was retail, was it not?"

"Well, yes," Fitzgerald said, with a broad smile. "I am not sure that I ever heard of a wholesale undertaker." There was a burst of laughter in which everybody, including the judge, joined.

From there Hill proceeded to the core of his case.

HILL: Now, do you recall the Maher contract incident?
FITZGERALD: No.
HILL: Do you remember giving your sanction to the contract?
FITZGERALD: I do not.

Flustered and confused by Fitzgerald's unexpected response, Hill handed a copy of the first Maher contract to Fitzgerald and asked again, "Do you remember having sanctioned this contract?"

"I do not," answered the ex-mayor.

Pressed by Hill, Fitzgerald admitted that by law the contracts could not have been made without his signature, but as to any of the details of this particular contract he repeated his claim that he did not recall. The mayor's repeated answer of "don't recall" exasperated Hill, and he used the grand jury testimony to refresh Fitzgerald's mind. "Do you remember saying this or that?" Hill would ask.

"No, I do not," Fitzgerald would reply. And on it went until the judge finally called an adjournment.

By seven o'clock the next morning, June 29, sprawling headlines in the city papers informed everyone of Fitzgerald's surprising lack of testimony. The cartoonists had a field day with his inability to recall. But Fitzgerald knew that he was caught in a trap of his own making. The decision to "forget" his grand jury testimony was the best strategy he could follow to protect both himself and Mitchell. He took the stand again, and several times during the day Hill made remarks about his "unfortunate lapse of memory," then finished his examination.

HILL: Did you not tell the grand jury anything but the truth?
FITZGERALD: Yes, sir.
HILL: Well, if you told the grand jury that you spoke to Mitchell about these flagstone prices, was it true?
FITZGERALD: If I so testified, it was true.

At this triumphant moment, Hill announced that he was finished with the witness. As he had intended, his questions had put Fitzgerald on the spot; for the mayor to admit that he had not told the truth would have been to admit perjury; yet clearly Fitzgerald did not wish to acknowledge—as he had to the grand jury—that he had spoken to Mitchell about the flagstone price.

Now it was time for the cross-examination by the lawyers for the defendants. Coakley kept Fitzgerald on the stand for nearly half an hour, eliciting from him the admission that during his term at city hall there was such a vast mass of business and so many people bringing him papers to sign, that he couldn't possibly remember who told him what in regard to one particular contract. With this established, Coakley then took aim at the prosecutor's final line of questioning, which had cleverly brought Fitzgerald to admit that whatever he had testified before the grand jury must have been true. Coakley attacked the problem head on.

COAKLEY: You are not infallible, are you, Mr. Fitzgerald?
HILL: I hardly think you should ask that. (laughter)
FITZGERALD: No, not infallible.
COAKLEY: I meant to show that many of these matters were negotiated by subordinates. At the grand jury the mayor may have testified *in good faith* that he thought he talked with heads of departments when it was really done by subordinates and he just signed papers.

Turning to Fitzgerald, Coakley asked, "Isn't it likely that some office attaché might have given you the information instead of Mitchell?"

"It is likely," Fitzgerald replied. "I may have made some mistakes in my testimony, of course."

Coakley had made his point. Fitzgerald was finally allowed to step down, and after that the trial moved swiftly to its conclusion. In his closing statement, before a hushed courtroom, Coakley spoke forcefully in Mitchell's defense. Assuming that it was upon the mayor's grand jury testimony alone that the district attorney was relying to prove a conspiracy, Coakley pointed out the inadmissibility of that testimony, saying that as far as Fitzgerald's evidence was concerned "it was as if he never appeared on the stand."

Then he burst unexpectedly into a savage attack on Fitzgerald. To the reporters in the crowd it seemed as if all his pent-up anger against Fitzgerald for days and days had simply exploded. Dismissing the former mayor's unfortunate lapse of memory, he said, "If Fitzgerald told the truth while on the witness stand in this trial, he gave false testimony before the grand jury. . . . I care nothing for mayors, ex-mayors, future mayors maybe. I appear for no man but Mitchell, whose reputation in the community stands head and heels over the reputation of any witness that has appeared here."

The sting of Coakley's attack, the strong language and irritability he displayed, were soft in comparison with the "scorching" attack of the district attorney. In his closing remarks, Hill declared that when Fitzgerald came into court he "did not come with the purpose of telling the truth to this jury" but "to throw the government's case." Hill continued. "Is there any reason for his coming here and practically refusing to testify except that he was afraid that if the whole truth came out it would not be only the defendants that would be there in the dock? I tell you, gentlemen, I don't know whether we have got all the conspirators or not, but I know we have proved a conspiracy here and proved it up to the hilt."

The jury began deliberation at three o'clock in the afternoon. The next morning they came back with their verdict.

In the strained silence, the clerk asked, "Do you find the defendants, Michael J. Mitchell and Thomas F. Maher, guilty or not guilty?"

The foreman spoke up. "We find the defendants guilty as charged in the indictment."

"Mitchell was almost overcome," reporters observed. "Tears sprang to his eyes." His friends immediately encircled him with sympathy, but he sat slumped in his chair, disgraced and inconsolable.

When the time for the sentencing arrived, on July 9, 1909, every seat in the courtroom was taken.

Maher's lawyer, Francis Carney, spoke first, telling the judge that Maher had asked him to make a special plea for Mitchell. "Mr. Maher wants you to know that absolutely no money went to Michael J. Mitchell. . . . Mitchell is innocent."

Then Coakley rose to speak. "If you feel," he said in part, "that Mitchell was an innocent tool of somebody else, I ask that you show him clemency."

After hearing both defense and prosecution, the judge delivered a remarkable speech explaining that the foreman of the jury had come to him after the verdict to speak on Mitchell's behalf. He had said the jurors thought that Mitchell "was not so deep in the matter as somebody else who was not charged . . . that they hoped the court would take this into consideration when sentencing Mitchell."

The announcement caused a commotion in the courtroom. Rapping for order, the judge went on to say that while he was willing to take the jury's plea into consideration, the facts were that Mitchell was a public servant, that the main object of a sentence is to protect the community from future crimes of the same kind and to keep others up to the proper standard. For that reason, he could not agree to a simple fine or to probation. Instead he sentenced both men to the House of Correction for one year at hard labor.

Then began for the loyal Mitchell what he later described to a friend as "a long nightmare" of monotonous days spent behind prison walls. "The curse of the place," he said, "was all the hours you had to sit there all by yourself, thinking and worrying and never really understanding how it had all happened to you."

6

THE MAYOR'S DAUGHTER

WITH MITCHELL SAFELY in jail, there was one piece of unfinished business Fitzgerald had to attend to: it was time to bring his daughters home from Holland.

From all accounts, the experience of a year at boarding school had not noticeably changed the shy and warmhearted younger sister Agnes. But Rose was changed in fundamental ways.

The two sisters were different in temperament. Agnes was softer and more easygoing than Rose, not so bold or so competitive, far more her mother's child. "I was the one with lots of ideas," Rose recalled. But a deeper affinity was unmistakable. Both girls had a vital interest in people, a perceptive cast of mind and an innate desire to please. And from all accounts they got on remarkably well, taking genuine comfort in each other's company—a comfort they both needed more than ever in the unaccustomed surroundings of Blumenthal.

In all things—in architecture, in ritual and in way of life—the Blumenthal tradition was one of monastic simplicity. All members of the community, including the teaching nuns and all the boarding students, were housed in the same building—a large granite structure, three stories high, with tall, arched windows. The Fitzgerald girls were assigned a small room, sparsely furnished. As there was no central heating, the cold could be numbing, and Rose reported that her hands had turned "a purplish bluish color" and that she had had frost on her feet for weeks. But if the girls talked aloud about their aches, they were told "to meditate on the sufferings of our Lord on the cross" so they would not be tempted to overestimate their own puny pains.

More difficult than the cold, however, was the rigid schedule, the ceaseless supervision of behavior and the mass of minutiae on which convent life was based.

The day began with the tolling of a bell at six a.m. The girls were expected to be washed, dressed and ready for assembly by six fifteen sharp, when another bell summoned everyone to prayer. During morning prayers, the girls were supposed to keep their eyes lowered and their backs straight. The slightest disturbance, the mere shuffling of one's feet, was noted. At the final amen, chimes announced the morning Mass, and with long black veils over their heads, the girls walked in step in ranks of two into the chapel.

Under the convent's strict rules there could be no conversation in the early morning. The ordered silence continued during breakfast in the refectory. At every meal either a lecture was delivered, usually on some aspect of character formation, or there was a reading in German or in French that the girls were expected to listen to without speaking.

"The hardest thing in the beginning," Rose later recalled, "was to learn all the small gestures which took the place of speech—the raising of the hand to ask for juice, the lowering of the middle finger to say, 'Napkin, please.' What a great relief it was to hear the gong which ended all these gestures by allowing us to speak for the last few minutes of the meal."

The class hours were long and the nuns were demanding. Nor was there any escape from the community; you might long to curl up on a bed and read a novel or take a walk through the woods with a friend, but this could never be. The regulations seemed to take it for granted that learning to live with oneself was more important than learning to make friends. The major recreational activity was "the promenade"—half an hour's walk up and down the terrace, which provided time to be alone and to meditate. For healthy, robust girls like Rose and Agnes, who had been swimming and skating, riding horses and playing tennis since they were very young, this concept of recreation was difficult to understand.

The grueling routine, the rigid surveillance that denied all spontaneous attachments—these were the aspects of convent life that proved the most troubling to Rose. Yet if it was the most exasperating challenge she had ever experienced, it was also the most compelling. For beneath the code of discipline lay a system for training in moral conduct, self-control, respect for authority and polished manners.

Every Sunday morning the entire school assembled in the chapel for a public examination of each girl's conduct. All during the preceding week the girls had been watched over carefully for the slightest imperfections—for walking too impetuously or forgetting to pass things at the table or for talking during a period of silence. Each imperfection counted for a certain number of "bad" points listed in a big black book. On the other side of the ledger, each student received "good" points for poise or politeness or for assisting at Mass, and each week a composite score was made for each girl and used to determine her ranking in the "weekly primes." The ceremony itself required each student, when her name was called, to walk up to the altar, curtsy before the mother superior and then stand on public display as her list of faults was read aloud.

Yet, for all its harshness, the Sacred Heart system relied on pride more than shame, on encouragement more than criticism. Any girl who came out at the top glowed with pleasure as her name was called to accept the coveted blue card, which signified that her performance that week had been *très bien.* Those who regularly received *très biens* were eligible for the next prizes— the blue ribbons. And then there were medallions; and beyond medallions, membership in sodalities—always a higher prize to reach for, a higher standard to meet.

For Rose, the experience at Blumenthal brought a gradual turning in her vision of herself and of her place in the world. During the long months of detachment from the bustle and activity of modern life, she gradually found within herself what she later called the gift of faith. "While I had always believed in God," Rose later said, "and had faithfully gone to church and confession, this was not really the same as the living faith I acquired at Blumenthal."

The first outward signs of Rose's growing piety were not taken too seriously by her Blumenthal friends. "I used to be behind her in confession," Margaret Finnegan reported when they all returned home. "My God, I used to have to wait an hour for her to come out of the confessional box." But if some friends thought her devotion a little funny, Rose was intensely serious. As wholeheartedly and as persistently as she had once pursued her academic ambitions, she was now determined to be all that the nuns wanted her to be. The process had a momentum of its own that took her beyond where even she could have guessed she would go. Step by step she became fully absorbed in the quest to become a Child of Mary, the highest honor a Sacred Heart girl could receive. The goals to be met were nothing less than the conquest of pride and self-will, the achievement of interior silence. Eventually the discipline showed, and on May 22, 1909, Rose was offered membership in the Children of Mary.

At the initiation ceremony each aspirant was asked to make a number of personal promises along with basic commitments. Among her pledges, Rose made two, to which she returned time and again in her long life: the first, "to make the effort necessary to practice those family virtues suited to my position as daughter, wife, mother, such as kindness, gift of self-abnegation and evenness"; the second, the promise "in the face of changes of fortune, to hold my soul free," and "in difficult moments, to obtain from Our Lady of Sorrows the courage to suffer as she did, standing at the foot of the cross."

In becoming a Child of Mary, Rose let a part of herself go, that part that had originally conceived of independent ambitions and career accomplishments, that part that had once wanted so fiercely to go to Wellesley College. The convent had done its work. "College is out of the question," she suddenly announced in a letter of May 23. "The convent girls may not know as much Greek etc. as the college girls, but I think in general they can hold their own, in the positions to which they are called." Had she been allowed to go to Wellesley, perhaps it all would have been different; perhaps she, as someone later suggested, might have become the first Catholic President instead of her son. Some might say it was fate that diverted her path, the result of a word to her father from the Archbishop of Boston. Yet it was she who decided to become what the nuns of the Sacred Heart wanted her to be. It was she who trod the path toward her religion that would give her life a new and irrevocable direction.

So it was a changed Rose who, with her sister, was brought home by their father at the end of the school year. "Our mother greeted us with tears in her eyes," Rose reported. "She had been terribly lonely." It was decided that the girls would not go so far away again. Agnes would continue her studies at the Sacred Heart Convent at Providence, Rhode Island; Rose, who had been hoping for another year with her books, would enroll at the Sacred Heart Convent in what was then known as the Manhattanville section of New York City.

AS THE AUTUMN OF 1909 approached, political observers began to speculate upon the political fortunes of John Fitzgerald, still the most visible Democratic contender for mayor. The Democratic Party bosses did not think, with all the baggage he carried, that he could be reelected, and had it been left to them to choose the nominee, Fitzgerald would have had little chance. But, by an ironic twist, the same finance commission that had collapsed Fitzgerald's chances of winning the support of regular Democrats had provided a new nominating procedure that opened a back door to his election.

The reform package, labeled Plan Two, called for abolishing primaries, removing the party label from ballots, extending the mayor's term to four years, and subjecting the mayor's departmental appointments to the approval of the civil service board. Party leaders fought hard to defeat Plan Two, but in a referendum, the reformers emerged victorious and a new city charter came into being. Encouraged by the popular vote for reform, the Good Government forces decided to run their own candidate for mayor.

They chose James Jackson Storrow, a blueblood patrician descended from the best of old Yankee stock, who was said to be one of the richest men in all New England. Tall and handsome, a Harvard man and a partner in a prominent banking firm, he projected the perfect Republican propriety. But he was, in fact, a Yankee Democrat—a community benefactor and a man with more conscience than most of his kind. His candidacy produced widespread enthusiasm, but those who believed he would coast to victory underestimated the formidable powers of John F. Fitzgerald.

Long before he announced his candidacy, Fitzgerald had planned his strategy. His biggest liability was the taint of corruption that had spread over his first administration. Denials of specific charges would be fruitless and would put him on the defensive. His aim, therefore, was to find a wholly different issue, one that would allow him to take the offensive, and he found it in Storrow's enormous wealth. On the day the campaign opened, Fitzgerald called for each candidate to limit his campaign expenses to $10,000 and to publish the contributions and expenditures before election day. Fitzgerald understood that Storrow would never accede to the scheme. Storrow needed the exposure that money could buy—the newspaper ads, billboards and posters. Yet, by making the dramatic pitch at the outset of the campaign, then following it up relentlessly day after day, Fitzgerald managed to simplify the election into a contest between "an Irish boy from the slums and a wealthy Harvard blueblood."

For a while, at least, Storrow's money had a devastating impact. In a brutally effective series of ads, he suggested that "Fitzgeraldism" was behind the scandals uncovered by the finance commission. The ads forcefully awakened all the unanswered questions regarding city contracts and coal frauds, leaving the clear impression that Fitzgerald and his friends had walked away with considerable cash.

Coming from a man of Storrow's reputation, these sensational accusations aroused public attention and submerged the entire Fitzgerald family in a new round of anguish and embarrassment. "I would awaken practically every morning," Rose recorded, "to find my father accused in headlines of being guilty of nearly every sin short of murder. My instinctive reactions were shock and outrage; I seethed." Yet, Rose recalled in amazement, her father "seemed to take it more or less for granted."

As the campaign progressed, Fitzgerald stepped up his own attacks. But, sensing that he also had to convince voters that he was *for* something, he began to talk of all the things he would do for the people of Boston. Countering Storrow's ads, he appropriated the phrase "Fitzgeraldism" for himself by linking it in the voters' minds with all the progressive programs he stood for. FITZGERALDISM IS CONSTRUCTIVE, declared the headlines in his own ads. IT MEANS BETTER SCHOOLS, BETTER STREETS AND BETTER HOSPITALS.

As the contest drew to a close, Fitzgerald's greater experience showed. Time and again, his dramatic oratory produced its desired result—tumultuous cheers from the audience. Then, typically, he would ask the crowd to join him in singing a

LIGHTNING CHANGE INTO EVENING DRESS EN ROUTE TO THE EVENING GRIND

CITY HALL (REAR)

Cartoonists had a field day during Mayor Fitzgerald's energetic days in office.

rousing song such as "When Johnny Comes Marching Home Again." It was now, during this most important campaign of his life, that the legend of Honey Fitz, the man with the golden voice, was born.

As election day approached, it was generally believed by most seasoned observers that Storrow was holding a slight lead. When the official results were calculated, however, Fitzgerald emerged the winner. Not surprisingly, in a battle so intensely emotional as this one, the results were deeply felt. "It certainly is a public calamity," wrote one reformer, "that such a discredited man should get back." For his part, Fitzgerald called it "the greatest triumph" of his political career. "My family appreciated the triumph especially, because there had been so much injustice in the attacks made on me."

As a vindication, Fitzgerald's victory was complete, and it was savored all the more as it helped Michael Mitchell to secure an early release from jail. But for Mitchell there was no vindication. He was a changed man. Tortured with sorrow, "he lived only a short time after that," one friend recalled. "And when he died, everyone said he had died of a broken heart."

WITH THE MAYOR'S triumphant return to power, a golden era dawned for the members of the Fitzgerald family. Ironically, his second term would be easier than his first, as a consequence of the reform legislation he had so vigorously opposed. By providing limits to the frenzied patronage seeking that had undermined his first term

WHIRLWIND CAMPAIGNING

in office, the new city charter protected Fitzgerald from some of his own greatest vulnerabilities and allowed him to concentrate on enacting programs that would improve the welfare of the people of Boston. And this time around, there was sufficient time to carry out his goals, since the charter change had doubled the mayoralty term from two to four years. As a result, Rose wrote, in her memoirs, "my father could relax a bit, which relaxed us all."

For Rose especially, as her father's favorite child and chosen companion, the years from 1910 to 1913 brought high adventure and glowing happiness. When, in June 1910, she graduated from Manhattanville and thereby finished with her formal schooling, she was free to spend most days with her father, who took her with him wherever he went—to "dedications, receptions, banquets, picnics, parades. . . ." She accompanied him on all manner of official trips as well, acting as "hostess-companion-helper." It was a special time for Rose, "a time to laugh and a time to dance." She was "the mayor's daughter again," and John

EXIT—"SWEET ADELINE"

IN THE EVE-
-ENING AS I SIT
ALONE A DREAMING
OF DAYS GONE BY
LOVE-E WHEN
YOU WERE
NE-AK,—

THE MUNICIPAL CARUSO

Fitzgerald delighted in her good looks, her intelligence and her superb social skills. Father and daughter, people said, had been cut from the same mold. Strikingly handsome, alike in their habits, each understood the other. And they adored each other.

All the while, according to Rose, Josie Fitzgerald remained contentedly at home. "Mother had a limited capacity for the official social whirl," Rose wrote. She declined most invitations and sent her willing daughter in her place. It was, in Rose's words, "a perfect arrangement" for everyone concerned.

Yet one wonders if this was really so. For, in delegating the role of companion to her daughter, Josie was giving up a part of her marriage, reducing her life with her husband to those moments when the political warrior chose to bring his tired body home. Perhaps Fitzgerald wanted it this way and perhaps Josie did, too. However, at times her stoic acceptance gave way to bitter outbursts of hostility toward both her frequently absent husband and the vibrant daughter who had all the charm and social skills she herself lacked.

Rose, for her part, was sharply aware of the constraints placed on her by her role as the mayor's daughter and she never allowed herself any unconventional or frivolous activity. A vivid portrait of this intensely serious, enchanting young girl at the age of twenty has survived in the newspaper accounts of her spectacular debut, held in her parents' home on a winter evening in 1911. It was considered "one of the most elaborate coming-out parties ever conducted in Boston." The Fitzgeralds' large white house was "ablaze with lights" as more than four hundred and fifty guests arrived by carriage and motorcar. "They found themselves confronted by a beautiful young woman whose frank, smiling face bade them welcome before they had hardly crossed the threshold."

Wearing a simple gown of the finest white chiffon traced with Italian embroidery over yellow silk ribbon, the debutante "stood revealed" as a natural beauty. "Not a jewel did she wear, not even a necklace or armlet of gold; only in the dark of her hair a silver ribbon had been twisted." Her thorough training in manners and poise came together in this moment, enabling her to do exactly what was expected of her, to smile, to talk, to dance. "She never lost her self possession or gave the least indication of being tired or bored. She had pleasant words for all and a laugh that was musical."

Amid all the descriptions of the party, however, one curious image stood out: the image of Fitzgerald wandering aimlessly about the house, his head bowed, his countenance betraying anxiety, the spirit in him suddenly quenched. His little girl was entering adulthood and would soon be gone from him forever.

The mayor's daughter christens a ship—one of her many official duties.

FOR THE MOST PART, Rose Fitzgerald had everything before her. Respected by the leading members of the community, surrounded by ardent admirers, she moved with elegance and ease wherever she went. Furthermore, she lived with the secret knowledge that the first love she had ever felt, for the handsome Joe Kennedy, was still the strongest love she had ever known.

From that romantic summer at Old Orchard Beach when she was sixteen, through all her years in the convent schools and all her adventures with her father, Rose had remained irrevocably drawn to the ambitious son of P. J. Kennedy. More commanding by far than all the other boys she knew, he was now a Harvard student, filled with dreams of glory, wealth and success.

Harvard College in the four years Joe spent there was a school in transition. Undergraduate life was still controlled by a select group of rich and fashionable families whose sons arrived to fill the places that had been waiting for them from the day they were born. But it was, at the same time, opening its doors to a more cosmopolitan student population. Of the nearly six hundred young men entering with Joe in 1908, more than sixty percent had graduated from public high schools. Yet the tone of college life was set by the enviable few: the golden boys who came from such prep schools as Groton, St. Mark's, St. Paul's and Middlesex, who knew one another by instinct and breeding, and who always seemed to associate with men of their own kind.

The social chasm was apparent the first day the freshmen arrived. Joe and others like him were herded into the only living quarters the college provided—a dreary set of dormitories, some of which still lacked central heating. The sons of the well-to-do, however, had luxurious private suites in one or another of the half dozen elegant residential halls clustered along Mount Auburn Street: Beck Hall, Claverly, Apley Court, Westmorley, Randolph and Dunster.

Joe would long remember his first encounter with the "Gold Coast" crowd. On a crisp autumn day he was walking down Mount Auburn Street when three young men approached. Dressed alike in white pants and blue jackets, their faces browned from rowing with the crew, they sauntered along the tree-lined street, their arms resting on each other's shoulders, smug expressions on their faces. Laughing and talking, caught up in the pleasure of their own conversation, they took no notice of Joe, but turned into Claverly Hall and closed the door. Nothing else happened, yet Joe later recalled feeling a strange longing as he watched the threesome go by, as if he were glimpsing a world he would never really know, a world he would never touch. It was a melancholy feeling he would experience again.

Not that Joe was lost or lonely at Harvard. On the contrary, he arrived with his own circle of friends from Boston Latin, including three other Joes—Sheehan, Donovan and Merrill—and as a warm and confident young man, a leader and a champion ballplayer, he reached out to create more friendships. He made friends with Tom Campbell, a fellow Catholic with a spontaneous wit. Through Campbell, Joe met Bob Fisher, a magnificent athlete who, to save money, was commuting to school from his home in the Boston suburb of Dorchester. Recognizing how difficult this was for Fisher, Joe invited him to share his room at Perkins Hall. Fisher happily took up the offer, and the two men became the closest of friends. It was, Campbell observed, the start of a lifelong triple friendship.

Then, through the freshman baseball team, which Joe easily made, he met Robert Sturgis Potter, a scion of an old Philadelphia family, a graduate of St. Mark's and a resident in Randolph Hall, perhaps the most sought-after dorm along the Gold Coast. Soon Potter became a regular visitor to Joe's quarters at Perkins Hall.

Joe, it was agreed by all, had a rare gift for friendship. Wanting all his friends to like each other, he took the time and the pains to keep the circle together. Every Sunday he engaged Campbell, Fisher and Potter in a ritual excursion to his family's home in Winthrop, six miles from Cambridge. The Kennedy house was huge and rambling, with a wide porch that fronted on a large green lawn and backed on Boston Harbor. Here they were able to enjoy the comforts of a warm and welcoming home. As Joe's sister Margaret recalled, these Sunday visits were always "the climax of the week." Mrs. Kennedy and her two girls prepared a festive supper for upwards of twenty people, including one or two neighbors and the young girlfriends of

Joe's sisters. Then, after supper, everyone would gather around the grand piano for a spirited evening of music and song. "Even as a youth," Margaret concluded, "Joe understood the meaning of life and loved it."

In their sophomore year, Joe and his friends emerged as leaders of their class; whenever committees were appointed or nominations announced, the names of Kennedy, Potter, Fisher and Campbell headed the lists. So it came as no surprise when all four young men were tapped, early in their sophomore year, for membership in the Institute of 1770—an essential first step in being considered for one of the small exclusive clubs that stood at the summit of Harvard's social hierarchy. There was a special honor in being chosen early, for then a man was admitted to an inner club within the club known as the Delta Kappa Epsilon, or the Dickey. It was a mark of distinction that Joe Kennedy and his three friends made the Dickey together.

But Rose Kennedy saw it differently. "I am now convinced," she said years later, "that being selected for the Dickey was the worst thing that could have happened to Joe, for it spawned in his heart the illusory hope that it qualified him as a good bet for membership in one of the exclusive final clubs. . . . It would have hurt him less, I believe, if he had accepted the social divisions at Harvard from the very start."

In figuring that the clubmen would be won over to him in spite of themselves, Joe failed to understand that for many of these men the decision to choose a member meant a lifetime commitment to seeing the man in a corresponding club in Boston or New York. So being club material meant not simply having a jovial personality; it meant having come from the right family, the right school, the same station in life.

Still, Joe persisted in believing that for *his* class and with *his* friends it would be different. After all, his gregariousness had allowed him, time and again, to cross the borders of class, wealth and standing.

Joe's illusions were finally dispelled in the late winter of his sophomore year, when the final clubs held their first round of elections for new members. It was the custom in those days for the entire membership of each club to march together through the streets with the treasured invitations in their hands while all the hopeful sophomores remained anxiously in their rooms, waiting for a tap on their door. Then, as each new member was informed, he would join the others as they wended their way to the quarters of the next person chosen, until everyone on the list had been notified.

All that day Joe had remained in his quarters, his proud soul undaunted as the hours slipped by. In the afternoon, a singing procession of Digammas had burst into their room and carried Fisher off into the street. Taking comfort in Fisher's good fortune, Kennedy redoubled his belief that it was only a matter of time until one of the clubs came for him. But as the day faded, he was forced to acknowledge that no one was coming. Finally, he put on his coat and went out. Walking mechanically through Harvard Yard, he found himself across the street from the most coveted of all final clubs, the Porcellian, which boasted a total of nine Adamses, seven Lowells and eleven Cabots in its hundred-and-fifty-year history. Joe, drawn like a moth to the lighted window above, tried to imagine what it was like inside. But the Porcellian would remain forever a thing of mystery and fascination to him, for its tradition dictated that no Harvard man who was not a member could ever step across the threshold.

Standing there, Joe later told Rose, he suddenly realized that Harvard was a tougher place than he had understood. What he had mistaken for a progressive campus was, in fact, an intolerant island on which the religion of the fathers was laid upon their sons. Was it sheer coincidence that Fisher and Potter, the two Protestants, were both taken into clubs while not a single one of Joe's Catholic friends had been asked? More than Joe had realized, there were dozens of places in *his* school where, no matter what he did, he would never be welcome. And the realization hurt him deeply. Harvard had ripped something out of him that night, and never again would he experience loyalty to any institution or any organization. In the place of that loyalty, resentment had crystallized hard as rock; whether he knew it or not, his siege against the world had already begun.

ALL THESE MONTHS while Joe was finishing up his freshman and sophomore years at Harvard, Rose Fitzgerald had been away—first at the convent school in Holland, then at Manhattanville in

New York. But the time apart only seemed to increase their affection for each other, and now that Rose had settled back into Boston, Joe could no longer tolerate merely carrying the relationship along. The time had come to get his girl.

And he did. Rose later remembered his final years at Harvard as the time she fell "more and more in love." In the afternoons she and Joe would meet on the steps of University Hall with the beautiful expanse of the college grounds stretching before them, and they would take long walks together—past the vine-covered walls of the venerable old buildings and out to the surrounding streets of Cambridge. One of their favorite rambles took them to the winding Charles River, where they would talk about their future life together. Anyone who knew anything about Rose or Joe could tell they were in love. Yet for years the seriousness of their relationship had to be kept camouflaged. The reason was that Rose's father objected strenuously to young Joe Kennedy. John Fitzgerald, it seemed, did not believe that the son of P. J. Kennedy was good enough for his treasured daughter. Some writers have suggested that Fitzgerald had his heart set upon a different suitor, a sensible, well-mannered young man by the name of Hugh Nawn, who was the son of one of Fitzgerald's best friends, a wealthy Catholic contractor. Fitzgerald believed young Nawn was just what a young man ought to be—solid, well bred and considerate, with a fine future before him as the heir to his father's firm.

Perhaps Fitzgerald truly did believe that Nawn would make a better husband for Rose than Joe Kennedy. But from all that is known of the powerful bonds that held Fitzgerald to his favorite child, it is more likely that he sensed in Joe Kennedy a formidable rival for his daughter's heart, a dark threat to his exclusive attachment to her. How much easier the thought of separation must have seemed if the entire courtship could be subject to *his* design.

In choosing Nawn, Fitzgerald never spoke disparagingly of Joe Kennedy. While he denied permission for Rose to accept most of Joe's invitations, he would relent on others. Moreover, while letting Rose know that Joe was not a welcome guest in their house, Fitzgerald would invite young Nawn to dinner, to the theater, to family outings. Fitzgerald's maneuvers, however, created a dilemma for Rose. "I adored Joe," she later wrote. "I also adored my parents and certainly didn't want to offend or deceive them."

But, more than she may have realized at the time, Rose had a will of her own; despite her attachment to her father, she would not allow his will to dominate her completely. So it was "with pangs of conscience" that she began to see Joe more often than she was supposed to, more often than her father knew.

For his part, Joe was at his best in a situation like this. Fitzgerald's opposition only sweetened the prize and strengthened his determination. Fitzgerald, for all his contagious charm, was up against a will far stronger and more single-minded than his own.

7

THE BALANCE SHIFTS

MUCH OF YOUNG JOE was pure P. J. Kennedy. He had his father's shrewd intelligence, his organizational ability and his good common sense. All his working life, P.J. had moved cautiously, never expanding his enterprises beyond his capacity to control them, always preparing his way carefully for the next move. It was a prudence rooted in his early life. While P.J. was still an infant, his thirty-five-year-old father had died from cholera. P.J.'s mother, Bridget, nearly destitute and with four small children to support, went to work in a notions shop to keep her family together. As the only son, P.J. had to grow up faster than many children, leaving school to take a job on the docks when he was only fourteen. Yet he had managed to keep his eye on the future, dividing his wages between his family's needs and a small savings account. When the time was right, he purchased a modest tavern in Haymarket Square.

With P.J.'s hard work the tavern prospered, and within several years, while still in his early twenties, P.J. was able to buy into two more. Before he was thirty he had established his own liquor-importing business. From this clever and cautious man, young Joe learned the value of looking forward before acting.

But Joe had a more adventurous, defiant strain too. Joe's

mother, Mary Augusta Hickey, was remembered by a grand-daughter as "an amazingly quick-witted woman with an exceptional mind capable of perceiving humor in almost any situation." Under her imaginative guidance, Joe's mind developed an irreverent quality, a rich counterpart to the sensible, conservative streak inherited from his father.

As the firstborn, Joe held a special place in his mother's heart, a position of privilege substantially fortified when his younger brother Francis died from diphtheria at the age of two. "The death of the baby was so unexpected and so senseless," the granddaughter recalled, "that her only way of coping was to pour even more love onto Joe." The death of young Frank affected P.J.'s relations with his only remaining son as well. "However busy P.J. was with his work or his politics, he always found the time to spend with Joe." As Joe grew older, his two younger sisters, Loretta and Margaret, responded to his primacy by "adoring him all their lives."

In light of his upbringing, it is no surprise that Joe walked through Boston Latin and Harvard with an assured step. This self-confidence found its expression at the end of school, when the moment came to choose his career. Although it was then the conventional wisdom that politics provided the surest road to power for an ambitious Irish youth, especially for the son of P. J. Kennedy, "I never felt I had the temperament to be a politician," Joe told a friend. "I couldn't stand to watch the incessant demands being placed on my father's time. Never was there a single moment when someone didn't want something from him; never was there a single stretch of peaceful time."

Joe's mother believed that people were sponging on P.J. because he was known as a soft touch for anyone with a hard-luck story. Yet, to P.J., personal generosity was simply part of his job as the boss of his district. Tall, lean and gentlemanly, he had about him an air of wisdom and dignity, and he took deep pleasure in helping others, whereas Joe always placed himself and his family first.

His rejection of politics as a young man, however, sprang from a source deeper than his temperamental dislike for the daily traffic with people in need. He was impelled by an irresistible longing for power, and from his personal observation, politics was not the surest route to real power. "It doesn't make any difference," he told a reporter in 1914, "how high a young man may rise in politics, nor how brilliant his future may seem, his ultimate defeat is inevitable." Joe spoke from experience, for he had seen his father deeply hurt by a stunning defeat. The upset had occurred in the fall of Joe's freshman year at Harvard. After serving eight successive terms in the state legislature, P.J. had left elective office to return to his position as boss of his local ward. But then, at the urging of both Mayor Fitzgerald and his friend Judge Corbett, the old warrior reluctantly agreed to run for the influential position of street commissioner. As a prominent figure in Boston politics, P.J. seemed a certain victor. It was this expectation of sure triumph that made his defeat—at the hands of a little-known opponent—so startling in its impact.

P.J. faced his defeat as he seemed to face almost everything in his life, with gentle dignity and good-humored complacency. But never again would he seek adventure in the larger political world. And in his tired eyes, the perceptive young Joe Kennedy saw that, underneath, the elder Kennedy was grieving like a child. To Joe, the experience suggested that nothing wears out faster than generosity and that political loyalty and gratitude were easily bought and sold.

It was then and there, it seems, that Joe determined to lay his foundation on what was under *his* control, rather than being dependent on the fickleness of public favor. As he saw it, the only way to guarantee power was to establish a base of financial success.

From that base a man of wealth could do as he pleased.

From the very first, young Kennedy had known how to make money. As a child Joe sold candy to excursion-boat passengers on the docks; at the age of ten he entered and won a soap-selling contest. As a teenager he organized his friends into a profit-making baseball team, and while still at Harvard he ran his first real business. Using the money he had accumulated from his smaller enterprises, Joe and his friend Joe Donovan bought a tour bus and went into the sight-seeing business together, with Donovan as driver and Kennedy as tour guide. By sprucing up their bus and by securing rights to Boston's choicest bus stands, the enterprising partners cleared a spectacular profit of ten thousand dollars in a single year of operation. Joe seemed to know instinctively how to use money to make money.

BY THE TIME Joe Kennedy graduated from Harvard on the sunny morning of June 23, 1912, he knew he wanted to be a businessman, and he intended to start out in the field of banking. "I saw, even in my limited dealings, that sooner or later the source of business was traced to the banks." He concluded that "banking was the basic business profession" and that it "could lead a man anywhere."

In this belief, Joe was not alone. Indeed, the turn of the century was the age of the banker, so much so that the leading bankers of the day had become legendary figures whose colossal power seemed to reach everywhere and who lived on a scale appropriate to their power. John Pierpont Morgan, the most towering of them all, possessed a luxurious mansion on Thirty-sixth Street in New York City, sumptuous apartments in the world's leading cities, a country house on the Hudson, and a lavish three-hundred-foot yacht; he entertained in a baroque style; he courted beautiful women and owned what was then considered the greatest art collection in the modern era, including magnificent paintings, porcelains, bronzes, precious manuscripts and jewelry. His partners and allies, too, moved in an extravagant world of conspicuous prosperity.

To a young man of Joe Kennedy's immense ambitions, the image of the banker was irresistibly attractive. For in Boston, even more than in New York, the leading bankers monopolized not only power but also prestige and privilege. Recruited almost exclusively from the oldest Brahmin families, they occupied the most favored place in Boston's social and cultural life. This financial elite had so concentrated its banking capital that over ninety percent of the city's banking resources were held by the two largest banks. All but six banks were connected by interlocking directorates cemented by mutual stockholdings, co-directorships and family ties.

The very existence of this closed economic circle suggests the enormousness of the task confronting young Kennedy. As one historian has written, Joe was choosing "an occupation where his Celtic name and church would always make him a stranger." It was an act of foolishness, it was an act of courage—it all depended on the outcome.

Joe's initial advance into the world of banking came a week before his graduation from Harvard, when he secured a position as a clerk in a small East Boston bank, the Columbia Trust Company. Joe's father, P. J. Kennedy, was one of the original founders of the Columbia Trust, which opened its doors in 1895 as a people's bank, dedicated to serving the small businessmen of East Boston. On its board mingled old Yankee, Irish, Jew and Italian, reflecting the highly cosmopolitan make-up of the local population. It was a small institution compared to the large downtown banks but a good place to begin.

Joe was apprenticed to Alfred Wellington, a man who had started as a clerk himself on the day the bank had opened in 1895 and who had risen by slow but steady promotions to the position of treasurer. He was kindly, honest and completely reliable, and Joe could not have hoped to find a better first teacher. As the two men worked side by side, the master gave his protégé the best of himself. But by summer's end, Joe's unbounded ambitions had already outstripped his mentor's expectations. Seeing infinite possibility in the young man, Wellington suggested that Joe take the civil service examination to become a bank examiner. As Wellington laid it out, the best way to master the routine of banking was to be a student of all banks and not a minor functionary in a single bank.

With Wellington as his tutor, Joe passed the examination and was appointed to the state bank commissioner's department at a salary of $1,200 a year. The department's work load was staggering. According to law, each of the state's five hundred and forty-nine banking institutions had to be examined at least once a year. As a consequence, Joe spent most of his eighteen months as a bank examiner on the road. "Inspection work took me to all parts of the state," Joe later recalled, "and gave me an opportunity for a field course in banking of many kinds: in mill towns, fishing towns and the bigger multiple-industry cities. I learned that . . . we make a mistake when we call money hard cash. It's lively and fluid—the blood of business."

Each inspection would begin with the sudden arrival of a crew of examiners bursting through the doors in the style of an old western movie, the most critical part being to descend "without previous notice." For if the bank's officers were given even one hour's time, they could cover up almost anything. Upon entering the banks, the examiners took immediate possession of all cash, notes, books of accounts and the like, until a complete check had been made.

Joe turned out to be one of the most industrious bank examiners the state banking commission had ever known. Within a matter of months, he knew the financial structure of many banks even better than the bankers themselves. He knew which banks had made questionable loans and which ones had failed to comply with the provisions of the law. He knew from what types of people different banks drew their depositors, and to which businesses they gave their loans. He knew which banks were expanding and which were retrenching and why. With his ability to make decisions unswayed by sentiment, he had found weaknesses and shortcomings in even the most established institutions. Never would the gleaming beauty of a bank's marble floors blind him to the possibility that the structure below might well be unworthy of the public's praise. Never would he delude himself with the ornamental appearances of institutions or people. "There are no big shots," he determined, coining an aphorism that was to guide him through the rest of his days.

WHILE JOE WAS becoming a familiar figure in the banking district, preparing the ground for all the dazzling conquests he would eventually make in the world of finance, the fortunes of John Fitzgerald were moving in the opposite direction. Ironically, in the final months of his mayorship, he appeared more popular with the people of Boston than he had ever been. Indeed, so much had been accomplished in his second term that many credited him with the commercial revival of the city. Now, nourishing visions of a contest against Henry Cabot Lodge two years hence for the U.S. Senate, Fitzgerald was saying he would not be a candidate for reelection to the mayor's office.

Taking him at his word, Roxbury's congressman, James Michael Curley, began planning his own campaign for mayor. Possessed of a blustering demeanor and superb oratorical skills, Curley had burst upon the Boston scene in the early 1900s.

After a term in the common council and a stint in the State House, he had made his name a household word when he was elected to the board of aldermen from the Charles Street Jail, where he was serving a sixty-day sentence for taking the civil service exam in place of a friend. Curley had turned his disgrace into a political blessing by defending his crime as an act of heroism in overcoming a system that gave the better-schooled Yankees discriminatory advantages over the Irish.

Curley's secret charm lay in his gorgeous flights of oratory and his ability to excite people's emotions, and the more indecorous and outlandish his actions seemed, the more the Irish loved him. Now, in November 1913, he defiantly announced for mayor, warning the bosses that when he was elected he would put an abrupt end to the outmoded system of ward politics.

Curley's announcement sent a shiver through the spines of the ward bosses, who had grown accustomed to Fitzgerald's more conciliatory style and his growing respectability among the lace-curtain Irish. Fearing that Curley meant what he said about dismantling the system, the bosses put great pressure on Fitzgerald to stand for reelection one last time. After all, they said, Curley was too much a realist to fight against Fitzgerald and the bosses too. He would end Curley's campaign, and could then look forward to an uncontested nomination.

Allowing himself to be persuaded, Fitzgerald announced that he owed it to Boston to run again. It was a calamitous decision. Instead of withdrawing as predicted, Curley redoubled his resolution to remain in the race. "For one hundred or more times in the last two years," he told the Tammany Club, "the mayor has told me that he would not be a candidate for reelection. I entered the campaign three weeks before Mayor Fitzgerald announced his candidacy. I am not opposing him. He is opposing me."

Curley's surprising obstinacy created a sensation, as seasoned observers predicted the most vicious campaign in the history of the city. Yet it is unlikely that anyone, least of all Fitzgerald, could have imagined the ugly turn the struggle would take.

THERE WAS AT THIS time another man in the city who had his own reasons for coveting Fitzgerald's defeat. This was Daniel Coakley, the small, handsome lawyer who had defended Michael Mitchell in the Coal Graft Hearings. All these years, as the story is told, the thought of Fitzgerald's treachery toward Mitchell had gnawed at Coakley, and nothing would content him until he had taken revenge.

Stories differ as to when Coakley first approached Curley with the astounding piece of information on which the election would turn. Whatever the details, it is clear that Curley listened with greedy interest.

Earlier that fall, Coakley reported, he had been visited by a triumphantly beautiful young woman named Elizabeth Ryan, who asked him to represent her in a $50,000 damage suit against a Mr. Henry Mansfield for his alleged breach of promise to marry her.

According to her story, she was a good girl corrupted by a bad world. Having grown up on a small farm in Connecticut, she had lived a wholesome life until one luckless day when she saw New York City for the first time. Lured by visions of bright lights and expensive clothes, she left her country ways behind, painted her lips, reddened her cheeks and found herself a job as a model in a department store. Then came "the event of her life." On a weekend jaunt to Boston she met the man of her dreams, Harry Mansfield.

Proprietor of the popular Ferncroft Inn in Middleton, outside of Boston, the forty-year-old Mansfield was an agreeably wealthy man, and witnesses agreed that he was instantly taken by Miss Ryan's beauty. While it was never proved that he had ever promised to marry her, he did shower her with costly gifts. She also spent months at a time at his Ferncroft Inn, where, under the name of Toodles, she was variously employed as a cigarette girl, a cashier and an entertainer. The importance of all this for Coakley came when Toodles listed the names of other admirers she had attracted, for among them was the mayor, John F. Fitzgerald. Often, she said, he would invite her to join his party, pulling her close to him when they danced, flirting with her for hours and smothering her with kisses.

No sooner had Miss Ryan volunteered this information than Coakley knew he had his weapon against Fitzgerald. The only question was how to use it. While there was nothing in Toodles' testimony on Fitzgerald that would stand up in a court of law,

John and Josie Fitzgerald vacationing in Palm Beach

the scheming Coakley, who was a master of insinuation, knew that just one cartooned image of Fitzgerald kissing the voluptuous Toodles—with her enormous chest daringly revealed—would be enough to transform this pillar of the community into a fool.

Mansfield's subsequent trial for breach of promise, which took place in January of 1915, received full and lurid treatment in the press: FITZ KISSING RYAN, TOODLES COLLAPSES ON STAND. But Fitzgerald was mentioned only once, in the testimony of a man who claimed that he had seen the mayor kissing Toodles on a September night in 1912. Yet if Fitzgerald was an innocent victim being drawn into a trap, it was, Coakley argued, precisely the kind of entrapment the mayor had committed against poor Michael Mitchell.

In deciding to go to Curley with his information, Coakley had gambled wisely. Not many politicians would have been willing to employ such a crass personal attack. But Curley was not a man to be limited by conventions of taste. He appreciated that the only chance he had of besting Fitzgerald was to *force* him to withdraw from the race.

On the first day of December, 1913, Curley had a black-bordered letter delivered to the house on Welles Avenue, informing Mrs. Fitzgerald that unless the mayor withdrew from the race, the family's reputation would be exposed to the scandal of her husband's relationship with a twenty-three-year-old cigarette girl named Toodles. From that moment on, everything was in confusion in the Fitzgerald household. While the family had weathered other storms before—popular rumors had long asserted that Fitzgerald chased after pretty women—this time Josie took it into her head that the only way to avert public humiliation was for her husband to get out of the race.

For Fitzgerald the situation was hopeless. As he later confided to a friend, the worst moment of his life was when he walked into the house and found his wife standing in the hallway with furious indignation on her face and the infamous letter in her hand. Worse still was the look of pain on his favorite daughter's face as she stood in silence behind her mother. Still hoping he could ride out the storm, Fitzgerald tried to persuade Josie that they could stand their ground with pride and call the blackmailer's bluff. To back away now would be to cut himself off forever from the respect of the bosses. But Josie was adamant. The one thing she refused to risk was her family's hard-earned aura of respectability.

Fitzgerald was trapped. He felt, he told his secretary, Edward Moore, as if he were walking in a nightmare. He was unable to sleep. Yet life had to be lived and engagements kept until he decided how to respond to Curley's threat. Eventually, the pressure was too much, even for a man of his strength, and he literally collapsed.

It happened while he was making a personal inspection tour of the city's cheap lodging houses, in the wake of a devastating fire that had trapped a hundred and seventy sleeping lodgers. By the end of the all-day tour, reporters observed, the fifty-year-old mayor was feeling unusually weak. But he insisted on making a second tour of the worst lodging houses, and it was at one of these that his body finally gave way. "Mayor Fitzgerald collapsed and narrowly escaped serious injury," the Boston *Herald* reported, "when he fell headlong down a flight of stairs" and "came within an ace of falling over the railing to a narrow hallway twenty feet below." He was caught by his secretary before he went over, but as it was, "he struck his head heavily against the rail and his helpless body fell limp into the arms of a reporter." According to another report, "an examination by his physician showed that the mayor had overtaxed his brain and body to such an extent that he must temporarily quit his activities if he wishes to fully recover."

In the days that followed, reporters and politicians alike monitored Fitzgerald's condition closely. To the surprise of those who knew him, he seemed to be rallying only slowly.

In this unquiet time, Curley determined to shed some further blood. He decided to deliver three public lectures as a means of contrasting Mayor Fitzgerald and certain famous men in history. The first of these was entitled "Graft in Ancient Times versus Graft in Modern Times." The second would be "Great Lovers in History: From Cleopatra to Toodles," while the third would deal with "Libertines in History from Henry the Eighth to the Present Day."

As it turned out, Curley found it unnecessary to deliver any but the first lecture. On December 18, with a great sense of melancholy, Fitzgerald announced that he was withdrawing from the race on the advice of his physician. With Fitzgerald out, Curley went on to become the thirty-eighth mayor of Boston and from there to forge an astonishing political career, which saw him elected mayor three more times, congressman twice and governor once.

The news of the mayor's withdrawal created a sensation. To withdraw at the height of his power cost him the esteem of his fellow politicians and left his name forever under a cloud of gossip. Having lost the respect of his peers, Fitzgerald lost his confidence in himself; despite a number of comeback attempts, in 1916, 1918, 1922, 1930 and 1942, he never won an election again.

The Toodles incident seems to have affected relationships within the Fitzgerald family as well. Rose was profoundly disturbed by the revelations about her father and a beautiful young girl who was, after all, only twenty-three years old—the same age as Rose herself. While Josie had long since made her peace with Fitzgerald's passionate nature, Rose had never allowed herself to imagine in him the existence of human weakness. Although she felt sorry for her father for having lost his kingdom, she also felt angry.

In the long run, however, the tawdry incident had a positive influence on her, for it left her freer to shape a life of her own.

For seven years she had been struggling with her father's displeasure with Joe, powerless to break away. But now the question of her marriage presented itself in a different aspect. As one friend suggested, "She began to realize that the choice of a husband was ultimately *her* choice and not her parents'. While she had given up Wellesley College for her father, she would not give up Joe Kennedy as well."

WHILE THE FITZGERALDS were absorbed in their own affairs in the fall of 1913, Joe Kennedy decided that the time had come to leave his job as an examiner and get a start on his lifework. Although his job was fascinating, he longed to be on his own, in a position where he could decide policies and direct others.

The opportunity came when P. J. Kennedy's bank, the Columbia Trust Company, found itself threatened by a hostile takeover by the First Ward National, the largest bank in East Boston. For P.J., the bank's vice president, and Alfred Wellington, its treasurer, the takeover presaged the end of a dream, the dream of a neighborhood bank run in the interests of local people. With the president of the bank lined up in favor of the merger, and without enough money of their own to buy out the other stockholders, there seemed little hope that P.J. and Wellington could block the deal. Still wanting to try, however, and believing it would be a good experience for his son, P.J. called upon Joe to organize a fight.

It was the perfect situation for Joe. Reckoning he would need at least $100,000 to stave off the takeover, he set to work, turning first to his relatives and then to his neighbors and friends, slowly building up the war chest he needed to mount his resistance. By appealing to local pride and ethnic identity, he managed to win the support of many stockholders, and finally, after two weeks of unremitting effort, he gained control of a majority of the shares. In the end, First Ward National, having been outmaneuvered, retired from the battle. That was on January 19, 1914. The next day, in gratitude to Joe for single-handedly saving the bank, P. J. Kennedy, Alfred Wellington and all the shareholders unanimously elected Joseph P. Kennedy president of the Columbia Trust Company.

The next morning Joe awoke to find himself the subject of admiring articles in all the Boston papers. Reporters hailed him as "the youngest man to hold the presidency of a banking house in the state of Massachusetts." Nor did the publicity stop in Boston. A large family scrapbook contains clippings about "the youngest bank president," from remote papers from all over the country.

Henceforth, Joe would be the guiding force in the family. His father, having declined reelection as vice president of the bank, would from now on stand by, his pipe in his mouth, proud and admiring but never interfering.

WITH JOE'S STRIKING CHANGE in status, Fitzgerald finally consented to the marriage. Though still troubled by the match, he conceded that his only hope in preserving a close relationship with his favorite child lay in accepting her desire to marry this remarkable young man.

Thus it was that on October 7, 1914, Rose Elizabeth Fitzgerald became the wife of Joseph Patrick Kennedy in a traditional Catholic ceremony performed by William Cardinal O'Connell in his exquisite private chapel. Only the immediate families of the bride and groom were present at the early morning Mass, which was followed by a wedding breakfast at the Fitzgerald house for about seventy-five guests. For a young couple descended from two prominent families, whose marriage was said to have excited "much interest throughout the city," the wedding was startlingly simple. Rose suggests that neither the bride nor the groom wanted "a public fiesta." But one wonders whether the plainness of the event did not also reflect a lingering political shame on the part of John Fitzgerald.

The young couple took their departure in the early afternoon under a bright autumn sky and traveled to White Sulphur Springs, West Virginia, to the majestic Greenbrier Hotel, surrounded by splendid mountains, winding streams and flowering meadows. There, for the next three weeks, Joe and Rose would spend hardly an hour apart, taking breakfast on the terrace, playing golf, dining in the evening by candlelight. And there, from the best one can tell by the timing of the birth, the first of their nine children was conceived.

On returning to Boston, the young Kennedys settled into a modest gray clapboard house on a shaded street in the suburb of Brookline, which Joe had purchased before the wedding. "From the very beginning," Rose later asserted, "home was the center of his world and the only place that really, finally counted in his plans."

With Joe working at the bank twelve hours a day, six days a week, there was little time for socializing. If Rose had envisaged her early married life as a continuation of her girlhood days, filled with parties and balls and first-night boxes at the theater, she must have been sorely disappointed. For while she continued to see her girlfriends at various luncheons and at her club, the life she was leading was undoubtedly quieter and more solitary than the life she had known as the daughter of the mayor and the belle of Catholic society.

There was little time to dwell on these matters, however, for Rose soon discovered she was going to be a mother, the "sacred role" for which she had been trained by the nuns of the Sacred Heart. The child was due at the end of July, and that summer, Joe rented an airy gray house in Hull, on a sandy hook of land that curved far out in Massachusetts Bay. There, in the fresh sea air, surrounded by her parents and their friends, Rose awaited the birth.

In common with the way most women gave birth in those days, Rose had her baby at home with the help of attendants, in her case two doctors, a nurse and a housemaid. Joe did what most expectant fathers were expected to do, paced the floor in a separate room. Finally, just as the clock struck ten on the morning of July 25, 1915, the doctors stepped out into the sitting room to announce the event. "A boy," they said to the father. Weighing nearly ten pounds, he was handsome and alert, his eyes bright blue, his complexion fair.

If reporters failed to record the father's response to the newborn child, it was because their eyes were fixed upon a different star. "It's Grandpa now," the Boston *Post* announced, setting the tone for a spate of stories about John Fitzgerald, who called the press to announce that he was quite "the happiest man" in the world. "No, I don't know what we'll make of the youngster. . . . He can yell all right and I'm sure he'd make a good man on the platform. . . . Of course he *is* going to be President of the United States, his mother and father have already decided that he is going to Harvard, where he will play on the football and baseball teams and incidentally take all the scholastic honors. Then he's going to be a captain of industry until it's time for him to be President. . . . Further than that has not been decided."

Reporters, that day, seemed genuinely struck by the radiant happiness they saw on Fitzgerald's face. And the best was yet to come. Compared with the pleasures of grandfathering, the experiences Fitzgerald had with his own children, particularly his sons, were filled with frustration. In his own household he was an overwhelming figure, and his sons would remain "Honey Fitz's boys" all their lives: one would eventually drink himself to death, another would stay at a low-level job with the Boston Edison Company and the third would serve as a bridge toll collector as his nephew prepared for the presidency of the United States.

But as the demands of his own life subsided, something gave way in Fitzgerald's heart that allowed him to let go and love his grandchildren with a nonjudgmental love that was impossible for him as a parent. All of his grandchildren spoke of him in glowing terms as "the warmest and most wonderful friend" and "the best grandfather a grandchild could ever have." With the magic of his companionship would come all the wonderful tales of the past, communicating to his young admirers a sense of the continuity of life as it sweeps from generation to generation.

All this, of course, was in the future. At the time of the birth, reporters speculated that the baby would be named John Fitzgerald Kennedy after his maternal grandfather. But if Fitzgerald was still the more powerful figure on the Boston scene, his son-in-law was indisputably the power in his own family. And Joe wanted his firstborn son to carry his own name—Joseph Patrick Kennedy—which would link this golden child of the bright blue eyes with three generations of Josephs and Patricks, stretching back to the homestead in Ireland whence the first Patrick had come.

BOOK TWO

THE KENNEDYS (1915–1940)

8

LEARNING THE TRICKS OF THE TRADE

So GENTLE WAS THE surf along the white sands of New England's shore that tranquil summer of 1915 that the happy young parents of Joseph P. Kennedy, Jr., could not possibly have comprehended the unremitting slaughter of the bitter war raging in Europe. As the first dispatches came to the United States, accompanied by photographs of uniformed soldiers marching to the front, most Americans viewed the struggle as just another of Europe's endless internecine squabbles, far from the primary concerns of their lives. But as the battles widened, the European crisis began to dominate the headlines, and, inevitably, Americans became emotionally involved.

Then came the succession of German submarine attacks on Allied shipping, culminating in the sinking of the great British liner *Lusitania.* Nearly twelve hundred people perished, among them a hundred and twenty-eight Americans, and the disaster stirred a strident outcry against Germany.

Joe Kennedy, however, refused to be swayed by the sound of the drum. "Joe could never accept the idea that war had a nobility of its own," Rose recalled. "He could never really believe that all that killing and bloodshed could ever settle anything." Cool and mature at the age of twenty-six, he was too realistic and too absorbed in his own ambitions to be swept away by a sentiment as vague and remote as patriotism.

Joe's early vision of the war comes down to us through Rose's vivid recollection of an embattled conversation that took place between Joe and his buddies Bob Potter, Tom Campbell and

Bob Fisher in 1916. Kennedy had brought them all together for a long Fourth of July weekend at his parents' house in Winthrop, and from the affectionate way the young men greeted one another at the start, Rose was certain it would be a joyous reunion.

There was much for these old friends to talk about. Campbell was coaching football at the University of North Carolina; Fisher had taken an executive job with a Boston department store, where his future seemed bright; and Potter had a plum job with the prestigious National Shawmut Bank, the third largest bank in Boston.

All other conversation was eclipsed, however, by news of the beginning of the great Allied offensive at the Somme, which was being reported in the press in spectacular detail. Described as the most extensive military action ever taken, this huge offensive was expected to be the decisive battle of the war. It promised once and for all to break through the bloody deadlock in the bitter trench warfare that had taken hundreds of thousands of lives since the winter of 1914. The most important element of the British plan was an immense artillery attack against the German frontline trenches, designed to destroy German guns and force their troops to withdraw. Then the Allied infantry could mount its offensive—could merely walk across the "no-man's-land" and occupy the deserted trenches.

The British artillery bombardment, unprecedented in its fury, had already begun when Joe's friends arrived in Winthrop on Friday night. The great offensive was expected to be launched at any moment.

Saturday morning, July 1, dawned hot and steamy in Winthrop, sending the Kennedy party to the beach, where, Rose remembered, "the boys had a wonderful time swimming, playing ball and joking around." But just as they were planning to go boating, a newsboy appeared with extra editions of the Boston *Globe,* announcing that the Allied offensive had officially begun. With copies of the newspapers under their arms, the men walked back to the house.

To a man, Joe's friends were deeply moved by the stirring accounts of the battle. "Great waves of men," the finest body of soldiers England had ever produced, rushed forward toward their goal, singing. Tearing across the uneven ground, they were met with an unexpected hurricane of German shells, but still they advanced, "cheering through the machine-gun fire as if it were just the splashing of rain." Thousands of young Britons dropped on the field, but the others went on, "with a spirit of self-sacrifice beyond the ordinary courage of men." According to *The New York Times*, it was a scene of "terrible beauty."

As Rose recalled, Joe listened to the enthusiasms of his friends and "merely shook his head with sadness." But as the hours went by, and the fortunes of the British Expeditionary Force became the only topic of conversation, Joe finally turned to his friends and said their "whole attitude was strange and incomprehensible to him." As he saw it, "thousands of young men were dying out there on that bloody field." He could not believe that "all those men would go to their deaths singing" and cheering. No matter how correspondents tried to romanticize it, Joe said, it "had to be intolerably painful and horribly lonely." Worse still, he warned them, "by accepting the idea of the grandeur of the struggle, they were contributing to the momentum of a senseless war, certain to ruin the victors as well as the vanquished."

The vehemence of Joe's outburst placed such a strain on the gathering that Rose heaved a sigh of relief when the weekend finally came to an end. "I can still remember how quiet the house seemed after Joe's friends had gone," Rose recalled. "When I went upstairs, I could hear only the even breathing of our baby in his crib. Just then, Joe, too, came into the bedroom and looked down at our sleeping child. 'This is the only happiness that lasts,' he said softly, and then he walked away."

Afterward, it became clear that the great Somme offensive was an immense human tragedy, more devastating than Joseph Kennedy in his most melancholy pessimism could have imagined. As one military historian has written, the week-long bombardment "for all its sound and fury, was inadequate to the task." The German guns were not destroyed, and the doomed British infantry, stumbling across no-man's-land with no support, were shot down in waves. Out of the 110,000 British troops who attacked on that first day, 60,000 were killed or wounded. Yet the British attack continued, and by the time it was over, casualties had reached an astounding 412,000—spelling the end of an entire generation of the nation's most promising men.

By Christmas of 1916 the war had lasted twenty-nine months, with no appreciable shift in the battle lines. A terrible gloom overcame the entire Continent as the realization set in that millions of lives had been lost to move the front a few hundred yards here or there. Still the dying went on, and the more the war cost, the more desperately both sides clung to the belief that they would win if only they could hold on long enough. Then, in April of 1917, the United States entered the war, and the nation began to mobilize at a phenomenal speed. To furnish the enormous number of men required, Congress, on May 18, enacted a selective service law authorizing the conscription of men between the ages of twenty-one and thirty.

While the vast machinery for registering, examining and classifying soldiers was being organized, the Kennedy household welcomed the birth of a second son. Born in the master bedroom of the Brookline house on May 29, 1917, the small blue-eyed boy was named John Fitzgerald Kennedy. The Boston *Post* reported that "Grandpa Fitzgerald is wearing a pleased smile" and that the day was "certainly a bright one" for the boy's father as well.

But for Joe Kennedy it was also a time of emotional distress. America's entry into the war, he feared, would shake the foundations of the world in which he and Rose had grown up. In recent weeks, first one and then another of his friends had enlisted in the armed forces. Campbell, Potter, Sheehan, Fisher, Donovan, Merrill—they all signed up. In the depths of his heart, Rose later said, Joe "believed he was right in not volunteering for the war," but increasingly he felt himself becoming "a stranger in his own circle of friends."

On June 5, one week after the birth of little Jack, as the baby was soon to be called, every man between the ages of twenty-one and thirty was required to register for military service. A massive lottery was being prepared to determine which of them would be called up and in what order. As chance would have it, Joe Kennedy was not chosen in this first lottery. And yet, as the days and weeks skipped by, Rose recalled, Joe began to feel "a sameness to his life," and a "feeling of sadness" stole into his heart. While citizens all over the country were geared into the immensity of things, as industries of every sort were converting their plants to the production of the materials of war, Joe's humdrum life at the bank was simply repeating itself. Increasingly he began to feel a desire for action. Since the war was now here, he argued, perhaps "there was nothing to do but accept the situation and turn all his efforts to winning it."

As it happened, Kennedy was presented with the ideal opportunity for joining in the action without having to expose his life to the course of a stray bullet. From the moment the United States entered the war, the primary need was for ships: for destroyers, the armed warships designed to combat German U-boats and protect Allied merchant ships; and for carrier vessels to ferry troops across the ocean and then keep them supplied. To meet this urgent need, contracts worth hundreds of millions of dollars were awarded to various shipyards, including those of the giant Bethlehem Steel Corporation. The company responded by centralizing the management of its separate plants, and as a consequence, their large Fore River plant in Quincy, Massachusetts, found itself in need of a new administrative team. Joe Kennedy was invited to apply for the office of assistant general manager.

While Kennedy had, as he later admitted, "absolutely no knowledge of shipbuilding," he did possess ripe experience in the world of finance, as well as a decisive temperament, qualities considered essential by Bethlehem Shipbuilding's vice president, Joseph Powell. Impressing upon the young man that it was "a patriotic duty for him to help in an undertaking of such national importance," Powell offered Kennedy a salary of $15,000. Accepting the offer without hesitation, Kennedy wound up his affairs by arranging for his father to succeed him as president of the Columbia Trust, then reported for work at the Fore River plant.

The plant was immense. Stretching over hundreds of acres of ground, it encompassed nearly eighty buildings and employed over seventeen thousand workers. No sooner had Kennedy arrived on the scene than he found himself caught up in the exhilarating atmosphere. The air was full of the sounds of thousands of workers laboring toward the common goal of building more ships in less time than ever before. Huge cranes hoisted and lowered flat plates of steel into the various shops, where they would be sorted out, marked and molded into shape. In each shop, teams of workers—machinists, riveters, electricians, plumbers, carpenters—competed with one another to finish their work in record time.

As assistant general manager, Joe worked harder than ever before in his life. He was involved in such varied tasks as managing the plant's railroad and settling accident claims. He also participated in the first stage of the construction of a second shipyard in nearby Squantum. It was a monumental undertaking, involving the building of huge construction sheds, a warehouse, a storehouse, a main office building, a service building, ten wooden shipways and four wet docks, as well as housing for nine thousand men and women.

Kennedy threw himself into his new duties with good temper and disciplined vigor. "The contractors began work on the 7th of October, 1917," reported the plant newspaper, and from that time on, things happened so fast that the new "Victory" plant was ready to lay the keel of its first destroyer by early the next spring.

While Kennedy was immersed in his new duties, the army was preparing for its second huge draft call. Recognizing the critical need for ships, the provost marshal had granted a special deferment for all registrants "engaged in building and manning ships," and Kennedy assumed that his claim for a deferment would automatically be granted. But his local board, apparently concluding that he was not essential to Bethlehem's program, rejected his claim and placed him in class 1, subject to immediate certification.

The news came as a shock to Kennedy. He appealed to the district board, but it upheld the local board's decision. At this point Powell reached out to his political connections in Washington. In a telegram to an official at the Emergency Fleet Corporation he argued, "There are not over six men in this establishment whose loss at this time would be felt as much as Kennedy's. . . . What can you do to help us out?" This produced the desired result. Kennedy was allowed to remain at his desk at Fore River throughout the war.

Though Kennedy achieved what he wanted at the time, there is reason to believe he felt a measure of guilt over his dealings with the draft. "He always knew," Rose later said, that "but for the grace of God and the powers of Washington" he, too, might have been among the hundreds of Harvard men killed in the war—men who had lived and loved and dreamed much as he. While he could have taken great pride in the phenomenal job Bethlehem was doing, he was increasingly disturbed by the growing gulf that divided him from his friends. And the feeling of alienation grew stronger still in the summer of 1918, when Campbell and Potter and hundreds of thousands of other American doughboys sailed away for the bloody battlegrounds of France. These fresh American troops, healthy and strong, would add the strength the Allies needed to repel the last, convulsive German offensives and to launch a counteroffensive of their own.

WHILE PEOPLE WERE preoccupied with the war, a deadly new virus was invading the United States. Known now as the influenza epidemic of 1918, it encircled the globe at frightful speed and killed more people in less time than any other catastrophe known to man.

Boston was the first city in America to be struck by the flu when, in August, two sailors reported to sick bay with a sudden illness, the passage from apparent health to near prostration having taken only one or two hours. On the next day eight new cases were reported, and, within two weeks, two thousand officers and men of the First Naval District had contracted the flu. From Boston the disease moved inland, and as doctors stood helplessly by, the killer flu spread throughout Massachusetts, reaching its peak in the fall. In Boston, all theaters, schools, churches, dance halls and other places of public assembly were closed. Five hundred doctors and a thousand nurses came to Massachusetts from the Midwest. But still the sick increased in number, overflowing the hospitals until there were no rooms and no ambulances left. Funeral bells tolled all day long.

The Bethlehem shipyard, with twenty-six thousand people now working and living together in close quarters, became a breeding ground for the disease. Within days, the most vigorous of them were unaccountably ill. "They'd be sick one day—gone the next," said one physician. But the urgent work of building ships had to go on. Joseph Kennedy was put in charge of coordinating the plant's response to the crisis. His task was to convert a large dormitory into an emergency hospital, gather beds, linens and medical supplies, and recruit a staff of doctors and nurses—all at a time when shortages of hospital supplies were endemic. Kennedy was not to be thwarted, however, and before he went to sleep that first night the first patients had been admitted to the hospital.

At the height of the epidemic, Kennedy's body began to register the strain he was under, and he fell victim to a severe attack of ulcers. And all the while he had another private worry, for when the flu first broke out in Boston, Rose was in her final weeks of pregnancy with her third child, and pregnant women were particularly susceptible to the disease. On September 13, 1918, however, she was delivered of a girl, Rosemary. It was, Rose later reported, "a normal delivery."

IN THE FALL of 1918, before the winter months set in, the flu epidemic finally subsided and the Great War came to an end. On the eleventh hour of the eleventh day of the eleventh month, an official German delegation met with representatives of the Allied powers and ended four years of the worst fighting the world had ever known.

With the ending of the war, the spirit that had guided the work of the Fore River shipyard disappeared, and the pace slackened. Now, without the common challenge of beating the German submarines and with scores of superfluous ships lying idle at their wharves, there was a bleakness in the air. Gazing one wintry evening over the deserted yard, Kennedy was struck with the stillness of the place: all the riveters, riggers and machinists had departed. Never in all the crowded hours he had spent at his wartime desk had Kennedy seen the plant so absolutely quiet. Aware that nothing short of another war would bring back the industry's spectacular productivity, he determined then and there that the time had come for a new adventure.

Already his mind was stirring with an uncannily intuitive

sense that a new economic age was in the making—a wildly prosperous era expressly inviting his exploration and conquest. "The key to Kennedy's spectacular financial success," said a longtime friend, "was his anticipation of the future. His vision of what lay down the road was simply phenomenal." Now, in the world's first peacetime spring in four years, he saw that things were shaping up for a great boom in the stock market, and he resolved to be at the center of the action.

Kennedy could not have entered the stock market at a more auspicious time. America was on the threshold of the twenties, a golden decade when her people would enjoy the highest standard of living they had ever known, an era when, thanks to innovations in mass production, men and women of moderate means were able for the first time to buy a dizzying multitude of consumer products. Purchased on the installment plan, automobiles, radios, vacuum cleaners, washing machines, iceless refrigerators and more would transform daily life in millions of households. At the same time, stimulated by the optimism of the decade, people who had never dreamed of entering the stock market now began to buy and sell shares on margin (that is, financing their purchases largely on credit and paying only a small "margin" in cash). Never before had a speculative boom engaged so many people or permeated the life of the nation so deeply.

With typical deliberateness, Kennedy charted his course. Anxious to make the most fitting entrance into the securities world, he determined to join the venerable Boston brokerage house of Hayden, Stone and Company. Founded in 1892 by Charles Hayden and Galen Stone, the company was a leading investment banking institution, specializing in financing young companies with strong growth potential. Kennedy's first acquaintance with Galen Stone dated from two years earlier, when Kennedy was appointed to the board of trustees of the Massachusetts Electric Company. Stone, who was a fellow trustee, had impressed Kennedy profoundly with his quiet wisdom, and the two men had established a warm relationship. In July 1919, Kennedy was offered a job as a customer's man at the prestigious brokerage house, and Stone became his mentor.

The old Yankee firm was located in a handsome white granite

building in the heart of Boston's financial district. On entering Hayden, Stone's offices, the visitor was drawn at once into the large and tastefully furnished customers' room, which, with its thick Oriental rugs and costly paintings, resembled a gracious library in an exclusive men's club more than a business office. There, Joe Kennedy executed buy and sell orders for his customers, arranged for bank loans to cover the securities, and looked after all the necessary details. In the adjoining room, reaching across an entire wall, was a large board containing movable blocks of figures representing the ever changing prices of dozens of key stocks and commodities. To keep the prices up to date, a crew of board boys kept posting and reposting the quotations as fast as they came out over the ticker.

Throughout the war Kennedy had been dabbling in stocks, maintaining a small margin account with a broker. In those years, the small investor had to put up only ten percent of the price of his stocks on margin, with the broker carrying the balance of the cost. It was a dangerous practice, for it allowed the lucky few with rising stocks to pyramid a small amount of money into a fortune while leaving tens of thousands of others vulnerable to losing everything if the prices dropped—for, the moment a customer's account seemed in jeopardy, the brokerage house would protect itself by selling out the stocks.

Operating on his own, Joe had had mixed results in the wartime boom market, netting profits in some areas, losing in others. His employment at Hayden, Stone marked an important change in his approach to speculation. In the course of his first months as a customer's man he realized that the only way to make real money in the market was to concentrate all his time and energy on a limited number of prospective companies, studying every fact and contingency that might affect the value of the stock before he bought even a single share. Guided by Stone, Kennedy learned that buying and selling stocks was not a bloodless science of facts and figures, but an art that demanded a skillful interpretation of the changing moods and emotions of thousands of individual investors. Kennedy came to recognize that the forces that drove stock prices down were not the vast impersonal forces or the changing events of politics, but the human reactions to those forces and events. Indeed, as the maddeningly human aspects of the craft unfolded before Kennedy's curious eyes, he became even more certain that the game of speculation was precisely the game he most wanted to play.

Kennedy's position at Hayden, Stone placed a subtle and significant power in his clever hands. Although he was paid only $10,000 a year, his real compensation came in other ways. As an insider in the wild, unregulated market of the twenties, he found himself among the charmed circle of men who won fortunes by using confidential information to speculate in the market, by being awarded large blocks of stock in return for services rendered, and by sitting on boards of directors at a time when it was a common practice for management pools to manipulate the market for their own benefit. If one looks at any of the celebrated traders of the twenties—from Jesse Livermore to Bernard Baruch and Percy Rockefeller—one can see that all of them were profiting in one way or another from connections and information. There was, for instance, nothing unusual in the fact that Galen Stone sat on the boards of twenty-two companies whose securities he sponsored; and in such a position, it was expected, he could best protect the corporations and investors he represented.

From the first, Kennedy realized that his association with Stone, if properly used, would give him enormous purchasing power. Recognizing that Stone never went into battle without some part of his forces held back, Kennedy set to building himself a strong cash reserve—both to protect himself from ruin and to be able to take immediate advantage of opportunity. He decided to buy the soundest securities he could find, ones that would be accepted as collateral at any bank, allowing him to pyramid his paper profits into lines of credit that he could then use to purchase more speculative stocks.

The first company that fascinated Joe was Eastern Steamship, which operated passenger steamships from Maine to Boston and from Boston to New York. Having taken the New York steamers himself, Kennedy had seen just how popular they were. Moreover, since Stone was chairman of the company's board, Kennedy knew he would be privy to anything that might affect its earnings.

Kennedy could not have chosen better. In the summer of

1919 he bought his first thousand shares of Eastern Steamship preferred, on margin, at $48 a share. It rose to 58, and it kept rising, reaching 75 in February of 1920. And all the while, Kennedy parlayed his earnings to buy more stock until he had accumulated several thousand shares. Then, in August of 1921, when Eastern Steamship crossed the line at 77½, Kennedy sold off one thousand shares, realizing $77,500 on his initial investment of $4,800—which represented the ten percent margin he had to pay for his first $48,000 worth of stock. With a sizable block of Eastern Steamship left on his account, as well as other stocks he had accumulated, there seemed no limit to the resources Kennedy now possessed.

Still, success did not come as fast as Joe had anticipated. The postwar boom market came to an end by November 1919. A sharp recession followed, and it lasted for nearly two years. As the Dow Jones Index plummeted, the young financier took some heavy losses. But under Stone's patient guidance, Kennedy learned from his mistakes.

As Kennedy watched and learned, Stone skillfully steered the firm through the recession, never losing confidence that recovery would soon be on its way. Stone was fundamentally correct. In mid-1921 the Dow Jones Index started to climb, and but for a few small dips it continued to climb through all the golden years of the twenties, reaching dizzying heights and bringing business, in the words of one historian, to "a perfect Everest of prosperity."

What a resource Galen Stone was for a man of Kennedy's ability! By spending hours with the master himself, listening and watching him make decisions, Kennedy acquired a decade of learning within the space of thirty months. The maturing apprentice was on his way.

WHILE JOE'S WORLD WAS lustily expanding, his wife's was contracting. Rose had been taught to believe that marriage was to be her great adventure, her journey's end. But with three children under five and a fourth expected, she began to feel, she later recalled, that the world outside was receding before the relentless demands of her growing family. While she reluctantly accepted her husband's need to be away from home much of the time, working long days, nights and weekends, her social nature was unprepared for the isolation of life in the quiet suburb of Brookline. As she approached her sixth year of marriage and her thirtieth birthday, she felt, in her own words, that her "life was flowing past" her.

Even harder to accept, Rose admitted long afterward, was the feeling that she was growing more and more distant from Joe. It had become increasingly clear that for Joe work existed in a special department of his mind into which he was unwilling to admit his wife. He disliked talking about business at home, and while Rose would brush off her ignorance—"My husband changed jobs so fast," she liked to say, "I simply never knew what business he was in"—there loomed within her an ancient fear: the terrible knowledge of the disintegrating effect on her parents' marriage of separate interests and concerns.

It is also possible, as some Fitzgerald relatives have suggested, that Rose was painfully aware that Joe, who enjoyed going out with his bachelor friends, was often in the company of other women. "Even in the early years of their marriage," one relative recalls, "Joe had a reputation for being a ladies' man, and some of this gossip must have caught up with Rose." In any case, her loneliness and isolation brought upon her a moody unhappiness, especially when she remembered the exciting days she had spent in her father's adventurous world.

One long wintry weekend in early 1920, while awaiting her fourth child, and with two of her three little children sick and Joe away from home, Rose suddenly wanted to be with her father again. She decided that after the children got well she would pack some clothes and go back to her girlhood home on Welles Avenue. There, in the big house where she had danced and dreamed on that sparkling night of her brilliant debut, there, surely, she could figure out what to do.

After three weeks at home, however, sleeping in the same room where she and her sister Agnes had whispered together in better, happier days, she understood that she no longer belonged in her parents' home, that she could never again lie down as a child, secure beneath her father's roof. For one thing, all her sisters and brothers were still single and still living at home. She noted how attentive and affectionate her father had become to her youngest sister, Eunice, who seemed, in turn, to know his every state and every shade of feeling. Eunice at twenty was, in Rose's opinion, "a beautiful young girl, intelligent as well as attractive, with the spirit and wit of my father." But that winter, Eunice was already desperately ill with tuberculosis, contracted during the Great War while she was with the Red Cross. No one in the family spoke much of the illness, but it was plain to Rose that, in her courageous struggle to live, Eunice had penetrated into her father's soul in a way that not even Rose had done.

Rose remained in her old home until one snowy night when her father came into her room and told her sternly that he believed the time had come for her to return to her family. "You've made your commitment, Rosie," he said, "and you must honor it now. What is past is past. The old days are gone. Your children need you and your husband needs you. You *can* make things work out. I know you can. There isn't anything you can't do once you set your mind on it. So go now, Rosie, go back where you belong."

Galvanized by the authority in her father's voice, Rose began thinking more sharply than she had done for weeks. Of course she could make things work. She could create definite goals for herself *and* have a clear vision of what she hoped to accomplish with her family. It was a question of accepting that her own desire to grow and learn deserved expression just as surely as that of her children.

In her new resolve, not surprisingly, it was to the church that Rose turned. She decided before going home to attend a religious retreat, a series of days passed in solitude and prayer, in order to reflect on the purpose of one's life. From this retreat, Rose would later recall, she brought home with her a renewed understanding of the ideals of Catholic womanhood. Her mission, she now realized, was to create a family: to provide her husband and her children with a feeling of belonging to something greater than themselves. She understood that the kind of family life she desired would have to be constructed by conscious effort, by instilling values and traditions so strong that every member of the family would know what to do and what to expect without having to ask.

Once Rose determined that her aim in life was to re-create

the strong family unit that had existed in the past, she was able to look on child rearing as "a profession that was fully as interesting and challenging as any in the world." From this point on, Rose rejected her mother's pattern of the martyred wife; instead of passively accepting her husband's role as an absentee father, she decided to encourage him to become more actively engaged at home.

Fortunately for Rose's plans, her separation had jolted Joe out of his preoccupation with his work and had propelled him more closely into the emotional center of his family's life. Then, in February 1920, within weeks of Rose's return, Joe was shaken by a second emotional crisis—the near death of his second son, two-and-a-half-year-old Jack, from scarlet fever. The disease, characterized by a sudden high fever, red congested throat, swollen tonsils, and a scarlet rash spreading over the entire body, assumed an intensely virulent form with little Jack. After nearly a week, neither the rash nor the fever had diminished, and the Kennedy household was plunged into a state of frantic terror. Scarlet fever is highly contagious, especially to pregnant women, and Rose was just hours away from the delivery of her fourth child. The new baby, a little blue-eyed girl, was born at home on February 20 in the midst of all this fear and confusion. She was named Kathleen.

There was nowhere that Jack could be taken to receive the proper care. In those days, Brookline's hospital did not admit patients with contagious diseases, and since the Kennedys didn't live in Boston, they weren't eligible to use the city's hospitals. With Rose convalescing from childbirth, the responsibility of caring for Jack fell upon Joe, who immediately determined that the only hope for his little boy, whose condition was worsening each day, lay in his being admitted to the Boston City Hospital, which was one of the nation's leading centers for the treatment of contagious diseases. Joe mobilized every source of influence at his command, until finally the hospital admitted Jack.

When Joe looked at his son's thin little form tossing about in the large white hospital bed, he suddenly felt he would strangle at the pain welling up in his throat. From this moment on, his conduct upset many settled notions about himself. Every morning he went to church to pray, promising that if Jack was spared he would give half of all his money to charity. Every afternoon, he left his office earlier than he had ever left any job in his life and journeyed to the hospital, where the love and attention he brought were no doubt magic to the child. Seated for long periods on the edge of Jack's bed, he realized that no amount of money could recompense him for a death in his family.

For Jack, the convalescence was slow and painful. Day after day his misery lasted, and by the time he was returned to his family, nearly three months had passed—a significant period of time in the mind of a small child. Yet the portrait of the little boy that emerges from the letters of the hospital nurses is that of an irresistibly charming child with an uncommon capacity to stir people's emotions. With his thatch of chestnut hair, his bright blue eyes and his irrepressible smile, Jack inspired a special affection in his nurses. "He is such a wonderful boy," one of them told Joe in the middle of Jack's hospital stay. "We all love him very dearly." Another wrote, "Jack is certainly the nicest little boy I have ever seen." Younger and smaller than his favored brother Joe Junior, Jack perhaps had learned at an early age how to reach out beyond his family for the affection he craved.

When Jack was fully recovered, his grateful father, to all appearances, fulfilled his pledge to God. He gave a check to a Catholic medical organization in the amount of $3,750, which, according to Rose, was exactly half of Joe's fortune at that time. How close she was in her estimate no one can say, though it is hard to imagine, from the large amounts of money he was then juggling in the stock market, that he was worth only $7,500. Unless, of course, in making up his balance sheet for God he considered only those assets that could be immediately converted into cash!

The importance of this dramatic family crisis lay in Joe's developing sense of fatherhood. From this time forward, according to Rose, he gave his children the best part of himself. "Joe was absolutely devoted to his children," Rose wrote in her memoirs. "He loved them and let them know it." True, his business activities still consumed most of his waking hours. To Rose's mind, however, there was a definite change. "After Jack's illness, Joe was determined to keep up with every little thing the children were doing," she recalled. "Every night we would spend hours together talking about the family and going over the children's activities. It made me feel that I had a partner in my enterprise." With Joe's vigorous backing, Rose dedicated her intelligence, her energy and all her talent to the tasks of making a total family life, molding her children's characters and encouraging their ambitions. Nor did Joe object to her spending money for additional household help. In Joe's eyes, Rose was an excellent manager and there was a general solidity in the household, an old-fashioned discipline that inspired his lifelong respect and admiration.

Joe also backed up his wife in her desire for a larger house, and on October 1, 1920, they moved into a two-and-a-half-story residence two blocks from the old house, on the corner of Naples Road and Abbotsford Road. The new house boasted twelve rooms, a porch that stretched halfway around the house, and, most importantly, enough extra space—even with the rooms set aside for the additional live-in help—so that Rose could have a room of her own when she wanted peace and privacy. All her life Rose would insist on such a place for herself, a place where she could assert her own needs and not feel she was continually on call for the children.

Joe spent weeks shopping with Rose for rugs and additional furniture for their new home. As further evidence of his involvement in the life of his family, his private papers reveal a number of occasions when he canceled engagements because of the family. On June 21, 1921, for instance, he wrote to a friend to cancel plans for a golfing trip to Bretton Woods in the White Mountains of New Hampshire. "Nothing I'd rather do, but on account of Mrs. Kennedy's condition I do not feel I would want to be away from home at this time." Soon after, on July 10, 1921, Mrs. Kennedy's "condition" resulted in the birth of her fifth child, a daughter named in honor of her dying sister, Eunice.

Seen from a distance, the structure of the family life the Kennedys created can be judged harshly, as hobbled by an excess of prescribed behavior and regulated activity. Yet, living in the twenties—the dizzying decade of flappers and bootleggers, of sensuous music, scandals and fads—Rose believed that adherence to daily rituals offered the best hope for the family's survival, and she established certain times of day as constants, including family meals eaten together, shared religious exercises and daily excursions, all of which she deemed essential for the maintenance of a secure, ongoing homelife and unchangeable ideals.

Every morning Rose would take the children for a long walk or for a visit to a historic place, the Bunker Hill Monument, Old North Church or the Boston Common, remembering how her own love of history had been fostered by the many expeditions she had taken with her father.

At the same time, she was determined to make the Catholic church a vital element in her children's lives. Unlike many of her Irish friends, reaching toward ease and comfort and shedding old-world customs in order to become more American, Rose embraced the ancient rituals, finding deep pleasure in the doing of things as they had always been done.

"I wanted them to understand that Church isn't just for Sundays and special times on the calendar," she wrote in her memoirs, "but should be a part of life." She insisted on the recital of grace at every meal, the saying of the rosary as a family

Rose sits for a portrait with Joe Junior,
Kathleen, Eunice, Rosemary and Jack.

venture and the practice of nightly prayer. On holidays she would take the children back to St. Stephen's in the North End, where the feast days were still celebrated in the old-fashioned way. By establishing a fixed time every day for meals, she made her children coordinate their engagements around the family instead of vice versa. And by organizing daily topics for the mealtime discussion—usually geared to the religious calendar or to current events—she encouraged an exchange of information and ideas in which even the younger children learned to speak up for themselves.

As both Rose and Joe became increasingly involved in sustaining the family life, their marriage seemed to settle on a different plane. From here on, they appear less like lovers than like partners in the common enterprise of creating a family group with its own standards, its own language and its own traditions. They made the family the object of their concord, the instrument of their togetherness. Instead of living for each other as they had done as young lovers, they now lived for the children and for themselves. Henceforth Joe had his world of business and his golfing buddies, a world Rose did not try to enter, while she had her clubs, her girlfriends and, most importantly, her love of travel. If Joe went off on golfing trips, as he did once or twice a year, Rose would have a trip of her own once he returned, and while she was gone he would arrange his business affairs so that he could be home with the children.

"Each time of life has its own kind of love," Tolstoy writes. If the excitement of the conquest was over, there was, it seems, an ease in the Kennedy's relationship that developed into a different kind of love.

9

"THE WALL STREET RACKET"

ON THE THIRD SUNDAY in June of 1922, Joe Kennedy motored to the Hotel Pilgrim in Plymouth, Massachusetts, where he joined over two hundred of his Harvard classmates for their tenth reunion. It must have been a happy occasion for him, for in the crowd of young men milling around and greeting one another with forced bonhomie were his three college buddies, Fisher, Campbell and Potter. With the return of peace had come an end to the tensions that had estranged Joe from his soldier friends. Then, too, among all his classmates, Joe stood out as one who had done exceptionally well in the ten years since graduation. He had made more money than most, and his association with the prestigious firm of Hayden, Stone added to his luster.

Yet, with all his success in the world of business, Joe Kennedy was still denied the full sweetness of social acceptance, as became evident that summer of 1922, when he rented a large shingled beach house overlooking a wildly beautiful beach at Cohasset. A heavily Protestant enclave, Cohasset was a private preserve of the old Boston families. Like most of his friends and acquaintances who summered there, including Bob Fisher and Dudley Dean, Kennedy looked forward to playing golf, and he made what should have been a routine request for a summer membership in the Cohasset Golf Club. But at a time when Irish Catholics were still looked down upon by the reigning Protestant establishment, the application proved anything but routine. In a letter to Fisher on the subject, Dean says, "It looks as tho it wouldn't be as easy sailing as I imagined when you broached the matter [of Kennedy's membership]. However . . . I will do all I can." And in the long struggle that followed, Dean remained true to his word. He promised personally to see members of the election committee with whom he had influence, and reminded others, in turn, to see to the same.

But as the days passed, Kennedy's application remained in limbo, and the time came when even Dean wearied of the stalling game the club's election committee was playing.

"It was petty and cruel," Ralph Lowell later said. "The women of Cohasset looked down on the daughter of Honey Fitz, and who was Joe Kennedy but the son of Pat, the barkeeper."

It is easy to imagine the embarrassment that Kennedy must have suffered all summer in knowing that his candidacy to the club had become a cause célèbre. He could no longer disguise from himself the melancholy fact that no matter what he accomplished in Boston, he was still unable to secure the social acceptance he craved. While in later years he denounced all social clubs as stupid and tiresome, there remained in his soul a bitter feeling that he would always associate with Boston. To strive so hard and reach so far and still be unable to get where one wanted to go seemed insupportable to him, so much so that he became all the more determined to live by his own standards in a world of his own making.

FROM 1922 TO 1929, the nation experienced a dynamic surge of productivity, bringing nearly seven years of unparalleled prosperity. Spectacular advances were registered in dozens of new industries; chief among them was the automobile industry. With the mass production of the cheap and sturdy Model T Ford, the auto's use, once restricted to the wealthy, spread to the middle classes, and with it came a boom in highway construction, remaking the face of America itself.

The soaring auto industry was destined to bring a significant increase in Joe Kennedy's fortune, and it was Galen Stone who supplied the lucrative connection. Stone was chairman of the board of Pond Creek Coal, a company whose stock had been performing admirably though not brilliantly. Knowing that Kennedy had taken some hard losses during the recession, Stone shared with him the privileged information that he had entered into secret negotiations with Henry Ford to merge the coal company with Ford's automotive operation. Stone understood that all he needed to do was drop a hint or two about the possibility of such a merger in order to attract a large following of new investors. Kennedy borrowed tens of thousands of dollars to purchase Pond Creek at about $15 a share. It was by far the largest amount he had yet gambled in the market.

Ford and Stone reached a final agreement just before *The New York Times* carried a story suggesting the possibility of a merger. Pond Creek stock immediately jumped seven points. The actual announcement made in the last week of December, 1922, pushed the stock up to a new high of 39. The following week Kennedy sold his entire block at approximately $45 a share, realizing a profit of more than $650,000 on his original investment. In the course of this single deal, Joe Kennedy thus amassed more than his father and his grandfather had accumulated in the course of two lifetimes.

On January 1, 1923, Galen Stone retired from the partnership of Hayden, Stone and Company. With his mentor gone, Kennedy's prospects with the firm, and particularly his chances of becoming a partner, were slim. Although he was now head of the stock exchange department of the Boston office, he knew that so long as he was not a partner, he would never be the master of his affairs. The time had come for him to travel his own road alone.

Kennedy elected to set up a private office in the familiar corridors of 87 Milk Street, connected by a short flight of stairs to the quarters of Hayden, Stone and Company. There, behind a door lettered JOSEPH P. KENNEDY, BANKER, the thirty-four-year-old Irishman went into business for himself. In choosing to call himself a private banker as opposed to speculator or trader, Kennedy sent a signal to the financial community that he stood ready to offer his technical experience in a wide range of market operations.

Kennedy had been installed in his new office scarcely six months when opportunity beckoned. His friend Walter Howey, the mercurial editor of Hearst's Boston *American,* came to him one night asking for help. He was facing financial ruin, he told Kennedy. Before coming to Boston from Chicago, he had invested nearly all his life's savings in the stock of the Chicago-based Yellow Cab Company, founded by his old friend John Hertz. In January 1924 the stock had been trading at 63; by the end of March it had slipped to 60; and now, in April, it was falling off nearly half a point each day. A similar fate had befallen the stock of the Yellow Cab Manufacturing Company, which Hertz had created to produce the taxis and buses used by the various transportation systems he operated in Chicago.

Yet while the two companies' stocks were falling, the profits and earnings of both were up from the previous year and stood to increase still more, inasmuch as Hertz was negotiating a merger with New York's Fifth Avenue Coach Company—a merger that would allow him to expand his operations into New York. Watching the ticker, both Howey and Hertz had concluded that a pool of New York operators was deliberately forcing the Yellow Cab stocks down, with the goal of thwarting Hertz's entry into New York by sabotaging his negotiations with the Fifth Avenue line.

Responding immediately to Howey's call for help, Kennedy journeyed by sleeper train to New York that very night and met with Hertz first thing in the morning to formulate the plan for Yellow Cab's defense. He was, he felt, poised on the threshold of what he considered the most difficult challenge of his financial career.

He met Hertz in the North Café of the fashionable Waldorf-Astoria Hotel on Park Avenue. When he arrived, the café was at the height of the breakfast commotion. Hertz, after shaking Kennedy's hand and introducing him to Yellow Cab's vice president, Charles McCulloch, promptly began explaining his plan for bolstering his company's collapsing stocks. Kennedy, with the backing of a vast treasure chest of $5 million, was to begin accumulating large holdings of the stock on the theory that it would drive the price up. For nearly three weeks now, Hertz confided to Kennedy, he had been trying to beat the raiders back by purchasing blocks of his own stock. But in spite of his best efforts the situation was steadily deteriorating. He and his fellow directors now knew they could not win without professional help. They needed Kennedy as their battlefield marshal.

John Hertz was not a man to accept defeat without a fight. The son of Tyrolean immigrants, he had grown up in the slums of Chicago. In his flight from poverty, he had turned to a variety of enterprises, including selling automobiles. Eventually, he began using the dealers' surplus cars to take passengers where they wanted to go for a fee. From this modest beginning Hertz moved on to create the Yellow Cab Company, America's first great fleet of public taxis. This was the remarkable enterprise Joe Kennedy was being called upon to preserve.

Kennedy heartily accepted the combat assignment, but only on the condition that Hertz abandon his absurdly expensive plan of attack in favor of a radically different strategy. Believing that fear was the only language the raiders would understand, Kennedy proposed to force them to respond to *his* moves instead of moving on their own. To carry out his plan, Kennedy demanded full authority to buy *and* sell Yellow Cab stock all over the country, pushing it up suddenly here, pulling it down swiftly there, until the raiders could no longer anticipate the future. Threatened with substantial losses if they guessed incorrectly, the raiders would have to halt their attack.

Hertz was attracted by the sheer effrontery of the plan, and he gave Kennedy unquestioned authority to go ahead, promising him all the money and stock he needed to carry on. Exhilarated, Kennedy set to work. Assisted by Edward Moore, a family friend and intimate associate who served as his secretary, Kennedy installed himself in the Waldorf, in a special suite of rooms equipped with its own automatic ticker tape machine and a bank of phones.

For the next weeks, Eddie Moore, who had earlier served as chief secretary to Mayor Fitzgerald, took calls, admitted visitors and ordered meals, while Kennedy grappled with the raiders. Staying on the telephone for hours at a time, he placed calls to brokers all over the country, instructing some to buy, others to sell. Shrouding his movements in secrecy, he left his suite only when absolutely necessary.

It took Kennedy some time to accomplish his goal, but by the second week it was apparent that his ingenuity was producing widespread anxiety in the other camp. As the stock jumped up and down from 46 to 53, from 57 to 52, the raiders found themselves in the position of reluctant riders on a sharply banked roller coaster. Never knowing what had hit them, they finally gave up, leaving the market to find its natural level once again.

Kennedy achieved a victory as complete as anyone could have won; in seven weeks he had preserved both the fortune of a friend and the life of a company. And since his scheme called for purchases to be offset by sales, he was able to bring the campaign to a close with Hertz's $5 million still intact. The strain, however, had been immense, as Kennedy's words attest. "I woke up one morning, exhausted, and I realized that I hadn't been out of that hotel room in seven weeks."

Kennedy's homecoming was joyous indeed. Not only was he father to a new baby girl, Patricia, born on May 6, but he also found himself, if not a multimillionaire, at least a very wealthy man. In return for halting the raid, he was given a large sum of cash, a fair proportion of Yellow Cab's stock, and also the opportunity to join with Hertz in his newest and potentially most lucrative project—the Hertz Drive-Ur-Self System, which would come to be known as Hertz Rent A Car. But the significance of his victory went further than money. It identified him to the inner circle of Wall Street observers as a financial genius.

Dealing now from strength, Kennedy got to know some of the shrewdest men of the financial world. One of these was Matthew Brush, president of the American International Corporation, who found in the vital Kennedy a man whose judgment he considered astonishingly sound. In the rich correspondence between the two, there is a strikingly frank exchange of confidential information that each man turned to his own advantage. At a time when insiders routinely operated with little regard for the effect of their actions on the ordinary stockholder, the only question—as Kennedy once put it—was how long the unregulated market would last "before they pass a law against it." Speaking with similar directness, Brush later admitted that "the Wall Street racket made Al Capone look like a piker."

FROM HIS FORAYS IN the stock market, Kennedy had accumulated by the mid-twenties a fortune estimated at about $2 million. But all along he eyed a different target: the burgeoning motion picture industry.

With eight hundred feature pictures being made annually, and with an investment of nearly $1.5 billion, the film business was the sixth largest industry in the country and one of the most profitable. Yet its financing remained almost entirely on a personal basis; certain individuals, known as bonus sharks, loaned money at excessive interest rates, or they participated in the profits. Only half a dozen banks in the country, most notably the Bank of America under Amadeus Peter Giannini, were willing to issue extensive credits to the movie industry. Here, Joe reasoned, taking note of both the spectacular profits and the primitive state of financing, was an industry in which to make a fortune.

The first operation with which Kennedy became associated was the Maine–New Hampshire Theatres, a chain of thirty-one small movie houses in which he bought a controlling interest. But as the years went by, according to one associate, "Kennedy learned [that] from the theater side of the business, Hollywood could wring you dry. He wanted to get where the wringing was done."

He found the opportunity he sought through a connection forged at Hayden, Stone with a large British trading house, the Grahams of London, which had a substantial investment in an American motion picture firm, the Robertson-Cole Company, producers and distributors of nearly fifty films a year. The R-C Company and its operational subsidiary, FBO (Film Booking Offices), had a national reputation for producing action-filled, fast-paced melodramas and adventure films.

As a small, privately held company, however, FBO was forced to borrow its working capital from private individuals at ruinous interest rates, which was why, for all its success, the company was losing money. Reluctantly its English owners decided to sell off the entire business to an American buyer through the venerable banking house of Hayden, Stone. Young Joe Kennedy was still with the firm at the time, and as the one Hayden, Stone broker who followed the movie industry religiously, he was given an exclusive option to sell the business. At first, nothing came of Kennedy's efforts, and after a while the English owners gave up trying to unload the company at a fair price. All along, however, Kennedy had harbored the dream of buying FBO for himself. Finally, in the summer of 1925, he was able to put together the capital he needed and he offered the Grahams $1 million for a controlling block of FBO's stock. The English owners balked, considering the offer far too small. But eventually they accepted, and in February 1926 Kennedy found himself the owner of a motion picture company.

The challenge at FBO was ideally suited to Kennedy. Having studied the company as an adviser for seven years, he recognized that while it was losing a good deal of money, the problem lay not in the company's productivity but in the shakiness of its financial structure. Before a month had gone by, Kennedy had set up an affiliate, the Cinema Credits Corporation, which succeeded in raising substantial capital for FBO by issuing stock. Next he established credit at four major banks, and with these resources at his command, FBO's credit squeeze ended. From then on, the company never lost money again.

With FBO's finances in order, Kennedy looked to the place where the money was made—the production studios in Hollywood. He boarded the elegant *Twentieth Century Limited* for the first leg of what was then a three-night-and-two-day train journey to California. For a man who enjoyed life as much as Kennedy did, his first transcontinental journey must have been a fascinating experience, though one wonders why Rose did not accompany him. Granted, he was heading west on business. Granted, too, there were children to consider. But surely Rose would have enjoyed the opportunity to participate in the high emotion that the trip promised.

Kennedy's offices were situated on the second floor of FBO's headquarters and looked out on Beverly Hills. From his windows he had one of the better views in the movie capital. At night he could see the famous HOLLYWOOD LAND sign outlined in lights.

It was often said, with some degree of accuracy, that Kennedy's success was due to his exquisite indifference to the business he was engaged in; thus he was never carried away by rash enthusiasm nor made foolish mistakes. Yet there is an unmistakable excitement that runs through his letters as he describes his first tour of the studio's back lot—thirteen acres of fairyland filled with locations ranging from a boxing ring on Broadway to an entire western village.

Under Kennedy's astute leadership, FBO concentrated on low-cost productions: a dozen westerns with lots of "action, riding and manly stuff"; a dozen dog pictures and twenty-five or more features each year. "Melodrama is our meat," Kennedy admitted, but, he said, it was "high-class melodrama" that allowed the public to weep and to sympathize with the handsome hero and the beautiful heroine. In the process, he established a definite niche in the film industry for FBO's films—and produced splendid profits for years to come.

10

GROWING UP KENNEDY

WHILE JOE WAS DEVELOPING his movie company, Rose cared for the children, now numbering seven with the birth of a third son, Robert, on November 20, 1925. Looking back on this period when her husband was away more than he was home, Rose claims that she never once felt that she was

THE FITZGERALDS AND THE KENNEDYS

being unfairly burdened by Joe's frequent absences. Yet one wonders if it really was as easy as Rose makes it sound to accept her growing distance from the exciting life Joe was leading.

For the Kennedy children, the immediate effect of Joe's journey to Hollywood was to add a touch of magic to the worshipful love they already felt for their powerful father. Here was a man standing at the center of so many fascinating worlds, and yet this same man was unfailingly interested in their swimming meets and football games, the movies they saw and the work they did in school.

Young Joe and Jack, eleven and nine when their father shifted his career to Hollywood, were perhaps the most vividly aware of the glamorous life he was leading. What boy would not be awed and delighted by a father whose business brought him face to face with cowboy star Tom Mix or baseball great Babe Ruth or football hero Red Grange, all of whom were negotiating with Kennedy for different FBO movies. When he was at home, the boys would listen intently to his every word; to be with him, to talk with him, to do things with him—all that was pure pleasure. While he was away, they would write him spirited letters, and Joe would usually respond by return mail. And when he came home from his Hollywood trips, Joe always brought a special present for each of his children. True, he was away from home now more than ever before. Still he managed, just as Fitzgerald had done in the previous generation, to make his children feel they were always on his mind; indeed, having achieved an almost primitive dominion over his children's youthful souls, he would rule his boys and girls for the rest of their lives.

Within the family, Joe Junior, as the eldest son, was accorded a position of primacy. Strong and glowingly handsome with his dark blue eyes and his sturdy frame, he emanated power, passion and promise, and a conquering poise that made him seem older than he was. Clearly this was a child of love. Emotions resonated between young Joe and his parents that none of the others would ever know or ever forget.

From his earliest childhood, Joe tried—in everything from throwing a ball to riding a bike—to attain success and perfection. A perceptive child, he grasped at once the critical role he was meant to play as the model son. In the process he acted as the little adult. Knowing that his mother, especially, depended on him to be an example to the others, he learned to suppress his spontaneous reactions. But as he did so, he walled off a part of himself as well. "I suppose I knew Joe as well as anyone," Jack wrote shortly after his brother's death, "and yet, I sometimes wonder whether I ever really knew him. He had around him a wall of reserve which few people ever succeeded in penetrating."

Jack grudgingly accepted Joe's occupying a place to which he himself could not aspire. The younger boy could not disguise his eager desire for his parents' praise and affection, yet he could be complacent about his own role in the family as the playful brother, as the "Pied Piper" who won the hearts of all his brothers and sisters. According to Lem Billings, Jack's oldest friend, Jack pardoned his father's preference for Joe because he believed his father always treated him fairly. But toward his mother, who found his irreverent and playful demeanor almost intolerable, he developed a lifelong detachment. As Lem later described Rose, she was "a tough, constant, minute disciplinarian with a fetish for neatness and order and decorum. This went against Jack's natural temperament—informal, tardy, forgetful, and often downright sloppy—so there was friction, and, on his part, resentment."

There is also evidence that Jack took an unorthodox attitude toward his religion, which was something of a trial to his devout mother. Never understanding why she took so many trips away from home, Jack told a friend he used to cry every time she packed her bags, until he realized that his crying only irritated her and made her withdraw from him even more. "Better to take it in stride," he said.

Perhaps the warmest moments little Jack spent with his mother were when he was confined to bed by the frequent illnesses that plagued him through his growing years. On these occasions Rose would spend an hour or more reading books to him, and Jack found a world he could happily inhabit for the rest of his days, a world of kings and queens, of heroes and adventures. Gifted with a fine intelligence and an active imagination, he was confident within himself that he surpassed Joe in one area alone, in mental ability, and he delighted in the look on his mother's face when he asked an intelligent question or showed a deep understanding of the story they were reading.

Jack's intellectual maturity set him apart from his brothers and sisters and proved especially irritating to Joe, who was accustomed to being the best. Of all the children Jack was the only one who ever tried to challenge Joe. Refusing to stay out of his way or to heed his commands, Jack was always full of mischief, provoking Joe and catching him off guard. For his part, Joe often turned bully, exercising far less patience with his closest brother than he exercised with others in the family. With Jack far more than with his other siblings, Lem Billings recalls, Joe's attitude was "sarcastic and overbearing and disapproving and challenging," almost as if the young Kennedy heir already sensed an implicit challenge to his throne. Yet, for all the difficulty between them, the two brothers shared an essential closeness, and when Joe first went away to sleepover camp in the summer of 1926, Joe Senior reported that Jack was "really very lonesome."

During their first years in school, Joe and Jack attended a public elementary school on Harvard Street in Brookline, but Joe Senior had a different plan in mind. He wanted his sons to meet the sons of Beacon Hill, and the perfect place for that introduction would be the Dexter School, a six-year country day school for boys. Comprising a social register of the area, Dexter at the time included among its students young James Jackson Storrow III (grandson of the Yankee politician who lost the mayoralty to John Fitzgerald in 1910), Leverett Saltonstall, Jr., and the two Bundy brothers, William and McGeorge. Looking back later, Jack thought of Dexter as a sort of "junior-grade Groton" and realized that he and Joe were probably the only Catholics in the school.

Rosemary followed her two older brothers to the public school for kindergarten, but when the year drew to a close her teachers could not recommend her for the first grade. While she had an uncommonly sweet and gentle disposition, she seemed unable to grasp even the simplest tasks, and the teachers' report confirmed all the lurking suspicions her mother had always harbored about her.

Born at the height of the flu epidemic of 1918, Rosemary had seemed to all appearances a normal baby. As the months went by, however, symptoms of trouble began to appear. She was slower to crawl, slower to walk and slower to speak than her brothers. Yet nothing prepared Rose for the heartbreak she would experience when she finally had to admit to herself that her beautiful and winsome daughter was retarded and had probably been so since birth, though no one understood how it had happened. "I went to the head of the psychology department at Harvard," Rose recalled. "I went to a priest from Washington who had made a study of retarded people. They all told me she had a low IQ, but when I said, 'What can I do to help her?' there didn't seem to be very much of an answer. For my husband and me it was nerve-racking and incomprehensible."

Still, when it was recommended that they send Rosemary to an institution, both Joe and Rose rebelled. They decided instead to keep her at home, and to shoulder themselves a large part of her unequal struggle for happiness. Determined to develop her capacities to the utmost, Rose hired a special governess as well as a score of private tutors to teach her how to print, play tennis, dance and read. And for a few years these ceaseless efforts seemed to work. In writing, math, dancing, she showed signs of progress.

Rose and Joe also saw to it that Rosemary was always one of the family, and the other children accepted the fact that whatever they did Rosemary would also do, even if it meant providing her with special assistance. But in a family governed by the desire to be extraordinary in everything, Rosemary was a constant reminder of the arbitrariness of destiny. Rose continually wondered why this one child alone had been given so few natural gifts while the others had been so abundantly endowed. But, after many searching questions, there was never a conclusive answer. And living as they did in an era when mental disability was regarded as shameful, the Kennedys decided to keep the nature of Rosemary's "condition" within the family. Surrounding her with the mantle of family affection, they projected her as a sweet but bashful little girl who was simply quieter than her rambunctious brothers and sisters.

At the same time, Rosemary became an instrument of their togetherness. All of the children, at a very early age, acquired a sense of responsibility for their sister. And in a family cushioned by wealth and privilege, her endless troubles provided a bridge of understanding to the ravages of everyday life. Years later,

Rose maintained that the key to her children's compassion for the poor and the underprivileged was unlocked by their sister's struggle for the smallest victory.

Because of Rosemary's handicap, Kathleen enjoyed the status of eldest daughter in the family. Five years younger than Joe and three years younger than Jack, Kathleen had curly reddish-blond hair, deep-set eyes, rosy skin and a playful, energetic disposition. As a small child she was like a high-spirited pony, so unafraid and full of fun that her family gave her the nickname "Kick."

Years later, thinking about her children, Rose reserved her warmest feelings for Kathleen, who seemed in many ways a reincarnation of Rose herself as a young girl. "She was lovely to look at, full of *joie de vivre* and so tremendously popular," Rose marveled. She could ski, sail and play tennis as well as her brothers, and at the same time she was a great dancer. She was, one of her friends maintains, "the sunshine" of her family.

Forming a family within the family, Joe Junior, Jack and Kathleen were the golden trio who shared all the inestimable advantages of being wealthy, good-looking, confident and intelligent. "They were the pick of the litter," says one Kennedy friend, "the ones the old man thought would write the story of the next generation."

Standing at the crossroads of the two clusters within the family, Eunice veered more toward the younger children, Pat, Bobby and eventually Jean and Teddy. Aware that she could not compete with her older brothers or her sister Kathleen, she spent most of her girlhood in games and sports with the younger

Summertime at Cohasset. From the left: Kathleen, Rosemary, Eunice, Joe Junior, and Jack— wearing a hat.

ones. Though suffering from her own bouts of ill health, Eunice early on assumed a leadership role in relation to her younger siblings, keeping them in line, often serving as the female counterpart of Joe Junior. She was also the child within the family who developed the strongest bond with Rosemary.

As the sixth and seventh children, Patricia and Robert must have experienced a trickling down of paternal attention. They were left more to fend for themselves, and as a consequence the two of them shared a special kinship. Of the five girls, Pat was considered by many to possess the best physical features, and she carried herself with an aristocratic poise reminiscent of her grandmother Josie Hannon Fitzgerald. Gifted with natural grace, she was also the best athlete in the family. But while the others seemed to take delight in the competitive spirit within the household, Pat would never, in her mother's words, "make the effort to achieve distinction."

As for Bobby, born into the household after a quartet of baby girls, he "had a lot going against him," Lem Billings noted. With his father away so much, and his older brothers off in school, his grandmother Josie feared that he would become a sissy, "stuck by himself in a bunch of girls." He was also the most open with his affections. But no one need have worried for long about Bobby's becoming a sissy, for he developed an external toughness that sustained him in his struggles. And struggle he did, possessing that same drive, sense of purpose and will to win that had propelled his father to success. Feeling, in Billings' words, "the least loved" of the sons, he became "a devoted observer of all the clan rules," the best behaved, the most punctual and the most religious of the boys. Yet he was also a full-blooded youngster who looked to his brother Jack for mischief and fun as if they were members of some forbidden society.

IT HAS BEEN SAID that aspirations are not inherited. When a man forces his way to the top, his most precious asset is his drive, his will, his indomitability. Yet that is the one asset he cannot easily pass on to his children. He can pass on his wealth, his knowledge and his influence, but he cannot pass on the memory of hardships, the will to win and the fierce determination born of struggle.

The experience of the Kennedy children seems to run counter to this theory. Perhaps that is because Joe and Rose Kennedy consciously chose to create an atmosphere pervaded by high expectations. As Eunice recalled, they were always taught that "coming in second was just no good." But part of the children's continuing drive for success must also be attributed to the peculiar conditions of life in Boston, where, for all of Joe Kennedy's wealth and accomplishment, the family was still unable to penetrate the inner sanctums of the city's insular society. In other large cities, surrounded by many ethnic groups, Kennedy's Irishness would have been much more easily blurred and diffused. But in Boston, where, for more than four decades, the Irish were the only major immigrant group, all social encounters were played out against a two-dimensional backdrop—the Irish versus the Yankees—and as a result, social antagonisms were not easily diverted.

Joe Kennedy believed he deserved better from the city of his birth. After the insult of his experience at Cohasset, he decided to move his family to Cape Cod, and in the summer of 1925 he rented a gracious white house on the beach at Hyannis Port. Here, he believed, in a new house in a new town, he could start afresh. But no sooner had the family settled in than Rose began to hear snide comments from the neighbors—about the noisiness and the gracelessness of the children, about the way the Kennedys pushed too hard to win.

Surely the family's style contributed to some of their social difficulties. From dawn to dusk the house and lawn resounded with yelling and laughter. They were very close, intensely loyal, and preferred each other's company to anyone else's. And the more they banded together, the greater the anger and the envy they aroused.

IN THE FALL OF 1927, Joe Kennedy evidently wearied of the frustrations he was still experiencing in Boston. The time had come to move his family to New York.

Years later, in an interview with Kennedy, a reporter asked, "I've seen you quoted as saying that the reason you moved your family out of Boston in the twenties was the anti-Catholic and anti-Irish prejudice in Massachusetts. Is that so?"

"That's exactly why I left Boston," Kennedy responded. "I felt it was no place to bring up Irish Catholic children."

Apart from his concern for his children, however, it was also true that Joe Kennedy was simply doing what many a successful businessman in the same position would have done—moving to the place where the action was.

To make the departure easier for Rose, whose roots in Boston ran the deepest, Joe sent Eddie Moore to New York to scout the area for a house to rent in a neighborhood with good schools. Moore produced a thirteen-room house in the exclusive Riverdale community, on the Hudson River just north of Manhattan. Then Joe hired a private railroad car for his family so that all his children, his servants and his possessions could leave Boston in splendor. In addition, to make his departure less total, he purchased the white house in Hyannis Port to allow his family to keep at least part of its roots in Massachusetts.

11

THE YOUNG MOGUL

As SOON AS HIS family was resettled, Kennedy moved to expand his movie empire by acquiring his own facilities for producing "talking movies." In that fall of 1927, Warner Brothers had just unveiled the wondrous new invention with the release of *The Jazz Singer,* using Warner's own Vitaphone sound system. At the same time, another system, Photophone, was being perfected by the Radio Corporation of America. Believing that Photophone excelled all previous efforts toward sound reproduction and synchronization, Kennedy opened negotiations with RCA's president, David Sarnoff, resulting eventually in a partnership between RCA and FBO.

The next step in the Kennedy-Sarnoff strategy called for FBO to take over a chain of theaters to form an initial market for the Photophone system. After extensive inquiries, Kennedy found that the Keith-Albee-Orpheum circuit, representing more than three hundred beautiful and commodious theaters scattered all around the country, would be a choice acquisition. It was indeed. Early in 1927, Keith-Albee-Orpheum, or KAO, had merged with Pathé–De Mille pictures. The general manager of KAO, John J. Murdock, became president of Pathé in charge of its lavish forty-acre studio in Culver City, California. A theater man with no experience in producing pictures, the canny Murdock recognized in Kennedy the strong, efficient executive he needed to bring Pathé's soaring costs under control. For years Pathé had enjoyed a near monopoly in the making of short comedies and newsreels, but with the coming of sound, many film producers were setting up their own newsreel departments, and Pathé was losing money. Now, with the KAO deal, Kennedy assumed the position of special adviser to Pathé films. Living up to his reputation, he boosted the company's sales while cutting overhead costs. Explaining his success, he later said, "Employees [in motion picture companies] were vastly overpaid. . . . [I] changed that."

With Cecil B. De Mille's half of the Pathé operations, however, Kennedy moved more cautiously, lest he cause the flamboyant director to leave the studio. A trailblazer, a pioneer in the technique of filmmaking, the virtual inventor of the epic film (among them *The Ten Commandments*), De Mille possessed an uncanny foresight into the temper of the public mind that the equally prescient Kennedy valued. Though the studio was being bankrupted by De Mille's grandiose style, lavish costumes and spectacular sets, Kennedy saw the genius in the man and was determined to come to terms with him. But in August 1928, De Mille signed an agreement to make three pictures at MGM and left Pathé. Kennedy was now free to merge Pathé with another company.

All the elements of the deal finally came together in October, when he and David Sarnoff brought RCA together with FBO and KAO to create Radio-Keith-Orpheum, or RKO, a new holding company with assets of more than $80 million. When Pathé was also brought in, Kennedy stood astride one of the largest mergers in the history of film. It was an exhilarating moment, for with the creation of RKO, Joseph Kennedy had reached the full height of success in Hollywood.

PROBABLY THE MOST talked about star in Hollywood at that time was Gloria Swanson. Joseph Kennedy first met her in November 1927, in the Renaissance Room of New York's elegant new Savoy Plaza Hotel, which stood on Fifth Avenue at the lower end of Central Park. It was a meeting that would alter the lives of both of them.

Miss Swanson had recently turned down a million-dollar salary with the Famous Players–Lasky Company in order to set up her own producing company under the banner of United Artists. Aware that she was suffering serious financial troubles, film executive Robert Kane asked Kennedy as a special favor to meet with her in New York. "Gloria needs handling," Kane advised Kennedy in early November, "needs being properly financed, and I am writing you now asking you to see her and find out if there is some way that we can get together on taking her over as a producing asset."

When two days passed without a reply from Kennedy, Miss Swanson took matters into her own hands. "Arriving New York Friday Century," she notified Kennedy in a telegram. "Shall appreciate a wire from you Blackstone Chicago advising whether you can see me Friday afternoon. Shall be at Savoy Plaza. Regards. Gloria Swanson." Sealing the bond in an exchange of telegrams, which remain today amid the private papers he kept all his life, Kennedy replied, "Will be very glad to see you Friday afternoon. Please telephone me Bryant nine four six naught after you arrive New York. Kindest regards."

For Joe, Gloria Swanson must have been, on first meeting, an enigma. Her headstrong spirit, her careless disregard for money and her three marriages must have seemed strangely out of place for a woman. At the time they met, Miss Swanson was twenty-eight years old, with more than a decade of successful films behind her. A deceptively small woman, she had bright eyes, high cheekbones and a large sensuous mouth. Her skin was white, her cheeks were painted red and her hair was dark. The contrasts were too odd, too striking to be considered natural beauty, but she had an aura of romantic glamour that produced a remarkable effect upon everyone she met.

The only child of an alcoholic father and an ambitious mother, Gloria was chosen at sixteen for the role of the young girlfriend in a series of light, homespun comedies centering on "the boy next door." Very much in command of herself, she rose quickly from an ingenue to a comic star to a glamorous woman of the world in a series òf Cecil B. De Mille's sophisticated marital melodramas. The De Mille films, which were designed to indulge the audience in the lavishness of gigantic four-poster beds, marble bathrooms and spectacular clothes, established Gloria as the all-time prototype of the movie star—temperamental, extravagant, dramatic, exciting and sensual.

Twice divorced by the age of twenty-three, Gloria bought one of the largest homes in Beverly Hills for herself and her four-year-old daughter. With its sweeping lawns, twenty-two rooms, private elevator and five baths, it soon became an inspired stage set for her personality and her well-publicized private life. She draped the enormous reception room in peacock silk, painted the breakfast room cream and gold, and next to her bedroom installed a black marble bathroom with a golden tub. "There is no star in Hollywood who lives in such gilded luxury as Gloria Swanson," proclaimed *Photoplay* magazine.

"In those days," Gloria later said, "the public wanted us to live like kings and queens. So we did—why not? We were making more money than we ever dreamed existed, and there was no reason to believe it would ever stop."

Yet it almost did. In the two years since she had turned down Jesse Lasky's million-dollar offer, Gloria had made only two films on her own, *The Love of Sunya,* which was not well received by the public, and *Sadie Thompson,* a daring and expensive adaptation of Somerset Maugham's celebrated story about a missionary who falls in love with a harlot. The big studios mounted a concerted protest against *Sadie's* release. Though Gloria was eventually allowed to release it, the months of litigation cost her thousands. By the time Joseph Kennedy came upon the scene, her situation was perilous.

When she and Kennedy met that day in the Renaissance Room of the Savoy Plaza, Gloria knew almost nothing about the attractive-looking banker with sandy hair and bright blue eyes. There was bluster and a boyishness in him, and with his solid build, his winning smile and his tendency to laughter, he proved himself a pleasing companion.

Amusing as their first conversation was, however, Joe was unable to find out much about her various obligations and agreements. He suggested that she grant him permission to look at her files so that he could see if he could be of any help. Swanson agreed at once.

The situation Kennedy uncovered when his men went swooping down upon Swanson's records was far more desperate than even she recognized. While she had made hundreds of thousands of dollars in the course of her acting career, she had consistently spent more than she made, and then, as Kennedy put it in a note to Kane, "she got herself all spread out with debts." Even worse, she was in serious trouble with the Internal Revenue Service. She had apparently deducted extraordinary expenses for clothing, trips and entertainment essential to her profession. The IRS agents disagreed. Going over her returns for 1921–26, they determined she had deducted more than a quarter of a million dollars more than she was entitled to.

To solve Gloria's financial problems, Kennedy proposed to replace her existing production company with a new one, Gloria Productions, which would be run by financial experts. "You're offering me all I've wanted for two years," Gloria told him, "freedom from the hassle of business worries. It's worse for me than for most star producers, because I'm a woman and I'm alone."

Next, according to Swanson, Kennedy proposed "a whopping deal" that would set all her finances straight at United Artists. In exchange for full distribution rights to both *Sunya* and *Sadie,* the studio would wipe out the debt she had incurred while making the two pictures. Taking steps to stabilize her overall finances, Kennedy also moved quickly to cover her short-term debts and to reduce what she was paying out every week to people in her employ. Her production manager was eliminated; her expensive accountant was replaced; her seamstress was laid off between pictures.

As all these changes were taking place, Gloria grew more dependent upon Joe. As for Joe, his new relationship with Hollywood's reigning sex goddess must have been intoxicating indeed. In the weeks that followed, their acquaintance ripened fast, and with Rose safely ensconced back East awaiting the birth of their eighth child, Joe felt free to spend as much time with his new client as he wanted.

Looking back at Joe's frequent absences at the moments when she was about to give birth, Rose laughingly claimed that giving birth was the one area where Joe had absolutely no expertise, so why should he feel compelled to stay at home? Yet, for a man who professed such deep devotion to his family, this rationalization seemed to go a little too far. While Rose accepted his need to be away from home on business, it seems that his definition of "business" was rather broad.

It happened that in the first winter of Gloria's relationship with Joe, she was still married to her third husband, Henri de la Falaise de la Coudraye, a French marquis. It was a "modern" marriage, separated often by an ocean and sealed by a written contract in which each party retained "ownership of all the property which belongs to him or her." But Henri had not found it easy to stand in the shadow of his wife's cresting career, especially since he had little money of his own.

When the Christmas holidays came that year, Joe Kennedy was in Riverdale with his family while Henri and Gloria headed west for California. "As soon as the holidays were over," Gloria recounted, Joe "was on the phone almost every day. He wanted Henri and me to meet him in Palm Beach. . . . He said there was lots to be settled, including an important place for Henri with an office in Paris."

In those days, Palm Beach attracted what was considered "the greatest aggregation of rich and fashionable notables" that ever gathered in a single place in America. In January, the weather was fair and dry, perfect for playing golf, and for several winters now, Kennedy had been visiting the resort, settling in for three weeks or more at the luxurious Royal Poinciana Hotel.

As Swanson later described her arrival at the Palm Beach train station, Henri was off arranging with Eddie Moore for her luggage to be sent to the Poinciana when "Joe Kennedy came charging down the narrow aisle from the other end of the car like a cyclone." The moment he reached Gloria he pushed her back into the drawing room, said a few excited words and then kissed her twice. Just as quickly he released her. "I missed you," he said, with no embarrassment at all. "And I wanted you to know."

"I missed you too," Gloria said, managing to keep her voice steady although her body was shaking. "Come out and meet my husband."

With this first stolen kiss, what had been a business partnership now gave rash promise of being much, much more. For three full days, however, the would-be lovers were so caught up in a crowded schedule of business discussions and dinner parties that they had no time to be alone together. But their meetings now generated an air of electricity, and a sense of silent complicity grew between them.

The affair was finally launched during an afternoon when Henri had gone off deep-sea fishing with Eddie Moore. As Gloria tells the story in her memoirs, Kennedy, having arrived at her hotel room, stood silently in the open doorway, staring at her for a full minute or more before he entered the room and closed the door behind him. "He moved so quickly," Gloria recounted, "that his mouth was on mine before either of us could speak. With one hand he held the back of my head, with the other he stroked my body and pulled at my kimono. He was like a roped horse racing to be free."

For the thirty-eight-year-old Kennedy, the affair with Gloria was a relentless pursuit of more, a quest to have it all, to live beyond the rules in a world filled with excitement and novelty. With her, he could still feel young; he could retain all the romantic dreams and pleasures of his adolescent days without forfeiting a single one of his adult privileges. Moreover, Joe had everything a man needed to be successful with a mistress—a great deal of time, considerable money and a capacity to live an almost schizophrenic existence.

To make it simple, Joe rented a house in Beverly Hills, on Rodeo Drive, five minutes away from Gloria's, on Crescent Drive. The house allowed him to maintain a certain decorum in his relationship with Swanson. "There is no question they had an affair," film director George Cukor recalls. "We all knew of it, that's all. But that doesn't mean they went around . . . holding hands or linking arms."

"Hollywood was the perfect place for an eastern banker to have an affair," observes film writer Cy Howard. "Separated from the East Coast by three days on a train, there was little worry of the accidental encounter between a wife and a mistress in a restaurant or on a street corner." Nor in those days, says Howard, would the press ever talk to the detriment of an insider. Under these conditions, Joe could enjoy his affair without feeling the need to choose one relationship or the other. The old love was home and family. The new love was romance, intensity and youth. And surely Joe must have been immensely flattered that Gloria Swanson, the most celebrated actress of the day, cared for him. Yet she also answered his need for companionship at a time when he was away from his friends for weeks and even months on end. Unlike Rose, she walked in the same world and was fascinated by all the details of his business dealings. She also had a keen sense of humor, a merry wit and a sharp tongue. "In an era of wonderful nonsense," director George Cukor recalled, "Gloria was always full of hell, always playing practical jokes, always able to find amusement in the most difficult situations."

How much Rose knew about Gloria remains an interesting question. At the age of ninety, Rose still asserted that she never worried, not even for a day, about Joe's relationship with Gloria. Indeed, throughout her life Rose spoke about Gloria with a strange solicitude, never publicly giving the slightest hint of jealousy or rage. She recalled simply that Gloria had needed Joe to straighten out "the financial morass" she had created for herself. Yet it is impossible to believe that Rose did not know the truth. From all accounts, however, it seems that she simply willed the repugnant knowledge out of her mind. After all, she seemed to have what she wanted in her marriage: children (her eighth, Jean, was born on February 20, 1927), as well as wealth and privilege. Better to suffer in silence rather than risk shattering the entire family and bringing public disgrace upon herself and her husband. So long as she felt secure about remaining Mrs. Joseph Kennedy, what did the rest really matter?

EARLY IN 1928, MOVING against the logic of his whole life, Joe Kennedy began insisting to Gloria that the time had come to take a big risk, to move beyond the mediocre movies he was turning out and produce a great one, an artistically ambitious film that would leave an indelible imprint upon the industry and upon Gloria's career. Joe also reminded Gloria that she had once said that *Sadie Thompson* was her best work because the Somerset Maugham story was the best she had ever had; if that was true, why consider anything but the next big artistic step forward—a great story *and* a great director?

For director, Joe selected the German master, Eric von Stroheim, and he could not have chosen better. According to producer Louis B. Mayer, Stroheim was "the greatest director in the world." Like D. W. Griffith and Charlie Chaplin, he was an original, a pioneer. Critics remarked upon the impeccable detail Stroheim lavished upon his films: the careful attention to costumes and scenery, the glances and gestures that indicated the depth of the characters.

For all his brilliance, however, Stroheim was embarked, it seemed, upon a curious pattern of self-destruction. He was determined to give the public what *he* wanted, regardless of the money it cost or the mores of the time. Flaunting contracts and censors, he shot reels and reels of material that could never survive a first cut and that no censor in the country would ever have passed. In choosing Stroheim, Kennedy was aware that the older man was, as Gloria warned him, "an undisciplined spendthrift, a hopeless egotist and a temperamental perfectionist." But, Joe told Gloria, "I also know he's our man. I can handle him." So long as Stroheim could be kept under tight control, Kennedy believed, everything would be fine.

The story Stroheim had in mind for Gloria's film was a curious tale of an imaginary German kingdom, a mad queen, a dashing prince and an innocent convent girl. In the lavish and romantic days before the Great War, a prince falls in love with a convent girl, and a mad queen places him under arrest and throws the girl out of the palace. The girl then journeys to German East Africa, where she becomes the proprietress of a low-down dive and the wife of an evil planter. In the midst of sin-drenched surroundings, she manages to retain her grace, charm and virginity, and becomes known far and wide as Queen Kelly. Meanwhile, back in Germany, the prince finally manages to escape from the mad queen and sets out to find the girl. A violent struggle erupts; both the evil planter and the mad queen die. In the final scene, the prince is crowned king and Queen Kelly becomes a genuine queen.

In this improbable tale, Gloria saw the part of the convent girl as a once-in-a-lifetime role that would allow her to portray both youthful innocence and more mature dramatic scenes. For his part, Kennedy imagined that with this story, with a director who was an acknowledged genius and with a star whom many considered the best actress of her day, he had everything he needed to enter the temple of art.

While Stroheim worked on the script, Kennedy negotiated with the director's lawyers for weeks to produce an ironclad contract. The agreement specified that if Stroheim fell behind schedule or ran over cost by more than fifteen percent, he would be terminated. Finally, the contract was signed and a great mood of euphoria settled over the project, which was named *Queen Kelly*.

The actual writing of the script was taking longer than anyone thought, but the early drafts seemed promising, and Kennedy felt relaxed enough to sail for Europe in August for a six-week vacation with his wife. When he returned to America, he was greeted with a present from Stroheim: a copy of the completed script, carried to his office on a silver platter by two black men clad as Nubian slaves in lions' skins. That night, bursting with excitement, Joe handed the massive script to Gloria. "Oh, I tell you, Gloria," he said, pressing her hand tightly, "this is going to be a major, major motion picture."

In the meantime, Stroheim was at work assembling a cast and supervising the construction of the sets. For the European sequences alone, six sets were constructed, including a royal palace complete with marble statues, a sweeping staircase and a sumptuous banquet room. For the second sequence, in German East Africa, the sets included the saloon-hotel known as the Swamp, the streets of Dar-es-Salaam, a jungle swampland and native huts. "Never," Swanson says Stroheim confided as he walked her proudly through the magnificent sets, "had he felt so utterly confident in the rightness of every detail." He declared that he would complete the film in ten weeks of camera work.

The filming of the European sequence of *Queen Kelly* began at the FBO studios in early November. Each night Gloria looked at the rushes from the shooting that day. As the lights went down and as Stroheim's first images flickered across the screen, she reported, the result was breathtaking. "Every scene was alive with glowing light play and palpable texture. You could almost smell the thin Havana cigars and taste the Viennese coffee."

But for all the élan generated in those early weeks, there remained the desperate pressures of time. As Gloria recorded in her memoirs, "Von Stroheim was so painstaking and slow that I would lose all sense of time, hypnotized by the man's relentless perfectionism. A scene that Raoul Walsh would have

Gloria Swanson, seen here on a movie set, was one of Hollywood's most glamorous stars when she and Joe Kennedy met. Their attraction was immediate.

wrapped up in an hour might take Von Stroheim all day, fondling and dawdling over the tiniest minutiae."

In December, it became clear that Stroheim's original fifty-two-day shooting schedule could never be met, and that it would take a hundred and three days to shoot, at a cost of at least $5,000 per day. Determined to control the budget, Kennedy worked on Stroheim to eliminate nearly half a dozen scenes, some of which would have required an extraordinary number of special effects. Somehow, in the clash and strain of many personalities fighting for their ideas, Kennedy managed to keep an open line with his director.

The first wave of exhilaration carried into the new year. But then came a period of anxiety. It began, as so many troubles with Stroheim began, with his obstinate unwillingness to speed up the pace of his shooting—and it deepened beyond control as the action of the film shifted from the imaginary kingdom in central Europe to the streets of Dar-es-Salaam in eastern Africa. In the original script the setting was a dubious hotel; in the shooting, the hotel had become a brothel. Gloria, who had been portraying an innocent young maiden, was called upon to shift her character to that of a hardened, sophisticated madam. Yet in spite of her capacity to run an establishment catering to flesh and the devil, she would not, as Stroheim envisioned her role, seem immoral. She would retain her chastity while flourishing amid thieves and drunken sots.

It was not an easy role to play, and during the filming of these scenes, the trust and confidence Gloria and Stroheim had originally placed in each other began to fly apart. Papers in Kennedy's files suggest that under the weight of Stroheim's demanding style of direction Gloria simply collapsed. As the situation deteriorated, Kennedy tried, from three thousand miles away, to keep things under control.

Meantime, a consultant was hired to look at the reels Stroheim had already shot and report on them "without prejudice." Failing utterly to appreciate either the fairy-tale quality of the film's beginning or the sordid realism of the African scenes, the consultant concluded that "in an attempt to be bizarre and unusual," Stroheim had been "vulgar. . . . To my mind, a woman who takes the profit from a bawdy house could scarcely be credited with possessing any of the higher virtues of her sex. The production is magnificent . . . but in my humble opinion it is mostly gilding the manure pile."

By this time Gloria's confidence in Stroheim was almost totally destroyed, but for Kennedy's sake as well as her own she agreed to continue. Then the time arrived to shoot the scene of Kelly's marriage to the repulsive planter, played by Tully Marshall. According to Gloria's account, "Mr. Von Stroheim began instructing Mr. Marshall, in his usual painstaking fashion, how to dribble tobacco juice onto my hand while he was putting on the wedding ring. It was early morning, I had just eaten breakfast, and my stomach turned. I became nauseated and furious at the same time."

"Excuse me," Gloria said to Stroheim. Then she walked off the set and called Kennedy, demanding that he come to California at once.

When Kennedy arrived, as he told Gloria's husband Henri in a long and surprisingly intimate letter, Gloria was "in very bad shape in the hospital, as the result of practically a nervous collapse. She was down to a hundred and eight pounds in weight and her attitude toward the picture, and everybody connected with it, was quite hostile." Leaving her in the hospital, Joe went to the studio, where, for ten hours, he sat watching the film taken over the past several months, knowing that these twenty-one reels represented nearly $800,000 of his own money. The European sequences flashed before his eyes with all the splendor he had expected in Stroheim's work. But then, as soon as he saw the African sequences, he agreed that the picture could not be released in its present form.

Still unwilling to abandon his original director, Joe offered Stroheim the opportunity to direct a new ending written by Ben Glazer, something Stroheim found impossible to do. So Joe was left with no alternative but to fire Stroheim and find another director.

THAT SPRING, WHILE everything was falling apart in Hollywood, Kennedy's father became seriously ill with liver disease. For six years, since the death of his wife, Mary, in 1923, P. J. Kennedy had been living with his married daughter Margaret and her husband. Joe visited him regularly and talked to him every week. Now, with the old man in critical condition, Joe put aside all matters of business in both New York and California and boarded a train for Boston. Then, in the middle of May, P.J.'s condition suddenly seemed to improve and the doctors agreed that the crisis had passed. Joe left at once for California, planning to return to Boston within three weeks. But on May 18, just a day after he had arrived in Hollywood, he received word that his father had died. Caught three thousand miles from home, Joe suffered what Rose later described as a "sea of despair" about having been so far away at the moment of death.

Given Joe's closeness to his father, however, it is difficult to understand why he did not drop everything and return to Boston for the funeral.

The funeral of P. J. Kennedy was, the Boston *Globe* noted, an impressive gathering, proving what P. J. Kennedy "meant in life to his legion of friends." The mourners included every prominent name in Boston politics, from governors and mayors to congressmen. But beyond all this there were hundreds of poor people who had been the recipients at one time or another of P.J.'s largesse. "With Mr. Kennedy," the *Post* reported, "public service meant public trust. . . . No man ever left his door in want or distress."

In Joe's absence, young Joe, age thirteen, stood in his father's place. According to Rose, he behaved with incredible dignity. "I am more than proud to have you there as my representative," Joe Senior wrote to the boy. "Help mother out and I'll be with you as soon as possible."

AFTER HIS FATHER'S DEATH, Kennedy tried to resume production on *Queen Kelly*. One new director after another was brought in to re-edit the completed reels, but it was impossible for anyone to recapture the original vision. Finally, Kennedy sent the actors home and suspended production. Joe was not in despair, Gloria recorded in her memoirs. "He was resigned. He said there was no sense in throwing more good money after bad." The time had come to cut his losses.

Not a man to brood on failure, Kennedy hired Edmund Goulding to direct Gloria in her first talkie, an original story with all the old formulas of popular entertainment—poor girl meets rich boy only to lose him when rich boy's father intervenes. *The Trespasser,* as the film was called, was completed in three months' time and was expected to be a great box-office hit. To help it along, Joe decided on a campaign of international publicity, with successive premieres in Paris, London, New York and Los Angeles.

Filled with excitement, Joe also decided that he and Rose would accompany Gloria at *The Trespasser's* premieres in Paris and London. In her memoirs, Gloria claims that she was appalled by the boldness of the scheme and resisted at first. But once Joe's mind was made up "there was not a big enough lever in the world to move him."

The trip brought Rose and Gloria together for the first time. Never once, Gloria later claimed, did Mrs. Kennedy treat her with anything but respect and friendship. "If she suspected me of having relations not quite proper with her husband, or resented me for it, she never once gave any indication of it." Was Rose a fool, Gloria asked herself, or a saint? Or just a better actress than she was?

Rose remembered the drama of those weeks vividly. While both couples were together in Paris, she recalled, Gloria received an envelope meant for her husband, Henri. When she opened it, she found inside a love letter from the actress Constance Bennett, which made it abundantly clear that she and Henri were having an affair. Furious at the discovery, Gloria announced that she intended to seek a divorce at once. "Poor Gloria," Rose said on looking back. "It was a very difficult time for her and I felt very sorry to see her so hurt."

How ironic to hear the phrase "Poor Gloria" coming from Rose to describe the woman who was her husband's mistress and who, now that she was on the verge of leaving Henri, must have presented at least some threat to the Kennedy marriage. The only explanation lies in the firmness of Rose's belief that no matter how involved Joe might be with Gloria, he would never leave his wife and children.

The London premiere of *The Trespasser* was a smashing success. "The crowd gave Miss Swanson a great welcome when she arrived," the United Press reported, "and cheered her again when she left. . . . Some critics said it was her best picture." Then, when the whirlwind days of the openings came to a close, Rose recalled, she and Joe sailed back to New York with Gloria. In a letter to Henri, Joe reported that Gloria was not at all well and had remained in bed for nearly the whole trip.

Back home, Gloria remained dispirited for weeks. While the New York opening of *The Trespasser* was considered a "triumph" and her performance was hailed as "brilliant," she was unable to cope with the loss of her husband. And indeed, by the fall of 1929 the sun of Joe's romance with Gloria was setting too. While they would still make one more movie together, Joe was already beginning to disengage from Hollywood, and with that disengagement his days with Gloria were numbered. Prompted perhaps by the added pressure now that Gloria was free of her husband, Joe decided to liquidate all his movie holdings and return to Wall Street.

Gloria Swanson was left behind. "It was," she recorded in her memoirs, "as if two men—my ex-husband and my ex-paramour—had in some mysterious way, through me, canceled each other out and moved on. I was completely on my own again, without love and without money."

12

RIDING THE *ROOSEVELT SPECIAL*

WHILE JOSEPH KENNEDY was winding up his affairs in Hollywood, frenzied trading on the stock market was making prices soar out of all relation to the country's economic reality. Believing there would never be a better time to get rich, tens of thousands of new customers had entered the stock market by trading on margin with the expectation that stock prices would continue to rise. A few voices warned that the market was already too high and no longer reflected the rise in earning power being generated by American business. But at a time when the public mood was invincibly optimistic, pessimists were brushed aside.

Cautious and questioning by nature, immune to most enthusiasms, Joseph Kennedy began, in the spring of 1929, to liquidate his stockholdings and withdraw from the market. So he was standing at a safe distance in September, when the great bull market finally began to crack. As stock prices fell, the smaller investors were hurt first. There followed weeks of uncertainty, but then, on October 24, as millions of orders to sell pounded the exchange, prices plummeted to all-time lows, crushing all the marginal traders and thousands of wealthy investors as well. A general panic set in. As stunned crowds gathered in the streets of lower Manhattan, the establishment decided to step in. Meeting in the offices of J. P. Morgan & Company, half a dozen top bankers agreed to create a pool of $240 million to support the market. Their plan was to shore up selected stocks and so rally the rest. For several days the medicine seemed to work. As word of the bankers' pool spread, prices steadied, and President Herbert Hoover issued a statement declaring that "the fundamental business of the country" was "on a sound and prosperous basis."

But words of reassurance were no longer enough; once basic confidence was lost, a crash was inevitable. It came on October 29, "Black Tuesday," the most devastating day in the history of the New York Stock Exchange. Thousands lost everything. For days afterward, the press would focus on dramatic accounts of the suicides of fallen financiers.

For his part, Joe Kennedy was "sitting pretty" in his new Georgian mansion in Bronxville, which he had purchased for his family the previous June. Having never been a member of Wall Street's inner circle, he felt no constraints now to save the system. Instead, he coldly calculated which stocks to sell "short," driving the market down still further and turning the situation to his own advantage. His maneuvers left him an even wealthier man after the crash than he was before.

But for most Americans the times were desperate. By the spring of 1930, over four million people were unemployed and millions more were working only two or three days a week. Across the country, unemployment and homelessness became a way of life. Once-proud men found themselves huddled together on breadlines, while every day, every week, more factories and stores were shutting their doors.

The Kennedys, by contrast, were experiencing what Rose later described as "a golden interval" in their lives, a time of family peace and economic security. Returning home from Hollywood, Joe Kennedy had become his old self again, warm, happy, and content to pour his affection and vitality upon his family. He spent hours on the furnishing of the new house in Bronxville, and with his overpowering presence he infused new life into his summer house in Hyannis Port. Rose apparently accepted her husband's return with no questions asked, rejoicing in the joy and cheer his presence brought.

"I think," a friend speculated, "that when Joe realized how close he had come to destroying his family, he determined that from there on in, he would keep his encounters with women at a more casual level. I think he simply decided that he would never again get so deeply involved with anyone. As far as I know he never did."

Hereafter, a renewed commitment to their marriage seemed to take possession of both Joe and Rose, bringing with it an absorbing affection for each other. Yet there is little denying that the Swanson affair had a permanent effect upon the family, for history would later record a link between the risks Joseph Kennedy took with Gloria Swanson and the sexual daring observed again and again in his sons as they repeated their father's behavior.

ON FEBRUARY 22, 1932, Rose gave birth to their ninth child, a sturdy little boy whom they named Edward Moore after Joe's faithful friend and companion. With their twentieth anniversary approaching, Rose must have realized she was living a life of great privilege. At a time when the average American was struggling to save the family homestead from foreclosure, Kennedy was purchasing his third estate, a magnificent ocean villa in Palm Beach.

In honor of their anniversary, he also presented Rose with the gift of a European vacation, including a sojourn in Paris to see all the new fall fashions and the leeway to buy whatever clothes she desired.

Prosperous as the Kennedys were, however, Joe could not rest secure so long as the staggering losses of the depression continued to spread, threatening eventual ruin for everybody. In the face of the continuing economic decline, the machinery of civilized life was breaking down. Kennedy, who saw that the business community could no longer cope with the situation, concluded that without substantial political intervention the situation would only get worse.

Strong political leadership, he believed, was the only solution to the uncontrolled economy. And as he looked ahead, he foresaw that the center of gravity in America would shift from big business to big government. And although he had forsaken politics for business three decades earlier, he now resolved to be at the center of action.

Searching for a leader, Kennedy found his candidate in Franklin D. Roosevelt, the popular governor of New York. Kennedy believed that FDR, more than anyone else in the country, had the resources, talent and personality to combat the nation's paralysis. "I was really worried," Kennedy later confessed. "I wanted him in the White House for my own security and the security of our kids—and I was ready to do anything to help elect him."

The first public indication of Joe Kennedy's evolving sympathies came with his journey to Warm Springs, Georgia, in May 1932, in the company of Eddie Moore. The visit, initiated by Roosevelt's aides, was intended to bring the wealthy Kennedy into the Roosevelt camp. The press found particular significance in the fact that Kennedy was just returning from a trip to California, where he had visited his old friend William Randolph Hearst, the newspaper magnate, who would control large numbers of delegates at the forthcoming Democratic national convention.

When the convention opened in Chicago in mid-June, 1932, Roosevelt held a majority but not the necessary two thirds of the delegates. His supporters, fearing a deadlock, hoped to win over the uncommitted delegates early on. In this situation Hearst's support was crucial. But Hearst, relishing his role, planned to hold out until the seventh ballot. Half a dozen people, including Joe Kennedy, tried desperately to change his mind, and when the publisher finally fell in line for Roosevelt, setting in motion a Roosevelt landslide, Kennedy claimed full credit for bringing Hearst around.

Following a night of wild celebration, Kennedy set to work raising money for the campaign. Beyond the $50,000 he himself contributed, it is said that he raised over $150,000 for Roosevelt in the space of four months. Little wonder, then, that his relationship with the candidate grew warmer.

Joe was just the kind of person FDR loved to have around him: intelligent, high-spirited, gregarious and affable. Moreover, the two men shared a sense of humor and an appreciation of the wonder and variety of life; and at night, when they got together to talk, the sound of their laughter would float through the halls.

IN THE FALL OF 1932, FDR invited Kennedy to join him aboard his campaign train on its thirteen-thousand-mile whistle-stop tour from the East Coast to the West and back again. Accompanied by the amiable Eddie Moore, who soon became a favorite of the entire Roosevelt entourage, Kennedy boarded the *Roosevelt Special* in Albany for the first leg of its journey.

The *Special* had a dining car and a lounge car, a car for the candidate and his family, cars for cameramen, radio announcers and representatives of the telegraph companies and a car for the newspapermen. There was a special car for what were known as visiting firemen—those dignitaries whose status called for one or two days of jaunting with the candidate—and two cars for the more or less permanent members of the troupe, including Kennedy and Moore. Later, Rose recalled the intense pleasure Joe experienced when he discovered that he and Eddie had been placed in the car carrying all the President's closest advisers and friends. In this gathering of vigorous, talkative men, Kennedy fit in perfectly.

As for the indefatigable Roosevelt, at every stop he would make his way to the back platform, accompanied by the strains of "Happy Days Are Here Again." Then he would smile his magical smile and say a few words of greeting, projecting his contagious warmth, vitality and confidence to the crowd. It wasn't so much what he said as the spirit of affirmation in which he said it. The crowds responded, growing larger and more enthusiastic at each stop. In Chicago, on the return trip, the candidate received what reporters described as "one of the greatest demonstrations ever accorded a candidate," with more than two hundred thousand people lining the streets. And through it all, Roosevelt never wearied or lost his good humor.

For Joe Kennedy that train journey was one of the best experiences of his life, providing him with a rare sense of group camaraderie and of participation in the great currents of the day.

On election night, Kennedy celebrated Roosevelt's victory over Hoover as though it were a personal triumph, staging a lavish party that spilled through two floors of New York's Waldorf-Astoria. Having tasted the pleasures of the campaign, he now looked forward to even greater excitement. Surely, if anyone was assured of an important administrative post, it was Joseph Kennedy.

All that winter he waited for a phone call that never came. One by one, the men who had contributed to FDR's victory were offered a place in the administration—all but Joseph Kennedy. He was mystified by the sudden change of heart in a man whom he had judged a friend. "He simply did not understand why he alone had been left out," Rose remembered. "He was pretty hurt and angry."

Unbeknownst to Kennedy, Roosevelt was caught in a conflict of loyalties, for Louis Howe, his best friend and closest assistant, was unalterably opposed to including a man with Kennedy's speculative background in an administration dedicated to reform. Apparently the brusque and diffident Howe was also jealous of Kennedy's special relationship with Roosevelt: their easy banter, their shared interests in movies and sports, their laughter.

A proud man, Kennedy did not find it easy to initiate contact with Roosevelt, but, in the spring of 1933, he sent the President several letters, all of which received polite notes but no mention of an appointment. Finally, after many months, Kennedy learned that Howe was the source of his undoing. That knowledge gave him some measure of optimism, for at least now he could begin working around Howe to influence Roosevelt.

Meanwhile, as he waited to hear from Roosevelt, Kennedy returned to Wall Street and his old ways. Why fight for reform when he was excluded from the reformist spirit in Washington? Besides, there was still good money to be made, particularly if one felt no compunction about manipulating the declining market at the cost of the ordinary investor. Although there is no way of knowing the full extent of Kennedy's maneuvers in the market of 1933, it is clear from his private papers that he was making enormous profits.

At the same time, Kennedy was also establishing himself as a major player in the emerging liquor industry. Roosevelt, he knew, was deeply critical of Prohibition and was pushing hard for repeal of the notorious Volstead Act—the law that for more than a decade had held legal drinks in America to less than one half of one percent alcohol. Kennedy figured that it was only a matter of time before the act was repealed. The only question was where and how he should enter the industry.

All through the "dry" twenties, Kennedy had been surrounded by rumors suggesting his involvement in the illicit liquor trade. For one thing, he seemed to have easy access to large private supplies of liquor whenever a festive occasion demanded it. In the early twenties, some of this supply undoubtedly came from P. J. Kennedy's private stock, rushed from his liquor store to the cellar of his Winthrop home during the last days of legal liquor in January 1920. Beyond his father's supply of liquor, Joe Kennedy also seemed to have access to a large supply of whiskey, which had been stored in a warehouse and sold to him by Honey Fitz's brother, James T. Fitzgerald. For James Fitzgerald and his brother Edward, both of whom had been profitably involved in the liquor business all their lives, Prohibition was a shattering experience. Knowing no other business when Prohibition came, they naturally drifted into the illicit liquor trade. James bought a building in Boston that he turned into a speakeasy drugstore, containing a soda fountain, a magazine stand and a corner where medicinal prescriptions for liquor could legally be filled—as they were in many drugstores all over the country. The Fitzgerald drugstore also had a back room where liquor was illegally sold at high prices.

With Rose's uncle providing a built-in market, it is possible, as some people have claimed, that Joe Kennedy got involved in financing illegal shipments of liquor from Canada or the Bahamas. If the stories are true, no hard evidence has yet been produced. It is known, however, that Kennedy's familiarity with sources of supply and distributorships provided him with a substantial advantage as the end of Prohibition drew near. Determining that his best entry into the liquor trade lay in securing the American distributorships for high-class English liquors, he made a trip to London in September 1933 and negotiated a deal with Haig & Haig, Dewar's and Gordon's—a deal that would be worth millions of dollars in the years ahead. On the night of December 4, 1933, with legal liquor sales only a matter of hours away, thousands of bottles of the best British whiskey were already making their way from his warehouse into the hands of hundreds of retailers.

WHILE KENNEDY WAS becoming richer and richer through his dealings in liquor and stocks, the Senate Banking and Currency Committee was just beginning its historic investigation into the whole pattern of stock exchange activity that allowed the few, time and again, to take advantage of the many. The investigating subcommittee's counsel, an Italian by the name of Ferdinand Pecora, was calling many of the nation's most prestigious financiers before the public. The hearings were sensational, producing amazing admissions of wrongdoing from a parade of leading bankers and brokers—admissions of the taxes they had avoided, and the bad investments they had passed off time and again upon an unsuspecting public.

Pecora, the son of a poor Sicilian shoemaker, was an indefatigable worker, brilliantly suited to the task at hand. The great success of the investigation—which resulted eventually in the Truth-in-Securities Act of 1933 and the Securities and Exchange Act of 1934—came primarily from his uncommon skill at collecting, analyzing and assimilating large quantities of data concerning his witnesses' activities, then genially eliciting from almost every witness the disclosures he wanted. As a consequence, the American public was treated to a shocking series of revelations about banking and securities practices. The Roosevelt administration put the subcommittee's findings to immediate use. Legislation was drafted creating the Securities and Exchange Commission, with power to compel disclosure of information, force investigations and control stock manipulations. For the first time, the authority of the federal government was asserted over the whole field of security markets.

Ferdinand Pecora could rightly take pride in his accomplishments and he was the obvious choice for chairman of the new commission. Many felt that the President owed it to him. But Roosevelt was considering a very different man—Joseph P. Kennedy.

Kennedy had been recommended by a presidential adviser because of his "executive ability, knowledge of habits and customs of business to be regulated, and ability to moderate different points of view." To Roosevelt's mind, the recommendation was an excellent one. As word of his thinking drifted out, however, a storm of criticism built up. Louis Howe complained that assigning Kennedy to police Wall Street was like setting a cat to guard the pigeons. But Roosevelt, having said all along it would take a thief to catch a thief, believed that only a man who knew Wall Street from the inside could put a clamp on its illicit practices. At the same time, with his great intuition at work, Roosevelt assumed that Kennedy, having made his pile, would now like to make a name for himself for the sake of his family. He told Kennedy that the appointment was set.

The decision to make an insider the first chairman of the SEC seemed to some a brilliant stroke, but to ardent liberals it was "grotesque" and "a slap in the face to his most loyal supporters." It was seen as an act of betrayal. But at the swearing in of the new commissioners on July 2, 1934, Kennedy disarmed his critics with reference to his family. "Boys," he said to the reporters, "I've got nine kids. The only thing I can leave them that will mean anything is my good name and reputation. I intend to do that and when you think I'm not doing so, you sound off."

During his days at the SEC, Kennedy lived with Eddie Moore on a lavish hundred-and-twenty-five acre estate called Marwood, deep in the Maryland countryside. He had rented it assuming that his entire family would move there for a year. But as he and Rose talked the situation through, they decided it made little sense to uproot the children. So Kennedy and Moore lived like potentates at Marwood, a beautiful thirty-three-room French Renaissance mansion on the Potomac, and it suited Kennedy well. He was able to steer clear of dinner parties in Washington while making his home a place of great warmth, relaxation and pleasure for his friends and, occasionally, various female companions. He also played host on several occasions to President Roosevelt, and as the President's confidence in Kennedy's ability deepened, the friendship grew stronger.

Wall Street, meanwhile, remained apprehensive about the SEC chairman, regarding him fearfully as "an erstwhile alley gamin eager to display and expose his old haunts and tricks to his newly found friends from the other side of the financial community." But in speech after speech, Kennedy's priority was new financing, and he promised that governmental supervision would be no hardship except to the crooked. If the new agency was able to protect the honest businessman from fraudulent dealers and stock swindlers, he predicted, then "a New Deal in finance will be found to be a better deal for all."

From the start, Kennedy's goal for the commission was the adoption of laws, regulations and enforcement proceedings to abolish the major evils of the exchanges. Defining his task as that of making Wall Street legitimate again to the American public, he sought to rally to his side all those "good" financiers who wanted to separate themselves from the "bad." Though he himself had stepped over the ethical line hundreds of times in the preceding decade, he was now willing to change the rules, even if it meant a short-term loss of profit, in order to preserve what he already had. Fearing that uncontrolled economic individualism would topple the entire capitalist structure, Kennedy was finally coming down on the side of the ordinary stockholder.

As it turned out, his chairmanship of the SEC would comprise his finest hours in public service. The Kansas City *Star* called him "a wizard" for sustaining the confidence of the business community while also earning the strong support of reformers and effecting their reconciliation in the process.

13

CHILDREN OF PRIVILEGE

BY THE TIME Joe Junior, Jack and Kathleen had reached their teens, they were welded together into an elite family, sharing intense loyalties that would bind them tightly for the rest of their lives. Strikingly good-looking, the three Kennedys were alike in their vitality, their sensuality, their cleverness and their particular brand of humor. Born within a five-year span, the three of them were enrolled in boarding schools in Connecticut, with Joe and Jack at the Choate School in Wallingford, and Kathleen not more than thirty miles away, at the Noroton Convent of the Sacred Heart.

Had Rose had her way, the boys would have gone to parochial school or, failing that, to public school. To Joe's mind, however, the advantage of the affluent, predominantly Protestant Choate lay in the social contacts it would offer. And beyond the contacts, he wanted them to walk in a world where preference and priority were assumed. Having freed them from material concerns, he hoped to create in them that aristocratic confidence and ease of manner he had first observed among the Brahmins at Harvard. But, even as he treated his sons as princes, he insisted that they work hard. The sense of privilege he inculcated in them did not allow for laziness or lack of effort. Setting the pace, as always, Joe Junior became a model student at Choate, respected by teachers and classmates alike. The school, founded in 1896 by Episcopalians and modeled after England's elite Eton College, was situated in beautiful rolling countryside, with a spacious, elm-shaded campus. The headmaster was George St. John, a tall, severe-looking man with hollow cheeks and a balding head, who presided over the students and faculty with a strong, authoritarian hand. The rules were strict, and serious study was expected.

At fourteen, Joe was physically sturdy, standing five feet six inches tall and weighing a hundred and thirty pounds, and was considered "one of the most promising" of Choate's younger athletes. The physical education director reported that he would be "watching his development with special interest."

Classwork was not easy for Joe, and in the first half of his freshman year his grades were poor. Yet, in all his letters to his father, he earnestly reported that he was studying hard, going every Sunday to Mass and staying out of trouble. Eventually, his persistence paid off. For the last quarter of his freshman year, in every subject his marks went up. His English teacher commented, "Joe deserves a great deal of credit for turning defeat into victory."

The headmaster, writing to Kennedy Senior, described Joe as "one of the most worthwhile people in the world. He has a high Academic Quotient, big heart and . . . I am betting on him 100%."

In time, young Joe fulfilled everyone's hopes. With astonishing self-control, and an eye capable of discerning how best to meet the expectations of others, he soon became a dominant power on campus, winning varsity positions on the football and hockey teams, becoming the editor of the yearbook and accepting the vice-presidency of the Andrews Society, a student association devoted to charitable works. Yet, for all his involvement with Choate, Joe's primary interest remained his family. He was the carrier of his family's ambition, and in him the desire for power and fame attained a force so intense that it tended to set him off from easygoing relations with his fellow students. At school, he talked about his family constantly, and to one or another of his sisters and brothers he wrote almost weekly.

WHEN YOUNG JACK arrived at Choate, in the fall of 1931, skinny and tall for his fourteen years, his older brother was already a fifth former, with all the special privileges that went along with this second-to-highest ranking. Wherever Jack went, Joe had already arrived before him and had attained such success that Jack could not believe he would ever catch up. He had responded in the oddly appealing way in which he had responded to similar challenges before—by refusing to emulate Joe, by taking himself out of the academic competition, and by using his charm to build a cadre of loyal friends with whom he could shape his own path in his own way. It was a strategy that brought him freedom and independence, but the price was high. For, once the habit of not working hard was deeply set, it was hard to break. To his parents, Jack's nonchalant attitude toward his responsibilities was a source of constant frustration. His father tried everything he could, from pressure to praise, to mobilize the boy. But the pattern continued, and Jack's freshman grades placed him in the second-to-last grouping.

On the playing fields, it was a different story. Here Jack did drive himself, trying especially hard to excel in football. But, given his frail physique and his continual health problems, which frequently landed him in the infirmary—his best was good enough only for the junior squad. Nevertheless, he fought hard and his father respected him for his fight.

In other ways, too, Jack was leaving his mark on Choate, by using a talent he had inherited from his father: the capacity for making friends. Possessed of a deep self-confidence, he was able to form many friendships, some of which lasted for years. "When he flashed his smile," the headmaster's son later recalled, "he could charm a bird off a tree."

His most enduring friendship was formed with Kirk Le Moyne Billings. The son of a Pittsburgh physician, "Lem" was a warm, bearish boy with unkempt blond hair and pale blue eyes. As he later described the relationship, "it was the closest friendship either of us ever knew. I was immediately captivated by Jack. He had the best sense of humor of anybody I had ever met. . . . No matter where we went he knew how to make the outing a special occasion: if we were at a show together, he'd somehow manage to sneak backstage to see the leading singer; if we were eating out, he'd be so charming to the waitress that we'd end up with an extra dessert. He enjoyed things with such intensity. . . ."

Jack reached out for other close friends as well, and soon he began to feel, as Lem later put it, "that Choate was *his*," irrespective of his brother's considerable presence there, for he knew that behind all of his brother's accomplishments there remained a certain loneliness in him, an absorption so deep with his father's great plans for him, that "he could never fully enjoy the present."

Yet, for all Jack's bravado and his real social success, there was no question that his failure to keep up with Joe, academically or athletically, hurt. One of Lem's most poignant memories of Jack revolved about the Prize Day exercises in 1933, when parents and students gathered to honor the graduating sixth formers. Joe and Rose Kennedy came, along with Grandpa and Grandma Fitzgerald, to enjoy Joe's moment of triumph and to applaud when he was awarded the coveted Harvard Trophy, given to the graduating sixth former who best combined scholarship and sportsmanship. As Lem tells the story, Jack was "very pleased for his brother," but at the same time, "when he saw the look of pride bursting from his father's face, he felt a little sad."

After the ceremony, Jack led Lem on a long walk across the campus to the athletic field, where they sat and talked openly. "This was the first time Jack ever admitted to me that underneath it all he believed he was smarter than Joe but that no one understood this, least of all his parents. His intelligence, he believed, simply worked along different lines—more questioning perhaps, and more imaginative, but less organized. . . . Nor could he help but wish that someday the roles would be reversed, that someday he would achieve supremacy in a family in which he had for so long felt himself in a subordinate role."

WITH YOUNG JOE'S GRADUATION, his father, who had fostered his talent and applauded his triumphs, now decided that the time had come to shape his character with a new experience. Joe Senior sought the advice of Harvard law professor (and later Supreme Court Justice) Felix Frankfurter, who suggested sending the boy to the University of London to spend a year with socialist Harold Laski, whom Frankfurter called the "greatest teacher in the world."

To Rose Kennedy, the idea of sending her favorite son to study under a socialist professor seemed "a little wild and even dangerous." But Joe Senior was captivated by the idea of exposing Joe Junior to a strain of political thought that was bound to have an impact on the social order for years to come.

It was an extraordinary opportunity for eighteen-year-old Joe, and it was during that year that his intellect caught fire.

Arriving in London with an introduction from Frankfurter, Joe found himself queuing up with a large group of students waiting outside the professor's door to consult him about everything from Marxism and socialism to constitutionalism and democracy. At his lectures, crowds jostled for seats and large numbers stood up in the back. A less confident boy might have found the situation intimidating, but as it turned out, Joe became one of Laski's favorite students.

Explaining his affection for the boy, the professor said that he had had innumerable students over the years far abler than Joe, but not many who had "his eager zest for life." Laski recalled Joe's astonishing vitality and enthusiasm. "He had set his heart on a political career and yet, with a smile that was pure magic he was willing to submit to relentless teasing about his determination to be nothing less than the first Catholic President of the United States."

Laski's real teaching took place at his celebrated Sunday teas, which he hosted for his students in a small book-lined study in his London flat. "Joe would always come to the teas," Mrs. Laski remembered. "He was tall and very good-looking and argumentative and very bright. . . ."

During Joe Junior's breaks from school, he traveled on the Continent, which gave him an opportunity to gauge the prevailing mood of the European democracies. Over Christmas vacation, he attended the Disarmament Conference in Geneva, and, in the spring of 1934, he journeyed to Germany, where Adolf Hitler was moving at an astonishing speed to recruit millions of volunteers into a new German army and to bring all of German life under the control of the Nazi Party.

Before starting his trip, Joe told his father, he had heard the greatest condemnation of Hitler and his party at Laski's teas and "had heard him and many German socialists tell of the frequent brutalities in Germany." But now that he had talked with Germans who stressed what life was like before the coming of Hitler, he had, he thought, reached a better understanding of the situation.

> They had tried liberalism, and it had seriously failed. They had no leader, and as time went on Germany was sinking lower and lower. . . . Hitler came in. He saw the need of a common enemy. Someone, by whose riddance the Germans would feel they had cast out the cause of their predicament. It was excellent psychology, and it was too bad that it had to be done to the Jews. This dislike of the Jews, however, was well-founded. . . .
>
> As far as the brutality is concerned, it must have been necessary to use some, to secure the whole-hearted support of the people. . . . It was a horrible thing but in every revolution you have to expect some bloodshed.

One might excuse Joe Junior's terrible insensitivity to the plight of German Jews on the grounds that he was young, that others, with far more experience, also misunderstood the nature of the Nazi phenomenon in its early years. But his letters reveal such a complete acceptance of the stereotyped image of the Jew as driving, unscrupulous and unethical that they betray a certain grounding in anti-Semitism that can only have come from his family background.

Joseph Kennedy had said, when he first went to Hollywood, that "a bunch of ignorant Jewish furriers" were running the movie industry, "simply because they had unethically pushed their way into a wide-open virgin field." Several of Kennedy's friends remember his arguing vociferously against letting too many Jews into Harvard, while others remember disparaging remarks about letting Jewish families into Christian country clubs. All these attitudes Joe Junior must have absorbed to the point where he knew that in his father, he had a willing listener for his negative observations. Nor, from what can be discerned from subsequent correspondence, did Kennedy Senior ever attempt to correct or soften Joe Junior's tone.

Had Kennedy seen his role as one of inculcating ethical standards in his nineteen-year-old son, he should have met this blatantly bigoted letter with a long letter of his own. But for a man whose dominant ideology was achievement, the importance of Joe Junior's experience abroad lay not so much in the substance of the beliefs he was acquiring as in the capacity he was developing to express them. And so it was. Joe returned home immersed enough in the ideals of socialism to be able to argue with his father on the comparative merits of capitalism and communism. In this discussion, in which Joe Junior took the socialist side of the argument, Jack sided with his brother. According to Rose, this did not bother her husband at all. "I don't care what the boys think about my ideas," he said. "I can always look out for myself. The important thing is that they should stand together."

IN THE AUTUMN OF 1934, Joe Junior began his freshman year at Harvard. It was a different college from the one his father had entered three decades before. In the early 1930s, a revolutionary "house" system had been inaugurated whereby all students, from their sophomore year on, would live in one of seven houses modeled after the colleges at Oxford. Beautifully constructed with large living quarters, elegant dining halls, spacious common rooms and comfortable libraries, the houses provided a home where young men of all social strata could mingle, work, eat and sleep. Although the clubmen still set much of the tone of undergraduate life, the house structure provided a vast improvement in living conditions for the majority of students and, it was hoped, a new and freer social pattern.

But at a place like Harvard the ties of background would never be eliminated, and to some extent they were simply transferred to the houses. Each acquired a certain character and admitted a certain "kind" of boy. Eliot House became known as the aristocratic house, the home of unfriendly socialites; Lowell attracted the grinds and academic highbrows; Winthrop, which Joe selected, was known as the house of the jocks.

Having graduated from a private prep school and come from a background of great wealth, Joe Junior started his Harvard career with far more social leverage than his father had enjoyed. He also had the advantage of entering Harvard as "the son of a famous father." Then, too, there was his appearance and his athletic ability. Standing almost six feet tall at around a hundred and seventy-five pounds, "he was so handsome," according to one observer, "he could have been in the movies." Joining the freshman football squad, he quickly made friends in the athletic crowd, and, when the time came for the clubs to choose their new members, he was invited into both Hasty Pudding and the Spee Club, which stood just below the top echelon of exclusive clubs.

But to Joe the social life mattered very little. While he formed some close friendships, he essentially operated alone. And while he often attended debutante balls, his tastes in girls, as he once admitted to his mother, ran to show girls and actresses.

"For Joe," Lem Billings observed, "Harvard was simply a way station, for he already had his heart set on a political future and he was so closely tied with his father's ambitions for him that there was little room for anything else."

WITH HIS OLDER brother away at college, Jack felt an enormous sense of release. "When he came back to Choate his junior year," Lem recalled, "he was really ready to give himself to his work and he even began to enjoy some of his subjects." His English teacher that year reported that "he had a very definite flair for writing" and advised a literary career. When a subject aroused Jack's interest, his lounging manner would give way to excitement and his mind would be totally engaged.

But once again illness returned to curb whatever strides Jack might have taken. In the winter of his junior year he was removed to New Haven Hospital, where a monitoring of his blood count revealed a serious condition—probably hepatitis; the family brought him home for the rest of the term.

Despite repeated illnesses, however, Jack enjoyed his final years at Choate. His spontaneous humor made him extremely popular, and even at sixteen he was beginning to develop a winning way with women that would last throughout his life. "The girls really liked Jack," Lem recalled. "I hated to admit it at the time, but it was true."

Jack spent a lot of time thinking about girls, according to Lem. Yet none of them could ever match up in his mind with his sister Kathleen. "God, was Kathleen a great girl," Lem recalled. "I can still remember how happy Jack was when she came to the convent at Noroton. The first week she was there he insisted we sneak up and visit her, and what fun we had! I think I fell in love with her right then and there."

Throughout their childhood, Jack and Kathleen had been especially close, sharing the same sense of humor, the same irreverence and the same vital curiosity about people. "They were so close," said one friend, "at times I thought of them as twins."

Kathleen looked extraordinarily like her mother, yet her features were illuminated by her radiantly joyous, self-confident sense of life and youth. Worried that her popular daughter was spending too much time with boys, Rose sent her to the same kind of convent school she herself had attended: a strict boarding school where, it was hoped, Kathleen would better train her mind and her body. Yet even there, where the rules prescribed that the girls entertain boys only at formal Sunday teas, "Kick" was amazingly popular. "There were more boys who thought they were in love with Kathleen than you can possibly imagine," one friend recalls.

Joe Senior took a special pride in the extraordinary closeness between Jack and Kathleen. "We had lunch with Kathleen Sunday," Kennedy wrote to Jack at Choate in February of 1935. "She really thinks you are a great fellow. . . . She is coming up on the 16th February and I told her if you and LeMoyne or another of your gang can get off, I will blow you all to a party." As it turned out, however, the plans for the party were

The Golden Trio

Joe Junior, acknowledged leader of the Golden Trio

Jack stretches out in the sun.

Kathleen, left, with schoolmates at Noroton

Jack and Kathleen share a dance.

forgotten in the wake of Jack's near expulsion from school.

The problem was a club formed by Jack, Lem and eleven other boys that had just come to the attention of the headmaster, Mr. St. John. Innocent enough as a loose gathering of high-spirited friends, the club had chosen to call itself the Muckers Club, appropriating a word Mr. St. John frequently used in chapel for the boys who were not diligent enough about their studies. Regarding the Muckers Club as a serious challenge to his authority, St. John threatened Jack and his friends with expulsion unless the club was disbanded. Then, to make sure everyone understood the seriousness of the offense, he devoted an entire chapel to the club, naming the members and characterizing their leaders as "public enemies" of the school.

Still thinking the whole incident a big joke, Jack called up Kathleen to let her know he was now public enemy number one. Responding in kind, Kathleen sent a funny telegram to Jack and Lem teasing them about their new status. Unfortunately, St. John intercepted the telegram and was furious. He summoned Mr. Kennedy for a talk.

Joe Kennedy arrived from Washington the following Sunday. According to Lem, Jack was in a state of considerable agitation. "It was one thing to take on St. John, it was quite another to confront his father. He was terrified that his father would lose confidence in him once and for all."

When Jack walked into the headmaster's study at the appointed hour, his father was already there, seated beside St. John's desk. Recounting the incident later to Lem, Jack said he feared his fate had already been decided and prepared himself for the worst. But then an amazing thing happened. The phone rang for St. John, and in that moment Joe Kennedy leaned over, winked and whispered, "My God, you sure didn't inherit your father's directness or his reputation for using bad language. If that crazy Muckers Club had been mine, you can be sure it wouldn't have started with an M." The moment Jack heard this, he relaxed. From then on, though his father officially backed up St. John in everything he said, Jack knew that in the end his father would be with him no matter what. And as it turned out, Jack was not expelled once he agreed to disband the club.

With the headmaster satisfied, Kennedy took his son to

lunch, where he gave him serious warnings about the importance of developing a sense of responsibility. Then, astonished that Jack had never recognized that the word muckers was a name of derision the Brahmins had given to the Irish boys in the days of their snowball fights on the Common—Kennedy wondered aloud if the proper Mr. St. John himself knew the word he used so regularly in his chapels.

In her memoirs, Rose Kennedy sees the silly episode as "a turning point" in Jack's life. He had discovered the depth of his father's support, but having come to the edge where he had almost lost it, Jack was determined not to risk it again. Under this impetus, he graduated with a record decent enough to afford him the chance to follow in his brother's footsteps and spend a year studying with Harold Laski at the University of London. And, in a final joke, he helped to manipulate the class elections, trading votes among his friends so that he was awarded the distinction "most likely to succeed."

JACK WENT OFF TO London, but he had little time to get to know Professor Laski, for within weeks of his arrival he was once again seriously ill, this time with an attack of jaundice, and it became evident that he would have to go home. Arriving back in the States, Jack felt better and thought he could manage at an American university. But soon his old hepatitis flared up again and he spent nearly two months in the hospital and more months recuperating in the sunny and dry climate of Arizona. Finally, by the fall of 1936, he was ready for college.

14

TEMPTING THE GODS

JOSEPH KENNEDY HAD promised President Roosevelt that he would stay on as chairman of the SEC only long enough to get the commission on its feet. Having done so, he decided to resign in September of 1935. "I'm proud of you," a friend wrote from Boston. "You're quitting at just the proper time. No big man stays too long in a job. Your resignation increases your stature ten times."

These were good years for Kennedy, years in which every-thing he touched seemed to become gold. In the spring of 1936, Paramount Pictures hired him as a special financial adviser to analyze why the company was failing. He performed similar work for RCA at a fee of $150,000, making him one of the highest-paid financial consultants in the country.

Kennedy's return to business did nothing to diminish his closeness to FDR, however, and he continued to receive numer-ous invitations to the White House from the President and his aides. As the '36 campaign got under way, Kennedy volun-teered to put together a defense of Roosevelt's policies in a small book that he called *I'm for Roosevelt.* Written by Kennedy's friend Arthur Krock of *The New York Times,* the book was a curious product, an embrace of the New Deal so uncritical that it credited the administration with every improvement in the economy since 1933. "Roosevelt must be gratified," one critic noted. And with Roosevelt's indisputable victory over Alfred Landon in November 1936, Kennedy's influence in the admin-istration increased tremendously.

In this otherwise happy and fulfilling time, sorrow arrived unexpectedly with the sudden death of Agnes Fitzgerald, Rose's younger sister. A pretty woman with blond wavy hair and clear skin, Agnes had married late, becoming pregnant for the first time at thirty-seven. She gave birth to a son, Joey, and then had two more children, born when she was thirty-eight and forty-two. Then, one morning in 1936, when little Joey came running into his mother's room, he could not rouse her from sleep. He knew at once that she was dead. At the young age of forty-three, Agnes had suffered an embolism. It was the third death in the Fitzgerald family: Eunice was first, dying of tuberculosis at twenty-three, then Fred, who drank himself to death at thirty-five, and now Agnes. For Rose, the death came as "a terrible blow," and for months she did not recover enough to leave her home.

At this same time, the Kennedys' oldest daughter, Rosemary, provided an additional source of sorrow. Given her limitations, she had done exceptionally well, having earlier reached about a fourth-grade level in reading, spelling and arithmetic. But her progress from then on seemed to stop, frustrating her teachers, her parents and, most of all, Rosemary herself. By the age of eighteen, she had reached only a fifth-grade level in English. Her tutor at the special convent school in Providence, Rhode Island, where she had been sent at sixteen, said in a letter to Rose, "She seems especially irritable the day after her lessons. . . . If she is allowed to continue in this, she will become more and more difficult to live with." Rosemary had never stopped trying to improve, but she could not catch up with her sisters and brothers, and, as the years went by, her frustration deepened.

THE PRESIDENT'S REELECTION brought Kennedy an offer of a job as chairman of the Maritime Commission. At first, Kennedy expressed reluctance about accepting the assignment, maintaining that his only experience in maritime matters was his work at Bethlehem Shipbuilding during the war. His hesitancy was merely a pose, however, a desire to appear in public as a reluctant maiden. In fact, as Rose later admitted, "He wanted nothing more than to return to the stimulation of public life." Telling Roosevelt he was "deeply honored by the suggestion," Kennedy prevailed once more upon his old friend Eddie Moore, and they returned to the Marwood estate and settled back into Washington life. And this time Kennedy's appointment was met with praise.

IN THE FALL OF 1936, as young Joe Kennedy entered his junior year, Jack became a freshman at Harvard, where he faced the same situation he had faced when he first entered Choate: his own presence on campus was overshadowed by his older brother, who was one of the emerging stars in the class of '38. The pages of the *Crimson* were filled with Joe's political triumphs. He was elected chairman of the Winthrop House committee; he beat out Caspar Weinberger, Nathaniel Benchley and others to win a position on the student council, and he was named business manager of the class album.

In contrast, Jack failed to win a freshman slot on the student council, nor did he achieve success in sports, though his failure was certainly not for lack of trying. Although recovered from his illness, he was still not robust; at six feet, he weighed only a hundred and forty-nine pounds. While he survived all the early cuts on the freshman football squad, his low weight worked against him. The following year, in a scrimmage, he was thrown to the ground and ruptured a spinal disk. It was an injury that was to plague him the rest of his life.

In spite of his difficulties with athletics and campus politics, Jack managed to create his own world at Harvard, just as he had done at Choate. Within months he had a loyal cadre of friends, and in Torbert Macdonald, a football hero, he found a best friend, the counterpart of Lem Billings at Choate. Also a second son, Macdonald intuitively understood Jack's personal struggle to win recognition from his family. And, like Lem, Torby also fell in love with Kathleen.

Toward the end of his first year, Jack joined the committee that sponsored the annual freshman smoker, a rowdy corncob-pipe affair that attracted more than a thousand freshmen. Agreeing to provide the entertainment, Jack counted on his father, and his father came through with Gertrude Niessen, a throaty New York stage and concert singer, and baseball stars Dizzy Dean and Frankie Frisch. On the night of the smoker, Jack was in his glory. With Memorial Hall filled to capacity, he was remarkably funny as master of ceremonies and the smoker was considered one of the most sparkling in many a year.

After this wildly successful performance, Jack's stature in his class increased, and when the time came to apply for admission to a house, he had no trouble gaining acceptance into Winthrop, where he was ranked "one of the most popular men in his class." Academically, Jack's record remained mediocre. But his tutors recall him as a vital student who thought deeply about political issues, who probed, read and asked questions. And when, in the summer after his freshman year, Jack traveled in Europe with his friend Lem Billings, his letters to his father revealed a far more sophisticated understanding of the Continent's complicated political situation than the analyses his brother Joe had made three years before.

IF IT WAS A TIME when Joe Senior could rightly be proud of both his sons, they could be terribly proud of him too. For, in the second week of December, 1937, Joseph Patrick Kennedy was appointed ambassador to the Court of St. James's, the first

347

Irishman ever named to that most prestigious of all diplomatic posts.

To Roosevelt, the appointment seemed ideal. The current ambassador was returning for health reasons, and while Kennedy merited a place in the administration, he was of too independent a temperament to be considered for the Cabinet; the London post, however, was a great plum and it was far away. "It was the kind of appointment he had been waiting for all along," Rose later recalled. Equally gratifying was the press reaction, which was overwhelmingly favorable.

From dozens of friends and acquaintances, Kennedy received praise. So at this glorious moment it was perhaps not surprising that he failed to absorb the one countering message, received in a remarkably thoughtful letter from a reporter friend, Boake Carter:

> You are a sincere man, Joe. You are a man of courage. You possess that great faith that so many Irishmen have—the faith that no matter what he tackles, he can't be licked. . . . But the job of Ambassador to London needs not only sincerity, faith and an abounding courage—it needs skill brought by years of training. And that, Joe, you simply don't possess. . . . You tempt all the Gods in diving into the Court of St. James as an expert. In so complicated a job, there is no place for amateurs.

Seen in retrospect, in view of how calamitous the ambassadorship would turn out for both the country and the man, Boake Carter's warnings give the Kennedy story the aura of dramatic tragedy. Indeed, had Kennedy been able to say no, had he remained in the States to finish up his work at the Maritime Commission and then returned to private life, the entire history of the Kennedy family might have been different.

JOSEPH KENNEDY TOOK possession of the American embassy in London on a brilliantly sunny afternoon in March, 1938. Situated in elegant Grosvenor Square, the embassy was housed in a series of three connecting brick town houses originally built in 1725 and just newly renovated. The ambassador's office was large and airy, but its decor left Kennedy with "a mixture of amusement and chagrin." In a letter to his friend Jimmy Roosevelt, he notes, "I have a beautiful blue silk room and all I need to make it perfect is a Mother Hubbard dress and a wreath to make me Queen of the May."

Kennedy spent the first days on the job becoming familiar with the staff. As was his custom, he surrounded himself with a few of his faithful friends, and, not surprisingly, Eddie Moore was his choice for chief secretary. The gentle Irishman, however, stayed in America until May so that he could accompany Rosemary and Eunice to England after they finished school.

Kennedy was scheduled to receive his formal accreditation as ambassador on March 8, 1938. Although the ceremony was to be carried out at Buckingham Palace, the home of the royal family, the official title of Kennedy's position remained Ambassador to the Court of St. James's in honor of the days when the court was situated at nearby St. James's Palace. At the appointed hour, three state carriages arrived at Grosvenor Square, complete with coachmen, footmen and outriders in top hats and long scarlet cloaks. Kennedy's entourage was driven to Buckingham Palace, where he presented his credentials to King George VI in a ceremony that was short and simple. Afterward, Kennedy chatted with the King, who, he later wrote, was "most gracious" and "a very pleasant chap."

In the days that followed, Kennedy called on all the foreign representatives of equal rank, as custom demanded. Unlike the previous ambassadors, who affected the stiff manners of English gentlemen, Kennedy retained his usual relaxed carriage. "You can't expect me to develop into a statesman overnight," he said engagingly, propping his feet up on his highly polished desk.

HAD EUROPE REMAINED in a state of peace during Kennedy's tenure, it is possible that he could have come and gone, leaving behind a reputation as a vigorous, capable ambassador. It was his own and his country's misfortune that he became ambassador at a critical hour in Europe's history, a time that demanded an uncommon understanding of history and a broad vision of responsibility—qualities that Joseph Kennedy, shrewd as he was in business affairs, simply did not possess.

Just as Kennedy arrived in England, "the curtain was rising on the final act of the tragedy of appeasement," as one Kennedy biographer has written. For years, Adolf Hitler had been putting Europe on notice that he saw himself as the protector of millions of Germans who had been cut off from the German Reich by the Treaty of Versailles and that he intended, by force if necessary, to bring all these people back into a new and remilitarized Reich. As early as July of 1934, his goal was to annex Austria, but when Benito Mussolini imposed restraint, Hitler temporarily shelved his "Anschluss" plans. A year later, however, he moved cautiously into the Rhineland, and when neither France nor Britain lifted a finger to stop him—so obsessed were they with preserving peace—he decided the time had come to reactivate his plans for the Austrian Anschluss.

During this critical period, the British Prime Minister was the aging Neville Chamberlain. Tall and lean, with graying hair, he was a stern, morose and humorless man. Profoundly affected by the horrible losses of the Great War, Chamberlain was convinced that his single purpose was to keep the peace in Europe. To that end he maintained a policy of appeasement toward Hitler and Mussolini, believing that almost any act of political accommodation was fully justified if it meant preventing another war.

In Chamberlain's Cabinet at this time, according to Winston Churchill, "there seemed one strong young figure standing up against appeasement." That man was Anthony Eden, the handsome young Foreign Secretary. But only days before Kennedy's arrival in London, Eden had resigned in protest. His departure was a great blow to the small body of resisters—including Churchill—who saw the peril of Hitler for what it was.

Kennedy tried at first to steer clear of all the confusing political currents. Arriving in England after Chamberlain had replaced Eden with Lord Halifax—a diplomat of the old school who viewed loyalty as a paramount virtue—Kennedy judged each development in Europe by the single yardstick of its possible effect upon America. He confessed that in spite of all the emotions surrounding Hitler and Mussolini, he could not see how "the Central European developments affect our country or my job." He remained convinced as he wrote to FDR, "that the US would be very foolish to try to mix in."

But events in Europe were moving too rapidly for the United

States to stand aside. For on the night of March 11–12, German troops crossed Austria's border and overnight the Austrian republic became a province of the German Reich. Again neither Britain nor France made a move on Austria's behalf. Without firing a shot, Hitler had gained a strategic position of immense value.

Within hours of the Anschluss, the arrests of Jews began— more than seventy thousand in Vienna alone. "The behavior of the Vienna Nazis was worse than anything I had seen in Germany," reported journalist William L. Shirer. "There was an orgy of sadism." Unaccountably, the Western democracies let the matter pass without incident—a decision with which Kennedy heartily concurred. In time, his isolationism would produce a storm of criticism, but, in the spring of 1938, his position found widespread support.

EVEN IN THE MIDDLE of his responsibilities in London, nothing mattered as much to Kennedy as news of his wife and children whom he badly missed. "Hurry that boat up," he cabled to Rose on March 12, "terribly anxious to see all especially you."

Rose finally arrived in the middle of March with Kathleen and the four youngest Kennedys, and the British reaction was extraordinary. The newspapers published dozens of pictures and stories of the family, involving their readers in the Kennedys in a manner usually reserved for the royal family. Hardly a day passed without a newspaper photograph of little Teddy taking a snapshot with his camera held upside down, or of the five Kennedy children lined up on a train or on a bus. As *Life* magazine told its readers: "When [Franklin Roosevelt] appointed Mr. Kennedy to be Ambassador to Great Britain he got eleven Ambassadors for the price of one."

The day the family arrived, Joe moved them all into the palatial thirty-six-room embassy residence, which stood at 14 Prince's Gate in fashionable Knightsbridge. In the weeks that followed, he and Rose were invited everywhere, sharing in the gaieties of English society. Kennedy was made an honorary member of all the most exclusive clubs in London, including the Royal Thames Yacht Club and the International Sportsmen Club. "According to my count I am now a member of at least six exclusive golf clubs," Rose later remembered him saying. "I wonder what the people in Cohasset would think if they saw me now."

If Rose's smile at this time was larger than usual, it was not surprising. After nearly twenty-five years of marriage during which her social life had markedly diminished from the glittering days of her girlhood in Boston, she now had what she wanted. Never before, she confessed, had the savor of social success been so sweet. The parties, the dinners, the races and regattas and the fancy clothes all were vivid reminders that the Kennedys finally belonged. Even more, they were an assurance to her that she was still young. Having kept her weight down and her face moisturized and protected from the sun, she looked younger than her forty-eight years. "How has this charming, unaffected, and typically American woman struck London?" a reporter for *Vogue* asked. "First, as a phenomenon. Those nine children must be changelings, adopted, borrowed . . . but not hers . . . or how to explain that lithe grace, that slim hipless elegance; that calm, unruffled gaiety?"

Responding joyfully to every social occasion, Rose was clearly in her element. "It was a wonderful time for the two of us," she later recalled, "so much excitement, so much anticipation, so much fun."

The high point of the Kennedys' social life in 1938 was the April weekend they spent with the royal family at Windsor Castle. The magnificent setting, the sumptuous meals, the extraordinary company—all these made it, in Rose's words, a "fabulous, fascinating" experience. For Joe, it offered his first chance to have a lengthy discussion of politics with Neville Chamberlain and his Foreign Secretary, Lord Halifax.

Tramping through the fields that Sunday afternoon, they made an oddly matched trio. Chamberlain's dour personality was in sharp contrast with that of the gregarious Kennedy. Lord Halifax, tall and handsome, an aristocrat by birth and breeding, was in Joe's words "a scholar, a sportsman and everything that an upper class Englishman who gives his life to public service ought to be." For all their differences, however, they were united in an abiding hatred of war and in their willingness to secure peace at almost any price.

In the course of their conversation, Chamberlain recounted for Kennedy how the British ambassador had heard of Hitler's demand for self-determination for the German peoples.

"It seems to me," Kennedy observed, "that the big question is whether Hitler means to limit his activities to helping his Germans or whether he has further objectives that will violate the self-determination of other nations."

"That is the important point precisely," replied Chamberlain. "Yet the only way we can find the answer is to wait and see."

In the weeks ahead, despite his intention to steer clear of British influence, Kennedy became more and more involved in Chamberlain's efforts to keep the peace. It was because he believed that he was buying peace for America that Kennedy chose to ally himself with Chamberlain rather than Winston Churchill. The choice would come back to haunt him, but for now, it was a choice with which the overwhelming majority of people in both Britain and America agreed.

15

THE LONG WEEKEND

IN JUNE 1938 KENNEDY returned to the United States to attend his son Joe's commencement from Harvard. From all indications, it promised to be an occasion of great pride for the popular ambassador—pride in his cherished son, who was graduating with honors, and pride in his own accomplishments, which, the papers predicted, would earn him a coveted honorary degree from Harvard.

Arriving in New York aboard the *Queen Mary,* Kennedy was met by a host of reporters all pumped up by a recent magazine story suggesting candidacy for the presidency in 1940. Once suggested, the idea had been picked up by a number of newspapers. The Washington *Post* observed that of all the contenders Kennedy had "the nearest to a Rooseveltian personality," and it concluded, "A mental picture of the White House with nine or ten Kennedys galloping about is most beguiling." But Kennedy was a realist who understood that his Catholicism militated against him. So he greeted reporters at the dock with a flat statement that he would not consider any presidential boom in 1940. "I enlisted under President Roosevelt to do whatever he wanted me to do," he told them. "If I had my eye on another job, it would be a complete breach of faith."

After traveling to Hyde Park to report to the President, Kennedy boarded a train for Boston. It was on that train that he heard for certain that he would not receive an honorary degree from Harvard. By one account, the nominating committee had considered Kennedy but decided that the rumors about his bootlegging activities in the days of Prohibition made it impossible to confer upon him such a distinguished award.

"It was a terrible blow to him," Rose later confessed. "Suddenly he felt as if he were once again standing in front of the Porcellian Club, knowing he'd never be admitted."

Joe spent the afternoon with young Joe at the Class Day festivities, a colorful mix of parades, speeches and skits, which Joe Junior had helped to organize. But as soon as Class Day was over, Kennedy retreated to his summer home at Hyannis Port, choosing not to attend the commencement exercises the following afternoon. Though he had come all the way across the Atlantic to see his son graduate, he must have decided that it would be too painful for him, after his hopes for the award had been raised so high, to witness the stately pageant during which the coveted honorary degrees would be conferred on others. There is no record of how Joe Junior felt about his father's sudden decision to forgo the graduation. But it must have been painful to realize that at the last minute Kennedy was unable to rise beyond his own personal disappointment to enjoy this day with his son.

WHEN KENNEDY RETURNED to London, he brought young Joe and Jack with him. Joe was to work for the year as his father's secretary, while Jack would remain only for the summer. Once the boys settled into the embassy residence, Rose took great joy in the thought that the entire family was together once more. Rosemary was happily situated at a special school in the country. Eunice, Pat and Jean attended a convent school outside of London but came home on weekends. Bobby and Teddy went to a day school in London. "I used to meet the boys at their school," recalled their nurse, Luella Hennessey. "We'd walk through Hyde Park and they'd kick pebbles, the way boys do. Teddy was always so bubbly and happy, always wanting to talk. Bobby was always the more serious one, a deep-thinking boy."

In London even more than in New York and Boston, Joe Junior, Jack and Kathleen set the pace for the younger generation. At twenty-three, twenty-one and eighteen, they were just the right age to enjoy the city's heady social life. Accepted without question among London's aristocracy, they were invited to country houses for weekends; they were asked to teas, balls and dances. But London was, above all, Kathleen's town. At eighteen her youth and freshness made heads turn, but more than that it was her vibrant personality, her sheer enjoyment of life that captured British hearts. She was genial and charming, and the beaux began pursuing her more than ever.

Kathleen's social life was dictated by the hectic activities of the debutante season, which was held between April and August. Through the endless rounds of parties and dances and lavish debutante balls, Kathleen gradually shaped her own circle of friends. Pasted into her scrapbook were dozens of letters and cards from boyfriends. At her own coming-out party, after a dinner for eighty young people, more than three hundred guests were received in the embassy ballroom, where a popular English swing band played into the night. All evening long Kathleen changed partners among noblemen and royalty, including Prince Frederick of Prussia, the Earl of Chichester and Viscount Newport. She had become the most exciting debutante of 1938.

Moving about in a world that was overwhelmingly Protestant, it was perhaps inevitable that Kathleen would fall in love with a non-Catholic man. At the time Rose was not concerned; she trusted that Kick would instinctively conclude that a mixed marriage could lead only to unhappiness. Besides, Kick was only eighteen, and before the time came for her to settle down the Kennedys would be back in America, where the number of eligible Catholics was far greater. And it all might have worked as Rose imagined had Kick not met William Cavendish, the Marquess of Hartington. Known as Billy, he was the heir to the Duke of Devonshire, one of England's wealthiest, most powerful men.

Kathleen and Billy first met in July 1938 at the annual garden party given by the King and Queen at Buckingham Palace. Kathleen arrived in the company of her friend Sissy Thomas and her brothers, Joe and Jack. It was in the royal gardens, as she was strolling with Sissy and David Ormsby-Gore, Sissy's boyfriend, that Kathleen encountered Billy, David's cousin and best friend. Billy had a well-bred air, a quiet ease that lent a certain grace to his tall, lanky frame. For nearly an hour the two stood talking amid a constant swirl of activity, and when the conversation was over they both knew, Kathleen later said, that something special was going to happen.

The week after they met, Billy invited Kathleen to his parents' coastal home, Compton Place in Eastbourne, a lovely ivy-covered house that was only one of the eight great houses belonging to the Devonshires. Initially, the Duke and Duchess seemed to have little objection to their son's relationship with Kathleen, undoubtedly considering it a novel friendship and nothing more. She was certainly no figure for marriage, since Billy, as the Duke's eldest son, was in line for the succession. Furthermore, the Duke's anti-Catholicism was legendary. Even so, Kathleen was so charming and so animated that Billy's parents could not help liking her. So long as the relationship remained casual, there was no great need to lay down the law. In the meantime, there was much to be enjoyed about this vital young girl.

For the month of August 1938, the Kennedy family took a house in Cannes on the French Riviera. While they were playing in the blue Mediterranean and lying on the sun-drenched beach, the situation in Europe was moving steadily toward the crisis that would soon culminate in the infamous Munich Agreement.

For years, Hitler had been claiming that the Treaty of Versailles had wrongfully and maliciously given Czechoslovakia the Sudetenland, the rich mountainous region bordering on Germany. Three million Germans lived there, and Hitler had long been encouraging the Czech Nazi Party to exploit the grievances of the Sudetens and to agitate for increased local autonomy. When Britain and France made it easy for him to subjugate Austria in March, Hitler was encouraged to pursue his designs more sharply against Czechoslovakia.

In late May 1938, reports of menacing German troop movements led to a partial mobilization of the Czech army. Since then, through all the summer months, negotiations had been conducted in Czechoslovakia, but by late August no agreement had been reached and Germany placed its army upon a war footing. The British Cabinet went into a series of tense secret meetings. As the situation stood, France was committed by treaty to come to the aid of Czechoslovakia if Germany invaded; and if France stepped in, Britain was bound to follow.

On the night of August 30, Ambassador Joseph Kennedy met with Prime Minister Chamberlain at 10 Downing Street. To Kennedy, Chamberlain admitted there were some in his government who strongly believed that unless Hitler was stopped now his prestige would so increase that it would soon be impossible to halt him. With this Chamberlain disagreed. "It is quite easy to get into war," he said, "but what have we proven after we are in?" Kennedy, with his own strong predilections against war, was relieved to find Chamberlain still standing firm for a peaceful solution.

Kennedy's views, however, did not sit well with Roosevelt and Secretary of State Cordell Hull. Both were troubled over Chamberlain's increasing dedication to "peace at any price." Yet neither Hull nor anyone in the State Department warned Kennedy directly about getting too involved in the details of the unfolding crisis. On the contrary, as events heated up, the State Department consistently praised the full and rich reports Kennedy was sending, reports that were possible only because of his closeness to the British government.

On the evening of September 12, people all over Europe sat close to their radios awaiting news of Adolf Hitler's speech at the Nuremberg party rally, a rally attended by hundreds of thousands of Nazi followers—storm troopers, elite guards, members of the Hitler Youth. Fearing Hitler's speech would be a declaration of war, Joe Kennedy sat listening to a radio with several of his aides, and translations soon enabled them to grasp the substance of what Hitler was saying.

Hitler took the offensive immediately, declaring that, "The Almighty . . . has not created seven million Czechs in order that they should supervise the three million five hundred thousand

Germans or act as guardians for them and still less do them violence and torture. I can only say . . . that if these tortured creatures cannot obtain their rights and assistance by themselves they can obtain both from us."

Kennedy interpreted the speech as "boastful, offensive, and threatening," which indeed it was. But at least Hitler did not demand that the Sudeten be handed over to him outright. Later that evening, Kennedy learned that the Prime Minister and his Cabinet were also gratified that "Hitler had neither closed the door entirely nor yet put his hand to the trigger." (It is now known that, even as he spoke, Hitler had already set October 1 for an attack across the Czech frontier.)

Seizing as usual the slightest opening to peace, Chamberlain made a stunning decision—to seek a personal interview with the Führer. Hitler, reported journalist William L. Shirer, was "astounded but highly pleased that the man who presided over the destinies of the mighty British Empire should come pleading to him."

The reaction of a large part of the world to Chamberlain's decision was, as Kennedy described it, one of "profound relief." But in Czechoslovakia, the people suspected a sellout, and rightly so, for during his meeting with Hitler, Chamberlain agreed in principle to the idea of self-determination, which in this case would involve a transfer to Germany of all areas in which ethnic Germans constituted a majority.

In the days that followed, British and French ministers met to draw up proposals as to which German districts within Czechoslovakia should be given to the Reich. The Czechs were told that if they rejected the proposals they would have to fight Germany alone. On the other hand, if they agreed to the Sudetenland transfer, both Britain and France would guarantee the borders of the new Czechoslovakian state. Thus deserted by their allies, the Czechs "had no other choice," an official communiqué stated, but to accept the Anglo-French proposals.

The Prime Minister promptly returned to Germany, and in a mood of great satisfaction began his meeting with Hitler by recounting his complicated but successful efforts at convincing all parties to accept the principle of the Sudetenland transfer, with an international commission to supervise the process. But, to Chamberlain's astonishment, Hitler responded by saying that the plan was no longer of any use, that he had since decided that Czechoslovakia must hand over the Sudetenland by October 1 with no nonsense of an international commission.

"It seems," observed William L. Shirer, "that Hitler has given Chamberlain the doublecross."

When Chamberlain returned to London, very tired and worn, he ran into strong opposition to the new Nazi demands. Both the French and the Czechs rejected them, and France ordered a partial mobilization. "Finally cornered," wrote Shirer, "Chamberlain agreed to inform Hitler that if France became engaged in war with Germany as a result of her treaty obligations to the Czechs, Britain would feel obliged to support her."

As the specter of war loomed larger, most people believed that London would be subjected to attacks from the air. The city quickened its preparations for war. At the embassy, Joe Kennedy had the children's belongings packed. As an oppressive gloom settled over Europe, Joe Kennedy found at least one glimmer of light in the Prime Minister's declaration that "I shall not give up the hope of a peaceful solution as long as any chance for peace remains. I would not hesitate to pay even a third visit to Germany, if I thought it would do any good." The nation listened admiringly but without much hope.

Then suddenly a message came from Hitler inviting Chamberlain to meet him at Munich. He had also invited Mussolini and the French Premier, Édouard Daladier. To the cheers of Parliament, Chamberlain declared that "the crisis has been once more postponed."

Amidst the general rejoicing, only a few understood the critical fact that though the conference would decide the destiny of the Czech nation, the voice of the Czech people would not even be heard. And indeed, at Munich, without the Czechs present, the substance of the deal was settled. There was no attempt to return to the Anglo-French plan, and when it was all over, Hitler had gained everything. He had threatened that his troops would enter the Sudetenland by October 1, and so they did—without firing a shot.

So relieved were the British people at not having to go to war that Chamberlain was treated, upon his return from Munich, as a conquering hero. Rose later recalled that Joe was so happy that "he kissed me and twirled me around in his arms, repeating over and over what a great day this was and what a great man Chamberlain was."

But within days the mood of the British people changed as they began to recognize that, as one historian has written, their "deliverance from war . . . had been purchased with the sacrifice of Czechoslovakia." The thought provoked feelings of humiliation and shame.

It was Winston Churchill who, in gloomy and unforgettable eloquence, proclaimed for history the meaning of Munich. "We are in the presence of a disaster of the first magnitude," he said. "Our brave people should know that we have sustained a defeat without a war."

In this highly charged atmosphere, Kennedy made the great error of committing himself fully and unequivocally to Chamberlain's policy. Having stood by the Prime Minister through all the ups and downs of the Munich negotiations, he now continued to stand by him as the flames of hatred and invective rose up everywhere. In a speech intended to give the British government a vote of confidence for having spared Europe the catastrophe of war, Kennedy launched into a plea for coexistence with dictatorships, hoping that in an atmosphere of tolerance the policies of the Munich declarations could work themselves out.

The speech provoked a storm of criticism on both sides of the Atlantic. As the New York *Post* editorialized: "To propose that the U.S. make a friend of the man who boasts that he is out to destroy democracy, religion and all the other principles which free Americans hold dear . . . that passes understanding."

FDR, who was trying to walk a delicate line between his growing distaste for the fascist dictatorships and the isolationist sentiments of the majority of Americans, hurried to counter the impression that the United States was prepared to coexist with the dictatorship "whether we like it or not." Within days of the Kennedy speech, he delivered a radio speech sharply critical of the dictatorships. To Kennedy, FDR's statement felt like a stab in the back.

Support for the theory of coexistence was further undermined on the night of November 9–10, when Hitler carried out his terrible pogrom against the Jews of Germany. Later known as *Krystallnacht,* the night of the broken glass, the Nazi rampage through the Jewish ghettos left thousands of shops, homes and synagogues destroyed. Thirty-six deaths were reported and twenty thousand Jews were arrested. On this flaming, riotous night, William L. Shirer wrote, "the Third Reich had deliberately turned down a dark and savage road from which there was to be no return." The Western world recoiled in horror.

A turning point was reached in March 1939, when Hitler's armies invaded Czechoslovakia. Despite repeated assurances that the cession of the German Sudetenland represented his last demand in Europe, Hitler was setting out to conquer non-Germanic lands. Now no one, not even Chamberlain himself, could ignore the Nazi threat.

Faced with howls of criticism from the press, with an impending revolt in the House of Commons, and with Hitler now making ominous threats against Poland, Chamberlain finally made up his mind to act. Sixteen days after Hitler entered Prague, Chamberlain told the House that if Poland was attacked, "His Majesty's government would feel themselves bound at once to lend the Polish government all support in their power."

"That statement marked a new shift in British policy," Kennedy later wrote. "I talked about it that night to President Roosevelt. 'Chamberlain's plan,' he said, 'is a good one, but it probably means war.' " Unlike Kennedy, FDR understood that there was a limit to the price that democracies would pay to avoid war. And with the destruction of Czechoslovakia, that limit had been reached.

16

HOSTAGES TO FORTUNE

I N EUROPE'S LAST REMAINING year of peace, Rose Kennedy and her children enjoyed some of the most exciting and stimulating experiences of their lives: traveling, attending parties and luncheons, fulfilling social obligations. Indeed, in reading Rose's diaries for 1938 and 1939, it seems impossible to imagine the awful calamity toward which Europe was heading.

For the events of the social world continued as regularly as the changing seasons, almost as if the upper class, filled with so many painful memories of World War I, was deliberately trying not to think about the future.

While Rose enjoyed her social life, young Joe was traversing the Continent from one crisis spot to another. Like his father, he had developed a remarkable instinct for being in the right place at the right time. Traveling to Prague, Warsaw, Moscow, Leningrad, Scandinavia, Berlin and The Hague, he wrote long reports to his father with summaries of the situation as he saw it. Wherever he went, he pushed his way into the center of things, displaying a certain rashness, a willingness to take unnecessary chances, almost as if he felt he was invulnerable. Over Christmas 1938, for instance, he traveled with his mother and his brothers and sisters to St. Moritz, in Switzerland, where he discovered the "terrific thrill" of bobsledding down an icy track at seventy-five miles an hour. On the ski slopes, his daring caught up with him. Skiing down a steep trail, he fell, breaking his arm. But the very next day he was out on the skating rink, his arm in a sling. Then it was back to London for a crash course in international banking, followed by a trip to war-torn Spain, where the long Civil War was coming to an end.

With all this extraordinary experience under his belt, as one friend observed, he emerged "a different Joe from the young man I knew a few months ago. There is the same smile, the friendly winning way, but he is now much older than 23."

JACK KENNEDY ARRIVED in England in the spring of 1939, having taken the semester off from Harvard so that he, too, could enjoy the opportunities the ambassadorship provided. In his luggage, he carried a pile of books he was reading in preparation for his senior honors thesis on Great Britain's lack of preparation for war. In the aftermath of Munich, Jack had hit upon the preparedness topic, which earned the enthusiastic approval of his teachers. The very fact that Jack had come up with a topic so early showed a certain diligence not previously noted in his character.

He started on a fact-finding tour with a stint in the American embassy in Paris. From there, he went to Poland, Lithuania,

Latvia, Russia, Turkey, Palestine and the Balkans, sending back detailed reports to his father. Taken as a whole, his letters revealed the working of a shrewd, perceptive, detached mind.

He returned in June to London, where he enjoyed an active social life for a month before heading back to the Continent with his Harvard friend Torbert Macdonald. After traveling through Germany, Jack wanted to visit Czechoslovakia. But with Prague in turmoil, such visits were forbidden. As Foreign Service Officer George F. Kennan recalled, Ambassador Kennedy made it clear to the embassy in Prague that "it was up to us" to find means of getting Jack through the German lines so that he could see what he wanted to see. The embassy staff was furious at having to waste time on this "upstart ignoramus," but they did as the ambassador asked. For Jack, the tour was an extraordinary educational experience. Not only did he gather the information he needed for his thesis, but he got the chance to witness the final rumblings of an entire continent moving toward war.

WHILE HER BROTHERS WERE touring Europe, Kathleen, following in her mother's footsteps, absorbed herself fully in the social life of London. By this time, her closest friends assumed she and Billy were semi-engaged. One Boston paper ran the tantalizing headline, KENNEDY GIRL MAY WED PEER. Both families immediately denied the rumor, and, in truth, the young couple had reached no such agreement. While they had been seeing each other regularly since their first meeting, and while their romance was intense, religion remained an insurmountable obstacle.

WITH THE ANNOUNCEMENT of the Nazi-Soviet Pact on August 21, Europe moved yet another step closer to war. Hurrying back to London from Cannes, where the family had been vacationing, Kennedy found Chamberlain "more depressed" than he had ever seen him before. "I have done everything that I can think of, Joe," the Prime Minister said, "but it looks as if all my work has been of no avail. The Poles can't be saved. All that the English can do is to wage a war of revenge that will mean the entire destruction of Europe."

The waiting was over on September 1, 1939; "the news came

with a rush," Kennedy recorded. "German troops had crossed the border; German planes were bombing Polish cities and killing civilians." The German army was on the march, and by the pledge Chamberlain himself had given, Britain was bound to come to Poland's aid.

On Sunday, September 3, Chamberlain prepared to speak to the British people. From the embassy residence at Prince's Gate, Rose, Joe Junior, Jack and Kathleen left for the House of Commons, where Parliament was scheduled to meet at twelve o'clock to hear the Prime Minister. A remarkable photograph shows the three young people en route. There is Joe Junior in a pin-striped suit, Jack in light jacket and striped tie, and Kathleen in a simple black dress, white pearls and white gloves, her pretty face framed by a large black hat. Captured in arrested movement, they have a look of high adventure, almost a jaunty appearance. As they walked swiftly toward the houses of Parliament, this golden trio could not have imagined how much they each would lose by the war that was about to begin.

Taking seats in the overflowing House chamber, the young Kennedys witnessed the dramatic moment when Chamberlain said, "This country is at war with Germany," and the entire chamber broke into sustained applause.

ROSE AND THE FAMILY returned to America soon after war was declared. For the ambassador, London became, he wrote, "rather a lonesome spot."

Though Kennedy would have liked now to resign his ambassadorship, he knew he could not leave his post in this time of crisis. So he settled in for what would be one of the most difficult periods of his life as he witnessed a diminution of his power. Where he had once been Roosevelt's right-hand man, now he was being bypassed by the President (who had opened his own secret correspondence with Churchill), and by the State Department. Having said repeatedly that England had little chance of winning the war and that he did not want his country involved, Kennedy had placed himself on a collision course with his British friends. He did not understand that no matter how they had argued before the war that Britain should stay out, once His Majesty's government was in the fight, everything was different. For while the British acknowledged the tough odds, they were inspired to fight harder. Even Chamberlain, Kennedy noted, "was now committed."

During these dark days, Kennedy turned to the one member of his family who was left in England—his nineteen-year-old retarded daughter, Rosemary. Still enrolled at a convent school deep in the countryside and thus safe from the bombing of London, she was happier and making more progress than she had made in many years. With all the rest of her family gone, she took it upon herself, as best she could, to be her father's companion. He visited her regularly and had her come to stay with him on occasional weekends. Even so, Kennedy felt increasingly isolated.

Then, in April 1940, Hitler suddenly invaded the neutral countries of Denmark and Norway. "The news is stupefying," William L. Shirer wrote in his diary. "Copenhagen occupied this morning, Oslo this afternoon . . . How the Nazis got there—under the teeth of the British navy—is a complete mystery."

In his memoirs, Kennedy recorded that in the wake of the brutal invasion "a revolution in British government broke with all its fury." The call for Chamberlain's resignation and for a new national government was sounded with bitter intensity. Finally, with his support rapidly eroding, Chamberlain agreed to resign and Winston Churchill became Prime Minister.

Events now moved swiftly. Hitler's forces occupied Belgium and Holland. The fall of France and the isolation of Britain were imminent. On May 13, Churchill appeared in Parliament as Prime Minister for the first time and made his historic "blood, toil, tears and sweat" speech, calling for "victory at all costs." Never losing faith that victory was possible, Churchill imposed that faith on the less confident. From a distance, he looked extraordinarily old-fashioned in his black coat, wing collar and bow tie, but his understanding of the Nazi threat was more profound than that of any other politician.

Perhaps in a different decade Kennedy would have appreciated Churchill's strength and inner vitality, but as events were unfolding in this momentous year of 1940 he perceived Churchill as a mortal threat to America's noninvolvement in the war; and

Churchill, fearing that Kennedy's pessimism would undermine the British cause in America, returned the suspicion in kind. As the weeks went by, Kennedy found himself increasingly cut off from 10 Downing Street.

With the fall of France on June 17, Britain had lost her closest ally, the nation with whom she had expected to fight until the bitter end. Yet, all through the summer of 1940, with the threats of invasion, aerial bombing and brutal warfare looming so large and so terrible, the British went about their business as if nothing untoward were happening. For their fantastic courage, Kennedy admired the British people greatly, but in his judgment, qualities of the human spirit could not be measured against Britain's lack of planes, tanks and guns to meet the German threat. "With the French out of the way and the Germans in control of all the ports I can see nothing but slaughter ahead," Kennedy said. And with each such dismal prediction, Kennedy's popularity fell still further.

BACK IN AMERICA, young Joe had enrolled at Harvard Law School, preparing for the day when he could begin his assault on the world of politics. Every Sunday he would journey into Boston to have dinner with his grandfather, gradually absorbing old Honey Fitz's understanding of Massachusetts politics.

Since 1940 was an election year, Fitzgerald suggested that Joe take his first political step by running as a delegate to the presidential convention to be held that summer in Chicago. Joe said he would relish the opportunity. He promptly took to the neighborhoods, knocking on doors, walking through saloons and barbershops. "I'm Joe Kennedy Junior. . . . I'd like to represent you at the national convention." Handsome and warm, he made an immediate impression on everyone he met.

On the ballot, Joe Junior was pitted against five candidates for two seats, and on voting day he and his running mate came in first and second, thus assuring Joe a seat at the convention. "Grandpa thought I did quite well," Joe told his father in a triumphant letter, "so I guess the Kennedy name is a pretty good vote getter. . . ."

As involved as Joe Junior was in politics, he continued to work hard at his studies. When the first-year grades were posted, his score was excellent. And then there was the wild experience of the Democratic National Convention, at which he saw FDR nominated by acclamation to run for a third term.

Jack, meanwhile, had been working hard on his honors thesis, and the final product, which he called "Appeasement at Munich," earned him a magna cum laude.

"Finished my thesis," Jack had written to his father back in March. "I'll be interested to see what you think of it, as it represents more work than I've ever done in my life."

As it turned out, the ambassador not only thought it a "swell" job but suggested that Jack send it on to Arthur Krock at *The New York Times* to see if he felt it could be published. Always ready to aid the Kennedys, Krock offered to help, suggesting the title *Why England Slept* and arranging for the book's publication. Jack then set to work polishing the manuscript.

In response to a letter from his father, Jack shifted the tone of his conclusion, adopting large portions of the letter almost verbatim. Probably the most significant difference between the thesis and the book related to the problem of democracy's response to crisis. Whereas the thesis had speculated about the limitations of democracy for national security, saying that democracy might be an unaffordable luxury, the finished book included lyrical endorsements of democracy and viewed its preservation as the very reason for rearming.

When the book was published in July, it rose quickly to the best-seller lists and the young author became an instant celebrity. Though he laughed at his own success, Jack did everything he could to promote the book—giving newspaper and radio interviews and autographing copies—and he was good at it. As one of his biographers observed, "Young Jack was finding the limelight to his liking."

FOR KATHLEEN, WHO had loved England so, the adjustment to life in the United States was difficult. During her eighteen months in England, she had bloomed into a woman, she had fallen in love and, for the first time, she told Lem Billings, she felt she was "a person in her own right, not simply a Kennedy girl." Upon her return to America, she enrolled in Finch College in New York. Her intent was to study art and design, but she lived mainly for the social events of the weekends. And, as always, the young men flocked around her.

Yet her heart was still in England, and she was unable to commit herself to any of the American boys who fell in love with her. Occasionally, Jack felt obliged to lecture her about her "insincerity" with his friends, but it was difficult for her to take her brother's counsel seriously when he himself was juggling any number of girlfriends. And when they really talked, as they often did, Jack understood the intensity of Kick's desire to return to England.

Joe Kennedy, however, was adamant about keeping his children safe from the certain catastrophe he saw descending. And, indeed, by the end of the summer, the Battle of Britain had already begun.

The German plan was to drive the Royal Air Force out of the skies within four days and to be out of the fight completely in four weeks. The RAF was valiant. Still, by the end of August, Hitler was within measurable distance of achieving his objective of superiority over southeast England. Then, inexplicably, the whole character of the German offensive was altered. The air attack turned from the RAF to the civilian population. For fifty-seven nights, the bombing of London was unceasing. Tens of thousands of Britons died in the Blitz, and more than a million buildings were damaged or destroyed. But the British did not waver. And after the first week of terror they adapted themselves to the fear. The shops in the heart of the city became a symbol of defiance. Big and small, they had their windows blown out, but business continued as usual. MORE OPEN THAN USUAL was a common sign, while one pub advertised, OUR WINDOWS ARE GONE BUT OUR SPIRITS ARE EXCELLENT. COME IN AND TRY THEM.

Kennedy expressed astonishment at the ability of Londoners to withstand the prolonged assault. Visiting bombing sites during the day, he confessed, "I did not know London could take it. I did not think any city could take it. I am bowed in reverence."

By the end of September, 1940, with the RAF still functioning effectively and with the threat of invasion diminished, Kennedy believed the time had finally come for him to resign and return to America. In mid-October, he sent a cablegram to the

President insisting that he be allowed to come home. Permission was received, and, on October 27, Kennedy arrived at New York's La Guardia Airport, where he was embraced tearfully by Rose and four of the girls. He had kept secret his intention to resign, and for days the press had been speculating about the reason for his return. Some reporters suggested that his fear of war was now so great that he was about to endorse the Republican presidential candidate, Wendell Willkie. Surely something dramatic was about to happen, for, as one newspaperman observed, "He looked for all the world like a man bursting with things to say."

But the President, anticipating Kennedy's arrival, had sent a wire to the plane inviting Joe and Rose to the White House that night for dinner. Knowing how much influence Kennedy could have if he turned against him ten days before the election, Roosevelt was determined to win back his support.

At the White House, after reporting on conditions in London, Kennedy launched into a diatribe against the State Department. He cited the ill-treatment he had received during recent months, including not being informed on vital matters and being consistently bypassed. The President listened closely, nodding occasionally. Kennedy concluded by saying that under these conditions he would not go back to London. To everyone's surprise, the President offered no rebuttal, but said that as far as he was concerned, Kennedy was being charitable. The officious men at the State Department should not be allowed to treat a good friend of his with such callousness, and after the election there would be a real housecleaning to ensure that a valued public servant like Joe Kennedy would never again be so abused.

Totally disarmed by the President's words, Kennedy unwittingly relaxed and Roosevelt turned to the subject of Kennedy's extraordinary sons, Joe and Jack, and to all their accomplishments. "I for one will do all I can to help if your boys should ever run for office," he said. Then, sensing that the moment was right, the masterful Roosevelt asked Kennedy if he would deliver a speech endorsing his reelection. "All right, I will," Kennedy replied.

As it turned out, Kennedy's speech to a nationwide radio

audience was a great success and a great boost to the President. While acknowledging that there had been some disagreements between himself and the President, he went on to praise Roosevelt's experience, wisdom, talent and diplomatic foresight.

"My wife and I have given nine hostages to fortune," he concluded. "Our children and your children are more important than anything else in the world. The kind of America that they and their children will inherit is of grave concern to us all. In the light of these considerations, I believe that Franklin D. Roosevelt should be reelected President of the United States."

Listening from the White House, FDR was absolutely delighted, and Kennedy received praise from all over the country.

On November 5, the American electorate went to the polls and gave FDR a third term. The following day, Kennedy celebrated by tendering his resignation. Roosevelt accepted, hinting that he would find something else for Kennedy to do in Washington.

Jubilant, Kennedy went off to Boston and, while he was there, he agreed to talk with Louis Lyons of the Boston *Globe*. He also agreed to see two journalists who had asked only for an off-the-record briefing for future editorial guidance.

Visiting Kennedy in his hotel suite, the three newspapermen found Kennedy relaxing in his shirt sleeves, and in an expansive mood. Apparently forgetting that Lyons had originally asked for an interview on the record, he spoke with startling candor, saying outrageous things, sharing all his pessimistic feelings about democracy and war, but commenting, too, on the British Cabinet, the stammering King of England and the President's wife. "She's . . . marvelously helpful and full of sympathy . . . she bothered us more on our jobs in Washington to take care of the poor little nobodies who hadn't any influence than all the rest of the people down there together."

Lyons printed practically everything Kennedy had said. Though he cast the story as a feature and downplayed its sensational news aspects, many of Kennedy's statements were so provocative that the interview created banner headlines around the world. Quoted out of context, his unguarded statements seemed worse than they were. In place of prescient ruminations on the impact of war on democracy, he was quoted as saying simply, "Democracy is finished in England." And his comments on Mrs. Roosevent came out as: "She bothered us more on our jobs . . . than all the rest of the people down there together."

For weeks, Kennedy was subjected to a barrage of criticism. After six years in public service, his unguarded talk had finally done him in, bringing his ambassadorial career to a humiliating close.

Kennedy reacted bitterly to the attacks that followed the interview. Indeed, were it not for his family, one friend observed, he might have become totally withdrawn and hostile. But once again his pride in his children kept him going. Writing to a friend the week his resignation became official, he declared, "Having finished a rather busy political career this week, I find myself much more interested in what young Joe is going to do than what I am going to do with the rest of my life."

BOOK THREE

THE
GOLDEN TRIO
(1941–1961)

17

THE CIRCLE IS BROKEN

AT TWENTY-FIVE, Joe Junior was a handsome young man, driven by a fierce ambition. "He had such a strong personality," Rose later claimed, "that anyone who met him knew at once that he was destined for great things." Joe Senior knew that Joe would like to be a candidate for public office. But he also realized that "to make any plans is just a complete waste of time" until "this mess is over."

But in 1941 the mess, as Kennedy Senior called the war, was far from being over, and it was only a matter of months until the United States would officially enter the conflict. Joe Junior knew that unless he volunteered for the navy or the air force he

371

would have to go in as a private once military service became compulsory. In May 1941, having completed his second year of law school, he signed up for the naval aviation cadet program and was assigned to Squantum Naval Air Facility in Quincy, Massachusetts. It was one of the most difficult programs in all the military services. During naval pilot training, the attrition rate for cadets was fifty percent, and Joe Senior was both pleased and worried. "Wouldn't you know," he complained to all who would listen, "naval aviation, the most dangerous thing there is."

Joe Junior found himself tested to the limits of his endurance and courage. After months of a grueling physical regimen and a tough academic course in navigation and flight theory, he was sent to the naval air station in Jacksonville, Florida, for flight training. With news of the Japanese attack on Pearl Harbor on December 7, the training pace was intensified. But, as Joe Senior wrote to a friend, young Joe "seems to be very happy and is anxious to do his bit."

Upon his graduation in May 1942, Joe Junior was sent to Banana River, Florida, for operational training. "We might just as well be in the middle of Africa as here," he wrote to his parents from the new base. "We are fifteen miles from the nearest town. It looks, however, as if it will be a good healthy life and a life without women." Then, in the middle of July, he reported that he had been out on several night patrols and that the place was shaping up better all the time. Some girls had come down from Jacksonville during his free days, and he had gone to Jacksonville one Sunday to play golf with the base chaplain, Father Maurice Sheehy, with whom he had become friends.

While Joe was in Florida, his father kept tabs on him by conducting a running correspondence with Father Sheehy. Everywhere his children went, it seems, Joe Senior managed to find someone—a friend, a journalist, a teacher—who was willing to keep him informed about the smallest details of his children's lives. The astonishing thing about this was not simply the intrusiveness of such a network of "spies," but rather the apparent acceptance of the system by the children, who treated it as "Daddy's prerogative."

WHILE JOE WAS ACCUMULATING the six hundred hours of flying time that would allow him to qualify as a patrol commander, Jack had enlisted in a naval officers' training course, and in September 1941, he had received his commission as an ensign. At first he had failed the physical, but after devoting a summer to back-strengthening exercises he tried again, and this time he made it. He was assigned to ONI, the Office of Naval Intelligence, in Washington, D.C., where he was given the task of preparing bulletins that distilled information from various foreign sources. It was not the kind of romantic job a young man dreams of in war, but it allowed Jack to be near Kathleen, who had recently moved to Washington to work as a reporter on the *Times-Herald*. Finding an apartment near Kathleen's, Jack became an instant member of her lively social circle.

In Kathleen's group were several friends from the past as well as new ones she had made on the paper. Among the new ones was John White, the paper's star feature writer. A handsome blue-eyed North Carolinian, White was the son of an Episcopalian minister. Years later, he could still remember the day Kathleen came into the office. "I liked pretty girls, and here was one pretty girl. . . . I found her so attractive and so much fun, I asked her to go to the movies that very night."

Thus began a warm, argumentative relationship that brought both Kathleen and White much pleasure and much grief. Considering himself a freethinking spirit and wiser than Kathleen— indeed, he was older by eight years—White was alternately attracted and appalled by the naïveté that caused her to fend off automatically even the most innocent advances. Although she had had dozens of boyfriends, White felt that she was totally inexperienced sexually. "Bickered with KK," he wrote in his diary in October of 1941. "Foolish Irish Catholic girl. She is best fun to argue with because she is always wrong."

As the weeks went by, Kathleen and White spent more time together: suppers in his basement apartment, movies, long walks, parties. Yet they were impossibly matched, for despite his uncommon intelligence and sharp wit, White at thirty admitted to no ambition other than maintaining a string of girlfriends and a reputation as an eccentric. Along the way, Kathleen got better about putting up with his rumpled clothes and his unconventional ways, such as walking barefoot through museums. But no matter how close they became, she refused to give in on the matter of sex. "She tells me what priest told her not to do," White recorded in January 1942. "I ask her to get dispensation." Then, "another fight," he wrote ten days later. "This is intolerable. . . . Too many words and no action."

For all their feuding, however, there were many tender moments, the best of which came at the end of evenings after he had escorted her home. They would chat in her room until she grew tired, and then she would run into the bathroom and return in her flannel nightgown. "She to bed," White described the ritual in his diary. "I rub her back and put cream on her face. Observe her put hair in pins and net. Prayers." It was a curious ritual in which Kathleen appeared like a little girl wanting nothing more than a mother to put her to bed. White would read aloud at her bedside until she drifted off to sleep, then let himself out.

While her relationship with White was wending its rocky way, Kathleen developed a close friendship with another reporter, Inga Arvad, who wrote a daily feature for the *Times-Herald*. Inga, who was in her late twenties, was a stunningly beautiful woman: a full-bodied blonde with large blue eyes and a healthy, glowing skin. Though she talked very little of her past, there were hints that she had led an exotic life in Europe, and it was known that she had been married twice. Inga was as warm and effervescent as Kathleen, and soon the two girls became inseparable. So it was only natural that Jack and Inga should meet, and somewhere along the way Jack fell into a passionate affair with her. According to White, "Papa Joe" found out the first time Jack dated her—suggesting the extraordinary efficiency of his spy network—but "he decided it was fine." However, as Inga was not yet divorced from her second husband, the affair had to be kept secret from Rose. Relishing the clandestine atmosphere, Jack covered his tracks by double-dating with Kathleen and John White. White's diary contains entry after entry about suppers at Inga's, after which he and Kathleen willingly exited, leaving Jack and Inga alone together.

Jack's romance took place at a difficult time. With the trauma over Pearl Harbor and the U.S. entry into the war, enemy sympathizers were believed to be everywhere. In this atmosphere Inga's past came under suspicion. One morning, in the morgue of the *Times-Herald,* a fellow reporter found a picture of her with Hitler at the 1936 Olympics in Berlin. Asked about the photo, Inga simply shrugged, explaining that she had been in Berlin as a correspondent for a Danish newspaper and that Hitler had granted her an interview. Apparently taken with her Nordic beauty, he had invited her to view the Olympic Games with him as a member of the press.

As it happened, the FBI had been watching Inga from her first year in America, and now, unbeknownst to Jack, the bureau began charting his romance with her on the grounds that at ONI he had access to secret information. Still, the affair continued until Jack was in real danger of being cashiered from the navy for his association with a possible Mata Hari. Some believe that at this point Joe Kennedy intervened to prevent his son from being thrown out of the service, persuading the navy brass to simply reassign him. However it happened, Jack was suddenly transferred to Charleston, South Carolina. White recorded that Inga was very gloomy and that Jack, too, seemed very sad. White remembers many phone calls from Jack when he would talk with Kathleen for hours about Inga.

Jack remained at Charleston for six long months before he finally got the sea duty he had wanted all along. In July 1942, he was assigned to the U.S. Naval Reserve midshipmen's school in Chicago, where he would learn the rudiments of seamanship in preparation for active duty. Although he saw Inga several more times—visits monitored by the FBI—pressure from his father finally ended the affair.

THE KENNEDY HOUSEHOLD was never the same after the golden trio left home. In 1941, Joe Kennedy made the decision to sell the Bronxville estate, preferring to divide his time between his homes in Palm Beach and Hyannis Port. For Eunice, age twenty, the decision had little impact; by then she had graduated from Noroton and was studying at Stanford University. But for all the younger ones, the move was a disorienting experience, for they no longer had a fixed base.

Later, the children's nurse, Luella Hennessey, claimed that

with the sale of the Bronxville home there was "a loss of stability" in the family, almost as if a dividing line had been drawn and the younger children fell on the wrong side. "After England," she recalled, "Mr. Kennedy began to withdraw more and more into himself. He was not as outgoing or as happy as he had been before, and the kids felt it."

During these years Pat was graduated from Rosemont College, Jean followed her older sisters to Noroton, and Robert was sent to Portsmouth Priory—a Catholic boarding school in Rhode Island—and later to Milton Academy in Massachusetts. Robert struggled hard to do well. "As a child," Lem Billings remembered, "nothing came easy to him, but he never stopped trying." For his persistence, Rose was forever grateful, and to her seventh child she displayed a special warmth. She called him her "little pet" and she monitored his schooling closely. His father's letters, however, reveal a subtly different set of expectations from the consistently high standards he had demanded of Joe and Jack. His mellower attitude had a paradoxical effect on his son, making Bobby struggle even more to win his father's attention and respect.

But it was Teddy who was hurt the most by the loss of a permanent home. From all accounts, he was a cheerful, loving child, but his cheerfulness was in part a protection against the tension of constantly being thrust into new situations and new schools. Before he reached thirteen, he had attended ten different day and boarding schools as his parents alternated summers and winters at the Cape and in Palm Beach. For any child, this constant transplantation would be hard. For young Teddy, unsure of his intellect and so overweight that his brothers called him "fatstuff," it was extremely damaging.

Rose continued to travel as much as she could during these years. Now past her fiftieth birthday, she was an amazingly handsome woman and still maintained her youthful enthusiasm for seeing new places and learning new things. And in Joe's letters to his wife when she was away, there is an extraordinary level of intimacy in the sharing of the details of family life. Yet it was during this period that Joe took it upon himself, without telling Rose, to make a devastating decision about Rosemary, one that he would regret for the rest of his life.

Following Rosemary's return from England, her mental skills had deteriorated. Having been forced to leave the only school where she had been happy, she was now, at twenty-one, giving way to tantrums, rages and violent outbursts.

"It had never been easy for Rosemary," Lem Billings observed, "but when she returned from England she became frustrated at not being able to do all the things her siblings could do. Every day there would be one terrifying incident after another: physical fights, long absences at night when she'd be out wandering the streets and violent verbal exchanges." She became, he wrote, "almost impossible to handle."

Something had to be done. "I was always worried," Rose later noted, "that she would go off with someone. . . ." Rose's niece, Ann Gargan, recalls, "Rosemary had the body of a twenty-one-year-old yearning for fulfillment with the mentality of a four-year-old." She was in a convent in Washington at the time, and many nights the school would call to say she was missing, only to find her out walking around the streets at two a.m." She was "the perfect prey."

Finally, Joe took matters into his own hands. He had talked with doctors about a pioneering operation called a prefrontal lobotomy, in which a hole about the size of a dime was drilled in the skull and a knifelike instrument inserted into the front part of the brain to sever the lobe areas from the rest of the brain. In the early 1940s the operation was considered a miracle treatment for certain types of intense worry, depression, frustration and violent behavior.

To Joseph Kennedy it was the obvious solution. If, as the doctors claimed, the lobotomy would not impair Rosemary's capacity to function on a daily basis, if her sexual drive could be calmed down and her violent moods contained, then she could remain with her family.

The family archives do not record where Rosemary had her lobotomy, for Joe kept it a secret not only from Rose but from the others as well. Something, however, went terribly wrong during the operation and Rosemary emerged far worse than she had ever been. "Her head was tilted and her capacity to speak was almost entirely gone," Ann Gargan later said. "There was no question now that she could no longer take care of herself."

Rose was simply told that the time had come for her daughter to be put into an institution and that for both their sakes she should not visit for some time. Even granting that at some level Joe was trying to protect his wife from heartbreak, it is also likely that he was protecting himself from her legitimate wrath at not having been consulted beforehand.

For years, in an astonishing act of control, Joe kept Rose from knowing the truth. It was only after he suffered a stroke in 1961 that Rose took it upon herself to go to St. Coletta's, in Jefferson, Wisconsin, where Rosemary had been placed. "Then she knew," Ann Gargan said, "though she had to piece the story together chapter by chapter."

In the years ahead, prompted perhaps by his guilt over Rosemary, Joe would devote a substantial amount of his money to research on the retarded, and his daughter Eunice would become a pioneering force in the field. But in 1941, the failed operation had to be one of the most heart-wrenching failures Joe Kennedy had ever experienced. And for Rosemary's sisters and brothers, her sudden disappearance must have raised dozens of questions that were never fully answered, surrounding the incident with the aura of forbidden mystery. Why, after all these years, did she have to be institutionalized? And why couldn't any of the family see her? And most ominously, why wouldn't anyone really talk about what was happening?

18

HERO IN THE PACIFIC

IN LATE SUMMER OF 1942, while Jack was at midshipmen's school in Chicago learning navigation, gunnery, semaphore and seamanship, his class was visited by two naval officers, John Harlee and John D. Bulkeley, who were recruiting reserve officers to man a new fleet of PT boats—fast, versatile, small combat craft—that would soon be operating in the Pacific. The PT service, more than any other, tapped a corps of wealthy young men, disproportionately Ivy League, whose families owned motorboats and cabin cruisers, and who spent their summers around marinas and yacht clubs. These men were considered especially capable of handling the small, maneuverable torpedo boats, and from the moment Jack heard Harlee and Bulkeley talk, he was hooked.

The two officers were favorably enough impressed with Jack's eagerness and his experience as an intercollegiate sailing champion to recommend him for the service. Had either officer known that he suffered from a bad back, it is unlikely that he would have been accepted, for these boats planed over the water at forty knots and more, with bows lifted, slicing great waves from either side of their hulls, and gave their crew "an enormous pounding." But except for his back, Jack appeared to be in better health than he had been for years.

From the first week Jack arrived at the PT school at Melville, Rhode Island, he was, Kathleen reported to Lem, crazy about it. For one thing, he shared his Quonset hut with his old friend from Harvard, Torby Macdonald, whose presence there was the result of the ambassador's intervention. But his back continued to give him trouble, and one of his classmates recalls that he now had to sleep with a piece of plywood under his mattress.

How much Harlee knew of this is uncertain, but when Jack was graduated on December 2, he was sent as a teacher to a training squadron. He was sorely disappointed. All his friends were going overseas and that's where he wanted to be. During a five-day leave, he went to Palm Beach, where he sought his father's help in pulling strings to allow him to see combat.

Jack's request was "causing his mother and me plenty of anxiety," Joe Senior confided to Father Sheehy. "I suppose that I should be proud that my sons should decide to pick the most hazardous branches of the service in this war, and of course, there is pride in my heart but quite a measure of grief in my mind." Nevertheless, he promised to do what he could, and, within weeks, Jack was ordered to report to the Solomon Islands, in the South Pacific.

When Jack reached the Solomons in March 1943, the war in the Pacific had been in progress sixteen months, and despite two substantial Allied victories—the Battle of the Coral Sea and the Battle of Midway—the Japanese were still in control. But the U.S. Marines had landed on Guadalcanal, and after a bitter and bloody engagement, the Japanese had given up trying to reinforce the island. By the time Jack arrived in the Pacific, there was a lull in the fighting.

Kennedy was stationed at PT headquarters at Sesapi, a primitive scattering of thatched-roof huts and makeshift docks on the island of Tulagi. As commander of his own boat, the *PT 109,* Jack had his first real experience as a leader, and from all accounts it seems that his men respected him. Never one to romanticize his situation, he wrote to Kathleen that the "bubble" he had had about "lying on a cool Pacific island with a warm Pacific maiden hunting bananas for me is definitely a bubble that has burst. . . . The glamour of PTs just isn't except to the outsider. It's just a matter of night after night patrols at low speed in rough water—two hours on—then sacking out and going on again for another two hours. Even with that however it's a hell of a lot better than any other job in the Navy."

In June, the lull in the fighting came to an end as the major staging bases—Guadalcanal, Tulagi and Nouméa—began preparations for the Allies' first major Pacific offensive. And in that offensive the night patrols of the small PT boats would be critical to preventing Japanese reinforcements from getting through. As Japanese aircraft struck almost daily at Allied ships and bases, Jack playfully wrote to his family that "to know that all nuns and priests along the Atlantic Coast are putting in

Jack at the helm of PT-109.

a lot of praying time on my behalf is certainly comforting."

The question of faith appears again and again in Jack's letters from the Pacific, though it is generally disguised in a humorous manner. But Jack's roommate Johnny Iles remembered that Jack was troubled about his religion. "We were both Catholics and we talked about it a lot. I clearly recall . . . Jack had lost his religion." But "He said he'd work it out someday."

Speculation about what this religious struggle meant to Jack leads to the recognition of the absolute irreconcilability between the contrasting messages the Kennedy children received from their parents. From their mother they were told: Be Irish, be Catholic, follow the rules. Yet the unconscious message suggested by every contour of their father's life told them never to let themselves be limited by anything, not by their Irish Catholic background, nor by convention, nor even by the rules of the game. Perhaps in trying to sort out his feelings about religion Jack was trying to shape his own identity within the family.

The pace of events, however, overtook his concern with religion, for on the night of July 17–18, a navy patrol bomber picked up the "Japanese express" nearby—three cruisers, six destroyers and two transports. *PT 109* and two others were ordered to go find them.

Jack kept the *109* in the water until three hours after midnight, but neither he nor his companion boats made contact with the express. Just as the decision was made to turn back, a Japanese plane came over and dropped a flare above the boat. Two large bombs fell on either side of the *109,* and Kennedy pushed the throttles wide open, zigzagging away and laying a smoke screen. Two of Jack's men were hit by shrapnel, and seeing them fall, Kennedy turned the helm over to his executive officer, Lennie Thom, grabbed a first-aid kit and attended to their wounds. At four a.m. the *109* returned to base.

Then, on the afternoon of August 1, word was received that another enemy express was expected to run that night, with the Japanese base on Kolombangara island as its destination. That night, fifteen PTs, including the *109,* left the base to patrol the area—by far the greatest PT force ever deployed against an express.

It was a starless night, black and overcast. At midnight, *PT*

159 picked up the express on its radar. The convoy consisted of four first-line destroyers.

With *PT 157* following, the *159* fired four torpedoes, but in the process its torpedo tube caught fire, lighting the sky like a beacon and giving the Japanese a fine target. After firing her own torpedoes, the *157* lay down a smoke screen so that the Japanese couldn't see the fire. With enemy shells falling all around, the two PTs moved quickly away.

Patrolling nearby, Kennedy's *109* saw gunfire and a light in the direction of the coast of Kolombangara, but Kennedy was unable to ascertain whether the light came from a shore battery or from ships close in. He intercepted *PT 162* and was incorrectly informed by the commander, John Lowrey, that the light was apparently from the shore. Then suddenly Kennedy intercepted a terse radio message: "I am being chased through Ferguson Passage! Have fired fish!"

At this point, both the *109* and the *162* made a hasty withdrawal, fearing that in the glow of the strong lights they could easily be fired upon. Had the two skippers recognized the lights for what they were, enemy destroyer fire, they might have trailed the source of the light and found a golden opportunity to engage the enemy. But as it was, both Kennedy and Lowrey sped off into the blackness until orders were received to resume their normal patrol stations.

It was now about two thirty a.m. In formation with two other PTs, the *109,* with its crew of twelve, was idling along on only one of its three engines, so as to leave a minimum wake. George "Barney" Ross was on the bow as lookout, Kennedy was in the cockpit at the wheel, and with him was John Maguire, the radioman. Raymond Albert was in the after turret. Suddenly a dark shape loomed up on *PT 109*'s starboard bow at a distance of two hundred to three hundred yards. Someone shouted, "Ship at two o'clock!" The dark shape was the Japanese destroyer *Amagiri,* bearing down at high speed, heading straight for the *109.*

Kennedy spun the wheel to port in preparation for firing torpedoes. But as the *109* was running on only one engine, it answered sluggishly. Up on the bow, Ross slammed a shell into the breach of the 37-millimeter antitank gun. Just then the huge

destroyer rammed the *109,* crunching across the bow and split-
ting the boat in two. Traveling at about forty knots, the *Amagiri*
vibrated sharply but continued right on course.

At impact, Kennedy thought, This is how it feels to be killed.
In a moment he found himself on his back on the deck, looking
up at the destroyer as it passed through his boat. Down below,
the engineer, "Pappy" McMahon, was thrown painfully against
the bulkhead. A burst of flame came at him from the exploding
gas tanks, and he put his hands over his face, waiting to die.
Then suddenly a cold splash of water hit him. His half of the PT
was sinking, and he was being sucked down into the sea. Struggling upward through the water, he saw a yellow glow—burning
gasoline—and he broke the surface, trying desperately to keep
away from the fire.

The destroyer had rushed off into the darkness, and now
there was an eerie silence broken only by the sound of gasoline
burning. Kennedy's half of the PT had stayed afloat, and when
he shouted "Who's aboard?" feeble answers came from five men
clinging desperately to the hull—the radioman, Maguire; the
quartermaster, Edman Mauer; the exec, Lennie Thom; and Barney Ross and Raymond Albert. But there was no time to rejoice
in being alive, for from the darkness came the cries of men who
had survived the sinking of the other half of the boat. "Mr.
Kennedy! Mr. Kennedy!" shouted Charles Harris. "McMahon
is badly hurt." Kennedy dived in and swam toward the voice.
Meanwhile, Thom and Ross struck out for the others. Kennedy
found McMahon with serious burns on his face and hands and
unable to swim. He towed the engineer back to the boat,
working against a strong current. Then he returned for two
others. It was five a.m. before the survivors, eleven in all, were
gathered on the tilted deck of the sheared PT.

Stretched out on the deck, the men speculated on how long it
would take the PTs to come back and pick them up. As it turned
out, the other boats, having seen the fiery collision from a
distance, assumed that no one had survived, and back at the
base, services were held for the thirteen men of the *109.* As the
day of August 2 dawned, a message was heading for the home of
Joseph P. Kennedy in Hyannis Port, informing him that his son
Jack was missing in action.

To the crew that first day, it became obvious that the *109* would soon sink, so Kennedy decided to abandon ship for a small atoll, which could be seen about four miles away. At two p.m., he again took McMahon in tow, clenching the ties of the man's life jacket in his teeth like a towline. The other swimmers followed, the stronger pushing and towing a make-shift float to which two nonswimmers were tied. It took five hours to reach land, but once on shore, the men discovered that the island was much smaller than they had realized—only seventy yards wide—and that it was south of Ferguson Passage, the only place where there was much hope of meeting other PT boats. Kennedy decided to swim out over the reefs to the edge of Ferguson Passage in the hope of flagging a passing boat. The men objected, arguing that he was too tired, but within thirty minutes of his arrival on the atoll, Kennedy was gone.

Making his way along the reefs with a lantern, he reached Ferguson Passage by eight p.m., and there he remained for hours. But he saw no PT boats. Giving up hope, he started back, but in the darkness a fast-moving current swept him past the little atoll where his shipmates waited. For hours his body drifted, his mind a jumble. Finally, he bumped up on a reef, crawled ashore and passed out. Later he awoke and made his way back to the island. The other survivors, who had given him up for dead, were overjoyed. Vomiting, feverish and exhausted, Kennedy passed out again.

The following day, he decided to change islands, hoping to get closer to Ferguson Passage. With the uncomplaining Mc-Mahon once again in tow, the eleven survivors made their way to Olasana, a larger island, which, it was hoped, might even have fresh water. For by now the men were suffering acutely from thirst. But the only water they found was the rain, which they tried to catch in their mouths during a storm. And so the next afternoon Kennedy asked Ross to swim with him to Nauru island, even nearer to Ferguson Passage, and there they found a treasure: a one-man dugout canoe, a fifty-five-gallon drum of fresh water and a crate of crackers and candy. Leaving Ross behind, Kennedy paddled the canoe back to Olasana to distribute the crackers and water to the men.

When he arrived, he found a fire going and two friendly island-ers helping the survivors. Returning to fetch Ross, Kennedy also brought back a coconut with a smooth shell. He scratched a message on it with a jackknife: "Eleven alive Native knows Posit and reefs Naura Island Kennedy." Then he said to the islanders, "Rendova, Rendova." They seemed to understand that he meant for them to go to the PT boat base there.

All that day Kennedy and Ross "lay in a sickly daze," and that night, fearful that the natives might not reach Rendova, Kennedy persuaded Ross to go out with him once more into Ferguson Passage. Caught in a sudden rainsquall, they were swept up onto a coral reef, where they remained the rest of the night. The next morning, the two officers were wakened by the noise of ap-proaching islanders. "I have a letter for you, sir," one of them said in excellent English. Kennedy tore the note open. It said:

On His Majesty's Service

To the Senior Officer, Nauru Island

I have just learned of your presence on Nauru Island. I am in command of a New Zealand infantry patrol operating in conjunc-tion with U.S. Army troops on New Georgia. I strongly advise that you come with these natives to me. Meanwhile, I shall be in radio communication with your authorities at Rendova and we can final-ize plans to collect balance of your party.

Lt. Wincote

Reading the formal message, Kennedy turned to Ross and smiled. "You've got to hand it to the British," he said.

The islanders took Ross and Kennedy back to Olasana to tell the others the good news. Then, in the middle of the night, moving in darkened canoes, the eleven survivors rendezvoused with a PT boat from Rendova. Kennedy jumped aboard first and hugged the men—all of them friends. The boat roared back to the base.

Meanwhile, halfway around the world, Joe Senior was living with the knowledge that Jack was missing in action. Having heard the news from unofficial sources, most likely through a connection in Washington, he decided not to tell Rose until he was absolutely certain. According to Rose, the first news she heard was a radio report that the missing John Kennedy had

Doing Their Part

December 1942: Jack and
Joe Junior, home on leave

Bobby is sworn into the
navy; his father looks on.

Kathleen, with the
Red Cross in England

been found. Joe heard the same bulletin over his car radio. He hurried home to Rose and the two of them fell into each other's arms.

The news of the *PT 109* affair made the front pages of the newspapers. All the accounts focused on Kennedy, if only because his name was the best known. Heroic versions of the incident, published in major magazines and newspapers, would become important in the development of John Kennedy's political career. Some critics would argue that the ramming of the *109* was anything but heroic and that the whole engagement that night was a great failure for the entire PT squadron. This is obviously true. Yet, if young Kennedy could take little pride in the humiliating destruction of his boat, it seems unjust to deny him praise for his part in the rescue of his crew or to blame him for the attention that focused on him. Indeed, through it all he seemed somewhat embarrassed by the fuss, stating right from the start that he never considered himself a hero.

And in the letters he wrote to his family after the incident, there is no indication that it had changed his own feelings about war. On the contrary, in responding to the news that his eighteen-year-old brother Bobby wanted to get into PT boats, Jack emphatically advised against it. Deeply saddened at losing his two men, he wrote, "It certainly brought home how real the war is—and when I read [in] the papers from home that we will fight Japs for years if necessary and will sacrifice hundreds of thousands if we must—I always like to check from where [the writer is] talking—it's seldom [from] out here."

19

FORBIDDEN ROMANCE

DURING THE TIME JACK was missing and then found, Joe Junior was in North Carolina learning to fly a new and strangely menacing plane, the B-24 Liberator. Considered "fast and dangerous," it was "a stable plane in firm hands," but in uncertain ones "it flew like a boxcar and landed like a weary truck."

In learning to fly the Liberator, Joe was preparing himself for a new assignment in England. Jim Reedy, his executive officer during his training, had been picked to command a new squadron scheduled to join the RAF patrols searching the English Channel and the Bay of Biscay for German U-boats. The moment Joe heard about the dangerous assignment, he volunteered and he was given the task of ferrying new Liberators to Norfolk, Virginia, from the factory in San Diego.

It was during a hectic period when he was making five cross-country trips in eight days that the news of Jack's encounter with the enemy broke. Apparently, Joe didn't call his parents at the time for news of Jack, much to his father's distress. Later he wrote a long, jaunty letter explaining his silence "about our young hero" as a consequence of his grueling schedule. Soon after, Joe was granted leave, and he arrived in Hyannis Port in time for his father's fifty-fifth birthday. An old friend, Police Commissioner Joe Timilty, was down from Boston. So, too, was Judge John Burns. At dinner that night, while Joe sat at his father's right, the judge proposed a toast: "To Ambassador Joe Kennedy, father of our hero, our *own* hero, Lieutenant John F. Kennedy of the United States Navy." According to Timilty, that was the end of the toast. The judge sat down and Joe lifted his glass to his father and his absent brother, a tense grin plastered to his face. But Timilty claims that that night, lying in his bed, he could hear young Joe crying, unable to hold in his hurt and frustration.

By THE TIME Joe Junior left for England in the summer of 1943, Kathleen was already there, working for the Red Cross. Though she had been doing very well on the *Times-Herald,* she had still wanted to return to England, and her longings grew stronger as she watched many of her friends leave home. In May 1942, John White had enlisted in the Marine Corps, bringing an end to their odd romance. Lem Billings was the next to go, leaving in July for North Africa, just in time for the Battle of El Alamein and the Allied march to Tripoli.

With her brothers away and so many of her friends leaving, Kathleen was more determined than ever to get overseas. And she was overjoyed when she was accepted by the American Red Cross, to serve in one of the rest-and-recreation clubs set up in

England for American servicemen on leave. Installed generally in hotels, the clubs provided snack bars, showers, barbershops, dancing and games and other recreation, in addition to sleeping quarters. The young American women who staffed the clubs were expected to live there, to greet the boys, dance and play cards with them, and listen as they talked of their hopes and fears.

Thanks to her father's friends "putting the squeeze on a few people," Kathleen was assigned to an exclusive club located in the heart of London rather than being farmed out to an airfield or camp in the country. As it turned out, however, the job was more than she had bargained for; it allowed only a day and a half off each week, and usually not weekends, since these were the busiest times. Still, Kathleen managed to lead an active social life. "I am really so pleased to be back," she wrote to her family. "Sometimes I feel I have more good, close friends here than in America." There were numerous men in her life, but among them, Billy Hartington remained the one she cared about the most. Stationed in Scotland when he heard Kathleen was back, he traveled all the way to London, and on July 10, 1943, they saw each other for the first time in four years. Kathleen later told her mother that they both knew that night that they still loved each other, more than they had ever loved anyone else, but until they could solve the problem of religion there was nothing they could do about it.

By the beginning of October, 1943, Joe Junior was flying with the RAF on the Cornish coast, and was finding it a great pleasure to work with the British airmen. In the middle of the month he managed, by what he described as "some deft arranging," to secure an assignment that would let him land near London so that he could see Kathleen. As soon as he got to London, he went to her club, where he found her surrounded by GIs who thought she was "easily the nicest girl there."

It was during this visit to London that Joe met Patricia Wilson, a beautiful young woman with dark curly hair and deep blue eyes. Finding himself seated next to her at a dinner party, he was immediately intrigued by her warm, open manner and infectious laugh. He soon found out that she had been married twice, the second time to a banker in his late thirties named

Joe Junior in England, with his girlfriend Pat Wilson.

Robin Wilson. Wilson, a major in the British Army, had been away from home for over two years.

Pat had three small children and was living in a tile-roofed cottage called Crastock Farm in Woking, about one hour south of London—and on the same train line as Dunkeswell, in Devon, where Joe's squadron would soon be moving. Before the evening ended, Pat had invited Joe to visit her on one of his leaves.

As much as Joe enjoyed the flying, he greatly anticipated his weekend leaves, for the conditions on the base at Dunkeswell were awful. Devon was experiencing one of its wettest falls, and the base was like "a mud hole." The officers and men of Joe's squadron lived in primitive Nissen huts, and in the perpetual dampness it was impossible to stay warm. After several hard weeks of straight flying on cold and miserable patrols that were ten to twelve hours long, Joe put in for a week's leave for his entire crew. With Jim Reedy joining them, they all went up to London, where Kathleen threw a big party for them, complete with a band, at the home of Marie Bruce, a woman her mother had grown close to during the ambassadorship. "It was the first party London had had for the young for two years," so people swarmed in, Kathleen excitedly reported to her parents. But if Billy Hartington or Pat Wilson was there, it was not mentioned to the senior Kennedys, for the two siblings shared secrets with each other but not with the rest of the family.

After that, Kathleen and Joe would often meet at Pat Wilson's cottage, which was conveniently located for everyone—including Hartington, now stationed in Hampshire. None of Kathleen's friends were scandalized by the relationship between Joe and

Pat. By 1943, many young married women whose husbands were away had taken up with American soldiers. In the chaos of war, everyone was in love with someone.

Still, Joe felt compelled in his letters to state that romance was "unknown in the life of this romantic, dashing naval airman." And while Kathleen mentioned Billy in almost every letter to her parents, she reassured them that she knew she could never marry him.

Nor could Billy bring himself to go against his family and agree to bring up his children as Catholics, which was the only way that Kathleen could marry him and still stay within the church. In a letter written to "mother and daddy only," Kathleen reported that she felt "most discouraged and rather sad. I want to do the right thing so badly and yet I hope I'm not giving up the most important thing in my life. . . . Poor Billy is very, very sad but he sees his duty must come first." The only hope, it seemed, lay in a special dispensation—"some stretch of the rules," as Rose described it—by which the marriage "could be sanctioned or at least tolerated by both the Roman Catholic and Anglican churches."

Joe Kennedy did everything he could. He went to see Francis Spellman, the Archbishop of New York. Together they worked out a means of reaching the Vatican. But it was soon clear that nothing could be done. Admitting to Kathleen that his efforts were unsuccessful, Kennedy tried to reassure his daughter. "As I've told you lots of times, you're tops with me. I'll bet on your judgment anytime for any amounts." Later that day he wrote to Joe Junior, asking him to give his sister "the benefit of your counsel and sympathy."

Rose, however, could support her daughter only so long as she believed that if a dispensation could not be found, Kathleen would renounce her love. But when Kathleen tried to persuade her that the marriage would still be a match of great love, even if the technicalities could not be resolved, Rose was furious. And she became more and more distraught as the possibility grew that Kathleen might go ahead and marry Billy.

Kathleen hated the idea of getting married in a civil ceremony, but that seemed the only alternative since, as she reported, "The church would not marry us." Writing sadly to Lem, Kathleen recalled the daydreams she used to have as a young girl about her wedding and all the bridesmaids she was going to have, and now she could look forward only to a ten-minute ceremony in a registry office. For a time she thought it might be better to convert to Anglicanism so that she could be totally accepted by Billy's church instead of simply living in lifelong estrangement from her own. But in the end, Kathleen realized that a conversion would hurt her mother even more than a registry wedding.

In the last week of April, after spending three days with Billy in Yorkshire, Kathleen finally consented to marry him on what were essentially his terms, agreeing to raise the children as Anglicans. As soon as she said yes, making them officially engaged, Billy wrote a letter to Mrs. Kennedy, saying in part, "I have loved Kick for a time. I do feel terribly keenly the sacrifices I'm asking Kick to make but I can't see that she will be doing anything wrong in the eyes of God. . . . Please try not to think too harshly of me."

Rose was, in her own words, "heartbroken and horrified." She had given her life to bringing up her children as good Catholics, and now, to her, this marriage proved that her job was not very well done.

In a move that would bring great sadness to Kathleen, Rose cabled, "Heartbroken. Feel you have been wrongly influenced. . . . Anything done for Our Lord will be rewarded hundred fold."

With the arrival of Rose's cable, Kathleen became terribly agitated. In her turmoil she turned to her brother Joe, and in him she found her best ally. "Once she had definitely made up her mind to

Kathleen and Billy Hartington on their wedding day. Behind them, the Duchess of Devonshire and Joe Junior.

do it," Joe later wrote, "I did the best I could to help her through. She was under a terrible strain."

The wedding had to be held almost immediately, since Billy's unit was soon to take part in the invasion of Europe. Joe came up to London, he saw the Devonshires' lawyer and helped with the marriage settlement. "Never did anyone," Kathleen later wrote, "have such a pillar of strength as I had in Joe. He constantly reassured me."

The wedding took place on Saturday morning, May 6, 1944, in a small drab room in the Chelsea registry office. On Billy's side were his parents, the Duke and Duchess of Devonshire, his aunt Lady Salisbury and his sisters Anne and Elizabeth. His best man was an old friend, Charles Manners, the Marquess of Granby. Kathleen was represented only by Joe, Marie Bruce and the Kennedys' old friend, Lady Astor. It was a ten-minute ceremony. But in spite of the austerity of the occasion, "everything was wonderful," Joe reported. Afterward, there was a reception for two hundred guests, and then Kathleen and Billy boarded a train for Billy's home at Eastbourne, where they received a private Anglican blessing and spent their honeymoon.

Back in the United States, when Rose finally received Kathleen's letter informing her of the marriage, she lost her composure and retreated to her room. She was inconsolable, and Joe Senior felt for her. On the other hand, he understood that Kathleen also needed his support, and so after several days of silence he finally sent her the cable she had been waiting for all along. "With your faith in God," Joe wrote, "you can't make a mistake. Remember you are still and always will be tops with me." He also talked with Archbishop Spellman, who assured him that Rose was being too hard on herself. "She has done the best she could," he told Joe. When Joe reported this to Rose she felt better. Indeed, according to Joe, the archbishop's words "carried her over the tough time."

After Kathleen and Billy had spent four weeks together in a country inn near where Billy was stationed, he received his orders to participate in the Allied invasion of Europe. "Although I've been expecting it daily," he recorded, "it is a shock now that it has come. I shall always remember this month as the most perfect of my life."

20

"NOW IT'S ALL OVER"

For over two years the architects of D-day had been haunted by the vision of German U-boats suddenly emerging in the waters of the Channel as Eisenhower's vast armada approached the coast of France with tens of thousands of men and millions of tons of equipment. To prevent this dreadful possibility, an ambitious plan was conceived, calling for hundreds of planes to fly hourly patrols over the Channel during all the days of the invasion. As soon as he heard about Operation Cork, as it was called, Joe volunteered. "I have finished my missions and was due to start back in about two weeks," he told his parents on May 8, "but volunteered to stay another month."

D-day was June 6, with an invasion force larger than any ever assembled in history. Joe's patrol that day was northwest of the invasion beaches and kept him aloft for almost twelve hours. It was an exhausting schedule, but in the end Operation Cork worked, for not a single ship of the invasion fleet was lost to a German U-boat.

For young Joe it was a heady time. Though his own role had not been a sensational one, he knew that he had done what was expected. "I am delighted that I stayed for the Invasion," he wrote to his parents. "I now have 39 missions and will probably have about 50 by the time I leave. It is far more than anyone else on the base, but it doesn't prove a hell of a lot . . . Don't worry about me. I don't think I am in as much danger now as I was (knock on wood)."

As a second-tour man, Joe had more leave time, which he regularly spent at the cottage with Pat. It was, of course, an impossible romance. Even assuming that Pat secured a divorce, it was inconceivable that a man with Joe's political ambitions could marry a twice-divorced Protestant. But there is no denying that Joe, at twenty-nine, was deeply in love, probably for the first time in his life.

Meanwhile, since the D-day invasion, London had been subjected to a terrifying barrage of German V-1 rockets, or

*Navy pilot Joe Junior
at the controls of a biplane.*

buzz bombs. Launched from giant concrete bunkers on the
French coast, they were dropping on London with horrifying
speed. Civilian casualties from
the new bombs were immense.
"People are absolutely terrified," Kathleen recorded in her
diary, and British morale was
seriously affected.

A plan was conceived. A
PB4Y plane, like those Joe had
been flying, had her insides gut-
ted. She was then loaded with boxes and boxes of explosives,
more explosives than were ever gathered in another single
plane. The top-secret plan was for two pilots to take the sacrificial plane and guide it across the Channel toward its target—a
gigantic concrete bunker set at Calais on the French coast. The
bunker was believed to be the launching site for Hitler's V-1
rockets, and while it had proven invulnerable to ordinary
bombs, the combined explosives in this mysterious plane promised to do the job. According to the plan, at a designated
moment the plane's controls would be switched to remote and
picked up by a mother plane flying nearby. At that point the
pilots were to parachute out, leaving the mother plane to guide
the suicide plane to its target.

It was clear that the mission was exceedingly dangerous. Yet
when Joe Kennedy heard about it, he begged to go. Believing
Joe to be his best pilot, his commander reluctantly gave his
assent.

"I am going to do something different for the next three
weeks," Joe wrote to his parents on July 26. "It is secret and I
am not allowed to say what it is, but . . . don't worry. I imagine
you are a bit disappointed that I haven't gone home, but I think
when I tell you the whole story, you will agree with me."

It was a mission so hazardous that its successful completion would have been one of the two or three greatest feats in the war. And it might have made him a greater hero than his brother Jack had been painted to be. Nor was this the first time Joe had pushed himself forward. "There was never an occasion for a mission that meant extra hazard that Joe did not volunteer for," a squadron mate later wrote. "He had everybody's unlimited admiration." It can be argued that in taking these risks Joe was simply responding to a lifetime of pressure, to the constant demand to be the best at everything he did. Perhaps, too, beneath his "model-child" behavior there existed a rebellious streak, a need to belong to himself before he belonged to his father's dreams. Perhaps, in this light, his risk-taking can be seen as a desperate attempt to shape his own life in his own way.

The secret flight was scheduled for sunset on August 12. On that day Joe displayed surprising calm. But there must have been a moment of fear, for at the last minute he called the wife of a friend at her apartment in London. "I'm about to go into my act," he told her. "If I don't come back, tell my dad . . . that I love him very much."

At eight minutes to six, Joe Kennedy sat in the plane with his co-pilot, Wilford Willy, behind him. Pushing the throttles gently forward, he lifted her into the air. Eighteen minutes later, at an altitude of two thousand feet, he engaged the autopilot. He then picked up the microphone and called the pilot of the mother ship, which was flying at his stern. Joe had only ten minutes more in the air before his part of the mission would be completed. Then at six twenty p.m., with no warning or explanation, Joe's plane exploded in midair. It was "the biggest explosion I ever saw until the pictures of the atom bomb," said a pilot in the mother ship. Not a single part of Joe Kennedy's body was ever found.

It was Sunday afternoon in Hyannis Port when two priests, one of them a navy chaplain, arrived at the Kennedy house to deliver the message. "It concerns your son Joe Junior, who is missing in action," the chaplain said. Then he told Joe Senior and Rose the whole story. Joe held on to Rose for a moment and then went into the living room to break the news. "Children," he said with tears in his eyes, "your brother Joe has been lost. He died flying a volunteer mission." With that he retreated into his bedroom and locked the door.

Back in London, when Pat Wilson received the news, she wrote a long and touching letter to Rose Kennedy.

> Loving him as much as I did, I can understand a little the agony you, as his mother must be going through. . . . Our love was strong, true and unspoilt. I now realize more than ever before how lucky I was to have been loved by someone so perfect as Joe and I thank God for the lovely times we had together.

Rose never acknowledged Pat's letter.

Kathleen was with the Devonshires in London when the RAF finally reached her with the news of her brother's death. She had a very hard time accepting it. In the last months, through so much turmoil, he had been her closest friend. Though determined to be brave, she found herself unable to control her emotions, sobbing openly. She realized that she had to get home. Arrangements were made to fly to the States, and when she landed in Boston, her brother Jack was there to greet her.

For Rose, these were "the blackest hours" she had ever known, and in her room she wept shamelessly. Joe had been the one child to whom she had given her unrestricted warmth and her deepest love, and in return he had been the perfect model for all the others, always reliable, always hard-working, always respectful. But now he was dead, and all that Rose could do was stay in her room, saying her rosary again and again, leaving it up to her husband to handle the arrangements, the letters and the telegrams.

At first, Joe Senior seemed to take comfort in reading and responding to all the letters that kept pouring in, especially from people who had known Joe Junior and who invariably spoke of his special radiance. But Kennedy's external composure shattered on an afternoon in late summer when he received the last letter Joe had written to the family. It "simply tore Joe apart," Rose later recalled. "He knew he would never again be able to hear his voice or to read his words. . . . Joe threw the letter on the table and collapsed in his chair with his head in his hands, saying over and over that nothing would ever be the same again, that the best part of his life was finished."

As the weeks wore on, the religious passion that had once allowed Rose to come to terms with her difficult experience at the Blumenthal convent now worked on her to forsake her grief and return to life. "As soon as I fully accepted that God had his reasons for taking Joe," Rose said later, "I began to recover."

Joe Senior seemed to sink into a deeper gloom with each passing day. For this man whose involvement with his children had become the primary motive of existence, the death of his firstborn son left a scar that could never be healed. "I just can't get in the mood" to do much of anything, he told one friend. "You know how much I had tied my whole life up to his and what great things I saw in the future for him. Now it's all over."

In his letters, the love Kennedy felt for young Joe is clear and powerful. But the letters also suggest that more was at stake than the loss of a son. In his open admission that all his own plans for the future had been demolished, Kennedy reveals a single-minded ambition that called for Joe Junior to make restitution for all that he himself had been unable to accomplish.

Of all Kennedy's children, Kathleen seemed to provide her father with the most comfort. Staying on into September, she would sit with him for hours, responding to all the letters about Joe, even as she worried herself to sleep each night thinking about Billy—Major William Cavendish, who was even then advancing with his company through the Low Countries, heading toward France.

By the end of August, with the Germans in retreat, Billy's Fifth Battalion had made spectacular progress. Indeed, in only a few days the battalion advanced to the Somme River, the site of the mass slaughter of the Great War. Reaching Brussels, the men were greeted by cheering crowds of liberated citizens. But the mood was suddenly shattered when, pushing on toward France, they encountered a German contingent of soldiers determined to fight with everything they had. That night his battalion of the Coldstream Guards suffered heavy losses.

On the morning of September 9, Billy's company set off to capture the village of Heppen. Calm and casual, Billy headed out in front of the tanks, calling back to his men, "Come on, you fellows, buck up," as he tried to sustain morale in a unit that had lost a quarter of its men the day before. Walking briskly, he had progressed just a few hundred yards when he was shot by a German sniper. The bullet pierced his heart, and he died instantly.

The terrible news reached Kathleen on September 16. As soon as she could, she arranged to go back to England, back to her new family, the Devonshires. "So ends the story of Billy and Kick," she recorded in her diary. "Life is so cruel. . . . Writing is impossible."

On September 30, Kathleen joined the Devonshires for a simple memorial service held in a little church near Chatsworth, where since the fourteenth century many of Billy's ancestors had been laid to rest. With the service over, the Kennedys assumed that Kathleen would return to the States, but she elected to stay in England. Though she had lost her legal claim to any portion of the Devonshires' holdings, the family opened their hearts completely to her.

She returned to the Catholic Church, which welcomed her back now that her Protestant husband was dead. "I guess God has taken care of the matter in His own way," she remarked bitterly. She also returned to the Red Cross, where her work now became vital to her existence. It took time, but gradually her native love of life reasserted itself and Kathleen began to be herself again. As she wrote to Lem Billings, "Luckily I am a Kennedy. I have a very strong feeling that that makes a big difference about how to take things."

For Jack, the months after his brother's death were a difficult time. For as long as he could remember, according to Lem, his competition with his brother had defined his own identity. Now Joe was gone and Jack did not know where to turn. After years of being the underdog, he had just begun to outperform his brother—at Harvard and in the navy. But now the possibility of victory was forever closed, for in his heroic death Joe was invulnerable, his superiority sealed forever in his father's heart. "I'm shadowboxing in a match the shadow is always going to win," Jack told Lem.

In the early months after Joe's death, Jack described himself as feeling "terribly exposed." For twenty-seven years he had lived with a protective shield. So long as Joe was there to attract the force of the family's intense ambitions, Jack could move about more or less freely, focusing on what *he* wanted to do. But with Joe's death came an abrupt removal of the protection he had enjoyed and he felt an "unnamed responsibility" both to his parents and to his brothers and sisters.

But with his father locked in his room, grieving, it was not immediately clear what Jack was now expected to do as the eldest surviving son. Legend has it that one day Joe consciously turned to Jack and ordered him to take Joe's place as the champion of the Kennedy clan in politics, and that then and there Jack answered his father's call. But for both father and son the struggle to create a place in each other's heart was far more complex than decisions about politics.

Having undergone a failed back operation immediately after his return from the South Pacific, Jack had endured months of disabling pain. To rebuild his health, he journeyed to Arizona, and while he was there his father called him every day. Gradually, they began to talk more fully and freely. For his part, Jack relished those talks, and Rose recalled how impressed Joe was when he came away from the conversations. "It was the one thing that seemed to make him brighten up."

Still, even as they circled closer, neither Jack nor his father was able, in the spring of 1945, to focus on whether Jack really could pick up his brother's mantle.

ON APRIL 12, 1945, Franklin Delano Roosevelt died in Warm Springs, Georgia. The war in Europe ended soon after, and by then the United Nations Conference had already convened in San Francisco. Through one of Joe's newspaper friends, it was arranged that Jack would cover the conference from a GI viewpoint for the Chicago *Herald-American*. He filed sixteen stories, and Joe Kennedy was very pleased with his son's work. The art of writing was something that never came easily to Joe, so it made Jack's success all the more impressive. And when Jack was then asked to go to London to cover the British elections in June, Joe Kennedy once again had reason to be pleased with Jack's performance.

Arriving home from England, Jack spent "hours on end,"

according to Rose, discussing his future with his father. By this time, nearly a year after young Joe's death, the older Kennedy was finally able to look more clearly at his second son. And he liked what he saw. Perhaps, with a little luck and a lot of hard work, the dream could be realized after all.

21

THE YOUNG CONGRESSMAN

ONCE JOE DETERMINED that he "had the goods," the pressure on Jack was fierce. In August of 1945, Jack made the decision to pursue a political career and almost immediately he became active in Massachusetts politics.

As one biographer has noted, Jack Kennedy was, in some ways, "a stranger in the city of his birth." He had been six when his family moved to New York, and the only person he knew in Boston, he would later recall half jokingly, was his eighty-two-year-old grandfather; so it was no accident that he set up his headquarters at the Bellevue Hotel, just down the hall from the suite where Fitzgerald and his wife, Josie, had been living for nearly a decade.

The idea was to move around the state, meeting people and making speeches, while avoiding as long as possible a declaration for a specific office. Joe Kennedy, meanwhile, was crisscrossing the state himself, having been assigned by the governor of Massachusetts to conduct an economic survey of the state. It was a fortuitous assignment, for it allowed the ambassador to meet every person of consequence in state government, politics and the media. Setting up his own headquarters at the Ritz-Carlton, Kennedy arranged to meet his son at the end of each day to analyze events and make plans.

Soon the momentum picked up and Jack, with his father's help, was invited to speak before an increasing number of organizations. His speeches had to be hurriedly prepared, and sometimes he lacked confidence in his delivery. Nor did he find it easy to approach people on street corners and strike up a conversation. Yet in the hurly-burly of local politics his reticence worked like a charm, setting him off favorably from the typical backslapping Irish politician. "There was a basic dignity in Jack Kennedy," an aide, Dave Powers observed, "that appealed to every Irishman who was beginning to feel a little embarrassed about the sentimental, corny style of the typical Irish politician."

At the beginning, Joe believed that his son's best shot would be to run for lieutenant governor of the state on the Democratic ticket. But when a congressional seat opened up in the Eleventh District—the same polyglot district Fitzgerald had represented at the turn of the century—Jack saw a rare opportunity to enter politics at a national rather than a local level. His father eventually agreed, and, in April 1946, Jack formally announced his intention to run for congress.

As it turned out, the primary race soon developed into a free-for-all with a field of ten candidates. At first, the others laughed young Kennedy off, calling him "the poor little rich kid," the "carpetbagger" and "an outsider trying to buy the election with his father's money." But Jack was undeterred.

Recognizing the narrow, localized strengths of the other candidates, Jack's advisers decided that the best strategy was for him to become the number-two man in all sections. But to run strongly throughout the entire district, Jack needed a large volunteer organization centered around a strong cadre of loyal, idealistic workers who had deep roots in their own communities. Once recruited, this inner circle developed a great feeling of fellowship toward one another and toward Jack, who drew them all together. "There was something about his personality that made you want to drop whatever you were doing and go to work for him," observed Dave Powers, an early member of this group. "It wasn't so much what he said but the way he reached into [people's] emotions."

However, no staff assignments and no alliances were final unless the ambassador approved, and he also controlled the disbursement of all funds. As Jack's campaign manager, Mark Dalton recalled, "The ambassador was the essential, real campaign manager." Though Joe remained behind the scenes, his influence could be felt everywhere.

As the weeks passed, Jack's speaking ability steadily improved, and as he visited firehouses, police stations, saloons and poolrooms, he found himself enjoying the process more than he ever could have imagined. And because he was already a celebrity, there were people all over the district who wanted to meet him. To them, the Kennedy name meant success, power and wealth, the fulfillment of the American dream. While it was clear to the voters that John Kennedy had lived his life in a different world from theirs, he was able to treat those differences with humor and grace, and so turned his wealth into an asset, making it something to aspire to, rather than be angry about. At one gathering, at which each of his opponents was introduced as the son of a poor man, Jack won over the crowd by saying, "I seem to be the only person here tonight who didn't come up the hard way."

As a way of bringing the campaign directly to voters in their own neighborhoods, an elaborate series of house parties was run with the help of sisters Eunice and Pat, who coordinated the volunteer hostesses. Each party accommodated between twenty-five and seventy-five people. After coffee and a brief entertainment, Jack would arrive, make a short speech and answer questions.

"Kennedy was at his best at these affairs," reported historian James MacGregor Burns, "coming in a bit timidly but with his flashing smile, charming the mothers and titillating the daughters, answering questions with a leg draped over the arm of his chair."

Before the campaign ended, almost the entire Kennedy family had joined in the fight. Even twenty-one-year-old Bobby, now in the navy, stayed for a while, working in East Cambridge, where he was remembered later for joining the neighborhood kids in pickup basketball and football games. But to the surprise of everyone except perhaps John Fitzgerald, Rose Kennedy proved to be the most effective campaigner of them all, bringing a special glamour and style to the campaign, telling stories about her children and her glamorous life at the Court of St. James's. To the socially conscious Irish, the Kennedys had now emerged as the "first Irish Brahmins," a position worthy of emulation.

On the evening of the primary, as the returns came in, it soon became clear that Jack had won a smashing victory. At Kennedy headquarters, his supporters went wild. It remained only for the irrepressible Honey Fitz, with tears in his eyes, to jump on a table and lead the crowd in a rousing chorus of "Sweet Adeline."

In November, as expected in a district where the Democrats held an overwhelming majority, John Kennedy won in a landslide. The die was cast, Joe Kennedy wrote to an acquaintance. "I find myself with a new occupation—that is, furthering young Jack's political career."

WHEN JACK FIRST ARRIVED in Washington, he rented an attractive town house in Georgetown, where he lived with an aide, William Sutton, the family cook, and his twenty-six-year-old sister, Eunice, whose experience as a social worker had led to a job with the Juvenile Delinquency Committee of the Justice Department.

The Georgetown house was a lively place, with guests likely to pop in at any moment. Among them were a parade of women. "Jack liked girls," his friend and fellow Congressman George Smathers observed. "He came by it naturally. His daddy liked girls. He was a chaser." All of the women in his life were bright, beautiful and amusing, but all of them were "safe": girls he could not or would not marry. In fact, so driven was the pace of Jack's sex life, and so discardable his conquests, that they suggest a deep difficulty with intimacy.

"The whole thing with him was pursuit," said one of the women Jack courted. "I think he was secretly disappointed when a woman gave in. . . . I once asked him why he was doing it—why he was avoiding real relationships, why he was taking a chance on getting caught in a scandal. 'I don't know, really,' he answered. 'I just can't help it.' He had this sad expression on his face. He looked like a little boy about to cry."

In the United States Congress Jack never came into his own. Although he was assigned to the Education and the Labor committees, and proved himself an able questioner at hearings, basically he did not relish servicing the mundane needs of his district. His real interest lay in national and international matters. And when, during the 1947 summer recess, a congressional fact-finding committee set off "to study education and labor conditions" in Western Europe and Russia, Jack was part of the group. On the way he stopped to visit with Kathleen, who was at the Devonshires' Lismore Castle in southern Ireland.

It had not been easy for Kathleen to make her peace with Billy's death. As the war drew to an end, she had confided to Lem that she was "rather depressed." But she told her family with characteristic spirit, "I try and do lots and that makes the days pass quickly." She had made up her mind to live in England and had bought herself a house in London, for as she wrote to Lem, "I feel I have terrific roots here." As her spirits returned, she found herself once more surrounded by beaux, including Anthony Eden, whose friendship she relished.

As Kathleen had hoped, Jack got along famously with all her friends. But in the days that followed, she and Jack spent a lot of time together. They took long walks through the Irish country-side, and it was during one of these walks, according to Lem, that Kathleen confided to her brother that she had fallen in love with a married man. His name was Lord Peter Fitzwilliam, and he was a war hero and one of the wealthiest peers in England. Peter was also something of a rake, a charming playboy who was married to Olive Plunkett, the beautiful heiress to the Guinness brewery fortune. But the marriage had broken down, and now Peter was planning to secure a divorce.

Kathleen had first met Peter at a ball, where her radiant beauty immediately attracted his attention. "It was overnight," one friend commented, "and it was the real thing—illicit, passionate, encompassing." Another found Peter much "like Joe Kennedy himself—older, sophisticated, quite the rogue male."

Always something of a romantic, Kathleen told Jack that in Peter she had found her Rhett Butler, the dark, handsome man who could tell her the most ribald stories and make her laugh. He was a man who knew how to play and who swept her along with him, a man with whom she could have fun again. She was blindly, recklessly in love.

Jack was a bit envious, admitting later to Lem that in all his relationships with women, except perhaps with Inga, he had never lost himself as Kathleen appeared to have done.

After his visit with Kathleen in Ireland, Jack traveled on to London. While there, he fell ill with acute nausea and low blood pressure. He was rushed to a clinic, where he was diagnosed as having Addison's disease, a serious illness resulting in general weakness, loss of weight, circulatory collapse and vulnerability to infection. His doctor gave him less than a year to live.

When the Boston papers broke the news of Jack's illness, there was no mention of his having Addison's disease. Fearing that the public would recoil from an aspiring leader with a life-threatening disease, the Kennedys had managed to characterize the illness as simply a recurrence of a case of malaria Jack had suffered in the South Pacific. And the deception worked. Back in Washington, though under a doctor's care for months at a time, he was able to serve his constituents adequately, through the hard work of his own and his father's staff.

At the beginning of March, 1948, all the members of the Kennedy clan—including Kathleen, who came for a two-month stay—gathered at their villa in Palm Beach. Kathleen was so in love by then and so determined to marry Peter that she spent much of her vacation gathering her courage to tell her parents, hoping against hope that they would accept her decision. But Kathleen had underestimated the depth of her mother's feelings about marriage to a divorcé. Rose told her that if she married a divorced man she would be disowned by the family. And this time the ambassador was silent, offering his daughter no support.

Profoundly shaken by her parents' reaction, Kathleen went to Washington to see her old friends Patsy Field and John White. "I don't know what to do," she confided to Patsy. But after talking it over, she made up her own mind. "It's my life," she said. "I'm going to do whatever I have to do so I can be with Peter."

Back in England, she and Peter were together constantly. With the plans proceeding for his divorce, they decided to announce their engagement in May. Still, Kathleen desperately wanted her father's blessing before making her decision public. Since Joe Kennedy was scheduled to be in Paris shortly, Kathleen called him to ask if she could bring Peter to meet him. She must have hoped that Peter himself, with all his charm, would be his own best advocate. When she hung up the phone, Kathleen's housekeeper recalled, she looked absolutely "radiant." Her father had agreed to meet them for lunch at the Ritz on Saturday, May 15.

On Thursday, May 13, the couple climbed into a De Haviland

Dove eight-seat plane at an airport just outside London and took off for Cannes, where they were to spend two days alone before going to Paris for the big meeting. The Dove landed in Paris for refueling, but Peter impulsively phoned a few of his buddies for lunch so that they could meet Kathleen. When they returned to the airport three hours later, the pilot announced that a thunderstorm had been predicted along their route to Cannes and the flight was far too risky. But Fitzwilliam was so insistent that the pilot found himself giving in. The Dove took off, and within a few hours, just as predicted, the small plane found itself in a violent thunderstorm, struggling against treacherous winds and heavy rain. After being tossed about wildly for twenty minutes, the plane suddenly shot out from the bottom of a cloud and headed straight for a mountain ridge. For about ten seconds Peter and Kathleen must have realized they were going to die.

In the tiny town of Privas, some farmers heard the explosion and climbed up to the ridge. Hours later, several gendarmes followed them to the wreckage. They found no survivors.

It was a Washington *Post* reporter who first brought word to Jack Kennedy and Eunice at the Georgetown house. Jack immediately got on the phone to an assistant and asked him to check out the story. When the call came a short time later saying Kathleen's body had been identified, Jack turned his head and began to cry.

Ambassador Kennedy heard the news from a Boston *Globe* reporter at his hotel in Paris. He rushed off to Privas and when he arrived, the gendarmes escorted him to the town hall, where he was obliged to identify his beloved daughter's disfigured body. When asked about his plans for the burial, Kennedy was unable to respond. "I have no plans," he said, his voice broken. "No plans."

Meanwhile, all the far-flung members of the Kennedy family were gathering in Hyannis Port, drawn to the sheltering protection of the big white house. When Joe Kennedy called home after his journey to Privas, he said nothing about Kathleen's mangled body, only how beautiful and peaceful she looked. This description made its way into the press along with a totally false account of her trip, a story that said Kathleen, on her way to Cannes, met Lord Fitzwilliam by chance and he offered her a ride in his chartered plane.

Joe Kennedy, hidden in his hotel, was unable to decide whether to bury Kathleen in England or on Cape Cod. But when the Devonshires suggested that she be buried in the family plot near Chatsworth, since she had died as Billy's widow and had so loved her life in England, the ambassador consented immediately.

Kathleen's burial took place on May 20. Some two hundred of her friends crowded into a special train and accompanied the coffin to Derbyshire. "I can still see the stricken face of old Joe Kennedy," someone recalled years later, "as he stood alone, unloved and despised, behind the coffin of his eldest daughter amid the hundreds of British friends who had adored her."

It was the Duchess who chose the epitaph for Kathleen's tombstone: JOY SHE GAVE / JOY SHE HAS FOUND.

OF THE BROTHERS and sisters, Jack was perhaps the most powerfully affected by Kathleen's death. "He was in terrible pain," Lem Billings recalled. Again and again he asked, "How can there possibly be any purpose in her death?" His Catholic faith had taught him there was a purpose to everything, but all he could see was a vital, high-spirited woman, cut down in her fullest flowering.

The deaths of his brother and sister, combined with the discovery that he had Addison's disease, plunged Jack into a terrible period of confusion. As the lone survivor of the golden trio, his emotions raw, his body weary, he talked constantly about death. And in the face of death, "the only thing that made sense, he decided, was to live for the moment," Lem Billings recalled, "treating each day as if it were his last, demanding of life constant intensity, adventure and pleasure." And for those around him, Jack's intensity was contagious. As another friend remembered, it was as if "he always heard the footsteps. . . . Death was there. It had taken Joe and Kick and it was waiting for him." Yet, as the months went by, Jack gradually began to accept his new situation. "Slowly," Billings recalled, "he began to fight back, knowing that to stand still was to stay in sorrow, that to live he had to move forward. He recognized he could never return to what he was—the younger brother of Joe and the older brother of Kathleen. So he began to establish a new

Jack, the naval hero, is greeted by his grandfather Honey Fitz.

and separate personal identity. And once he focused on what *he* really wanted to do with his life, he realized that it really might be politics after all."

As 1949 gave way to 1950, Jack's physical condition also took a marked turn for the better, due to the discovery that cortisone could be a "miracle drug" for Addisonian patients, allowing them for the first time to lead fairly normal lives. Patients treated with the drug generally experienced "a markedly increased sense of well-being . . . a real increase in energy . . . strength and endurance." For years, Jack had struggled against a series of mysterious illnesses—high fevers and hepatitis, jaundice and malaria—illnesses that had left him tired and weary, without his ever understanding what was wrong. Now, in his thirties, he finally knew why he was so vulnerable to infection, and with treatment he experienced a whole new lease on life. And with it came a new seriousness and a renewed commitment to politics—a commitment that was reinforced during a visit he paid to his grandfather at the Bellevue Hotel in February 1950.

The old man had visibly aged—his hair was now white and his face deeply lined—but he was still possessed of his full faculties and his phenomenal energy. During this visit, Fitzgerald openly encouraged his grandson to carry on the family's political tradition. Indeed, what Jack remembered most about this last, long conversation with his grandfather was how the old man's eyes still burned when he talked of the richness of political life. "You are my namesake," Fitzgerald told him, and he again described the long road that had taken him from the tenement on Ferry Street to the happy years he had spent in the political arena. "You are the one to carry on our family name.

And mark my word, you will walk on a far larger canvas than I."

Eight months later, with his wife and two of his sons at his bedside, John Fitzgerald died. He had outlasted all his brothers except the youngest, Henry. He had buried three of his six children and had lived to see ambition's death in his two older boys. But there was always Rose, his favorite child: her accomplishments had lifted his own name to greater heights than he could have imagined.

But at the time of his death his "rambling Rose" was in Paris. She was, the Boston *Post* reported, "grief-stricken, and distraught because she could not arrange immediate plane passage home in time for the funeral." Years later, Rose still deeply regretted not being there at his death.

The day of the funeral, October 5, more than thirty-five hundred persons crowded into the Cathedral of the Holy Cross. "Bankers knelt side by side with laborers," the *Post* reported. "State and national dignitaries shared the same pews in the church with unpretentious housewives from the North End, South End, Dorchester and Roxbury." Seated next to his sisters Eunice, Pat and Jean, Jack saw the funeral as "the final triumph" of his grandfather. "All his life he had loved his city of Boston, and now Boston was returning that love."

Jack Kennedy later told Billings that he decided to stick with politics just about this time. "It was," Billings recalled, "as if he were seeing for the first time that he really might be able to touch people as a politician and that if he could, then they could give him something back—something to make up for his terrible sense of loneliness and loss."

22

SHOOTING FOR A STAR

NOW THE STORY OF the Fitzgeralds and the Kennedys, the century-long ascent from the immigrant slums of Boston's North End, was to become something different: the personal and political journey of John Fitzgerald Kennedy. The family was to become celebrated as never before, elevating the family saga past the borders of mythology. Parents and siblings were to play a large and well-publicized role in John Kennedy's success, but in the largest sense it was his own triumph.

Emotionally and materially Jack was always a Kennedy. Yet there was also a sense—especially as he neared the summit—in which he needed no one else at all. Because he was so much his own man, so armored in his solitude, he could belong—if not to anyone, to everyone.

Of all the Kennedy children, Jack was the one to notice that "the idea of the family" served to substitute for his parents' absence. There was nothing dearer to his parents' hearts than their children, yet both Rose and Joe spent substantial amounts of time away from home, leaving the children with various surrogates. Yet, precisely because he was left alone so much of the time, Jack had the freedom to be a child, and to develop his own emotional life. In contrast to Joe Junior, the model brother, Jack became the warm and playful brother, the Pied Piper, and at least for some of his family, the center of attention.

Jack's intelligence and imagination were also stimulated by his childhood isolation. The books his mother read him during his days of youthful illness—those rare times when he alone occupied the center of Rose's attention—were charged with high intensity. Camelot, or the concept of a Camelot, the joys of adventure, the glory of high deeds, were conceived in the fevered brain of a sick child. As he became older, books also offered him a retreat from the continual rivalries and tensions of his family surroundings. And from the worlds of adventure, history and biography, which were his favorites, came the values and ambitions that were to guide him as he entered into public life.

His struggle for independence within the family was also reflected in his almost complete lack of ideological commitment. "Some people have their liberalism 'made' by the time they reach their late twenties," he told James MacGregor Burns, his biographer. "I didn't. I was caught in crosscurrents and eddies. It was only later that I got into the stream of things."

The statement is both revealing and misleading. John Kennedy was never to subsume himself under a coherent political philosophy, liberal or conservative. He never fully identified with a cause or an institution except in pursuit of goals. His vision, unobstructed by ideological preconception, was continually reformed by personal experience. His mind welcomed divergent views. He had the capacity to admit mistakes and to modify his approach without feeling personally threatened. It was, in fact, his mounting confidence in the powers of his own mind that became the most important component of his defense against the basic insecurities of his relationship to parents, family structure and life itself.

To describe these qualities is not to summarize the man. There is always something more—an indescribable compound of self drawn from the experiences of the generations who lived before. From his namesake, John Fitzgerald, Kennedy inherited a driving will, and a radiant warmth that he projected onto crowds and individuals alike. Yet beneath this exterior he carried his grandmother Josie's coldness. From P. J. Kennedy, he inherited a certain self-possession and dignity that his father never achieved. And from both his parents he inherited curiosity about the world and the people around him.

But of all the influences that shaped John Kennedy, his father's absolute commitment was probably the most important. Jack was now experiencing all the insight, understanding and affection that had once been focused on Joe Junior. It had been a long time in coming, but precisely because it had taken so long Jack was able to absorb the force of his father's personality without losing his own.

WHETHER HE DECIDED to run for governor or the Senate—a question that was still unresolved in the spring of 1951—Jack Kennedy began a ceaseless, grueling pursuit of the statewide constituency either office would require. Every Thursday he flew to Massachusetts for a three- or four-day weekend of speaking engagements. "Jack told me," Dave Powers recalled, "to let everybody know he was available as a speaker. No town was too small or too Republican for him."

Driving himself and his staff relentlessly, he rose before dawn, then rode in a car for hours in rain or snow to make a dozen speeches in three or four different towns, and all with continuous pain in his back.

Meanwhile, the ambassador was working to establish a state-wide organization far broader than the traditional Democratic structure. From the start, Joseph Kennedy felt that Jack should run for the Senate against the incumbent Henry Cabot Lodge II—grandson of the isolationist who had defeated John Fitzgerald for the Senate thirty-six years earlier. "When you've beaten Lodge," he said, "you've beaten the best." For Jack, too, the Senate seat had much more appeal than the lieutenant governor post, since it would allow him to focus on foreign affairs. "He asked me what I thought," Justice William O. Douglas recalled. "I told him I believe in every young man shooting for a star and this was a star."

To some in the Kennedy camp, the quest seemed impossible. For nearly two decades the handsome blue-eyed Lodge had dominated political life in the state. Like Kennedy, Lodge had graduated from Harvard and dabbled in journalism before settling into a career in politics. And like Kennedy, he was a war hero with a reputation for appealing to the women's vote. "Rarely in American politics," historian James Macgregor Burns observed, "have hunter and quarry so resembled each other. Not only were they both tall, young, handsome and winning, each a Brahmin in his own way, but their careers were remarkably parallel."

During the campaign, Joe Kennedy rented an exclusive apartment on Beacon Street and there he mobilized his aides. Only Eddie Moore was missing from the inner circle, for at seventy-seven years of age, Joe Kennedy's partner was largely confined to bed in his home on the Cape. Even so, Eddie did his bit in the campaign, making sure the Cape was completely covered.

It was no secret that Joe Kennedy was providing money for the campaign. It was expensive to spread the Congressman's name across the state, to hire the cars and charter the planes and print the invitations for the dozens of teas attended by more than fifty thousand women. With the money came power over campaign decisions, and Joe Kennedy wielded his power with a heavy hand, as was illustrated most damagingly in the callous treatment of Mark Dalton, the quiet, intelligent young man who had managed Jack's previous campaigns for the House. Jack "felt a great affinity toward Mark," one aide remembered. By 1952, however, Dalton's law practice had grown to where he could no longer afford to work as an anonymous, unpaid volunteer. So a press release was drawn up announcing that Dalton was now the full-time campaign manager. But though Jack trusted Dalton completely, Joe did not. Or perhaps the old patriarch could never place anyone except a Kennedy in a position of authority. In any case, he blocked Dalton's appointment, a move that came as "a grave disappointment" to Dalton, who departed soon after, leaving the staff leaderless. Jack's aide, Kenneth O'Donnell, thought the campaign was bound for "absolute disaster" unless Jack's brother Robert took over.

Robert was working for the Justice Department, and when O'Donnell called him, he responded angrily. "Don't drag me into it," he said, explaining that he loved what he was doing and didn't know anything at all about Massachusetts politics. "I'll screw it up," he warned, "and . . . I just don't want to come." But when O'Donnell said, "Unless you come, I don't think it's going to be done," Robert agreed to talk to his father.

In the years after the war, Robert had gradually attracted his father's attention and respect. After his graduation from Harvard and through his years in law school, his modest store of self-confidence had begun to grow. Nevertheless, he had never strayed far beyond his family orbit, and now, a few days after talking with his father, he gave up his job in the Justice Department and headed for Massachusetts. His entrance into the campaign proved to be a turning point. "Bobby could handle the father," said O'Donnell, "and no one else could have. . . . If Bobby had not arrived on the scene and taken charge when he did, Jack most certainly would have lost the election."

The more Kennedy's advisers studied Lodge and his record, the more they despaired of winning the support of the party's indifferent and suspicious liberal wing. The decision was to have the candidate take strongly liberal positions, while his father worked to attract conservative support. But despite strenuous efforts, Lodge, who had the backing of the Republicans' popular presidential candidate, General Dwight D. Eisenhower, began to gain momentum. Many years later, Lodge recalled "a growing feeling of confidence as the election approached," and he added, "I think I could have made it if it hadn't been for all those fancy tea parties the Kennedys sponsored."

The idea of the tea parties was a masterstroke, for it brought the entire family into direct contact with thousands of women who looked upon the Kennedys as royalty, and saw their own dreams of success mirrored in that family's achievement. In all, there were thirty-three teas, and from the start, recalled Polly Fitzgerald, who organized them, "we decided to rent the fanciest rooms in the nicest hotels and to set up the rooms with lace tablecloths and silver candelabra. We wanted it beautiful, as if it were an exclusive party in someone's estate."

The entire Kennedy family would stand in a receiving line while the guests poured in. As Polly reminisced, "Mrs. Kennedy was a key element in our success, known for her style in clothes and her rich experiences in travel. All the women wanted to meet her. And what a terrific speaker she turned out to be."

On election day, the early returns foretold an uncertain contest between Kennedy and Lodge. But in the early hours of the morning, Jack began to pull ahead, and at seven thirty-four a.m., Lodge conceded. At the news, the tumultuous crowd at Kennedy headquarters burst into shouts and whistles and enthusiastic applause.

For the entire Kennedy family, Jack's victory was a great triumph. For Jack and Bobby, it forged a blood partnership that would last until Jack died. But for Rose, the victory brought back a special memory. "I kept thinking about my father and what this victory would have meant to him. In my mind, I kept picturing him as a little boy, huddled in the servants' quarters at old Henry Cabot

During Jack's 1952 Senate race, Rose campaigns for her son at a tea in Worcester.

Young and in love: Jack and Jackie sailing off Hyannis Port.

Lodge's home as he warmed his shivering body from the cold of his newspaper route. In his wildest dreams that winter's night, could he ever have imagined how far both he and his family would come?"

THE NEW SENATOR from Massachusetts attended President Eisenhower's inaugural ball on January 20, 1953, with Jacqueline Bouvier, whom he had met at a dinner party in 1951. Now twenty-three, she had dark, luxuriant hair and wide-set deep-brown eyes. The daughter of stockbroker John Bouvier III and Janet Lee Bouvier, Jackie had attended Miss Porter's School in Farmington, Connecticut, before spending two years at Vassar, one at the Sorbonne in Paris and a graduating year at George Washington University in Washington, D.C. When she met Jack, she was working as a photographer for the Washington *Times-Herald*.

"Jackie was different from all the other girls Jack had been dating," Lem Billings recalled. "She was more intelligent, more literary, more substantial. And her mother's second marriage, to Hugh Auchincloss, carried the family into *The Social Register*, which gave Jackie a certain classiness." But, in fact, what Jack and Jackie had in common had less to do with their backgrounds than with the loneliness each of them had experienced as a child. Jackie, a vulnerable and sensitive child, was six when her parents separated and nine when they divorced. Crushed by the breakup of her home, trusting less in people than in animals and in nature, she sought her deepest pleasures in solitary acts: riding a horse, reading a book, listening to music. Jack's loneliness, born of continuing illness and the preeminence of his older brother, was more subtly shaped; it took a practiced eye to see the reality beneath his gregarious exterior. But "they were kindred souls," Billings romantically observed.

Yet, having been so private for so long, neither of them found it easy to give of themselves, especially at a time when Jack was so totally absorbed in his race for the Senate. "It was a very spasmodic courtship," Jackie said, "conducted mainly at long distance with a great clanking of coins in dozens of phone booths."

Nevertheless, by the spring of 1953, Jack's romance with Jackie had progressed further than any of his other relationships. And in May, while Jackie was in London covering the coronation of Queen Elizabeth II, Jack proposed by telegram. The wedding was scheduled for September.

"For the Kennedy family, it was a strange summer," Billings recalled. "Ever since Joe Junior's death, Jack had been the focal point of the family's ambition, and now that he was marrying they feared that he'd be drawn away from them. They perceived Jackie as a threat. This was especially true for Jack's sisters, who

Jack and Jackie strolling to Joe Kennedy's house at Hyannis Port.

called her 'the Deb,' made fun of her babylike voice and worked relentlessly to engage her in the family's physical activities, where they knew she could never excel."

If Jackie was intimidated by the raucous atmosphere of Hyannis Port, she never let on, determined to hold her own against the overwhelming pressures to become a Kennedy. Of all the family, Joe Senior appreciated Jackie the best, finding in her independence a quality he much admired. So while others played touch football on the lawn, Joe and Jackie would sit on the porch, "talking about everything from classical music to the movies."

The spectacular wedding of Jacqueline Bouvier to John Fitzgerald Kennedy took place in Newport, Rhode Island, on September 12, 1953. Almost three thousand people, *The New York Times* reported, broke through police lines at the church, "nearly crushing the bride."

The first year of marriage was very difficult for Jackie. Night after night Jack arrived home from his office tired and ready to sleep. On weekends she sat alone in their small Georgetown house while Jack traveled through Massachusetts. "It was all wrong," Jackie recalled. "Politics was sort of my enemy and we had no home life whatsoever." But Jack never seemed to comprehend the invidious effect his absences were having upon his marriage, nor the devastating effect on Jackie of his continuing involvement with other women. "Jack kept assuring us that she didn't suspect," one friend said, "when it was obvious that she knew exactly what was happening."

Clearly Jack was following a pattern established by his father, but while Rose had willfully turned her attention from her husband's dalliances, knowing that her first priority was to keep her marriage alive, Jackie belonged to a different generation—one in which one marriage out of every five was ending in divorce. Moreover, having suffered through her own parents' breakup, she could not rely on the permanency of the marital bond as a salve for the disappointment in her relationship with her husband.

DURING THE SPRING and summer of 1954, Jack had increasing trouble with his back. Suffering pain more acute than he had experienced before, he was forced to use crutches as he willed his thin frame along the corridors of the Senate. His best hope was a complicated operation, a double fusion of spinal disks. Two operations were required, the first performed in October 1954, the second in February 1955. For a time the doctors could not say whether he would ever walk again. Afterward he was exhausted from the constant pain. Gradually, however, he began to mend.

Jack spent part of his long convalescence at Palm Beach working on a book. Published under the title *Profiles in Courage,* it was a collection of stories about eight political leaders—from John Quincy Adams to Thomas Hart Benton—whose political courage had led them to defy their constituents and their colleagues in order to serve the national good. Each story reinforced the confident belief that one man counted, that one man could change the course of events.

Within weeks of its publication, the book became a smashing best seller and a literary triumph as well. In years to come, however, questions would arise about the extent of Jack's authorship of the book, given the help he received from staff members and historians. "This kind of political production is normal," columnist Garry Wills has observed, "not only for an officeholder's speeches but for his books." But when Kennedy allowed his father's friend Arthur Krock to lobby the Pulitzer advisory board for a *writer's* prize, and then accepted the Pulitzer as if the work were wholly his own, he aroused suspicions about the extent to which his substance was fabricated by illusion, suspicions that would linger for most of his life.

JACK KENNEDY WOULD remain in the Senate for only eight years, spending at least half that time campaigning for national office. He realized, almost from the moment of his election, that the road to the summit did not lie in establishing a reputation as a hardworking senator but in creating an image of himself as a broad-gauged politician whose concerns transcended the parochial interests of Massachusetts. So he kept his interest in foreign affairs alive by traveling abroad as often as he could—to analyze the workings of NATO or to study the effects of totalitarianism in Eastern Europe—and he became a widely publicized spokesman against what he publicly described as "the hopeless internecine struggle" in Vietnam. Yet for all his clever-ness in cultivating a national image, Kennedy made a major mistake when he failed to recognize the moral issue at stake in the Senate censure of Wisconsin Senator Joseph McCarthy, who had been a friend of Jack's since he first arrived in Wash-ington as a young Congressman.

In the early 1950s, McCarthy's crusade against communism had turned into a witch-hunt, jeopardizing the careers and repu-tations of thousands of Americans. When the Senate finally got around to censuring McCarthy in December of 1954, Jack Kennedy was in the hospital recuperating from his first back operation. He was, however, in communication with his Senate office and, under the rules, could have put himself on record against McCarthy. But he was the only Democrat who did not. Whatever the reason—preoccupation with his health, his fa-ther's influence, his own loyalty to McCarthy or political calculation—it was a decision he would live to regret, for it deepened the suspicions of the party's liberal wing, which would prove the greatest obstacle to his pursuit of the presidency.

In an earlier era, Kennedy's national ambitions might thus have come to a halt, but the fifties was a decade marked by the decline of political parties, the rise of television and the trans-formation of politics into public relations—a decade perfectly suited to the engaging personality of John Fitzgerald Kennedy, who projected an image of youth, glamour and excitement. With his open smile, his careless perfection of dress and his self-deprecating humor, he was fast emerging as the most sought-after speaker on the national scene. "It was the damnedest thing," Senate Majority Leader Lyndon B. Johnson later said, "here was a young whippersnapper . . . he never said a word of importance in the Senate and he never did a thing. But some-how he managed to create the image of himself as a shining intellectual, a youthful leader who would change the face of the country."

As election year 1956 approached, the press speculated that the young Massachusetts Senator might have a place on the national Democratic ticket as the vice-presidential nominee. As the speculation increased, Joe Kennedy tried to hold his son back, arguing that presidential nominee Adlai Stevenson would be badly beaten in his second run against Eisenhower in November and that "defeat would be a devastating blow to your prestige." Nevertheless, Jack found himself caught up in the excitement of hearing himself described as a leading candidate, even though sentiment in Stevenson's headquarters favored either Senator Estes Kefauver or Senator Hubert H. Humphrey.

Jack arrived for the Democratic National Convention in Chicago accompanied by his pregnant wife and numerous members of his family—with the notable exception of his father, who was vacationing on the Riviera but staying in close contact. On August 13, the opening day of the convention, eleven thousand delegates watched the presentation of a propaganda film on the history of the party, produced by Dore Schary and narrated by Jack Kennedy. Schary later recalled that "the personality of the Senator just came right out at you. The narration was good, and the film was emotional. He was immediately a candidate. There was no doubt about that."

Kennedy became an instant hero, surrounded by crowds on the streets and on the convention floor. But still it seemed that Kefauver would be Stevenson's choice as a running mate. Then, unexpectedly, Stevenson made a decision that stunned veteran politicians. He declined to name a running mate, leaving the choice to the delegates. The would-be candidates now had only hours to fight for the nomination. Jack immediately decided to run.

"The next twelve hours were a nightmare," his secretary recalled. His staff worked all night having banners, buttons and leaflets printed, making the case for Jack's candidacy, persuading and appealing.

The hastily assembled Kennedy campaign achieved remarkable results. His strength on the first ballot was a big surprise. On the second ballot, it grew even more. The convention was in a tumult. On the third ballot, however, a number of delegations began to shift back to Kefauver. Watching from his suite, Kennedy recognized that Kefauver would now win. Heading for the convention hall, Jack made his way to the rostrum, receiving a long and emotional ovation. Then, in graceful, controlled tones, flashing an infectious grin seen on TV sets nationwide, he moved that Kefauver be nominated by acclamation. And then he was gone—the underdog candidate who had intrigued and captivated millions of Americans. The handsome, vigorous young man who fought valiantly and accepted defeat with a smile had touched the hearts and minds of people in living rooms across the nation. "In this moment of triumphant defeat," James MacGregor Burns wrote, "his campaign for the presidency was born."

When the convention ended, Jack flew to Paris, then on to the Riviera, an exhausted son needing the comfort of his father. The trip was poorly timed. Jackie, in the final months of pregnancy, was unable to leave her doctors, and had asked Jack not to go. But he went nonetheless. After long talks with his father, Jack left for a week-long sailing trip, and while he was away Jackie began to hemorrhage. Rushed to the hospital, she underwent an emergency cesarean operation. The baby, a girl, was stillborn.

It must have been a terribly lonely moment for Jackie, facing the loss without even knowing where to reach her husband. It was three days before Jack heard the news and flew back to the States.

"The death of the baby produced a real strain on Jack and Jackie's marriage," Lem Billings recalled. "Jackie . . . blamed her problem on the crazy pace of politics and the constant demands to participate in the endless activities of the Kennedy family. The only answer, she decided, was to separate herself even more from the rest of the family." This wise decision allowed her to keep a part of herself intact.

ON NOVEMBER 25, 1956, surrounded by his wife, six children and a dozen grandchildren, Joseph Kennedy presided over the traditional Thanksgiving Day feast at Hyannis Port. "After dinner," Rose recalled, "Jack and his father went into the little study off the living room to talk about the future." It was a crisp autumn day on the Cape, a day that would long be remembered by the family as the day Jack decided to run for President.

The decision was an act of daring. John Kennedy was less than forty years old, inexperienced in party affairs, and few experts would have given him much of a chance. But they could not know that he was finally at ease with himself. He had, with the help of cortisone, triumphed over a life-threatening disease. And he had, in that moment of high drama in Chicago, become a national figure, acknowledged and admired in his own right. He was no longer a surrogate for his brother; he was ready to shape his own destiny, ready to forge, in the fire of his ambition, a campaign of unprecedented duration, single-mindedness and popular appeal.

Constructing his campaign within the tacit limits imposed by the conservative Eisenhower presidency, Kennedy adopted a relatively cautious and moderate approach to domestic affairs. Only later would he receive the wholehearted support of the party's liberal wing. In foreign affairs, where liberal and conservative divisions were confused, he used the Senate as a forum to speak out for a strong American leadership against decaying colonialism and expanding Soviet totalitarianism. In this arena, he could establish that he was neither a dilettante nor a playboy, but possessed of qualities of statesmanship that entitled him to seek the very highest rank of public office.

IN NOVEMBER OF 1957, Jackie gave birth to a seven-pound baby girl who was named Caroline Bouvier Kennedy. Having a baby seemed to complete Jackie's life. Being a mother gave her an inner peace and security, which nothing else ever had. It opened her heart. In the forty-year-old father the baby girl produced equally strong emotions. "When he showed me the baby," Lem Billings observed, "he looked happier than I had seen him in a long time. With this child, he finally had a family of his own."

The following year, Kennedy was up for reelection to the Senate. His Republican opponent was Vincent Celeste, an Italian American from the waterfront district of the North End. This was no fight at all, most observers agreed. Yet the Kennedys set to work, running so hard that it seemed that Jack's entire future turned on winning a large margin of victory. Once again the ambassador was behind the scenes. And on November 4, 1958, a record turnout gave Kennedy nearly seventy-four percent of the total senatorial vote, the greatest margin ever recorded in the history of Massachusetts. "The vote was beyond our fondest dreams," the ambassador told a friend. "Keep in shape—there may be more work to be done."

ON JANUARY 20, 1960, Senator Kennedy entered a crowded press conference in the Senate Caucus Room. "I am announcing today my candidacy for the presidency of the United States," he began, projecting from the start a tone of confidence that America was entering a new era of forward movement in contrast to the Eisenhower years of passivity and acquiescence.

John Kennedy realized that to succeed he would have to impress future delegates and their leaders with his qualities, make alliances, incur debts. But many political leaders were ambivalent, even hostile, toward his candidacy. Many thought his youth and religion might be insurmountable obstacles to a Democratic victory. They had to be persuaded, through the presidential primaries, that his victory was politically possible.

In 1960, as before, campaigning would be a family affair. Bobby was again drafted as campaign manager. Brother-in-law Stephen Smith, Jean's husband, was assigned to coordinate Jack's schedule. Teddy was given the Rocky Mountain states to organize. Eunice, Pat and Jean put in weeks at a time. And Rose, at seventy, once again proved herself to be the daughter of Mayor Fitzgerald, delivering remarkably effective personal speeches that included comments on Jack's youth, his dislike of war, his early training and success.

Joseph Kennedy, meanwhile, fearing that his presence would be controversial, remained in self-imposed exile at Hyannis Port throughout most of the primary season.

In many ways, the years had not been kind to Joe and Rose; beset by devastating personal losses, they had gradually moved apart. While Joe committed himself to the secular success of his family and enjoyed a wide-ranging set of friendships, Rose retreated more and more into her own world, taking spiritual solace in her church and her books. But once Rose was out on the campaign trail, her vision suddenly expanded. In every appearance, she betrayed her political origins—the perfect use of a phrase, the perfect sense of timing, the perfect choice of dress. It was as if she possessed a buried chord of vitality that needed only to be struck.

After victory in New Hampshire, the campaign moved on to Wisconsin, Indiana, West Virginia. As Kennedy added sweeping victories in Nebraska, Maryland and Oregon, the country heard "the unmistakable sound of a bandwagon calliope," according to *The New York Times*. Indeed, by the time the convention opened in Los Angeles in the second week of July, victory seemed close at hand. Adlai Stevenson was emerging as the candidate of a growing and impassioned movement. But while the emotions belonged to Stevenson, the votes were Kennedy's. The balloting began at eight p.m. on Wednesday, July 13. Earlier in the day Kennedy had slipped away unnoticed to visit his father, who was staying at the Beverly Hills home of a friend. Ann Gargan witnessed the afternoon's events. "There was no question that day of the strength of the bond between these two men. They . . . had worked together for this and now the pieces were all falling in place. It was an incredible moment of high anticipation, an intimate moment in which Jack understood so clearly everything his father had done."

After the nomination became official with Wyoming's announcement that its fifteen votes belonged to "the next President of the United States," Kennedy decided to offer the vice-presidential spot to Lyndon Johnson. As Joe Kennedy saw it, simple arithmetic made the Majority Leader the natural choice: add the votes of New England to the votes of the solid South and only a small percentage more was needed to carry the election. Johnson, who had fought hard to secure the presidential spot for himself, startled the political world by accepting Kennedy's offer.

For two months, beginning just before Labor Day, Kennedy traveled throughout the country, carrying with him the slogan of his campaign, the need "to get the country moving again" after its long period of stagnation. But no sooner would he begin to articulate his hopes for a new day than the religious question would arise. Said a typical public letter: "We cannot turn our government over to a Catholic President who would be influenced by the Pope and the power of the Catholic hierarchy." Kennedy decided to meet the issue head-on. In a major speech to a group of Protestant ministers in Houston, Texas, he began by saying that because the religious issue was obscuring all other issues in the campaign, he recognized the necessity to state once again, as he had throughout the primary campaign, "I believe in an America where the separation of church and state is absolute." His speech was patient, good-tempered and unfailingly clear, punctuated by the dramatic statement that he would resign the presidency before he would allow religious pressures to violate the national interest. Although anti-Catholic prejudice remained a factor in the election, the Houston speech made it difficult for well-intentioned voters to believe that Kennedy's Catholicism represented a threat to America's separation of church and state.

Shortly after the speech, Kennedy appeared in his first televised debate with Richard Nixon. When it was over, columnist Joseph Alsop wrote, "Neither man fell flat on his face. Neither even stumbled . . . It is hard to believe the debate was at all decisive."

But it had been decisive. A new type of politician—a new politics—had emerged. As columnist Ralph McGill put it, "Maybe the audience looked more than it listened." Nixon looked sick and the camera betrayed the nervous awkwardness of his movements. In contrast, Kennedy looked charming, and his movements had "a patrician grace." Moreover, he spoke forcefully and coolly, whereas Nixon's private self—sweaty and edgy—kept poking through.

Seventy million Americans received their first exposure to Jack Kennedy as a presidential candidate during that debate. And from that point on he was met by huge, wildly enthusiastic crowds at nearly every stop. The entire campaign took on an air of confidence.

In Boston, election day was crisp and clear. Accompanied by Jackie, Jack descended to the basement of an old branch library in the West End, Martin Lomasney's old domain, to cast his vote. Then they flew to Hyannis Port, where the rest of the clan was gathered. Over the years, most of the children had purchased homes near their father and mother at Hyannis Port and now they were all together: Joe and Rose; Bobby and his wife, Ethel; Teddy and his wife, Joan; Pat and Peter Lawford; Jean and Steve Smith; Eunice and Sargent Schriver.

The long wait began. Dinner was served at the ambassador's house, and afterward, most of the crowd went to watch the returns at Bobby's house, which had been established as a command post with direct access to operators at Jack's head-quarters in Washington.

The early returns brought elation to the Kennedy compound, but by midnight the shape of the election was not as the Kennedys had anticipated. It was much closer than privately predicted. Just before four a.m., when it had become clear that the election would not be decided for hours, Jack Kennedy decided to go to bed. It was not until almost nine a.m. that the key state of Illinois went to Kennedy, and by then the news from other undecided states was equally positive. After twenty-four hours of waiting, victory was certain.

The time had come for Jack to go to the armory in Hyannis Port, where television cameras were waiting, to acknowledge his triumph to the country. Ann Gargan recalls that he tried to persuade his father to come, only to have the ambassador refuse. Piling into the car without him, the family started off; then Jack ordered the car stopped so that he could make one last appeal to his father. When Jack appeared at the armory as the new President-elect, his father was by his side, their first public appearance together in over a year.

IN THE WEEKS BEFORE the inauguration, almost as if he were making up for lost time, Joe Senior seemed intent on drawing his family around him. Jack willingly complied, making Palm Beach his headquarters for the transition planning. Jackie remained in Washington, for her second baby was due in mid-December. Flying back and forth between Palm Beach and Washington, Jack was returning to Florida on November 25 when he received word that his wife had gone into early labor and had been taken by ambulance to the hospital. "I'm never there when she needs me," he said, and boarded a fast plane back to Washington. During his flight, Jackie gave birth by cesarean section to a baby boy. This time, however, the premature baby survived, and when the President-elect arrived at the hospital, it was announced that both the baby and the mother were doing fine. The boy was given the name John Fitzgerald Kennedy, Jr.

In the weeks that followed, Jack spent many hours with his father, playing golf and taking walks. But the ambassador recognized that once the inauguration took place everything would be different. To reporter Hugh Sidey, Joseph Kennedy sadly admitted, "Jack doesn't belong anymore to just a family. He belongs to the country. . . ."

Joe knew he had to move quickly. As he saw it, the victory was a victory for the entire family, and the family had a right to share the spoils. From all accounts, it was he who insisted that Jack appoint his brother Bobby to the post of Attorney General, arguing that the President needed someone in his Cabinet whom he knew intimately and trusted completely. And it was Joe who insisted that the family clear the way for Teddy to run for Jack's seat in the Senate.

There were many who would see in Joe Kennedy's design for his sons a monstrous arrogance, just as years before the press had criticized the Fitzgeralds for their "imperial dynasty." And arrogance it was. On a grand scale, with ambition, passion and will attaining in them a terrifying yet wondrous force, both the Fitzgeralds and the Kennedys seemed to live their lives with an uncommon intensity. . . . Striking against the existing order of things in pursuit of their ambitions and their passions, they achieved more than they had ever dreamed, lending a magic to their family story that no tale of ordinary life could possibly rival. But the very nature of their search was for success of such towering proportions that, as history records, a terrible price was paid.

23

A TIP OF THE HAT

FOR MORE THAN one hundred years a thick Catholic Bible with a gold cross on its brown leather cover had accompanied the Fitzgerald family on their journey from the narrow streets and small rooms of the North End to the stately mansion on Welles Avenue and to the Bellevue Hotel. With the death of Mayor Fitzgerald, the old Bible was brought to the dusty attic of the Dorchester home of Thomas Fitzgerald, the mayor's youngest surviving son. There it remained until, in January 1961, it was brought to Washington for the swearing in of the thirty-fifth President of the United States.

The Bible had originally belonged to Thomas Fitzgerald, the Irish farmer with one cocked eye who heard the summons to America in the late 1840s and sailed westward to a new life. Its front pages, used as a family record, chronicle the births and deaths of the twelve Fitzgerald children, beginning with the birth of Michael in 1858. Recorded in a large, florid hand, the twelve children of Tom Fitzgerald and Rosanna Cox are followed by the five children of John Fitzgerald and Josie Hannon, who are followed in turn by the nine children of Rose Fitzgerald and Joseph Kennedy.

Some of these children died before they had a chance to live, others lived to see their dreams corrode, still others survived to bury their young. But on the twentieth of January, 1961, they would share in a collective moment of glory as the old Bible recording their names would play a central role in the inauguration of the first Catholic President in the history of the country.

During the years of the Kennedy family's rise in America, thirty-five million immigrants had entered the United States. Westward from Ireland came four and a half million people; from Great Britain, from the lands that became the German Empire, from Scandinavia came millions more. Then Italians, Poles and Jews, Hungarians and Slovaks came, and by the turn of the century millions more were on their way from the Balkans and Asia Minor. For these people and their children, John F. Kennedy's dazzling rise to power was a recognition that the great immigrant revolution was finally complete. In almost every field, the new immigrants had already broken through the barriers of fear and prejudice to reach the top of their professions. Now the final barrier had been breached.

But John Kennedy was not simply a member of an excluded ethnic group whose time had come. As author Garry Wills has observed, "It is the old story, for one of your own to get elected, he has to go out of his way to prove he is not just one of your own." John Kennedy had been inculcated from birth with the privileged sense that he could walk wherever he chose. His father had given him a prestigious secular education and had provided him with the opportunity to travel to dozens of countries before he reached the age of thirty-five.

The Kennedy children had heard conflicting messages from

their parents throughout their lives. From their father, whose internal battle for assimilation had never been resolved, they were taught to live beyond convention, to bow to no man and no institution, to act as if the land had always been theirs. From their mother they were told to remain true to the Catholic faith, to accept the limits and the pieties of the church, to live by the rules. Detached in some measure from both of his parents, John F. Kennedy was able to draw strength from both traditions. And by shaping his own integration in his own way, he suggested a means of reinvention and identification for millions of others.

The close structure of the Kennedy family had a special appeal to the imagination of the American people. For nearly a quarter of a century, ever since Joseph Kennedy had become a source of public interest, reporters had invariably focused attention on the esprit de corps of the Kennedy family, the loyalties and commitment and rituals that bound them together. In the early days, their rituals were in the form of religious celebrations, obligatory mealtimes, discussions, shared vacations. But with the emergence of John Kennedy as a public figure, the rituals of politics had replaced the others as the means by which their collective bonds were strengthened. And now, after years of common effort, the family was about to witness the flourishing of the family tree.

THE DAY BEFORE THE inauguration, a raging snowstorm brought the capital to a standstill. All night the snow continued as workmen labored with plows to clear Pennsylvania Avenue for the inaugural parade. But then at dawn the snow stopped and soon the sun flooded down from a cloudless blue sky.

Long before noon, an immense crowd began to gather. There came the sons and daughters of John Fitzgerald's brothers; the Duke and Duchess of Devonshire, the first members of British nobility to attend an American President's inauguration; the crew of Kennedy's *PT 109,* along with the commander of the Japanese destroyer that sank the boat.

Just before twelve, the Kennedy family and their guests took their seats on the inaugural platform. Joe Kennedy, still vigorous at seventy-two, was handsomely dressed in a dark blue topcoat with a blue-and-white dotted scarf at his neck. At his side, Rose Kennedy looked elegant in a mink hat and coat.

At a few minutes past twelve, the marine band struck up "The Stars and Stripes Forever," and John Kennedy walked onto the Capitol steps wearing a cutaway coat and a silk top hat. When General Eisenhower was inaugurated, he had elected to wear a business suit and a black homburg, but Kennedy believed the occasion called for something more elegant. "He recognized," Lem Billings said, "that even as the people would reject a king, their hearts tugged for the symbols of royalty. For that reason, he deliberately decided to invest his inauguration with pomp and ceremony. He wanted to use the moment to appeal to the imagination. . . . It worked."

Richard Cardinal Cushing, Archbishop of Boston, gave the invocation. It was followed by the recital of a poem by the nation's unofficial poet laureate, Robert Frost, whose participation had been suggested by Jackie. Frost's recitation of his poem "The Gift Outright" provided the most moving moment in the inauguration. When he finished, there was thunderous applause.

It was now time for the climax of the ceremony, the swearing in of the new President. Placing his left hand on the family Bible and holding his right hand in the air, John Kennedy repeated the oath: "I do solemnly swear," he said in a loud, clear voice, "that I will faithfully execute the office of the President of the United States and will, to the best of my ability, preserve, protect and defend the Constitution of the United States. So help me God."

Several people saw tears glistening in Joe Kennedy's eyes. In so many ways, it was the father's triumph as well as the son's, and it was surely an extraordinary end to a journey that had begun one hundred and eleven years before, when his grandfather left Ireland to sail across the ocean.

As soon as the oath was completed, the President delivered his inaugural address, his Boston accent and his clipped voice now familiar to millions. "Let the word go forth from this time and place, to friend and foe alike, that the torch has been passed to a new generation of Americans—born in this century, tempered by war, disciplined by a hard and bitter peace, proud of an ancient heritage." In the famous peroration, "Ask not what your country can do for you, but what you can do for your country," Kennedy evoked a theme of obligation that lay deep within the American tradition. But even more impressive was the image of youth and vigor he conveyed, at forty-three, to a world whose leaders seemed tired and old.

After the speech, Jackie whispered to her husband, "Oh, Jack, what a day," and softly touched his face.

As the inaugural parade made its way down Pennsylvania Avenue toward the White House, the crowds were sometimes eight and ten feet deep despite the freezing temperatures. The President and his wife rode at the front of the parade to the White House, where they would go to a special presidential stand to review the rest of the parade. Waiting in the front row of the reviewing stand were all the members of Kennedy's family. As the President approached, Eunice saw her father stand up and take off his hat in a gesture of deference to his son. "It was an extraordinary moment," Eunice said later. "Father had *never* stood up for any of us before. He was always proud of us, but he was always the authority we stood up for. Then, just as Jack passed by and saw Dad on his feet, Jack too stood up and tipped his hat to Dad, the only person he honored that day."

After the inaugural, the family Bible was returned to the Fitzgeralds in Boston, where it was largely forgotten until the opening of the John Fitzgerald Kennedy Library in Dorchester. There, resting in a Plexiglas cradle, it remains today, its worn pages open to Ecclesiastes, one of Rose Kennedy's favorite books of the Old Testament:

> *All things have their season, and in their times all things pass under heaven.*
>
> *A time to be born and a time to die; a time to plant, and a time to pluck up that which is planted.*
>
> *A time to kill, and a time to heal; a time to destroy, and a time to build.*
>
> *A time to weep, and a time to laugh; a time to mourn, and a time to dance.*

In the family record at the front of the old Bible, the list of family deaths remains frozen where it was at the time of the inauguration.

January 20, 1961: Jack
delivers his inaugural address.

A replica of PT-109 stars in
the inaugural parade

The inaugural ball, the family
celebrates Jack's triumph.

The new President
takes command.

EPILOGUE

ON NOVEMBER 22, 1963, President John Fitzgerald Kennedy was assassinated in Dallas, Texas. He was forty-six. On June 6, 1968, Robert F. Kennedy, campaigning for the presidency, was assassinated in Los Angeles, California. He was forty-two. The following year, Joseph P. Kennedy died.

BEETHOVEN

A CONDENSATION OF

BEETHOVEN

by
ALAN
PRYCE-JONES

Young Beethoven was not an exceptional pianist. Still, his music helped make ends meet in an impoverished household.

But it was the Age of Napoleon, and a revolutionary fervor was sweeping Europe. To the arts it brought a new and romantic spirit, one that fired Beethoven's imagination. His music, always moving, now turned tempestuous. It could bring an audience to tears.

Soon Beethoven's fame was assured, and despite a clumsy bearing and country accent, women sought him out and the rich opened their doors to him. Yet he remained a lonely and driven man. Of the fears that haunted him—of the demons that pursued him, like jackals at his heels—few would ever know and fewer still would understand.

CHAPTER I

BONN: 1770-1792

THOUGH Ludwig van Beethoven allowed the Viennese to imply from the "van" that his family was of the nobility, beyond the fact that his great-grandfather was a merchant from Mechlin we know little about it. His grandfather, however, another Ludwig, was so competent a musician that as a very young man he was engaged to the court of the elector of Cologne, who appointed him kapellmeister at Bonn. Possibly because he ran a vintner's business to supplement his income, his wife, Maria van Beethoven, drank to excess—a weakness which recurred in their son Johann, also a musician attached to the elector.

Of Johann we hear little good. In the years that have elapsed since the composer's death, the character of his father has been blackened by successive biographers. The truth appears to be that he was a weak, jovial man, a good enough musician to succeed the elder Ludwig and not, during the lifetime of Maria Magdalena, his wife, too dissolute to instruct his children in an art which might be profitable to themselves and to him.

Maria Magdalena, the widow of the elector's chief *valet de chambre* and daughter of his head cook, was a colorless personality, and consumptive as well. Three years after her marriage to Johann, on the fifteenth or sixteenth of December, 1770, Ludwig was born, and after him Karl Kaspar, Johann Nikolaus, and Margarethe. There also were four children who died early.

Of the surviving children, Ludwig was said to be his mother's favorite. But his feeling for her was mixed at best. Though he loved her, she was unable to keep the home together and was a bad-tempered and melancholy woman, as well as a disillusioned one, who disliked the institution of marriage and the cares of running a family. Moreover, in view of the tenacity with which he later asserted his own right to noble rank—a right which did not in fact exist—it is possible that he resented his mother's modest birth.

At the time of Ludwig's birth the Beethoven family was already in seeming decline. Old Ludwig, then nearly seventy, could deplore his own unhappy marriage to a woman who was confined in her last years to an insane asylum; he could regret that his son's good qualities were only pale reflections of his own, and disapprove his son's choice of a wife.

It is perhaps significant that Ludwig showed a particular affection for his grandfather, who died when he was only three. Until the old man's death, life in the Beethoven household had been at least tranquil. The elder Ludwig van Beethoven had been a person of consequence in Bonn; he was a cultivated musician whose ordered life had held the family together. But after his death matters went from bad to worse.

The young Ludwig's childhood could not have been happy, in any case, if only because even in youth his temperament was not a happy one. He was a silent, shy, unattractive child. In addition, his parents were miserably poor; his education was limited to music and to what an inferior school had to provide. It is suggested that his father brutalized him in an attempt to create an infant prodigy. It is certain only that Ludwig hated his music lessons and that it was decided to drill him into early proficiency on both the piano and the violin. But it is easy to imagine that an ugly, rebellious little boy was not likely to endear himself to a handsome and profligate father.

As a young child his musical ability was unremarkable. At eight years old he made a public appearance, but his performance was not to be compared with that of Mozart at the same age. Yet he was quick at his lessons, quick enough to read Cicero's *Letters* six weeks after he had begun to study Latin; and, whatever he may have suffered in his early years, at the age of nine he became a pupil of Christian Gottlob Neefe, court organist

Left, the elder Ludwig, Beethoven's grandfather. Above, Beethoven's birthplace. Right, Bonn in the 1770's.

to the elector Max Friedrich, with such effect that two years later he was allowed to publish three pianoforte sonatas.

The electoral court at Bonn deserves a word of homage; and not merely the court of Max Friedrich but those of innumerable contemporary German princes. A royalist society, unburdened by heavy responsibility, uncorrupted by excessive riches or power, asserted its superiority by the fineness of its civilization; and until they were blown to pieces in the Second World War innumerable little palaces survived as a memorial to the enlightenment of these minor courts at the close of the eighteenth century—an enlightenment due not to any extraordinary power on the part of the princes but to a general opinion in favor of intelligence.

Thus at Bonn, after the death in 1761 of the elector Clemens August—an archbishop who died, uniquely perhaps, of dancing—Max Friedrich supported as a matter of course admirable operatic and theatrical companies. Bonn had fewer than ten thousand inhabitants and no commerce of any kind. Beyond the presence of the court the city had no reason to exist, since even the military importance, which had caused it to be wholly enclosed by walls, had vanished. Yet its intellectual diversions were far more adventurous than those of twentieth-century London.

In one year (1779) plays of Lessing, Beaumarchais, Garrick, Voltaire, and Goldoni were performed; and in accounts of the

Christian Gottlob Neefe

One of the picturesque villages near Bonn Beethoven visited as a young man. Right, a church organ on which Beethoven played.

archbishop's birthday in 1767 we can see how agreeably the arts were mixed with royal gaiety which now nowhere survives. For at the celebrations there was not only a concert of serious music but also a comic opera, in which Johann van Beethoven sang; with the High Mass there were salvos of artillery; the court and the public were "graciously permitted to kiss His Transparency's hand"; and the whole concluded with a supper of more than a hundred persons. On other nights operas would be performed—operas whose names are now wholly forgotten.

In this atmosphere Beethoven passed the first seventeen years of his life. In order to make his son appear more remarkable,

Johann van Beethoven falsified Ludwig's age by two years, a fact which upset the whole chronology of the Bonn period and for many years deceived even the composer himself. But, though now a notable with a "mixed talent for music," he was apparently not a preeminent performer. It was not possible to canalize such questing energy as his, even in childhood, into one form of expression.

That he was a good performer on more than one instrument, however, is proved by his appointment in 1784 as assistant organist and, a year before that, as cembalist in the theater orchestra. As assistant organist he had, in Neefe's absence, to

take entire control of the musical services, and as cembalist he found an excellent opportunity of discovering, through the extraordinary variety of the scores performed, the technique of orchestral writing.

In 1784 the elector of Cologne died and was succeeded by Max Franz, son of the empress Maria Theresa. Each member of the empress' family was a capable musician, and the new elector took the keenest interest in the arts.

He was very fat, very pleasant, and at the same time a good moral example to the people of Bonn, who had lately become somewhat lax, we are told. Though he was at first accused of being niggardly—the state was nearly bankrupt—he was at any rate more popular than the neighboring elector of Hesse-Kassel, who had sold his subjects to King George III of England to put down the revolt in America. The petitions of Johann van Beethoven for an increase of salary and the reports on the conduct and capabilities of the royal musicians show the charming intimacy that existed between the elector and the least important dependents of his little court. The singing men, the theater cembalist, the assistant organist, were evidently in direct touch with their prince.

It seems likely that Beethoven's notorious disregard of differences of rank arose from the free and easy atmosphere of the electoral court at Bonn. It was also probably at about this time that he formed an intimate acquaintance with the rich and cultivated family of Court Councillor von Breuning, whose second son, Stephan, remained a friend for more than thirty years.

It was through the Breunings, too, that he met Franz Wegeler, a lifelong friend who later married one of the Breuning daughters, and made the acquaintance of Count Ferdinand von Waldstein. Thus he found himself in a society at once young— Waldstein was not above twenty-five, and the Breunings were younger than himself—intelligent, and influential. Frau von Breuning, no doubt sorry for the boy on account of the unhappy circumstances of his home, established a strong and comfortable influence over

Beethoven at sixteen, and his earliest musical notation.

him. Besides herself there were Reicha the violinist, who later taught Berlioz; Ries, whose son became Beethoven's only professional pupil in Vienna; and Simrock the horn player—his colleagues in a very notable orchestra. All of them were young, and all were sympathetic to one who, however graceless, had an abundant talent for making friends.

The common picture of Beethoven in the last years of his life—soured, furious, vindictive, suspicious—is so familiar that it is not easy to imagine him in extreme youth. The pride that always made him reserved was less marked; a heavy jocosity, which is almost more frightening in his late life than the usual bitter tempers, was thought pleasantly rough. At his best Beethoven was coltish, and coltishness in one who has given promise of rare abilities is not unattractive at seventeen. The clumsiness of his nature was emphasized by his appearance—so dark that his friends nicknamed him "the Spaniard," red-faced, pock-marked, squat in figure, with small but brilliant eyes. Already, however he might overflow in passionate love affairs (Wegeler says that he was seldom not in love), his real nature was a secret one. We must suppose that his slow and irresolute discovery of himself was translated into an attraction that could not be resisted. Otherwise it is impossible to account for the affection in which he was held by the sophisticated friends he was now beginning to make.

It was due to their influence with the elector that Beethoven was given leave of absence in 1787 to study in Vienna. The elector did not expressly send him there and provided no allowance beyond his salary. The object of his visit was probably to study under Mozart, but, except that he impressed Mozart by his improvising, we know nothing of his activities. Nor was he in Vienna for more than a few months, for the fatal illness of his mother recalled him to Bonn only in time for her death.

Thus at the age of seventeen he found himself in charge of a father now free to give himself altogether to drink, and of three younger children, one of whom, Margarethe, died a few months later. The family had no money; Beethoven had had a tantalizing glimpse of the full life of Vienna without any prospect of being able to return to it. His state of mind, at once incoherent and sentimental, is indicated in the earliest letter we possess, written to Councillor van Schaden:

"Oh! Who was happier than I, when I could still utter the sweet name of Mother, and heed was paid to it; and to whom can I say it now? . . . Since I have been here I have enjoyed only a few pleasant hours; during the whole time I have been troubled with asthma, and I much fear that it will lead to consumption."

Except in his music, Beethoven found it hard to express himself. The rhetoric of this letter, so conventional in manner, so obviously sincere, may be found in others written thirty years later. He never learned to use words, so that any emotion could be laid down only for future music; he ran small risk of disseminating his feelings in the ordinary intercourse of humanity.

This kind of dumb unhappiness, which later in life could break out into hysteria, nevertheless allowed him to look back on his last years at Bonn as the happiest of his life. During these years his father's condition became such that Beethoven was forced to petition the elector for half his father's salary to be paid separately to himself for the education of the children. As a warning which was not meant to be executed, Johann was even ordered to leave Bonn. But the Breunings offered Beethoven a perpetual refuge in Vienna, and in 1789 there occurred a trip to the electoral palace at Mergentheim which seems to have been one of the unforgettable pleasures of his life. In October the electoral orchestra traveled down the Rhine and took part in

a daily routine of excellent music. An octet of oboes, clarinets, flageolets, and horns played to the elector during dinner—after which an opera was performed. In these operas the chief soprano was Magdalena Willmann, to whom, five years later, Beethoven proposed marriage. Members of the band provided a concert later in the day. Even now it is pleasant to think of the conditions under which music was heard and played by this body of young men, bright in the scarlet-and-gold electoral uniform.

Earlier in the year, Beethoven had been taken to see the abbé Sterkel, one of the most famous of German pianists and the first of national reputation that Beethoven had heard. The abbé's style of playing inclined to that of Mozart, a style in which delicacy counted above all. Beethoven, who played tempestuously, was sufficiently impressed by the abbé, although later he confessed himself in general disappointed by all the famous pianists of the day. He found the prim staccato, the amazing clarity of Mozart's touch, old-fashioned, and shocked some of his contempories by the thickness of his own manner.

So far he had nourished his creative faculty in silence. He possessed an extraordinary gift for improvisation, and that seems to have satisfied him as long as he remained in Bonn. His reputation as a pianist, due to tours made by the elector's order,

enes of Vienna in the late 1700's.

was increasing, and his personal reputation was that of an amiable if eccentric young man. But he was in no hurry to publish.

His genius was of an order that acquired constant enrichment. Each year added its accretion to the substance of his music. He took nothing from books; he declared, during his first years in Vienna, that he would not hear any music but his own for fear of spoiling his originality; he felt no need of friends possessing exceptional gifts. So we are driven to believe that the minutest circumstances of his life were perpetually building music, and the aggregate of cold coffee, the slam of a door, a present of wine, a country walk, fed a richer stream in the hidden sources of his music than any conscious intellectual process.

447

CHAPTER II

VIENNA: 1792–1802

ALL PERIODS of history seem full of peril to those who experience them at first hand, but the Europe of Beethoven's day was in an unusually prolonged and intense state of upheaval. At few periods of history, moreover, has the effervescence of events been matched by so much talent. The two intellectuals whose influence was most potent in sweeping away the old order, Voltaire and Rousseau, were still alive at the time of Beethoven's birth. Napoleon was Beethoven's contemporary. And in the world of music Haydn was thirty-eight and Mozart fourteen. Liberty, fraternity, equality: the words glowed with meaning. The Romantic movement, which brought a new spirit in the arts to all Western Europe, was in its essence no more than a translation of revolutionary fervor into thought and feeling.

Not surprisingly, Beethoven's ardent imagination was fired by the tumult of the age in which he lived and, specifically, by the unique atmosphere of the city of Vienna.

Though musical interest was high in Bonn in 1792 and Beethoven was more favorably placed than he would have been in most cities of today, it was with a natural delight that he accepted a plan to return to Vienna. The elector granted him indefinite leave so that he might study under Haydn, who, on a chance visit to Bonn, had commended one of his earliest scores.

The other capitals of Europe were centers of a homogeneous nationalism, but Vienna, though its population was no more than a quarter of London's, ruled an empire of extraordinary diversity. From the southern borders of the empire, and from what is now northern Italy, an Italian lightness and volatility braced the basic German stock of the Austrian people. Men from the mountains lived in Vienna beside men from the eastern plains. There were Polish and Jewish minorities, increasing in size and power.

At the end of the eighteenth century Vienna was the most

cosmopolitan city in Europe and so in the world. But it was much less solid than it seemed. The changes to be felt everywhere in Europe after the French Revolution could not easily be resisted by a many-nationed empire divided by passionate jealousies and sharp inequalities of wealth. Yet at the time of Beethoven's arrival in 1792, Vienna was about to embark on one of the calmest, least clouded periods in modern history.

Nothing had altered a feudal class system of great rigidity, closely dependent on the imperial court for all matters of taste and habit. There was no effective middle class. It was not money but court patronage which marked the successful man, and a basic assumption of Viennese society that the rich should pay the bills of those better born than themselves. Certainly there was poverty and disaffection, but in general the people of the city followed devotedly where their betters led them, warming themselves, if they could, in the sunlight of imperial favor.

In the late eighteenth century and the early days of the nineteenth, this was made easier by the innate simplicity of the imperial court. The great summer palace of Schönbrunn was anything but private. On his walks through its pathways, the emperor was always ready to stop and talk with any of his subjects. And the baroque palaces of the city might be splendid without, but indoors they were hardly luxurious—uncarpeted and furnished with stiff-backed chairs.

Though no outsider has ever felt entirely comfortable with the Viennese, the city suited Beethoven. He was no intellectual; neither were the Viennese. If he found them lazy and treacherous, he also appreciated their tolerance and high spirits. His instinctive radicalism, romantically linked to the idea of the preeminence of the artist, was well suited to the informality of those great houses that afforded him their patronage.

To understand the role of the nobility in the life of a musician in Beethoven's day, it is important to know that there was then virtually no professional standard of music making, no permanent orchestras or chamber-music ensembles. The time coincided with one of those rare moments in history when the term "amateur" was a title of honor, for in the hands of amateurs lay almost all executive musical art. People made music because they loved to, and they played a great deal at home, often fortified for an evening by trained instrumentalists. There was no way for a young musician to make his way in the world unless he attracted the patronage of the great, for where except in the spacious houses of a music-loving nobility could a routine of music making be established? If the same noble names recur again and again in the history of music during Beethoven's lifetime, it is because the nobility alone possessed the space, the leisure, and the means to promote a musical performance.

Thus, letters from Count von Waldstein were sufficient to admit Beethoven, on the merit of his playing alone, into the grandest of the houses where chamber and orchestral music was performed, as soon as he cared to present himself. Within two years, although he had a strong provincial accent, deplorable manners, and coarse clothes, Beethoven was living in the house of Prince Lichnowsky; dining, not on terms of equality but of a self-elected superiority, among princes, playing only when he chose, and paying not the slightest attention to ordinary rules of politeness. Yet throughout this side of his character appear veins of capricious kindness—a real generosity, a quick acknowledgment of a fault. In 1792 we can put down most of his faults to an inverted snobbishness, though, if he was sturdily maintaining the dignity of art against the aristocracy of its patrons, his sturdiness far surpassed the plain Flemish independence which his ancestry had bestowed upon him. We know that he was exceptionally sensitive; it is not unlikely that his bad manners were the bad manners of the shy. From his rage twenty-six years later, when the Upper Austrian provincial courts publicly declared him not noble, it can be assumed that his country accent and clumsy appearance were misery to him at the age of twenty-two.

As for his new acquaintances in an idle, witty, and eccentric society, we must credit them with a sufficient perception to see the genius that underlay this unpromising behavior, and with enough toleration to think the genius a good exchange. They even may have been amused by Beethoven's antics. Most important of all, he evidently had some psychic power of dominating people. A certain wildness of aspect, coupled with his reputation as a musical virtuoso, brought women toward him, to the point, according to Wegeler, that he made many conquests "which an Adonis would have found difficult." As to his response, those who write from experience express contradictory views. One of them, his pupil Ries, says that "he was frequently in love but generally only for a short time." We have no certain evidence that he ever dared to translate ideal love into action. It is probable that, at least as a young man, he allowed himself some anonymous adventures—adventures which soon began to disgust him, as his private notes testify.

THE LESSONS with Haydn were not a success. Beethoven had too confident an opinion of himself to wish to acquire knowledge. His only aim was to see how far academic theories coincided with his own. A charming and courteous old gentleman, Haydn cannot have cared much for his pupil, and Beethoven imagined that Haydn was careless in correcting his exercises. When Haydn liked least his own favorite of three trios, Opus 1, he even doubted his good intentions. At the end of 1793 their association was broken off. But for some time Beethoven was careful to keep in Haydn's good graces, and there was never any open breach between them. In fact, there was even a question of accompanying Haydn to England, and we have entries of the price of chocolate, to which Beethoven used to treat his master in the cafés of Vienna.

Yet, owing to Beethoven's dissatisfaction, he took secret lessons with Joseph Schenk (a now forgotten opera composer) and lessons in counterpoint with Albrechtsberger, both of whom found him assiduous but self-willed. After 1795, when he published his three trios, he studied only by himself.

Scarcely had Beethoven reached Vienna when his father died and the repercussions of the French Revolution destroyed the electorate of Cologne altogether. Little over a year later the elector was chased out of Bonn by the French and forced to take refuge in his bishopric of Münster. After 1796, Beethoven had no further dealings either with him or with Bonn. By these events Count von Waldstein also was ruined.

This meant that Beethoven had to rely wholly on what he

earned. But the Lichnowsky family alone bought thirty-two copies of his Opus 1, and he played constantly in the great houses of Vienna. He even seems to have made an effort to smarten his appearance by spending the greater part of his money on clothes, and by learning to dance. If, as is likely, these efforts were made to attract the singer Magdalena Willmann, they were wasted. She would not even reply to the offer of marriage he made her at this time, on the grounds that he was "too ugly and half mad."

Nonetheless, his social life appears to have been full. Garden parties occupied the afternoons and musical parties the evenings. Beethoven was a great punster and made a number of jokes among his intimates. Among all his acquaintances, almost his only close friend was Baron von Zmeskall, some ten years older than himself, who for years was charged with cutting the pens Beethoven used. Zmeskall was a tolerant friend who supported such whimsicalities as a note addressed to "Mr. Muckcartdriver," and another ending with the words, "Adieu, Baron Ba . . . ron ron|nor|orn|rno|onr—"

A dedication to his teacher, Haydn.

By 1796, Beethoven had good reason to be merry. He had, in three years, risen to comparative affluence; that is to say, he had his own servants and a horse. The horse, a present from Count Browne, he did not ride more than once or twice, after which Beethoven was much annoyed at having to pay for its food. Yet he had enough money to summon his two brothers to Vienna, where he secured a position in a bank for Karl, and Johann became an apothecary. To the latter Beethoven wrote a typical letter from Prague, whither he had accompanied Prince Lichnowsky: "First of all, I am getting on well, very well. My art wins for me friends and esteem. What more can I want? I am also earning this time a fair amount of money. . . . I hope your residence in Vienna will please you more and more—only beware the whole tribe of wicked women."

Whether urged by experience or not, Beethoven could never resist giving gratuitous advice or refrain from criticizing the moral conduct of others. His musical success was principally due to his talent for improvisation. He did not hesitate to compete with the best pianists of the day, and, though his improvisations were usually thought by the fashionable world to be turgid and too abruptly modulated, his audiences were often so affected that the ladies were in tears. When Prince Lobkowitz remonstrated with him for his rudeness to someone who had suggested that he ought not to compare himself with Haydn, he merely replied, "With men who do not believe in me because I am not famous, I cannot associate." We need not call this a pose. Beethoven's conception of himself as an artist was quite separate from his conception of himself as a man. He was absolutely sincere in what he said of himself as a musician; it never occurred to him to argue about his own merit.

He was intolerant of other musicians, and offended several of his hosts by walking about, talking, or turning over music during the performance of a rival. He was never forgiven by the pianist Hummel for asking him, apparently in all innocence, when Hummel had improvised for some time at Beethoven's own request, when he was going to begin.

He could be charming, however, to an artist whom he admired. In 1797 he published "Adelaide," his first real success, a song which ran through fifty editions, and in August 1800 wrote the following letter to Friedrich von Matthisson, who had written the poem:

"Highly honored Sir, Herewith you receive a composition of mine which was published some years ago, and of which, to my shame, you as yet have no knowledge. To excuse myself and say why I dedicated something to you which came warm from my heart, yet without letting you know anything about it, that I am unable to do. Perhaps, at first, it was because I did not know your address, also partly from timidity, fearing that I had been over hasty in dedicating something to you without knowing whether it met with your approval. . . . My most ardent wish is gratified if the musical setting of your heavenly 'Adelaide' does not altogether displease you, and if thereby you feel moved soon to write another poem of similar kind, and, not finding my request too bold, at once to send it to me. I will then put forth my best powers to come near to your beautiful poetry."

Beethoven's praise of the poem reflects more credit on his heart than on his judgment.

In 1796 a precocious and brilliant musician, Marie-Thérèse von Brunsvik, came to Vienna with her mother and sister to see Beethoven. Every afternoon Beethoven used to give her a music lesson, and in the summer he went with the family to their castle of Martonvásár in Hungary. Their father, Anton, had a sister, the countess Guicciardi, whose daughter Giulietta was a good singer and a pupil of Lazarini. Of Beethoven's relations with these girls at this time little is definitely known.

We know, however, that at Martonvásár Beethoven had his tree in a certain lime grove where every tree bore the name of a friend; and there is every indication that Marie-Thérèse, a romantic bluestocking, was warmly attached to him.

Her sister Joséphine, after marrying Count Deym, used to give musical parties at which Beethoven presided and which were attended by the whole circle of notable amateurs among whom Beethoven moved. A celebrated quartet at this time in the service of Prince Lichnowsky produced, as a matter of course, Beethoven's chamber music. The prince also had an orchestra which Beethoven, owing to his privileged position in the household, could hold at his own disposition.

As a composer he still showed more promise than accomplishment. But as early as 1793 his name had been brought to England by a certain Mrs. Bowater, who had taken with her from Bonn a manuscript copy of Beethoven's E flat trio, with which she had a considerable success in the musical circles of Leicester. In Vienna his success was less marked. Italian opera was a more usual field for the Viennese. Nevertheless, in his own circle, Beethoven's music, especially after the success of "Adelaide," was heard with much the same wondering sense of revelation as, later, the early music of Wagner and of Stravinsky. The first symphony, the first two piano concertos, the earliest sonatas, of which the most important is the *Pathétique*, were thought to put a cruel strain on the faculties of their audience, but the septet, Opus 20, written in 1800, marks the beginning of Beethoven's extended fame. What had until then been considered eccentricity was recognized for an idiom. After 1800, Beethoven was a composer to be criticized as such; before, he was a pianist who had written some abstruse things.

ALTHOUGH the first mention of Beethoven's deafness occurs in a letter to his friend Karl Amenda, dated 1800, he had been troubled by it for two years previously. In the letter he writes: ". . . Your Beethoven is most unhappy, and at strife with nature and Creator. The latter I have often cursed for exposing His creatures to the smallest chance, so that frequently the richest buds are thereby crushed and destroyed. Only think that the noblest part of me, my sense of hearing, has become very weak. Already when you were with me I noted traces of it, and I said nothing. . . . *Please keep as a great secret what I have told you about my hearing; trust no one, whoever it may be, with it. . . .*"

It was not until the last ten years of his life that Beethoven became wholly deaf; for some years his hearing actually improved. But the fear of his deafness becoming known, and the necessary effort to conceal it from all but his most intimate friends, quickly brought about the sour and terrible humor of which so many contemporaries have written. Even at Martonvásár, where he was enjoying provincial gaieties among an intelligent and beautiful family, he was liable to fits of irascibility. No doubt these were partly congenital. Frau von Breuning, in the Bonn years, spoke of how he would withdraw at will into a private world in which he was absolute in suffering no interference.

A great deal has been written about Beethoven's heroism, his conquest of infirmity, his titanic resolution. The affirmatory ring of his music lends itself to such glosses; but the legend does not stand examination. It conceals not resolution but a touching bewilderment. From the beginning of his deafness onward, his letters and his conversation are full of loud, and sometimes desperate, complaint. His illness, his servants, his friends, his patrons, the musical taste of Vienna, everything that touches him, are a reason for lamentation. This is perfectly excusable. Few men of genius had greater excuse for lamenting.

The cause of his deafness is uncertain. Beethoven himself told, among others, an extraordinary story of throwing himself on the ground in a fit of rage and getting up deaf. But, in fact, it was not so much the final atrophy of his hearing as the fear of its slow approach which so unnerved him. For nearly twenty years he hoped, by   baths, ointments, or the application of herbs, at   first to conceal and later to delay his infirmity; he seems fairly soon

Giulietta Guicciardi

Beethoven at thirty.

to have given up all hope of curing it. He had been in Vienna only five years when it became difficult for him to hear the high tones of an instrument, and a characteristic fear of "enemies" made him unable to show this. He could often hear only the timbre of a voice and not the words, and, although he was little enough at ease in a drawing room, he had to pretend to be absentminded in order to conceal that he had heard nothing. Worst of all for one who made his living as a pianist, he feared he might soon become too deaf to take part in concerted music. These anxieties, acting on a naturally somber habit of mind, began to poison his shyness with suspicion, his intolerance of other people with active hatred, his egotism with savagery.

The first crisis of his deafness was lightened by "an enchanting maiden who loves me, and whom I love," as he says in a letter to Wegeler, written in 1800 or 1801, a "maiden" to whom it is supposed that he wrote his famous letter to the Immortal Beloved. Some biographers believe the Immortal Beloved to be Giulietta Guicciardi, to whom he dedicated the *Sonata quasi una Fantasia*, Opus 27, No. 2, in the spring of 1802, when she was sixteen or seventeen years old. Others think it more probable that the letter was written to Marie-Thérèse von Brunsvik; and yet others, since the letter has no date beyond July 6, attribute it to quite another period of Beethoven's life and therefore to one of the other women whom Beethoven is known to have loved.

Whether or not the letter was intended for Giulietta Guicciardi, it is probable that she would have married him at this time had not one of her parents forbidden her on the ground of Beethoven's scarce and uncertain income. It is a touching detail that he would accept no money for Giulietta's lessons, but only linen, under the pretense that Giulietta herself had sewed it.

The letter, to whomever it may have been addressed, reads in English like an embarrassing pastiche of romantic tags:

"My angel, my all, my very self, just a few words today, and indeed in pencil—(with thine) only till tomorrow is my room definitely engaged, what an unworthy waste of time in such matter—why this deep sorrow where necessity speaks. . . . Oh! Gaze at nature in all its beauty, and calmly accept the inevitable —love demands everything, and rightly so. . . ."

The letter is continued the following day in much the same disjointed manner:

"Yes, I have resolved to wander in distant lands, until I can fly to thy arms, and feel that with thee I have a real home; with thee encircling me about, I can send my soul into the kingdom of spirits. . . . Be calm, only by calm consideration of our existence can we attain our aim to live together—be calm— love me—today—yesterday—what tearful longing after thee— thee—thee—my life—my all—farewell—oh, continue to love me—never misjudge the faithful heart of Thy Beloved, L."

Were the letter written by anyone else, it might well be called childish if not insincere. But it is Beethoven who writes:

a being in whom power of expression could be achieved in music only. His letters, however deeply felt, reflect the dilemma of wholly specialized intelligence unable to come to terms with the demands of everyday life.

This love, this "tearful longing," had nothing, therefore, in common with the ordinary, still less with the sublime, love of a man of thirty. Beethoven could do no more than construct a working human emotion out of a passionate musical emotion; his natural simplicity gave him no encouragement to translate life deliberately into terms of art; it was the contrary, rather,

which occurred. Whatever it was that projected music into his waking brain was so pervasive that it left no faculty over to conduct the human Beethoven. Wagner calls him "a world, walking among men," and this is scarcely an exaggeration. But the counterweight to this disproportionate power of the subconscious self was a strange simplification of the conscious. Beethoven could not show any emotional control, since the elements which composed his emotions were curiously indistinct. This is why, when he attempted to write to a program, as in *The Battle of Vittoria*, even in the *Pastoral* symphony, the program is felt as an imposition rather than the groundwork of a logical structure. He himself seems to have perceived no

difference of kind between those works and the supreme master-
pieces in which the music was allowed to follow its natural
course.

In the first months of 1802 he became seriously ill, partly,
it appears, because of the emotional disturbance of his unhappy
love affair with Giulietta, and, on his recovery, he moved to
Heiligenstadt, outside Vienna. Here, in despair, he wrote a will,
addressed to his brothers. The
tenor of the will is a lament that
his deafness cuts him off from all

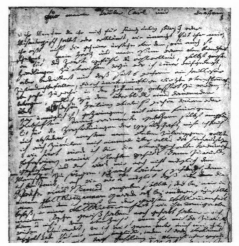

Left, a view of Heiligenstadt.
Above, the house where he stayed.
Right, the Heiligenstadt will.

society, a declaration that he was wronged by those who thought
him misanthropic, and a resigned hopelessness.

"O you, who consider or declare me to be hostile, obstinate
or misanthropic, what injustice you do me! You know not the
secret causes of that which makes such an appearance to you. . . .
Enjoined by my intelligent physician to spare my hearing as
much as possible, I have been almost encouraged by him in my
present natural disposition; though, hurried away by my fond-
ness for society, I sometimes suffered myself to be enticed into it.
But what a humiliation, when anyone standing beside me could
hear at a distance a flute that I could not hear, or anyone heard a
shepherd singing and I could not distinguish a sound! . . .

O me! When you shall read this, think that you have wronged me. . . . Recommend virtue to your children; that alone—not wealth—can give happiness; I speak from experience. . . ."

This is the zero of Beethoven's life. Not only had his love affair gone wrong, his health broken alarmingly—for his eyes were much affected—but because of his growing deafness his career as a pianist was coming to a close. This, and increasing expenses, are the principal reasons for his sudden poverty.

The years from 1799 to 1809 were, nevertheless, the most productive of his life. After an early preoccupation with chamber music, and after publishing the first symphony and two piano concertos, Beethoven was working in 1800 upon the third piano concerto, the septet, Opus 20, and the six quartets, Opus 18. The septet made his name abroad, though later he came heartily to dislike it. In 1801 he produced a ballet, *The Creatures of Prometheus*, and in 1802 he was busy with the second symphony, which did not appear for two years, and *The Mount of Olives*, which was not published until 1811.

But before any of these works, in 1798, a friendship with Bernadotte, who had been appointed French minister to Vienna, as well as his own strong republican ardor, resulted in the idea for his third symphony, the *Eroica*, at which he was working in 1803 and 1804. Beethoven was accustomed to work at several compositions simultaneously, partly owing to his habit of keeping a sketchbook in which themes were developed and partly because, once an idea germinated in his head, it acquired the shape of a whole movement and could therefore be written down at leisure.

Since 1796 his brothers Karl and Johann had been in Vienna, where they had come after their father's death. The composer reserved for Johann, the apothecary, and Karl, who eventually acted as his secretary, most of the affection of which he was capable. But, as in later loves and friendships, he could not experience affection without a dominating possessiveness. Both brothers were of limited intellect; both were eager to stand well with their far more successful elder. Both in turn fell from favor, less from undoubted personal faults than because Beethoven declined to share their affection.

Though it has been asserted that Karl and Johann were in league against their brother to swindle him as much as possible, both suffered more at Ludwig's hands than he at theirs. For, in his anxiety at their possible contact with the "tribe of wicked women," he harried them both into unhappy marriages. Johann had a confessed mistress, which so outraged Ludwig that he denounced the girl to the police and, by exaggerated efforts to evict her, drove Johann into marrying her. His hatred of Johanna van Beethoven, his other sister-in-law, was such that it later gained for him the reputation of being eccentric and rancorous to the point of madness.

But at the time of Johann's marriage, and in the first years of the century, his rancor was little more than a contempt for his fellows and an emotional bias toward women that was probably due to his own experiences at the hand of "the tribe." Still Beethoven could be charming. When Ignaz von Seyfried, a contemporary composer, met him at this time he got the impression that Beethoven "was altogether too generous and tolerant to offend anyone by condemnation or contradiction."

But there are others who write of him already as a sort of ogre. The truth appears to be that he was much at the mercy of a casual mood. Loving popularity, he disliked people, and the contradiction made it impossible to adapt the rhythm of his private world to the world in general. In terms of action, the private world was not less capricious. Beethoven could do nothing for himself; he had not even the ordinary acumen of the artist. In the confusion of his rooms, for example, he imagined himself a slave to order.

To quote Seyfried:

"Books and music would be scattered in all the corners; in one place the remains of a cold snack, in another a wine bottle, on the desk the hasty sketch of a new quartet . . . on the piano some scrawled pages containing a glorious symphony in embryo, private and business papers strewing the floor . . . and then, despite this confusion, our master would take every opportunity of extolling with Ciceronian eloquence his accuracy and love of order. . . . He only changed his tone when for days, or even weeks, fruitless search was made for some object; then he would blame the innocent, murmuring in a complaining tone: 'Yes, it is unfortunate! Nothing will stay where I put it; all my things are mislaid; everything is done to vex me.'"

The contradiction holds good wherever we look. Because he had noble aspirations, Beethoven imagined himself of noble stature. In his will he recommends virtue *out of his own experience;* and in his letters he is always ready to assume the unctuousness of a good child. Yet there was never a man to whom the word "virtuous" applied less, never one less likely to call himself

Franz Gerhard Wegeler

virtuous out of priggishness. Beethoven's sincerity is often alarming; he can be as embarrassing as a confidential adolescent.

Uncertain in judgment, he was also infirm of purpose. His conviction of his own superiority, coupled with laziness, made him wrong his friends—probably only by some show of bad manners; but, directly he had done so, the conviction failed. A passionate apology would be sent, as though he could not feel sure of himself except insofar as he was sure of this friendship. There is a letter, written about 1796, to Wegeler:

". . . I do not deserve your friendship. You are so noble, so kindly disposed, and now for the first time I do not dare to compare myself with you; I have fallen far below you. . . . I scarcely venture to beg you to restore your friendship. Ah, Wegeler! My only consolation is that you knew me almost from my childhood, and—oh, let me say it myself—I was really always of good disposition, and in my dealings always strove to be upright and honest; how otherwise could you have loved me. . . . Impossible that these feelings for what is great and good should all of a sudden become extinct. . . . Oh, Wegeler! Do not cast off this hand of reconciliation; place your hand in mine—O God!—But no more—I might come to you and throw myself in your arms. . . ."

Wegeler himself says that Beethoven's fault had been a trivial one. And there are the two famous notes sent to Hummel a few years later, on consecutive days: "Do not come any more to me. You are a false fellow, and the devil take all such." And: "You are an honorable fellow, and I see you were right. So come this afternoon to me. You will also find Schuppanzigh, and both of us will blow you up, thump you, and shake you, so you will have a fine time of it."

These are not letters written out of a merely changeable humor. The robustiousness of the second note is a symptom of timidity—the timidity of

Marie-Thérèse von Brunsvik

Joséphine von Brunsvik

someone who knows he is wrong and is too lazy and too shy to attempt more than to drown his fault in the noise of a hearty welcome.

But the mental and physical illness of Beethoven in 1802 hastened these natural changes. In a few months his illness did the business of several years; it had an icy effect on whatever in his nature was fluid. It is remarkable that, although he was only thirty-two, we feel toward him as if he were a middle-aged man. The only sign of youth about him is this fluidity, which made him equally likely to enchant a stranger by his simplicity or shock him by his roughness. The Heiligenstadt will is the chief turning point. It coincides with the first check in Beethoven's professional career and marks his first, perhaps his chief, emotional crisis. When Beethoven returned to Vienna in the autumn, therefore, he had not only to recover his own world but also to recover a place in the common world; because of his deafness, to exchange his reputation of pianist for that of composer.

CHAPTER III

VIENNA: 1802–1815

AT HEILIGENSTADT the *Eroica* had been begun, and soon after his return to Vienna Beethoven began *Fidelio*. He also, it appears, transferred his affections to Countess Deym, née Joséphine von Brunsvik, whose husband died during the winter of 1803 and who herself was picturesquely consumptive. (Was there not a certain comfort in the fact that some of his female friends were invalids and thus safe from any erotic aspirations on his part?) Among these activities the disillusionments of the year before might be softened; yet it is only fair to say that the course of those disillusionments is by no means certain. It is important to remember that the Immortal Beloved letter may have been written as late as 1812, that the woman who made Beethoven unhappy may be someone wholly unknown to us.

Indeed, nothing is known of his love for Joséphine beyond letters between her sisters, Marie-Thérèse and Charlotte, and her brother Franz, in the winter of 1803–04, when they apprehend "danger" from the close friendship of the two. Whether he loved sensually or ecstatically, dishonorably or tragically, we cannot know. It is important only that he was able to smash through his despair with the immense power of the *Eroica*.

It is unwise in the extreme to attach a literary gloss to music, to interpret in concrete emotional terms the movements of musical thought. But if ever this danger can be run, it is in the matter of the *Eroica*. If ever Beethoven deserves the name of hero, it is at the moment when, poor, ill, and unhappy in love, he was able to write such positive, such sure music. The poverty, the illness, the unhappiness, floated on the world we know; Beethoven's private world remained untouched. Obviously that inner world was nourished by the stress and tragedy of daily life; but it obeyed its own logic and preserved its own independence.

Yet the *Eroica* upon its completion made no stir. Two publishers refused it. When the first performance took place in the Theater-an-der-Wien, Beethoven insisted on unusually high prices being charged, so that the concert was not a very notable success and the symphony no success at all. It is true that at the time the French were advancing on Vienna, leaving little room

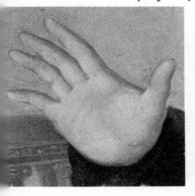

About the age of thirty-four, Beethoven sat for this portrait by Willibrod Maehler. Above, detail of the right hand.

for the arts in the breasts of the Viennese. And even in time of peace, serious music was so far an aristocratic privilege that the ordinary person did not look on the rare public concerts as an entertainment within his sphere.

The most satisfactory of the Beethoven portraits, that by Willibrod Maehler, shows him about now. The face is almost handsome, with eyes wide apart, a firm mouth, and a broad nose. The hands have curiously short fingers, and we know that Maehler was much struck with them because of their stubbiness and because Beethoven kept them "so very still" when he played. This stillness of his hands was a sign of his absorption; he never played for effect, except when he was improvising in competition. That all his improvisations were not spontaneous, however, is shown by the story that when Amenda regretted the loss of one which was especially beautiful, Beethoven replied by playing it straight through again. Probably the improvisations supplemented, or developed, those themes in his notebook which were the foundation of all his finished works.

The oratorio, *The Mount of Olives*, a ballet, *The Creatures of Prometheus*, and the continuous popularity of the septet had, by 1804, gained for Beethoven a reputation equal to that of Mozart and Haydn. There is, indeed, no truth in the assertion that he was neglected by the Viennese. Despite the rarity of public concerts, he was held in high estimation; and, despite his unending complaints of the obtuse attentions of a neglectful aristocracy, no sooner did he threaten to leave Vienna than its purses were put at his disposal. At all times, no matter what his ingratitude or rudeness, he was greeted with the friendliest hospitality. At a dinner given to Prince Ludwig Ferdinand of Prussia he was so enraged at not being put at the royal table that he publicly insulted his hostess and left the house; yet we do not hear that any grudge

Beethoven in the rain.

was borne against him. In 1805, while he was staying at a country house of Prince Lichnowsky, a French officer also staying there was rash enough to ask Beethoven if he "also understood the violin." This question so annoyed him that he flatly refused to play for the party, quarreled with his host, and left the house on foot there and then, carrying the manuscript of the *Appassionata* sonata under his arm through heavy rain. On his arrival in Vienna he wrote to the prince: "What you are, you are through accident and birth. What I am, I am through my own efforts. There are princes and there will be thousands of princes more, but there is only one Beethoven."

Yet, though this is only one example of his churlishness to Lichnowsky, one of his earliest and kindest benefactors, their friendship was eventually restored.

Beethoven's private world, which had been reclothed and repeopled by the unhappy events of 1802, was now discovering its riches in his music. His extraordinary power of withdrawing entirely into music, of allowing his work to control every thought and every movement, made his recovery the more rapid. The suspicions that clouded each friendship for him, the supposed villainies of his household, and all his other physical circumstances did not seem the permanent bases of his daily life, but so many blows which now and again disturbed the real, the almost unconscious, life he was leading. Even his love affairs, except when they led to a nervous eruption, appear rather unreal; and his aspirations for married life, however passionate, are probably the more vocal because he knew he would never be married. Apart from the fact that he was totally unfitted for family life, rigid class barriers left small question of marriage for himself. Beethoven, as a grown man, spent much of his time among the talented aristocracy of Vienna, but he could not, under the conventions of the day, marry into it. And he spent so much time and energy railing at his brothers for marrying, as he saw it, inferior women of dubious morality that he could hardly follow their example.

In any case, apart from the preeminence of spiritual over physical life in him, his health was too infirm to have allowed any wife to be much more than a nurse. For, strong as he looked and conscious as he was of a certain animal strength, his liver, his bowels, his ears, his eyes, gave him almost endless trouble. Already the misanthropy which at length barred him from all public life had begun. Yet, when he was happy, he could be droll among his friends, or equally alarm and entertain them by his sarcasms; and when he was unhappy, the childlike bewilderment which then confused him made him long for their actual presence. Not for nothing did he once write: "I consider [certain friends] mere instruments on which, when it pleases me, I play. . . . I value them according as they are useful to me."

We have in Beethoven's letters a fairly complete account of

one of those unbalanced quarrels in which he was ever involving his friends. In July 1804 he was sharing a house with Stephan von Breuning—in something more like "middle-class comfort" than at any other period of his life.

One day he writes to his pupil Ries: "As Breuning did not scruple by his behavior in your presence and that of the landlord to represent me as a wretched beggarly mean man, I therefore select you first to give my answer by word of mouth to Breun-

ing. . . . To Breuning I have nothing more to say. His way of thinking and acting, as regards myself, shows that there ought never to have been friendly relationship between us, and also that there certainly never will be. . . ." Again: "He is small-minded, a quality which from childhood I have despised. . . ."

Afterward he wrote to Breuning: "My good dear Stephan, Let what for a time passed *between us* lie forever hidden behind this picture. I know it, I have broken *your heart*. The emotion which you must have noticed in me was sufficient punishment for it. . . . Men came *between us* who are not worthy either of you or of me. My portrait has long been intended for you. You know well that it was intended for someone, and on whom better could I, with warmest feeling, give it than to you, faithful, good, and noble Stephan. . . ."

Sooner or later almost all his friends were likely to undergo an identical scene. Even Ries was the victim of a strange piece of rudeness when he had driven with Prince Lichnowsky to hear Beethoven play one part of *Fidelio*, and Beethoven inexplicably refused to play any of it until Ries had been put out of the house. By the time *Fidelio* was produced, Beethoven's rupture with Lichnowsky had already occurred.

The history of *Fidelio* is curious. Beethoven had long been approached to write an opera, but it was not until 1803 that a suitable libretto could be found. The subtitle, *Married Love*, was just what would appeal to one who had always a weakness for pointing a moral. But his experiences during the production were such that he never wrote again for the stage. By caring little whether or not his music were singable he antagonized the singers, who subsequently used to alter the music and rely on his deafness to cover their alterations. Because he liked to conduct the first performance of his works and yet was too deaf to do so easily, he led the orchestra into chaos.

Fidelio did not, therefore, begin luckily, and the week of its production, in November 1805, coincided with Napoleon's entrance into Vienna. On the thirteenth, Napoleon issued a proclamation from Schönbrunn; on the twentieth, and for two successive nights, *Fidelio* was performed with small interest. The Austrian empress and the better part of the nobles had fled. General Hulin had made Prince Lobkowitz's palace his

Left, Napoleon's entrance into Vienna, 1805. Above, program for Fidelio.

headquarters, and the audience was principally of French officers.

The overture gave considerable trouble. At a trial performance at Prince Lichnowsky's house it was considered too light, and for the first performance Beethoven wrote the overture which we know as "Leonora No. 2." In the spring of the next year the opera was reduced to two acts, and a fresh overture, "Leonora No. 3," written. A proposed performance at Prague in 1807 would have been given with "Leonora No. 1"; and for the final 1814 revision, which left the opera as we now hear it, Beethoven wrote the *Fidelio* overture.

To induce Beethoven to make these alterations was not easy. For the 1806 revival he had to be tricked, after a party in one of the Vienna palaces, into allowing certain excisions, for he found it difficult to believe that any suggestion, made to him by no matter whom, could be disinterested. As to his troubles with the singers, we can surmise that they were considerable from a letter to one of them: "Please request Herr von Seyfried to conduct my opera today; I myself want to see and hear it at a distance; by that means, at any rate, my patience will not be so severely tried, as when close by I hear my music murdered. I cannot help thinking that it is done purposely. . . ."

Sensibility distrusts the unknown. The chief cause of Beethoven's distrust of his environment was his lack of knowledge of the world. Helpless by nature, and deaf into the bargain, he was living—when he became wholly aware of his surroundings —in an environment which to his imagination reflected chiefly cold and silence. His letters, however, throw a little light on the extent of his deafness in 1806. His left ear was much stronger than the right; occasionally he could hear tolerably well, and occasionally scarcely at all. Yet if he could hear from the back of the theater he must have been far from totally deaf, and there is additional proof that he was less deaf than is sometimes supposed, from the fact that he enjoyed operatic music so absurd that he could laugh at it. It gave him much the same kind of pleasure as throwing out the players when he was rehearsing a scherzo. But his deafness could no longer be concealed, and for this reason he was less and less willing to play the piano publicly.

By 1806, although Beethoven's reputation was high, he had

not had a success for some time. *Fidelio* was still unappreciated. The extent of his glory is the more remarkable when we remember that he had in all published very little, owing to a scrupulousness which, until 1809, prevented his publishing anything which did not fully satisfy him. However, he never lost confidence in his own worth. There is a story of his saying about Napoleon: "It is a pity I do not understand the art of war as well as the art of music. I would conquer him."

Among the new names which now appear among his acquaintances is that of the countess Erdödy, a rich widow of twenty-five, brilliant and remarkably good-looking, albeit half paralyzed, who in 1809 was living with her three children in the upper part of Beethoven's house. There was nothing beyond an affectionate friendship between them, though she is mentioned as a possible Immortal Beloved. The countess played the piano extremely well, and surrounded herself with the somewhat frilly atmosphere of luxury most attractive to Beethoven. She went so far as to build "a handsome temple" in his honor at Jedlersee, and, although the comfort and sympathy she kept for him did not prevent his quarreling with her, she was able to do him a more substantial service.

When he sold the English rights of six works for two hundred pounds, or contracted with an Edinburgh publisher to harmonize some Scottish songs, Beethoven was in funds. But betweenwhiles he found it hard to live, and was therefore likely to accept an offer made in 1809 by the king of Westphalia that he should be kapellmeister at Cassel, on a salary of six hundred ducats in gold, with few concerts to direct and plenty of leisure for his own work. As he had given another unsuccessful concert in Vienna the year before, it is all the more probable that, but for Countess Erdödy, he would have accepted this comfortable proposal. But that lady, perhaps scandalized at the loss to Vienna of so great a man, perhaps afraid of the loss to herself, prevailed on the princes Kinsky and Lobkowitz and on the archduke Rudolf to settle an annual stipend upon Beethoven, on condition that he remain in Vienna.

Two years before this, however, at the beginning of his friendship with Countess Erdödy, Beethoven had made friends with a court official, Baron von Gleichenstein, and, through him, with Theresia and Anna Malfatti, who were renowned as the loveliest sisters of their time in Vienna. Gleichenstein later married Anna Malfatti, and Beethoven had more serious intentions of marrying Theresia than ever he had had, so far as we know, of marrying his earlier loves. He did not, however, definitely propose to her for five years, and then only through Gleichenstein. As in any case Fräulein Malfatti aspired to someone more imposing than an ill and impoverished composer, his proposal was in vain.

Left, title page of Two Trios, 1805.
Above, Countess Erdödy.
Right, Baron von Gleichenstein.

For his music, however, the years 1806 and 1807 were unusually fruitful. The fourth piano concerto; the fourth symphony; the violin concerto, Opus 61; the three quartets, Opus 59; the Mass in C; and the fifth and sixth symphonies were all written then. This burst of composition was Beethoven's final liberation after the setback of Heiligenstadt; the zenith of the second period of his life, and the first of his full maturity. Whatever reception his works may have had, and however small his output might be, there was a general conviction of his greatness in the air, and as many performances were given in Vienna of his works as of Haydn's or Mozart's. His mental equilibrium was more stable than it had been for some time, and far more stable than it would be again. A young man called Baillot, whom Anton Reicha took to see Beethoven in 1805, commented on his visit that "he did not have the bulldog, gloomy expression" which he had expected "from the majority of his portraits"; he even thought he recognized "an expression of good nature in the face of the composer." It was the bulldog who was forever accusing his acquaintance of cheating him, the bulldog who threw a mess of lungs and gravy at a waiter, swore and laughed when the gravy ran down the man's face. But Baillot saw an aspect of Beethoven that the composer hid more closely every year—that played with the Erdödy children and that wrote to Gleichenstein of the Malfattis' little dog: "You are mistaken if you believe that Gigons only follows you. No, even I have had the fun of seeing him keep close to me. He sat beside me at dinner in the evening, he followed me home. . . ."

In trying to reconcile the indifference of Beethoven to the feelings of others with his occasional delicacy, his boorishness with his pathetic attempts to be charming, we must remember that he was easily irritated. By nature he resented even the most tactful patronage, so that the rich who befriended him were likely to put him in a temper. And in his friends unconsciously he demanded genius, or at least an acute sensibility; whereas these same friends, on the whole, were in fact a wonderfully mediocre lot. Those with whom he was in constant touch—Gleichenstein, Breuning, Zmeskall, Schindler, Malfatti, Ries—were at the best cultivated and at the worst devoted; most of them could play an instrument well; none had the faintest gleam of inspiration, nor had they any intelligent perception of the kind of man Beethoven was. Goethe, the other great emancipator of the German Romantic world, was fortunate enough to move easily among men of genius. Beethoven seldom met, and certainly never intimately knew, anyone with any claim to genius. He was too inarticulate and too far from the world to claim the friendship of his equals. His horizon was bounded by Austria; that love of nature of which we hear so much was founded on excursions into the suburbs; his reading was conventional, and where it showed personal taste, as for Oriental mystics, the taste was unsure; among authors he read Kant, à Kempis, Goethe, Schiller, Plutarch, but without much apparent enlightenment.

During the first decade of the century a new patron had arrived in Vienna as Russian ambassador. Count Rasoumowsky was an ingenious seducer whose charm had brought him from the humblest origin to eminence and an enormous fortune. His embassy was, in some measure, an exile, but he did not allow this to prevent a splendid ostentation, the building of a palace, and the engagement of the Schuppanzigh quartet. From 1808 to 1815 Beethoven ruled the music of the house, and Rasoumowsky's quartet was always at his disposal. Furthermore, Beethoven had undertaken to teach the young archduke Rudolf, already a good musician and, for the rest of Beethoven's life, a warm friend. It is comical to see how violently Beethoven came to resent his obligations to the archduke, how casual he became in his lessons, what false excuses he raked up to avoid giving them; nevertheless, the archduke, who was one of the abler members of this able imperial family, remained obstinately friendly.

Theresia Malfatti

During the winter of 1808–09, the quartet gave a concert every Thursday. Apart from the music and the comfort of the palace, Beethoven had discovered an additional attraction in Marie Bigot, wife of the count's librarian. He had even found it necessary in the previous summer to write her a pained letter, evidently meant to be shown to her husband as well:

"You must think me very vain or small-minded if you

suppose that the civility itself of such excellent persons as you are could lead me to believe that—I had at once won your affection. Besides, it is one of my first principles never to stand in other than friendly relationship with the wife of another man. . . . It is perhaps possible that sometimes I have not joked with Bigot in a sufficiently refined way. . . . Dear Bigot, dear Marie, never, never will you find me ignoble. From childhood onward I learned to love virtue—and all that is beautiful and good. . . ."

In addition to these Thursday quartets, Zmeskall, who was slowly dropping into the background of Beethoven's life, gave a quartet party every Sunday at noon, in which another young and brilliant friend of Beethoven, the baroness von Ertmann, used often to play. And in the many salons of Vienna concerts were still almost universal. These concerts were short. First there would be a Haydn quartet, then an air by Paër or Salieri, then a sonata for the piano, and lastly an operatic chorus, probably of an Italian. Most delicious of all, there would be small dinners given by Countess Erdödy or whomever it might be, after which one or another would play. When Beethoven was in good temper, he would improvise with a breadth and passion on which all his hearers agree.

Just before Christmas 1808 Beethoven gave a benefit concert of his own works. The concert was long and badly rehearsed, which, as his music was thought to be of the utmost complication, made the playing of each number worse, until in the eleventh and last the players broke down altogether and had to start over again. The concert opened with a first performance of the sixth (*Pastoral*) symphony. The cold was so great that the singers in what followed could scarcely sing; and then the fifth symphony was also given a first public performance. The ardor of Beethoven's conducting upset the candles on his stand; the audience, half frozen, laughed. Had it not been for Countess Erdödy this last setback would have made him wash his hands forever of the Viennese.

However, as we have seen, her efforts assured him the prospect of a tolerable income, a prospect which was not, however, fulfilled. For the Austrian exchequer began to suffer, as is usual after a protracted war, and Beethoven's pension was reduced to one-fifth. In 1814, Prince Lobkowitz, who provided the smallest part of the pension, went bankrupt; Prince Kinsky was temporarily embarrassed by the Austrian crisis and shortly afterward died of an accident (though the account books of his family show that they made up for the delay in his early payments and continued the pension up to the death of Beethoven).

It is noticeable that these were all young men. Beethoven's patrons were usually as young as or younger than himself—which shows, unless we are to assume a high degree of intellectual snobbery among them, the same curious physical compulsion

that, from the Bonn days, drew the most unexpected people into his orbit; especially those who, because of their youth, would be most likely to drop away from a sour invalid at the first contact with his sourness.

The fact that he was a radical, if not a republican, makes it even stranger that he prospered at the Austrian court. He invariably criticized the government in public, yet he was allowed freely to exercise his opinions. They did not, however, make him welcome the approach of the French in 1809. Throughout the bombardment of Vienna he lay in a cellar of his brother's house, his head covered with pillows; furthermore, it was hot, and the prospect of a radical era in Vienna did not recompense him for the loss of his summer holiday in the suburbs.

The year 1810 marks the close of his career as a virtuoso; in a few years more he would be totally deaf. Theresia Malfatti would not marry him; his income was going to be taken away before he could enjoy it. All his standards were to be relaxed. It is noticeable that henceforward he will cheat any publisher, publish any rubbish—even if it is an early work long discarded. He will do anything for money. Also, because in his looking-glass world it was the conscious mind that dreamed and the unconscious mind that worked with severe application, he will write more glori-

Left, the resort of Teplitz.
Above, Bettina Brentano.
Right, Goethe.

ously than before, after a pause of seven years between 1809 and 1816, during which he publishes almost nothing but two sonatas and *The Battle of Vittoria.*

In 1810, over a performance of *"Kennst du das Land,"* he met Bettina Brentano. She was a gay, brilliant girl of twenty-two, a clever bluestocking who was also saucy. In 1839 she published three letters purporting to be from Beethoven, the authenticity of which has never been proved. An authority on Beethoven's letters believes that they are mainly genuine, but probably touched up, with the enthusiasm of a woman who was determined that the letters of a man of genius to her should fully look like the letters of a man of genius, and, furthermore, to someone as sympathetic as herself.

The first letter, dated August 1810, is pleasantly affectionate, though one sentence announces the more inept, more muddled Beethoven. He describes his deafness, and laments: ". . . I could only understand the great, intelligent look of your eyes, which so impressed me that I can never forget it. Dear friend, beloved maiden! Art! Who comprehends it? With whom can one consult concerning this great goddess?"

Meanwhile, Bettina had written enthusiastically to Goethe, with whom she was in close friendship:

"He [Beethoven] accompanied me home, and on the way he said many beautiful things about art, speaking so loud, and stopping in the street, that it took courage to listen to him."

Beethoven's "beautiful things," as quoted, are not striking; and Goethe cautiously replied: "A layman must have reverence for what is spoken by one possessed of such a demon"; and again still more cautiously: "It would give me great pleasure if Beethoven were to make me a present of the two songs of mine which he has composed, but neatly and plainly written."

But Bettina Brentano's chief importance is that she had brought Beethoven into touch with Goethe.

They met at Teplitz, a fashionable resort, in July 1812. Some idea of the brilliance of that season can be given by the other principal names in the list of arrivals, which, in a week or two, included Napoleon's empress, Marie Louise, and her retinue, the duke of Saxe-Weimar, the king of Saxony and his household, the emperor of Austria, and the prince of Courland. The meeting was conspicuously a failure.

Later Beethoven said, "Court air suits Goethe more than becomes a poet"; while Goethe said of him, "Unfortunately he has an utterly untamed personality, not altogether in the wrong in holding the world detestable. But he does not make it any more enjoyable either for himself or for others by his attitude."

Among others at Teplitz was Amalie Sebald, another possible claimant to the name of Immortal Beloved. Beethoven had met her there the year before, and his letters during the autumn of 1812 leave no doubt that she replaced some of his other affections. But in the following year the defects of his emotional life were partly balanced by a brilliant musical success. To the order of Maelzel, inventor of the metronome, Beethoven wrote the battle symphony on Wellington's victory at Vittoria. It could not have been more loudly applauded, though it had originally been written for a freakish instrument called the panharmonicon and only then rescored for orchestra. There was an inevitable quarrel, in which Maelzel said the work was his property and Beethoven refused him any share of the profits. Yet Maelzel gave it in another version a year later at Drury Lane, and probably during its travels it was most useful of all agents for making the world abroad admit the greatness of Beethoven.

In 1814, Beethoven had a further notable success with a revival of *Fidelio*. The revisions were excellently received, although Beethoven's conducting was so incoherent that the bandmaster had to stand behind him and give insistent directions to the orchestra.

Finally, this period of his life closes with a great personal triumph at the festivities for the Congress of Vienna. Beethoven was presented to the monarchs, and at a concert in January 1815, for the Russian empress' birthday, he played in public for the last time—pathetically changed, no doubt, for since his deafness his *forti* were such that the strings nearly cracked and his *piani* were inaudible. During these festivities the Rasoumowsky palace was burned to the ground.

CHAPTER IV

1815–1827

FROM whatever cause, Beethoven now reached the climax of his misanthropy, a misanthropy which, coupled with increasing physical illness, prevented his working until, in 1818, he localized its power into the *Hammerklavier* sonata. When Bettina Brentano met him, only five years before, the vigor of his appearance had made her think him no more than thirty. It is not easy to show Beethoven's slow change from a proud and slightly extravagant youth to a passionate middle age, veined with the bitterness of bad health and a frustrated emotional life.

It is still less easy to show the quick change, between 1810 and 1815, of that already sour yet vigorous humor into a desperate, an almost insane, decay. He was inclined to distribute his own ills among all humanity; but, even so, melancholy is not so much the epithet for him in these latter years as formidable. His hopelessness was not blank but furious. Greed for money, suspicion, irritation against his neighbors, were goads rather than the blows they had once been. Hitherto, when something had

Concert hall of the Streicher piano firm.

gone wrong, he had been likely to bow to it with the conscious resignation of one who had never expected anything better. Now, except when he was composing, his wrongs kept him in a long ferment. The instability of his character helped to darken his miseries.

When he was working, he always neglected his appearance—at one time he was even arrested as a tramp—and people avoided his table in a restaurant because of his manner of eating and the dirt on his linen. It required a love affair, or the encouragement of someone's taking an interest in him, to replenish his vanity. As in so many other matters, his intentions were always admirable, but their execution was too much trouble.

Probably the most satisfactory of his women friends was Nannette Streicher, the daughter of the celebrated piano maker

Stein, who had made him several pianos during the years of his increasing deafness. In 1813 she had found Beethoven with no linen, no domestic economy, and henceforth she made it her business to order his establishment. From a number of letters he wrote her, it is clear that the calm and asexual kindness which was all she had to offer was precisely what he needed. Frau Streicher acted as a mother substitute. She helped

Nannette Streicher. Above, Beethoven's questions on household matters to Frau Streicher, with her answers.

him run a household and held herself in readiness to answer such questions as "How many pounds of meat is enough for three people?" or "What does one give two servants for dinner and supper? Both in quantity and quality?"

Many of Beethoven's letters to Frau Streicher complain about Nany and Baberl, his servants:

"Nany has improved, but I really do not think she has any real wish to be better. . . ."

"As soon as the other maid arrives, I will, the first time you pay me a visit, call her in, and *in your presence* express my doubts about the kitchen book. . . . I beg you so to instruct the kitchen maid about to enter my service, that she *must take sides* with you against N. . . ."

"The new kitchen maid made an ugly face when asked to

carry up wood, but I hope she will remember that our Saviour carried His cross to Golgotha."

And finally he writes to Zmeskall: "God have pity on me—I look upon myself as quite lost. The servant steals."

IN 1806 A SON, named Karl, had been born to Johanna and Karl van Beethoven. As with the other members of his family, the composer was demanding, interfering, and overemotional with his nephew, now a boy of nine.

Beethoven spoke of his plans for turning young Karl into a musician. In 1815 the child's father had died of consumption, leaving himself and the mother as joint trustees. The elder Karl had expressly asked Beethoven to make up his differences with the mother in order to share with her the child's upbringing. Nevertheless, one of Beethoven's first acts, on the death of his brother, was to suggest to the authorities that he had been poisoned and to forbid little Karl to have any truck with his mother. And, since the litigation over this action lasted until 1820, it may be well to give the facts at once.

Beethoven's nephew, Karl.

Beethoven's complaint was that Johanna van Beethoven's notorious unfaithfulness made her an unsuitable guardian for a young child. To support his opinion of her he did not allow himself to be bound by the truth. Set on keeping the boy to himself, Beethoven threw any accusation at her which occurred to him; and he had this much right on his side, that she had in other times been unfaithful to her husband. That was enough to damn her forever in the eyes of Beethoven, whose abhorrence of the sexual behavior of others was already loud and vindictive. He had never approved of Karl's marriage, although he himself had brought it about. His dislike of his sister-in-law had, probably, so blinded him that the original cause of it was now only a weapon in a fight which must, at all costs, be won against her.

In 1816 the Upper Austrian provincial courts gave him the custody of Karl, who was sent to a fashionable school. In 1818, as the school was too expensive and as Karl, who was entirely neglected by his uncle, had never learned enough manners to keep on good terms with masters and pupils, he was given a private tutor. Beethoven tried to weight the boy's mind against his mother, and Karl discovered that by abusing her he could ingratiate himself with a deaf, exacerbated man who otherwise scarcely spoke to him. Since the servants were sorry for him, they used to allow him to see his mother occasionally, but at last he ran away. Again the matter came before the courts. As it was now shown that Beethoven, despite the "van," was not of noble birth, the matter was devolved to a lower court, which gave a verdict in favor of the mother. The unscrupulousness of Beethoven's evidence only destroyed his own case; a new guardian was appointed. After further litigation Beethoven regained the guardianship, and although, in 1820, Johanna van Beethoven appealed to the emperor, she was not able to alter this decision.

In Beethoven's actions throughout the case he is shown in a bad light. His intentions, as so often, were excellent. "I confess," he wrote in a letter to the magistracy after Karl had run away, "that I feel myself better fitted than anybody else to incite my nephew to virtue and industry by my own example." But, apart from the children of his friends, he had never seen a child at close quarters; he had no other ideas of bringing one up than to beat it when it annoyed him and caress it when it pleased him. His deafness made easy intercourse impossible, and preoccupation with his own affairs left him no time to see that Karl's clothes were changed or that his person was in any way attended to. It seems never to have occurred to him that Karl would not be a man of genius. In point of fact, he became a very normal young man, cultivated without brilliance, handsome without beauty, well disposed without special virtues. But in the middle of 1826, worn out by his uncle's reproaches, he tried to commit suicide. When Beethoven came to see him in the hospital and implored him to confess to the worry that was distracting him, Karl turned his face angrily to the wall. It was a cruel thing to do, but excusable after being harassed for ten years for not being another man than himself. "I have become worse because my uncle insisted on making me better," he wrote, and when he had recovered he became, as he had always wished, a soldier.

This long conflict and eventual failure is the saddest part of Beethoven's life. He was proud of Karl; he spent money on Karl; he looked so high for Karl that little below his own accomplishment would have contented him. But, by a neglect which he never realized, he spoiled Karl's childhood; by a persistent malignance against his mother, he terrified him and drove him to lies. What affection that uncle gained by foolish indulgence he lost by foolish severity; and only because Karl was a simple fellow who liked the ordinary pleasures of a gay and intelligent city. Yet Breuning sacrificed Beethoven's friendship for a time in 1817 when he said, as any outsider must have said, that Beethoven was not fitted to direct a child.

Beethoven's financial position was made more solid, in the year after he adopted Karl, by the fixing of his allowance from Kinsky and the archduke Rudolf at thirty-four hundred florins. Prince Lobkowitz was now bankrupt, but the archduke was generous enough to make good the difference between the original sum and its depreciation after the financial reorganization of the country in 1811. With the archduke, Beethoven never had an open quarrel. He used to complain, without foundation, that his allowance was not paid. His elastic duty of playing the piano with his benefactor was often intolerable to him. But the archduke was so gentle and considerate that Beethoven never had an excuse to attack him.

Beethoven was also able to make a fair amount of money by publishing small works written and discarded many years before, and by playing off one publisher against another until he had raised the value of his manuscripts to a large sum. Charles Neate, later one of the directors of the Philharmonic Society, who was in Vienna in 1816, was useful as an unofficial agent for Beethoven in London, where his music was still scarcely known. Beethoven kept a particular love for the English, and often declared that next year he would positively pay a visit to London.

Sir George Smart had whetted public opinion in London by

playing *The Mount of Olives* and *The Battle of Vittoria*, and Neate was able to prevail on the Philharmonic Society of London to pay a considerable sum for three new overtures. For some time nothing happened; and at length the society found itself insulted by the arrival of three old overtures, among them *The Ruins of Athens*, which were unacceptable to an audience that had already heard the C minor symphony. Such a clumsy trick as this did great harm to Beethoven's reputation among those who were most able to put money in his pocket; but the consideration of his English admirers was shown a little later, in 1818, by the present of a Broadwood piano. Beethoven was so pleased with it that he would allow nobody to touch it, though this care diminished until once he hit the keys with a bootjack to show that some strings were wanting.

Up till 1822, Beethoven could still hear a little music with his left ear, although conversation was impossible. In 1819 he had started to carry the Conversation Books. At his death his biographer Schindler sold a hundred and thirty-seven of these books to the Berlin Library. They underline the strange mediocrity of Beethoven's friends. The only name of distinction is that of the poet Grillparzer, whom he never knew well. Most of his old friends had vanished. Zmeskall was an invalid, Schuppanzigh had left Vienna, Breuning was estranged; Waldstein, ruined, had disappeared many years before. Lichnowsky was dead. Only Schindler, who seems to have been a jackal at the heels of genius, and a new friend, Oliva, could constantly support his humors. Haslinger, an ex-choirboy whom Beethoven had placed with Steiner the publisher, was scarcely less an intimate. Beethoven amused himself by giving his friends military titles: Haslinger was the adjutant and Steiner the general-lieutenant.

During these years, among depressions, jokes, and fulminations, Beethoven's inner world suffered an eclipse. But in 1818 he

Beethoven's Broadwood piano.

found himself able to work again, and gave a public that was beginning to accuse him of artistic sterility the sonata Opus 106. In spite of its amplitude and intensity of feeling, this sonata, the *Hammerklavier*, strains the listener, because it appears to have strained the composer. The release of energy is too tumultuous. The *Hammerklavier*, the ninth symphony, the Mass in D, and the Diabelli variations, which are the largest works of Beethoven's third period, are saying in splendid fragments what the last quartets, his final works, say more exactly. In the same year, 1818, he was busy with the sketches of the ninth symphony and also with the mass, intended for the archduke Rudolf's enthronement as archbishop of Olmütz but only finished, two years too late, in 1823. So huge a work meant that Beethoven had no time for the daily tasks which supplied him with most of his income, so that again he found himself in poverty.

At a certain degree of celebrity, however, it is not easy to starve, and between the terror and the admiration which Beethoven's reputation now inspired he had attained that degree. Thus, commissions were abundant, so that Beethoven's poverty must be called a poverty of choice, until the mass was finished and he had to decide what to do with it. He elected in 1823 to offer it in manuscript to the European courts for a subscription of fifty ducats, and at the same time played off one publisher against another. To Simrock, in lieu of this *Missa Solemnis*, he offered an alternative mass immediately (which in fact was not even begun), and he importuned the kings of Europe with an eagerness hard to reconcile with his theoretical republicanism. Ultimately, when the king of France sent him a somewhat cumbrous medal, his friends with difficulty prevented his wearing it around his neck.

Other events, too, show Beethoven in a sad condition—a condition which goes far to excuse any practical faults. Schindler tells a terrible story of a rehearsal of *Fidelio* in 1823. Beethoven, though almost totally deaf, wished to conduct himself; but, owing to the unusual *tempi* which he tried to impose on an orchestra and singers whom he could not hear, fatal confusion once more ensued. Beethoven perceived nothing, nor did anyone dare to tell him that he must stop, until Schindler passed him a note: "Please do not go on; more at home." Beethoven, understanding, left the theater abruptly, ran home, and was found later in an almost desperate melancholy.

His nervous irritability had increased to the point that he left a villa, which he had taken from Baron Pronay at Hetzendorf in the summer of 1823, because of his annoyance at the good manners with which the baron lifted his hat to him whenever they met. There are peculiar anecdotes of his being discovered by friends thumping on a stringless piano, composing almost naked, shouting and stamping as he scribbled music on walls and woodwork. Among his landlords he was unpopular, if only because of the habit of pouring jugs of water over his head, wherever he might be, to cool the humors of composition. His furniture was splendid but disordered, his clothes fashionable, his stockings white, but all untidy and blotched. His pockets were stuffed with a heavy carpenter's pencil, an ear trumpet; his voice was rough and very loud. It was only in the company of Karl Holz, a gay young man whose friendship he gained in 1824, that the bearish gaiety of his own youth reappeared. Despite the anxiety he felt for his nephew, despite the atmosphere of cotton wool, medicine bottles, purges, and eye lotions in which his precarious health kept him, his letters to Holz are full of the old jokes:

"Friday is the only day on which the old witch, who would certainly have been burned 400 years ago, cooks tolerably—for on this day the devil has no power over her—therefore come or write . . ." and he was so enchanted with his charming friend that he wished him to write his biography.

In the new pleasure of being amused he allowed himself to drink liberally—to the danger of his liver, already weak and at last the cause of his death. He was already complaining of Schindler, both to Holz and to his nephew, as an incompetent, treacherous, and deceitful boor—allegations wholly beside the mark. Schindler was jealous of Beethoven's friendship, unscrupulous in pretending that he was the main prop and the most disinterested servant of Beethoven's last years; but he deserved no greater reproaches. Nevertheless, he was insulted both behind his back and to his face, especially after a concert in the

Court Theatre on May 7, 1824, at which the *Missa Solemnis* and the ninth symphony were presented to the public.

There had been great difficulty in arranging the concert at all. Disgusted with the taste of Vienna—though he shared with it an admiration for the better work of Rossini, Cherubini, and the singing of the Italian opera—Beethoven wished to produce his new works at Berlin. But a petition signed by more than thirty friends so moved him that he consented to a first performance in Vienna. There is something touching about his unwillingness to believe in the affection of others. A little music shop he frequented would be jammed with admirers; he was renowned throughout Vienna; his fantasies were described in

detail by the musical press of all Europe; his residence in Austria was accounted a glory by the Austrians. But these testimonies he seems to have taken as his due; his emotions offered them no response; therefore, when a small group of friends

Haslinger's music shop, Vienna, frequented by Beethoven.

showed an interest in keeping his work in their own city, it affected him with as much surprise as though he were totally neglected. He noticed appreciation only when it became particular.

Even when it was decided to give the concert in Vienna, it was not easy to decide where to give it, and it was only after the most acrimonious discussions, during which Beethoven repeatedly canceled the whole affair, that Prince Galitzine arranged for it to take place in the Court Theatre.

The success of the concert was immense, but, notwithstanding the volume of applause, Beethoven perceived none until one of the principal singers turned him around that he might see his own triumph. The audience, for the first time understanding his total deafness, responded by the most prolonged and tumultuous shouting; but such pleasures as Beethoven may have gained from their ovation he forgot in the disappointment of a small financial profit—depleted by the heavy expenses of the concert. In the hope of increasing that profit, the concert manager arranged a second performance, with the additional attraction of Rossini's *"Di tanti palpiti."* The hall was half full and the management suffered a heavy loss.

The conjunction of these disappointments made Beethoven suppose that he had been cheated by his friends, and in particular by Schindler. Schindler was banished for several months and was received, even when he was forgiven, with the coldness shown by the following phrases from a letter:

"I must confess that the purity of my character does not permit me to recompense new favors with friendship, although I am ready willingly to serve your welfare."

Another example of his savage irritability at this time is given by the comments scrawled over a dignified letter from one of the copyists with whom he had quarreled. Not only is the letter itself crosshatched but in great lines upon it is written:

"Honor Mozart and Haydn by not mentioning their names. . . . Stupid fool! Scribbler! . . . Correct your own faults caused through ignorance, arrogance, self-conceit and stupidity. This is far better than to try to instruct me; for this would be just like a sow trying to teach Minerva. . . . Conceited ass of a fellow . . ."

In 1825 an excellent picture of Beethoven is given by Ludwig Rellstab, the poet. Already sick, Beethoven had become sunken and yellow in face, and because the violence of his personality had colored Rellstab's conception of his appearance, he was surprised at the smallness of the face, the small sharp nose, the small gray eyes. Nor could he discern any but soft, or at least melancholy, qualities in Beethoven's expression. A change had come suddenly upon him. Apparently he now gave way to a passive, an almost animal, hopelessness. All his stamina was needed to preserve a private world; therefore the last eighteen months of his life are, for the most part, a picture of silent ruin, pathetic because of the noise of previous years. The scattered fragments of dull conversation, the few scenes in Beethoven's rooms which are recorded by Rellstab, are hollow, are almost dead. Beethoven could still be whipped into animation, but he had no longer enough energy for the old excitement, scarcely enough even for the inevitable business of life. Thus, in an attempt to show the beauty of a Broadwood piano, Rellstab says that he "struck a chord softly. Never will another fill me with such melancholy. He had C major in the right hand, and struck B in the bass; and, looking at me steadily, repeated the wrong chord several times that I might hear the sweet tone of the instrument." This is the act of a listless, not of a deaf, man.

At a performance of one of Beethoven's quartets, Rellstab met Johann van Beethoven, to whose property at Gneixendorf, near Krems, the composer retired for the summer of 1826. Johann told him that he had offered six thousand gulden to any doctor who might cure his brother's deafness, an offer which makes it appropriate to rebut once more the allegations of lack of feeling brought against Johann van Beethoven. The Conversation Books alone testify to Johann's constant willingness to

Beethoven's studio.

help, both by his time and his money, despite the composer's animosity to his wife.

Early in 1826, when the nephew, Karl, made his attempt at suicide, Beethoven was so unwell that he began to spit blood. It was to Gneixendorf, therefore—reassured by news that Frau van Beethoven was treated more as a housekeeper than a wife—that uncle and nephew went to convalesce. The visit was pleasant for nobody. Beethoven was determined that Johann must make a will in favor of the nephew; but he could not prevent himself from renewing those complaints and accusations which had already driven Karl to desperation.

The Conversation Books show that Karl had a most unhappy time of it. He writes for his uncle:

"Why do you make such a disturbance? . . . I'll come again later—I only want to go to my room—I am not going out, I only want to be alone for a little while. Will you not let me go to my room?"

Both Karl and Johann van Beethoven must have shown exemplary patience with a grotesque and arbitrary invalid whose egotism overlay, at any rate for his family, all other qualities. Genius is seldom welcome at home, and the Beethovens had to support not only ill humor but also such eccentricity that

Above, Gerhard von Breuning. Right, deathbed sketch of Beethoven.

the neighboring peasants usually believed Ludwig to be out of his mind. He would walk about the country, waving his arms, stamping and shouting, consternating the herds; or sit, scarcely speaking to his relations, over hurried meals. The life he led was simple and regular. He rose at five thirty and wrote for two hours before breakfast. Next he walked quickly about the fields, notebook in hand, until twelve thirty, after which, having eaten, he worked and walked again till sundown. At seven thirty he dined, and at ten, after more work, he went to bed.

By the late autumn, life at Gneixendorf became intolerable; and Karl had to join his regiment. At length Beethoven set out for Vienna, in the full cold of December, and on his arrival fell ill at once with pneumonia. His whole system gave way together. Potations with Holz had completed the sickness of his liver; as soon as the pneumonia was cured, dropsy set in, and

Beethoven's body became yellow with jaundice. The dropsy made rapid progress. After a week or two it became necessary to draw off the water, and again, owing to a quick accumulation, to draw it off in greater amounts on three later occasions.

The details of these winter months of 1827 are alarming. His stomach became much swollen and was tightly bandaged; the pain was such that Beethoven was often bent double. He suffered much from suffocation at night, and from outbursts of grief or rage, after one of which the puncture in the abdomen reopened and water streamed to the middle of the floor. Sweat baths filled with birch leaves were prescribed, and frozen punch was given him to allay the pain, until he drank so much of it that the treatment had to be stopped. Dr. Malfatti, the uncle to Theresia Malfatti with whom Beethoven had quarreled some years before, was reconciled enough to supervise the case; and with Stephan von Breuning Beethoven was now sufficiently friendly for the Breunings to have an apartment in the same house—a Benedictine convent converted to secular purposes by Joseph II. The little son, Gerhard von Breuning, was one of Beethoven's most constant visitors; his questions are recorded in the Conversation Books:

"Has your tummy become smaller? . . . You ought to sweat more. . . . Your cello is getting full of dust. . . . What soup would you like tomorrow?"

The invalid was tortured by bedbugs, and so badly looked after that his bedclothes were often soaked through. Little gave him pleasure beyond a present of all Handel's scores and—in pity for his wretched condition—a present of a hundred pounds from the Philharmonic Society of London. By the end of February he could no longer always think consecutively. It was plain that he was dying; and since, though he never spoke of religious matters—he once wrote to Schindler that "religion and thorough bass [continuo] are both things that settle themselves" —since, notwithstanding, he was a Catholic, he gladly took the Sacrament. On the evening of March 26, 1827, in the midst of a violent storm and in the presence of Hüttenbrenner the musician and Frau Johann van Beethoven, his old enemy, the composer sat up and, immediately after a bright flash of lightning had fired the room, lifted his hand and remained rigid. Hüttenbrenner supported his head and closed his eyes. Frau van Beethoven cut a lock of his hair.

After his death, bank shares and considerable cash were discovered, saved for his nephew; two days later, on March 29, in beautiful spring weather, the body was taken in procession, accompanied by an immense crowd, to its burial place.

CHAPTER V

A SUMMING-UP

MORE than a century after Beethoven's death, it is especially appropriate to recall the speech made by the poet Grillparzer at Beethoven's grave. "He was an artist, and what he was, was he through his art alone."

Unlovable, and yet in such need of love that it is hard to read of him without affection; speechless and clumsy, yet with an unforced grandeur of aspiration which preserves him from ridicule; ungrateful, loutish, untruthful; by no means exempt from snobbery and a harsh self-righteousness, yet built to a scale so large that these qualities are relegated to a province of him, we can watch him from a safe distance without either awe or repulsion. Like the slow building of coral, his barren, ugly life of every day sufficed to carry forward an invisible process of creation. Just as it is a waste of time to speculate on whether or not Beethoven's love for this or that lady ever went very far, it would be a waste of time to speculate on the drives which compelled him to distill a singularly unfruitful emotional life into an art of often seraphic fulfillment.

The simplicity which all who knew him remarked in him allowed room for his greatness. It is, perhaps, essential to such greatness that he should have been so little of a clever man. When he rose at five thirty in the morning, and bawled and stamped over his music, and kicked the desk in contrapuntal rhythms, we need not pretend to explore very far his conscious processes of thought. The apparent discrepancy between all that

Beethoven seemed to *be* and all that we know he has *done*, becomes less when we remember that the conscious mind of a creator works chiefly as a powerhouse for the unconscious; a mechanism for collecting, storing, and later transcribing impressions. The significance of these impressions is never wholly perceived until they are stabilized in a work of art.

Beethoven's contemporaries were quick to perceive the paradox that a life such as his has to be reconciled with music both lucid and noble. They accepted the sense of liberation in his manner of writing; they recognized the difference in range between his work and that of his ablest forerunners, such as Bach or Mozart or Haydn. After his death they went so far as to canonize his technical procedures and to identify the dimensions of his music with the ideal. Thus, his symphonies became, for the better part of a century, the unquestioned model for all symphonies; to rival Beethoven on his own ground became the hallmark of an elevated musical gift; and Vienna itself, as the home of Beethoven, acquired a position not unlike that of Rome in the religious world.

The extent to which Beethoven influenced the entire nineteenth century can be gauged by the welcome given to the classical revivalism that succeeded it. A large public, nourished on the symphonic shapes and colors which derive from Beethoven, discovered—largely through the prompting of Richard Strauss and of Stravinsky—that Handel and Mozart and Haydn offered musical thought as rich and varied.

In consequence of this discovery it became fashionable to admire that part of Beethoven's music in which he gave a special subtlety to universal emotions without losing the sense of their breadth—in particular, the quartets. To ears accustomed to the sensuous scoring of the Russians, to the astringency of Central Europe, to French delicacy and Spanish rhythm, the symphonies inevitably lost their original air of powerful innovation. The quartets, however, by the nature of their medium, have proved timeless. And so, as the symphonies recede, little by little, in critical estimation, the chamber music—and not the quartets only—is generally accepted as the supreme example of Beethoven's art.

Of all the great composers, Beethoven wrote the least. At the time of his death he was only beginning to satisfy himself that he had mastered his material. In a sense, therefore, his end is more tragic than that of Mozart or Schubert, young as they were, for he had set himself a more difficult aim than they, and was finding his way out of a hampering obscurity when he died. This obscurity is the harder to penetrate in that it arises less from complexity of emotion than from the personal nature of that emotion. Beethoven speaks from his own heart; his forerunners had applied their gifts to the common condition of humanity. Our greater familiarity with subjective art may make us unduly impatient of his solutions; we are aware of a struggle, yet unconvinced that the conflicting forces have been properly assessed. Nevertheless, it is impossible not to perceive the intensity of his struggle. Above all, Beethoven changed the course of European music by inventing what today is called a tune; that is, a combination of cadence and surprise which can be extended or varied at will to conclude, in terms of musical logic, a recognizable emotional situation. The tunes of the earlier masters have not the same autobiographical flavor; they are more dispassionate statements, polite, less authoritative.

It may be objected that much of what Beethoven had to say is now commonplace or antiquated. The concept of personal nobility—the concept which inspired the subtlest Romantic art—is out of fashion; the concept of man as the central product of the universe—a doctrine which alone makes Romanticism intelligible—has few defenders; the world of 1820 has been reproved or overlaid or simply put aside by succeeding generations. Beethoven was himself too little of an intellectual to codify his own intentions; nevertheless, he could not wholly escape the metaphysical preoccupations of his own time. His music is occasionally absurd, occasionally irritating, never negligible.

Although Beethoven paid small attention to the forms of religion, he was passionately interested in those expressions of ethical conduct by which the early nineteenth century hoped to reconcile reason with the divine. We know that he wished to impregnate his music with high moral purposes—an attitude which reflected a general insistence in his time upon the importance of the individual. He saw himself as a regenerative force. His private world had much in it that was as noble, yet warmer, more approachable than Goethe's. And at the same time he possessed an unequaled power of suggesting grandeur; a power that might be applied to an occasion as intimate as the opening of a small theater, yet would not appear forced at the dedication of an imperial city.

There is no likelihood, therefore, that the clearer light in which his personal life can now be viewed will interpose an unnecessary distraction between his admirers and his music. The legends which have often surrounded him do not easily bear investigation. His complaints may appear, on the contrary, extravagant; his independence may be called rudeness; and his family may be conceived to have suffered more at his hands than he at theirs. But these evidences of human weakness, if they obtrude upon his music at all, only give it a sharper poignancy; so that the almost unquestioned position of Beethoven at the summit of musical creation can be ascribed to a general recognition of his power to erect the somber fragments of human fallibility into a monument. It transcends and compensates us all.

The funeral procession, March 29, 1827.

GOOD EVENING EVERYBODY

From
Cripple
Creek
to
Samarkand

GOOD EVENING EVERYBODY

From Cripple Creek to Samarkand

A CONDENSATION OF THE BOOK BY

Lowell Thomas

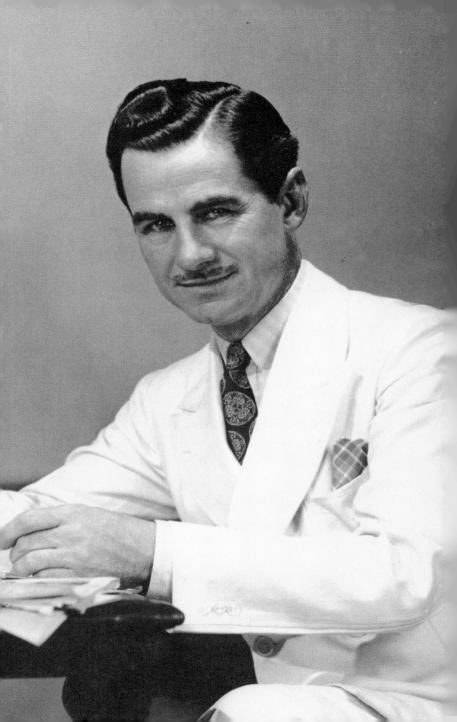

In his fabulous career as a journalist, Lowell Thomas would see it all.

In World War I, he tracked the elusive T. E. Lawrence across the Arabian desert, and the story he found catapulted him to international fame. After that, the world was his beat. Whether dodging bullets in Berlin or crash-landing in the desert . . . when Thomas covered a story, he *lived* it.

Then, on September 29, 1930, he stepped up to a microphone and said, "Good evening everybody." It was his first radio newscast and the start of a long career on the airwaves. All of America came to know his voice and to love his special brand of broadcast journalism. Here, the man who brought the news to so many millions tells his own incredible story.

Chapter I

THE FIRST TIME it ever occurred to me that I might have gained a certain prominence was in the 1920s when someone sent me a snapshot of a large road sign that said, GREENVILLE: HOME OF ANNIE OAKLEY AND LOWELL THOMAS.

Greenville is the seat of Darke County, Ohio, and I was actually born nearby, at the village of Woodington. By the time I arrived on the scene, April 6, 1892, Annie had become the sharpshooting star of Buffalo Bill's Wild West show. Just about then, in fact, Buffalo Bill had taken his troupe to London, where Grand Duke Michael of Russia had come to choose a bride from among Queen Victoria's granddaughters. The grand duke, doubtless thinking to have some sport with the rustic little American, challenged Annie to a match. It was a mistake. While Michael was missing fourteen of his fifty shots, Annie plunked forty-seven bull's-eyes. It is said the humiliation drove Michael back to St. Petersburg—still single. So I bask in reflected glory on that Greenville road sign.

My parents were both country schoolteachers, working to put by enough money so my father could go on to a medical college. Benjamin Harrison was President at the time of my birth, and Grover Cleveland was elected for his second term seven months later. There were forty-four states in the Union and the population stood at fewer than sixty-seven million. Except for its handful of cities, the United States was a scattered community of farmlands with plenty of unexplored territory west of the Mississippi.

But in that last decade of the nineteenth century America was losing her frontier innocence, changing from a self-contained agrarian nation to an industrial world power. In 1893 the Duryea brothers drove the first successful gasoline-powered automobile in the United States. (Not long after, the Chicago *Tribune* told how a pedestrian had been knocked down by an "auto cab," the first such accident on record.) Soon, Orville and Wilbur Wright were tinkering with an airplane in their bicycle shop in Dayton, Ohio. But I suspect these events made no immediate impression on my parents. A few weeks after I was born we moved to Cincinnati, where my father attended medical school until his money was gone and he had to drop out. It was not then necessary to have a license in order to practice, and as some relatives in western Iowa had written of a shortage of doctors, we moved on to Kirkman, a little town on the Rock Island railroad. And my first memories, shadowy and jumbled, are of that time and place.

THE SUMMER DAY is dark and oppressive. There is tension in our house, some nameless threat. My father is away. My mother stands at the open door and looks out into the distance. Suddenly a man runs down the street shouting, "Cyclone!" My mother pulls me out the back door, across the yard, down into the dank vegetable smell of the storm cellar. But I have seen it—that twisting black plume whipping through the sky—and I wish it would come even closer and that I could be outside to watch. . . .

I am sitting on a fence with some other children and the street is crowded with people. A band is playing, too far away for me to see, but the sound has charged our placid little village with excitement: the circus is here! Then—oh, endless wait!—it comes parading by, the tubas and their tantalizing *oompa-pa, oompa-pa;* the horse-drawn wagon cages full of monkeys and lions; and then the clowns, juggling, somersaulting. When they have all disappeared, I gaze after them. The circus is passing through Kirkman on the way to Harlan, the county seat, and Harlan is ten miles away over a bad road. The only time we went there, the buggy got bogged down in mud and my father said never again. . . .

The railroad whistle floats on the summer night, calling, as I lie in bed. Everything is still but that whistle, and then the rush of the train as it shoots through the junction. Another day, sitting in the buggy with my father, I watch as the train plunges by, all black roar and billowing smoke. When it has passed and my father clucks the horses forward, I ask whether the train goes all the way to Harlan, and he says yes, and beyond that. . . .

In autumn the corn is everywhere. The men go from farm to farm to harvest. At Uncle Sam Slates's farm, the aunts bustle about in the kitchen, overseeing roasting chickens and endless pumpkin pies. Someone gives me a piece of pie and I go out to watch the husking bee. My uncle hoists me high so I can see the men rush through the rows, slashing at the stalks with hooked husking gloves and throwing the ears up into the wagons. Then I hear the train whistle somewhere out on the prairie and am lost in the sound, and at last my uncle jostles me and says, "Well, boy, cat got your tongue?". . . .

We are in Omaha now, for my father's graduation from Omaha Medical College, later the University of Nebraska's medical school. He takes me walking. I have never dreamed that there could be so many people in one place or such grand buildings. We start across a bridge spanning the Missouri. Rafts of logs are drifting downstream, guided by crews so far below as to seem unreal to me. My father stops to watch and, idly, I pry a loose red brick from the roadbed. Then I drop it over the side. At once I am overcome with horror—surely my brick will hit one of those men below! I want to run. But I am condemned to watch, trembling with remorse, as the brick grows tinier and tinier, and finally splashes into the water. My father has not noticed, and all alone, age five, I have learned something about right and wrong.

At five I began school in Kirkman. That winter it turned bitterly cold. The prairie wind battered our small frame house; my mother tacked wrapping paper around the foundation to keep the wind from whipping up through the floor. My father, who drove an open buggy to call on rural patients, would be blue with cold by the time he returned. Still, life was pleasant enough. We were hardly well off, but as many people paid their medical bills in produce, we had plenty to eat. I believe I have eaten corn in every one of its guises—soup, mush, hominy, fritters, popcorn, parched—and sometimes, it seemed, all on the same day. Yet, I was perfectly content and couldn't even imagine what it might be like to live in some other place.

But my father had an older brother, Cory, a mining engineer. He had sought his fortune in the gold camps of the Far West and Alaska, and now he had moved to a place called Cripple Creek, in the Rockies. The opportunities there were fantastic, he wrote. There were hundreds of gold mines—he was chief engineer at one of the largest—and a crying need for doctors. Almost at once, it seemed, my father was gone, traveling on ahead to find us a place to live. Then before the end of summer my mother and I, too, climbed aboard the Rock Island on our way to Colorado.

It was a trip filled with memories. I remember the hypnotic sound of iron wheels clattering westward and the nights of sitting up in the coach—there were sleepers, of course, but only rich people rode them. I remember the look of the land as it rose from endless flat prairie to foothills and their wooded valleys. And when the train made a wide turn, I saw the magical peaks far ahead. The year was 1900 and I was eight years old.

ZEBULON M. PIKE, a young army officer and explorer, discovered the mountain that eventually was to bear his name in November 1806. "Grand Peak . . . bare of vegetation and covered with snow, appeared at the distance of fifteen or sixteen miles from us," he wrote, "and as high again as what we had ascended. I believe no human being could have ascended to its summit." It was a reasonable judgment, considering the time of year and the distance Pike had already covered as the first man to map this remote region of the Rockies. But though Pikes Peak is more than fourteen thousand feet high, it is not a difficult climb. A lady wearing bloomers reached the summit in 1858, and eventually, innumerable tourists would each year make it to the top on foot, by auto or on the cog railway. No, the enduring American fascination with Lieutenant Pike's mountain is the simple fact that it has always been so unmistakably *there,* a reachable star. During the gold rush in 1859 thousands of dreamers swarmed into the Rockies, the call "Pike's Peak or bust!" emblazoned on their Conestoga wagons. Few of them found gold, but they established the city of Denver.

Twenty-five years later a man named Bradley started another boom by sprinkling some imported gold dust into a hole on nearby Mount Pisgah. When the bubble burst, Bradley fled with the few hundred dollars he had conned from others for his "discovery." Some of the disillusioned prospectors moved on and some others, like Levi Welty, from Ohio, turned to ranching.

Welty found a high valley with a creek running through it and, with his three sons, built a log house and set his cattle out to feed. One day, while the Weltys were putting in a fence by the creek, a log got away from one of the boys and struck another, who responded with a bawling obscenity. Old Levi wheeled around to see what had happened—and accidentally fired off his gun, peppering his hand with buckshot. At this, an agitated calf tried to jump the fence and broke a hind leg. When calm was restored to the Welty homestead, Levi muttered ruefully, "Well, boys, this sure is some cripple creek." The name stuck.

Big, shambling Bob Womack, an old friend of the Weltys', was certain that infinite riches lay somewhere along Cripple Creek. So he prowled around, assuaging bouts of discouragement with liberal applications of whiskey. And one October afternoon in 1890, in Poverty Gulch, Bob found a chunk of rock that assayed out at two hundred and fifty dollars a ton. Elated, he staked his claim, named it the El Paso and set about raising money.

But the memory of the Mount Pisgah hoax was still fresh, and as for Bob Womack—well, everyone liked him, but he was a souse. So there was no money forthcoming, and eventually Womack sold his El Paso claim for a few hundred bucks and died broke.

Two years would pass before the boom took off with a rush and a roar. Before it was over, half a million men and women had stampeded into the small Cripple Creek district. Eleven towns sprang up and three railroads came snaking up the craggy mountainsides. There seemed to be a new bonanza every day: the El Paso paid out three million. The West had never seen anything like it, nor ever would again. When the golden era ended in 1918, more than three hundred million dollars' worth of ore had been taken from the ground; another two hundred million would come out later. That's more gold than California's forty-niners got from the mother lode, more than came out of the Klondike.

Cripple Creek was the gold camp's social and financial center. Victor, a few miles around Battle Mountain, was where the miners lived, and our first home was a three-room frame house on Sixth Street in Victor. The town had an ornate city hall, many brick buildings and a handsome opera house, but no one would ever mistake it for anything but a mining town. Wherever you looked, mine-shaft houses rose from the mountainsides. Our streets were quite literally paved with gold, for in those early years low-grade ore was crushed and some of it became a part of our roads.

Iowa quickly faded in memory, and I came to believe that every town had more saloons and gambling halls than stores, and a red-light district—a tenderloin. At school, where the third grade was full, I was shunted into fourth grade and thereafter was always the youngest in my class.

My first friend in Victor was my cousin Carl, Uncle Cory's boy. He was a year older. We played marbles with steel ball bearings picked up around mine-shaft houses and threw rocks at every target in sight. Carl was burrowing out a miniature gold mine in his backyard and let me join him. Under his sure direction—he became a Puget Sound bridgebuilder and railroad engineer—we dug an underground shaft and set a frame on top, with a cage to hoist the rock. Our mine had everything but gold, and we expected to hit that any day. When I couldn't find Carl, I would trudge up Seventh Street to a spot where one had a clear view of the snowy Sangre de Cristo range. I don't remember a time when I wasn't yearning to find out what lay beyond them.

In April 1901, Vice-President Theodore Roosevelt came to Victor. The streets were festooned with flags and bunting, and an expectant crowd hung around the depot waiting for his train. It was a far cry from his first visit less than a year before.

He had been campaigning then for William McKinley and the gold standard, which would fix the price of gold at $20.67 an ounce. This did not endear him to miners, who wanted to see William Jennings Bryan in the White House and the free coinage of gold and silver as the law of the land. TR stepped off the train into a sea of anti-McKinley posters and never did make his speech. He got his glasses knocked off, and except for the quick intervention of the Republican postmaster, Danny Sullivan, he would have been crowned with a two-by-four. For years afterward, Danny sported a gold watch inscribed, "To the man who saved my life," that Teddy sent him.

But now even the diehards were ready to concede the gallantry of the old Rough Rider. At noon he came up from Colorado Springs on the new Short Line, with its inspiring panorama of the Sangre de Cristo range and the Continental Divide. Said TR, "This is the ride that bankrupts the English language."

This time TR was ceremoniously marched to a luncheon at the Gold Coin Club. There, after shuffling forward on a long line, I shook his hand. He handed me a lump of sugar from the bowl on the table beside him. So I went outside and got on line again. On that second time around he said, "Does this mean you'll be voting twice at election time?" When McKinley was shot by an assassin and TR became President, he was already my number one hero. My father bought me TR's four-volume *The Winning of the West,* and I read it again and again.

Cripple Creek lured a gaudy cross section of humanity. Bob Ford, the outlaw who shot Jesse James, brought his guns to town—and was promptly run back down the mountain by Sheriff Hi Wilson. The sheriff, or his deputy, Pete Eales, also relieved plenty of tenderfeet of their six-shooters. "I'll just take that for the school fund," Pete would say, and the sale of assorted weaponry did pay a portion of the district's educational bill. They say Cripple also had a large number of college graduates, as well as remittance men from England—a well-educated, hard-drinking bunch.

And on the heels of this freewheeling crowd came some soul-saving luminaries. We had a traveling evangelist at least once a year, and my mother never missed a revival. She took me along when Billy Sunday, the most colorful of them all, came to

Cripple, crying out for the devil to rise up then and there and fight like a man. And when Billy sounded the call to "hit the sawdust trail" for salvation, up the aisle she went, pulling me along. I was glad to have my immortal soul saved, although I had believed the rush forward meant an offer of free candy.

Carry Nation, the hatchet-swinging temperance agitator, made the biggest splash of all when she swept into Cripple Creek. So awesome was her reputation that every saloonkeeper boarded up his place. That is, every one but Johnny Nolon of the Manitou, who announced that he was not about to be buffaloed by Carry.

After a sermon at Army Hall, and followed by the Salvation Army band, Carry marched down to Johnny Nolon's—six feet of scowling sobriety, cape flowing behind. The first thing in Johnny's place that caught her eye was his pride and joy, a life-size painting above the bar called *Venus Emerging from the Sea.* Venus was amply proportioned and alluringly garbed in the altogether. "Hang some blankets on that trollop," said Carry.

"We got no blankets," said genial Johnny. "What kind of a place do you think this is?" Then he went after her, as she suddenly began tearing down his red velvet draperies.

"Take your foul hands off me!" she boomed, elbowing poor Johnny and sending him sprawling. She pulled the famous hatchet out from under her cape and hacked away at the offending picture, stopping only to sweep every bottle of whiskey in reach to the floor. Johnny's clientele scrambled to rescue what bottles they could. The Salvation Army fled, and the Manitou looked as though it had been hit by a cyclone. Finally the police arrived, handcuffed Carry and led her off to jail.

There she would have spent the next thirty days, had it not been for the intervention of bighearted Johnny Nolon. Still bemoaning the loss of his *Venus,* he appeared before the judge and offered to pay Carry's fine if only she'd take the midnight train to Denver. So the story had a happy ending—and Johnny even managed to get the Manitou open for business the following day.

The list of those who lived anonymously in Cripple Creek and went on to catch the public's notice is a long one. Groucho Marx took a job driving a grocery wagon when the show he was traveling with folded in Victor. A future baseball commissioner, Ford Frick, covered the district for a Colorado paper. Youngsters named Jack Dempsey and Bernard Baruch worked in the mines.

But of all the then undiscovered notables, my personal favorite was a vivacious woman from Waco, Texas, named Marie Guinan, who taught Sunday school at Anaconda and played the organ. I wasn't the first twelve-year-old to be smitten with a teacher, but in my case love required hiking around the mountain to Anaconda on Sunday to be in Miss Guinan's radiant presence. In view of my lack of enthusiasm for Sunday school in Victor, my parents no doubt were puzzled at the lively interest I took in the one at Anaconda. But this was nothing compared to my surprise years later when my demure teacher metamorphosed into the brassy blond queen of speakeasy nightlife, "Texas" Guinan, of the famous "Hello, sucker" greeting.

I GOT MY FIRST job when I was in the sixth grade, delivering newspapers in Victor and Goldfield. I needed fifteen dollars to buy a burro. There were hundreds of them running wild in the mountains, but I was still some years short of the strength required to lasso and break one. So the thing was to buy a burro from some older boy who was moving up to a horse.

Burros are remarkable little animals. Brought to the New World by the Spanish conquistadores, they hauled stone to build the missions of California and endless supplies for the explorers of our American West. They carried gear for prospectors and sniffed out waterholes. Old-timers said, "A mule knows three times as much as a horse, and a burro is smarter than a mule."

Every burro had a mind of its own, and sometimes the only way to get it moving was to bite its ear, but I didn't know a boy in school who didn't have or hanker for one. So one autumn afternoon I presented myself at the Victor *Daily Record*, was assigned a route and began saving my earnings in a tin box labeled BURRO. Anxious to do well, I woke up at three in the morning and hurried over to the *Record* to fold newspapers. By first daylight I was hustling through the business district, all pinkish gray and eerily silent, leaving my papers in the doorways of locked houses.

The only people awake at that hour were some weary-looking women on First Street who came to their doors in wrappers, and appeared relieved to find only the newsboy. They often chatted with me, and I answered respectfully, as I had been taught to do, and this seemed to please them inordinately. One even invited me inside for a glass of milk, but I politely declined, explaining that I still had papers to deliver before school started. I came to look forward to exchanging a word or two with the women, maybe because I was still a little uneasy about being abroad at that lonely hour and their friendliness helped.

I'm not sure when I first realized that I was in Victor's red-light district and affably passing the time of day with its daughters of joy. I suppose my larger education had something to do with it—listening to the stories of the older boys; understanding, at last, my father's disquiet when, as town physician, he had to make his "inspections." He must have thought that I was still too young for a frank talk about sex—that came later—but boys come to understand such matters. I remained respectful to the young women, and they were always nice to me. When I finally got my burro, I led it over and showed it to them. They seemed proud, too.

A YEAR OR SO after we arrived in Victor, my mother gave birth to a little girl who, soon after, died of pneumonia. Then, in 1904, when I was twelve, my sister, Pherbia, was born. Meanwhile, my parents—paragons of rectitude in that bluff mining camp who didn't drink, smoke, swear or play cards—concentrated their attentions on me. And I, younger and perhaps more innocent than some of my classmates, tried to find my niche among them.

It was not easy. As we had come from corn country, the boys inevitably dubbed me Rube. Later, when they heard that my father was giving me elocution lessons, my nickname became Windy. Not until I was well into high school and had proven myself one of them—at the cost of some wear and tear on the rules of conduct set down by my parents—did they begin calling me Tommy, the name used by my closest friends.

I began smoking when I was around ten. You didn't necessarily like it, but when everyone else began puffing away at corn silk, or even a section of buggy whip, why, you joined in. Then I graduated to Bull Durham and Duke's Mixture, pinching just enough tobacco out of the little cloth sack to roll into my own cigarettes. When I finally learned to perform this intricate feat with one hand, I hardly minded the nausea that followed the cigarette. Then there was Rosser's poolroom, with six tables and a tempting array of slot machines. I became fairly adept with a pool cue, but I am afraid the one-armed bandits gobbled too many of the nickels and dimes I ought to have dropped in the collection plate at church. Nor could I take any comfort from the fact that my parents, who often inveighed against cards, had never mentioned slot machines.

Chapter II

O N MONDAY, JUNE 6, 1904, the Colorado Springs *Telegraph* rushed an extra to press describing the most "diabolical crime in the history of Colorado." Twenty-five miners on the night shift of the Findley mine were waiting at the Independence depot, just around the mountain from our home, for the Florence & Cripple Creek Railroad train to take them to their homes when hundreds of pounds of dynamite exploded under the platform. My father was called there in the middle of the night. Thirteen miners were already dead, their dismembered bodies strewn across the dark hillside. Nearly all the others were badly hurt. Thus did the bloody ten-month strike of the Western Federation of Miners (WFM) come to its decisive hour.

It had begun as a power struggle between the leaders of labor and management. The WFM, very strong in Cripple Creek, was dominated by "Big Bill" Haywood, a one-eyed giant of a man who stomped the West bellowing for the overthrow of the capitalist system. In 1903, Big Bill had ordered our thirty-five hundred WFM miners out on strike to cut off the supply of ore to some nonunion mills in Colorado City. But the Mine Owners Association was dedicated to smashing the union. They imported scab labor and called on the state militia to drive the WFM out of town.

Feelings ran high, and nearly everyone in the district was on one side or the other. My uncle Cory was a member of the union. Both he and my father sympathized with the plight of the miners, caught in the struggle between the owners and the WFM leadership, but they grieved at the excesses of both sides. Few others were so dispassionate and many an old friendship ended in bitterness.

Neither side had anything to be proud of—WFM hirelings planted bombs in working mines; a shift boss and a superintendent were murdered. Militia, paid by the mine owners, struck back by imprisoning hundreds of union men in a huge bull pen at Goldfield, and by deporting another two hundred and twenty-five, the innocent along with the guilty. They were taken in locked boxcars across the state line and dumped on the empty plains of Kansas and New Mexico. When the Victor *Daily Record* protested these cruelties, its presses were smashed. And so we came to Bloody Monday, when a professional terrorist named Harry Orchard blew up the twenty-five nonunion miners.

Nobody went to work that day. A mass meeting was called for three o'clock, and soon angry men, many of them armed, headed for the site, an empty midtown lot. The militia lined the bluff above, rifles ready, and WFM men watched from the union hall across the street. My cousin Carl and I were with my father and we knelt at the side window of his office, which overlooked the meeting place. Uncle Cory was at the union hall.

At three o'clock a bantam of a man, Clarence C. Hamlin, secretary of the Mine Owners Association, climbed up on a wagon and began addressing the crowd. A fiery orator, he had just one purpose—to whip the crowd into a mob. Arms outflung, he summoned up the image of the gold camp's orphaned children and beseeched "every man with guts" to drive the cursed WFM out of town. A union sympathizer yelled something back at Hamlin and was immediately beaten up. Then a shot was fired and the wagon horses bolted, tumbling Hamlin to the ground.

Suddenly shots rang out from the edge of the crowd and, some said later, from union-hall windows. The terrified mass of men were soon trampling each other in a mad rush to save themselves.

"Get down on the floor!" my father shouted at Carl and me; then he bounded down the steps and out into the melee.

But we clung to the windowsill and gaped out at the nightmare scene as militiamen swarmed down the bluff and, swinging rifle butts, charged headlong into the crowd. In minutes the packed lot was empty—except for the men who lay motionless on the ground. My father clutched one wounded miner by the armpits and, with someone's help, dragged him toward the office.

The militiamen had surrounded the union hall and ordered the WFM men to come out with their hands up. The answer was no. Someone barked an order and rifle volleys echoed up and down the street as round after round was pumped into the building. I prayed that Uncle Cory would be spared. When the shooting stopped at last and the men came out, Cory was among them. They were rushed away by the soldiers, Carl flying after his father. The mob stormed into the hall, smashing everything in sight. Then they set off to wreck and loot every union store and meeting place in town.

Meanwhile, my father had gotten the unconscious miner up to the office and onto his operating table. He called for me to take the man's gun belt. As I reached for it, I caught sight of the bloody bullet hole in his stomach. I threw the holstered .45 behind a bookcase and tried not to be sick. Then I stood staring at the wall as my father probed for the bullet, announcing every step of the procedure as though he were addressing a class of medical students. When it was done we took the miner to the hospital—where my father spent the night tending the injured.

The strike changed the Cripple Creek district for all time. The WFM was driven out, but a great wound of the spirit remained. Uncle Cory and his family left, as did hundreds of other miners. Nobody profited. The mine owners, momentarily triumphant, were soon to see the gold camp's long decline. Big Bill Haywood was discredited in the eyes of fair-minded laboring men. He became the motive force behind the militant International Workers of the World (IWW), called the Wobblies. In 1921, awaiting trial for wartime sedition, Haywood fled to Soviet Russia, where he was lionized but died lonely and embittered, to be buried at the Kremlin Wall. The depot terrorist, Harry Orchard, wandered the West for a year or so, hiring out as a professional killer. In 1905 he planted the bomb that killed Frank Steunenberg, former governor of Idaho. Caught and sent to prison, Orchard claimed to have undergone a great reformation. He lived to be eighty-five but spent all the rest of his long life—forty-five years—growing flowers in the Idaho state penitentiary.

For a while longer, things went on much as they always had for us. The miner whose life my father saved recovered, then, typically, neglected to pay his bill. When Dad casually mentioned this some weeks later, I remembered the .45 behind the bookcase. "You could sell that and keep the money," I said, proud to make this indirect contribution to the family finances. But not Dad. He fished out the gun and returned it to the miner.

WHEN I WAS TWELVE or so, I began to notice girls. One of the first was Lucille McAvoy, who, though only thirteen, could really fill out a middy blouse. Unhappily for me, nearly all the boys in the neighborhood were similarly smitten, and there never seemed to be room for me on her porch. Then, at a birthday party, I was introduced to the charm of a game called post office. Pining to deliver a "letter" to Lucille, I was paired instead with a sweet girl, Bessie, whose kiss—my very first— convinced me that life without Lucille could be worth living after all.

For a while a girl named Dale Latimer and I were supposed to be an item, maybe because her father was a doctor, too. I don't think Dale and I had any grand passion for each other, but when everyone in our group began to pair off, it was convenient to pretend. Once, in the McAvoys' barn, the others persuaded me to take Dale up into the haymow. I did, but when we were alone in that seductive, sweet-smelling dimness, we sat a good three feet apart, afraid to so much as hold hands.

Gertrude Oliver, who came into my life a couple of years later, bowled me over. She acted older than any of the other girls in school, and when she seemed to respond to my fumbling attentions I was transported with joy. I went to her house often, and stayed until her father, a prosperous mine operator with an antic sense of humor, signaled that I'd better be gone, sometimes by lowering a ringing alarm clock down over the upstairs railing.

One night, when I'd left even later than usual, I heard footsteps in the street behind me. It was Gertrude's father. I felt sure he would want to discuss the long good-bye Gertrude and I had just shared in the darkness at their front door. But Mr. Oliver didn't seem angry. In fact, he put his arm around me in the friendliest way. Then he said, "My boy, do you think you can support my daughter?" That was the end of the romance! Her wise father must have foreseen Gertrude was about ready for a husband—and, indeed, got one barely a year later, right after we got our diplomas. She married the principal.

In high school some of my friends began experimenting with demon rum. I stuck to root beer, but I was often present when my friends broke open a bottle of whiskey—and sometimes had to lead them home. Maybe that's why they invited me to accompany them to the Port Wine Club ball at the Elks Hall.

As my father would not approve, I sidled out of the house in my good suit, mumbling something about meeting the boys. I had second thoughts myself when we arrived; the smoky hall seemed to me to be a den of iniquity. But soon my interest was piqued by a girl. She was attractive in a flamboyant way, and squeezed as she was into a shiny black dress, it was easy to believe what my friends said about her being "available."

By ten o'clock I had worked up the nerve to ask her to dance, and at eleven—the hour I was due home—I was still waltzing her around the floor, concocting wild tales about my adventures as a young man-about-town. My breath came fast as I held her closer and closer, until around midnight some inner sensor picked up a warning. My father was standing in the doorway.

Gone my painfully fabricated poise! Without a word I left my prize in mid–dance floor and marched out the door in front of my father. All the way home two questions were on my mind: first, whether my father had recognized my intentions toward that girl; and second, whether he considered me too old for a licking.

He didn't say a word until we were inside. Then he quickly made it clear that the answer to both questions was yes. For the next two hours he gave me the dark side of the facts of life. He didn't use any street words—I never heard my father say anything stronger than "Hmph!"—but he made the hazards of casual sex graphically clear. I took the lesson to heart, especially as it was vividly punctuated by one of my pals at the Port Wine ball. He later told me that he had tangled with the girl in the shiny black dress on that fateful night—and wound up taking a long series of distressing treatments at my father's office.

My FATHER REMAINED a scholar all his life. He probably knew almost as much geology as any mining engineer in Cripple Creek, and he was a dedicated student of philosophy, literature, astronomy, botany and comparative religion. When most of the people in our town had an extra dollar they bought a drink; when my father had an extra dollar he took a course or bought a book. Two of the leading medical schools in the United States were Johns Hopkins in Baltimore and Rush in Chicago; by 1914 Dad had degrees from both. (In 1951, when he was in his mid-eighties, he was still at it, sending us a note from England to the effect that he had just signed up for some graduate courses at Oxford.)

My sister, Pherbia, and I were the lucky beneficiaries of his insatiable quest for knowledge. Dad read aloud to us from Shakespeare, the Bible, Kipling, Mark Twain. He and Mother had me reading by the time I was three, and thereafter my father drilled me in the art of elocution. He had the good old-fashioned idea that life was enhanced for anyone who could speak clearly and explicitly. "Your voice is the expression of your personality," he would say. "Don't cringe behind it."

At ten, I was frequently called on to declaim at church and club affairs. Once, my father ushered me inside our empty church, stood me up in the pulpit and had me recite "Paul Revere's Ride." Sitting in the back pew, he kept calling out, "Louder! And put more fire into it—the British are coming!" My voice has enabled me to earn a livelihood, but I don't know how often my wife has had to shush me in a restaurant, reminding me that when I whisper I can be heard clearly on the far side of the room.

My father took me on long hikes to gather flower and rock specimens for his collections, and often, on a winter night, when the heavens shone with particular brilliance, he would wake Pherbia and me to come and gaze at the stars, which he identified with proprietary affection.

He was of two minds about religion. My mother could hardly be kept out of church, but Dad came late and took a seat in the back, the easier to slip away when the sermon palled. I think that he is probably best described as an open-minded agnostic, willing to be convinced but unable to accept hard-line fundamentalism. Yet he was a devoted student of the Bible, and whenever we got a minister who agreed that not every line in the Good Book need be taken as literal fact, Dad would invite him to join the Century Club, a literary circle he had organized.

Other doctors came to Cripple Creek, salted away goodly sums and eventually moved on to Colorado Springs or Denver, but not Dad. For one thing, he seemed incapable of pressing anyone for payment and had devised a simple strategy for dealing with delinquent accounts: he forgot about them. So we were never affluent, although my father was one of the busiest men in town. Between mine accidents and shooting scrapes he practiced more surgery in a year than most doctors did in a lifetime.

I suppose my father would have liked me to follow in his footsteps. He never actually said so, but he did once undertake to stimulate my enthusiasm by inviting me to observe him at the hospital, where a miner, struck by a falling rock, was to undergo a trepanning operation to relieve the pressure on his brain. I was scrubbed and garbed by a nurse and then was ushered into the operating room, where white-shrouded figures were clustered around a shaved, shining skull. Somebody urged me to move closer so I could see better. One of the mysterious figures—my father, I suppose—was cutting a neat hole in the skull. I remember the brain being exposed and that's all I remember, because at that point I keeled over. Not long after, my father suggested that perhaps I would be interested in pursuing a career in the law.

I LOOKED FORWARD to holidays like the Fourth of July and Labor Day as though they were my birthday, for then the gold camp burst into dawn-to-dawn celebration—fireworks, prizefights, hard-rock drilling contests and rodeos, each with its favorites and heroes. One of the greatest was a horse named Steamboat. Steamboat had gotten his name by throwing a local cowhand, who vented his frustration by whacking the horse across the snout. Unfortunately, Steamboat breathed with an audible whistle thereafter, but his bucking power was unimpaired: he threw every man who ever got a leg over him. Cowboys from all over came to try a hand at taming him. Whenever one bit the dust, the Cripple Creek crowd cheered lustily. Steamboat was, after all, one of us.

The most gifted performers of the time toured the mining camps. We saw Lillian Russell, Anna Held and—greatest night of all—John Philip Sousa. Miners, those who wouldn't have paid ten cents to see the Statue of Liberty play the fiddle, lined up to buy dollar tickets when the March King came to town.

Not all the excitement in Cripple was scheduled. One afternoon, working in our backyard, I heard a tumultuous clanging behind me and looked up to see a whole string of boxcars tumbling down Squaw Mountain. They had broken away from a locomotive and, plunging down the steep incline, had jumped the tracks at the first sharp turn. That sort of thing happened often enough in our mountains. One summer night a coach loaded with Fourth of July celebrants returning from Colorado Springs broke loose and, after a terrifying runaway ride, crashed into an embankment. Miraculously, only three were killed.

As for me, I continued to generate my own excitement—mischief may be a better word—mostly, I suppose, because I was still the youngest in my class and felt obliged to somehow emphasize my presence. Some teachers reacted by giving me the stony-faced silent treatment. I didn't like that; I didn't want anyone mad at me. I preferred the more direct response, painful as it might be. When it was over, you had the feeling that accounts were squared and you could be friends again.

In high school my mathematics teacher was named Mr. Lady, and I suppose some sophomoric remark I made about that led to the mayhem. Mr. Lady, who definitely wasn't, worked me over in front of the class, then sent me to the principal's office for more. But as the principal was engaged, he suggested I return the following afternoon and, in the meantime, confess my villainy to my father. Honorably I did so, and got a second licking, with the third delivered, as promised, by the principal next day. I would like to believe this established a Victor High record for corporal punishment for a single offense.

My favorite teacher was Mabel Barbee. First she captivated me—along with every other boy in class—with her cool good looks. Then, head over heels in love with her, I followed willingly as she led me into history and Spanish. She had come to Cripple as a child in 1892, by stagecoach. Her father, known as "Honest" John, discovered a rich mine, but was so hard up for cash that he had to sell out before it began producing. When he died, a coffee can labeled FOR HONEST JOHN'S GIRL appeared on the counter of Griff's drugstore. With the dollars and dimes tossed in, Mabel Barbee had paid for her education.

While teaching at Victor, she met and married a young mining engineer, Howe Lee. They went off to a remote mining camp in Oregon and there he died, leaving Mabel with a small daughter and no money. She went back to Colorado College, her alma mater, and became dean of women. Then she moved east to Radcliffe and eventually helped launch Bennington College in Vermont. When she retired, she wrote *Cripple Creek Days,* a best seller, with two fine sequels.

In my first summer job I worked for a cattle rancher named Kennedy who had a scraggly spread south of Victor. My job involved clearing and plowing a boulder-strewn field that seemed to stretch into eternity. At the end of a week, when I had tilled a strip about four feet wide, my back ached and my brain felt scrambled from the plow's constant collisions with huge, malevolently hidden rocks. I stopped in midfield and evaluated my situation. True, I had not yet been paid. True, I had no prospect of another job. But, on the other hand, what could be worse than endless boulders? I turned up the trail for home. And found out.

My father listened to my tale of woe, then put his arm around my shoulder and walked me outside. I knew he was displeased, but he didn't say so. Instead he pointed to a load of freshly cut piñon pine, brought in by some rancher to pay his medical bill. "I was planning on hiring someone to cut this into firewood," my father said, "but as you are unoccupied, it will keep you busy."

It did. Piñon pine oozes pitch, which makes it burn well even when green, but sawing through it, with that gooey tar grabbing at the saw blade, was sheer hell. I hacked away, day after day, sometimes groaning with fatigue and frustration, but at last the mountainous pile disappeared, and though my father never paid me a cent, I came to realize that I had been otherwise rewarded: all the physical labor I have ever done since has seemed easier by comparison.

The following summer I went to work at the Empire State mine, swinging a pick and shovel and pushing ore cars out to the shaft from the Buena vein. It was the richest single vein of ore ever discovered, thirty-six thousand dollars in gold to every ton of rock, and it was an irresistible temptation to miners. Each day they chipped out rich bits and smuggled them out in boots and secret body belts. This was appropriately known as high-grading, and the driller for whom I worked, a boisterous bull of a man named Ed Cody, was getting rich at it. Soon he was able to

***Lowell Thomas grew up** amid the mine shafts of Cripple Creek, Colorado. He recalled his father, the town doctor, and mother (cameo) as "paragons of rectitude" in that roisterous gold*

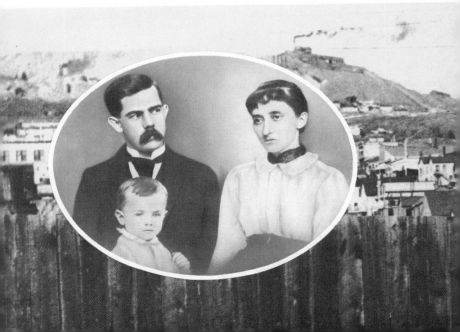

realize a longtime ambition. He chartered a private train and took his pals to Los Angeles for a month-long celebration.

Both the government and the mine operators tried hard to put an end to high-grading. But it was so much a part of the life in Cripple—high grade was often dropped in the church collection plate—that even the local law winked at it. In one celebrated case a miner was caught red-handed with a load of rich ore taken from the Independence. The judge ruled that ore was real estate and how could anyone "steal" real estate? Not guilty. The practice ended only when the high-grade ore petered out.

Accidents were common in the mines—cave-ins, fires, falls, premature explosions—and people tended to become hardened to them. But that summer Cripple suffered a disaster of such tragic magnitude that nobody in the district was unaffected. Somehow, something went wrong with the hoist at the Independence mine. At dawn, loaded with men coming off the graveyard shift, it shot to the top with terrific speed, then, completely

camp. The saloons were shut down briefly by temperance crusader Carry Nation (cartoon, left). In high school (right), Lowell quarterbacked the football team.

out of control, dropped thirteen hundred feet to the bottom of the shaft. The bodies of twenty-two miners were brought to Hunt's Mortuary in Victor that morning, and people watched in silence as the big Clydesdale horses pulled wagon after wagon through the street.

In time I held nearly every job there was to be had in a mining camp—mucker, trammer, driller—and sorting ore was one of my favorite jobs. The ore house was on the surface, and as I sifted the various grades of rock I listened to the gaudy tales of men who had searched for gold in the Klondike. It was those stories that sent me to Alaska only a few years later. And later still, when I would speak to black-tie audiences, I could always break the ice by telling them that I had gotten my start in an *ore house*.

I suppose the peak of my mining career was riding assay for the great Portland mine. Its assay office on Battle Mountain serviced smaller mines and "prospect holes" all around. For two summers, nine hours a day, I rode horseback over the mountains, my saddlebags filled with ore samples and the high hopes of prospectors and independent operators. The ore was roasted in the assay-office furnace and the residue of pure gold weighed. Next day, on my rounds, I would report the results. The miners were nearly always disappointed, for there is a harsh equation in the quest for gold: dreams are boundless, but gold is rare.

Sometimes, in a long afternoon, when the sun was hot and the snow-covered peaks shimmered hypnotically in the distance, I would doze in my saddle. And one day, following a late night of dancing, I fell into a sound sleep. The trail was familiar and the horse surefooted, but as we crossed the entrance to a railroad tunnel, a train entering the other end blew its whistle. The horse leaped across the tracks. That woke me. In fact, I found myself hanging from the horse's underside, tangled in the girth and saddle straps. Luckily the horse stopped—I suppose he, too, was unsettled by this unorthodox alignment of steed and rider—and I was able to crawl free and remount.

Years later, when I'd return to Cripple Creek, I'd manage to find a moment to visit the mountain above. At my favorite place, Windy Point, I'd sit in the saddle and marvel at the spectacular array of peaks, the spine of our continent, stretching all the way from New Mexico to Wyoming. A metal marker there noted the names of the highest mountains of the Sangre de Cristo and the Collegiate Range. Unmarked were other places I'd remember, mines like the Bluebird, the Lost King, Joe Dandy, the Doctor Jack Pot, trails overgrown and forgotten, and forgotten with them the dreams of thousands of hardworking men and women. But as I stood for a moment at Windy Point, they would all come to life again for me.

IN THE SUMMER of 1907 my father concluded that boom times were over. He sent Mother, Pherbia and me back to relatives in Darke County, Ohio, while he set off to look for a new opportunity somewhere in the Northwest. Ohio seemed a foreign place to me, and in my western clothes I felt much the young barbarian. My mother finally rented a house in Greenville and there, in September, I was enrolled in the junior class of the high school. For a few miserable days I tried to make myself invisible among those effete Easterners who wore cotton shirts and ties to school, and they obliged by treating me accordingly.

Then our English teacher decreed that each of us was to memorize a famous oration and deliver it before the school assembly. For the others in class the assignment had the ring of doom. But I never gave it a thought beyond brushing up on the piece I'd decided to do, Wendell Phillips's tribute to the Haitian patriot, Toussaint L'Ouverture.

On the appointed day a parade of unhappy young men stumbled up to the platform, mumbled into their neckties and fled back to the oblivion of their seats. I did better—I had, after all, been doing this sort of thing for years—and the reaction was astonishing. There was a burst of applause when I finished, and the rest of that week boys and girls with whom I'd never exchanged a word greeted me as though I were a lifelong friend. I was even elected captain of the football team, though I won by default—the team was evenly split on two other chaps, one of whom should have had the honor.

From then on I belonged. In Cripple, I had striven to keep up with the rough, tough sons of miners and saloonkeepers; though I sometimes broke family rules in an adolescent effort to be one of them, I never had their easy grace. In Greenville, my oratory plus the aura of my western background stood me in good stead. The local newspaper, reporting our first football game, listed the captain and quarterback as Lowell "Two-Gun" Thomas. I was cast into a position of leadership, and it was heady and gave me more self-confidence than I had ever had.

The following summer we returned to Victor, because my father hadn't found any place that suited him as well. In my last year in high school, I organized and edited our first school paper, *The Sylvanite,* and spent a lot of time sending inquiries to colleges. I had an acceptance from Valparaiso University in northern Indiana, and suddenly there was a flurry of packing, advice and kisses. Then I was climbing aboard the train, waving goodbye to my parents and, age seventeen, setting off on my own.

Chapter III

SOME CALLED VALPARAISO the poor man's Harvard, but to those of us who studied there during its golden era, the years before World War I, it was plain old Valpo. Its strength was a straightforward attention to the matter at hand—education. There was no athletic program, not even a gymnasium; there were no accommodating courses in ballet or leisure-time management. There was no leisure time. The student body worked!

This industrious attitude must have impressed me. Without consulting anyone, I signed up for both the freshman and sophomore years. By the time this monumental arrogance was discovered, the semester was half over. Vice-President Kinsey, who had sent for me with every intention of throwing me out of the sophomore class, could only stare at the record and, his big red mustache twitching, mutter, "Well, you seem to be managing."

"Yes, sir," replied Two-Gun Thomas, straining to hide self-satisfaction.

"But look here, young man," Kinsey exclaimed, "at this rate you'll have your bachelor's degree in little more than a year!"

"Then I'll stay two and take a master's," I replied. One of my many weaknesses has been an oversupply of confidence.

I had to provide for myself, as did so many others at Valpo.

My first job was as a janitor, tending a furnace, sweeping, even milking a cantankerous old cow. I couldn't have been luckier in my roommates. The first was a poker-faced Spanish-American–War veteran named George Washington Vilain. He was the scion of a well-to-do New York City family. Years before, he had broken his parents' hearts by spurning a university education and running off to join the army. After a distinguished career with the Corps of Engineers, rising to the rank of major, he realized his parents had been right. Without a word to them, he decided to study law and to surprise them with an invitation to his graduation. But shortly before he graduated, they died, never to know of the dramatic turn in their son's life.

To escape the attentions paid him by our landlady's daughter, Vilain would flee to the library to study, leaving me alone. When he graduated, I was assigned a roommate who was equally considerate—for the opposite reason. He had discovered the charms of a lady known as "Mabel the Campus Widow," and he was at her place day and night, so again I had a room to myself.

Valpo tolerated no fraternities, but one, Alpha Epsilon, flourished sub rosa and attracted some of the most gregarious students. I was invited to join and soon made friends with a handsome and persuasive young man from Kansas—Preston Burtis, known by everyone as "Cap." Cap, as the cliché goes, could sell iceboxes to Eskimos, and he sold me on a new way to make money. The national census of 1910 had left nearly all town and county maps out of date; we would take time off that summer and tour the countryside selling revised maps. "Tommy," he assured me, "we'll clean up." Well, we didn't, but we had a lot of fun clip-clopping along in a horse and buggy.

We made our headquarters in Elgin, Illinois, home of the Elgin road race. Automobile racing was just coming into its own, with a new kind of hero, the racing driver. Cap and I got to know three of the top racers.

The first was a starchy little man with icicles for nerves, named Ralph DePalma. In the next four years Ralph won the national racing championship twice, then took the Indianapolis 500 in 1915 with an average speed of just under ninety miles an hour. One evening DePalma introduced us to Barney Oldfield, a cigar-chomping daredevil who bewitched us with stories about his early days in racing.

It had all begun for him in 1902, when Henry Ford hired him to race against a competitor, Alexander Winton. "I had never even been behind the wheel of an automobile then," Oldfield said, grinning around the ever present cigar—which, incidentally, he bit into while speeding over the jarring tracks of the day to keep from breaking his teeth. "But I guess Ford had heard that I'd try anything once." With only a few weeks' practice, Oldfield beat Winton's record-setting car with room to spare.

The third member of that daring trio was Eddie Rickenbacker. Though he was only a year or so older than Cap and I were, he was already dreaming big dreams. History has recorded how well he succeeded—America's greatest air ace in World War I, builder of a major airline, survivor of devastating crashes, one of which cast him adrift in the Pacific for twenty-two days—one of the towering figures of the twentieth century. He remained my close friend until his death in 1973, when his wife and sons asked me to deliver the eulogy at his funeral.

THE TIME AT Valpo went swiftly. I remember the exhilaration as I was drawn into unsuspected realms of knowledge, challenged to imagine the unimaginable, to let my mind wander freely. Valpo's faculty was studded with teachers who could *teach*, inspire, uplift. I was lucky to have been there in their time.

America's foremost orator in those days was William Jennings Bryan, and I heard him deliver his famous oration, "The Prince of Peace," to the student body. All I remember of my interview with him afterward was his saying that he invariably made his best speech when on the way back to the railway station.

In June 1911, I returned to Colorado with a bachelor of science and a master of arts. There were no Cripple Creek employers out beating the woods for young scholars of nineteen. I did what young scholars in mining camps have always done: I took a job swinging a pick and shovel in the mines. But before I'd even had the chance to work out my aches and pains, the telephone rang. George Khyner, the fast-talking owner of the Victor *Daily Record*, was on the line.

"I hear you've got a job mucking at the Portland. Is that what you went to college for? How much do they pay you? Three dollars a day? Well, I'll give you ninety-five a month as a reporter. Room for advancement. Take it or leave it."

"Why, sure, Mr. Khyner." My heart leaped into double time. "When should I come to work?"

"Right now," he said, and hung up.

That was George Khyner. He had turned up shorthanded that night—employees didn't always stay long. For ninety-five dollars a month Khyner expected me to turn out the *Record* almost single-handedly. Reporter? I was to be a reporter, legman, rewrite man, editor and front man for readers' complaints.

But Khyner gave me a chance to get started in journalism in a place where zesty news stories broke outside the front door or just down the street. In any ten-day period, I could count on a shooting spree, a holdup, a fire, a mine accident and an indignant reader proposing to horsewhip the editor. It was an opportunity to intrigue any young man with a taste for human drama.

I made a fair number of mistakes. Once, after a fire, I pulled out a typeface of the size usually reserved for posters and handbills, and the *Record* proclaimed, BLAZE SWEEPS LOCAL BUILDINGS! That afternoon one of my predecessors returned for a visit. He glanced at the headline.

"Do you think it's too big?" I asked.

"How many local buildings were swept by this blaze?"

"Three."

"Well, I tell you what, kid," he said, "I'd try to hold something back for the Second Coming."

In about six months a group from Denver started a second newspaper in Victor, the *News*, and offered me the job as editor. The salary was a hundred and thirty-five a month and I would have a staff. I never regretted moving to the *News*, but nothing much changed at first. I was still covering all the action in Victor. The staff consisted of mining editor Sam Vidler, a general manager, "Honest" John White—he was always called that, I don't know why—who looked after circulation, advertising and bills, and a series of itinerant linotype operators.

Vidler had a weakness for the ladies, a failing his wife viewed with some heat. As Honest John put it, "This could lead to quite a misunderstanding." It did. One day Sam's little boy misbehaved at school and was given a whipping. Mrs. Vidler thought this unjust and went out to find Sam. Alas, she found him in a room in the National Hotel and, approaching the door, heard inside the sighs and banterings of her Sam and a woman named Nellie Smith. Mrs. Vidler marched to a nearby store, purchased a revolver and had the accommodating clerk give her a quick lesson. She went back, flung open the door of Sam's room and shot the undraped Nellie dead. Sam dived under the bed. It took a jury only ten minutes to acquit Mrs. Vidler—Cripple always deferred to outraged womanhood—and she and Sam went home together.

Every now and then an unfortunate peace settled on the Cripple Creek district. And that's how I got in trouble. One very quiet Saturday night nothing happened in Victor, Cripple, Goldfield or Independence. There was a possibility from Denver—man shot by paramour—but no pictures. Then a similarity in names struck me—the victim was the nephew of our mayor! In no time at all I had the story written—MAYOR'S NEPHEW SHOT IN LOVE NEST—and prominently placed on page one, with a picture of the mayor grinning as he received the returns from the last election. Then, feeling the honest exhaustion that comes after a hard job well done, I went home to bed.

Before breakfast Honest John called me. "Lowell?" he said. "Are you still in bed? Well, you'd better stay there. The mayor is out looking for you, and he's got a gun."

I concluded the mayor had cause to be angry and, since I was in no position to leave town, I'd better apologize. I went to his home, where his wife agreed to serve as intermediary. When the mayor returned, she calmed him sufficiently so he would allow me to express my contrition. I mentioned the possibility of doing an interview with him for the paper, extolling the progress he had brought to our fair town. He finally put away the gun.

IN THE FALL OF 1912 a yen for more schooling overtook me. I quit the paper and, with my savings, enrolled for graduate study at the University of Denver. The chancellor of DU suggested that since I had gotten both my degrees in only two years, it might be wise to take some senior courses as well. When the year ended I had another bachelor's and another master's degree. I also worked as part-time reporter for the Rocky Mountain *News* and the Denver *Times*, and at night I clerked at a small hotel, where I studied and even got in a little sleep.

And there was a young woman, a freshman named Fran. Although I never took her out—we spent no time alone—we met occasionally at parties and at school. There was something about her, a certain look, a kind of heightened sensitivity to life's promises, that sent messages to my brain. I didn't do anything about it. But something was happening to me.

Meanwhile, I still had no clear idea of my future. I had a general education in the liberal arts, essential for the enrichment of soul and spirit, but only a bare foundation on which to build a career. Did I want to be a newspaperman? A lawyer? A university theologian urged that I consider the ministry.

I thought about all these and half a dozen other callings, and when school ended I went off to a ranch my father had acquired in the seven-thousand-foot-high valley of the Los Pinos River, in the San Juan Mountains of southwestern Colorado. And I thought some more.

My father had once said to me, "Son, when it comes to land, the easiest marks are doctors, lawyers and preachers." He was no exception. When an old friend ran into stormy financial weather, Dad bailed him out by taking the ranch off his hands.

The ranch was run by my uncle Ira, who had been advised to get out of Chicago to cure a persistent cough. Much of the San Juan area was open range then and still roamed by bands of Ute Indians. Uncle Ira, like the other ranchers, depended mainly on state-owned rangeland to graze his cattle. So I helped with summer brandings and roundups, sleeping on my saddle blanket under the stars. Sometimes, riding along, the cool breeze in my face, I wondered why the life of a cowboy wouldn't suit me.

And then, suddenly, for reasons that remain a mystery to me, I decided that I would go to Chicago and study law.

CHICAGO. IT WAS THEN the center of our midwestern universe: bustling, important, but rooted in America's heartland, unlike those Gomorrahs at the edges of the continent, New York and San Francisco, awash with bizarre philosophies and moral codes.

Before I found a place to live, I went down to Market Street—newspaper row—in search of a job. I chose to try the *Evening Journal* first. It was written and put together in the daytime and I could attend law school at night; also, I was attracted by the massive double doors, invitingly open in the summer heat. Inside, there were a dozen reporters at their typewriters, the horseshoe copy desk and, overseeing it all from his corner looking out on Market Street, a young city editor, cool, decisive, absolutely in command. It was a moment I've never forgotten.

Apparently I had been noticed. "I looked up," Dick Finnegan, the city editor, said later, "and saw this young fellow from the West standing outside, wearing a Stetson, and I said to the assistant city editor, 'Find out what he wants; it if it's a job, he's got it.' "

A dark, handsome man with a law degree, Dick Finnegan knew everyone in the city. He *was* the *Evening Journal.* Seated next to his desk, I was enthralled by the incisive way he went at things: "Any experience? Good. You'll start at fifteen dollars a week. The assistant city editor has an apartment and he's looking for a roomer. You want to attend law school at night? See Guy Guernsey, Chicago-Kent College of Law. Tell him I sent you." And so my future was settled in ten minutes.

Guy Guernsey turned out to be on the board of trustees of Chicago-Kent, a flourishing institution with over a thousand students. He seemed interested in my debating and oratorical experience. A few days later the president of the college told me there was an unexpected vacancy in the department of forensic oratory—the techniques of courtroom debate. Could I take over until they found a replacement? I said yes and they kept me on. So I studied law, worked full time on the *Journal* and taught public speaking.

I lightened my load by inviting notable legal figures to address my pupils. One was Clarence Darrow, already the best-known criminal lawyer in America, though this was years before the famous "monkey" trial on the right to teach evolution. Darrow believed in shocking juries, and audiences, to attention. Opening his talk at Chicago-Kent, he announced, "All lawyers are crooks." Then he launched into a dazzling examination of the principle that every defendant has the right to qualified counsel. This meant, he said, that not all lawyers could have virtuous clients all the time. And *this* meant that any lawyer could find himself using the law for undesirable ends. And yet the principle was central to our constitutional rights.

I can still see him standing there, the rumpled clothes, the shaggy, leonine head thrust forward in perpetual challenge, and his eyes shining with the fire of his beliefs. He came back several times, his wife always sitting in front, lips apart in adoration. Every time he came the auditorium was packed, some even sitting in the aisles. There has been only one Clarence Darrow.

SOMEHOW I COULDN'T get excited about torts and wills, but my heart sang when I reported to the city room. I sometimes think that no city has ever been so full of color and life as Chicago was in those years. The mayor was William Hale Thompson, a cartoon caricature of a machine politician, with such henchmen as saloonkeeper "Hinky Dink" Kenna and "Bathhouse" John Coughlan, who ran the First Ward. Thompson was returned to office again and again by cornering the Irish and German immigrant vote. One year he did it with a one-plank platform: "If the king of England comes to Chicago, I'll punch him in the snoot!" On election night he didn't bother to stay up for the returns. When, early next morning, I was the first to bring him word that he'd won, he snorted. "I knew that before the polls opened. Come on in and have some bacon and eggs." That was the first time I ate grapefruit—a new thing in American stores.

Some of my colleagues made history. Floyd Gibbons covered so many invasions, revolutions and sieges that it was said no war was official until Floyd arrived. Richard Henry Little gained a certain immortality by always reporting on his expense account the cost of replacing a horse shot from under him in battle— even when he did a stint on a battleship. There were reporters who did more lasting work: Carl Sandburg, Marquis James, Ring Lardner. "Talk about your fiction!" Carl Sandburg once said. "The first page of today's newspaper has human stuff in it that puts novels in the discard."

One summer morning I got to work early. Dick Finnegan was

there alone, on the telephone. When he hung up, he told me to get down to the Chicago River; the Great Lakes excursion steamer *Eastland*, with two thousand passengers, had capsized at the dock in one of America's worse maritime disasters.

I was among the first to reach the scene. Men and women, some clutching children, were flailing toward shore; the *Eastland*, like a stranded whale, was turned on her side. I clambered aboard and joined those trying to haul the living out of portholes and the drowning from the river. I'd have had a scoop if I'd rushed back to the office, but I finally got back around noon. My face no doubt reflected my emotions at having been there when more than eight hundred people met their deaths. Dick Finnegan said, "Go some place and forget it, Tommy. See you tomorrow."

Another morning Finnegan handed me a name: Carlton Hudson. "Dig up what you can," he said. "Some old people have been uncommonly nice to him in their wills."

Hudson had a handsome office on Dearborn Street, and though I never seemed able to catch him in, it was not hard to flesh out his background from other sources. People in the building volunteered that he was a financier and philanthropist. A lawyer told me that he was a pillar of the evangelical Moody Temple. There I found a good many elderly ladies with solid bank accounts who vouched for Hudson's integrity. Several had made him their financial adviser; three had remembered him in their wills.

I kept digging. Hudson had turned up in Chicago in 1892, nobody knew from where, but a few mentioned his "eastern" accent. I wrote to every college in New England, describing Hudson and explaining that I was looking for him because he was heir to a gold-mining fortune. Soon I struck pay dirt. A letter from a college in Vermont told me that my description fitted the writer's former roommate, who had gone to New York. But I had the name wrong. It was Carlton Hudson *Betts*. Two hours later Finnegan handed me a train ticket to New York and a hundred dollars for expenses.

In the morgue of the New York *World* I found two fat folders marked CARLTON H. BETTS. Five minutes' reading told me we had our man. Betts, a con artist, had victimized New Yorkers years ago. When arrested, he had gotten out on bail and vanished.

The city's former district attorney, Charles S. Whitman, was now governor of New York. I went to see him. "Governor," I said, trying to sound self-assured, "I have something the people of New York want. In exchange, I want something for my paper." Then I told him the whole story.

He was several steps ahead of me. "So you want time to write your story before the other papers get it. I'll give you twenty-four hours, young man; also the thanks of the people of New York."

The following afternoon, when Carlton Hudson Betts stepped out of his office building, the police were waiting for him. So were the newsboys, with our extra edition of the *Journal*. I got a bonus and a raise, and Silas Strawn, head of a large Chicago law firm, asked me to drop by his office.

"Lowell," he said, "you have saved some clients of mine a lot of grief." Some time before, the great meat-packing houses of Chicago—Swift, Armour and Wilson—had been involved in a Texas oil venture and had inadvertently broken a federal statute. Somehow, Betts had gotten wind of it and was trying to blackmail them. "My clients have asked me to tell you," Strawn said, "that if there is ever any way in which they can be helpful to you, you have only to say so."

I would remember that.

Chapter IV

I BEGAN TO FEEL a restlessness, a sense of having been too long in the same place. Throughout my life, it would catch up with me, this urge to see some other part of the forest. I never did anything either to cause or accelerate it; I just went on doing what I was doing. But before long there always came to me a logical, irresistible reason for taking a trip. And so it was to be this time. Meanwhile, I continued to work, teach and study.

I still had trouble making ends meet, so Dick Finnegan assigned me to cover a banquet every Saturday night, thereby assuring me of at least one square meal a week. As a bonus, I also got some valuable insights into why most banquets are a bore. There is, to begin with, a direct ratio between a speaker's oratorical ineptitude and the length of his speech. (President Hoover used to amuse himself by clocking the interval between the time a speaker reached his conclusion and the moment when, having restated it four or five times, he finally sat down.) Another speaker's sin is to read from a script. People who cannot remember what they want to say ought to send letters to the audience. The only man who ever used a manuscript with real effect was Theodore Roosevelt; he crumpled it in his fist and waved it dramatically.

So I learned some things about public speaking that not even my father could have taught me. Besides, I gained twenty pounds.

In Chicago, I had an overnight visit from Paul Chamberlin, a playboy friend from the University of Denver. He was in a wheelchair, having walked out of a party and into an open elevator shaft. Now he was on his way to convalesce in New Orleans. His visit had a great effect on me, for we fell to talking about the old days at DU, and Paul was soon regaling me with accounts of his amatory exploits. Suddenly he said, "Tommy, of all the girls we knew at DU, which one did *you* like best?"

"Fran Ryan," I replied at once. "She's pretty and has a brain and—I don't know, but of all the girls I've *ever* known, she's the one who's stuck in my mind."

"Did you ever tell her?"

"Well, no. We just saw each other at parties now and then."

"It's not too late, you know."

I suppose Paul's words watered a seed that had lain dormant in my consciousness. Now it bloomed and crowded every other thought from my mind. I put Paul on the southbound Wabash Cannonball that Sunday morning, and spent the afternoon and evening composing a letter to Fran Ryan, a girl I barely knew and had suddenly decided I wanted to marry. I didn't tell her that. I just said I wanted to come out to Denver and have a little "talk."

I hadn't the money for such a trip, but I managed to persuade some railroad advertising managers to send me on a longer one, via Denver. I reminded them that the Panama-Pacific Exposition in San Francisco was being planned, and told them I was prepared to write a series of articles about the scenic wonders people should see on the way to the fair, which would boost passenger traffic. Building passenger service was important in those days, so they sponsored me. I arranged a leave with the paper, and as soon as that semester ended at Chicago-Kent, I was off on a euphoric cloud that swept me right into Fran's living room. I wasn't there fifteen minutes before I asked her to marry me.

In the end, I took heart from the fact that she wasn't outraged, but at the time her response sounded pretty final. "Why, Tommy," she said, "what do we know about each other? When you were at DU you never even asked me out on a date."

There was no arguing with that sort of logic. But I did get her to say that she would give this outlandish idea some further thought and that I could see her again. And with that for encouragement I set out for the far West.

MY RAILROAD CREDENTIALS opened all sorts of doors. In Los Angeles the president of the chamber of commerce invited me to a luncheon because he was touting an arid little suburb called Hollywood, which, he said, would someday be the motion-picture capital of the world. In San Francisco, I made some notes about the fairgrounds. Then I went on to Seattle and met executives of the Chicago, Milwaukee and St. Paul Railroad, who organized a climbing expedition for me on Mount Rainier, a trip across the Cascades in a new electric locomotive, a tour of the Olympic Peninsula in a Stanley Steamer automobile, and a sea lion hunt in a dugout canoe with a band of Quileute Indians. Those Pacific rollers had our frail little canoe standing on end, and I've never been so seasick. The Indians kept apologizing because we hadn't sighted any sea lions, but to me our return to the beach was the high point of the trip.

Next came an unforgettable steamboat trip to Alaska, stopping at each fishing town in the Alaska panhandle until we reached Skagway. There I was introduced to Harriet Smith Pullen, a famous old Alaskan character. She sat in a carriage on the dock, a handsome, well-corseted Amazon, red hair massed atop her head, holding the reins of a team of horses and waiting to conduct her guests, including me, back to the Pullen House.

"Ma" Pullen told me her story as we sat on the memento-filled sun porch of the Pullen House one afternoon. A penniless widow, she had brought her four toddlers north from the state of Washington in 1897 and made a home for them in the midst of the ruffians who swarmed to Alaska in the gold rush. She started out by baking apple pies for the hordes of cheechakos—newcomers—bound for the Klondike over murderous White Pass. (There was an easier way for a woman to make money in a boomtown full of lonely men, but Harriet slept alone.)

Soon she had enough money to start running a packtrain up the steep switchback to the summit of White Pass. The gold seekers bought her supplies at twenty-five dollars a load, grateful not to have had to haul them up "Heartbreak Trail," and her capital mounted. But not everybody loved her. She once came upon a wild-eyed sourdough beating a horse that had a broken leg. "That animal is in misery," she said. "It can't go any farther."

As a cub reporter Thomas went to Alaska, where he met the legendary "Ma" Pullen (cameo) and "Sourdough" Jack McCord (right). Later, Dale Carnegie (far right),

"Mind your own damn business," was the reply.

She fetched out her revolver and shot the suffering horse through the head. When the man turned on her, she pointed the gun squarely between his eyes and said, "You look in a misery of sorts, too." He quickly vanished up the trail.

Eventually she saved enough to buy a big white house just off the street they called Broadway. She had a giant sign painted— PULLEN HOUSE—and for fifty years it was Alaska's most famous hotel. The likes of Jack London, Warren G. Harding and Herbert Hoover stayed there. But more important in a way were the thousands of ordinary men and women who passed through—and I was one—each of us brushed with Alaska magic by the legend known as Ma Pullen. They closed Pullen House after she died in 1947, age eighty-seven, because nobody could take her place.

After Skagway, I headed north for Dawson, in the fabled

helped LT develop a lecture on his Alaskan adventures. Then Thomas was off to cover the war in Europe. In Italy he donned skis to keep up with a crack Alpine troop.

Klondike. Until 1896, Dawson was a muskeg swamp on the east bank of the Yukon River. Two years later the gold rush was on. A hundred thousand men started for Dawson, and half actually made it. Overnight the mud flat boomed into the glittering metropolis of the North, where the sounds of revelry rang from dark to dawn; where fifty million dollars in gold was sluiced from the Klondike's storied creeks in five years; and where ten thousand people all but starved to death in one bitter winter. Then, in 1899, word came that they'd found gold in Nome, and a stampede there was on. The big mining companies moved in and huge dredges took the place of sluice boxes. But eventually even the dredges lay still, and Dawson became a ghost town of perhaps five hundred stubborn souls, the wind blowing down empty streets and rattling the loose boards on long-deserted saloons.

I RETURNED FROM Alaska determined to go back—and that's all I knew for certain about my future in my second year of law school. My job at the *Journal* provided lots of excitement, but I had that restless feeling again. I continued writing to Fran—with only tepid encouragement—and applied to the graduate college at Princeton, without much hope of being accepted.

Then the railroads and the Alaska Steamship Company sponsored a trip to Fairbanks and Nome, and early that summer I was on my way, this time with a very cumbersome camera. The voyage was enlivened by twelve young women from Vassar College, shepherded by their geology professor, who were to study the natural wonders of the North. Among them was a captivating blonde with the unlikely name of Al McIlravey, to whom I paid considerable attention. In feeble defense, I can only say that she never told me she was already engaged.

I arranged an itinerary that coincided with the route of the Vassar class, which seemed to do little studying of geology. From Skagway we crossed the St. Elias range and took a sternwheeler down the Yukon to Dawson and eventually on the Tanana River to Fairbanks.

One morning our ship was hailed from the shore by a bedraggled young man, and in true Alaskan tradition the captain pulled over to pick him up. His name was Jack McCord and, with his ragged beard and torn clothing, he looked as though he had been in a hand-to-hand go with a grizzly. He had been prospecting far up toward the Arctic Circle, and I suspect he had a gold-dust pouch on him, for "Sourdough" Jack seldom failed at anything.

Raised in the Dakotas, he had taught school in western Canada, then heard the cry of gold from Alaska and had had a hand in the epic construction of the railroad along the Copper River over the mountains to Cordova on the coast. He never smoked or drank and was one of the most powerful men I ever met. His favorite trick was to pick up a woman at a local dance-hall, sit her in the palm of one hand and muscle her straight up over his head. But Jack's real gift was promotion. He became one of Alaska's most energetic lobbyists, heading "outside" each year to talk up the opportunities in the Big Land. Irritated by Alaska's dependence on food shipped north from Seattle—at exorbitant rates—he bought an island off the Aleutians and stocked it with beef cattle.

In the 1940s, well along in years, he went to England, where he met Grace Doering, a lawyer from Cleveland, and married her. Not until statehood came was there such a hullabaloo in Alaska as the day *Life* magazine appeared with a picture of their own Sourdough Jack striding from the church, bride on arm, and wearing spats, tailcoat and a silk topper. Jack lived on until his mid-eighties and was in San Francisco when his final illness caught up with him. Somebody sent for an ambulance; when it came, Jack insisted on riding up in front with the driver.

In Fairbanks, I was detached from the Vassar students by a persistent fellow named Bobby Sheldon. Bobby planned to drive his Model T Ford over the trail to Valdez, the dogsled route over which supplies went north each winter. He had already done it once, and if he could do it again, he'd be entitled to call the trail a road. Then, if there was a road between Valdez and Fairbanks, they'd have to give a mail contract on it to the only man in town who owned an automobile—Bobby Sheldon!

Bobby pressed two improbable passengers into service: the kindly, generous Episcopal bishop of Alaska, the Right Reverend P. T. Rowe, and me. After we'd started out, Bobby announced that he was charging us *only* a hundred dollars for the trip. Years later Bobby became a member of the state legislature and one of his favorite after-dinner stories was about that epic journey. "I should have paid *them*," he'd say, laughing, "because they pushed me a lot of the way." But Bobby got the mail contract.

I went on down the Yukon and then to Nome, boarding the last steamer south before ice closed the river for the year. Also aboard—as I knew they would be—were Al McIlravey and the other Vassar women. By the second evening out, Al and I had rekindled our friendship and were up on deck watching the red sun disappear into the sea. Suddenly a United States marshal appeared, clapped a pair of handcuffs on my wrists and ordered me below. There the evening's entertainment had been laid out—a breach-of-promise trial, with me as the culprit and a young male passenger, costumed to look like a streetwalker, preferring the charges. Al McIlravey, of course, was cast as the "other woman." After some lurid testimony, I was sentenced to buy every female passenger aboard a box of candy at the first port of call.

Unfortunately the fake trial attracted the geology professor's notice to what he conceived as a genuine romance between Al and me. Knowing that she was already engaged, he sent a cable, when we stopped at Cordova, to Al's parents in Tarrytown, New York. When our steamer reached Seattle, not only were Al's parents on the dock, but so was her roiled fiancé. I was the only one who wasn't there. In Cordova someone had told me that the final salmon run of the season was about to begin, and on the spur of the moment I decided to stay behind and film it with a big Ernamann camera I had been using all through Alaska. Smartest decision I ever made.

BEFORE I LEFT Cordova, I wrote to Fran and said I would stop off to visit her as I headed east. On the way, I made a side trip to see the Grand Canyon. There I met a cowboy camed Carl, from a ranch on the Utah side of the canyon, who offered to take me across on his way home. I was full of anticipation as we started into the rocky gorge, its walls a marvelous violet color. Near the bottom, Carl showed me a rusty cable which ran across the great chasm. The early Mormons had strung it, he told me, and, in a cage suspended below, transferred themselves, their animals and their belongings from Arizona to Utah. Now the cable was so old that broken strands popped out of it.

Then Carl said, "That's how we're going across."

From his pack he produced two pairs of heavy work gloves and two lengths of wire. He threw the wires over the cable and hooked their ends under a couple of narrow boards. Then he installed himself on one, tested its balance and, almost as an afterthought, said to me, "There's nothing to it. Just grab the cable and pull yourself across on that board, hand over hand." And with the wild Colorado a white-flecked blue below—once we sagged to within thirty feet of it—I crossed the Grand Canyon.

When I finally arrived in Denver, a day behind schedule, I found Fran concerned enough to make me hopeful that I was making progress. She seemed intrigued by all I had to tell her about Alaska, and when I promised to take her there, her eyes seemed to light up. But she still had a year to finish at DU.

Encouraged, I returned to Chicago to find a letter from Princeton. I had not only been accepted, but also had been awarded a scholarship. I suspected my lawyer friend Silas Strawn of having something to do with this, for I had given him as a reference. In any event, I closed out my affairs in Chicago and headed east.

PRINCETON'S LOVELY CAMPUS wore its prestige like an invisible shield of excellence. The new graduate college building, a mile or so from the main campus, seemed in splendid isolation, as required for the most elevated intellectual pursuits. And all of us, even when dining, wore black scholastic gowns.

When I had been at the university only a few weeks, the president, John Grier Hibben, called me to his office. Would I, he asked, be willing to take over the speech department? The professor in charge was retiring soon and Dr. Hibben was prepared to offer me the job on a permanent basis. I gulped and thanked him, but told him I wasn't yet settled on a career. If he wanted me for a couple of years, I'd give the department my best.

And so I was off again on a frenetic program—teaching and study during the week, with still another job on weekends. I had been bombarding nearby colleges and clubs with a brochure about an illustrated talk on Alaska—and bookings were coming in. Soon I was earning much more from my films and talk than from teaching. Furthermore, I enjoyed it.

When the summer of 1916 arrived, I invited my mother and Pherbia to come East. Dad, a devoted Anglophile, had volunteered his services soon after war broke out in Europe, and was now on the staff of a London hospital. So I took an apartment in Princeton, where the three of us lived for a year.

Mother brought happy news. Fran had visited her in Victor, and they had taken to each other from the first. Was there a wedding in the offing? Mother inquired. "Ask the lady," I answered. But I had been asking her myself. She had won her degree and, in September, she set off to teach in a one-room schoolhouse at Jackass Ranch, near Castle Rock, south of Denver. Would she marry me in June? I wrote. Yes, she replied. I must have been an optimist, for I was broke.

Shortly after the beginning of 1917, I received an unusual speaking invitation from Franklin K. Lane, Secretary of the Interior. Lane was an ardent booster of the American West. Now, with Europe at war and closed to tourism, he decided to launch a coast-to-coast campaign promoting our national parks and scenic splendors. He had called a conference of governors, congressmen, naturalists and national park superintendents in Washington, and a western railroad executive had suggested that I represent Alaska.

I headed to New York in search of a public-speaking coach to help me shorten my talk, for my guess was that I might be introduced at the end of a long roster of speakers, when brevity would be golden. The man I found had a studio in Carnegie Hall, which was appropriate, as his name was Dale Carnegey. (Later, he changed it to Carnegie and won fame and fortune with his book *How to Win Friends and Influence Poeple*.) He helped me reshape my talk, and later we would work together.

When I reached Washington, I found Lane presiding at the conference, held at the Smithsonian Institution. During a lull I placed my card on his table, and I could tell from his expression that he thought I was a page announcing the professor's arrival. "Um—I'm Lowell Thomas," I said.

He looked again—hard. "I see. Well, you're to show some films. We don't want to darken the auditorium in midsession, so we've scheduled you last."

Finally my moment came. The other speakers had showered the audience with superlatives that had a soporific effect. Showing only my choice pictures, dwelling only on the high spots from my usual talk, I made my thirty minutes count. And when I was finished, the audience stood to applaud. Afterward, governors and senators came up to shake my hand. It was a heady moment for a young fellow. Then Franklin Lane asked me to run the tourism campaign, starting in June, and I floated back to Princeton on a cloud. Fran and I could be married.

But on my twenty-fifth birthday, April 6, the United States declared war on Germany, and Lane again summoned me to Washington. "Our national travel campaign is out for the duration," he said. "But how about going to Europe for us? Congress is appropriating all sorts of money to fight the war, but they may be slow in allocating funds to *tell* about it. Why not take a cameraman and get what you can? It might help with the war effort here at home. Could you raise enough privately to finance such a mission?"

I said I believed I could, for I remembered that Silas Strawn had said, "If there is ever any way in which they can be helpful . . ." So to Chicago I went. I sat in Strawn's oak-and-leather office and laid out Lane's proposal as forcefully as I could, adding that it would cost seventy-five thousand dollars.

After a long moment's contemplation he said, "I'll put myself down for three thousand and I'll give you a list of others to see. If you're still short, come back here."

With Strawn's name as the passkey, I got into the executive offices of Chicago's most important business firms. Not one man turned me down. Arthur Meeker, of Armour & Company, was being shaved in his private office when I was shown in. He listened; then, through the lather, he said, "Would ten thousand be helpful? We owe you at least that, young man." E. P. Ripley, the patriarchal head of the Atchison, Topeka and Santa Fe Railway, sat expressionless while I made my pitch, and then said, "I'll match the top amount on your list." And so it went with the heads of Swift, Wilson, International Harvester,

Weyerhaeuser, Quaker Oats. In two weeks I had a hundred thousand dollars.

Then I went looking for the best cameraman around. I found him in a soft-spoken veteran named Harry Chase. He was not only a crack cameraman but a mechanical marvel, and he stayed with me for ten years.

While Harry rounded up equipment, I hurried to Washington to get our credentials. Secretary Lane took the matter up with President Wilson, and within hours, while thousands scurried about the war-frenzied capital seeking this or that, I was on my way out with impressive letters addressed to all military commanders and embassy personnel.

Chapter V

F RAN AND I WERE finally married in Denver on August 4, 1917. And a few days later, along with Harry Chase and his padded trunks full of camera gear and fragile glass negatives, we sailed for France. More than a thousand soldiers and civilians were crowded aboard the *Chicago*. We came to know Mrs. Theodore Roosevelt, Jr., and Mrs. Kermit Roosevelt, TR's daughters-in-law, whose husbands were "over there." Both had joined the Red Cross, and as I watched Fran studying their crisp gray uniforms, I could tell an idea was taking shape in her mind.

When we landed at Bordeaux, we went the first evening to dine in a fine restaurant. I'd heard there was some question about French water, and being inexperienced and a trifle gauche, I put it to a gentleman at the next table. Was the water fit to drink?

He was a white-bearded patriarch, surrounded by an array of wineglasses, and was somewhat startled by my question. "I can't say," he replied. "I have nevaire tasted eet."

The following day we went on to Paris. After I installed Fran at the Regina Hotel, I went off to see General Pershing, commander in chief of the American Expeditionary Force (AEF). He had been in Europe a bare two months and obviously had other things on his mind, but my Washington letters were persuasive and I was soon ushered into his austere presence.

I have met many professional soldiers in my time, but never one who so completely looked the part as "Black Jack" Pershing. He sat stiffly behind his desk, his eyes cold and his uniform immaculate, planning strategy. Even this interruption was accepted as a duty. What, he inquired crisply, were the specifics of my mission and how could he assist me? I told him my assignment was to help bring the realities of the war home to the American people, perhaps by focusing on the experiences of a single infantryman, with films and firsthand reporting. And perhaps he could tell me something of his plans for the AEF?

His only plan, he replied, was to use the American army as the spearhead of a coordinated Allied drive. Nor did he intend, as some had suggested, to dissipate this attack force by parceling it out to every Allied commander who ran into trouble. This may have been the first public exposition of Pershing's doctrine of holding his forces intact, hotly debated later. Despite intense pressure, he relented only once. During the savage German attacks in the spring of 1918 he released his forces to Marshal Foch, the Allied commander, but got them back in time for the final counteroffensive.

At the mammoth American supply center in Tours, I interviewed Colonel Merritte W. Ireland, who would later be surgeon general of the AEF. Afterward, I asked if it wouldn't be a good idea to give commissions in the U.S. Army to American doctors who had been serving with our Allies. Yes, he replied, we are considering the idea.

"Well," I went on, pressing my luck, "may I suggest an excellent surgeon, now with the British in Italy?"

"Who is he?"

"My father. Major Harry G. Thomas."

He made no promise. But he smiled, and in a short time Dad was transferred to France as a colonel with the AEF.

After several requests, I was granted permission to visit the trenches with a staff officer. I had barely looked around before the German artillery opened up. "Your reception committee," the officer said sardonically as we crouched low in the mud.

The barrage was a heavy one, shells whining as they closed in, thunderous explosions when they burst, showering us with rocks and dirt. Twenty yards to the left, our trench disappeared under a direct hit, and from the rubble came the anguished cry, "Aid man! Aid man!" And so I came to know that this war left a man trembling in helplessness, naked to the unseen guns; that no matter how far down against the earth you pressed, there was no place to hide. When there was a lull in the barrage, my guide muttered, "Let's get out of here." I scrambled to obey.

Back in Paris, I tried to find a doughboy to film. A classmate from Chicago-Kent was at the front, so I decided he would be my man. Alas, a German shell came over with his name on it. Next I tried to film a young flier, Tommy Ward. But it turned out that we could not get our heavy gear into the air with him. After more than two months in France, we weren't getting anywhere.

Then the war in Italy came to a shattering climax. At Caporetto the Austrian army, reinforced by German divisions, launched an offensive. The Italians retreated more than seventy miles to the Piave River, north of Venice. Now the urgent question was whether the remnants, with Allied reinforcements, could stave off complete collapse. It sounded like the place for us to be.

After a contretemps in Italy over our passports, I asked AEF headquarters if they could assign us an officer able to cut through such bureaucratic vagaries. They sent us Colonel Webb Hayes. He was apparently not a vital cog in the war effort. In fact, his high rank may have had less to do with his soldierly skills than with his relationship to President Rutherford B. Hayes. Distinguished-looking and skilled in the niceties, for our purposes he was perfect. When I introduced him simply as the son of the President of the United States, it provoked looks of awe and an immediate solution to our problems.

We made our base in Venice, which was being hastily evacuated, glassworkers to Florence, laceworkers to Genoa, and so on. The American Red Cross was trying to assist the refugees, and one night, returning from a trip to the front, I found Fran in a Red Cross uniform. She had signed up and was off to Genoa in the morning. I bade her good-bye with mixed feelings: our meetings would be few and far between now, but I knew she longed to work among the bereft and uprooted victims of the war.

Harry and I went scrambling through the trenches, recording the faces of men under fire and, with the help of an Italian aide, putting together a word picture of the precarious front. The only Americans in active combat in Italy were some airmen under the command of a round little major who had left Congress to join the fighting. I made a note of his name, Fiorello La Guardia, because I had an idea I might be hearing it again. Years later, I often featured "the Little Flower," then the colorful mayor of New York, in my broadcasts.

That December we were taken to the thirteen-thousand-foot-high Alpine lair of the crack Arditi, one of the first military ski outfits, near one of the summits of Monte Rosa, on the Austrian frontier. To get there we were hauled one at a time across a gaping chasm from another summit in a hip-high basket suspended from a cable. I had had an indoctrination into this sort of thing at the Grand Canyon, but Harry Chase arrived looking as though he had been pummeled by the hammers of hell.

The Arditi were nerveless young men who climbed cliffs with knives in their teeth and went silently down the powder-snow slopes on nine-foot skis, rifles slung, and using a single pole for braking. Clad entirely in white, they simply vanished from sight in a scant two hundred yards. When would they finish their training? I asked. Arched eyebrows: their training *was* finished. Then when would they fight? A shrug: fighting could be dangerous; across the valley was an equally well trained Austrian ski troop.

The Arditi leader was a dashing young cavalry officer who was obviously chafing under these restrictions handed down by headquarters. During the day Austrian artillery would open up and we would retire to safety in galleries blasted out of the mountain wall. Later, the Italians would return the fire, but the enemy guns were equally secure. It was as though each side had developed a new secret weapon and didn't care to risk losing it in combat. Finally, Chase and I left.

By December, Venice was all but deserted, but one afternoon, in the Piazza San Marco, I saw three British officers. One seemed vaguely familiar. I walked over to say hello and realized he was the young Prince of Wales, sent to Italy to shore up morale. When he heard I had just returned from the front, he questioned me; he had not been allowed up front for fear he might be captured. Harry photographed us in earnest conversation against the background of the wintry and desolate piazza.

Late one day we stopped at the cathedral, where military bulletins were posted. A dispatch noted that General Sir Edmund Allenby had been named commander in chief of the British army in Egypt. Allenby had fought brilliantly in France, but his efforts to introduce mobility and surprise on that static front had not endeared him to the orthodox general staff. That the generals were willing to entrust the Near East command to him seemed to herald dramatic doings there, and I decided it was where I wanted to be. I sent off a long cable to the Foreign Office in London, quoting in full my impressive letters from Washington and pointing out that, while the war in Europe was being thoroughly covered, the world knew little about the British campaign against the Turks.

I was in Genoa, spending Christmas with Fran, when a message from the British ambassador to Italy, Sir James Rennell Rodd, asked me to come to see him in Rome. Kissing my bride good-bye, I took the next train south. Later I learned that the sheer length of my cable had caught the attention of John Buchan, director of information. Author of *The Thirty-nine Steps* and other best sellers, he would end a distinguished career as Lord Tweedsmuir, governor-general of Canada.

His message to Rodd had been terse: "Do everything possible to help this young man." By the time Chase and I arrived in Rome, the ambassador had arranged for a converted destroyer to speed us across the Mediterranean to Egypt. And so I was off on the most profoundly affecting experience of my life.

CAIRO, THE LARGEST city in Africa, was a bedlam of activity as thousands of British, French and colonial troops thronged the streets. General Allenby, we learned, was somewhere in the Sinai Desert with his army, but a whirlwind appearance he had made in Cairo had sent morale soaring. Seeing numbers of British officers lounging in the great hotels, he replied to their salutes with a crisp, "Stand by for orders to leave for the front." And off they went.

THE FITZGERALDS AND THE KENNEDYS

by Doris Kearns Goodwin

They were two families with a common dream. And by their drive and charm and sheer force of will, they made that dream come true.

Rising from the Irish slums of Boston, the Fitzgeralds and the Kennedys reached the pinnacle of American life in just three generations. Here a noted historian takes a new look at the families—at their great achievements, their noisy scandals, and their heart-rending sorrows. There is the rise and fall of John "Honey Fitz" Fitzgerald, the colorful mayor of Boston; the wooing of the mayor's spirited daughter Rose by the ambitious young Joseph Kennedy; Joe's shady business deals, and the grooming of his son Jack for the presidency. A vibrant telling of a classic story, in all its triumph and tragedy.

Both the Fitzgeralds and the Kennedys seemed to live their lives with an uncommon intensity. . . . Striking against the existing order of things in pursuit of their ambitions and their passions, they achieved more than they had ever dreamed, lending a magic to their family story that no tale of ordinary life could possibly rival. But the very nature of their search was for success of such towering proportions that, as history records, a terrible price was paid.

—from The Fitzgeralds and the Kennedys

A PILLAR OF IRON
by Taylor Caldwell

A *Pillar of Iron* takes us back to the days of ancient Rome, to the turbulent days of Caesar, Brutus, and Mark Antony. It is a majestic story, of the great Roman democracy slipping inexorably into decline. The villains are many, but the hero is Marcus Tullius Cicero, a poet, a patriot, a brilliant lawyer, fighting to save a nation on trial for its life.

Based on prodigious research, Taylor Caldwell's book is an historical work in novel form, and it captures in extravagant color the life and times of one of the greatest Romans of them all.

BEETHOVEN
by Alan Pryce-Jones

Beethoven was only thirty-two in the year 1802, but every sign of youth had fled him. A love affair had gone wrong. Growing deafness threatened to end his career as a pianist. A man of naturally somber moods, Beethoven now turned churlish, even savage. To his brothers he lamented, "O you know not what a humiliation, when anyone standing beside me could hear at a distance . . . a shepherd singing and I could not distinguish a sound!"

Beethoven withdrew into his music and made the fateful transition from performer to composer. And if ever a man deserved the name of hero, it is Beethoven at the moment when— poor, ill, and unhappy in love—he went on to create the mighty music for which he is revered the world over.

GOOD EVENING EVERYBODY
From Cripple Creek to Samarkand
by Lowell Thomas

With an unquenchable curiosity, Lowell Thomas followed wherever a good story led him—from his home in Cripple Creek, Colorado, to the Silk Road of Samarkand. As world events unfolded, he was always in the thick of things, his daring and energy helping him uncover stories others missed. And so his autobiography, illustrated here in the richest detail, has everything—adventure and romance, comedy and drama and, above all, excitement. Novelist Faith Baldwin said, in reviewing Thomas's life story, "I can put it all in just three words: glamour, glory and guts."

Late in October, Allenby had struck Beersheba, at the southern end of the Turkish defense line. The Turks reeled back, with no time to destroy the town's wells, assuring Allenby of vital water for his desert campaign. Then, turning north, Allenby had rolled up the Turkish line, taking Gaza and Jaffa in November and Jerusalem in December. It seemed he had a chance to drive Turkey out of the war.

While Harry and I waited in Cairo for permission to move up to the battlefront, weeks passed. A minor battle royal, I learned later, had resulted from our request to be allowed to cross the Sinai. Allenby, known as "The Bull"—it was said that you could hear his roar all the way from Dan to Beersheba—had been incensed to learn that an American observer and his photographer had been sent to Egypt. He cabled, demanding to know who was running the war. If it got out that members of the press were joining his army, every state and sect in the West would want to be present at the liberation of the Holy Land. He was in no position to accommodate a small army of newsmen and religious zealots. Buchan cabled back that civilization deserved to have the details of the general's brilliant campaign, as there was no good news from France. And the Foreign Office would not send any more "observers" without Allenby's approval.

Meanwhile, I questioned those who had been to the front. A few mentioned a mysterious young Englishman who had gone into the desert and was leading Bedouin tribesmen against the Turks. When I pressed for more information, that was all anyone in Cairo seemed to know.

I also wangled my first airplane ride. I have probably lived through more great technical and scientific advances than have occurred in all the rest of recorded history, yet no landmark in my life has seemed so remarkable as the moment when a Breguet biplane lifted free of the earth and I realized I was flying.

The headquarters of the Royal Flying Corps was at Heliopolis, a few miles from Cairo. An ancient seat of learning, where Moses had been a student, it now echoed to the impudent roar of frail, fabric-covered, open-cockpit planes. My South African pilot put his Breguet through every acrobatic maneuver he knew. I loved every second of it—looking at the pyramids upside down as we looped over them again and again, seeing a whirling Sphinx rush up at my face as we spun down in a whirling tailspin.

"Are you all right?" the pilot asked after we'd landed.

"Yes," I replied at once. "When can I go up again?"

A few days later I went aloft again. I flew in one plane, with Harry and his motion-picture camera in the cockpit of another, and we took the first pictures of the Suez Canal ever made from the air. When we returned to Cairo, we found that our clearance from Allenby had arrived. Harry and our equipment would travel to Jerusalem via the railroad between Sinai and Palestine—The Milk and Honey Express it was called—but I was to be *flown* there!

My pilot was Major A. J. Evans, an engaging young man with a bent for adventure. We flew over the Suez Canal and then started across the Sinai Desert. There, stretched out below us, was a land where men had fought and died throughout the ages. It was here that Moses received the Ten Commandments; here that the children of Israel wandered for forty years before they reached the Promised Land. With a swing out over the Dead Sea, we circled over Jerusalem and landed in a meadow. We taxied over the very plain where Richard the Lion-Hearted had camped during the Third Crusade, longing for the Holy City he would never enter. And so between morning and noon, three thousand years of human history had flashed beneath our wings.

In Jerusalem, I learned that Allenby's force had been depleted by a call for manpower from the Western Front. His spring offensive was off, but he was hoping to reach Damascus by summer. He was now in his field headquarters.

When Harry arrived, we photographed the bleak hill country and ancient towns, now swarming with British and Australian cavalry, Indian lancers and camel corps from Rajputana. Jerusalem had been in Moslem hands for a thousand years. Allenby, having outflanked the Turkish position, had surrounded the city and marched in without firing a shot—which was as he had planned it, for he had a horror of damaging any of the holy places. General Otto Liman von Sanders, the German com-

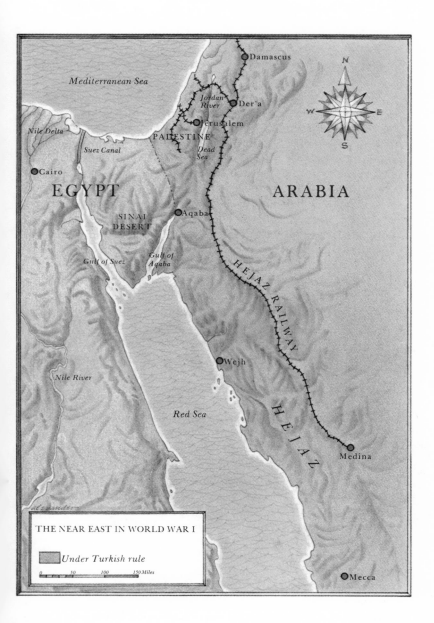

THE NEAR EAST IN WORLD WAR I

Under Turkish rule

0   50   100   150 Miles

mander of the Turkish force, had been awakened to be informed that British cavalry had enveloped the city. He fled in his pajamas.

AGAIN I HEARD rumors of that shadowy Englishman among the desert tribes. The story was that his Bedouins were harassing the enemy behind the lines and that the Turks had put a price of fifty thousand pounds on his head. I asked nearly everyone I encountered about him, but learned little.

One day as I walked alone in Jerusalem's Old City, fascinated by the swirl of faces and exotic dress, a group of Arabs approached, their half-hidden faces swarthy and bearded. All but one. That one man was smaller, clean-shaven; though he was sunburned, his eyes were a startling blue. And he wore the short curved sword of a prince of Mecca. As they moved down the street, I could see that the others deferred to him.

A blue-eyed Arab? Perhaps he was a Circassian, one of the storied people from the Caucasus Mountains who had abandoned Christianity for Islam more than two centuries ago. One of their early leaders was Saladin, who led the armies that threw back the Crusaders. I felt sure there was a story in this mysterious figure. I went to the military governor, Sir Ronald Storrs, and told him about my encounter. Was the blue-eyed Arab, by any chance, the desert fighter I'd been hearing about? Somehow I wasn't surprised when, without a word, Storrs opened a door, and there, sitting in the adjoining office and looking at us quizzically, was my blue-eyed Arab, still dressed as a Bedouin. Sir Ronald said, "I want you to meet the uncrowned king of Arabia."

I spent only a short time with Thomas Edward Lawrence that first day, and I found him reluctant to talk about himself or the desert campaign. He kept looking at Storrs, as though begging to be rescued from this American. Casting about for something—anything!—to say, I mumbled a few words about my enchantment with the antiquities of the Holy Land. Instantly I was tuned in to an entirely different personality. For Lawrence, an archaeologist, had originally come to study the crusader castles. Now, his blue eyes shining, he spoke eloquently of his explorations into the past.

We arranged to meet again the next day. When he was gone,

Sir Ronald told me that not only had Lawrence and he been together at Oxford, but in 1916 both had been on a mission to Hejaz [later a part of Saudi Arabia] that had persuaded the Arabs to support the British in the Near East. The two were among a tiny minority of British officials who believed in an enlightened future for the Arabs. Lawrence had been rejected for military service, but now, not quite thirty years old, he was the legendary leader of the Bedouin revolt against the Turks. He had become, quite simply, Lawrence of Arabia. Not long before, he had been captured by the Turks in Der'a and before escaping had undergone a gruesome experience, about which Sir Ronald would say no more.

Recently, Allenby had called him in from the desert. Wounded in each of his last five battles, exhausted, Lawrence had returned to headquarters convinced that he had made a mess of things, and begging Allenby to find him some smaller part elsewhere.

"Will Allenby let him go?" I asked Storrs.

"Impossible. Lawrence is an inspired tactician and the only man we have to whom the Arabs will listen. He must go back."

When he does, I decided, Chase and I would join him. Next day Lawrence told me ruefully that he was ordered to return to the desert. When I told him I wanted to report on the Arab effort, he said he had no objection. But he had to return through the Turkish lines and it was not feasible for us to attempt this.

After Lawrence left, Harry and I went to the Plain of Esdraelon, where the British correspondents—two reporters, a photographer and an artist—were encamped. Four men to cover a war involving hundreds of thousands of troops! But it was their attitude that made it clear I virtually had the field to myself. Lawrence and his Arab irregulars were just a diversion, they said. No one would ever hear of him again.

Had they tried to get his story?

What! Travel halfway across the Arabian desert to see a bunch of Bedouins on camelback?

The exception in this fog of indifference was a gentle, whimsical Scot, James McBey, Allenby's official artist. Our tent and the sand outside were strewn with his sketches. If I had only picked up a few! McBey quickly became known as one of the greatest etchers of our time.

I might have never gotten acquainted with Allenby if it hadn't been for King George V's uncle, the Duke of Connaught, who had come to Palestine to give out decorations to Allenby's army. When the duke arrived at the Plain of Esdraelon via the Milk and Honey Express and emerged on the train platform, he faced thousands of Allenby's troops, all wearing helmets.

But he saw a blot on the landscape. It was my American campaign hat, the same as those worn by the Royal Canadian Mounted Police. The duke had served in Canada as governor-general. He asked Allenby who I was, and this reminded the C in C of me. A few days later Allenby invited me for luncheon.

When I arrived, I was surprised to find I was to be alone with the duke and Allenby. Here was my chance! I said I'd been disappointed not to accompany Lawrence back to Arabia. Allenby replied that the British had tried to keep Lawrence's role a secret. They hoped to have the revolt in the desert appear strictly an Arab affair, so that men of Arab blood would desert from the Turkish army. Now that the plan had succeeded, Lawrence's accomplishments could be revealed, and Harry and I could join him.

When I told Allenby we wanted pictures of him and his staff, he told me to bring Chase the next day to the Augusta Victoria Stiftung, a hospice and sanatorium built by the Germans, its high tower dominating the Mount of Olives. We found Allenby and some of his staff officers waiting for us on the tower. We talked briefly about his campaign, but he seemed totally taken up with Jerusalem's history and its conquerors and defenders.

For the Jews, Allenby said, the Wailing Wall, all that remains of King Solomon's Temple, marks Jerusalem as the heart of their homeland. For Christians this is the City of God, for here Christ was crucified and buried. And for Moslems the Dome of the Rock, whence Mohammed is said to have ascended to heaven, makes Jerusalem holy. Allenby had received a delegation of quarreling Greek Orthodox monks, Roman Catholics, Copts and Nestorians, each sect convinced it should control the Shrine of the Holy Sepulchre. Each beseeched Allenby's support. But he was a solider, not a magistrate. He said to them, "Who am I to set the world aright?" Peace would come to the Holy Land, he added, not by fiat, but only when men began to live their religious faith.

Before heading back to Egypt, Harry and I had our first home-cooked meal of the war, in the American colony in Jerusalem. Bertha Vester, then about forty, was a striking blonde, utterly lovely and with an abiding composure. Her husband ran a mercantile establishment just inside the Jaffa Gate, and she directed the social services the American colony provided to Jerusalem's sick and poor. Bertha Vester told us her story.

Her father, Horace Spafford, had been a prominent Chicago attorney. Then tragedy: his wife and four daughters aboard a steamer that went down in mid-Atlantic, the mother rescued but the children drowned; a year later, an infant son dead of scarlet fever. To the bereft parents, life seemed to mock them for their concern with material things. In 1881, three years after Bertha was born, they gave up everything and moved to the Holy Land, to live close to the presence and spirit of the Saviour. Soon a few friends followed, settling in what came to be called the American colony. Then others joined them, fundamentalist Protestants, some Swedes, perhaps fifty in all, all convinced that God's love was given most freely to those who served their fellowmen.

Bertha moved spontaneously into a lifetime of benevolence. She was to live eighty-seven years in Jerusalem, through many upheavals that racked history's most tormented land. She came to know kings, presidents, princes and uncounted thousands of Moslems, Jews and Christians, who called her *Ommona*—Mother of us all. The enduring capstone of her life is the clinic she established. Its beginnings go back to Christmas Eve, 1925.

On her way to lead the carol singing in a field outside Bethlehem, Bertha met an Arab whose sick wife had just been turned away from the general hospital. The reason? It was the Christians' holiday. The woman slumped weakly on the back of a donkey. The man, walking alongside, carried an infant in a bundle of rags. The mocking analogy to that holy night of two thousand years before struck Mrs. Vester like a blow to the heart. She arranged to have the woman admitted to the hospital, but on Christmas morning the man stood sadly at her gate; his wife had died. Now, he said, holding forth a ragged bundle, unless someone took his baby, it, too, would die, for he could not care for the boy in the cave that was his only home.

"I will take him," Bertha Vester said. That moment began a career of many decades, caring for more than a million mothers and children. Eventually, I was to succeed Dr. and Mrs. Norman Vincent Peale as president of the charity association Mrs. Vester had established. Bertha Vester died in 1968 at the age of ninety. I am proud to have been her friend.

Chapter VI

LAWRENCE OF ARABIA was born in Wales in August 1888. His parents were an Irish baronet, Sir Thomas Robert Chapman, and a talented Scottish governess, Sara Maden. Sir Thomas had abandoned his wife and children to run off with the governess, and the two lived together as Mr. and Mrs. Lawrence. They had five sons, of whom Thomas Edward ("Ned") was the second.

Amateur analysts have made much of Lawrence's illegitimacy, ascribing to it a warping of his psyche. They have conjured up a character of dark introspection, a man who masked his feelings of inferiority by plunging himself into dangerous situations and then, having won worldwide fame, by renouncing the honors and the fortune offered him. How else did it happen, they ask, that he had no interest in women? Why, after the war, did he twice enlist in the military under assumed names? Why did he appear to court death so assiduously? Why, indeed? I don't think anyone knows.

Lawrence was, above all, possessed of a clear and penetrating intellect. At Oxford he took first-class history honors. Then, fascinated with the Near East, he wandered there for five years before the war, part of the time excavating sites of ancient civilizations. He was a natural for British intelligence, and early in 1914 he was reporting to the War Office on Turkish troop dispositions along the Egyptian border. Once the fighting began, he was posted to Cairo. In November 1916, after Husein ibn-Ali, emir of Mecca, led an Arab revolt against four hundred years of Turkish rule and proclaimed himself king of Hejaz, Lawrence set off on his singular desert mission. Thereafter he dressed like the Arabs, shared their food and their tents. Almost his sole contacts with British officialdom were requests for money and ordnance for his Bedouin warriors.

Officially, Lawrence was attached to the army of Faisal, ablest of Husein's sons, as political and liaison officer. In fact, he was the leader and inspiration of the rebellion. He harried the enemy where they least expected him to appear, then vanished into the desert. His strategy violated textbook precepts, but worked perfectly for undisciplined irregulars operating in a trackless desert. He cut railroad lines, blew up bridges and struck down strongholds the enemy considered impregnable. His raids diverted thirty thousand Turkish troops which could otherwise have been thrown into the fight against Allenby. And now, as Harry and I journeyed west, south, east and then north to join him, he was poised for the final blows.

Our ultimate destination lay little more than a hundred and fifty miles south of Jerusalem, but to get around the Turkish line, as well as to preserve the secrecy of Lawrence's whereabouts—Palestine swarmed with spies for both sides—we were obliged to travel a devious route of nearly three thousand miles. First we took the Milk and Honey Express back to Cairo. Then we boarded a paddle-wheeler for the long journey up the Nile. Some days later, at Wadi Halfa, we transferred to a train to continue our journey south to Khartoum.

In Khartoum, Harry and I dined with the head of British intelligence. Suddenly his face tightened and he said, "I don't mean to rush you, but do you see what is coming in the distance?"

The air was ominously still. The sky remained cloudless, but to the east we saw what appeared to be a mountain range moving toward us. It was a *haboob*, our host hastily explained, a fierce storm that whips up sheets of sand, blinding and choking anyone caught abroad. Probably we had just enough time to get back to our hotel.

We said a quick good-bye and ran for our donkeys. Although the hotel was only half a mile away, the black wall was on us before we got there. We urged our little mounts forward, but by the time we arrived I had a vivid idea of what it must be like to get caught out in the desert by such a storm. Inside, with windows closed tight, the heat was stifling, and sand sifted through every crack and crevice, coating the beds and floors, turning our eyes red and our mouths gritty. It lasted for hours. I have lived through blizzards, cyclones and monsoons, but none as unforgettable as that Khartoum *haboob*.

From the Nile we crossed the Nubian Desert by train to Port Sudan on the Red Sea, and then boarded a much torpedoed wreck of a steamer bound for the Arabian coast. Our shipmates included several hundred sheep, horses and mules, a platoon of Gordon Highlanders and some Turkish deserters. We bunked on deck with the animals. Somewhat testy in these odd surroundings, they didn't sleep much. Neither did we.

In Cairo we had stocked up on chocolate bars against the possibility of being confronted with a steady diet of dried dates and fried locusts. And on the advice of a colonel—"If you offer Bedouins a gasper, they'll love you; if you don't they might go through your pockets while you're still wearing them"—we had also stuffed our bags with cigarettes. But the temperature shot straight up and one hungry afternoon I opened my kit to find a fluid mass of chocolate, notebooks, bullets and tobacco.

At the Gulf of Aqaba we transferred to a big barge, with the livestock, for the trip to the beach. If we had any complaints about the crowded quarters, we kept them to ourselves after one of the mules fell overboard and was torn to pieces by sharks. We heard the crackle of rifle fire on land, but as we scraped ashore we saw, to our relief, that a thousand Bedouins were blazing away at the sky, in exuberance over our arrival.

They were, in fact, part of Lawrence's army. They led us to a nearby tent, and soon Lawrence himself, just back from a raid, appeared. He seemed glad to see us. He introduced us to Husein's son Faisal, and to the handful of British officers who were fighting the lonely desert war with him. And before many days had passed, we were mounted on camels and off to the interior to see the action. There, standing on a mountaintop with Lawrence and Faisal, we watched the bombardment of Ma'an, a station on the Hejaz Railway north of Medina.

Though Lawrence was reluctant to talk about himself, I pieced together an account of his astonishing desert campaign from his comrades-in-arms. In March 1917 he had made a six-day camel ride across the desert to the camp of Abdullah, Faisal's older brother, carrying with him a plan of attack devised at British headquarters. Stricken with dysentery, burning with fever, Lawrence feared at every stop that he would fall into the hands of well-meaning tribesmen whose treatment for every ill was to burn holes in the patient's body at the sites where they believed the malady lurked.

As it turned out, his sickness changed the course of the war in the Near East. Until then, Lawrence had been too caught up in the fighting to see with clarity the complex nature of the Arab campaign. In Abdullah's camp he collapsed and for ten days lay sick and shivering, sometimes delirious, but finally coming to understand that the desert was an ally, and that the very massiveness of the Turkish army could be its undoing.

Until then the recapture of Medina, the second holiest city in Arabia, had been an obsession with the Arabs and the British. To the Arabs, who had already taken Mecca, it was an emotional issue, and to the British, schooled in orthodox war—big battles for big objectives—Medina seemed the biggest prize around.

"One afternoon," Lawrence wrote in his account of the desert war, *Seven Pillars of Wisdom*, "I woke from a hot sleep, running with sweat and pricking with flies, and wondered what on earth was the good of Medina to us?" The city did not threaten the Arabs nor was it situated to serve as a base. In fact, it was contributing most to the Arab-Allied cause just as it was—a remote enclave tying down a Turkish garrison that required huge quantities of supplies. And even if the Turks came to recognize Medina as a liability, pride would keep them from abandoning it. Why should the Arabs do their work for them?

Now Lawrence's agile mind leaped ahead to further heretical questions. Why should desert tribes challenge a numerically superior Turkish force led by war-wise officers? "Battles in Arabia were a mistake," wrote Lawrence. "Our cards were speed and time, not hitting power."

And Lawrence's trump card was thousands of square miles of desert terrain that the Arabs knew intimately. Instead of pitched battles, he planned a hit-and-run campaign "to destroy, not the Turk's army, but his matériel." Lawrence conceived detailed tactics, so carefully reasoned that they never had to be revised. When the war ended, the defeated Turks were still in Medina, and Medina had remained a liability to them to the last.

THE HEJAZ RAILWAY, built by Sultan Abdul-Hamid II as a monument to Moslem power, was known as the Pilgrim Railway for the great number of the faithful it carried to Mecca and Medina. It also served for the swift transport of Turkish troops. Now it bore a steady stream of soldiers and supplies for Medina. Lawrence could have put it permanently out of commission, but he did not want to dishearten the Turks and have them quit Medina; he only wanted to keep them off-balance. And of course he could replenish his own stores of food, weapons and ammunition with the booty taken from derailed trains.

The target of his first raid was the railway station at Aba el Naam, within a hundred miles of Medina. While his artillery opened fire from the hills, destroying the station and distracting the Turkish garrison, Lawrence planted explosive charges—what he called his "tulips"—under the tracks. A train touched off the charge and traffic was blocked for three days. The raiders also inflicted nearly a hundred casualties on the Turks and

During World War I, T. E. Lawrence (left), a scholar turned soldier, led the Arab revolt against the Turks. Thomas was the only reporter to follow this mysterious young

took thirty prisoners, at the cost of one man slightly wounded.

In the months that followed, travel along the Hejaz line became a terror, and people paid up to five times their normal value for seats in the rear carriages. Lawrence slipped into Damascus and posted a notice that Arabs would use the railroad at their peril. Civilian traffic all but stopped. Engineers went on strike. So much rolling stock had been destroyed that the Turks could not have evacuated Medina if they had wanted to. And supplies for their Jerusalem garrison were badly pinched, just as the British began their march on the Holy City.

By the time Harry Chase and I came to Arabia, Lawrence was calculating his explosions with such devastating acuity that if a train were carrying foodstuffs and ammunition—which of course he spied out in advance—he could make the locomotives buckle so that the boxcars spilled their contents onto the right-of-way for the Arabs to scoop up. And so meticulously did he

Englishman into the desert. There LT rode an armored car through the Dead Sea valley and conferred (right) with General Allenby, the British commander.

plan the raids that if Turkish guards came out of the train fighting, they found themselves raked by strategically placed machine guns.

Lawrence usually set the charges himself. It was characteristic of him to choose the most dangerous assignment; but he was also concerned that if his Arab friends became familiar with the use of high explosives, they would blow up trains for fun and profit long after the war was over. He was always close by when the targeted train hove into view, staff in hand, looking very much like a Bedouin shepherd. The Turks began shooting even at innocent-looking shepherds, and Lawrence was hit several times.

Late in the campaign Lawrence touched off his charge under an unusually long train. As it careened off the tracks, more than a thousand soldiers poured out, firing wildly—the train was carrying the Turkish commander in chief. Lawrence, who had only sixty men hidden in the hills, ran for his life, bullets kicking up the sand at his heels. But as he ran he counted his steps and, reaching his machine-gun positions, he gave the gunners the precise range. They killed a hundred and twenty-five Turks, and the little Arab band got away safely.

Liddell Hart, a foremost military expert, was particularly struck by Lawrence's capture of the port of Aqaba. Held by the Turks, Aqaba commanded the Red Sea approach to both Palestine and northern Arabia. It could provide a splendid base to support a British drive east from Egypt. But taking it would not be easy, for Turkish guns bristled along an impregnable shoreline to the south and west; and to the north and east King Solomon's mountains provided a natural defense.

Lawrence and his handful of warriors set out on camelback from Wejh, six hundred miles to the south, swung across the desert in a great counterclockwise arc, and two months later stood poised to strike from the heights behind the town. The journey had been an incredible odyssey; his ragged band had been reduced to eating their camels. But Lawrence had gathered new adherents, retaking Arab villages long dominated by the Turks. And when at last they swept down into Aqaba—sheikhs, tribesmen, nomads—the Turks and their German commanders were stupefied with surprise and overwhelmed.

LAWRENCE WAS OFTEN called on by his followers to adjudicate disputes. With antagonistic tribes suddenly thrown together against the common enemy, there were assaults, thefts, arguments over loot—even cases of bewitchment, which Lawrence resolved by counterbewitching the accused. But killing left Lawrence shaken and torn, though he never spoke of these feelings, as he avoided talk of all things that touched him most deeply.

One time murder had been done. A Moroccan, Hamed, had shot one of the Ageyl tribe, and the dead man's relatives and friends demanded "blood for blood." Lawrence wrote:

> There were other Moroccans in our army; and to let the Ageyl kill one in feud meant reprisals by which our unity would have been endangered. It must be a formal execution, and at last, desperately, I told Hamed that he must die for punishment, and laid the burden for his killing on myself . . . no revenge [for it] could lie against my followers; for I was a stranger and kinless.

Lawrence made the man enter a dank, narrow gully. He gave Hamed a moment's respite, then shot him through the chest. The bullet knocked him down, but it did not kill him. Lawrence shot again, but was so undone that he managed only to hit the man's wrist. Finally he put his .45 under the Moroccan's jaw and fired. He called the Ageyl and they buried the body, but he did not sleep that night, and long before dawn, burning to be gone from that place, he woke the men and bade them load up. In his agony of the heart, he had to be lifted into the saddle.

Not long before I met him, Lawrence had undergone his most lacerating experience. He had slipped into the key railroad junction, Der'a, as a spy, and almost at once was seized by the Turks. They did not doubt his story that he was a Circassian; their mission was to provide a comely young man for the perverted pleasure of the bey, the governor of the province.

That night, soon after dark, Lawrence was taken to the bey's quarters and, in a dimly lighted room, thrust toward a bed where a squat, sweating man in a nightgown sat trembling with passion. Lawrence endured the frantic pawing as long as he could, then thrust his knee hard into the man's groin. Lawrence was whipped bloody and left, barely conscious, in a wooden shed. He escaped, but those hours left harrowing scars on his mind and body. In Der'a, he wrote, "the citadel of my integrity had been irrevocably lost."

"WHAT WAS LAWRENCE *really* like?" People continued to ask me the question long after the war was over. It was a mark of Lawrence's lasting appeal. He was the giant of a particular time and place, perhaps the last of his kind, and the world could not seem to forget him.

But my answer to the question was: I don't know. For the question implies that one can have some magical insight into the soul and spirit of another man, and I don't think this is possible. Certainly, he had a tremendous personal effect on me. If I had thought of the desert before, it had been as something forbidding, to be avoided or endured. And my first experiences with it reinforced this. For there before me stretched an immense and arid land of rock and shifting sand; and when you reached the top of one ridge, there ahead was another, and then another—endless, barren, all the way to some distant horizon.

Lawrence finally enabled me to see the desert through Arab eyes: dangerous to any who challenged it in ignorance, but a refuge to those who respected its awesome breadth, and a source of nourishment to those who knew its oases and the wadis that in season rushed with fresh water. The noted Arabist, Gertrude Bell, wrote that the Arabs know "how to rejoice in the great spaces and how to honour the rush of the storm."

My book, *With Lawrence in Arabia*, went into more than a hundred printings. But Lawrence changed my life in ways that had nothing to do with fame or fortune. With him I was in the presence of greatness. I remain eternally thankful.

Lawrence turned aside a promotion to general's rank, had friends sidetrack a recommendation that he be awarded the Victoria Cross, and declined a knighthood. When I asked him why, he laughed and replied that if he were knighted his tailor would double his bills. "I have enough trouble paying them as it is."

During the long marches, or sitting by his tent as day faded, his exhilarating talk seemed to separate us from the world. He was gloomy about the Arabs' chances of winning nationhood and independence. Even as Lawrence led them in the struggle against the Turks, he knew in his heart that the old bondage would only be replaced by a new one. The French were determined to have Syria; the British wanted Mesopotamia. Self-interest had led nations to secret agreements; how were commitments of honor to the Arabs to be redeemed?

In the end, when the promises had been broken, when he came face-to-face with his personal tragedy—that he had been used as the instrument of an Allied policy inimical to the hopes of his friends and followers—he made a final effort to win public opinion to the side of simple justice. In a poignant letter to *The Times* of London he wrote:

> The Arabs . . . did not risk their lives in battle to change masters, to become British subjects or French citizens. . . . Whether they are fit for independence or not remains to be tried. Merit is no qualification for freedom. . . . Freedom is enjoyed when you are so well armed, or so turbulent, or inhabit a country so thorny that the expense of your neighbor's occupying you is greater than the profit.

So he foresaw the chaotic course of events in the area now called the Middle East. The truth of his judgment would be confirmed by history, but not until long after he was dead.

THE WAR IN THE desert now began moving swiftly toward its end. All during the spring and summer of 1918 Allenby rebuilt his depleted army until he had a striking force of nearly a hundred thousand. With several incursions across the Jordan, he persuaded the German general Liman von Sanders that the main British thrust would be aimed at the Jordan Valley, and Lawrence's raids strengthened this belief. Liman von Sanders massed almost half his troops on his inland flank, while Allenby secretly prepared to strike along the coast.

This plan depended on the element of surprise and was known to only four people. Lawrence was one. He was to cut the three rail lines radiating from Der'a, isolating its defenders.

Lawrence struck on September 17. Like maddening wraiths, his little band appeared south, north and west of Der'a, and each time, they left a railroad in shambles. Two days later Allenby attacked. His infantry punched a hole in the Turkish line and the cavalry poured through. The Turks scrambled toward Damascus, harassed by British aircraft and Lawrence's Arabs. Together the British and Bedouins marched into Damascus on October 2, and on the thirtieth the Turkish government requested an armistice.

Lawrence stayed in Damascus only four days, its virtual ruler until Allenby's arrival. Then he begged the commander in chief to let him go, to give the Arabs a chance without him. In the end, Allenby agreed—"and then at once," Lawrence wrote, "I knew how much I was sorry." By November 11, 1918, the day the armistice was signed, he was back in England. Knowing he would go, I, too, returned to Europe.

Chapter VII

Paris in November—biting wind and rain—was a raw contrast to the desert heat. One evening, returning to my hotel room after a long day, I felt the stairway moving under my feet, like some surreal escalator, and I passed out. A colleague, Webb Waldron, then European editor of *Collier's Weekly*, caught me by the lapels of my trench coat and gently lowered me to the steps. When I came to, some forty hours later, I was in the American Hospital. That winter an influenza epidemic would sweep over Europe, taking millions of lives.

I had returned from Palestine via Genoa, to collect my bride. But Fran, having completed her Red Cross work and having heard nothing from me during my weeks in the desert, had returned to Denver. I had written her at length, and then had gone to France. There, on November 11, in a railroad car pulled into a woodland siding at Compiègne, German representatives signed the articles of surrender.

I had sent Harry Chase back to the States to begin processing our film, but I was not yet ready to go home. Wild rumors were seeping out of Germany, its borders sealed by order of the Allied supreme commander, Marshal Foch. Kaiser Wilhelm II had fled, and there was a crucial struggle going on inside the beaten land. That had to be a story!

One evening, when Webb Waldron came to the hospital to

see me, I put it to him: Why didn't we go to Germany? Webb said the German border was closed tight. Foch didn't want any softhearted stories out of Germany to rouse a gullible public in Britain and the United States, since the French intended to press for a rigorous peace treaty. Some correspondents had gotten to Koblenz, but our military people had hustled them back to France. But there had to be a place along the Rhine where two enterprising reporters could cross into Germany, I said.

Webb humored his sick friend. He said, "Let's see how long it takes you to get well, LT. That's the important thing."

It was all the spur I needed. Two days later I was up and about, and soon Webb and I were on a train bound for Alsace, the Rhine province newly retaken from the Germans.

We arrived in Strasbourg, the provincial capital, with our hopes high. But the Rhine bridge was heavily guarded and Germany, so close we could see children playing on the far bank, remained beyond our reach. We pondered the possibility of a night swim, but the river looked so swift and cold that we continued south. In Mulhouse, we sat in a café bemoaning our luck—we had not found a single unguarded crossing—and wondering what to try next. Confident that no one could understand us, we made no effort to keep our voices down. Suddenly a French soldier, who had seemed to be devoting all his attention to a bottle of white wine, brought his bottle over to our table and, in impeccable New Yorkese, said, "Sounds like you got a problem."

We parried. It was heartening to hear an American voice, but how could we be sure he was as sympathetic as he sounded? After another glass of white wine, he told us he was an ambulance driver serving with a French unit. His name was Tony, he came from Staten Island and he was on a dull assignment, driving along the frontier and picking up prisoners of war, now streaming out of German prison camps. What were we up to?

Webb and I decided to tell him; maybe he could be our ticket into Germany. We were reporters, Webb said, trying to get the straight story of what was happening inside Germany, but kept out by idiotic red tape. If we hid in his ambulance . . . ?

He took another swallow. "Let's see your map."

Not only was he willing to help, but he provided us with a

plan. It was impossible to cross the Rhine between France and Germany; but a few miles to the south, both banks of the river were within Swiss territory. If we could get into Switzerland, all we'd have to do would be to cross one of the bridges in Basel.

We ate a hearty meal, then walked through empty streets to his ambulance. He had us stretch out in the back and buried us under a pile of blankets. Then we felt the creaky vehicle lurch forward. It was stopped twice by road patrols. We heard Tony's laborious French—*"Je retourne à l'hôpital"*—and they passed us. Shortly before two a.m. he stopped again. "The Swiss border's right here," he whispered as he let us out. "Good luck."

We shook hands. The ambulance lights vanished around a curve and we were alone in the pitch-darkness. We picked our way through the brush until we tripped over a low barbed-wire barrier and fell heavily into Switzerland. We got up and stumbled on, crouching in a ditch as a pair of sentries went by. Soon we could see the lights of Basel ahead, and just about dawn we found an untended bridge and crossed the Rhine. At the German land border beyond, we watched as people were waved through the checkpoint, and I guess that went to our heads. Why should we try to sneak into Germany? We could just walk across.

Well, we didn't. Everyone else was known to the guard. When he saw two strangers in American uniforms he slammed the gate. Ten minutes later Webb and I were sitting in a Basel prison.

Though it hardly seemed so at the time, this was one of the luckier things to happen to us. The jailer gave us a decent breakfast and sent for an imposing-looking American consular official. "What the hell do you two think you're up to?" he said.

We told him. In fact, we bombarded him, giving him no chance to answer. When we finally ran out of breath, he said he thought we were on a worthwhile mission and wished he could join us. He would help us, if only we'd shut up for a minute.

He returned around noon with the Swiss military commandant in Basel, who asked us a few questions and then produced some papers. A few hours later, after we had stocked up on coffee, chocolate and cigarettes, we were placed aboard a train. Without anyone seeming to notice our presence, we were deposited well inside Germany, in Freiburg.

LITTLE MORE THAN four years had passed since Kaiser Wilhelm II sent German armies smashing into Russia and Belgium. Eight and a half million soldiers died in those four years, nearly two million of them Germans. Despite the awesome casualties, despite winters of near starvation, protests and spreading strikes, the war had ground on. With the home front sliding toward chaos, the kaiser at last appointed a humane chancellor, Prince Max von Baden, who moved for peace. But even as the articles of surrender were being signed, the despairing land burned with the fires of revolution. As radicals and reactionaries wrangled over who was to blame for the downfall of the proud nation, rioting erupted across Germany, a cry of anger by a defeated people broken by the intolerable demands of the war. The kaiser fled to Holland. In Kiel, navy crews mutinied and dockworkers and troops joined them. The revolt spread.

With Rosa Luxemburg, a brilliant speaker and pamphleteer, Karl Liebknecht led the Spartacus League, a revolutionary Marxist party. Liebknecht called for a government patterned on the new Russian soviets, and as his strength swelled, there seemed no way to forestall the Spartacists but to proclaim a republic. On November 9, 1918, Prince Max turned his shaky control over to the moderate Social Democratic leader, Friedrich Ebert. And Ebert began his monumental effort to save Germany from herself.

It was only a month or so later that Webb and I wandered the streets of Freiburg. A red flag flew over the *Rathaus*—the city hall—and a revolutionary council ruled the city. Its members told us what they could about the political ferment in southern Germany. As we were in uniform, perhaps they thought we were an advance element of an occupation force.

Prince Max, who had returned to his Baden estate after divesting himself of the chancellorship, graciously welcomed us to his home, so Webb and I sat in his comfortable study and listened to him talk. During the war he had devoted himself to the Red Cross and the welfare of war prisoners on both sides, refusing to accept a political role until the kaiser told him he alone could save Germany from ruin. Ruefully he told us that he seemed not to have succeeded. "I believe the Allies want vengeance more than peace." He was also concerned about the

German high command's pretense that the fatherland had been betrayed on the home front while the army was still fighting strongly. Someday, he predicted, the myth of the "stab in the back" would be seized on to start another war.

AT THE BAYERISCHER HOF in Munich, one of Europe's great hotels, we seemed to be the only guests. Outside, the streets were eerily still. In the shops, only ersatz—substitutes—appeared to be for sale: ersatz tobacco and coffee, even ersatz food. Our Swiss chocolate and cigarettes didn't last long; we kept passing them out to pinched, hungry-looking people.

Goaded by reactionary elements in Bavaria, demobilized soldiers in Munich would soon turn to violence in a scramble for power. One of them was a thirty-year-old Austrian corporal named Adolf Hitler.

Just before the New Year we came to Berlin, where the war for the control of Germany was moving toward a shattering climax. The telephones worked and the streetcars were running, but gunfire crackled from the rooftops and people were killed in the streets while Chancellor Ebert struggled desperately to restore order. A mob of three thousand sailors had seized the royal palace, and when Ebert called on loyal troops to drive them out, Liebknecht and the Spartacists urged the citizenry to defend the palace against the "counterrevolutionaries." Thousands of shouting students, veterans and angry women heeded the call, and the soldiers could not bring themselves to turn their guns on unarmed civilians. So the troops withdrew and, flushed with victory, the Spartacists united with other radicals to form the German Communist Party. One of its leading theoreticians was Rosa Luxemburg, then an overweight lady of middle years. She did not believe the German working class was ready for revolution, but events were outpacing theory; she and Liebknecht, who sought to ride the tiger, would soon be devoured by it.

WEBB AND I CHECKED into the Adlon Hotel, not far from the Brandenburg Gate, which divided East and West Berlin. Once again our American uniforms were a passkey. Ignoring the curfew, we went walking and were stopped by a sailor carrying a rifle and wearing an ammunition belt festooned with grenades. Who were we? he asked in English, and I had visions of a summary execution. But as we haltingly told him that we were American journalists, he laughed. He was from Hoboken and had been visiting relatives when the war broke out. The next thing he knew, he had been drafted into the German navy.

As we stood there shaking hands, a machine gun opened up across the street. The bullets ricocheted around our ears and we dived into the nearest doorway, huddling close. When the gun quit rattling, we invited the sailor to the Adlon for a drink.

We sat up most of the night, pressing cigarettes and brandy on our new friend. He was one of the sailors occupying the royal palace. Most of them had no better place to go, he said. Next day, as if to prove his companions were the most cordial of revolutionaries, he took us on a tour of the palace. We even had a glass of wine from the kaiser's swiftly dwindling private stock.

Webb and I were blessed to be in Berlin at precisely the moment when the contending political leaders were most anxious to get their versions of events out to the world. We saw Friedrich Ebert. Not quite fifty, plump, but with haggard eyes, he looked like a man on the edge of a breakdown. For two months he had held Germany together with his bare hands, and now the whole thing was getting away from him.

Ebert's deputy, Philipp Scheidemann, was present at the interview, and told us how he had come to proclaim the republic almost by accident. He had been having a bowl of soup at the Reichstag when a swarm of workers and soldiers came rushing in looking for him. Liebknecht, they said, was at the royal palace, about to declare the establishment of a soviet republic. "I went upstairs to a window. There was a great crowd in the Koenigsplatz and I addressed them. 'The war is over,' I said. 'The kaiser has gone.' They cheered wildly, and before I quite realized it, I cried out, 'Long live the new Germany! Long live the republic!' And so it was done."

Ebert had been furious; he had hoped for a restoration of the monarchy. But the two had since worked together tirelessly. "I cannot even tell you what will happen tomorrow," Ebert said. "But if my government falls, Germany will turn to a dictator, and then you Americans will have to come back."

Next day Webb and I went to see Karl Liebknecht and Rosa Luxemburg. When the rebels had finally evacuated the palace in exchange for eighty thousand marks and a promise of amnesty, Liebknecht and Luxemburg had moved on, setting up new command posts, whipping up street demonstrations. But for what? we asked them. What was their program?

Rosa Luxemburg spoke first. She was not an unattractive woman, despite her plumpness, for the intensity of her feelings fired her eyes, and her eyes illuminated her whole face. She opposed the use of force in pursuit of a political end, she said. The Bolshevik regime in Russia had become a dictatorship by an elite. The *people* must bring down Ebert's government; then the Spartacists would take charge. Speaking clearly and looking straight at Liebknecht, she said, "The Spartacus League will never take power except with the clearly expressed will of the proletarian masses."

Unable to contain his agitation, Liebknecht jumped to his

In postwar Berlin, *Thomas found widespread unrest. Crowds demonstrated in the streets while refugees (far right) jammed temporary shelters. Suddenly, revolution. Radicals*

feet. "We will heed the will of the people later. But we have to *have* power before we can offer it. We have to *lead!*"

It was almost as though Webb and I were no longer there; the two were replaying an old argument for each other. They wrangled on, Luxemburg coolly intelligent but Liebknecht stronger, more caustic, wearing her down. He looked like a bank clerk, with his clipped mustache and stiff collar, but he smoldered with passion. At the first break in their fiery dialogue, I interrupted to ask what they meant by calling on the people to "arm for the final battle" and "destroy" the existing power structure.

"That is political rhetoric," Rosa Luxemburg replied.

"It is an incitement to revolution," Liebknecht said flatly.

He was right. On the morning of Monday, January 6, the bloody rising known to history as Spartacist Week began with a general strike called by Liebknecht and a hastily formed national revolutionary council. In a ringing statement the Spartacists "dismissed" Ebert and declared themselves to have "provision-

led by Rosa Luxemburg (cameo) tried—and failed—to overthrow Chancellor Friedrich Ebert (far left). When the fray was over, LT sailed home on the SS Leviathan.

ally taken over." When Rosa Luxemburg heard the news, she was stunned; but, utterly convinced of the rightness of their cause, she committed herself to the revolution.

But by then Ebert was no longer the discouraged leader Webb and I had seen only a few days before. He had taken a strong man into his cabinet, a master butcher named Gustav Noske, who had put down the naval mutiny at Kiel and was now defense minister. With Ebert's nervous concurrence, Noske took over the Freikorps—Free Corps—an army of antirevolutionary volunteers controlled by fanatic officers. In Berlin, electricity and public transport stopped, factories and stores closed down. Hundreds of thousands of demonstrators, soldiers and ordinary citizens, desperate for food, swarmed through the streets.

Once, as I scurried back to the Adlon, a bullet whipped through my hat. This "news" was promptly sent out by a German reporter and reached the United States in garbled form: "Lowell Thomas was shot through the heart today during a street battle." A Denver *Post* reporter telephoned poor Fran, who wept and, for the next two weeks, considered herself a widow.

On January 9, Noske sent the first Freikorps troops into Berlin. They blasted the Spartacists out of their strongholds with cannon and grenades. More than a thousand on both sides died. Liebknecht and Luxemburg hid in a working-class district, but they were ferreted out and taken to the Eden Hotel for questioning. Later, a chambermaid told how the "questioning" had consisted mainly of "knocking the poor woman down and dragging her about." Liebknecht was badly beaten, too. Curiously, Wilhelm Pieck, a young Communist who had brought them false identity papers, was not harmed at all. He had answered Freikorps' questions all too willingly; he may even have betrayed Liebknecht and Luxemburg. These facts were never mentioned in official biographies of Pieck, who in 1949 became the first president of Communist East Germany.

Webb and I heard about the arrests and hurried to the Eden Hotel. From a block away, we saw two cars speed off from a side entrance. At the hotel no one seemed willing to answer questions, so we started back. We thought we heard some shots from inside a nearby park, but there was sporadic shooting all over Berlin, so we gave it little thought. Those shots, we later learned, ended Karl Liebknecht's life.

Rosa was in the second car. An officer put his pistol to her head and pulled the trigger; when the car reached a bridge over the Landwehr Canal, her body was thrown in. In their cover story the men said they had surrendered her to an anti-Communist mob. This led to tales of her escape, but in May her battered body was washed up at a lock. Neither followers nor foes could pretend any longer. Only one man ever went to prison for the crime. He served four months.

Elections were held immediately, and the Social Democrats won a smashing victory. Ebert then led the elected assembly to Weimar to draft a new constitution. It was humane, idealistic and democratic—and pleased no one. The Weimar Republic infuriated the old imperialists and the new nationalists by "pandering to the rabble," and the feverish left was incensed because industry and the great estates had not been turned over to the masses. The seeds had been sown for a black harvest.

One thing the German people agreed on: a massive and galling wrong had been inflicted on them at Versailles. Ebert's struggling nation lost twenty-seven thousand square miles of territory, including the rich Saar coal basin. The Rhine's left bank was occupied and the army reduced to a police force of a hundred thousand volunteers; and reparations began at once with a payment of twenty billion marks in gold. The terms were staggering in their vindictiveness; worse, the economic and emotional burden they pressed down on the German people all but guaranteed the undoing of the peace.

As long as Ebert was alive, he managed to keep the wallowing ship of state afloat. But when he died in 1925, to be replaced by timeworn Marshal von Hindenburg, the extremist parties gained strength year by year until in January 1933 the weary old marshal turned the chancellery over to Hitler. Two months later the Weimar Republic was dead.

IN LATE JANUARY, 1919, Webb and I made our way to Hamburg, where we hitched a ride on a French cruiser bound for Le Havre. Well out to sea, we confessed that our papers weren't precisely in order. The captain was a good sport. He anchored offshore of Le Havre in the dead of night and put us over the side in a longboat. We were landed on a deserted beach miles from the city and left there with nothing more than our luggage and a cheery *"Bonne chance!"* Films I had bought in Germany weighed a lot. So did the souvenir helmets I had gotten at the chancellery and the palace, and the ersatz suitcase full of ersatz goods I had found too fascinating to resist. As we set out toward the lights of Le Havre, I seriously considered dumping the whole lot. But in a couple of hours we came, finally, to a railway station, where we caught a train, packed with demobilized soldiers, to Paris. It deposited us at the Gare St. Lazare, and even in the gray of a winter morning that Paris station was a welcome sight.

But we still had a problem. Here we were, sitting on a sensational firsthand account of the German revolution, and Webb was anxious to start filing it at once. But how would the French and American military commands react to an admission that we'd defied their orders against crossing the frontier? President Wilson and the American delegation to the peace conference had arrived in Paris, so we decided on a rather brazen strategy. We would bring our information to the President's attention. It seemed our only chance to finesse the military authorities. We stuffed a briefcase with our notes and headed for the Hotel Crillon, where we asked to see Colonel Edward M. House, Wilson's intimate adviser. To our immense relief he agreed to see us.

We started talking as soon as we were shown into his suite and didn't stop for an hour and a half. Then House called in two other members of the delegation, Herbert Hoover and General Tasker H. Bliss, and gave them a twenty-minute briefing.

There were a few questions; then House thanked us for our report. "I will convey it to President Wilson this evening," he said. "It is going to be very valuable to all of us. Now, is there anything I can do for you?" When we said we were anxious to return home but knew shipping space was at a premium, he said, "Let me take care of it."

I unequivocally recommend allowing a presidential assistant to make your travel arrangements. The *SS Leviathan* had been the flagship of the Hamburg-American Line. Converted to a troop carrier, it held eighteen thousand doughboys, most of them forced to sleep in shifts. But not Webb and I. We were assigned to the kaiser's lavish imperial suite, with two bedrooms and a private dining room. The other bedroom was occupied by a Chicago tycoon, but we saw him only when he came out to complain because we had invited some of the troops up to share our luxury. He said he didn't know why he had to be inconvenienced by having all those chaps cluttering up his quarters.

Chapter VIII

PEOPLE IN AMERICA, in their typically all-or-nothing way, seemed totally uninterested in anything to do with the war. They had won it. Now they wanted to forget all about it. This didn't bode well for showing my hundred thousand feet of war film, as I had hoped.

I had cabled Fran and asked her to meet me in Chicago, since I felt obliged to report to Silas Strawn and the other generous men who had made the trip possible. I told Harry Chase to keep on processing the film, and I tried to forget the problem of what we would do with it, while Fran and I enjoyed a brief second honeymoon. Back in New York, I could see that the country was in a wild postwar mood of merrymaking. Theaters and nightclubs were packed with people hungry for amusement, as though America were saying, "We did our bit; now make us laugh." Well, why not? I quit thinking of my films as a somber chronicle and began to see them as entertainment, transporting audiences to places they'd only imagined, while I told them the stories that could never be conveyed by news dispatches, with music in the background. The result could be a wholly new form of entertainment.

Exhilarated with the idea, Harry, Fran and I went to work editing the film. But theatrical producers, playing to full houses, weren't interested; studio executives, hearing that the film had been shot in the war zones, shook their heads. Then Harry Chase had an idea. The New York *Globe* had sponsored travelogues before the war. Maybe they would take us on. I hurried there, and Fred B. Taintor, the editor, *was* interested; he saw our show as a circulation builder. However, only one theater was available in all Manhattan, a huge white elephant called the Century, well out of what was then the theater district. No production had ever turned a profit there, but at this point I was willing to try anything, and we shook hands on the deal.

Taintor gave the show plenty of space in the *Globe*, and for promotion, contrived to have my war souvenirs—helmets, flags and all—showcased in the Lord & Taylor windows on Fifth Avenue, flanking a Century Theatre broadside. The windows drew such crowds that Lord & Taylor had to put someone outside to keep people moving.

The Century was nearly sold out for my opening night, featuring the Near East. I was nervous—I always am. When the lights dimmed, a swell of Levantine music, chosen by Fran, filled the darkness. Then I stepped into a spotlight and said, "Come with me to lands of history, mystery and romance. . . ." My show was on at last. With only another sentence or two, I stepped back into the shadows and the screen was lit with a sweeping, panoramic picture from the air. I could hear gasps out front: it was, remember, well before the age of television, and the movies were still silent. Dr. Frank Crane, one of the best-known clergymen and columnists of his day, gave his reaction in a hundred newspapers, ending: "My head is in a whirl. . . . This is the most smashing picture I ever saw."

Though the mile between Times Square and the Century near Columbus Circle seemed an obstacle course not all theatergoers dared traverse, we had a three-week run. Taintor went looking for another theater, but what he found seemed like another white elephant. Madison Square Garden (the original one, at Madison Avenue and Twenty-sixth Street) was even farther from the theater district than the Century. It was the habitat of spectaculars like the Barnum & Bailey Circus and those other traditional circuses, the Democratic and Republican national conventions. How could I fill it? But it was the only place available. We took it—and we played to capacity audiences for eight weeks.

It was pretty heady stuff, and I began planning a coast-to-coast tour. But Taintor's interest in us stopped at the Hudson River, so I had to serve as my own manager. The only places with open dates in the fall were cavernous opera houses and out-of-the-way auditoriums, but I took six of them, paying some twenty thousand dollars in deposits.

Then, on the last night of the Madison Square Garden engagement, a stranger came to the dressing room and turned our lives completely around. He was Percy Burton, a British impresario, who was in New York scouting new talent. He was, so he said, "thunderstruck" by having an American telling of a British hero—Lawrence—of whom he, a Briton, had never heard. I must come to London with my Lawrence and Allenby productions.

Actually, I was as eager as he was, but not knowing how to get out of my tour commitments short of sacrificing twenty thousand dollars, I told him there would be several impossible conditions. I would come only during the worst theatrical period of the year, the summer, and only if he could book me at a great national institution like Covent Garden—the Royal Opera House. When he didn't blanch, I threw in still another: "How about an invitation from the king?" I was pulling his leg, but he took it seriously. Some days later, I had a cable saying he had booked Covent Garden. The cable included an invitation from King George. (Later, I learned that the management had been loath to lease the esteemed theater to a Yankee. Sir Thomas Beecham, the famous conductor who held the lease on Covent Garden, warned Burton, "You stand no more chance here than a snowball in the Jordan Valley.")

We didn't have much time. The opening was the first week in August and I was preparing a radical change in my presentation. The separate Allenby and Lawrence shows I had been giving were really part of the same story, and with Burton's encouragement I decided to combine the two. This meant heavy cutting and complete rewriting. Once more I sought out Dale Carnegie, and he quickly put aside for a while his own plans for giving public-speaking courses at the YMCA.

I saw little of the sea and not much of Fran during the Atlantic crossing; Dale, Chase and I huddled all day and far into the night. But by the time we docked in Southampton we had put together a tight, swiftly moving show: *The Last Crusade—With Allenby in Palestine and Lawrence in Arabia.*

Burton had been busy, too. When we got to Covent Garden, all red plush and glittering crystal, the scenery was in place and it was perfect, a Nile set from an opera. Burton had hired the Royal Welsh Guards band. One look at them in their scarlet uniforms and I decided to put them onstage before the show to play for early arrivals.

And so the opening night rushed in on us. Peeping out from the wings into the resplendent house, filling with men and women in formal dress, I was suddenly conscious of how recently I had come down from our Colorado mountains. Then the Welsh Guards began the overture, the curtain opened on the faintly illuminated Nile set and a dancer glided onstage in an oriental dance. Fran had set to music the Mohammedan call to prayer and, from the wings, a tenor sent out this haunting, high-pitched melody. Then I stepped into the spotlight.

"I never dreamed," I said in part, "that you British might be interested in hearing the story of your own Near Eastern campaign and the story of your own heroes—told through the nose of a Yankee." That remark, thrown in on the spur of the moment, drew a burst of laughter. After a few more words, I stepped aside, the screen came alight and we were on our way.

None of us, in our wildest fantasies, could have conjured up the reaction. Afterward, the audience stood and applauded for ten minutes, and next morning, front-page newspaper reviews were full of such ardent tributes as to require even a prudent man to be helped back down to earth. Within hours, scalpers had bought up blocks of seats, and soon it was almost impossible to buy tickets at the box office for current performances. When I went down to Covent Garden, I found lines waiting on all four sides of the building. Later, people even brought campstools. Burton organized special trains to bring people in from the provinces, plastered posters on the sides of London's big double-decker buses and doubled our advertising in the evening papers. Alongside an ad for *The Wild Widow,* a highly successful comedy, he took one twice as big: WHY IS THE WIDOW WILD? BECAUSE SHE HASN'T MET LOWELL THOMAS. . . .

I was astonished by the warmth of the British audiences, who were aware that I was an outlander. I couldn't see beyond the second row, but any performer will tell you that an audience's reaction is a tangible thing. And each time I appeared, I felt the flow of enthusiasm from out front.

Each night, too, Burton would tell me the names of famous personalities in the audience. Rudyard Kipling, Winston Churchill, George Bernard Shaw, Georges Clemenceau, premier of France, came; and my old friend Emir Faisal with a suite of Arab dignitaries. Members of the royal family, theatrical stars, the titled elite of Mayfair—they all came, and some asked Burton to escort them to my dressing room afterward. Late one night, heading back to our apartment, I said to Fran, "Is this really happening to us?"

"I suppose it is," she replied, "since I read about it in the newspapers. But I can't believe it, either."

When three or four weeks sped by with no letup in demand for tickets, Burton said I could probably continue the extraordinary run indefinitely. Did I still intend to leave at the end of August for our American tour? I had been pondering that question. I wanted to stay. Still, it takes a special sort of effrontery to forfeit a small fortune. Until Burton put it to me, I wasn't sure I could do it. But I did. I cabled the theaters I'd rented, canceling our tour and forfeiting twenty thousand dollars in deposits.

ONE MORNING THERE was a note from Lawrence in the mail: "I saw your show last night and thank God the lights were out!" A day or so later he came around for tea. With a wry smile he begged me to pack up and go home: I was making life impossible for him. When he ventured out on the streets, he was stopped by strangers, then swiftly surrounded by a crowd. He had a hundred letters a day, many from women proposing marriage and other, less formal, couplings. "And it's all your doing," he said, again hiding his true feelings behind his smile.

When I told him I had just signed a long-term contract with Burton, Lawrence shrugged and smiled. Neither Fran nor I could decide if he was serious. He said the only way out now was for him to leave London, but there is reason to believe he had already made such arrangements. In any event, he went up to Oxford, where he became a fellow of All Souls College. There, still plagued by idolators, he retreated behind a schedule he would follow for most of his short life, sleeping by day, writing by night and going out only when absolutely necessary.

Two things finally convinced me he had forgiven me for the part I played in turning him into a celebrity: first, we continued seeing each other from time to time, although I always had the feeling that each visit might be the last; and second, his mother telephoned to say she would like to meet us. We invited her to tea, and found her an attractive, gray-haired lady filled with maternal pride in her son, whom she called Ned. She thanked me for bringing his achievements to public notice. We later corresponded for some years.

The engagement at Covent Garden ran on into the autumn. I threw myself into each performance, six evenings and two matinees every week, and eventually I felt the strain. One evening the bright beam of the projector seemed to dance crazily in my eyes, and as I sagged back into the wings, it vanished in a frightening darkness. Luckily, Burton was on hand. He produced a bit of brandy that brought me around, and somehow I got through the rest of the performance. Meanwhile, Burton and Fran, thoroughly alarmed, had rounded up London's leading heart specialist, who examined me in the dressing room and again the next morning in his office.

"I find nothing physically wrong," he finally said, "but from what I've heard of the pace you've set for yourself, I must tell you that you may be dead of exhaustion in a very short time. I recommend that you take your wife on a three-month holiday."

"But, Doctor, this is the opportunity of a lifetime!"

"Very well," he said. "Do your shows, if you must, but remain in bed all the rest of the time. Around the clock."

He prescribed a diet consisting largely of raw eggs and sent me off to adjust to a strange new life, half invalid, half theatrical athlete. To make it easier, Fran and I moved out of London to the edge of Wimbledon Common. A Daimler limousine chauffeured us back and forth. It was a graphic reminder of the affluence within my reach and, as such, maybe a help in keeping me to my stiff regimen. I did not want to die just then.

Early in October, Allenby returned to England for the first

time since the end of the war. He and Lady Allenby sent word they would attend a matinee. Hours before his arrival every approach to Covent Garden was jammed with thousands of people. Inside the opera house, Fran had banked two first-tier boxes with roses. When the Allenbys entered, every head in the packed house turned in their direction, and the audience gave them an ovation. Again there was a burst of feature articles in the press, and Burton said he believed we could play Covent Garden for the next five years. But Beecham and his company were due back in another week. Where could we go?

Every legitimate theater in the West End was booked, but Burton came up with a bold idea. How about huge Royal Albert Hall? With a seating capacity of over six thousand, it was used for exhibitions, major sports events and the like; no one had ever attempted an extended engagement there. Said Burton, "Let's give it a try."

We did, playing to several thousand people every day. But we did have some problems. London was famous—if that is the word—for its midwinter fog, a fog so dense it could even creep right inside buildings. This is precisely what it did at the vast, domed Royal Albert Hall, sometimes filling it with a haze that made it seem as though Allenby and Lawrence had driven the Turks from the Holy Land through a dense smoke screen.

I had also been cautioned about strange acoustical problems and was advised always to address myself to the Prince of Wales's box. But this did not entirely solve the problems. One night a major who had been sitting in the center came around and insisted on shaking hands with me three times because, said he, "I heard every ruddy thing you said three times."

LATE ONE SUNDAY morning Lawrence turned up unannounced at Wimbledon Common. Fran and I engulfed him with questions. Patiently he sorted them out and brought us up-to-date on his life. He was writing an account of his wartime experiences, although he assured us his book would not be published in his lifetime. (*Seven Pillars of Wisdom,* a literary masterpiece about the desert war, was issued privately in 1926, then published in a general trade edition after Lawrence's death. It has never gone out of print since.)

A long, late talk followed, and Lawrence came frequently after that. He had attended the Versailles peace conference as a member of the British delegation, with Emir Faisal; and he still blamed himself for having made promises to the Arabs that were broken as soon as the shooting stopped. He expected never to return to the Near East.

Only afterward did I wonder if I might have missed an opportunity to do something for him. Suppose I had offered to back him in an expedition to, say, Central or South America, to study the Maya or the pre-Inca cities of the Andes? At the time, I had the money. Would it have changed the downhill course of his life? Probably he would have refused. Even so, it is one of the moments in my life I wish I had back, to do differently.

All through our London season, publishers kept after me to write something about him, a magazine article, a book, anything. Sometimes I told Lawrence of these offers and he assured me he had no objection. But at the time I did not have the energy for such an undertaking, nor had I yet properly sorted out my impressions. Once I asked him to verify an anecdote I'd heard from someone who had known him in Cairo. He laughed and said, "Use it if it suits your needs. What difference does it make if it's true? History is seldom true."

After I left London, we corresponded. He once told me that he tossed away most of his mail unopened, yet whenever I wrote to him he responded. And so I knew when he enlisted in the RAF under the name of Ross, obtaining a discharge a few months later when a newspaper revealed his secret. Soon, though, he reenlisted, this time as T. E. Shaw, still trying to lose himself in the anonymity of the military.

From his cottage at Clouds Hill in Dorset he used to blast around the winding country roads on his powerful motorcycle, the Blue Mist, named for the armored car he had used in Arabia. And on a spring afternoon in 1935, overtaking some children on the road, he wrenched his wheel to one side to avoid hitting them and crashed. Six days later, he died of his injuries.

WHILE WE WERE still playing to full houses at Albert Hall, I ran afoul of a movie tycoon, Sir William Jury, who had fought the war in the British Ministry of Information. Sir William discovered, as I had never realized, that I was using a few hundred feet of War Office film. As a result, he managed to extract from me most of my share of the box-office receipts. Not wanting to become involved in a legal battle, nor to appear an Ugly American, I paid, and never regretted the decision. Life, after all, is a game of high stakes. Surviving, bouncing back—isn't it what life is about? The great danger in hitting the jackpot when you are young, as I did, lies in coming to believe this is all there is to it. You sit on your jackpot, living from it, living *for* it. Then when you lose—and we must all lose sometimes—you haven't the strength or the will to bounce back.

Early in the New Year, 1920, we moved to a more manageable theater, Queen's Hall, and there Burton, following an inscrutable calculation understood only by publicists, announced that I was about to present *The Last Crusade* to our one-millionth patron. He had reporters and photographers on hand for the historic occasion, and by—ahem—great good luck, number one million turned out to be a highly photogenic Anglican prelate, the bishop of Gloucester. When I congratulated Burton he replied, "We'd have done even better with a good-looking blonde, but his Lordship was the best I could manage."

Finally the fabulous London run came to an end, but we went out in a blaze of glory. King George V and Queen Mary came to the theater and, following the show, invited Fran and me to the royal box. I was somewhat intimidated by Queen Mary's celebrated hauteur; if I said anything beyond, "Good evening, your Majesties," I have forgotten what it was.

In the United States, the Shuberts were unwilling to release me from my dates in their Washington and Philadelphia theaters. Rather than pay the full rental they demanded, we made a quick round trip; putting on two highly successful performances. A road tour of England and Scotland which followed produced sellout crowds, and then a cable from the prime minister of Australia caught up with us, inviting us to present our show as guests of the Commonwealth government. I sat staring at the ceiling for a long time. Our plan had been to take up our long-postponed American tour—financially, by far the more sensible thing to do. "What do you think?" I asked Fran.

"Well, Australia is another corner of the world," she replied. "And it's been a long time since we had an invitation from a prime minister."

I smiled happily. "I like the way you think," I said.

And we went out to cable our acceptance.

Chapter IX

EVEN BEFORE THE great voyages of discovery, some European geographers theorized that there had to be a continent in the Southern Hemisphere, since the earth would be "unbalanced" without it. They even put it on their maps: *Terra Australis Incognita*—unknown southern land.

And that was all most people knew about it when the twentieth century was young. But during my Cripple Creek days I had devoured a series of lurid thrillers about Australia; I knew about cobbers, bushrangers, sheep stations and billabongs. It was only the rest of the three million square miles—its people, cities, culture, government—that I needed to learn something about. I looked forward to it, and so did Fran.

On a rainy morning in April, our cumbersome equipment stowed aboard a Pacific & Orient steamer, Fran, Harry and I stood at the rail and waved good-bye to Dale Carnegie, who had come back to England to organize two road companies of our show. I remember thinking he looked a little overwhelmed.

I suppose I should have felt the same. We were bound for a strange land half a world away, without any idea of when we might be back. Fran and I were delighted with the prospect; Chase was poker-faced as usual. It was another adventure; we were young and unburdened by any of the conventional cares.

Our first stop in Australia was Perth. A few nights later, the captain staged a moonlit costume party, a gay affair, with dancing on the decks. Suddenly a chill cry—"Man overboard!" shattered the make-believe. As the ship reverberated under the stress of reversed engines, then began circling, a sad tale circulated among the passengers. On board was a group of war veterans, so badly wounded that only now were they able to return home. One, blinded and despondent, unable to face his family, had confided in a comrade and then, before he could be stopped, had gone over the rail. We circled for hours, in vain.

THERE WAS BAD NEWS waiting for us when we docked at Melbourne—the British road companies had folded. The show had been so identified with me in the public mind as to defy substitution. We lost a good deal of money, and poor Dale, blaming himself, had suffered a nervous breakdown. There wasn't a thing I could do about it except to cable him my absolute confidence that he had done all anyone could expect.

We were welcomed with a dinner at Government House, given by the prime minister, and I made my opening appearance before a special session of the Commonwealth Parliament. With such sponsorship, I could hardly fail; again we played to full houses. I found Australian audiences extremely cordial but more outspoken than their English cousins. One night, after my line about being surprised to find that Australians would want to hear the story "through the nose of a Yankee," a voice from the balcony boomed out, "That's quite all right; just don't try to sell us your Yankee Prohibition." It got the best laugh of the evening.

I remember also one Australian less-than-rave review. Lowell Thomas, it said, "appeared in dapper waiter's garments that seemed a little shy of his boot tops, and poured out his talk with an occasional jest to prevent the populace brooding unduly on his nasal inflections. . . . The lecture is illustrated with lantern slides and cinema films. The films are good." Other notices were lavish enough to soothe my ruffled ego, but the one I appreciated most was about Harry Chase, who, it said, "must be nothing less than a wizard . . . the world's foremost projection engineer."

Harry also had the insights of an artist. He had begun in the days when film ran through the projector and collected in a basket on the floor, to be rewound by hand. He fixed that. Now he could fill the largest screen with a brilliant picture, grind his own lenses, design equipment, take his camera apart to clean it after a desert sandstorm and put it back together—and do the same thing to your wristwatch. Eventually Harry and I would travel a quarter of a million miles together, but he alone would see to the crating and transporting of our half ton of projectors, film and other equipment, never complaining, rarely speaking, but forever there when you needed him.

WE SAILED AWAY from Australia vowing to come back—which we were to do, many times. Now we were bound for that international crossroads, Singapore, first stop on a planned tour of the Malay Peninsula and India. Singapore particularly fascinated me because Sir Thomas Stamford Raffles, the audacious Englishman who won it for his king and the East India Company, has always ranked in my imagination with Marco Polo. Arriving in 1819, he built a new metropolis on the ruins of an ancient city and made it the commercial center of southern Asia. In 1921, Singapore was the Gibraltar of the Pacific, and the memory of Raffles was everywhere—the Raffles Hotel, the Raffles Museum, Raffles Square. The waterfront was an ever changing panorama of ocean liners, tramp steamers, Chinese junks and sampans.

Among our largely British audiences at the Victoria Theatre, we could count on a generous sprinkling of wealthy Malays and Chinese, Americans from Standard Oil or General Motors, and a broad spectrum of missionaries. Touring Singapore's sin section, we got the flavor of the city's nether reaches. British sailors seeking escape, Chinese merchants trying to sell it to them, sidewalk peddlers hawking drugs, gold and anything else that men come by in shadowy ways, crowded the narrow streets. In an opium den we watched skeleton-gaunt Chinese rolling pills, lighting their pipes, inhaling deep puffs and then slipping into oblivion.

We were preparing to move on to Malacca when Harry, a fanatical fisherman, sailed out into the lagoon to try his luck. Alas, poor Harry! In the bush, snakes made for his bedroll; in the desert, scorpions found his shoes; in London, he had had a perpetual cold. And that day off Singapore, he let himself in for the most blistered, swollen sunburn I had ever seen.

An American couple offered us their guesthouse while Harry recovered. It was a thatched-roof cottage on stilts, amid lush coconut palms and with the South China Sea rolling gently up the beach a few yards away. During our peaceful interlude there

I decided that since we had all our camera equipment along, we could film Asia's exotic sights and human drama and put together a new production. When I broached this idea to the officials in Singapore, they offered me a special train to carry us up the Malay Peninsula in style—a private locomotive, lavish sleeping quarters and a diner. The following morning Harry tottered out of bed and pronounced himself ready to go.

Our first stop was the ancient city of Malacca. Along with a full house of rubber planters, traders and colonial officers, squadrons of immense bats were attracted to our performance in the town hall, zooming in through the unscreened windows and making straight for the brightly lit screen. Now and then one dive-bombed into an electric fan the size of an airplane propeller suspended from the ceiling and came crashing down into the audience, adding some extra sound effects to the performance.

Moving up-country in a series of one-night stands, we reached Ipoh, where the sultan of Perak invited us to a festival in the jungle. We rode out in a procession of elephants. There was no howdah on ours, just a pad secured by broad straps, to which Fran, Harry and I, riding together, clung as we jounced along the trail through the dripping dense growth. The feature attraction was a hundred-foot waterfall: Malays tobogganed down the churning water on huge leaves, howling with glee. An Afghan with a trained Himalayan dancing bear entertained the non-swimmers until the sultan commanded the Afghan to take his bear down the waterfall. Both seemed terrified, but after one swoop, even the bear wanted to do it again.

Harry and I slid off our elephant to film the spectacle. The bear was coaxed closer to our camera, and the elephant, either offended at our interest in another creature, or just plain frightened, suddenly went lurching off into the jungle. The last we saw of Fran, she was hanging on for dear life.

"There goes my wife," I said to the sultan. "What can we do?"

"Nothing," his most gracious Majesty replied.

We had gone only a hundred yards into the torn underbrush when we came upon the elephant calmly feasting on young bamboo shoots. Fortunately, Fran was none the worse for her adventure. "If you have that bear with you," she said, "please leave."

She was a good sport always. On our next expedition, to the Sakai pygmies deep in the interior, she turned down the opportunity to stay behind. We set out from Ipoh in a forty-foot houseboat skippered by a native opium addict. Every couple of hours he would order the crew into a cove, roll a pill or two and drop off into a world of dreams. But eventually he put us ashore and we entered the Malay interior. It would live up to anyone's most nightmarish vision of a jungle. Towering trees closed over our heads; thick creepers and vines surrounded us; and it took an advance guard of machete-swinging Malays to enable our rented elephants to go crashing through. In this dank wilderness lived the king cobra, the gaur—a fierce wild ox standing six feet at the shoulders—and the Malay tiger, which stalks human beings.

In a clearing with a dozen palm-leaf huts, we found a Sakai village. The café-au-lait people seemed a lighthearted, friendly group, though each man carried a long bamboo blowgun and a quiver of poison-tipped darts. The first sight of a whole tribe of undersized people is a bit unsettling, but I soon forgot their stature. Indeed, I imagined a pygmy sage describing *us* to his people: "Too bad for them! They must suffer from some glandular disorder that leads to gigantism."

FROM MALAYA WE went on north to Burma, whence we proceeded by stern-wheeler up the Irrawaddy, a thousand miles to the China frontier. After we returned to Rangoon, we crossed the Bay of Bengal to Colombo, capital of Ceylon [now called Sri Lanka]. It is said that when the Lord banished Adam and Eve from the Garden of Eden, they found a new paradise in this land. Here were immaculately maintained coconut plantations and tea terraces, first-rate hotels and superb beaches—all enlivened by the warmhearted Sinhalese in colorful costumes and bejeweled headdresses.

But in Colombo, that most oriental of cities, we could not find an oriental dancer for the prologue. Hesitantly, Fran said, "I've watched the dance so often, maybe I . . ." And so, in addition to her chores as company manager, she did the dance.

During our performances a monkey would occasionally throw a coconut onto the tin roof, where it landed with an explosive clang; and when the tropical rain thundered down on that roof, it sounded as if the world were tearing apart.

From Colombo we sailed on to India, where Harry's wife joined us. Except for brief intervals, they had been apart ever since 1917, and I thought it would be in order to invite Emma to share this adventure. She was most helpful at looking after the box office, but she was not what you would call a born traveler. In fact, almost from the day of her arrival she pined for home.

In the Punjab, the governor invited us to tour the Lahore bazaar by elephant, and so we came to know and love Primrose. One morning she was waiting outside our hotel, a tall elephant painted and gaily caparisoned, with a howdah on her back impressive enough for the lordliest of maharajas. We climbed aboard and went lurching down the narrow streets.

Primrose had toured the bazaar before. While Fran, Harry and I enjoyed the spectacle—and Emma Chase's stiff upper lip turned rigid—Primrose swept her great trunk left and right and wreaked havoc on the sidewalk stalls. Nuts and fruit, baubles and beads, came cascading to the ground, to be eagerly snatched up by the youngsters who followed in our wake. One of the governor's retainers ran behind to hand out copper and silver largesse to the shopkeepers on our route.

We were all having a fine time until we noticed poor Emma crying bitter tears. It was awful, she sobbed. She was frightened and hated it and wanted to go home.

Stricken, Harry cried out, "But, honey, what could be more fun than riding your own elephant through a bazaar in India?"

"Riding the East Orange streetcar to my mother's house!" the good woman wailed.

And that was it. We put Emma on a train for the coast and, alone, she began the long voyage back to her own particular Garden of Eden—East Orange, New Jersey.

IN CALCUTTA, WE visited the site of the infamous Black Hole, where in 1756 a large number of Europeans died of suffocation when they were imprisoned in a single cell by the nabob of

Bengal. The Black Hole incident was the spark that touched off the British conquest of India. Robert Clive, the moody young military genius, subdued the nabobs and established the supremacy of the East India Company, which led to direct administration by the British Crown. At the time of our tour, Mohandas Gandhi was already revered by Indians, half scorned, half feared by the British for his passive-resistance movement against British rule. We felt the reverberations, both of a turmoil centuries old and of the trouble to come.

In Peshawar, at the eastern end of the Khyber Pass, fabled gateway to central Asia, our hotel was surrounded by barbed wire, and at every performance there was the threat of violence. The rugged country west to Afghanistan was inhabited by fierce, well-armed tribes. Raiding was their way of life. Towns were surrounded by twenty-foot walls; inside, each family had its own walled enclosure, for when people were not battling outsiders they were engaged in blood feuds with each other. It was not

During the early 1920s, Lowell Thomas and his wife, Fran, toured the exotic Far East. They filmed rickshaws in Singapore and relaxed under palms in Malaya (left). They

uncommon for a man to sit perched in a tower atop his mud wall for months, eating and sleeping there, peering through a slit, rifle always ready, just waiting for a shot at his particular foe—who lived nearby. In the Khyber, British troops couldn't keep tribesmen from blazing away from the cliffs and mountaintops, and the Tommies called the pass the Valley of Sudden Death.

The British were not entranced with the prospect of three Americans moving into the Khyber, but after we persuaded the governor it was essential for the film we were planning, a British captain went along with us in our borrowed Model T Ford. He said Fran would have to stay at Peshawar. I could have predicted the outcome; but he finally won a minor point—Fran agreed to disguise her sex in a soldier's uniform.

It was a spectacular trip. Camel caravans wound along the floor of the gorge, bearing the silks and rugs of Samarkand—Tamerlane's fabled fourteenth-century Mongol capital—to India. British motorized traffic traveled a road cut into the cliffs,

braved the jungle on elephants and encountered Sakai pygmies (lower right). Thomas's faithful camera-man, Harry Chase, sits in the front row, hat in hand.

and above the hairpin turns, snow-covered peaks rose into the sky. We sped through a narrow gorge to a British fort, then dropped to the desert floor. The frontier was guarded by poker-faced Afghan soldiers. An emphatic sign read: IT IS ABSOLUTELY FORBIDDEN TO CROSS THIS BORDER INTO AFGHAN TERRITORY.

We had come to the end of the world as we knew or could imagine it. Beyond was a proscribed land where—except for a British military invasion—only a bare handful of Westerners had ever set foot. As we turned back, I wondered if I would ever have a chance to cross this forbidden boundary.

And so, after nearly a year in Asia, our tour was over—and I didn't want to leave. India seemed to me the most exciting place in the world, and I wanted to see it all. But first we had to return to England to make necessary financial arrangements and re-stock our film supply. Then Fran joined her mother for a leisurely European tour, while Harry and I went back to New Delhi, hoping to enlist the support of the British government.

The viceroy's aides, as sometimes happens with those in lesser positions of authority, showed caution, even resentment, and blocked me at every turn. But the newly appointed viceroy, Viscount Erleigh (later Viscount Reading), invited me to luncheon. I told him that I wanted to film India, but it was so enormous and its transportation so uncertain that I needed help with special trains and steamers. Most of all I wanted to borrow the services of an officer I had known in England, a remarkable man who spoke a number of Indian languages and knew more about the country than anyone I had ever met.

"Who is this paragon?" the viceroy asked with a smile.

"Major Francis Yeats-Brown of the Bengal Lancers."

"Well, you shall have him, and everything else. I heard you at Covent Garden. If you can do for India what you did for Palestine, possibly I can justify my appointment." He was pulling my leg a bit, but Harry and I were on our way.

YEATS-BROWN—YB, as everyone called him—was delighted with the prospect. In the months that followed he would be our guide and our guru. As with many men possessed of both soaring intellect and considerable physical prowess, he was not prepossessing. Of average height but with a stoop that seemed to shrink him, he had a remote, even ascetic expression and spoke with a slight stammer—perhaps because his family had bound him over to an army career despite his feelings for literature and the arts.

YB downed his share of whiskey and sodas, but he was a rare individual. He had become a crack officer, a member of the all-India polo team and a wartime RAF pilot who crashed into the desert, was captured and escaped to fight again. But YB's fellow officers considered him an oddball, for he had a habit of donning native garb and disappearing among the people. While his comrades were off pigsticking, YB conversed with holy men or pored over classical Hindu texts. He had already written a couple of books. Later, he did the one closest to his heart: *Lives of a Bengal Lancer.* It became a spectacular movie, starring Gary Cooper and Franchot Tone, and made YB famous.

YB brought along a six-foot-four noncom named Naim Shah, who wore a peaked hat that made him seem as gigantic as Aladdin's genie. Wherever we went Naim Shah, in full regimental regalia, walked in front of us clearing the way; at night he carried a lantern and a heavy stick, peering sharply ahead, and if ever a cobra crossed our path, I didn't know about it.

We went first to Cape Comorin, southernmost tip of the Indian peninsula, so I could fulfill my dream of traversing the entire length of the subcontinent. I stood at the water's edge looking off into the empty distance. Then I faced north and tried to comprehend the immensity of that land. Feeling dwarfed and intimidated, I climbed into a bullock cart with my companions, the driver cracked his whip and we went plodding north up the trail.

Toward evening we stopped to let the bullocks drink from a roadside pond. Nearby there was a shrine to Kali, goddess of death, portrayed as a four-armed demon dancing on the dead body of her husband. Why, I asked YB, did this female monster number her Indian worshippers by the millions? "Answer that and you may have a clue to the Hindu mind," he replied.

Within the memory of men living then, a sect that worshipped Kali and practiced thuggee—the art of ritual murder—had roamed the land, strangling their victims with a ceremonial scarf. The British executed hundreds of Thugs, but they never made much headway against the whole enterprising criminal caste. Estimated to be ten million strong, they believed the soul's needs are satisfied by strong-arm burglary and intricate confidence games. At Bapatla, on the Bay of Bengal, we met an old, emaciated but celebrated member of this caste. He and his men had once kidnapped six policemen sent to arrest them, donned their uniforms and, thus disguised, proceeded on a crime spree of epic magnitude. He came to be revered as The Man Who Stole Six Policemen.

As every traveler does, we journeyed to Agra, city of the Taj Mahal. The Taj is a masterpiece of white marble reflected in an oblong pool. Over the years, I returned to it some thirty times, by day and by night. But one man's wine is another man's vinegar. I knew an American colonel whose duty it was to escort visiting dignitaries to the Taj. After doing this many times, he would take them to the vicinity of the Taj and, from where he couldn't even catch a glimpse of it, sit reading a newspaper until his VIPs returned.

In New Delhi, I sought the help of British officials and American envoys for permission to cross the forbidden border into Afghanistan. Nowhere were the answers encouraging. I also sent messages to the Afghan ruler, Amir Amanullah Khan, at Kabul. No answer. We moved on.

Our tour took us to Puri, on the Bay of Bengal. Puri gave us a word meaning an object that crushes everything in its path—juggernaut. The original juggernaut is a twenty-foot-high temple on sixteen gigantic wooden wheels in which the Hindu divinity Jagannath rolls through the streets of Puri once a year. In former times the streets were littered with the bodies of worshippers who sought nirvana by throwing themselves under the wheels, but the British called a halt to this manner of showing religious devotion.

A police inspector led us to a housetop from which we could film the ceremony. Suddenly a chant went up from hundreds of thousands of throats: "O Jagannath, lord of the world, have pity on us, release us from our woes!" Then the juggernaut was on its way. The god's sister's car came first, then his brother's and then his own. People in the vicinity surged forward to get their hands on the heavy ropes pulling it. Guiding the first car was a

European, the Puri superintendent of police. We saw him signal for the emergency brake when devotees threw themselves in front of the huge wheels. A log dropped and brought the car to a stop just in time.

We journeyed on to the Black Pagoda at Konarak, which we hesitated to film at close range. Around the outside of it ran a series of explicit tableaux representing every conceivable sexual pleasure. It was impressive, but we could not have shown a single segment in the West—how different today!—without attracting the attention of the police. Yet, inside, the artistic motif changed, the statues and bas-reliefs expressing the soaring metaphysical and moral precepts of Hinduism. YB explained that Hindus believed a man must face the crudest level of experience before taking off into the loftier reaches of reflective thought. Such was the moral of the Black Pagoda.

WITH MY CASH supply near zero and still no word from Afghanistan, we had to pack and get to Bombay, where Harry and I booked passage on a P & O steamer for England. Then, a few hours before we were to sail, we had a message from the American chargé d'affaires in Persia [now Iran]: he had just been informed that Amir Amanullah Khan would welcome our visit.

YB and I exchanged a discreet cheer. He thought it might be possible to drive an automobile across the Afghan desert. Ford and General Motors were competing for the Indian market, and I remembered an American I had met in Calcutta, a jute broker named David King, who might help us. Furthermore, King, one of the sixteen survivors of the original French Foreign Legion in World War I, would be an ideal companion on the journey.

King was intrigued by the chance, and a friend of his at General Motors agreed to furnish us with a new Buick. Soon, if Allah willed it, and if Amanullah Khan, Light of the World, did not change his mind, and if his zesty subjects did not shoot holes in our car, we would journey into Afghanistan. The size of Texas, the country was locked between Russia and India. It was fought over for a hundred years by Great Britain and the czars, and all through the ages violence within the country had maintained a bloody pace. As an object lesson to other warring tribes, Amanullah's grandfather once built a tower of skulls.

But first, Peshawar, a caravan stop for five thousand years. Standards of morality differ, but of the thousand and one sins of Peshawar, most are unmentionable and some are unbelievable. They are the sins of dancing boys and acquiescent girls of every libidinous persuasion, of jealousy and intrigue and the deviltry which gets into men's blood in certain latitudes; of gluttony and gambling and strange intoxications; of the passion of blood feuds and sudden, satanic death. We visited the serai of the dancing boys, the streets of the daughters of Jezebel. We heard the labored coughing of those who smoked charas.

Out of curiosity, we tried some charas, a resin made from the flowers of the hemp plant; it is smoked in a water pipe, and one puff was all I cared to take: I felt as though I were riding through bumpy air on a magic carpet. Abdul Ghani, a friend of YB's, told us a tale that illustrates the mental aberrations that come from smoking charas. Three travelers from Afghanistan are anxious to reach Peshawar before dark. But night comes on them before their arrival; the gates are locked. One of the three is a whiskey tippler, the second an opium smoker and the third smokes charas. They sit down outside the city wall to drink and smoke and talk the matter over. Soon the whiskey drinker says, "Let's break down the gate." The opium addict yawns and says, "No, let's sleep and wait till morning." Then the charas smoker speaks. "I have it! Let's crawl through the keyhole!" One puff and I found I understood the story.

At the very last we had bad news. Yeats-Brown, perhaps because he was a British officer, was denied permission to enter Afghanistan. We bade him a sad farewell, and in the cool of early morning we set out for the Khyber Pass.

By nine o'clock the sun was beating down fiercely, and it took us until midafternoon to pierce the mountains and cross the desert. Miles of road had been washed away by floods, and tacks from the heavy shoes of Asian caravanners punctured our tires at the rate of one an hour. But at last we reached a cluster of tents and huts, the barbed wire and the forbidding sign at the frontier. This time the soldiers let us through. Ahead, the scorched, shimmering terrain was like the wasteland we had just crossed. But we were in the forbidden kingdom, and now not even the long arm of the British raj could protect us. Dave King remarked that recently, at about this point, a German engineer, returning from Kabul after completing a project for the amir, had been murdered by his Afghan escort.

A soldier crisscrossed with bandoliers climbed up on the running board and directed us to a nearby fort. There an officer said he would accompany us; we would spend that night at the amir's winter palace in Jalalabad. On we rolled through the harsh glare until—all at once—we found ourselves bowling along a tree-shaded avenue. It was as though we had been shot up from the fires of hell into a suburb of paradise.

Jalalabad was half a mile above sea level, and date palms, orange groves and pomegranate orchards flourished there. At the palace we felt like Sinbads in a modern Arabian Nights. We were handsomely fed and we slept on voluptuous silken sheets, not thinking about Amanullah's father, Habibullah Khan, who had been assassinated in this palace three years before.

In the morning we drove to Kabul. Here we were quartered in a strange octagonal palace, and a court chamberlain assigned to us began keeping a record of every person we spoke with and every move we made. On our first evening we sat down under a huge, glittering candelabra at a table laden with spicy pilaf, cheese, mysterious sweets, unleavened bread and mountains of delicious fruit. Suddenly there was a rumble as of heavy artillery. The building rocked, the candelabra swayed and the dishes crashed to the floor. The servants fled through the door, and we were hot on their heels. The awesome rumble lasted more than a minute, then all was silent. There would be other earthquakes during our stay in Afghanistan, but none like that.

After some days of filming, we were driven north to Paghman, in the Hindu Kush mountains, to meet the amir. There we saw, kneeling in front of a gathering of robed Afghans, a heavyset young man wearing a black tunic, riding breeches and black boots. We had come upon the royal court at Moslem devotions; leading the service was none other than his Majesty, Amir Amanullah. Afterward, he greeted us and introduced his brothers and some cabinet ministers. He seemed a jovial man, though accustomed to having his way. He had dark, questioning, protuberant eyes and a penchant for the good things of life.

"I am very glad you have come to Afghanistan," he said

through the interpreter. "Tell me if there is anything you want."

"I want to go to the headwaters of all the rivers of Afghanistan," I replied.

He laughed. "It is better that you do not. I could not guarantee your return, for we are in a disturbed state here."

After the assassination of his father in 1919, Amanullah had ascended a precarious throne, menaced by treason and conspiracy. He was so closely guarded that once, during filming, when I took his arm to shift his position, rifles snapped up and were trained on me. "It is better if you *say* where you want me to stand," he said gently.

Still, he seemed to be taking forceful steps to modernize his remote land, building schools and seeking trade links with the West. He was a fanatical believer in home industries, insisting his people wear clothing made in Afghanistan. He had his own ideas about how to enforce this. He carried a razor-sharp knife, and whenever he spotted someone wearing clothes of foreign fabric or design, he would slip up behind and cut out a piece.

"This country is rich in resources but undeveloped," he said to me. "I hope that you will tell Western people something about us. But tell them that Afghanistan is for Afghans; my people, not foreign capitalists, will enjoy the fruits of their labor."

One day we filmed an exhibition of tent pegging. Cavalrymen galloped ten abreast, coming on like rolling thunder, calling on the name of Allah. *"Ye de!"* they cried when their hands struck true, looking up at the pegs impaled on their lance tips, and *"Wa! Wa!"* when they went wide. A sham cavalry battle followed, and a display of horseback wrestling. The heat was terrific, and the foreign minister began to wilt in his tight-fitting court dress. Finally he took off his fez and collapsed into the arms of an attendant. A stretcher carried him away, and when we left Kabul the poor man had not yet recovered.

In the afternoon Chase was to photograph the amir in formal dress. His Majesty was in a playful mood and posed as we suggested. But once, out of the corner of my eye, I saw him stick out his tongue at me. When we were finally finished he said to me, "You have ordered me about more than any other living man. I hope you have everything you want." I assured him we had.

Amanullah Khan was to hold the throne only a few more years. His efforts at modernization stirred up violent opposition, and in 1929 Kabul was seized and he went into exile in Italy, where he died some thirty years later.

Chapter X

IN THE WINTER of 1922, Harry and I returned to London. Fran was waiting patiently, and we had a gala reunion. But we were broke—almost. A banker agreed to advance me the cash to put together a new show. However, he ahemmed, there was the matter of collateral. I went back to the hotel, and like a valiant heroine in fiction Fran brought out her jewels and said, "Go get the money." The jewels consisted mainly of pearls I had bought her at Australia's famous oyster beds. I was never at ease until I got them out of hock.

We edited our film with the speed born of necessity. Once again Percy Burton booked us into Covent Garden, and once again people came by the hundreds of thousands to see our show.

One day, when I was somewhere between Peshawar and the Khyber Pass, an irate woman suddenly stood up in the main aisle and began shouting protests against British rule in India: "Down with the salt tax! Down with the viceroy! Down with Lowell Thomas!" Attendants, in the gentlemanly British manner, led her outside. Next day she was back, and the day after that. By the fourth day she was getting a bit of applause, which spiced up the proceedings. I began to think about hiring her, but someone called the police, who took away our gray-haired rebel and locked her up. I bailed her out and testified in court on her behalf. She was released without fine. But apparently we had offended her; alas, she never came back.

After London, we toured England and Scotland, then took the show to Paris. My speaking part there lasted only one week, despite the efforts of a Berlitz professor. At the first Saturday matinee, I noticed a gentleman in the second row cupping his ear as though he were having difficulty hearing. He turned to his companion, and in one of those whispers you can hear yards away, he asked, *"En quelle langue parle-t-il?"* I turned the narration of all future performances over to our Parisian producer.

Fran was going to have a baby within a few months, so we moved out to Versailles, and in that romantic town we whiled away the summer. When Fran's time drew near, we returned to London. I was signed for a twelve-week tour in Ireland, opening in Dublin on October 7, and it looked as though there might be a conflict in scheduling. But Lowell, Jr., didn't let us down; the morning before I was to leave for Ireland, he made his debut.

Something else made October 6, 1923, memorable. In the afternoon Harry came to see Fran and the baby. He had rigged up a contrivance of earphones, wires and whatnot, called a crystal set, and thought it might amuse Fran. When she put the earphones on, a look of astonishment crossed her face. She passed them over to me and I heard Lord Curzon, the former viceroy of India, addressing the House of Lords, miles from where I stood. It was a strange sensation, listening to my first radio broadcast. I sensed some of the potency, the possibilities, of this instrument. But I had no idea of the extent to which it was to affect my life.

JUST AFTER CHRISTMAS, Fran, Harry, young Lowell and I sailed for home. We moved in with my parents in Asbury Park, New Jersey, where Dad had established a practice. I decided the time had come to put the Lawrence story on paper. I worked at full speed to meet a magazine-serial deadline; later, in book form, *With Lawrence in Arabia* enjoyed heartening reviews.

By this time we had moved to Forest Hills, on Long Island. Fran and I talked constantly about establishing ourselves permanently somewhere. A real home is little enough to provide for a baby. But we hadn't come to a conclusion about the one place where we'd be happy to spend the rest of our lives.

One evening we were walking through New York's theater district when I noticed a familiar name on a marquee. I stopped to stare at it, and said, "Beulah Bondi! I knew a Beulah Bondy at Valpo. I wonder if this is the same one, only with an *i*."

"It certainly isn't an everyday name," Fran said.

Beulah Bondy had not been an everyday girl. She had been something of a mystic, and it had been a little weird to hear divinations from someone who looked more attuned to a prom than a crystal ball. But Beulah had also been a drama student. I steered Fran toward the stage door, and sure enough, my Beulah it was—and the one who was to become a famous stage and movie actress. It had been nearly fifteen years since our Valpo days, but she didn't seem in the least surprised to see me. We chatted a moment, then Beulah said, "I knew you'd be coming soon, Tommy."

I didn't know what to say. "Well," I managed finally, "it was a pleasant accident."

"It was no accident." Then she told us that she had been spending some time on Quaker Hill, near the village of Pawling, in Dutchess County, New York, and that she had noticed a house there, a lovely white house with a wide porch. "I've seen you and your wife living there," she said.

"But . . ."

"I know—I hadn't even heard that you were married. But there are some things we *know*. Will you go and see the house?"

I laughed. "Sure, Beulah. I'm taking off on a tour, but when I get back we'll all look at 'our' house in—where?—Quaker Hill."

Same old Beulah. When I asked her why she had changed Bondy to Bondi, she said something about the numerological advantages of *i* over *y*. Fran and I walked up Broadway chuckling about lovely, talented Beulah Bondi—the mystic!

I'd signed to do a coast-to-coast tour; we took the Allenby-Lawrence show to just about every American city and town of more than five thousand people, and afterward we did the same thing all the way across Canada. By then I was so tired of the sound of my own voice and the seas of anonymous faces that I vowed never to face an audience with that production again.

IN 1924 EIGHT AMERICAN army aviators set out to become the first men to fly all the way around the world. They took off from Seattle in the best equipment available—four Douglas single-engine amphibious biplanes with a speed of seventy miles an hour. One crashed on an Alaskan mountaintop and it took the pilots ten days to hike out through snow to a cannery on the

Bering Sea. The others flew on, island-hopping across the Pacific, scraping over Asian jungles at treetop level amid vicious air currents. By the time they reached London they were so exhausted that they had to turn down an invitation from King George to visit Buckingham Palace. Then they were off on the most dangerous leg, history's first east-to-west flight across the Atlantic. One plane went down in the ocean, but the pilots were picked up, and the remaining planes flew on to Boston. Now, with a third replacement plane, they had only to cross the United States to complete the epic trip, and I joined them for the final few thousand of their twenty-six thousand miles in the air. Thanks to General "Billy" Mitchell, I had been appointed the flight's official historian and assigned an army plane.

Today it is hard to grasp the tremendous excitement that gripped the world at those early feats of airmanship. The sky was then as much of a challenge as outer space is today; in addition, the planes of a dozen nations were in the race to be first to circle the globe. Everyone wanted to see the successful Americans. As one admiral who rose to toast them said, "Other men will fly around the earth, but never again will anybody fly around it for the first time."

Major Corliss C. Moseley, who winged me cross-country, was as good a flier as the army had, but the planes were still a long way from measuring up to their pilots. Taking off from New Orleans, the engine of our DH-4, known among airmen as the Flying Coffin, cut out at a hundred feet and we almost went right back into the hangar—the hard way. At the last second "Mose" coaxed it back to life and we sputtered up into the air. A couple of hours later we had to make a forced landing in a cotton field near Natchez. Some field hands were working nearby. One approached, looked us over, and with a certain wisdom said, "Mister, before I ever got into one of those things, I'd write a letter to the Lord. And I wouldn't go until he wrote back!"

We had another forced landing, a close call in the dark, at San Francisco, and a thrill a minute in between. But we finally made it to Seattle. Afterward, I put together a film and narrative and, with one of the world fliers, did a coast-to-coast tour. A radio station in Pittsburgh invited me to do a one-hour impromptu show, March 21, 1925, on the flight. It was the first time I stepped up to a radio microphone and began talking.

BY SPRING, 1926, I had finished writing *The First World Flight* and *Beyond the Khyber Pass*. Having been desk-bound for a year, I felt an urgent need to pack a bag and get going. I had been reading about the development of airlines in Europe, and I suggested to Fran a journey that no one had ever made before: crisscrossing Europe by air via every available route.

We left young Lowell at Locust Farm, a country home and school with experience looking after children whose parents needed to be away. It was in Dutchess County, north of New York City, and as our train passed through Pawling, I remembered Beulah Bondi's vision of the Thomases living in a white house near there. But I was too preoccupied with leaving Lowell, Jr., behind to think about it much. I would have given anything to take him with us, but two and a half is young for barnstorming by single-engine plane. We sailed for England with heavy hearts. I still remember the sad look in his eyes, but in light of his own fabulous adventures later on, I take comfort in the hope that he came to understand why we left him.

Europeans had gotten the jump on Americans in commercial aviation—nearly all the planes were being built in Europe. Now the World War I aces were pioneering routes between dozens of cities. Before our tour was over, Fran and I would break the record for passenger miles flown. We often traveled in open-cockpit planes held together with baling wire, and in more than one white-knuckled hour it seemed likely we would never see our son again. But it was a unique adventure and neither of us would have missed it.

In London, the general manager of the newly organized British Imperial Airways, G. E. Woods-Humphery, offered to start us on our journey with a flight to Amsterdam in a six-passenger plane. But the weather turned foul and stayed that way. On the fourth day, though it had not noticeably improved, a Rolls arrived to drive us to Croydon airfield.

We took off in a driving rain. The ceiling was low, and we came in over Holland at minimal altitude. As one of the unhappy, airsick passengers said, "We were looking up at the windmills." Years later I learned the true depths of their misery—they were British Imperial employees who would have to turn right around in Amsterdam and go home. After the delay, Woods-Humphery, sure we would get a bad impression of Imperial Airways service, had ordered the pilot to fly us to Amsterdam, no matter what the weather. There were no other passengers booked, so to make a showing he sent four office employees to fill up the seats. I can only hope they forgave us.

From Amsterdam we flew to Paris, and from there to Bucharest in a French Spad. The pilot's face was swathed in bandages, but I made a point of not asking him what had happened. Landing, the Spad bounced hard, spun and went over on its nose. "Are you well?" asked the bandages.

"*Oui,*" said Fran, who was looking straight down at the back of his neck.

Next day another Spad, another French pilot. As we prepared to take off for Istanbul, I asked, I hope casually, what would happen if our single engine conked out over the Black Sea. Frankness, not reassurance, was this pilot's strong point: "*Oh, on tombera quelque part dans la Mer Noire.*" No matter how I twisted the translation around, it still came out as a flat assertion that we were bound to come down somewhere in the Black Sea.

Well, we made it to Istanbul, and moved on from there. We were among the first ever to land at Tempelhof, in Berlin, and got permission to fly into the U.S.S.R. Our plane this time was a Fokker with a small cabin under its single wing. We were kept company by the flight engineer, who opened a forward port to check the engine. The engine was lubricated with castor oil and the fumes filled the cabin. For the first and last time in millions of miles of air travel, I was good and ill. Nor could I forget my malaise by looking out at the scenery; the Russians had the window curtains drawn, as if the endless miles of forest below might reveal dark secrets of their latest five-year plan.

We had gone to the opera wherever we could, for Fran had an insatiable enthusiasm for music. She watched bright-eyed and absorbed while I slept through great arias. So when we returned to Paris with Fran ready for still more opera—as well as some serious shopping—I started for Morocco on my own. And on this jaunt I almost, as many fliers put it, "bought the farm."

I was to fly Latécoère, a small airline, later absorbed by Air France, which was pioneering routes from France to North Africa. Our plane, which was flying mail to Morocco, was a Breguet, a two-seater left over from the war. Crammed into the rear cockpit between my knees was a Latécoère mechanic, bound for a new assignment in Fès. We landed at Lyon and Marseille, and finally set course for Spain. Somewhere over the Andalusian desert the engine suddenly quit, and in a frightening silence we came down to earth in a hard, dead-stick landing. After the mechanic failed to coax the engine back to life, the pilot went for help. He knew of a mine a few miles away.

The mechanic and I crawled under a wing to take shelter from the blistering heat, and soon the pilot returned. He had found the mine and telephoned. The airline's chief pilot himself was on his way with another plane. Little more than an hour later, there he was above us. We lighted a small fire to indicate wind direction, and he dropped down beside the crippled Breguet. The mail was transferred and the three of us prepared to take off: the *pilote en chef* would wait for a new engine.

But our substitute plane was overloaded. After racing five hundred yards toward some boulders without getting off the ground, the pilot taxied back again. There followed a good deal of gesticulating and spirited French. Our pilot wanted the mechanic to remain behind, and the mechanic was wailing his resistance. The *pilote en chef* seemed to favor whoever currently had his attention. With the mechanic still on board, we tried again, but only succeeded in coming even closer to those boulders. This time we dropped some mail sacks, and while the *pilote en chef* gestured encouragingly, we staggered up.

Only a few hundred feet off the ground, the plane bucked and began falling. The pilot cut the switch, twisted in his seat and shouted, *"Garde à vous, monsieur!* We are going to—how you say?—crash!"* An instant later we hit like a bursting shell, sand exploding all around us. Somehow we tumbled out, but I was the only one to get up from the ground. Frantically, I dragged the other two away. But the plane did not burst into flame. We sat in the sand and surveyed it. It was a wreck, and mail was strewn over the desert for fifty yards. We were too badly hurt to move, so we waited for someone to come to our aid.

The *pilote en chef* and some peasants who had seen the plane falling arrived about the same time; the peasants took us to a hospital in Murcia. Days later another plane came for the pilot and the mechanic and flew them on to Morocco, but I had had enough. I stayed in this land of oranges and good red wine and let my battered bones heal. By the time I got back to Fran in Paris, I could make the crash sound like a joke, but I was glad transatlantic air service was still in the future. We sailed home on the leisurely old *Rotterdam*.

IN THE FALL OF 1926, Fran and I again took up our hunt for a permanent home. We were drawn back to lovely Dutchess County, and one day found ourselves driving along a dirt road leading to the place called Quaker Hill. When we came to a big, handsome white house, we both thought, *This could be it!*

There was nothing to indicate the house might be for sale, but I jumped a fence and knocked at the door. A butler answered and showed me into a charming sitting room. There I was joined by a serene older woman, Mrs. Wise. I introduced myself and told her that after traveling for many years, we wanted to settle down. By any chance was this place for sale?

Her eyes widened. "This is the strangest thing," she said. "My husband and I lived here for thirty years. Our children were born here. And now you come along and . . ."

My heart sank. "I'm sorry. I didn't mean to offend you."

I started to get up, but she motioned me to stay. "My husband passed away several years ago," she said, "and now the children are grown. Just this morning—I haven't mentioned it to a soul—I made up my mind to sell the house and take an apartment in the city. And suddenly you knock at my door. It's as though you were fated to be the new owners of Clover Brook Farm."

I brought Fran in, and Mrs. Wise showed us around. Then she invited us to stay with her for a while so we could be absolutely sure Clover Brook Farm was where we wanted to live.

We were sure. One day Fran and I picked up Beulah Bondi and told her to direct us to the house she had envisioned. She went straight to Clover Brook Farm, as we'd known she would.

THE FARM CONSISTED then of a thirty-two-room house, two barns, and eighty acres of fields, to which we added another three hundred and fifty of woodland. The house had been built in colonial days; we were only the fifth family to own it.

So Fran, Lowell, Jr., and I had a home at last. But I also had a commitment to write six books, none of which had been researched or even outlined. I figured I needed help; and it came in the person of a round little man—he measured about five feet two in any direction—with the unlikely name of Prosper Buranelli. Behind Prosper's engaging wit was a computer brain that seemed to have absorbed the total sum of human knowledge and stood ready to call forth even the most obscure bits on demand. He was an authentic genius, a marvelous companion, altogether one of the most remarkable men I have ever known. Our meeting, through a friend with whom he had collaborated, was one of the luckiest things that ever happened to me.

When I explained my problem and invited him to join me, he said, "Let's give it a try." He was with us for thirty-four years, until the night of June 19, 1960, when he died in our house.

Prosper came from Temple, Texas, one of seven children born to an Italian immigrant and a Wisconsin girl of German-Scottish parentage. His schooling was interrupted in the sixth grade. Having borne as much as he could of rote and repetition of things he already knew, he stood up in his classroom one day, broke a ruler over his knee and walked out, never to return. When he was still in his teens, he spent three years in New York experimenting with musical composition. He became a favorite with Greenwich Village writers and artists, and soon a wealthy friend, awed by his mind, offered to sponsor him at Yale. So "Pros" went to New Haven. He lasted one semester, then returned to New York. He had enjoyed Yale, he reported, but there was little they could teach him that he couldn't learn more easily by himself. The rich friend persisted. What about Cornell then? But Prosper didn't even make it through the first marking period—and this time he came back with a wife. That was the end of his formal education and he decided he'd better go to work.

The editor of the New York *World* hired him to do cerebral pieces, and then, in 1919, put him to work devising the *World's* crossword puzzles. Pros was not happy about this, he said, because "the crossword puzzle was regarded in the office as beneath a sensible man's consideration." But he developed a new numbering system and elevated the level of the crossword puzzle until it intrigued even intellectuals. In fact, he helped father the crossword-puzzle craze in America, turning out new puzzles for the next ten years and joining in editing the first crossword books.

He was also a chess master who could play five men at the same time while discussing archaeology with a sixth. He haunted the Metropolitan Opera, knew most of the singers and musicians and, apparently, almost every line of music ever written. If you hummed a few bars for him, he would identify the composition, then proceed with a brief account of the composer's life. He was a brilliant conversationalist, always able to pluck a gem of relevant information from his incredible memory and offer it with wit. President Hoover later called Pros his favorite fishing companion, and I suspect Franklin Roosevelt tried at least once to lure him to Washington.

Prosper also had some shortcomings, most having to do with practical things. Our relationship may have flourished partly because it meant he no longer had to concern himself with finances, which bored him. A main task of Mary Davis, who ran my New York office, was to retrieve and pay the bills Pros threw into the wastebasket. Mary also periodically sent to the laundry the soiled socks and shirts he stuffed into filing cabinets.

He had an ideal if unusual marital relationship. Although he and his Mina loved each other dearly, and Pros took an inordinate pride in his family, he was rarely home. He stayed at Quaker Hill or, during my radio and Fox-Movietone years, in a small hotel across from the office.

Meanwhile, Mina was at their house in Ridgefield Park, New Jersey, somewhat disconsolate because the house seemed to shrink as the nine Buranelli children grew. In the 1940s I bought a larger place for them in Tenafly. Weeks later Prosper told Mary he was going home and asked her to write down his new address. He gave it to a taxi driver, who drove him all the way to Tenafly. But when Pros saw the expansive grounds and the big house he said, "Somebody's made a mistake. This must be where the mayor lives." And he taxied back to New York.

OVER THE YEARS we had quite an array of guests at Quaker Hill—three presidents, a Supreme Court justice, governors, actors, military men, artists, authors, explorers and opera stars.

Soon after surrendering the White House to Roosevelt, Hoover, forsaken and even reviled, came to Clover Brook for quiet and some fishing. Thereafter he was a regular visitor, for the Chief, as he was known to his friends, knew that no one at Quaker Hill wanted anything from him. He treated his friends with a warmth he could never convey in public; he was a gifted storyteller, and his visits were a high-water mark for all of us.

Time heals all wounds. Eventually, Hoover came to be loved once more by the American people he served so valiantly. He was a football fan, and on one memorable Saturday we took him to the Army-Cornell game at West Point. Leaving the game early so Hoover would not be held up in the postgame traffic jam, we were in full view of the crowd. All forty thousand of them stood and applauded. It was a thrilling moment: the first time Hoover had been given such an ovation since he had left the White House.

IN THOSE EARLY YEARS I invited the subjects of my books to stay at Clover Brook so I could start them talking. One such guest was Fred Harmon.

I was speaking in Cleveland and had been invited to the book department of Halle's department store to autograph *With Lawrence in Arabia* and *Beyond Khyber Pass*. I was sitting at a table behind tall stacks of books when a man thrust his scarred face between the stacks and muttered, "Mr. Thomas, would you be interested in writing my story? I am one of fourteen survivors of a shipwreck. We drifted thirteen hundred miles across the South Seas in an open boat. When we ran out of food, we ate the chief engineer."

As opening gambits go, it was a blockbuster, and we arranged to meet later in the day. When he came to my hotel, his scarred face looked more menacing than before. But Fred Harmon, lately the first assistant engineer of the merchantman *Dumaru,* was not a menace. He was a tormented soul, unable to exorcise the demons of his memory. He had survived a horrible tragedy, living through an ordeal that claimed a score of weaker men, but he had not yet finished paying the price. Yes, I wanted to do a book about the *Dumaru*, and I invited Harmon to Clover Brook.

He arrived early in January. Fran didn't even make it through lunch the first day. As Harmon began telling us about the cannibalism practiced by the *Dumaru*'s survivors, she paled. So did Helen Hamlin, my fragile-looking secretary. When Harmon described how some men had drunk the blood of a corpse, Fran took a last look at the leg of lamb on the table, rose, put young Lowell in the car and drove off to New Jersey to spend the week with my parents. Poor Helen had to stay and make notes. But *The Wreck of the Dumaru*, the story of that incredible open-boat voyage of thirteen hundred miles, became one of the six books I had promised Doubleday.

Doubleday was already pleased. My first book for them, *Count Luckner, the Sea Devil*, had been the hit of their 1927–1928 season. Luckner was a fantastic man—six feet three inches of supercharged energy and high spirits. I first saw him when Fran and I were making our survey of the budding European airlines. One day, delayed at Leipzig, we watched a silver plane circle the field and glide to a gentle landing. Then a big man opened the door and a scattering of applause swept the field. He wore a chinchilla coat and a rakish naval cap, and as he bounded down a ladder to the ground, a blond woman who looked like a fairy princess brought to earth on a sunbeam appeared behind him. She leaped daintily into his arms, he set her down and they made a triumphal procession across the field as he boomed out *"Wiedersehen! Wiedersehen!"* to mechanics, attendants and travelers.

"Who is he?" I asked the field commandant.

He looked at me as though I had just arrived from outer space. "Why, the 'Sea Devil'—Count Felix von Luckner—with the countess. He commanded the *Seeadler—Sea Eagle*—during the war."

The Sea Devil was making a tour of Germany, seeking to reinvigorate his defeated countrymen. Wherever he went, half-holidays were declared in his honor and great crowds turned out to hear the amiable buccaneer who had sunk twenty-five million dollars' worth of Allied shipping without taking a single life.

We invited von Luckner and his countess to visit us at Clover Brook. They stayed two months, as lively a time as the old homestead was ever to know, for the irrepressible von Luckner regaled us with salty tales in which he acted out every role, his dialogue studded with vigorous exclamations of "By Joe!" his substitute for the profanity of his youthful days at sea. In between, Prosper and I drew from him the story of his remarkable life.

He was the scion of an old military family. At thirteen he ran away from home to become a cabin boy on a Russian schooner, roaming the world under an assumed name, surviving shipwrecks and suffering the beatings and deprivations that the merchant marine visited upon its children in those days. He took a few turns ashore, too, trying his hand as an assistant to an Indian fakir, a kangaroo hunter, a prizefighter, magician and beachcomber, in the Salvation Army and as a soldier in Mexico.

But inevitably he went back to sea and rose in rank to command a series of rust buckets under sail. As a result of saving several lives, he came to the attention of the kaiser, who enrolled him in the German navy. The kaiser, fascinated with his gifts for comedy and legerdemain, also made him his Falstaff for a time. Von Luckner even plucked eggs out of the czar's beard.

In the third year of the war, as one of the few officers in the navy with long experience under sail, von Luckner was given the desperate mission of running a windjammer through the blockade to prey on enemy shipping. The vessel was a captured American three-master. At twenty yards, the *Seeadler* looked like an innocent vessel, perhaps of Norwegian registry, but in fact she bristled with hidden cannon and machine guns and had been fitted with two powerful diesel engines, provisions for two years and quarters for a large number of prisoners.

Two days before Christmas, 1916, she slipped out of Hamburg harbor and sailed straight into a North Sea hurricane. While Allied patrol vessels ran for cover, the *Seeadler,* unmolested, bucked her way into the open sea. In January the Sea Devil struck for the first time. Intercepting the British steamer *Gladys Royal* west of Gibraltar, von Luckner ordered his German colors raised and a false rail dropped, revealing a heavy gun. One shot across the steamer's bow and the battle was over. The stunned crew of the *Gladys Royal* was transferred to the *Seeadler,* along with the best of the cargo. Then the captive vessel was sunk by gunfire and the raider sailed on, racking up a mounting toll of enemy ships, taking their crews aboard and providing them with three solid meals a day. The captains were shown to a special Captains' Club and treated as deferentially as they had been on their own ships. The other prisoners also had the run of the *Seeadler,* and as each of their prizes contributed its stores, food and drink remained plentiful. The voyage was more like a holiday cruise than a war patrol.

But all good things must end. By late March, 1917, von Luckner had taken aboard two hundred and sixty crew members and passengers from eleven sunken enemy ships. An earlier pirate skipper might have cleared the decks with a plank-walking ceremony, but the Sea Devil hit on a happier solution. Up over the horizon came a French barque, the *Cambronne,* to become his twelfth trophy. But this one was not sunk. Instead, von Luckner transferred all his prisoners to the *Cambronne.* He asked for the captain's promise not to reveal the *Seeadler*'s existence until he reached Rio de Janeiro, the nearest port. In light of von Luckner's chivalry, the promise was gladly given and kept.

There was a gala farewell party. In accord with international convention, von Luckner paid the prisoners for the time they had spent aboard the *Seeadler,* and they gave him three cheers from the deck of the *Cambronne.* Then the *Seeadler* made for Cape Horn under every stitch of canvas she had.

By the time the Sea Devil reached the Pacific, the United States had declared war on Germany, and in short order he captured three American merchantmen. But now the fates turned against the *Seeadler.* For weeks she roved the Pacific without sighting another vessel. As stores of fresh food vanished, some weary, discouraged men came down with scurvy. Finally, late in summer, they landed on an uninhabited atoll in the Cook Islands. It was a palm-shaded paradise of wild fruit and, in the lagoon, excellent fish. Quickly all hands regained their strength. But one morning a tidal wave drove the *Seeadler* high up on the coral reef: the raiders were marooned. They set about building themselves huts, but after two weeks of languid existence, the Sea Devil declared that he was a naval officer, not a beachcomber, by Joe. With five volunteers he set sail in one of the lifeboats. His destination was the Fiji Islands; his goal, to capture a sailing ship, come back for the others and continue raiding.

It was one of those incredible epics of the sea, six men naked to the weather in a cockleshell of a boat, fighting wind, hunger and ravening thirst. And all in vain. After covering twenty-three hundred miles and landing at Wakaya, they were arrested by a patrol and taken to a prisoner-of-war camp in New Zealand. Twice they escaped, only to be recaptured. "If the war had lasted another week," said von Luckner, "there would have been another escape."

Ending his account, the Sea Devil told me, "I suppose we inflicted only small injuries to our foe. But we had done everything you could expect of a lone windjammer. And"—he leaned forward—"no mother, wife, child or father ever had to shed a single tear because of any harm we brought to a loved one."

THE YEARS PASSED. Von Luckner, idolized in Germany and decorated by Allied governments for his unfaltering humanity during the war, married the beautiful Swedish heiress Ingeborg Engstroem. When my book about him appeared in 1927, he made a triumphant tour of the United States. A Chicago friend, Burt Massee, a former newsboy who had made millions as an executive of the Palmolive Company, heard him speak and never forgot it. Two years later Massee told us he was getting married and invited us to go along on a honeymoon cruise. Indeed, he wanted me to arrange it. He wanted nothing less than to charter von Luckner's four-masted sailing ship, the *Vaterland,* for a leisurely cruise of the Caribbean. I cabled Burt's slightly wild idea to Hamburg, and a day later received a typically Lucknerian reply: BY JOE! CAPITAL IDEA! SEND DETAILS!

In midsummer, 1929, the von Luckners set sail for Bermuda to pick us up for what was to be a fantastic voyage. Massee ordered the ship stocked with enormous quantities of luxurious food and drink—two hundred Westphalian hams, six thousand bottles of wine and champagne and ten thousand bottles of Munich beer. By the time we finally set off, the honeymoon party numbered twenty-six, for the beaming groom, who brought his Katie East to spend a weekend with us before sailing, insisted on inviting everyone in sight. I was working on a book with Dan Edwards, a swashbuckling AEF sergeant who had gone into a World War I court-martial for insubordination and come out with a Congressional Medal of Honor, having deserted from a military hospital to get back to the trenches. He had lost an arm and wore a gruesome facial scar from a gunshot wound, but none of this dimmed his zest for life. Massee promptly invited Dan to join us. He also invited Prosper, three more of my staff, the explorer Carveth Wells, the artist McClelland Barclay, and a clutch of his friends from Chicago.

We arrived in Bermuda late in July. The *Vaterland* stood offshore in a flaming red sunset, gleaming white hull resting lightly on the water. Von Luckner greeted us—by Joe!—with a champagne supper and showed us to lavish staterooms. The *Vaterland* carried a crew of thirty and a full-time captain so the Sea Devil himself need never be distracted from his social obligations.

It was the era of wonderful nonsense, and prosperity was supposed to last forever. Such were the enchantments of the lovely British crown colony that no one was anxious to hoist anchor. By day we swam and sunned, one-armed Dan Edwards terrifying the rest of us by climbing up to the crow's nest and diving fifty feet into the sea. By night, after dinner at the Hamilton Hotel, Massee and his Chicago friends sat around matching hundred-dollar bills. Von Luckner loved every minute of this phenomenal foolishness. On the night we finally set sail for Santo Domingo, we stood together at the rail and he said to me, "You know, Tommy, we all came into this world crying while everyone else was laughing. By Joe, I mean to go out laughing—and let the others do the crying!"

Santo Domingo, the oldest city in the Americas, is the capital of the Dominican Republic, which shares the island of Hispaniola with Haiti. In many ways it still looked like the Spanish colonial town founded by Columbus's brother Bartholomew in 1496. But neither the look nor the lore of Santo Domingo particularly intrigued Dan Edwards. He had heard there were wild pigs in the hills behind the town, so one day he set off with a rifle slung over his shoulder. No one was surprised when word came back to the ship that he had been arrested for carrying a loaded firearm. Dan demanded to be taken to the military commandant. He never told us what passed between them, but the charge was dropped and the commandant was invited to dine aboard the *Vaterland.*

This was only the beginning of their friendship. Before we sailed on, the commandant made Dan a colonel in the Dominican army—which passed in review for him—and presented him with a thousand acres of inaccessible but beautiful land on a mountaintop. These were lavish gifts for a young officer to be passing out, and we all wondered about the source of his power. Then Dan, only half joking, invited him to sail away with us, and only half joking the Dominican replied, "If I leave island for a day or two, the president, he dies of fright."

In this land where revolution was practically a semiannual occurrence, the commandant and his troops were the main prop of the current regime. But before another year passed, our new friend—whose name was Rafael Trujillo—had seized the presidency for himself; he established a corrupt, ruthless dictatorship that lasted until he was assassinated in 1961.

But to us Trujillo was the soul of kindness. He arranged for the president to receive us, came each night to dine and dance with us, and solved all our problems. When a local orchestra Massee had hired tucked the cost of formal evening wear in with their bill, Massee had only to mention it. The orchestra was arrested, but as we sailed off to Jamaica they stood on the wall of the white prison fortress overlooking the harbor, wearing their new tuxedos, with picks and shovels on their shoulders, to give us a salute.

We sailed on, and summer passed into fall. Then, one morning, after a late breakfast, someone brought Massee a wireless message. He read it quickly, took Katie's hand and, with a rueful smile, said, "I guess the party's over."

It was, and not only for Burt Massee. Wall Street had been hit by the greatest stock-market crash in history. An era ended and a far grimmer one began. Massee had lost sixteen million dollars and was wiped out. He would go into the insurance business and make a partial recovery, but no man ever had a finer moment than Burt Massee did that morning. "Cheer up," he said to us, "we've had a good time, haven't we? I don't have a thing in the world to worry about—all the bills for this trip are paid."

Chapter XI

ONE DAY IN AUGUST, 1930, my telephone rang and an overwrought voice said, "Mr. Thomas, I'm with the Columbia Broadcasting Company and I figure you're the only man in the world who can save my job. I heard you speak at Covent Garden and—well, if you can come to New York at two p.m. tomorrow I'll explain everything. You may be doing both of us a favor."

A little mystery, the promise of something new and exciting . . . "Where?" I asked.

"The Columbia Broadcasting building," he said.

And so began my more than forty-five years in radio.

ON TUESDAY, NOVEMBER 2, 1920, station KDKA, Pittsburgh, the nation's first commercial radio station, had gone on the air with returns from the presidential election. It was clear before midnight that Warren G. Harding was the winner, and that broadcast introduced a revolutionary new entertainment and information medium. Within two years, more than five hundred commercial stations had been licensed, and in 1928, with the National Broadcasting Company already operating three stations in New York, William S. Paley bought the fourth, originally the Columbia Broadcasting Company. His Columbia Broadcasting System set out to capture NBC's prize program, the only daily news broadcast. It was sponsored by the staid *Literary Digest,* but its newsman was the hard-drinking, colorful war correspondent Floyd Gibbons. This had been an unlikely marriage from the start. The *Literary Digest* and its parent company, Funk & Wagnalls, had put up with Gibbons's flamboyance because magazine circulation had begun to climb. But the company president, a fervent teetotaler named R. J. Cuddihy, found it increasingly difficult to smile at Gibbons's irrepressible ways.

Then, at two o'clock one morning, Floyd, a pal and a pair of women friends found themselves in the vicinity of Cuddihy's Long

Island home. Pounding on the door until RJ appeared in night-gown and cap, Floyd said, "How's about a li'l old drink for my friends?" Cuddihy asked them in. I never heard what drinks he served them, but Gibbons's radio days were numbered. Cuddihy auditioned dozens of lecturers and journalists for the spot. Dissatisfied with all of them, he was about to cancel the program.

I knew none of this when I went to the Columbia Broadcasting building. My mysterious caller introduced me to William Paley and disappeared. (Months later, when I tried to find him, no one remembered who he was.) Paley took me to a studio, put me in front of a microphone and said, "When you hear the buzzer, start talking. Talk fifteen minutes. Then stop." Then *he* disappeared.

Three musicians, obviously standing by in case of a programming emergency, watched me from the corner of the room. "Did you hear what the man said?" I asked them. They nodded. "Well, I don't know what this is all about, but if you would play something oriental when I start talking, it could help."

The buzzer sounded. The musicians played "In a Persian Garden" and I started. I talked about Lawrence, Afghanistan—whatever came into my head. Fifteen minutes later I stopped. Paley reappeared and said, "I want you to meet some people."

Cuddihy and eighteen of his editors and executives had been listening as my voice was piped out from the studio. And so I found out that the *Literary Digest* wanted to replace Floyd Gibbons, but that I didn't have the job locked up. Cuddihy, a rather stern-faced man, told me that he had soured on the whole project because neither network had been able to bring him anyone who came close to Gibbons's distinctive style.

"Why replace him at all?" I asked. I was feeling indifferent, and radio meant little to me.

As if I hadn't spoken, Cuddihy went on to say that I had made no attempt to imitate Gibbons, had spoken in my own, more casual style and—would I come back Thursday at six and do a news summary? "We'll listen to you, then we'll listen to Gibbons, who is still on the air, and give you our decision."

"Yes, of course!" Bill Paley answered. He hustled me off. "We'll get the best brains in the business to prepare this broadcast!"

For him, luring the *Literary Digest* away from NBC would be a million-dollar triumph. For me, it was a little confusing. How many brains did it take to prepare a fifteen-minute newscast? I said, "Okay, Mr. Paley, you round up the best brains you can find and I'll round up the best brains I can find and we'll make an event of this audition."

I called my publisher, Russell Doubleday, and asked if he had any brains to spare. He asked if I was sober. Backtracking, I explained the story, and Mr. Doubleday—who also wondered aloud how big a brain pool it took to tell the day's news in fifteen minutes—promised to send me some people nonetheless.

Thursday morning at nine we assembled in strength at the Princeton Club. Three men came from Columbia. My own contingent consisted of Prosper, Dale Carnegie, a Doubleday editor and a young manuscript reader named Ogden Nash. I also brought along a stenographer and a couple of jugs of applejack.

Rural Dutchess County, New York, became the Thomases' home in 1926. One of their neighbors (left) was later elected President. In 1930, LT began his nightly newscasts. At center, he goes over listener mail with writer Prosper

Everyone dived into it, and soon the geniuses paired off for a lengthy debate on the best way to begin a news broadcast. And there we stayed, hung up in the starting gate, until poker-faced Ogden Nash, scribbling away in the corner, produced a couple of lively paragraphs. His work already had the qualities that would make him one of America's best-known humorists.

When at four o'clock we still had lots of noise and fury but no script, I quietly walked out. I don't think anyone even missed me. I picked up a couple of evening newspapers and headed to the Columbia building. At the studio I made a few notes and at six I walked up to the microphone and said, "Good evening, everybody." Then I told the news. At the end of fifteen minutes I said, "Good night," and sat down.

Paley came in beaming. After Gibbons's broadcast, he rushed me down to R. J. Cuddihy and his aides.

And Cuddihy was beaming, too.

Buranelli. Thomas went on the air in the time slot preceding Freeman Gosden and Charlie Correll (right)— better known as "Amos 'n' Andy." Their popular comedy show helped raise LT's audience to millions.

AT SIX FORTY-FIVE on September 29, CBS *and* NBC announcers introduced me on the air as "the *Literary Digest*'s new radio voice, informing and entertaining you with the latest news of the day." My report dealt with Adolf Hitler.

Looking back, it is hard for me to believe that one broadcaster ever had the world's airwaves all to himself. I had both networks, for Cuddihy kept NBC for the eastern half of the United States, with CBS taking the West. Actually there was one news analyst broadcasting then—Hans von Kaltenborn. But he was on only twice a week, with commentary, and not only was I the lucky heir to the audience of the immensely popular Gibbons, but on NBC the program was in the time slot immediately preceding "Amos 'n' Andy." So powerful was the lure of radio's first situation comedy that after six months Cuddihy moved the program back to NBC altogether. And soon along came competition, with the impressive likes of Gabriel Heatter and Boake Carter on the air. One day there would be thousands of newscasters around the country.

My own voice, say those who calculate such irrelevancies, was probably heard over the years by around a hundred and twenty-five billion people. After a year and a half, the *Literary Digest* dropped out of radio, but I was taken over by the Sun Oil Company. In 1946, I switched over to CBS and stayed until 1976—one of the longest-running daily programs in the annals of broadcasting.

In the beginning, we simply bought the afternoon papers and rewrote the stories we wanted for the broadcast, giving full credit to the newspapers and wire services. At first they were enthusiastic about getting the credits, but one day the head of Hearst's International News Service called me and said that Hearst had decided to build his own chain of radio stations and saw no reason to help the competition. Soon after, the Associated Press and United Press also cut me off. Roy Howard, head of UP, said the news services had to "destroy this radio monster before it destroys us!" So we subscribed to Reuters and other foreign press agencies, and then hired Abe Schechter, a newspaper reporter, who later became head of NBC's news department.

Every day we would comb the newspapers and decide

which stories to feature. Then Abe and Prosper would telephone the people who were making headlines. Flattered to have attracted the notice of a New York radio station, they would provide us with fresh and exclusive material. The system gave us the kind of last-minute deadline no paper or wire service could match, and one by one the press associations came around to make peace, and began providing news services for broadcasting, a tremendous new business for them. The networks learned a lesson, too, and soon built up their own news departments.

People who worked with me delight in telling tales about how I would come dashing to the microphone at air time with hardly a second to spare. The tales are true, but the circumstances were extenuating. For example, our location was a problem. For a time our office was high up in the RCA Building in Rockefeller Center, which also housed NBC. There was no way to get to our studio except down forty-one floors in one elevator, across the lobby and then up eight floors in another elevator. Several times I arrived to hear the announcer intoning my name in introduction. And one day during the Christmas season I snatched some packages from my desk, dashed for the studio, reached the microphone in time to say, "Good evening, everybody"—only to realize that I had forgotten my script in the rush. There was some wild ad-libbing regarding the joys of the holiday season until a breathless Mary Davis arrived with the sheets of news.

In winter, when heavy snows buried our country roads, I had difficulty getting to the Pawling railroad station. Usually, I could manage it with a horse-drawn wagon on runners, but once, in a record blizzard, I had to ski. Cutting overland, I finally reached the railroad tracks well south of Pawling, where I flagged the train down with my ski poles.

Soon I persuaded NBC to let me do my broadcasts from a studio at Clover Brook. I wanted to work near the skiing. Neither NBC nor, later, CBS objected. On a routine day I'd check the news by phone with Prosper, rough out a broadcast, head for the slopes. By late afternoon I was going over dispatches sent up by phone, redoing them to suit my style. At six forty-four I would hurry out to the studio beyond the barn, where I would climb up a ladder to the mike just as the engineer, in a room below me, yanked on a cord to signal my "Good evening, everybody."

Of course, if you play on the same fiddle for forty-five years, you're bound to hit a sour note now and then. Once, I dropped the script and recovered it with the pages completely out of order. For a while I had the abdicating King Edward VIII involved in the Miss America pageant—as if the poor guy hadn't enough trouble. Another time I transposed the *a* and the *i* in the first and last names of the eminent British statesman Sir Stafford Cripps, tried again, did it again—and burst into such a paroxysm of laughter I knocked the microphone over.

Fluffs or scoops could bring ten thousand letters in a given week. But no broadcast ever generated such a massive response as the one we did from Western Union headquarters. It all began with a phone call from Newcomb Carlton, the Western Union chairman, questioning my occasional references to Mackay Radio, the overseas arm of Postal Telegraph, his arch-rival. I told him I was simply crediting Postal for relaying some shortwave messages to me from Admiral Byrd in Antarctica, with no favoritism intended. Mr. Carlton adroitly turned the conversation around to the virtues of Western Union. One word led to another, and within a week our NBC crew was down at his headquarters in lower Manhattan. While scores of telegraph keys tapped out marvelous sound effects, and wire baskets bearing messages spun overhead, and young women on rubber roller skates zoomed noiselessly by, I did my broadcast. Carlton, assuming I'd hear from some relatives, told my announcer, Jimmy Wallington, to invite anyone in the audience to send me a free wire.

Before the night was over we were buried under 265,567 telegrams, more than ever summoned up by any event before in history. The messages ranged from thrifty expressions like "Keep up the good work" to a whole chapter from the Book of Job, sent along by a pious skeptic who doubted it would go through. It did, as did several thousand sent in error via Postal Telegraph, for which Western Union had to pay in hard cash. Had the whole lot been charged at the regular rate, the bill would have come to around five hundred thousand dollars.

I was going to answer every telegram, so I had them carted away to a rather ancient frame building at Quaker Hill. I had loaned the building to Dr. Norman Vincent Peale and my brother-in-law, Raymond Thornburg, when they launched a new magazine, *Guideposts*. One day the building caught fire and the telegrams all went up in flames; so did the *Guideposts* subscriber list. When I told about this on the air, many people wrote in, and overnight the *Guideposts* list of subscribers doubled.

Our mail was fascinating in those early years. Radio was an intimate medium then; all around the world, people tuned in as though opening the door to an old friend. And like old friends they felt free to scold, for radio also made it possible for a broadcaster to step on millions of toes at the same instant.

Of course, not everyone wrote to complain. Some, like a lady in Broome, Australia, and a sea captain off the Madagascar coast, only wanted to tell me I was coming in loud and clear. A Canadian Mountie on Ellesmere Island said that the broadcast was being heard by the farthest-north man on earth—him. An American geologist came in person to thank me for making him rich. Deep in the Canadian bush, he'd picked up my report about a gold strike in northern Ontario. He had immediately chartered a plane and staked a claim before anyone else could get there.

One day a former United States naval attaché, Harold Grow, who had been imprisoned in Peru during a revolution, told me that for weeks my broadcasts had helped him hang on to his sanity. When I began reporting the excesses of the revolution, he persuaded his jailers to listen in; they were so concerned by their unfavorable image in the outside world that they released him. In World War II, Grow made a brilliant record and wound up accepting the surrender of three Japanese-held islands in the Pacific.

As the years passed, observers, expert and amateur, have submitted their analyses of why, of all the thousands of programs on the air since 1930, mine alone survived so long.

Damon Runyon said it was because I gave the impression of saying, "Now here is the news with some human slants on it and you can interpret it to suit yourself." Columnist Cy Caldwell, a caustically comic sort who was irreverent about everything except "Amos 'n' Andy," came up with a piece of doggerel which he said explained everything and was also suitable as my epitaph:

> *Here lies the bird*
> *Who was heard*
> *By millions of people—*
> *Who were waiting to hear*
> *"Amos 'n' Andy."*

Chapter XII

RADIO CAST ME in a new role, which sometimes left me ill at ease. When strangers rushed toward me with slightly glazed eyes to say, "What a *thrill* it is to meet you!" I tended to look over my shoulder to see whom they meant. My name seemed to pass into the public domain. A pun making the rounds in the early 1930s had an aristocratic young potato seeking her parents' permission to marry Lowell Thomas. "But that's impossible, dear," they replied, aghast. "He's just a commen-tater."

I was swamped with invitations to speak at banquets and commencements, to endorse commercial products and candidates for public office, to invest in esoteric inventions—and to edit and narrate commercial films. I had been on the radio only a few months when someone from the Jam Handy company got in touch with me. Jam Handy, to my surprise, was not in the business of preserving strawberries; it was one of the largest filmmakers in Detroit, shooting sales and promotional movies for business concerns. Would I be interested, asked Jam Handy, in appearing in a film they were about to make for Frigidaire?

Sure! That was a whole new arena for me. But, I said, I always prepared my own scripts and had reservations about speaking someone else's words. They assured me Jam Handy would be open to suggestions, and sent the script off to me at once.

I had never seen anything quite like it. It was full of the verbal twists we later came to associate with Madison Avenue—verbs wrenched into nouns, like "freezability"; euphemisms in place of plain, reliable words, like "home food center" for kitchen. Still, I was sufficiently intrigued to take a train to Detroit—where I promptly antagonized everyone. Introduced to a dozen gentlemen in the Jam Handy boardroom and asked my opinion of the script, I said, "Well, first of all, why isn't it in English?"

This produced weak smiles. Then the scriptwriter asked what I found so obscure about it. I told him. There followed a babble of sound out of which I comprehended that, as a neophyte, I couldn't be expected to understand the need for specialized language in commercial movies. I said English was almost always best understood when used according to the rules of grammar; so eventually changes were made and we got down to work.

A pleasant aspect of my first venture into commercial films was the young woman cast as my secretary. She was so charming and efficient that I tried to hire her as my real secretary. She smiled. Her office skills were make-believe; all she really knew was acting. Next time I saw Martha Scott she had become a Hollywood star.

Enter the Cohn brothers—Harry and Jack, movie moguls in the making. In those days they were still seeking a foothold for their fledgling company, Columbia Pictures, grinding out obscure features and documentaries, sometimes combining the two and leaving it to the audience to figure what was fact and what fiction. I knew nothing of this when Jack Cohn telephoned me. He said Columbia had a picture that they were convinced needed my touch. It was about the Australian aborigines, filmed by a University of Hawaii professor of anthropology, authentic but exciting, a revelation. Anyway, it would only take me a few weeks. Many in the film world regarded Harry Cohn as a brigand and Jack a buccaneer, but I did not yet have an agent or a lawyer, and in my innocence I agreed to the deal and signed an unrealistic contract to edit the film, write the narration and record it, all for a sum I'm embarrassed to set down.

627

When months, not weeks, had gone by and Prosper and I were working on the last of the ten reels they had given me, and when I was already deep in the red on the whole project, the Cohns presented me with two more reels. The early reels at least had the virtue of having been shot in Australia, but the last two were as phony as a Cecil B. DeMille sunset. To juice up the story, the Cohns had sent to Harlem for some black extras—who looked about as much like aborigines as I did—for the "breathtaking and sensational climax." Are you ready to hear it?

It seems this pearling vessel is wrecked off Australia. The captain's beautiful blond wife, separated from the others, is captured by the aborigines. Naturally she is wearing very little. The frantic captain searches for his beloved wife. One day he spots an aborigine chieftain wearing a pair of familiar silk panties. Aha! He follows the panties and they lead him straight to the hovel where his blond darling is held prisoner. Swelling music! Rescue! Clinch! The end!

Apart from my contractual commitment to finish the thing, I suppose I did it because I never believed anyone would actually pay money to see it. I had failed to gauge the ingenuity of the brothers Cohn. They entitled their epic *The Blonde Captive;* they plastered the country with billboards showing me watching benignly as the flimsily clad lady was dragged off in chains by elephants. Elephants! In kangaroo land! The Cohns netted half a million right off the bat, and every five years or so they would send it around again. After a while I didn't pay attention anymore; I finally decided there was no point in going into hiding every time it turned up.

BEFORE THE AGE OF television, movie newsreels enabled people to *see* and hence understand their times. Five hundred staff cameramen and thousands of stringers regularly turned in miles of raw film from which the big companies culled maybe ten minutes' worth, to provide sixteen thousand theaters from coast to coast, twice a week, with news stories.

Fox was the giant of the newsreel field. When sound was introduced, it became Fox-Movietone, and for seventeen years, beginning in 1932, I was its "voice." I brought Prosper in with me to write our scripts.

Twice a week, around ten or eleven in the evening, we repaired to the Movietone studios to screen the film, cut it and begin preparing the script. As new film came in, pressure intensified. We cut, spliced, rewrote, rerecorded. Toward dawn, when everyone was ready for a hot bath and a warm bed, we did the final version.

It was a pressure-cooker business, and periodically a banner-line story would blow the lid off altogether. In October 1934, King Alexander of Yugoslavia arrived in Marseille to begin a state visit. The French premier, scholarly Jean Louis Barthou, was on hand to greet him, and two Fox cameramen were shooting away as the motorcade moved down the broad avenue. Suddenly, pandemonium. A blurred figure breaks through the police line, leaps up on the running board of the royal car and begins firing a pistol at the king and Barthou. The camera trembles as the crowd surges toward the assassin, but the cameramen keep grinding away. We see Alexander and Barthou, with stunned expressions, slump down on the seat, mortally wounded. Next day, black headlines about the Croatian terrorist—and in only a few days our film arrived and all America *saw* it happen.

In 1937 those sensational pictures were topped. Early in May, cameraman Al Gold was grousing because he had to cover the arrival of the zeppelin *Hindenburg*, pride of the Nazi air fleet, at the Lakehurst, New Jersey, naval air station. It was an out-of-the-way location and, besides, it was just another transatlantic crossing by a dirigible. As the *Hindenburg* dropped her landing ropes to the ground crew, Gold routinely turned the handle of his camera. Then it happened. In an incredible instant there was a muffled detonation, and the airship, filled with hydrogen, turned into a mass of flame. In less than a minute, thirty-six were dead in the inferno that marked the end of lighter-than-air travel, and our reluctant cameraman, Al Gold, got it all.

Then in December, Japan, busily devastating China without a declaration of war, bombed and sank the *Panay*, an American gunboat, in the Yangtze River, killing two. The Japanese claimed it was an accident, but two cameramen were aboard and shooting away. Their film was delivered directly to President

Roosevelt. It showed the American flag flying in plain view as the Japanese airmen swept low over the *Panay*. Japan paid a large indemnity, and the American people had striking notice that they faced a ruthless foe in the Pacific.

THERE WAS A GOLDEN age on Quaker Hill in the years before World War II. It was neither the sleepy little community of colonial days nor the summer resort that boomed just before the coming of the automobile. Instead, for a few old-timers and newcomers, like us, the high ridge above the Harlem Valley became a haven of tranquillity. Fran and I built sheds, remodeled barns, moved stone walls, put up miles of fencing, planted tens of thousands of trees and endlessly landscaped the grounds.

There had long been touchy feelings between the country "squires" on the hill and the merchants and townspeople below in the valley, at Pawling. When several of us organized a softball team called the Debtors, our number one opponents were the Creditors, from Pawling. For a while all went well enough, hill-versus-valley rivalry expressed only in the swings of our bats. Then came a day when one of our players, with too many under his belt, started needling the Pawlingites. His caustic remarks set them seething. Following a close play at home plate, fists flew and, but for a few cool heads, what had started as a friendly game would have ended in a donnybrook. So I proposed to merge our two teams, using the name Debtors *and* Creditors, and henceforth to play only in competition with teams from nearby towns. We had some fair baseball and a lot of fun.

Then came the summer of 1933. President Roosevelt had declared a bank holiday and orchestrated a pyrotechnic display of legislation and executive acts aimed at stemming the worst depression in American history. As the dog days of August began smothering Washington, he decided to escape for a few days to Hyde Park. After him trailed a hundred and thirty reporters.

The unhappy press corps was jammed into an ancient hotel in Poughkeepsie while the Hudson Valley was languishing in the grip of a heat wave. Meanwhile, twenty miles away at Quaker Hill, a refreshing breeze blew. I felt sorry for my sweltering colleagues, so I phoned one of the President's secretaries, Marvin McIntyre. "Mac," I said, "if some of your flock want to beat the heat for a couple of hours, come on over here." I expected six or eight old friends to accept. Instead, all hundred and thirty showed up—plus FDR's four sons and his daughter, Anna.

How do you entertain a hundred and thirty-five unexpected guests? Applejack and other spirits were the obvious answer, but by midday we ran out. Then someone found the key to our wine cellar, and at the first gurgle a stampede of thirsty humanity thundered down the stairs. I had a flash of inspiration. "Everybody outside!" I said. "We're going to have a ball game."

I phoned my Debtors and Creditors teammates and we had a hilarious game. The correspondents, many of whom hadn't done anything in years more athletic than climbing a barstool, floundered to a 10–0 deficit. When we loaned them some of our men to even things up, ineptitude overtook *them*, too, and we soon quit keeping score so players and spectators alike could concentrate on watching two grown men slide into the same base, several brilliant pundits wandering together under a fly ball until it hit one of them on the head, and an overstuffed columnist swinging so vehemently at a third strike that he popped his belt and went down, entangled in his own trousers.

I would like to believe our laughter was heard clear across the valley at the summer White House. At any rate, the Roosevelt boys carried the tale of our merrymaking back to FDR. His one-of-a-kind voice boomed over my phone early the next morning. "Lowell, how come I wasn't invited to your ball game?"

"My apologies, Mr. President. Your team could have used some extra encouragement."

"Well, I need a good laugh. So round up your team and come over to Hyde Park next Sunday."

As it turned out, the game was not played at Hyde Park. Someone asked the President how it would go over in the Bible Belt if they heard he staged a baseball game on Sunday. So FDR sent Secret Service men to a neighbor's place to lay out the diamond. The neighbor: Ogden Mills, Secretary of the Treasury under Hoover, and an implacable political foe.

The President's big open car was parked by first base, and from this vantage point he ran his team as though it were a federal agency, boasting of its virtues while constantly changing the lineup. In and out of the game went a bewildering array of White House correspondents, brain trusters, Secret Service men and Roosevelt sons. FDR exhorted them all, while Mrs. Roosevelt sat on the running board, stoically knitting.

Naturally, everything in the game was endowed with sham political overtones. The brain trust—professors and reformers whose advice shaped the New Deal—suffered the most ribbing. Harry Hopkins, chasing a home run into the next field, was confronted by a nettled bull and came tumbling back over a centerfield fence—to be greeted with the cry, "The capitalists' revenge!"

Then FDR's starting pitcher, Rex Tugwell, ran into hot water. Farthest left of the brain trusters, Professor Tugwell had become a celebrity, and now extra-base hits were whistling past his ears. Finally, Roosevelt, laughing so hard he could barely get the words out, yelled, "Tugwell, you're through!" and sent him to the showers. Next day an editorial in the Chicago *Daily News* congratulated the President for this. "Now," the editorial urged, "finish the job and get him out of the administration altogether."

Virtually every newspaper in the country ran a front-page story about the game, so what had begun as a pastime became almost a national institution. Every summer when Roosevelt came to Hyde Park he challenged the Debtors and Creditors to another game. After the first they were played at Quaker Hill to minimize political repercussions. They attracted nearly a thousand spectators eventually, as well as news coverage.

In 1937 we renamed our team the Nine Old Men. It was the year Roosevelt came up with his court-packing scheme, shedding crocodile tears for the nine elderly justices of the Supreme Court and their heavy burden of work. What he really wanted, as everyone knew, was to pack the high court with new members who shared his political philosophy. Someone leaked our new name to FDR, and when his team trotted out on the field, on their sweatshirts was *their* new name: The Roosevelt Packers.

Celebrities drifted in and out of the lineups. Jack Dempsey, who looked fearsome at the plate, popped up or fanned out. He confessed that at the age when most kids play baseball he had been working or fighting. Gene Tunney liked to pitch, and took the game seriously. He bought his chauffeur a catcher's mitt, and on the way to Quaker Hill they would stop so Gene could warm up. Then there was Branch Rickey, who won innumerable championships as manager of the Cardinals and the Dodgers, and broke baseball's color line by signing Jackie Robinson. Rickey was a devout man and never appeared at the ball park on Sunday. However, he did come to the hill and played with us. And now and then we had a lovely star like Gloria Swanson umpire for an inning. The women loved it—all but glamorous Anna May Wong. A line drive sailed through the pitcher's box, and *gong!* Down went Umpire Wong, out cold.

During the summer of 1940, when we assembled at Quaker Hill, the campaign was heating up. Wendell Willkie was the Republican nominee, and it was an open secret that Roosevelt would run for a third term.

FDR said, "Lowell, I hope you don't have any false notion about why I'm here. I know I can't get ten votes on Quaker Hill." Then he told me that when he had first gone into state politics, he had driven all over the hill, trying to drum up support. But it was a Republican stronghold then and it remained so, as did the entire area. Not once in his political career had Roosevelt ever carried Quaker Hill, Dutchess County or even his own Hyde Park township. "You know," he said wistfully, "I'd give Willkie almost any three western states if I could carry Dutchess County."

Of course he defeated Willkie soundly in 1940, and our neighbor Tom Dewey much more narrowly four years later—the only time in American history that both candidates came from the same county. But he never did carry Dutchess.

THE NINE OLD MEN were bombarded with challenges, many of them from similar softball practitioners, hoping to have some fun or maybe raise a little money for charity. For many years we were at it almost every summer Sunday afternoon. Among our opponents were Robert L. Ripley's Believe-It-Or-Nuts, the Connecticut Nutmegs and the Oystervelts, a team of Republican Roosevelts from Oyster Bay, Long Island, led by TR's son Ted.

One afternoon Tom Dewey, recently moved to Quaker Hill, stopped by to watch the game for a few minutes. He was on his way to a speaking engagement and was dressed in his Sunday best. Soon, though, he had shed his jacket and I put him in as a pinch hitter. Whereupon he lashed one into left field and stretched it into a double with a slide that tore his pants. I have always believed that Tom Dewey—who was the warmest guy in the world, but, some said, projected the public image of a suspicious department-store floorwalker—would have beaten FDR if only someone had taken a picture of him barreling into second base and put it on all his campaign posters.

We played a series against the Oystervelts, both at TR's Sagamore Hill and at Quaker Hill. Of course FDR was never present: there was a longtime antagonism between the two families, both personal and political.

There was a vaudevillian in those days named Billy B. Van, who bore an eerie resemblance to President Roosevelt. Cleverly made up to enhance the illusion, wearing a felt hat and waving a long cigarette holder, he had made a nightclub success imitating FDR. Secretly, I arranged for Billy Van to come to Quaker Hill for a game with the Oystervelts. The grandstand was packed and hundreds stood on the foul lines. Suddenly, with Ted Roosevelt at bat, into the outfield rolled a black open touring car flanked by state troopers; inside, beaming at the crowd and waving the ever present cigarette holder was—was it? Yes, of course!—President Roosevelt.

Ted's jaw dropped. Obviously he couldn't leave—not even a Roosevelt can turn his back on the President. For a moment I thought he would crown me with his bat. Then, as the car was driven across the infield, players and crowd bowing, I went up to the plate and whispered in Ted's ear. With a broad grin he ran to the car, hopped up on the running board and shook the "President's" hand. While the crowd cheered, the newsreel cameras filmed the scene. I have always wondered whether FDR ever saw this "reconciliation" between the estranged branches of the Roosevelt family.

THOSE WERE GLORIOUS DAYS at Quaker Hill, a glorious era that ended on a December Sunday in 1941 with the news of the Japanese attack on Pearl Harbor. And the next spring the end of a golden age for all Americans was poignantly underscored by a brief letter I received from President Roosevelt.

Dear Lowell, I am afraid Hitler has ended our ball games for the duration. . . . As ever yours, F.D.R.

ACKNOWLEDGMENTS

The condensations in this volume have been created by The Reader's Digest
Association, Inc., and are used by permission of and special arrangement with
the publishers and the holders of the respective copyrights.

BEETHOVEN by Alan Pryce-Jones, copyright © 1957 by Gerald Duckworth & Co., Ltd., is
reprinted by permission of Gerald Duckworth & Co., Ltd.

GOOD EVENING EVERYBODY: From Cripple Creek to Samarkand, copyright © 1976 by
Lowell Thomas, is reprinted by permission of Lowell Thomas, Jr.

THE FITZGERALDS AND THE KENNEDYS, copyright © 1987 by Doris Kearns Goodwin,
is reprinted by permission of Simon & Schuster, Inc. and George Weidenfeld & Nicolson
Limited.

A PILLAR OF IRON by Taylor Caldwell, copyright © 1965 by Reback and Reback, is reprinted
by permission of Doubleday, a division of Bantam Doubleday Dell Publishing Group, Inc., and
William Morris Agency, Inc.

ILLUSTRATION CREDITS

COVER: Lowell Thomas and Rose Kennedy, Wide World Photos, Inc. Ludwig van Beethoven and
Cicero, The Granger Collection, New York. John F. Kennedy, The Bettmann Archive.
INSERT: Front, back bottom right: *Handbook of Early Advertising Art* by Clarence P. Hornung,
Dover Publications, Inc. Back bottom left: Beethoven-Haus, Bonn.
THE FITZGERALDS AND THE KENNEDYS: *Pages 221, 230, 254, 306, 342 top left, top right,
bottom left, 386 bottom, 390, 409, 415:* Kennedy Family Collection. *188, 224:* courtesy of The
Bostonian Society. *199:* Boston Public Library. *252, 253:* "Norman," Boston *Post. 292:* Bachrach,
Watertown, Massachusetts. *319:* United Artists. *342 bottom right:* Gordon Morris, New York. *380:*
Pictorial Parade Inc. *386 top:* Frank Turgeon. *386 middle:* U.S. Navy. *392:* Portman Press Bureau.
395: George Woodruff. *416, 417:* Hy Peskin/FPG. *433 top left, top right, bottom right:* Time-Life.
433 bottom left: U.S. Army Signal Corps.